D1563886

CRIMINAL BEHAVIOR

A PROCESS PSYCHOLOGY ANALYSIS

CRIMINAL BEHAVIOR

A PROCESS PSYCHOLOGY ANALYSIS

Personal Constructs — Stimulus Determinants — Behavioral Repertoires

NATHANIEL J. PALLONE
Rutgers University

JAMES J. HENNESSY
Fordham University

Transaction Publishers
New Brunswick (U.S.A.) and London (U.K.)

Library of Congress Catalog Number: 91-36914
ISBN: 1-56000-044-9
Printed in the United States of America

Library of Congress Cataloging-in-Publication Data

Pallone, Nathaniel J.
    Criminal behavior: A process psychology analysis / Nathaniel J. Pallone, James J. Hennessy.
    p.cm.
    Includes bibliographical references and index.
    ISBN 1-56000-044-9
        1. Criminal psychology.   2. Criminal behavior.   I. Hennessy,
James, 1942-   . II. Title.
    [DNLM: 1. Criminal Psychology.   HV 6080 P168c]
    HV6080.P33   1992
    364.3 — dc20
    DNLM/DLC
for Library of Congress

Contents

DISPLAYS, FIGURES, TABLES

to RAYMOND B. CATTELL, *the Last Giant*

Preface

The criminologist usually begins with the question, "What accounts for crime?" In contrast, the psychologist interested in criminal behavior starts with rather a different inquiry: Why does *this* person commit *that* crime, but not some other crime — or no crime at all? For the most part, the responses to that question to emanate from scientific psychology have remained fragmentary and incomplete. It is the immodest aim of this volume to respond by integrating such scientific data as have been adduced in contemporary psychological research, within the overarching framework of process psychology.

This volume is intended for the working professional in psychology, the behavioral and mental health sciences, criminal justice, corrections, and the law, as well as for graduate and advanced undergraduate students in these disciplines. Without losing touch with the bedrock of scientific data on which any psychological conception of crime and its engines must rest, we have endeavored to compose this work according to the principles of sound pedagogy. The volume thus follows a format more typically encountered in textbooks than in scholarly monographs.

Since the conceptual domain the work addresses is vast, we have incorporated enough in the way of description of scientific methodology in psychology that the student or practitioner from other disciplines will feel comfortable enough to function as a reasonably informed reader of psychological research. Similarly, we have incorporated enough in the way of description of the principles of criminal law and the operation of the criminal justice system that the student or practitioner from psychology and the behavioral and mental health sciences will feel comfortable enough to function as a reasonably informed reader of criminal justice research. Since psychological knowledge vastly pre-dates the invention of scientific psychology as a formal discipline in the late nineteenth century, a recurrent subtext reminds us that poets, dramatists, and writers of fiction have provided an incredible array of insights into the engines for human behavior that have only much later been empirically verified. The text is punctuated with some frequency by material set in a different typestyle and surrounded by a double box; consider these punctuations as "marginal glosses," intended to illustrate, amplify, or exemplify issues discussed on adjacent pages.

Though only two names appear on the title page, any volume that aims at comprehensiveness owes huge debts to other hands and minds. Raymond B. Cattell, that giant upon whose shoulders we stand, dwarfed, has never been less than inspirational. We learned much and were challenged mightily in our conceptions by Willard Heckel, late dean of the School of Law at Rutgers — Newark, a senior academic statesman in legal education, and one of the founders of "advocacy law." In the interpretation of data from the neurosciences, we have continued to benefit from the assistance of Robert Pandina of the Center for Alcohol Studies at Rutgers

— New Brunswick, Kirtley Thornton of the New Jersey Center for Health Psychology, and Eugene Loveless of St. Joseph's Hospital, Yonkers.

Adeline Tallau of the Library of Science and Medicine on the New Brunswick campus and Phyllis Schulze of the National Council on Crime and Delinquency Library at the Newhouse Center for Law and Justice on the Newark campus, both at Rutgers, responded marvelously in helping us locate obscure references. Joanne Williams at Rutgers, James J. Hennessy (the Younger) of Shared Medical Systems, and Elisabeth Hennessy, Teresa Hernan, and Laurie Kepecs-Schluesl at Fordham provided assistance in ways too varied to enumerate, as did the editorial and productions staffs at Transaction, but most particularly Esther Luckett and Larry Mintz. Letitia Pallone continued to be supportive to one of us even as she chided another for his peculiar work habits.

Nathaniel J. Pallone
James J. Hennessy

Chapter 1

A Process Psychology Paradigm for Criminal Behavior

WE AMERICANS SEEM NOT TO BE A NOTABLY LAW-ABIDING PEOPLE. IN A typical year, some 14 million episodes of serious (felonious) crime are reported to law enforcement authorities in the United States, with many million more episodes of minor crime, and with perhaps as many as 21 million additional criminal victimizations which are not formally reported (Maguire & Flanagan, 1991, pp. 251, 353). On any given day, more than 1,000,000 of us are incarcerated in state or Federal prisons as a result of conviction for felony crime, with another nearly 3,250,000 of us in jails or juvenile reformatories or otherwise under the supervision of correctional authorities through probation or parole (Bureau of Justice Statistics, 1990, 1991; Maguire & Flanagan, 1991, pp. 564-565, 567, 578, 606; Langan, 1991).

If one assumes (and the assumption is barely warranted) a single perpetrator in each episode of serious crime *reported,* it appears that one of every 17 of us commits a crime each year; victimization data suggest that one of every eight of us is victimized each year; and something approximating 3% of those of us beyond infancy are either in custody or under correctional supervision each day as a result of criminal behavior.

Hence, it is not surprising that few topics engage the public attention or stir the public imagination more compellingly than the dynamics of criminal behavior. In the information media, accounts of criminal activity (especially of violent crime) and of apprehension and trial are almost invariably accompanied by facile observations about individual motivation and/or about the pathogenic social circumstances surrounding the crime. It is not atypical that the enterprising crime reporter spices his or her account with quotable observations from psychologists and psychiatrists in the community who, despite the ethical urgings of their principal professional organizations (American Psychological Association, 1978; American Psychiatric Association, 1974, 1984; Stone, 1976) are not reluctant to comment on the psyche of a real, alleged, or imagined perpetrator whom they have never personally observed, clinically or otherwise.

As is to be expected, crimes that achieve notoriety on a national scale — ranging from attempted assassinations to economic crimes like "insider trading" — energize the press to ever greater inventiveness (Hamilton, 1986). For their part, the entertainment media (television, motion pictures, fiction) have become incorrigible in offering easy interpretations about the interplay between internal psychological forces and criminal behavior, to the horror and delight of viewer and reader.

☐ CURRENT STATUS OF A SCIENTIFIC PSYCHOLOGY OF CRIMINAL BEHAVIOR

Volume and ubiquity alone might thus readily elicit the impression that the psychology of criminal behavior is well understood scientifically, that an integrated body of theory and empirical evidence undergirds the facile psychological interpretations that everywhere regale the reader and viewer — and hence represent but its "pop" outcroppings.

But that impression proves illusory. Despite more than a century and a half of careful study since the English physician Joseph Pritchard invented in the 1830s a mental illness he termed "moral insanity" to explain criminal behavior (Pichot, 1978, p. 56), and many more centuries of non-empirical speculation by insightful philosophers, physicians, and litterateurs, formulation of a broad-gauged, widely applicable, and *scientifically-anchored* psychology of criminal behavior remains at a relatively primitive stage. Though insightful and expert experimentalists and conceptualists have developed well-integrated psychological explanations for *specific types of criminal behavior* (e.g., homicide, arson, rape, shoplifting), few have attempted to construct a comprehensive psychology of criminal behavior which fits equally across the variant species of crime.

Criteria for a Comprehensive Psychology of Criminal Behavior

Such a comprehensive psychology of criminal behavior should both meet the requirements of psychological science *and* prove serviceable to the interests of the enforcers of law and the administrators of justice. To do so, that comprehensive psychology should simultaneously provide *both* a reliable understanding of the psychological factors that antecede criminal behavior of various sorts, ranging from minor offenses to those of the greatest gravity, *and* signposts leading to prediction and control. Judged by these stringent criteria, a quick reading would suggest that the process of formulating a comprehensive, scientifically-anchored psychology of criminal behavior remains fragmentary and incomplete (Janeksela & Miller, 1985).

Nor are the reasons for this state of affairs difficult to discern. As succeeding chapters on boundary conditions in the conceptual and empirical domains which constrain the empirical base for the scientific study of criminal behavior suggest, there are limitations inherent in the enterprise. They originate in the variant *conceptual* domains in which scientific psychology operates, on the one hand, and that demarcated by the legislative definition, regulation, and formal adjudication of behavior as criminal on the other. They extend into the *empirical* domain as well, affecting both the charac-

---

⇨ *Retrospective Clinical Analysis by Long Distance*

Illustrative of the eagerness to perform clinical analyses retrospectively is a study by Marohn (1987) of John Wesley Hardin, an adolescent cowboy-killer of the 19th century much celebrated by Hollywood. According to Marohn (p. 271), Hardin "never established the capacity to regulate internal tensions and strong affects," so that "he used self-objects for regulation instead." Thus, his string of killings is attributed to an undiagnosed and untreated case of narcissism.

No less fantastic for its proximity in time to the criminal events is Bailey's (1985) "paleopsychological" rendering of mass murderer Ted Bundy, who had sexually brutalized and murdered some three dozen young women and was executed in Florida, with the governing dynamics attributed to a "breakdown of neopsychological inhibitions, which [breakdown] allowed extreme phylogenetic regression to occur."

In the same wildly speculative vein, Montanile (1986) analyzed at long distance Bernhard Goetz, the so-called "New York subway vigilante" who crippled a would-be assailant by means of an unlicensed revolver. According to Montanile (p. 55), "Goetz expressed the group fantasy feelings of many persons in the US and acted out the public's own murderous desires, providing a release for many persons for the pent-up feelings of frustration, anger, and fear." Montanile continues by asserting that "Persons in a group (all of whom share the same fantasy) go through four group-fantasy stages (strong, cracking, collapse, and upheaval)" and that "the US was in the upheaval stage" at the time of Goetz's actions — with the quite obvious implication that he was merely an actor in a sociodrama which had its origins elsewhere than in his psyche.

ter of the subjects upon whom scientific studies of criminal behavior can be carried out and the methods of inquiry thereby available to psychologists who study criminal behavior.

But in some large measure the current state of affairs obtains because those psychologists who have studied criminal behavior empirically (in common, to be sure, with a wide array of investigators in other areas of human behavior) have typically adopted the assumptions, biases, and investigatory methods of *differential psychology* rather than those of *process psychology*.

EMPHASIS ON DIFFERENCES OR COMMONALITIES?

By definition, differential psychology takes as its province the illumination of *differences* between people that result in variant behavior between different behavers. Virtually by definition, differential psychology is not particularly interested in those *commonalities* between people or within situations that are likely to elicit *similar* behavior.

For these reasons, it is a fair assessment to say that differential psychology has consistently displayed at least an implicit preference for *univariate* explanation over *multivariate* explanation — not in the sense that differential psychologists have sought to discover the sources of behavior in single variables, but rather in the sense that it has been their belief that the sources of behavior can be discovered in *singular and unitary sets* of variables.

Thus, differential psychology formulations are likely to hold that Behavior *A* is attributable to measurable differences between persons in *personality traits* denominated X, Y, and Z *or* to measurable differences in intelligence, *or* perhaps even to interaction between level of intelligence and the "amount" of traits X, Y, and Z. The bias has remained even after the introduction of sophisticated means for data analysis by means of computerization.

BEHAVIOR AS A FUNCTION OF INTERACTION

At the diametric polarity, those convinced that the determinants of behavior lie in the characteristics of the stimuli which elicit behavior and not at all in differences between behavers (a set of assumptions which undergirds much of contemporary empirical sociology) are likely to formulate *equally* univariate statements that attribute behavior exclusively to stimulus determinants.

And, in the *via media,* there stands the conceptual position that holds that behavior is a function of the dynamic calculus through which intra-person and stimulus characteristics interact. That position, virtually by definition, represents a multivariate stance.

Though the differential tradition is (accurately) said to have given birth to psychology as a science, there is a fallacy inherent in regarding the two as coextensive. To assert (quite correctly) that psychology has not yet successfully differentiated, on the basis of measurable intra-person traits or characteristics, those who have behaved criminally from those who have not — much less proved itself capable of identifying in advance those whose internal traits will compel them to behave criminally at some future time — is *not* to assert that psychology has failed to illuminate the *process* by which criminal behavior is emitted.

Hence, the pivotal position in a process psychology interpretation of criminal behavior holds that the process by which criminal behavior is emitted results *not* from single antecedents that can be identified by focusing *either* on intra-person variables alone *or* on extra-psychic properties inhering in stimulus situations that seem to elicit or invite behavior of one sort rather than of another sort. Instead, such an interpretation focuses on the *process* by which criminal behavior is emitted, construing that process as a dynamic interchange between the person and the environment — between intra-

---

⇨ *Criminal Personality Profiles*

One of the newer "techniques" to emerge in the field of "forensic psychology" has been denominated *criminal personality profiling.* According to Pinizzoto (1984), "profiling focuses attention on individuals with personality traits that parallel traits of others who have committed similar offenses. Close examination of the crime scence and the extrapolation of certain relevant psychological material leads to a profile." As Douglas, Ressler, Burgess & Hartman (1986, p. 401) describe it, this "developing technique" is intended to reveal "the kind of person most likely to have committed a crime by focussing on personality characteristics. A basic premise is that the way persons think directs their behavior. The profiling process moves from input through a decision models stage considering the type and style of the crime. After further assessment, a generated profile is applied to the investigation.' '

Quite clearly, such an approach absolutely demands the existence of a rock-solid body of empirical evidence linking "personality characteristics" to criminal behavior of one or another sort, a condition sharply contrary to fact — or to the present state of the science. Instead, the procedure operates largely through unwarranted over-generalization from clinical evidence that may be systematically biased rather than representative of the offender groups whose "profiles" are to be drawn on the basis thereof. In addition to failure to meet generally accepted scientific canons (a topic further explored in Chapter 4), the procedure is likely to yield wildly high proportions of "false positives." Despite the fictionalized popularity of such techniques when they are displayed in films like *The Silence of the Lambs,* doubtless the courts and opposing counsel will have a field day when "criminal personality profiles" are adduced as evidence in trials — perhaps equal to that enjoyed when clairvoyants give testimony.

person propensities to behave toward certain objects (and in certain ways; and in certain ways toward certain objects, but not toward other objects) and those situational cues and variables which highlight certain objects and seem to invite, permit, or tolerate certain ways of behaving.

☐ UNIVARIATE vs. MULTIVARIATE EXPLANATIONS FOR BEHAVIOR

Suppose that you and I and your brother Sam (or sister Sal) have each purchased a new automobile within the last month — and that each vehicle has been manufactured by the same automaker. Who among us would believe that *your* "reasons" for purchasing your vehicle are the same as mine — or that either of us have reasons that are identical with those of Sam or Sal?

For one of us, purchase price may have been paramount; for another, fuel economy; for another, brand loyalty; for two of us, but not the third, ease of financing, or accessibility to service facilities, or whatever, may have been an important consideration; availability of an acceptable model ready for delivery (in contrast to a long wait for a custom order to be placed with the factory) may have played a role in my decision, but not in yours — and the examples could multiply endlessly. That is by way of illustrating that, even in our daily lives, we tend toward multivariate explanations of relatively complex behavior, so that the tendency of many investigators in psychological science to prefer univariate explanation is the more curious.

A Search for Multiple Causation

Briefly (or even simplistically), a *univariate* explanation would hold that a phenomenon of interest results from a specific antecedent variable (that is, from *this and this alone*), with little or no contribution made by any other variable. Alternately, as the term suggests, a *multivariate* explanation would hold that a phenomenon of interest results from a mixture or blend of several antecedent variables, each of which has a particular weight; implicitly, unless each variable is present as an antecedent condition, the phenomenon will not occur.

In the normal course of human events, we very likely tend to prefer univariate explanations — precisely because they seem to account for things so simply by permitting us to attribute, say, Behavior X to antecedent condition or variable A, even at the expense of oversimplifying what may be quite complex phenomena.

Doubtless, the attractiveness of univariate explanation inheres in this very quality of simplification at a level that seems to permit easy answers and facile explanations.

But a moment's reflection may convince us we typically do *not* perceive human behavior as so unidimensional that it can be explained univariately.

Let's take as another example the matter of how we might go about summarizing coherently the research evidence bearing on the mastery of the Russian language by a person who was born and bred in the United States and who, further, monolingually spoke and read English in his or her own home.

Surely, it will not surprise us that the evidence indicates that reasonable cognitive capacity is necessary for such persons to learn Russian — but few of us would, even without a body of research evidence to limit such an attribution, be willing to predicate the mastery of Russian univariately on cognitive capacity (or intelligence) alone.

Instead, we are likely to believe, more or less intuitively, that some other antecedent conditions are also necessary, including exposure to adequate instruction, some discernible motivation on the part of the learner, and very probably real or implied rewards anticipated by the learner once mastery has been achieved. For purposes of our example, let's assume that the accumulated research evidence does indeed indicate a positive relationship between each of these variables, in isolation and in various combinations, with mastery of Russian as the criterion.

Yet there probably lingers the temptation to segregate and to serialize each antecedent, so that an unsupportable statement may be made: *Mastery of Russian is attributable to the degree of motivation on the part of the learner* or *to the learner's cognitive capacity* or *to the quality of instruction provided to the learner,* and so on, for each antecedent variable. Now, if we take this example apart variable-by-variable, we must admit that it is certainly *not* incorrect to make a statement like *[Bright people]* or *[People with better motivation]* or *[People who receive better instruction] . . . are more likely to master the Russian language.* But a more *comprehensive* (and therefore even "more correct") statement would link each of these antecedent variables in some fashion such as *Bright, well motivated people are likely to master the Russian language, provided they receive competent instruction.*

Or, if we were to clothe the same sentiment in language more redolent of scientific formulations: *Mastery of Russian on the part of a native English speaker / reader without previous exposure to that language will occur* if, but only if, *the learner has sufficient intelligence, sufficient motivation, and has been given adequate instruction.*

Appropriate Attention to Extra-psychic Determinants

Moreover, we tend to believe (and the relevant evidence from studies of the instructional process will demonstrate) that the contribution made by each of several antecedent variables to producing a particular behavioral outcome may vary (i.e., that, technically, the weights assigned to each variable may differ) between behavers. For example: A particularly bright and very highly motivated learner may master Russian even though the level of instruction (albeit at least "adequate") could not be denominated as stellar — but truly stellar instruction may yield mastery of that language even among learners who (albeit at least of average intelligence) could not reasonably be denominated as intellectually brilliant.

In each of our two examples, both *extra*-psychic and *intra*-psychic variables are seen to contribute to behavior, whether the purchase of a particular brand of automobile *or* the mastery of a complex foreign language. Further, the imputation is that extra-psychic variables *interact* with intra-person variables; to that extent, the relative "weight" of a particular extra-psychic variable may also shift from one behaver to another.

Thus, the fact that an auto dealer is offering a particularly attractive financing package (a low down payment and sharply reduced interest rates) represents a set of extra-psychic conditions; that I am a particularly miserly sort who places great emphasis on the opportunity to hoard money represents an intra-person condition that *in combination with* a given extra-psychic condition will the more readily predict *my* inclination to purchase — particularly if my sense of brand loyalty (another intra-person condition) is low and the brand of automobile represents a change for me.

In explaining *my* behavior, then, very great emphasis is to be placed on the favorable financing package, an extra-psychic variable, *in interaction with* what may be my "characteristic" interest in availing myself of a bargain (whether in the matter of an automobile purchase or otherwise), construable as an intra-person "trait" that I carry around with me, from one behavioral situation to another as part of my "psychological baggage." But you have purchased the same brand essentially as a matter of brand loyalty; in explaining your behavior, very great emphasis is to be placed on that intra-person variable, with little contribution made by extra-psychic conditions.

On the other hand, those who are oriented to the design and manipulation of *extra*psychic conditions which are likely to compel the behavior of purchasing an automobile of a given brand *across* purchasers whose *intra*-psychic characteristics may be quite different will, perforce, be primarily interested in determining whether each of the several extra-psychic conditions enumerated — alone, or in combination with each other — compel purchasing behavior among a wide array of prospective purchasers whose intra-person properties are widely dissimilar.

Among psychologists who have studied criminal behavior, not only has there been a preference for univariate explanations (shared to be sure with psychologists who study other kinds of behavior); but there has also been very heavy reliance on *intra-personal traits or characteristics* (or, more simply, personality variables) as the antecedents to which criminal behavior can be attributed. A *process* psychology approach to an understanding of criminal behavior avoids at least two pitfalls — that of reliance on univariate antecedents and that of reliance on intrapersonal characteristics.

☐ AIMS & METHODS IN DIFFERENTIAL PSYCHOLOGY

Differential psychology is a school of psychological thought that holds that different persons behave in different ways largely in consequence of measurable differences in their psychological characteristics and/or personality traits.

Behavior Springs from the Inside Out

As Cattell (1985) observes, the overarching goal of differential psychology is to determine what measurable differences on some specified (or hypothesized) trait or characteristic between persons *A* and *B account for behavior X,* which person A is observed to emit but which person *B,* in similar context, is not observed to emit.

The inherent, and usually unspoken, assumption is that *behavior springs from the inside out,* that its genesis lies primarily in *intra*psychic factors and forces, and that *extra*psychic forces play only a minor role.

In respect of criminal behavior, it is but a few conceptual steps from that inherent assumption to the conclusion that those who behave criminally do so in consequence of internal proclivities or disordered psychopathological conditions, rather than (as many criminologists and sociologists who study crime might argue) in response to a set of environmental conditions that might almost uniformly elicit criminal behavior from a variety of persons with dissimilar traits or characteristics.

Measurable Differences in Characteristics

The pivotal theoretical anchor in differential psychology holds that *behavior is a function of measurable differences in psychological characteristics* between different behavers. The primary aim in differential psychology is to determine the measurable psychological characteristics (whether these be personality attributes, genetic and/or constitutional or neurophysiological factors which influence behavior, even variations in patterns of psychological development or socialization experiences) which differentiate persons who regularly or sporadically emit a particular behavior or pattern of behaviors from those who do not.

A comprehensive psychology of criminal behavior rooted in the methodology of differential psychology would have as its goal to reliably differentiate persons who have committed crimes from others who have not — with perhaps reliable differentiation between persons who have committed crimes of one sort and those who have committed crimes of other sorts an added bonus.

Implicitly at least, since criminal behavior is invariably regarded as socially deviant, whatever specific traits or characteristics are found to differentiate those who commit crimes from those who do not are often, virtually by definition, regarded as indicia of psychological deviance — though, as we shall see in Chapter 2, there is no particularly strong reason to group psychological deviance either with criminal deviance nor with other forms of social deviance.

The Failure to Post-Dict

In practice, the psychological study of criminal behavior following the methods of differential psychology can, at best, hope to determine whether those who have committed, say, Crime Y differ in Characteristic A from those who have committed no crime — and, on the same characteristic, from those who have been judged guilty of Crime Z.

Such a methodology, of course, inevitably leaves unanswered the question of whether all those persons who display certain levels of Characteristic A are destined to commit Crime Y — or whether Characteristic A must interact with other determinants of behavior to produce Crime Y. A current application of such a process centers on what has been called "criminal personality profiling" (*Note* 1) intended to reveal "the kind of person most likely to have committed a crime by focusing on personality characteristics" (Douglas, Ressler, Burgess & Hartman, 1986, p. 401).

A system of prediction and control founded on the methods of differential psychology would, perforce, seek to identify those who are prospective committers of crime on the basis of measurable personal characteristics, yielding to a system of *a priori* identification of those who are predicted as likely at some future time to commit criminal acts. The continuing attempts by the world's civilian airlines and regulatory agencies to develop a reliable profile of prospective hijackers and/or terrorists attests the obstacles in developing such a system.

For a variety of conceptual and empirical reasons to be clarified in later chapters — reasons that inhere not only in the methodology of differential psychology but, even more pertinently, in the operation of the criminal justice system — efforts to find specific differences between those who behave in *formally* criminal ways and those who do not have thus far yielded only fragmentary conclusions.

Nor have the methods of differential psychology yielded evidence that formal psychopathological disorder is reliably associated with criminal behavior, or that the absence of such disorder (i.e., mental health) is reliably associated with crime-free behavior.

At this juncture, and despite the major strides made by Eysenck (1977) and Megargee (1979) and their colleagues, suffice it to say that neither 150 years of more-or-less scientific psychological research nor many more centuries of psychological speculation have yet produced methods or instruments capable of reliably identifying, on the basis of differentially measurable psychological traits or characteristics, those who are adjudicated as guilty of legally criminal behavior from those who are not. Megargee's (1970) trenchant observation of two decades ago — that no method or instrument has yet "been developed which will acceptably *post-dict*, let alone predict" criminal behavior — continues to apply.

To assert that the customary methods employed in differential psychology have thus far not yielded a comprehensive psychology of criminal behavior, however, is not to assert that there are not discernible psychological elements in formally criminal behavior, though these elements may more appropriately be construed as *process* variables than as differential variables.

☐ *AIMS & METHODS IN PROCESS PSYCHOLOGY*

In contrast to differential psychology, *process psychology* is a school of psychological thought that seeks not primarily to differentiate persons from each other, but instead to inquire into the psychological processes that antecede and maintain the emission of behavior of one or another sort. The controlling term was coined by the preeminent theoretician Raymond B. Cattell (1979, p. 31), and process psychology as a cohesive school of thought has been developed principally by Cattell and his associates.

Differential psychology attributes individual differences in behavior to "traits" that inhere within; bundles of such traits differentiate one person from another. Broadly speaking, experimental psychology (as well as empirical sociology and empirical criminology in the sociological tradition) focuses on the formulation of laws that relate primarily to the influence of external, or environmental, causes on behavior. Process psychology, in contrast, is concerned with the *interaction* between intra-person and extra-person variables.

For Cattell, the proper focus in psychological inquiry should be the *process* whereby extra-personal variables interact with rather deep-seated fundamental predispositions to behave (which he terms *source traits* and which themselves result from the individual's past learning history) to yield what are essentially temporary *states* of readiness-to-act with regard to a particular, concrete opportunity to behavior or with regard to a class of behavioral objects.

Process psychology thus recognizes that the contributions of specific internal or intra-person variables to the emission of behaviors may vary. But it further recognizes that external stimuli and situations also change, that external stimuli and situations may have different meanings for different actors *or* that they may have essentially invariable meanings for all actors, and that, therefore, their relative contribution to the emission of a specific behavior is non-constant — but may be amenable to measurement. Hence, in its attempts to explain with some precision the contributions of intra-person and extra-person factors, process psychology seeks to integrate the psychometrics of personality theory with the experimental rigor of social psychology and the psychology of learning and social learning. Cattell, who has displayed a fondness for neologisms, terms such an integration an "econetic model" for understanding the complexities of human behavior.

Inquiry into the Engines of Behavior

The aim of process psychology is to explain a particular behavior (say, behavior *X*) by inquiry into

- ❑ what psychological *processes* are involved in the emission of behavior *X*,
- ❑ under *what* conditions,
- ❑ in response to *which* environmental stimuli or contingencies
- ❑ activating *what* internal sensitizations and predispositions,
- ❑ subject to *which* internal and external controls, *and*
- ❑ whether these processes occur in both persons *A* and *B* or only in one or the other.

The goal of process psychology, in short, is *to explain behavior X in comprehensible conceptual terms* in respect both of *the processes involved in its emission and their antecedents,* whether these antecedents lie in differences in personality, in developmental history, in genetic endowment, in neuropsychological functions, in psychopathological disorders, biochemical particularities, or in external stimuli of sufficiently compelling character to elicit virtually uniform behavioral responses among and across different behavers.

Thus, a comprehensive psychology of criminal behavior rooted in the methodology of process psychology would have as its goal to "model" in comprehensive conceptual terms the psychological processes activated in the emission of an act of formally criminal behavior *among and across* behavers who may or may not differ significantly from each other in measurable psychological characteristics.

Incorporating Data from Differential Psychology

Process psychology seeks to incorporate contributions made to the scientific psychology of criminal behavior by investigations that proceed along the lines of differential inquiry. Granted, for example, that persons who have committed Crime *Y* display measurably differential levels of Characteristic *A,* but that it is not in evidence that all persons who display similar levels of that characteristic commit Crime *Y* or any other crime, *what other variables* contribute to the emission of that criminal behavior we have labeled *Y*?

Stimulus Determinants of Behavior

A system of prediction and control founded on the methods of process psychology might then focus on those *stimulus determinants* of behavior that are likely to elicit criminal activity, while at the

➡️ *Raymond B. Cattell on Traits, States, and Processes:*
Complex Conceptual Models for Complex Phenomena

The search for single causes for specific behaviors has in most instances proven fruitless. Only quite primitive reflexes now seem "caused" by single provokers; but, even in this domain the apparently simple may be amazingly complex, as recent findings in the neurobiology/chemistry/physics of reflexes have suggested.

Perhaps no other psychologist has more consistently underscored the shortcomings of the "single cause' model than the eminent theoretician and empiricist Raymond B. Cattell. Since his days as a graduate student at the University of London, where he studied with Charles Spearman, through his long career at distinguished institutions in the U.S., Cattell has been guided by the conviction that an understanding of human behavior of any and every sort can be found only in the study of complex arrays of data that are usually undetectable by the methods of univariate and bivariate analysis.

From his first published work in 1936 through hundreds of books, chapters, articles, reports, and papers since then, Cattell has mapped human behavior on the axes of the theoretical principles of psychoanalysis, trait psychology, and experimental learning theory integrated with a wide array of research data from the biological and social sciences. Very early in his career, he recognized that reliance on simple correlation and/or analysis of variance as statistical devices for the analysis of data would prove insufficient to the task of understanding differences in the expressions of behavior. Hence, Cattell sought to develop methods for analyzing information that do not sacrifice sources of interaction that are difficult to detect by means either of correlation or analysis of variance. In his quest, he became a pioneer in the use of factor analysis, multivariate analysis of variance, discriminant function analysis, and other advanced data analytic procedures employed widely today in sophisticated psychological research.

As a student under the preeminent British empiricists of the early years of this century, Cattell held firmly to his belief that advances in science are accompanied by advances in the *methods* of science; his interest in methodology, however, was subsidiary to his abiding interest in uncovering lawful principles of human behavior.

No brief synopsis can do justice to Cattell's rich theoretical system. It is fair to say that its scope includes:

❏ the most complete taxonomy of personality traits, states, and motivations yet developed;

❏ a hierarchical theory of intelligence, first formulated in 1941 and expanded in 1971, that is now a cornerstone in the interpretation of the Wechsler intelligence tests and that provided the theoretical rationale for the most recent revision of the classic Stanford-Binet Intelligence Test;

❏ *and* a model for analyzing and understanding interactions among elements in groups that has usefulness in psychotherapy, organizational development, and international relations.

It is Cattell's recognition of the complex interaction between intra-person and environmental variables (or stimulus determinants) that is of greatest concern to a psychological understanding of criminal behavior; we turn briefly therefore to Cattell's conceptualization of process psychology.

Cattell's theory is sometimes categorized as a "trait theory" because of the import-ance it ascribes to stable, enduring, and consistent ways of responding to events that characterize much of human behavior. These consistencies are observable as clusters of manifest or overt constellations that are called "surface" traits. In Cattell's view, beneath such surface traits lie more fundamental intra-person qualities he terms "source traits." One might conceive an analogy that runs something like *surface : source trait :: molecule : atom.* Both surface and source traits can be assessed by instruments developed and validated by Cattell and his associates; the most widely known of these is the 16 Personality Factor Questionnaire, known more simply as the 16PF (Cattell, Saunders & Stice, 1950). Cattell differentiates "traits" into those he calls "temperamental traits," which are said to be rooted in the biological composition of the individual and related to the energy, speed, and reactivity of responses to stimuli; those he calls "ability traits," said to affect the effectiveness with which goals are reached; and those he calls "dynamic traits," which set the individual into action and serve as internal motivators. Each of the three "types" of traits is held to be activated to some degree in all behavior beyond the simple reflex.

To this point, Cattell's process psychology seems not to be dramatically different from other trait theories and indeed to have much in common with differential psychology perspectives. It is at this juncture, however, that Cattell systematically describes, as-sesses, and accounts for even *temporary* changes in trait strength that occur in interac-tion with certain environmental variables. Cattell terms these temporary changes "states." In Cattell's view, traits represent as sort of matrix for behavior, but states influence behavior directly. Following Cattell, Smith (1988, p. 722) put it that *process psychology* is the study of those processes that "occur as behavior changes over time and across state dimensions as a function of environmental encounters."

Thus, the goal of understanding specific actions (such as criminal behavior) must begin by detailing the process elements both within the person and in the specific circumstances in which the person is acting. Cattell has been singular in his devotion to mathematical notation to express such interactions and relationships, producing a variety of quite complex (and sometimes intimidating) algebraic formulae — which he terms "specification equations" — to depict the multiple determinants of any single behavior. A relatively simple specification equation might hold that *the behavior of person X on occasion Y in relation to object Z is a function of the interaction between source traits A, B, and C, from which surface traits D, E, F, G, and H derive, and stimulus determinants I through K — as potentiated by the second-order interaction effect, say, between stimulus determinant L and the "cluster" of surface traits represented by E/F/G.* Alter-nately, however, on another occasion *W*, stimulus determinant *M* might enter the equation, with the effect that quite a different behavior results.

From the perspective of Cattell's process psychology, the expectation that a singular or exclusive "cause" of criminal behavior can be found either in a flaw in the character structure of the actor, or in hardships in the social environment, seems highly improbable.

same time identifying those persons who are *at greatest risk* for criminal activity in the face of those, presumably externally-controllable, extra-psychic determinants, because they display those intrapersonal characteristics which sensitize the behaver to opportunities for criminal behavior of one or another sort.

An Anchor in Personal Construct Psychology

Though a number of theoretical explanations founded upon, or akin to, a process psychology perspective have been offered to account for limited classes of criminal behavior (usually, of crimes of the greatest violence and social disruption), few comprehensive attempts have been made to develop a psychological model of criminal behavior across the spectrum of such behavior — with the notable exceptions of the conceptualizations proposed by the distinguished psychoanalyst Franz Alexander (1931, 1956) and the distinguished behaviorist-*cum*-differential psychologist Hans Eysenck (1964, 1977, 1989).

Yet we believe that the general conceptual framework which undergirds *personal construct psychology*, the exemplar nonpareil of the methodology of process psychology, is sufficiently robust conceptually to serve as an anchor for a process model of the psychology of criminal behavior.

The body of research and clinical inquiry developed through the methodology of differential psychology has yielded little reason to suppose that the psychological processes observable within persons who behave in formally criminal ways are *not* also operative within persons who do not so behave. In part precisely for this reason, there appears to us sufficient conceptual justification to formulate a synthesis that approximates a comprehensive psychology of criminal behavior, resting to be sure in research on criminal behavior but strongly anchored in research and theory on the acquisition and maintenance of behavior in general.

☐ THE PERSON-ENVIRONMENT INTERACTIONIST FRAMEWORK

This conceptual synthesis will be multi-rooted, with its deepest sources to be found in

❏ Paradigms for the *experimental analysis of social learning* pioneered by such seminal thinkers as Skinner (1938, 1961), Mischel (1973-*a*, 1973-*b*, 1979), and especially Bandura (1962, 1963, 1969, 1973, 1978, 1985, 1986, 1989);

❏ *as interpreted within a person-environment interactionist framework* for understanding human behavior-in- general,

❏ which anchors primarily in the Cattell's (1963, 1985) *structured learning theory* and Kelly's (1955) *personal construct psychology* paradigms for behavior.

❏ with a proper appreciation for the impact of what Sells (1963) labeled the *"stimulus determinants of behavior"* inhering in the psychosocial and physical environments on the elicitation and maintenance of particular classes of behavior, as frequently encountered in what Clarke & Cornish (1985) have labeled "opportunity-based" criminogenesis.

The resultant conceptual synthesis, we believe, models in general process terms the psychological antecedents to the emission of an act of criminal behavior which inhere both in the person [P] and in the environment [E] in which the person "finds" himself or herself *or selects for himself or herself*, outlines the boundary conditions that govern relations between the relevant process elements, and suggests how the continued emission of criminal behavior is maintained or extinguished.

An interactionist framework, in its baldest terms, holds that "behavior is not accounted for by either inner or outer forces separately, but by their interaction" (Sells, 1963, p. 3). Thus, as Sells has it:

the principle that behavior represents the interaction of the individual and the environmental situation implies that the variability observed in behavior between different behaving persons is only partially accounted for only by individual differences [between those persons].

Or, as Bandura (1989, p. 1175) put it in slightly different terms:

Social cognitive [i.e., interactionist] theory subscribes to a model of emergent interactive agency. Persons are neither autonomous agents nor simple mechanical conveyers of animating environmental influences. Rather, they make causal contribution to their own motivations and actions within a system of triadic reciprocal causation. In this model of reciprocal causation and action, cognitive, affective, and other personal factors and environmental events all operate as interacting determinants.

Since the characteristics of the psychosocial and physical environments are relatively stable when judged objectively, the sources for variations in behavior are to be found in the network of *interactions* between the behaving person and the environment, with equal focus on those characteristics of the environment that represent cues to behavior and those characteristics of persons that *sensitize* them to cues of one or another sort and that incline them to behave in one or

⇨ *George A. Kelly: The Process of Construing as Organismic, Not Merely Cognitive*

If one defines construing as a process that follows the conventional principles of logic and conceptualization, or if he has already classified the psychology of personal constructs in his own mind as a "cognitive theory," what follows won't make much sense.

Some construing is consistent. It may not be logical but it can still be consistent. Of two objects one is always construed as darker than the other, or heavier, or more beautiful; that is to say, whenever the construct *dimension* is applied to a pair of objects the outcome is the same. This is tight construction . . .

But there is loosened construction too. The inconsistency of the dreams one tries to recall in the morning is a good example. Language may play a part in such dreams but it usually fails to keep their construction tight. Some of us don't have to be asleep to construe loosely. We can even make our spoken words clatter along with our loose construction in a way that would give Noah Webster the jitters.

Actually, construing can be tight or loose, regardless of whether words are tied to constructs or not . . . When we construe tightly, we can subject our constructs to experimentation and various other kinds of tests, but it is very hard to rotate them into new positions so as to get any new slant on our personal affairs. A tight construct tends to be brittle, and it stands firm or is shattered by the outcome of the predictions it involves.

It is almost impossible to test a loose construct, or, to put it better, a construct loosely used. In an elastic sort of way, it seems to apply to almost everything — or to almost nothing — that happens. That, too, can be good, for if every idea we ever laid hold of remained rigid and either stood firm or collapsed in the face of every test it got, mental processes would all be guesswork, and any progress that happened to take place in human thinking would depend on the sheer accident of hitting on something useful.

• *Source:* George A. Kelly, A psychology of the optimal man. In Alvin W. Landfield & Larry M. Leitner (editors), *Personal Construct Psychology.* New York: John Wiley, 1980. Pp. 33-34.

another way in response to those cues. An interactionist framework, then, holds that *the engines for behavior inhere both in the person, in the environment, and in the network of interactions between the two.*

☐ AN INTERACTIONIST PARADIGM FOR BEHAVIOR

Cattell's *structured learning theory* and Kelly's *personal construct psychology* jointly epitomize the interactionist framework.

As developed by Cattell (1965, 1985) and his associates during the past fifty years, structured learning theory interprets behavior as a function both of predisposing tendencies within the behavior that sensitize him or her to certain stimuli (a tendency akin to the meaning of "trait" in popular usage) and the specific potency of those stimuli in a particular situation to elicit a particular behavior.

As initially formulated by Kelly (1955, 1967, 1970, 1980) and refined by later contributors (Bannister & Fransella, 1971; Maher, 1969; Niemeyer, 1985, 1990; Niemeyer & Niemeyer, 1987; Pervin, 1975), personal construct psychology interprets behavior as a function of the way the behaving person "construes" *both* an object of behavior *and* the ways of behaving accessible to him or her in relation to that object.

On the conceptual foundations developed by Cattell and Kelly, expressed in somewhat variant terminology, our conceptualization of personal construct process psychology yields the following paradigm as a general model for the explanation of behavior:

   ❑ *Any person P who is either required by external contingencies or impelled by internal contingencies to behave in regard to a particular object of behavior scans the ways of behaving toward that object which are open and accessible to him/her — i.e., scans his/her "behavioral repertoire" with respect to that object.*

   What is generally termed *motivation* to act may thus inhere in compelling external stimulus conditions *or* arise intra-personally. In the latter case, such motivation itself may be construed as the accumulation of past learning experiences *either* in relation to similar objects of behavior *or* in relation to particular ways or patterns of behaving.

   When the motivation to act arises *intra-* personally, it may be that certain persons have developed particular sensitivity to particular stimuli — i.e., may have learned habitually to respond to certain types of objects of behavior *or* opportunities to behave; or it may be that biochemical particularities (e.g., sensitivity or insensitivity to particular stimuli mediated by mood-altering substances) or neuropsychological processes (e.g., typical level of neural arousal) incline the behaver *either* to behave in respect of certain stimuli *or* to behave in certain ways in respect of certain stimuli.

When the motivation to act arises from what appear to be *extra*-psychic factors (or "stimulus determinants"), it may be that certain persons have become *sensitized* to certain cues in the environment that elicit certain behavioral responses, *or* to certain environments that are *tolerant* of certain ways of behaving, and have *elected* to place themselves in those environments with more-or-less conscious deliberation.

❑ *As P scans his/her behavioral repertoire, he/she calculates the costs, risks, and benefits he/she construes to be attached to each accessible way of behaving.*

❑ *P selects that way of behaving toward the given object*

❑ that is most readily accessible to *(i.e., most easily performable by) him/her* and

❑ *that is also construed as exacting the least significant cost and/or involving the least risk* and

❑ *that is further construed as yielding the greatest benefit,* both in the immediate behavioral situation and in respect of the maintenance of a reasonable and economical balance (often called "equilibrium") in P's behavioral repertoire, or at least of requiring only minimal change in P's typical pattern of behaving.

❑ *Costs, risks, and benefits may be calculated in psychological, social, or financial terms, or, more frequently, through some combination of these dimensions.*

How *P* construes the costs, risks, and benefits attached to particular ways of behaving may itself be the result of past learning experience reflected in habitual ways of behaving but is modifiable through manipulation of environmental variables so as to increase or decrease the costs, risks, and benefits attached to particular ways of behaving (*Note* 2). Not incidentally, it is to be noted that the *assessment* of costs, risks, and benefits associated with particular ways of behaving is notoriously susceptible to influence by mood-altering biochemical substances.

These calculations occur so rapidly and often with so little discernible deliberation that they are often imprecisely described in the psychological literature as "unconscious" processes.

Phenomenologically, *P* may be unable to trace those processes in detail and may, when inquiry is subsequently made as to why he/she behaved in a certain way toward a certain object on a certain occasion, declare that "It seemed a good thing to do at the time." That response, in fact, is very nearly an accurate approximation in non-scientific terms to the process as it is experienced by *P*.

❑ *The ways of behaving accessible to P clearly result from a blend both from P's past learning history and physical capacities (if P does not know how, or is physically unable, to perform a particular behavior in relation to a given object of behavior, for example, that way of behaving is simply not accessible to him / her, however much he / she may construe it as desirable for himself or herself or as accessible to another actor or behaver) and psychophysiological particularities (P may behave quite differently from what is the norm for him / her when particularly fatigued or under the influence of biochemical substances which affect mood and / or central nervous system functioning) and of such other factors as the general attitudes held by P toward the behavioral object in question, toward other objects*

➪ *Fragments: Process Psychology Perspectives on Criminal Behavior*

A number of investigators and commentators have adapted certain perspectives from process psychology to the study or analysis of criminal behavior, often without situating those perspectives within a comprehensive conceptual framework. Thus:

❑ Williams (1982) utilized the perspectives of personal construct psychology in an analysis of violent crime among adolescents. While employing terminology somewhat variant from that of Kelly, the process Williams proposes as antecedent to the emission of an act of criminal behavior is fully congruent with a personal construct framework: "Every action is preceded by a conscious and/or unconscious fantasy; the action visualized is subjected to a process known as reality testing . . . an intrapsychic buffering process operates . . . so that a successful pilot experiment is conducted in the mind [before] the individual is committed to the deed."

❑ Finding their sources in Ellis' rational-emotive therapy and not acknowledging Ellis' debt to Kelly or to Cattell, Zastrow & Navarre (1979) propose that "the reasons for a criminal act can be determined by examining the offender's self-talk (what the offender tells himself) before and during a crime."

❑ In an analysis that highlights the interaction between how the behaver construes himself or herself as well as how he or she construes external objects and stimuli, Oysterman & Markus (1991) attribute the initiation, maintenance, and cessation of delinquent behavior among a sample of Israeli adolescents to the role of "possible selves," identified as those selves "expected, hoped for, and feared."

❑ Similarly, Keltikangas-Jarvinen (1982), in a study of violent offenders in contrast to those convicted of non-violent offenses, found evidence in the responses of the former group of subjects to projective devices of "alexithymia," or the inability to fantasize — a deficit which may be akin to an impaired capacity either to construe alternate responses to stimulus situations or to foresee the consequences of one's behavior. A roughly parallel finding is reported by Buikhuisen (1982) on cognitive disorders in relation to aggression.

that P construes as similar to that object, and toward particular ways of behaving.

❑ *Those ways of behaving either in respect of a particular object of behavior, in respect of classes of behavioral objects that P construes as similar to each other, or in general across a wide spectrum of classes of objects that have become habitual in person P, are often imprecisely called "psychological characteristics" or "personality traits."*

But these terms, at bottom, *merely refer to habitual ways of behaving in general or in relation to a class of behavioral objects* which *P* construes as similar to each other. Operationally, the term *personality* has as its principal empirical referent *the sum of those ways of behaving* toward classes of behavioral objects *that have become habitual in P in respect of those objects and similar behavioral objects.* From Cattell's perspective in particular, "personality" might be viewed as the sum total (i.e., source traits of various sorts which underlie surface traits of various sorts) of that which permits a prediction of how a particular person is likely to behave in a particular situation.

❑ A PROCESS PSYCHOLOGY PARADIGM FOR CRIMINAL BEHAVIOR

When we apply the framework of personal construct psychology to behavior that is specifically and formally criminal, we make several assumptions:

❑ That the behaver is aware that a particular prospective way of behaving toward a particular object is in fact, or is likely to prove, contrary to the law; that certain probabilities are attached to detection and apprehension; and that certain costs are to be exacted in the way of societally-imposed sanctions should the illegal and formally criminal act be detected and the actor apprehended.

But we do *not* make the assumption that those who behave criminally are measurably different in "personality" or other psychological characteristics from those who do not (and implicitly similar to each other), *nor* that criminal behavior issues from psychopathological disorder — that is, that crime results from mental illness.

On the basis of what must be regarded as fragmentary evidence (Stewart & Helmsley, 1979), we incline to believe that among many criminal offenders there obtains *a generalized tendency to underestimate the costs and risks* attached to behaving in formally proscribed ways and that this generalized tendency is often *imprecisely* described as a psychological characteristic or personality trait rather than — more economically and more directly — denominated as a habitual way of behaving. But we find little evidence to support the notion that the selection of formally criminal ways of behaving *generalizes* from one class of behavioral objects to other, dissimilar classes of behavioral objects.

Thus, we propose what follows as a statement of the probable process elements and boundary conditions that are *psychologically necessary* for the emission and continuance — that is, for the acquisition and maintenance — of behavior that is formally criminal. The paradigm which follows puts the matter simply but schematically.

⇨ *Opportunity + Risk Assessment = Rational Choice?*

The opportunity to act without deterrence is a property inherent in the stimulus determinants for criminal behavior, which range from social factors and group norms (Kudryavtsev, 1974) to such physical characteristics as lighting in a parking lot and the relative isolation of a dwelling.

A panoply of investigations have considered one or another of these stimulus determinants. Among many other studies, those of Sampson (1983) on structural density, Pfuhl (1983) on police strikes, Kelley (1985) on population density in relation to crime rates, and of Steinmetz (1980) on social isolation in relation to criminal child abuse, are relevant. Research investigations on the stimulus determinants of homicide and larceny are reviewed in Chapters 7 and 10, respectively.

But the most ambitious and comprehensive conceptual work on what we have called the stimulus determinants of criminal behavior, however, is that of Ronald Clarke (1980, 1984, 1985, 1987) on what he terms "situational crime prevention" in relation to "opportunity- based crime." Clarke concludes that an adequate understanding of the genesis of criminal behavior requires attention to "the circumstances and conditions under which different forms of crime take place" and "a deeper knowledge of the decision-making processes of people at the point of [criminal] offending."

Under those circumstances, whether to commit an offense or not becomes a matter of "rational choice" (Clarke, 1987) — one that is, in our terms, dependent largely on interaction between stimulus determinants *and* on the capacity to appraise the costs, risks, and benefits of a particular prospective criminal act fairly realistically.

Elements in the Process

For formally criminal behavior to be emitted, four process elements that interact with and potentiate each other in varying ways must be present and activated in the behavioral situation:

❑ *Inclination or predisposition on the part of the behaver to behave in ways that are construed by the behaver, and held by the society, to be formally and legally criminal,* whether aggressive or not, in which one (and, in isolation from other predisposing variables, not necessarily particularly weighty) variable is a willingness to break the law. On the basis of the current evidence, we believe that this predisposition obtains in respect of a *specific* behavior or class of behaviors and is typically not generalized across the spectrum of behaviors customarily or characteristically emitted by the same person.

❑ *The opportunity to behave without direct deterrence* — that is, in the absence of observation by another who may act to deter.

❑ *The expectation of reward,* which may be either tangible or symbolic — and in the latter case may be no more than the internal experience that one has "beaten the system" (Rosner, 1992).

❑ *The expectation that the act will remain unobserved or will go unpunished.*

Boundary Conditions

These boundary conditions confine the psychological processes activated in the emission of formally criminal behavior and regulate the interaction between process elements:

❑ *In a specific criminal offense, the weights attached to each of the four process elements vary, but in no case is the weight attached to any element zero* — that is, each process element influences the behavior emitted during a specific criminal offense and in no case is any single element inoperative.

❑ *In any criminal act, there obtains a relation between "predisposition" and "opportunity" such that opportunity potentiates predisposition in what is likely an exponential manner.*

❑ *Expectation of reward likely varies in inverse relation to the other three elements.*

❑ *Expectation of impunity is likely geometrically potentiated by what the prospective behaver observes in the psychosocial environment as others who emit criminal behavior of whatever sort go undetected and unpunished.* A specific act of criminal behavior may thus be vicariously reinforced by an act of criminal behavior of the same (or even of a different sort) not emitted

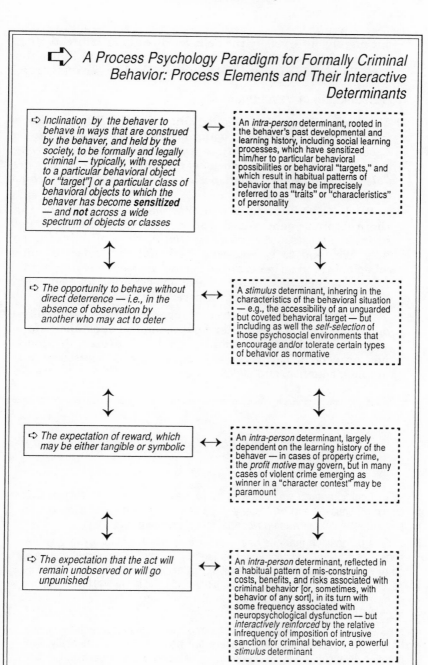

A Process Psychology Paradigm for Formally Criminal Behavior: Process Elements and Their Interactive Determinants

⇨ Inclination by the behaver to behave in ways that are construed by the behaver, and held by the society, to be formally and legally criminal — typically, with respect to a particular behavioral object [or "target"] or a particular class of behavioral objects to which the behaver has become **sensitized** — and **not** across a wide spectrum of objects or classes

↔ An *intra-person* determinant, rooted in the behaver's past developmental and learning history, including social learning processes, which have sensitized him/her to particular behavioral possibilities or behavioral "targets," and which result in habitual patterns of behavior that may be imprecisely referred to as "traits" or "characteristics" of personality

⇨ The opportunity to behave without direct deterrence — i.e., in the absence of observation by another who may act to deter

↔ A *stimulus* determinant, inhering in the characteristics of the behavioral situation — e.g., the accessibility of an unguarded but coveted behavioral target — but including as well the *self-selection* of those psychosocial environments that encourage and/or tolerate certain types of behavior as normative

⇨ The expectation of reward, which may be either tangible or symbolic

↔ An *intra-person* determinant, largely dependent on the learning history of the behaver — in cases of property crime, the *profit motive* may govern, but in many cases of violent crime emerging as winner in a "character contest" may be paramount

⇨ The expectation that the act will remain unobserved or will go unpunished

↔ An *intra-person* determinant, reflected in a habitual pattern of mis-construing costs, benefits, and risks associated with criminal behavior [or, sometimes, with behavior of any sort], in its turn with some frequency associated with neuropsychological dysfunction — but *interactively reinforced* by the relative infrequency of imposition of intrusive sanction for criminal behavior, a powerful *stimulus* determinant

but merely observed by the behaver directly or indirectly (e.g., through the journalistic or entertainment media) that either actually remains undetected or unpunished or is so construed.

No Assumption of Psychopathology

❑ *No assumption need be made that criminal behavior issues from psychopathological conditions embedded within the behaver or from the inability to distinguish right from wrong, though in any specific instance of criminal behavior such variables may influence predisposition or inclination to behave criminally.*

We have already indicated that we harbor the view that there obtains a generalized tendency to misconstrue by underestimating costs and risks associated with specifically criminal acts. We tend to believe that such habitual misconstruing, when observed as generalized across ways of behaving in relation to a given class of behavioral objects or on an even wider basis, is often *mislabeled* as a personality trait or defect.

Similarly, as we have already suggested, the psycho- physiological effects of mood-altering biochemical substances (or, at even more biologically primitive levels, of severely disordered neuropsychological processes) frequently yield a misconstruing of costs, benefits, and risks.

⇨ *Criminal Child Abuse by Parents Free from Mental Illness*

In later chapters, we review in some detail the research evidence on criminal homicide and on larceny in particular. In each case, there is little support for a link between psychopathology and criminal behavior.

The proposition that one need not assume psychopathology as an antecedent of criminal behavior is supported in a number of studies of crimes of other sorts including those of Heller, Taylor, Ehrlich & Lester (1984) on psychosis and violent crime other than homicide and in several investigations of parents who commit criminal child abuse (Kinard, 1982; Williams, 1983; Main & Goldwyn, 1984; Webster, Goldstein & Segall, 1985; and Wolfe, 1985).

Steinmetz (1980) put the general tenor of the relevant research succinctly: "As a group, [criminal] child abusers are no more or less mentally ill or emotionally disturbed than any randomly selected group of parents."

⇨ *Seriousness Progression and Recidivism: Paradoxical*
Data on Probation vs. Imprisonment

The high rate of recidivism among *incarcerated* felons may be largely an artifact of a system of justice administration whereby — as we shall see in detail in Chapter 3 — only 40% of *convicted* felons are sentenced to confinement, with the remaining 60% placed on probation. In cases in which there is judicial discretion in sentencing [in some jurisdictions for some offenses, prisons terms are mandatory], the offender's prior record is assuredly a determinant of incarceration. Hence, it is likely that the majority of those offenders sentenced to prison terms are not "first offenders" (Langan, 1991), while the obverse obtains for those sentenced to probation.

Thus, it may *simultaneously* be the case that the majority of *convicted* felons do not recidivate and that the vast majority of *incarcerated* felons recidivate repeatedly (Witte & Schmidt, 1979; Haapanen & Jesness, 1982; Holland, Holt, Levi & Beckett, 1983; Buikhuisen & Meijs, 1983; Wormith & Goldstone, 1984).

Current evidence appears to suggest that offenders sentenced to *probation* are less likely to recidivate than are those (likely, already "repeat") offenders sentenced to prison (Lindquist, Smusz & Doerner, 1985). Thus:

❑ In a discerning review of research data from four longitudinal studies of criminality, Petersilia (1980) concluded that only half of all those arrested once were ever arrested for a second offense.

❑ In a review of 55 studies of recidivism among 138 samples of parolees and 39 samples of probationers, Pitchard (1979) found that "auto theft is the only specific offense category consistently and significantly associated with recidivism."

❑ Schneider, Schneider & Bazemore (1981) reported that only 9% of juvenile offenders remanded to a community services program rather than incarcerated had committed a subsequent offense.

❑ Roundtree, Edwards & Parker (1984) reported a recidivism rate of only 14% in their sample of 17-54 year old probationers.

❑ In a study of releasees from a forensic psychiatric hospital ("for the criminally insane") in Canada, Pruesse & Quinsey (1977) found that only 46% of even this highly volatile and unpredictable group had recidivated during a four-year follow-up period.

In contrast, in a follow-up study over a quarter century of the offense records of nearly 1600 subjects who had been convicted of violent crimes or of robbery in 1950, Miller, Dinitz & Conrad (1982) found a mean of nearly 8 re-arrests, with half of these resulting in conviction. Their data appear to support Blumstein & Moitra's (1980) contention that a very small proportion of persons (perhaps on the order of 6% of all those ever convicted) are responsible for a very large proportion (perhaps on the order of 52%) of all criminal activity. Whether these and similar data will support the contention that prisons are themselves schools for the perfection of the skills required for future crime is another topic for another place.

Reinforcement and Maintenance

❏ *It is likely that, once emitted, criminal behavior that is rewarded (i.e., reinforced positively), directly or vicariously and
whether through tangible or symbolic reward, will be repeated.
In its turn, positive reinforcement, direct or vicarious, increases
"predisposition" to behave criminally.*

❏ **THE PROCESS MODEL IN CONTEXT:
VARIABLES AND WEIGHTS**

We posit the four *antecedent* elements as *interactive* among and
between themselves and as *potentiating* each other. Thus, the prospective behaver who is heavily predisposed toward criminal behavior will be particularly vigilant to evidence of lack of deterrence and
to evidence of impunity in the world around him or her, while the
experience of impunity directly (or *vicariously*) will strengthen even
a mild predisposition toward criminal behavior.

Predisposition as a Function of
Infrequent Intrusive Sanction

We believe that *inclination* or *predisposition* may inhere either in
learned or culturally-acquired patterns of behavior, in genetic factors that determine physique and body size in relation to age, or, in
the most recent frontier to be explored, in neuroanatomical, neurochemical, bioelectrical, or even biomolecular processes which influence behavior (*Note* 3).

We hold that, at minimum, formally criminal behavior is widely
reinforced vicariously by a system of detection and adjudication such
that, as we will review in greater detail in Chapter 3, convictions
result in barely 6% of the episodes of serious crime reported, with
imprisonment the sanction in only 2% of all cases of serious crime.
In turn, the sequelae to criminal behavior reflected in such data also
reinforce the expectation that a formally criminal act is unlikely to
be deterred or detected, with subsequent adjudication and intrusive
sanction.

Varying Weights and Sources

We propose as a boundary condition that, in a specific criminal
offense, the weights attached to each of these four elements vary, but
that each element contributes to the process; if the weight of any
element is zero, *formally criminal* behavior will *not* be emitted.

⇨ *Evelyn Waugh: Mr. Loveday's Little Outing*

With great regularity, consummate writers of fiction anticipate themes that only later become the objects of scientific inquiry among those who study behavior empirically. In his short story "Mr. Loveday's Little Outing," originally published in 1937, Evelyn Waugh (1983) offered a fictional account that well illustrates focused predisposition for one type of criminal behavior only, along with quite specific propensity for recidivism for that behavior — but not for other criminal behaviors.

The account begins with a visit by Lady Angela Moping to her father, who is confined to the County Home for Mental Defectives as a result of what today could be identified as senile dementia (perhaps even hastened in its course by heavy alcohol consumption). She finds that her father is well attended by a Mr. Loveday, who functions as butler-*cum*-secretary.

Lady Angela is quite shocked to learn that Mr. Loveday is not an employee, but rather has been confined as an inmate at the Home for a period of 35 years. The medical superintendent's account of the reasons for Loveday's incarceration: "When he was a very young man, he killed somebody — a young woman quite unknown to him, whom he knocked off her bicycle and then throttled. He gave himself up immediately afterwards and has been here ever since." While there is the implication of sexual assault as well as murder, the ever-circumspect Waugh leaves the matter unclear.

In Lady Angela's view, Loveday is by now perfectly sane and safe; the medical superintendent appears to concur. "Oppressed by a sense of injustice," she organized a whirlwind campaign to achieve his release: "She read a great deal in the library, she cross-examined any guests who had pretensions to legal or medical knowledge, she showed extreme good will to old Sir Roderick Lane-Foscote, their Member [of Parliament]. The names 'alienist,' 'barrister,' or 'government official' now had for her the glamour that formerly surrounded film actors and professional wrestlers. She was a woman with a cause, and before the end of the hunting season she had triumphed. Mr. Loveday achieved his liberty."

But Loveday's freedom proved short-lived in the extreme. Within two hours, he returns to the Home. He tells the Medical Superintendent: "I've enjoyed myself *very much*. I'd been promising myself one little treat, all these years. It was short, sir, but *most* enjoyable. Now I shall be able to settle down again to my work here without any regrets." Waugh's concluding paragraph: "Half a mile up the road from the asylum gates, they later discovered an abandoned bicycle. It was a lady's machine of some antiquity. Quite near it in the ditch lay the strangled body of a young woman, who, riding home to her tea, had chanced upon Mr. Loveday."

Even cursory and superficial consideration suggests that "predisposition" and "opportunity" not only vary but are likely themselves comprised of very different sub-elements in such cases as

❑ the pot-smoking youth who chances upon an unattended late-model sports car, its key in the ignition and its motor running while its owner has dashed from the curb into the corner store *vs.*

❑ the "professional" car thief who equips himself with sophisticated tools before he selects a likely prospect parked in the far corner of a public lot after the close of the business day;

❑ the bank clerk who steals $1000 in cash from a mail deposit envelope when the depositor has failed to include a deposit slip *vs.*

❑ the bank employee who coolly and deliberately devises a scheme to skim by sophisticated tampering with computer programs small amounts each day from each of many accounts;

❑ the middle-aged drifter who starts by trying to pass a bad check in a liquor store but ends by assaulting the clerk with the jackknife he habitually carries *vs.*

❑ the hold-up artist who carefully selects a particular clerk in a particular store at a particular time of day and purposively arms himself with a particular weapon.

Inclination toward Specific Criminal Behaviors

"Inclination" or "predisposition" seem to us less an embedded trait of personality than a term conveniently applied to denominate a pattern of behavior. We see inclination or predisposition as related to a variety of specific factors within the behaver — including, in the case of the car thief or burglar, such factors as mechanical ability and physical agility — which may be quite independent of his/her traits of personality or state of mental health, save that he or she be willing to disregard the mores of the society embodied in formal or positive law, whether habitually across a spectrum of behavioral objects or in relation to a given object or class of objects. In short, we regard "predisposition" as a psychological characteristic *that recapitulates a pattern of past behavior,* but not necessarily as a symptom of mental illness nor indeed as a "trait" of personality, any more than the consumption of cigarettes or pistachio ice cream is a "trait" rather than a habit or pattern.

The currently available data, further, incline us to the view that, except for this fundamental difference in "predisposition," no other reliable differences are dependably observable between those who emit formally criminal behavior and those who do not.

⮕ On Specialized Predisposition for Criminal Behavior:
Blumstein & Cohen vs. the Conventional Wisdom

The conventional wisdom holds that an offender progresses inexorably through graduated acts of criminality and is doubtless supported by what are generally interpreted as high rates of recidivism.

But the conventional wisdom is not supported by the research of Loeber (1982, 1990) on delinquent adolescents; that of Holland, Holt, & Beckett (1982) on recidivism among violent and non-violent offenders; that of Gibbs & Shelly (1982) on commercial thieves who specialize in truck hijacking; nor that of Holland & McGarvey (1984) on adult felons. In these instances, the researchers not only found no evidence for progression but instead some evidence of retrogression.

Thus, after reviewing the relevant published research, Loeber concludes that "Patterns of antisocial behavior tend to change during preadolescence and adolescence: the number of youths who engage in *overt* antisocial acts *declines* whereas the number of youths who engage in *covert* antisocial acts increases." In a study of 300 adult male offenders utilizing sophisticated statistical analyses, Holland & McGarvey found that "there was specialization in nonviolent offenses and little tendency toward consistently violent behavior. Seriousness progression from nonviolent to violent misconduct was infrequent; however, there was substantial retrogression from violent to nonviolent offenses." There is also some evidence that the "specialization" phenomenon is international in dimension, at least among non- violent offenders (Goeppinger, 1975).

In an impressive study (which, however, relied on data reflecting *arrests* rather than *convictions*), Blumstein & Cohen (1987) studied what they called the "criminal careers" of some 13,000 arrestees in Detroit and Washington, D.C., concluding that participation in crime tends to stabilize in early adulthood. At this point, many who commenced delinquent behavior in adolescence or earlier apparently forsake the criminal lifestyle, but those who do not apparently continue to commit crimes at a relatively constant rate for the remainder of their lifespan. Buikhuisen's (1982) finding that, as a group, what he called "persistent" offenders tend to suffer more frequently from central nervous system dysfunctions implicated in learning, and therefore in impaired ability to profit from experience, may offer some explanation.

But what is germane to the question of specificity, however, is that even in this highly sophisticated statistical analysis, no evidence emerges of "graduation" from one sort of crime to another, so that Blumstein & Cohen's data do not support the conventional notion that there obtains a generalized (as distinct from specialized or focussed) predisposition toward criminal behavior.

Moreover, since the current research evidence on recidivism fails to portray a generalized progression or graduation from one sort of criminal behavior (e.g., car theft) to another (e.g., rape), but instead indicates that the offender who "recidivates" is more likely to commit subsequently an offense of a character similar to his/her previous offense or offenses rather than one of a different character, we find scant evidence to support the belief that there obtains a generalized predisposition toward criminal behavior of any and all sorts.

Rather, we hold that the specific mix of predisposing factors, including always willingness to break the law as one component, incline the behaver toward one or another *limited range* of formally criminal activity.

⇨ *Ronald V. Clarke: Opportunity as a Complex Stimulus Determinant for Criminal Behavior*

Opportunity is not merely the necessary condition for [criminal] offending, but it can provoke crime and can also be sought and created by those with the necessary motivation . . . opportunity is a rather more complex concept than implied by simple counts of available targets. Whether opportunities are acted upon depends upon their ease and attractiveness, and these qualities must be subjectively perceived and evaluated. Moreover, these subjective processes are affected by motivation as well as knowledge and experience — which explains why opportunities may not only provide the cue for offending in those with an established propensity (as when an untended handbag tempts the sneak thief), but may also provoke crime in the previously law-abiding (as when an accounting loop-hole proves to be the bank clerk's downfall). In addition, opportunities are not merely presented and perceived, but can also be sought. [Thus] not only can crimes be the result of presented or sought opportunities, but they can also be the outcome of opportunities which have been created or "planned" . . .

A variety of data . . . would force [one] to accord a greater role to the circumstances and conditions under which different forms of crime take place. An understanding of how these situational contingencies achieve their effect is in turn likely to demand a deeper knowledge of the decision-making process of people at the point of offending . . . knowledge of this kind might permit a more realistic assessment to be made of the potential for, and limits to, policies in regard to deterrence, prevention, and rehabilitation.

• *Source:* Ronald V. Clarke, Opportunity-based crime rates: The difficulties of further refinement. *British Journal of Criminology*, 1984, 24, 75, 80-81.

⇨ *"Tightening the Bolts" — Police Foot Patrols +*
Increased Surveillance = Deterrence?

For some two centuries after the British decided to put their constables on patrol (a decision that gave the language the acronym *cop*) by foot or on bicycle, the familiar figure of a uniformed policeman plying his (or her) "beat" in the cities of the US functioned as an omnipresent reminder of societal authority and, one presumes, served to deter criminal behavior that might otherwise have occurred.

That means of behavioral surveillance seemed well suited while we remained an urban nation. In the quarter century following the end of World War II (and for a panoply of reasons which also produced the "baby boom" of that era), we became a suburban nation, with the suburban population surpassing the urban population for the first time in the 1970 census. In contrast to the compactness of the city with its relatively high density in residential housing, however, the sprawling character of the suburban community dictated the demise of the foot patrol and the substitution of the police cruiser criss-crossing the streets of the suburb. In the wake of suburbanization, the populations of many central cities were decimated, with vast residential areas converted to commercial or industrial purposes, so that, except for normal working hours, these cities became virtual ghost towns. Accordingly, the foot patrol largely disappeared from the urban centers as well.

Yet a conviction has been growing among both policy makers and the citizenry that the return of the "cop" to his or her beat could well restore the prospect of immediate behavioral surveillance that deters crime. As a result of an experiment undertaken by the New York City police department, to their voices have now been added the expert opinions of actual or would-be felons themselves. According to a report in the *New York Times:*

❑ According to data released by the New York City Police Department, crimes against both persons and property have declined since the Department has increased the number of foot patrol officers in the midtown region. Robberies, said to be the single best gauge of overall street violence, were down 18% from the same period a year earlier. All persons interviewed, including ranking and patrol-level police, merchants, business leaders, and criminals themselves attribute the decline to the visible deterrent effect of the additional police. One 28-year old self-described street hustler and convicted felon is quoted as saying "Too many cops in sight — it's intimidating," and added "They're tightening the bolts, and crime is definitely down." Both City and Transit Police stated that the fewer crimes in midtown, above and below ground, have not resulted in more criminal activity in other areas; the deterrent effects of increased surveillance has led to a dramatic reduction in criminal activity.

• Source: [Unsigned] As Crime Drops in Midtown, Even Criminals Credit Police, *New York Times,*
Wednesday, April 24, 1991, pp. A-4, B-4

Inverse Relationship between Opportunity and Predisposition

Another boundary condition posits that there obtains an inverse relation in any criminal act between "predisposition" and "opportunity," such that when there appears to obtain maximal opportunity to act without deterrence or observation, there need be only minimal predisposition to trigger criminal behavior — that is, that opportunity potentiates predisposition in what seems to us greater than a simple linear progression.

Similarly, we posit that the expectation of reward geometrically potentiates other elements, so that expectation of sizable tangible or symbolic reward will elicit criminal behavior when opportunity to act unobserved is perceived to be great and even when internal disposition is slight.

Expectation of Impunity Potentiated by Vicarious Conditioning

As a final boundary condition, we posit that expectation of impunity is vicariously potentiated by what the prospective behaver observes in the psychosocial environment as others who violate the law remain undetected and unpunished. In this sense, the behaver's psychosocial environment is not limited to his/her immediate "surround," but is as wide as the information and entertainment media to which he/she is habituated (*Note* 4).

For the person who repetitively violates the law, escape from meaningful sanction, whether intermittently or recurrently, may represent as powerful a symbolic reward as the tangible rewards associated with criminal activity itself.

Conceptual and Utilitarian Value

We propose the model here formulated as prospectively capable of meeting both the conceptual requirements of psychological science and the practical requirements of the enforcers of law and administrators of justice. To the extent that it is achievable at all, the task of predicting criminal behavior, whether in general or on the part of a specific prospective behaver, will require specification of the component variables which comprise what we have here called "predisposition" and the determination both of their weights in any given behavioral situation and of the dynamics by which weights vary, a task in which the accumulated evidence developed through the methodology of differential psychology will prove valuable.

But, in contrast to those approaches which rest only upon the identification of prospective offenders through the methods of differential psychology, this conceptual model addresses as well the control of criminal behavior through the identification and manipulation both of deterring factors and of the expectation of impunity as variables which impinge upon the construing of the costs, risks, and benefits associated with criminal behavior and, to that extent, may prove more serviceable to the enforcers of law and administrators of justice than models which are exclusively intra- person in their focus. If the model here sketched is conceptually valid, it should apply equally to criminal behaviors that are diametric or at least orthogonal — for example, to both homicide and to larceny. Later chapters test the model against the accumulated research evidence on those who have committed those very different kinds of crimes.

☐ SUMMARY

This chapter has presented a brief overview of the incidence of crime in the U.S., suggested the sources of popular interest in the psychological explanation of criminal behavior, characterized the effort to produce a differential psychology of criminal behavior as thus far incomplete and fragmentary, and proposed, within the framework of personal construct psychology, a tentative formulation which conceptually models the process by which formally criminal behavior is initiated and repeated, or, more technically, acquired and maintained. The model proposes four mutually interactive process elements of varying specific weights in any given situation — i.e., *inclination; opportunity; expectation of reward real or symbolic; expectation of impunity* — as *psychologically necessary antecedents* to the emission of behavior that is *formally criminal* and suggests the boundary conditions which govern interactionion between these elements.

Later chapters examine data derived from the empirical psychological study of very different types of criminal behavior against which the validity of this process model as a general conceptual statement should be tested. First, however, we should examine boundary conditions in the conceptual and empirical domains transversed by the psychology of criminal behavior, to which we turn our attention in the next three chapters — for an overview both of the methods by which such data have been obtained and the limitations necessarily imposed on the empirical study of criminal behavior by the inherent character of law and justice.

☐ NOTES & COMMENTARY

☐ *1. Biological Profiling of Offenders through DNA Typing*

Proponents of criminal personality profiling will argue that, despite its lack of adherence to customary scientific canons and its long-standing love affair with the *post hoc, propter hoc* logical fallacy, the technique is, in combination with other forensic methods, nonetheless an aid in detection. In some sharp contrast to the over-generalization from limited data endemic to criminal personality profiling, the process of *biological profiling* (Lewontin & Hartl, 1991) employs sometimes minute "biological markers" (in some cases, no more than a strand of hair) to develop, through analyses of DNA traces, a portrait of likely suspects who can be described fairly precisely as to gender, race, height, weight, age, and the like, along with specific genotypic anomalies. According to Chakraborty & Kidd (1991), more than 2000 DNA polymorphisms have been defined and catalogued and are usable in forensic applications.

☐ *2. Cost-Benefit and Transactional Cost Analysis Technique*

"Cost-benefit analysis" and "transactional cost analysis" are techniques more typically associated with scientific economics than with psychology, so it is not surprising that specialists in econometrics rather than psychologists have applied such analyses to criminal behavior. Ehrlich's (1975-*a*) analysis of the deterrent effect of the death penalty, published in the *American Economics Review,* is a *tour de force* in the cost-benefit analysis of criminal homicide, which sets forth the proposition that an act of murder depends on the "costs" and "benefits" perceived by the potential murderer in relation to the probability of apprehension, conviction, and execution, concluding somewhat controversially that each execution for criminal homicide deters eight or more murders. Though these techniques were developed in order to study economic and managerial issues, they deserve to be better known among those concerned with the psychosocial procrocesses that precede particular focal behaviors.

☐ *3. Biological Bases of Criminal Behavior*

As a result of the major technological advances in methods of investigation in the neurosciences, substantial research had been reported during the past two decades on what Mednick & Christiansen (1977) have labeled the biological bases of criminal behavior, especially in relation to violent crimes; representative studies relevant to the neurogenic aspects of criminal violence will be outlined in Chapter 6. Pallone (1990, pp. 63-69) has elsewhere outlined the current research evidence on neurogenic facets of sex crimes.

☐ *4. Bandura on Vicarious Conditioning*

In an inventive series of experiments, Albert Bandura and his colleagues at Stanford (Bandura & McDonald, 1963; Bandura, Ross & Ross, 1963; Bandura & Kupers, 1964; Bandura, 1965; Bandura & Rosenthal, 1965; Bandura, Grusec & Menlove, 1967-a, 1967-b; Bandura, 1977, 1985, 1989) demonstrated the efficacy of vicarious conditioning more than a quarter of a century ago. But these investigations did not generally consider what one might term *long-distance vicarious conditioning* — i.e., conditioning that occurs when one observes the reward or punishment not of others in his/her immediate psychosocial environment but rather of others of whom he/she learns through the communications media. Relevant studies (primarily undertaken by social psychologists who investigate the effects of mass media) on the phenomenon we have called long-distance vicarious conditioning in relation to violent crime are reviewed in Chapter 7, along with Bandura's social learning theory.

Chapter 2

Conceptual Constraints in Studying Criminal Behavior

AS A SCIENCE, PSYCHOLOGY SEEKS TO UNDERSTAND, RATHER THAN TO predict or to control, behavior. Such understanding may well arise *post hoc* and bear little relationship to the prediction of future behavior, even in the case of a particular person whose behavior is under study. Although in clinical application professional psychologists may develop means to help their clients control particular behaviors which those clients have *self*-defined as undesirable or inimical to their own welfare, it is not the aim of psychology as a science to control behavior — but merely to *understand in precise and scientific terms*.

Rather in contrast, the enforcers of law and the administrators of justice seek (and appropriately so) to control behavior that is *societally*-defined as undesirable or inimical to the welfare of the polity. Such control could well proceed in the absence of significant scientific understanding of the psychological engines of criminal behavior and indeed so proceeded for many centuries. The mutual, but thus far largely unrealized, hope is that a scientific psychology of criminal behavior can provide both rational understanding and rationally-anchored bases for prediction and control.

❑ DIVERGENT CONCEPTUAL DOMAINS

A variety of boundary conditions thus demarcates the conceptual domain which the psychology of criminal behavior transverses. *Scientific psychology* claims as its domain the study of behavior which is:

❑ *psychogenic in its origin* — that is, that arises in cognition, emotion, or volition or which originates in somatic processes but has discernible sequelae in cognition, emotion, or volition;

❑ *and* that is *recurrent* rather than occasional or indeed observed in a single occurrence only;

❑ *and* whether or not such behavior violates positive law, moral principle, or social convention.

But *criminality* is a legal rather than a psychological (or even moral) construct, and its referent is invariably a single episode or act. Hence, in contrast to the domain demarcated by scientific psychology as the primary object for inquiry and analysis, the domain of criminal behavior includes *only* that behavior that:

❑ specifically *violates positive law,*

❑ *whether or not* such behavior simultaneously violates moral principle or social convention,

❑ *even if* that behavior is observed only in a single occurrence,

❑ *and* whether or not such behavior originates from what others would label psychogenic sources.

Clearly, only a subset of human behavior falls properly into the intersection between these divergent conceptual domains.

The enforcers of law and the administrators of justice are not likely to concern themselves, for example, with the machinations of an acquisitive financier who (by ruthlessly shrewd business tactics which nonetheless violate neither criminal law nor the regulations of the Federal Securities Exchange Commission) engages in a series of corporate takeovers which financially ruin the owners or operators of the companies he has acquired; but the motivations of that financier clearly fall within the domain of psychology and may prove intensely interesting as the object of scientific analysis to the psychologist who specializes in the study either of personality or organizational behavior.

Alternately, psychology takes no particular interest in the noisy reveler who, during an infrequent "night on the town," is enticed into a barroom brawl during which he mauls his opponent. But this behavior even in a single episode is clearly a matter of interest to the criminal justice system. And the aggressive bully who verbally intimidates his classmates in school may be an object of concern to the psychologist, scientific or professional, but only when his behavior becomes physically assaultive does it enter the domain of concern to criminal justice.

❑ **CRIMINALITY AS A LEGAL CONSTRUCT APPLICABLE TO A SINGLE BEHAVIOR**

The examples might be multiplied endlessly, but the key line of demarcation between the domain of scientific psychology and that of the enforcement of law and the administration of justice is to be drawn precisely at the boundaries of a comprehensive, inclusive, and legally precise definition of criminal behavior. Such a definition would hold that

> *criminal behavior is that behavior formally proscribed by the positive or formally promulgated laws of society, to the emission of which formal negative sanctions have been attached.*

To place this definition in the appropriate context, one needs immediately to define *law*, again in the customary and precise way, as *the formal institutionalization of social convention* (Fagothey, 1953, pp. 146, 198-208). As attorneys Marshall and Clark (1962, p. 14) put it:

> A crime is any act or omission prohibited by public law. Crime concerns transgression against the public order rather than against the moral or private order.

Criminality Follows Adjudication

Moreover, the pivotal principle for the system of criminal justice in every civilized nation on the globe — i.e., the presumption of innocence *until* formal adjudication of guilt — urges that no act (not even a palpably illegal act in which the behaver has been observed by a reliable witness and to which the behaver has admitted guilt) be denominated as criminal until it has been so declared by a court or tribunal duly empowered to so declare. Many acts emitted by a person may be morally or socially "wrong" and perhaps deserving of punishment, but *no act is criminal and deserving of societally-prescribed punishment until it has been officially so adjudicated,* including those acts formally proscribed by law for which no legal declaration of criminality is made because the law-breaker is either not apprehended, not prosecuted, or not convicted.

For these reasons, *criminal* is used as an adjective rather than as a noun throughout this volume, to convey the strong conviction that *only behavior is properly labeled criminal.* As a noun, *criminal* suggests a state-of-being inherent in a *person;* as an adjective, it indicates a property which a particular *behavior* acquires *in relation to a particular body of law* in a particular society. The observation that a person occasionally or recurrently behaves criminally tells us less about his state-of-being than about the relationship between his behavior and the *enforcement* of the body of law which regulates the society in which he lives.

The motive in emphasizing this point so sharply is not to hammer the reader with a civil libertarian banner, but rather to emphasize that *the only proper focus for the study of criminal behavior in scientific psychology is that behavior which has been adjudicated as criminal by properly empowered courts,* not that which is alleged, assumed, or even self-confessed to be criminal in the absence of such adjudication.

A psychology of aggression is not necessarily a psychology of criminal behavior; psychology and the other sciences of behavior may study behavior that is aggressive and/or anti-social (as well as that behavior that is passive and/or societally-supportive or societally-advancing) as presumed *antecedents* to behavior that is formally criminal; but they do so within a sector of their domain that does not necessarily overlap that of criminal justice. Nor should it be assumed that what is discovered about behavior that is aggressive and/or anti-social but *not* criminal is simultaneously true either of criminally aggressive behavior or of criminal but non-aggressive behavior.

It may be useful at this juncture to reconsider our observation in Chapter 1 concerning the failure of differential psychology (thus far) to reliably post-dict not only the emission of behavior that is formally criminal, but more pertinently that a specific behaver will be apprehended, prosecuted, and convicted of a particular behavior that is formally criminal. The nub of the matter lies not in the essential character of a particular behavior but rather, in the first instance, in how society has defined its character through its formally promulgated criminal laws — and, in the second instance, in how effectively the processes of detection, apprehension, and adjudication are applied, with the latter clearly properties *extrinsic* to the behavior itself.

Thus, the distinguished sociologist Kai Erikson (1966, p. 6) has observed that "Deviance is not a property *inherent in* any particular kind of behavior; it is a property *conferred upon* that behavior by the people who come into contact with it." Though he phrases his analysis in technical language and grounds it within the context of the psychometric substratum that undergirds differential psychology, distinguished psychologist Jerry Wiggins (1973, pp. 88-89) echoes Erickson's observation:

> [A]ll socially relevant criterion classifications are based on the notion of *statistical* deviance, that is, every member of a criterion group is *by definition* "deviant" in that he is different from individuals who are not members of the criterion group. In this sense, the criterion group of suicide attempters, successful physicians . . . are *all* deviant because members of these groups have been designated as being different from the norm or average. The important point with respect to [statistically] deviant groups is that they are *socially* defined, rather than defined on the basis of

psychological theory . . . the critical condition for being assigned membership in a deviant group is *not* a psychological condition of the individual but the *circumstances* which led to labeling on the part of society. Hence, when we study "murderers," we are studying not a psychologically homogeneous group of individuals but rather a group of individuals who have been *convicted* of the crime of murder by one jury or another . . . groups formed by social definition are highly heterogeneous [on focal psychological characteristics]. Although members of a criterion group are homogeneous with respect to the defining characteristics of the criterion class, *they are most likely heterogeneous with respect to personality characteristics.*

⇨ *Jerry Wiggins: On the Inverted Logic in Personality Research*

Distinguished personality psychologist Jerry Wiggins (1973, pp. 88-90) argues that most personality research proceeds from an inverted logic. Customarily, individuals who have been designated by one means or another as members of a socially-defined criterion group are compared to "non-members" of that group to determine whether or not there are differences in measurable personality characteristics between the groups.

According to Wiggins, findings to emerge from such research (if any) have little actuarial value, for they *begin* with the criterion class (e.g., murderer vs. non-murderer) already known and attempt (almost tautologically) to "postdict" psychological explanations for group membership or non- membership.

As Wiggins has it, a more appropriate formulation would analyze patterns of responses to psychological measures, identify patterns or profiles that differentiate among subjects, and then examine the frequency of occurrence of the criterion behavior within subgroups of subjects clustered according to the similarity of their psychological profiles.

Wiggins (p. 90) terms this model the process of *predicting from taxonomic classes,* or estimating the probability of criterion group membership as a function of responses to psychological (or other types of) evaluation, expressed as *P(Ci/Rj),* or the *probability of criterion group membership given a particular pattern or profile of responses to a psychological assessment.* This is a radically different endeavor from that more frequently encountered in clinical practice, where the effort is typically made to estimate the probability of responses to evaluations as a function of criterion group membership, a formulation Wiggins expresses through the notation *P(Rj/Ci).*

A few steps along, the reasoning of Erikson and Wiggins will yield the conclusion that only a very broad, very general model for criminal behavior that does *not* rely heavily on differentiation in psychological characteristics among behavers could pretend to be comprehensive in character.

Shifting Definitions of Criminality

And — to anticipate briefly merely one facet of the boundaries of the empirical domain to be discussed more fully in the next chapter but which inheres in the very conception of criminality — therein lies a major reason why the psychology of criminal behavior has remained in its infancy. For the same behavior at one point in time and in one place may be of no concern to the law and at another point in time or another place be (or become) clearly and patently crimi-

---

⇨ *Herbert C. Quay: On Psychological Heterogeneity among Juvenile Delinquents*

. . . juvenile delinquency is a legal construct. Thus, the label "delinquent" cannot automatically be considered to carry with it any information about the behavior of the individual beyond [his or her] having committed some act(s) which have violated the law. Put another way, since delinquency is not a psychological construct (such as "extravert," "anxious personality," or "conduct disorder"), the label does *not* imply that those who carry it are behaviorally or psychological homogeneous.

However, the assumption that all delinquents exhibit some common set of psychological characteristics has been the basis for most of the early research . . . If, in fact, delinquent youth are behaviorally and psychologically heterogeneous, the search for single psychological variables that can reliably separate delinquent youth from non-delinquents is not an effective research strategy. Neither will the search for the causes of or cures for delinquency which proceed on this assumption be effective. Searching for *the* cause of or *the* cure for delinquency is much like searching for *the* cause and *the* cure for fever. Clearly, fever is caused by many different infections, and these different infections are susceptible to different interventions.

• *Source:* Herbert C. Quay, Patterns of Delinquent Behavior, *Handbook of Juvenile Delinquency*, (New York: John Wiley, 1987), p. 118.

---

nally illegal: What has changed is not the nature of the behavior, but rather its *relation* to the corpus of positive law.

Consider, as exemplars of one class of behavior the criminality of which varies by time and jurisdiction, such issues as:

❑ Marriage between persons of different races today and in most jurisdictions in the U.S. 50 or 100 years ago.

❑ The consumption of alcohol in most states by a U.S. citizen who is 18 years old *vs.* similar consumption by one who is 21.

❑ Alcohol consumption by a native citizen of any age in the Western nations *vs.* similar consumption by a native citizen of the fundamentalist Moslem nations.

❑ Homosexual liaison between an adult male of 45 and a boy of 14 *vs.* the same liaison with a boy of 16 in those Eastern seaboard states where 15 is the age of consent and where homosexuality is not violative of positive law.

The on-again/off-again oscillation in the "legal drinking age" in the northeastern states over the past dozen years, even before the leveraging effect of Federal intervention, presents a convenient case for illustration. Presume that, as recently as five years ago, a psychological study was completed in one of these states of the dynamics of early initiation into systematic alcohol consumption (as distinguished from alcohol abuse) among subjects aged, say, 18-20 at a time when 18 constituted the legal age. To assume the generalizability of the results of that study to similarly-aged persons who today break the law by similar consumption is unwarranted; and, worse, to include those subjects in a grand pool of subjects who are labeled "criminal" in the aggregate is likely to yield some quite erroneous conclusions about the dynamics of criminal behavior. There is simply no sound reason to believe that the dynamics that explain such early initiation into alcohol use when there is no legal prohibition thereto are identical with similar attraction under conditions of legal proscription.

Similarly, ignorance of the criminal character *imposed* on a behavior by positive law is held almost universally not to exculpate the behaver of the consequences of his or her act before the law, but such ignorance surely represents a variable of importance in psychological analysis. In each case, willingness to transgress or disregard positive law itself represents a variable of interest to the psychologist concerned with criminal behavior as an *additive* factor to the dynamics of similar behavior emitted in the absence of legal proscription.

☐ POSITIVE LAW, SOCIAL CONVENTION, PRISTINE MORALITY

The illustrations just offered suggest the interplay between positive law and the norms prevalent in a given society at any given point in time. As Sir Gerhard O.W. Mueller (1961, p. 204), a leading international scholar of criminal law, has observed, the formally-promulgated positive laws of a society reflect the conventions

---

⇨ When Is Behavior Moral, But Nonetheless Criminal?

That positive law represents primarily the institutionalization of the conventions of society, that those conventions are subject to change, and that those conventions may or may not reflect pristine moral standards can be illustrated by considering the case of Caroline, Arthur, and the Reverend.

☐ Here's the basic paradigm: Arthur meets and falls in love with Caroline, who reciprocates his affection; after a suitable period of courtship, they are wed by the Reverend. Thus far, the behavior of all three *personae dramatis* not only does not seem criminal but indeed quite conventional — and it surely does not violate, but instead seems to support, pristine moral principles.

☐ Now let's vary the paradigm: Add that the time is 1920, the place one of the Southern states, that Arthur is Black but Caroline is Caucasian. Under these conditions, we conclude to a violation both of miscegenation laws and of the local social conventions reflected and institutionalized in those laws.

☐ Vary the paradigm again: Change the time to 1980, but let all other conditions remain the same. Now Arthur, Caroline, and the Reverend have violated social conventions (so long as the locus remains the American South) but not positive laws, since local miscegenation laws have been declared unconstitutional.

☐ In another variation, let the time remain 1920, change the locus to one of the major industrial cities of the Northeast, but let all other conditions remain the same. We now conclude to a violation of social conventions held by a relatively smaller proportion of the local populace than in the American South in 1920 — and probably one less serious than the identical behavior under identical circumstances in the South in 1980. If we permit the locus to remain the industrial Northeast, and change the time once again to 1980 but leave all other conditions unchanged, we shall notice barely a ripple among the guardians of social convention.

In any of the variations sketched, could the behavior of either of the three principals be regarded as the product of a "criminal personality"? In the first instance, the will to violate the miscegenation laws of 1920 might provoke the interest of the psychoclinician as an exemplar of a fierce and unbending determination not to be bound by what Arthur, Caroline, and the Reverend must have construed as an unjust law — but that determination does not necessarily spring from a generalized need to behave contrary to law. In the other variations, the willingness to behave contrary to a particular social convention similarly may or may not spring from a generalized need to behave contrary to social convention.

adopted by that society to regulate and maintain itself: "What ought to be criminal is in itself influenced by the cultural factors from which a nation selects its scale of values and makes its decisions as to how such values should be protected." Because societal values inevitably undergo change, the corpus of positive law eventually reflects such change, predictably after a period of lag-time during which support and acceptance wax or wane. Cases in point:

❑ The decriminalization in many jurisdictions in the U.S. during the past two decades, of sexual behavior of any sort (including that which, in the inimical language of the British tradition, was once universally called "the unspeakable crime against nature," whether heterosexual or homosexual and whether within the confines of legal marriage or not) between persons of any sex or combination of sexes, provided only that all involved are consenting adults.

❑ The reduction from the status of felony punishable by imprisonment to that of misdemeanor punishable by fine, over the past decade and in a smaller number of jurisdictions, of the possession of marijuana in small enough quantity to suggest only an intent for personal "recreational" use.

❑ The current situation in respect of voluntary, but not medically therapeutic, abortion of the human fetus represents another variation, in which a behavior is long held in the laws of the several U.S. states (but not in the laws of many other nations) to be criminal, presumably because that behavior violates the social norms of a broad segment of the society in this nation (though not in others). The nation's highest court declares that such state statutes violate the Federal Constitution, with the decision widely applauded by a large and vocal segment of the society whose values are presumably reflected in *that* decision. But, because abortion appears still to offend the values of another large and vocal segment of the society, efforts are made to alter the Constitution and/or to redraft legislation so as to permit the re-institution of prohibitory laws at state or Federal levels.

Some laws change in response to changes in social convention, but others remain in force even after the corresponding social conventions change.

In this situation, a particular behavior defined by law as criminal may no longer be offensive to the majority of members of the society and hence no longer violative of social norms; the behavior officially remains illegal and liable to criminal prosecution, but the law is typically simply not enforced — a process which itself entails a cost to the society in what it says about the obligations of citizens and the enforcers of the law alike.

⇨ *Cultural Relativity and the Penalty for Drug Possession: Marijuana and Capital Punishment*

The role of cultural relativity in the formal declaration of a given behavior as criminal is perhaps nowhere better illustrated than in the network of legislation that defines some substances as "controlled and dangerous" (e.g., marijuana) but does little to regulate the distribution and use of other substances even with similar biochemical properties (e.g., beverage alcohol). Certainly, there are many distinguished scientists who would prefer, on the basis of deleterious biochemistry alone, to see beverage alcohol declared a controlled and dangerous substance and to see marijuana become as available as beverage alcohol is today (Hofmann & Hofman, 1975, pp. 203-212, 311-315; Royal College of Psychiatrists, 1987, pp. 122- 142, 210).

Moreover, the lack of international correspondence in laws regulating the distribution and use of mood-altering substances itself illustrates the major role played by cultural relativity. Thus, what is illegal in one nation may be quite outside the interest of the law in another; what may be a relatively minor offense in one nation may be a major offense in another or no offense at all in a third.

A journalistic account of the trial of an American professor at a university in Malaysia serves as an apt illustration (Kaplan, McKillop & Cohn. 1990, p. 42):

❑ Eleven months ago, Kerry Lane Wiley, a 37-year-old . . . Californian, went to Malaysia . . . to teach computer science at a local university. Today he faces death at the end of a rope. Wiley spent last week in a Kuala Lumpur courtroom on trial for his life. The crime: possession of more than a pound of marijuana. Malaysia hangs plenty of Malaysians, but Wiley stands to become the first American ever put to death abroad for a drug offense — in this case, one that would barely merit jail time under U.S. law. Unlike other countries with harsh drug laws, Malaysia makes no exception for foreigners. Since 1975, when . . . death sentences were introduced, 30 foreigners have been put to death, as well as 82 Malaysians, despite pleas from prime ministers and, in one celebrated case, the queen of England.

Because the Wiley trial coincided with a major expansion of the Federal "war against drugs," little assistance was in prospect from diplomatic quarters:

❑ The Bush administration is in a particularly awkward position: how does the United States help one of its own without seeming to contradict a new offensive against drugs at home? American diplomats are especially concerned about jeopardizing growing efforts at cooperation between Drug Enforcement Administration agents and their Asian counterparts in halting the drug trade in the Golden Triangle — Burma, Laos, and Thailand — which grows most of the world's opium.

Contextually, it might be observed that Malaysia is a constitutional monarchy with considerable ethnic diversity in its southeast Asian population (Malay *vs.* Chinese) that is largely Moslem or Hindu in terms of religion. Its economy depends primarily on the exporting of tin and rubber; Malaysia accounts for 35% of the world's output in each. The nation shares a long border with Thailand, doubtless a factor in the adoption and implementation of its harsh laws on the possession of drugs. Unlike Thailand, which in 1987 received some $68 million in aid from the U.S., Malaysia is no longer a recipient of such American largesse; instead, in 1987, it *returned* to the U.S. Treasury some $11 million in aid funds previously conveyed in the form of loans.

Alternately, some behaviors which are offensive to a majority of members of a society and hence violative of newly emerging or newly identified social values may not — or perhaps not *yet* — be legally defined as criminal. The disparity in legal treatment between physical abuse of spouse or child, which universally constitutes legally criminal behavior, and the psychological abuse of the same victims — which constitutes in most jurisdictions adequate cause for the dissolution of the relationship but not for criminal prosecution — illustrates the latter case.

Behavior That Is "Wrong in Itself"

But there are some behaviors — usually those that are threatening to life or that deprive another of his or her property without justification — which seem to offend what ethicists call pristine moral principle not colored by the tinctured norms of specific societies and which *may or may not* violate the positive laws of a given society. Some (and arguably most) of these behaviors may be universally recognized as inherently "wrong" by pristine moral standards *and* by positive law, but others may not be incorporated into the formal proscriptions of positive law.

Even though the tradition of British common law that informs the system of justice in most English-speaking nations putatively recognizes as legally sanctionable violation of pristine moral principle even in the absence of specific positive law (in contrast to those nations which follow the traditions of Napoleonic positive law, in which only those behaviors formally proscribed by law are sanctionable), in practice the "unwritten code" of British common law (or, in some formulations and particularly among those who follow the metaphysics of Aristotle and Aquinas, the "natural law") is rarely cited as grounds for criminal prosecution.

Hence, some behaviors (as in our example of the psychological abuse of spouse or child) may be very nearly universally regarded as wrong by pristine moral standards embedded in ethical codes of varying origin — but not proscribed by the standards of positive law.

Whatever the origin or specific content of our personal set of moral standards, few of us would hesitate to identify as inherently wrong such behaviors as murder, rape, or theft committed without adequate and compelling justification (most of us would exempt the "theft" of an auto to be used to transport an injured party to a source of emergency medical treatment), and we would likely consider such behavior as gravely wrong even in the absence of proscriptive law. As Marshall and Clark (1962, p. 17) put it, these behaviors seem to us "*mala in se* or *wrong in themselves*."

Behavior That Is Merely Proscribed

But few of us would regard it as gravely wrong to operate a high performance automobile at 70 miles per hour on a sparsely traveled, limited-access freeway with adequate natural light, even though that behavior is specifically (currently and perhaps temporarily) proscribed throughout the U.S. Behaviors of the latter sort are "*mala prohibita,* or wrong merely because they [are] prohibited and punished by statute" (Marshall and Clark, 1962, p. 17). We have already met behaviors which are *mala prohibita* but not *mala in se* in our examples of miscegenation and alcohol consumption.

This class of legally criminal but morally neutral behavior is also well illustrated by the *status offenses*, a term that refers to behavior that is licit in some circumstances but defined in other circumstances as criminal in consequence of the "status" of one or another of the participants therein (Newman, 1975), as in the example of homosexual liaison between adult and adolescent males already cited. Curfews imposed on young people or the *sale* of beverage alcohol to underage consumers represent further examples.

Between the extremes illustrated by behaviors that are (almost) universally regarded as *mala in se* under terms of any code of pristine moral standards and those that are legally *mala prohibita* but nearly universally regarded as essentially morally neutral, there are many behaviors that counter the conventions of some segments of the society and, therefore, the positive law in some jurisdictions: the sale or purchase of sexual intercourse, in any U.S. state but Nevada; homosexuality in Virginia, but not in the northeast; topless dancing, but not the sale of magazines celebrated for their centerfolds, in many jurisdictions.

One could conceive a special area of inquiry within scientific psychology which would take as its focus the study only of those behaviors which are universally held to be *mala in se* (that is, the psychology of unquestioned immorality) — but such is *not* the psychology of criminal behavior if it is to reflect faithfully the domain demarcated by the legislative definition and judicial determination of criminality.

☐ FIXING CULPABILITY FOR CRIMINAL BEHAVIOR

Once a particular behavior emitted by a particular behaver under finite circumstances has been identified as criminal, the question of culpability arises; in turn, the manner in which this issue is resolved dictates the sanction to be applied. Granted that a behavior has been

⇨ *Antecedents to the M'Naghten Principles*

In his remarkable treatise *Crime and Insanity in England: The Historical Perspective,* Oxford criminologist Nigel Walker (1968) traces the remote antecedents for the principles announced at M'Naghten's trial to Saxon jurisprudence, well before the Norman conquest — and, indeed, opines that even earlier sources may be found in the laws of Rome applied during the Roman occupation of Britain in the first century. Certain provisions of the Roman code, it is reasonable to believe, may be been preserved orally and were thus incorporated into the first written laws for what was to become modern Britain. It seems clear that the antecedents for the M'Naghten principles have long, though perhaps imprecisely articulated, roots that extend well over a millennium prior to that landmark trial.

According to Walker (pp. 16-20), the "Penitentials" of Egbert, the eighth-century Saxon archbishop of York, contained a provision that "If a man fall out of his senses or wits, and it come to pass that he kill someone," such an unfortunate would be personally exculpated from the penalty, which then stood at a year's fasting for accidental homicide and five years' fasting for a killing done "in anger and with premeditation." In such cases, although the person who was in effect found not guilty by reason of insanity was to be excused from the normal penalty, the "Penitentials" insisted that the penalty be paid by someone: "let his kinsmen pay." Similarly, the laws of the Saxon king Ethelred prescribed leniency (but not exculpation) "if anyone does anything unintentionally" or "when a man is an involuntary agent . . . because he acted as he did from compulsion."

Walker sees the distinction between leniency and exculpation as quite congruent with Roman law and rather at variance with later formulations (pp. 27, 247):

❑ one of the justifications which Roman law offered for treating the insane offender with leniency [was] that his madness was punishment enough (*satis furore ipso punitur*) . . . in the minds of Roman jurists, *excusing the madman because he was punished enough* by his madness took the form of leniency. . . . The justification on which the codes of Western Europe and America have based their reasoning is that *the madman is not to blame* for the harm he does . . . it is a fundamental principle of our criminal law that one should not be liable to its penal measures unless one has, without sufficient cause, [voluntarily] infringed one of its prohibitions.

Whether its sources lay in the Roman occupation or in the Christian tradition of Egbert or in some commingling, by the time Henri de Bracton compiled a compendium of positive law and long- standing custom to serve as a veritable lexicon in the thirteenth century, he was able to formulate a version of *mens rea* (i.e., the doctrine of "evil intent") that has a remarkably contemporary ring: "In misdeeds, we look to the will [i.e., intent], and not the outcome . . . for a crime is not committed unless the will to harm be present: *Quia crimen non contrahitur nisi voluntas nocendi intercedat" (Ibid.,* pp. 26, 33).

Moreover, Walker (p. 67) cites some 222 trials at one British court alone — albeit, London's central criminal court (the celebrated "Old Bailey") — in the century preceding M'Naghten at which either the matter of the accused's mental state at the time of the criminal act *or* his or her mental fitness to stand trial was raised. According to Walker, the pleading of incompetence to stand trial prevailed in 83% of the 12 cases in which it was raised, while what amounts to an insanity defense prevailed in 45% of the 210 cases in which it was raised. For the United Kingdom as a whole, there were perhaps four times as many insanity defenses during that period (p. 72). Thus, Walker contends (p. 74), "Successful defences of insanity had been a regular feature of Old Bailey trials" well before the M'Naghten case, including even the empaneling of physicians to offer what we would today call "expert witness" testimony as to the defendant's state of mind at the time of his or her allegedly criminal behavior.

found to be criminally violative of positive law, what blame is to be attributed to the behaver? What punishment — or other sanction, such as fine and restitution — should ensue?

Ethicists have long held that culpability hinges primarily on the *voluntariness* of an act (Fagothey, 1953, pp. 82-100, 301- 308): Was the prohibited act intentional — that is, emitted in what most reasonable people, such as those who comprise a jury, would regard as a willful or deliberate attempt to injure another (or oneself) or deprive another of property? Or, in another variation, was the "wrong" or "evil" result of an otherwise neutral act foreseen, but the act nonetheless performed willfully?

To fix culpability legally rather than ethically or morally, it is necessary that the behaver also had prior knowledge, or could reasonably be expected to have prior knowledge, that his or her behavior was specifically *proscribed* by law, or (in the case of criminal behavior resulting from failure to perform one's duty) *required* by law.

The M'Naghten Rule and its Descendants

The *M'Naghten Rule* has long been precedental in determining criminal culpability in nations that follow British common law. Promulgated in the decision of an English court in 1843 (and doubtless influenced by the views of Dr. Pritchard) in a case in which a cabinet officer was murdered by a disappointed office seeker who declared that he had been commanded by God to kill the Prime Minister, the M'Naghten Rule holds that legal culpability attaches to an otherwise criminal act only when the behaver knows in advance that the contemplated behavior counters moral principle and/or positive law *and* when he or she is *free to choose* to behave or not to behave (Reid, 1976, pp. 169-170). Thus, under M'Naghten, a person who is incapable of distinguishing "wrong" from "right" is not to be held legally culpable (West & Walk, 1977; Schopp, 1991, pp. 27-70).

On this side of the Atlantic, two cases in the last quarter of the last century — *Parsons v. the State of Alabama,* adjudicated in 1887, and *Davis v. United States,* adjudicated a decade later — added the "irresistible impulse" test, which exculpates a person who is incapable of resisting an impulse propelling him or her to a wrong or legally criminal act (Stone, 1976, p. 229). In 1954, the U.S. District Court for the District of Columbia specifically included prior mental illness in the catalog of acceptable justifications for a claim of non-culpability under M'Naghten by holding that "an accused is not criminally responsible if his unlawful act was the product of mental disease" (Mears & Gatchel, 1979, p. 330). Following the name of the defendant (Durham) and the presiding justice (Bazelon) in the case, the resultant principle is called the *Durham Test* or the *Bazelon Rule*.

Over the course of nearly a century and a half, a variety of other justifications have been accepted by the courts under M'Naghten to explain either the incapacity to distinguish right from wrong or the incapacity to resist the impulse to behave criminally, including intellectual deficiency and even habitual criminal behavior itself (Yochelson & Samenow, 1977, pp. 19-20; Rogers, 1986, pp. 39-90).

A COMPREHENSIVE MODEL DEFINITION FROM THE AMERICAN LAW INSTITUTE

The American Law Institute (ALI) exerts considerable influence on the operation of the civil and criminal law through the drafting of "model legislation," which the appropriate legislative bodies (the Federal Congress, state legislatures, or, in some cases, even county or municipal legislatures) may adopt in whole, in part, or not at all. In its model penal code, the American Law Institute proposed a rather comprehensive statement for the insanity defense, that, however, effectively eliminates habitual criminality as a basis (Stone, 1976, p. 230):

> A person is not responsible for criminal conduct if at the time of such conduct as a result of mental disease or defect he lacks substantial capacity either to appreciate the criminality of his conduct or to conform his conduct to the requirement of law. [But] the terms "mental disease or defect" do not include an abnormality manifested only by repeated criminal or otherwise anti-social conduct.

THE AMERICAN BAR ASSOCIATION: SEVERITY OF DEFICIT

In its model statement, the American Bar Association (1989), through its Commission on Criminal Justice Mental Health Standards, added important limitations concerning the *severity* of the disorder said to underlie an insanity defense (or a pleading of incompetence to stand trial) that tend to function as operational guidelines (p. 330):

> When used as a legal term . . . *mental disease or defect* refers to: (i) impairments of mind, whether enduring or transitory; or, (ii) mental retardation, either of which substantially affected the mental or emotional processes of the defendant at the time of the alleged offense.

AGGRAVATING AND MITIGATING FACTORS

The ALI formulation, or a close variant, has by now been legislatively adopted in most states, both as the legal definition of insanity and as part of a catalog of "mitigating factors," the presence of which may not exculpate an alleged offender but influences the severity of the sanction imposed upon conviction. Other mitigating factors may include such variables as the influence of mood-altering drugs or alcohol, the prior relationship between the victim and the alleged offender, whether the victim in some way invited or colluded in his/her own victimization, etc. A litany of mitigating factors may be offset by "aggravating factors," such as the degree of demonstrable pre-meditation, whether the alleged criminal act was performed during the commission of another criminal act, etc.

⇨ *Recognizing the Permanent Effects of Alcohol Abuse:*
From Hale to the ABA

The position adopted by the American Bar Association's Commission on Criminal Justice Mental Health Standards in 1989 in excluding those "temporary" periods of insanity which have been induced by the ingestion of alcohol and/or other mind-altering substances seems remarkably similar to the position taken by Sir Matthew Hale in his *History of the Pleas of the Crown,* which Nigel Walker dates to approximately 1676.

According to Walker (1968, p. 39), Hale, who had been Lord High Chief Justice of England, "is insistent that mere drunkenness cannot excuse." But Hale provides that "if a man's toxic state were 'due to the unskilfulness of his physician or the contrivance of his enemies, his phrenzy' is to be judged like any other."

More important is the concession that, "if heavy drinking had caused 'an habitual or fixed phrenzy,' [the accused] should be treated by the law as if it were involuntarily contracted — a principle that was to save several Victorian alcoholics from the gallows."

That view of things is not only more forgiving than the American Psychiatric Association formulation but indeed in greater congruence with the state of neuropsychiatric knowledge today.

Even if we grant that "voluntary misbehavior" may have been responsible for the spiral that led to a permanent, alcohol- induced, *organically-based* mental disorder like Korsakov's psychosis, once the brain has been damaged by repeated onslaughts of alcohol, there is very little misbehavior that can properly be labeled as voluntary.

We discuss the linkages between substance abuse and violent crime in Chapter 7.

Predictably, expert witnesses for the defense tend to find evidence of insanity or of mitigating factors, while expert witnesses for the prosecution typically fail to find such evidence, so that closely contested trials sometimes resemble three-ring circuses abounding with conflicting testimony (Saks, 1990). Such was the case in the trial of John Hinckley after his attempt to assassinate Ronald Reagan, and the press coverage of this aspect of the Hinckley trial served to underscore emphatically deep divisions in the mental health community (Stone, 1984).

THE AMERICAN PSYCHIATRIC ASSOCIATION AND VOLUNTARY INTOXICATION

Virtually as a direct result of the Hinckley trial, or at least of the press reports thereof, the American Psychiatric Association (1984, p. 17) issued a statement on the insanity defense which in essence endorsed the American Law Institute definition but added important contingencies concerning aberrational mental states induced by voluntarily self-administered mood-altering substances, viz., that

> the terms mental disease or mental retardation include only those severely abnormal mental conditions that grossly and demonstrably impair a person's perception or understanding of reality and that are *not* attributable primarily to the voluntary ingestion of alcohol or other psychoactive substances.

For its part, the American Bar Association's Commission on Criminal Justice Mental Health Standards (1989, pp. 346-347) proved rather more lenient. While the ABA's argument similarly pivots on the "voluntariness" of intoxication, so that the drug or alcohol user who voluntarily becomes intoxicated by his or her own actions assumes the risks of behaving criminally consequent to such intoxication, the Commission recognizes a number of situations that fall "on the moral border," such as those cases in which

> drug use precipitates psychotic deterioration in a predisposed person, alcohol use results in organic brain pathology, or a person has an excessive (or "pathological") reaction to a small amount of alcohol insufficient to induce intoxication in most people.

Whatever the specific terms of the relevant legislation, in virtually all cases the M'Naghten Rule is pivotal. Like criminality, however, *insanity* is fundamentally a legal rather than a psychological or psychiatric construct; its meaning, even in the world of criminal law and adjudication, is highly variable.

⇨ *The Hadfield Case and Its Consequences: Confinement of the NGRI Acquittee, Introduction of Expert Neuropsychiatry*

Of those cases tried in the Old Bailey in the century before M'Naghten, perhaps the most significant for several reasons is the Hadfield trial of 1800 (Walker, 1968, pp. 73-83).

In May of that year, Hadfield fired a pistol at George III as the king entered the Royal Box at the Drury Lane Theatre. Though the shot went a foot wide of its mark and landed harmlessly in the orchestra pit, the event amounted to attempted homicide; but an attempt to kill the king itself constitutes treason.

For the latter reason, Hadfield was permitted greater latitude in the preparation and presentation of a defense than was the custom in ordinary criminal matters. A jurist named Erskine, whom Walker (p. 75) describes as "at the peak of his career" and as having "mastered the literature of his subject," appeared for the defense. To examine the defendant, Erskine engaged "Sir Alexander Crichton, whose recently published *Inquiry into the Nature and Origin of Mental Derangement* included discussions of insane motives for murder" and who later become personal physician to Czar Alexander. I and, in that position, organized the first department of health for Imperial Russia.

According to Walker, those physicians who had testified in earlier trials had typically known the defendant for some time, either as patient or as a member of the community whose "peculiarities" had become common knowledge. But Crichton did not meet or examine Hadfield until well after the attempt on the king's life, so that his activity perhaps constitutes the precursor for the role and function of today's "expert witness" in mental health.

Moreover — and, as a consequence of the knowledge explosion in the neurosciences of the past three decades, this point is perhaps more significant today than it was when Walker composed his treatise — the pivot for Hadfield's madness was not primarily psychological, but rather *neuro*psychological: Hadfield "had obvious and disfiguring wounds in the head, acquired in action against the French six years before. One of these had penetrated the skull, so that Erskine was able to invite the jury to inspect the membrane of the brain itself . . . The regimental surgeon [testified] how he had been compelled to have Hadfield tied to a bed for a fortnight . . . incoherent, with 'manifest symptoms of derangement.' Crichton's evidence was to the effect that the prisoner's madness was probably the result of his wounds" (pp. 76-77).

Apparently, both the jury and the Lord High Justices were persuaded by Crichton's testimony — which had rather clearly designated a neurological basis for Hadfield's mental condition, and thus very likely stands as the originating point for forensic neuropsychiatry. But Hadfield had made an attempt at the life of the monarch, an act that might have gained him popularity among the American colonists who had fought a revolution against the same monarch; and, from Crichton's testimony, it was clear that Hadfield might, at any moment and without warning, emit what we shall describe in Chapters 6 and 10 as impulsive neurogenic violence.

Yet the state of the law at that time contained no provision for the confinement even of dangerous persons who had been found not culpable on mental grounds. Very likely because the object of Hadfield's attack had been the monarch rather than a lesser personage, "a hastily drafted Bill was . . . passed by Parliament in order to provide a clear-cut and foolproof procedure for such cases . . . Whether the Act of 1800 'for the safe custody of insane persons charged with offences' would have been drafted and passed with such urgency if Hadfield's target had not been a royal one . . . is doubtful" (Walker, *op. cit.,* p. 78).

The Act of 1800 made it plain that "the only possible verdict in cases in which the jury was satisfied that the accused was insane at the time of his crime was to be the special verdict . . . that the acquittal was on the ground of insanity; the alternative of plain acquittal was no longer open to them" (*Idem*). Upon such acquittal, the defendant was "to be kept in strict custody, until His Majesty's pleasure be known." In addition, the Act provided the same disposition for persons found not competent to stand trial *and* to any person who might be brought before two Justices "under circumstances that denote a derangement of mind and a purpose of committing an indictable offence." The latter provision encompasses rather sweeping powers for preventive detention. Walker observes that, under the Act of 1800, expert witness testimony concerning the accused's mental status was *not* required. Moreover, the Act apparently applied only when the actual or prospective offense carried the death penalty — but at a time when "the penalty for all felonies was capital" (*Ibid.,* p. 80). Once the precedent for the involuntary confinement of the mentally deranged felon was established, of course, there was but a short step to legislative provision for what we would today call civil commitment of mentally disordered persons who were not dangerous but simply incompetent to care for their own affairs.

The historically-minded may also wish to consult Pankratz's (1984) account of 19th century views on criminal insanity in the United States, derived from a content analysis of the *American Journal of Insanity,* the official publication of the "alienists" who studied such phenomena from the 1860s to the 1880s. In a related context, Shapiro (1984, pp. 28-50) has provided a succinct history of the development of the construct of criminal responsibility.

Psychopathic Deviation and Its Referents

The closest analogue one finds to *insanity* as a legal construct in the lexicon of psychology and psychiatry is the term *psychopathic deviation*, included in the first edition of the American Psychiatric Association's (1954) *Diagnostic and Statistical Manual of Mental Disorders* as a mental illness clearly reminiscent of Pritchard's formulation, but excluded from the roster of mental illnesses in the second (1968) and later (1980, 1987) revisions. But the analogue largely begged the question by providing essentially only a circular definition, in which insanity was defined by psychopathic deviation and psychopathic deviation by insanity. The current edition's successor term, *anti-social personality disorder,* appropriately avoids notions like the incapacity to form moral judgments in favor of a focus on patterns of socially responsible and irresponsible behavior — that is to say, "habitual criminality" itself is a principal criterion for such a diagnosis.

As we implied in Chapter 1, the only discernible empirical referent in these varying terms is likely *a generalized tendency to underestimate the costs and risks,* both for the behaver and for others affected by his/her behavior, *attached to behaving in formally proscribed ways,* implying an element of reckless disregard for the consequences of behavior — for which the construction "psychopathic deviation" may be as useful a piece of intellectual shorthand as any other.

Retrospective Diagnoses

In clinical practice, psychologists and psychiatrists seek to assess the general mental health of a client as reflected in his or her *recurrent* behavior and in the patterns of behavior which are typical of him or her; single episodes, especially when atypical, are of little interest. But the courts are concerned, under whatever specific formulation of the insanity defense or in the search for explanatory or mitigating circumstances, *only* with a person's state of mind *with respect to a particular proscribed behavior*, whether observed in a single episode or recurrently.

When professional psychodiagnostic evaluation is requested either in the prosecution or defense of criminal behavior, it is customarily the case that the examination of the accused occurs long after the emission of the particular behavior the criminal culpability and sanctionability for which are at issue, so that professional judgment can be only retrospective and thus speculative at best [*Note* 1].

"Guilty, but Mentally Ill"

From the perspective of psychology and psychiatry, a plea of "guilty, but not fully culpable" or one of "guilty with diminished responsibility" might be more precise than an insanity plea under whatever specific formulation (Walker, 1968, pp. 138-164; Fersch, 1980, pp. 94-132; Rogers, 1986, pp. 16-20).

Distinguished Oxford criminologist Nigel Walker (1968, p. 138) has traced what the British term the "diminished responsibility"

⇨ *Gerhard O.W. Mueller on Psychological Normality vs.*
Criminal Responsibility

In law, we have to make the far-reaching decision whether or not, at some time in the past, when the defendant has committed what looks like a criminal act, he should and could have made a decision not to violate the law. We are interested in the defendant only insofar as a particular act or a particular sphere of human activity is concerned. When we try a defendant for larceny, it is of no interest to us that he has also raped. The question of rape will be taken up at the next trial. At stake, therefore, is only the defendant's "responsibility" insofar as his larcenous conduct is concerned. Moreover, we are not interested in whether the defendant would be responsible for larceny today, or would have been ten years ago, but only whether the defendant was responsible for larceny at the given time during which he is said to have committed the act charged.

An otherwise completely normal taxpayer and voter may be completely irresponsible to any normal communal stimuli in another sphere of human activity, i.e., an otherwise normal and responsive citizen may be a compulsive doorknob-wiper, a compulsive hand-washer, or, perhaps, a compulsive thief of baby buggy rubber mattresses.

A fully psychotic, cannibalistic killer who slaughters and eats babies in a state completely withdrawn from reality, a state in which the legal stimulus against homicide means nothing to him, may be completely reality-grounded in driving his automobile or in doing other chores of daily life. He may meticulously stop at every stop sign and operate his automobile as a fully responsive and responsible traffic participant. He may meticulously pay his electric bills on time. An income tax defrauder may prove to be a perfectly responsive and responsible businessman who manipulates his books for the purpose of defrauding the government in full awareness of the unlawfulness of his activities. Yet the same businessman may be a paedophiliac to whom the stimulus of the law means nothing in his relation to children. No threat of punishment, no reasoning can deprive him of his morbid urge to abuse children. He is as relatively free as you and I when it comes to filling out his income tax returns. But he is completely unfree in his sexual behavior toward children.

• *Source:* Gerhard O.W. Mueller, The public law of wrongs — its concepts in the world of reality. *Journal of Public Law*, 1961, 10, 203-244.

⇨ *Criminal Sexual Psychopath Legislation: Both Guilty and*
Mentally Ill

In the usual case, the issue of the mental health or illness of a defendant to charges of felony crime arises *if and only if* the defendant *elects* on his or her own initiative to plead *not guilty by reason of insanity.* Should the status of the defendant's mental illness rise to a level that meets the legislatively-defined criteria for an insanity defense in the relevant jurisdiction, a judicial finding reflecting that plea is entered, so that the defendant is formally declared *not* guilty of the felonious act, with the customary result that he or she is confined to a public mental hospital (often, a hospital "for the criminally insane") until he or she has been declared no longer psychologically disordered, usually both by the mental health authorities responsible for treatment and by the court which declared the defendant "not guilty by reason of insanity." The usual case, therefore, involves a neatly compartmentalized *disjunction* between mental illness (or, at the least, between mental illness serious enough to rise to the level of an insanity defense) and criminal guilt.

But, in more than half the states of the union, these neat compartments collapse under the weight of legislation governing sex offenders that implicitly creates a third, and *conjunctive,* category — that is, *both* guilty *and* mentally ill.

In these states, the criminal codes distinguish between two categories of sex offenders: (1) those who commit sex offenses incidentally to other felony offenses (e.g., the burglar who rapes) or who are first- time sex offenders *and* (2) those who are identified as "repetitive, habitual, or compulsive" sex offenders. The relevant legislation typically refers to the former as *felony sex offenders* and the latter as *criminal sexual psychopaths.*

As legal scholar Josephine Bulkley (1981, p. 92) put it in an American Bar Association review on the issue:

❑ Sexual psychopath statutes generally define such offenders as possessing a mental condition or defect which falls short of insanity. *Such persons are considered socially maladjusted or mentally disabled, but not legally insane* or mentally ill so as to render them irresponsible for the criminal acts. Underlying these laws is the premise that the offender is unable to control his sexual acts because of this particular mental defect . . . A typical definition of a sexual psychopath [extracted from the laws of the District of Columbia] is "a person, not insane, who by a course of repeated misconduct in sexual matters has evidenced such lack of power to control his sexual impulses as to be dangerous to other persons."

The distinction between *sexual psychopathy* and *insanity* is capital in the legal definition in several dimensions, for it creates a sort of Twilight Zone at the intersection of the law and the mental health sciences. In the first instance, the legislation raises *a priori* — and *not* on the motion of the defendant — the issue of his or her mental health.

The relevant laws customarily *require* examination of the accused by mental health clinicians responsible to the court prior to trial or prior to sentencing, while the laws governing the insanity defense render submission to such examination entirely volitional. Usually, there is no provision for *waiver* of examination, with the implication that the offender thereby voluntarily opts for what is virtually uniformly presumed to be the "harsher" penalty of sentencing as a felony sex offender.

A variety of issues related to Constitutional guarantees to privacy and against self-incrimination might seem thereby to be engaged. Nonetheless, the U.S. Supreme Court has upheld, in its *Allen v. Illinois* decision of 1986, the right of the state to require defendants to submit to such examination, ruling that legislatively-mandated (or, at minimum, legislatively-approbated) procedures for determining whether a particular offender should be classified as a "sexually dangerous person" in need of treatment were essentially *civil* rather than criminal in nature, holding therefore that plaintiff in the case "was not entitled to self- incrimination warnings prior to a court ordered psychiatric examination pursuant to the Illinois statute" (Wettstein, 1986, p. 330). Since such proceedings for determining classification as a sexual psychopath arise *only* within the context of adjudication of *criminal* charges, however, as distinguished forensic psychiatrist Paul Appelbaum (1987) has argued, one is hard pressed to understand the reasoning of the Court.

In the second and conceptually more salient instance, the legislation implicitly sorts those who commit sex offenses into *three* groups:

❑ Those who are unable to control their behavior *only* in the sexual sphere and thus are "properly" classified as sexual psychopaths — that is, as *both* guilty *and* mentally ill.

❑ Those who are unable to control their behavior in *any* sphere and thus meet the relevant legal criteria for insanity, with the result that they are exculpated from any penalty for criminal behavior — that is, those who are adjudicated as *mentally ill but not guilty*.

❑ Those who are neither so mentally disordered as to be classified as legally insane nor as sexually psychopathic but are "merely" guilty of felony crimes which are sexual in nature and thus are adjudicated as *guilty but not mentally ill*.

A succinct history of what he calls "special sex legislation" not only in the various states of the Union but throughout the "first world" is provided by the late Alfred Vuocolo (1968) in his landmark volume *The Repetitive Sex Offender*. Pallone's (1990-b) *Rehabilitating Criminal Sexual Psychopaths: Legislative Mandates, Clinical Quandaries* traces the pathways for the current legislation, including calls for its repeal by the Group for the Advancement of Psychiatry and the American Bar Association's Commission on Criminal Justice Mental Health Standards, the antecedents and consequences of repeal in California and in Canada, and the research evidence on the effectiveness of clinical treatment of sex offenders.

pleading to a trial in Scotland in 1554, in which the defendant was said to be, for legal purposes, comparable to "ane infant, pupill or beist . . . [wherefore] he could nocht contract, trespass or do any sic deid." A plea of "Guilty, but with diminished responsibility" (roughly equivalent to the "Guilty, but mentally ill" formulation in the U.S.) was formally recognized in Britain by means of the Trial of Lunatics Act adopted in 1883. Clearly, the concept is not a newcomer.

Nonetheless, the American Psychiatric Association's statement (1984) dismissed in strong terms (as fraught with "moral, legal, and psychiatric problems" that the Association neither cataloged nor defined) the proposal to introduce a "guilty but mentally ill" defense, advocated by its supporters as a reasonable and professionally

---

⇨ *California's Legislative Reforms Reduce the Frequency with Which an Insanity Defense Is Invoked*

In 1982, the California legislature undertook substantial revisions in its formulation of the terms of an insanity defense, in the process eliminating a defense of *diminished capacity* altogether. According to McGreevy, Steadman & Callahan (1991, p. 745), the action of the legislature was "generally seen as an attempt to make the insanity defense more restrictive."

In a major research undertaking, McGreevy, Steadman & Callahan (1991) investigated similarities and differences both in the *rate* at which the insanity defense was invoked before and after legislative reform *and* in the *characteristics of defendants* who invoked that defense before and after legislative reform. Focusing on six populous California counties over a six-year period (three prior to reform, three subsequent to reform), the investigators found that:

❑ The *rate* at which the insanity plea was *invoked* (p. 746) *declined* by ten-fold, from a high point of 10 per 1,000 indictments (i.e., 0.01%) — for criminal activity of all sorts, not only crimes of violence or crimes against persons — in 1981, the last year before reform, to only 1 per 1,000 in 1985 (i.e., 0.001%)

❑ The rate at which the insanity plea *prevailed* hovered at or near 40% for most of the years under study — until it declined dramatically in 1985 to approximately 20% (pp. 746-747).

❑ The median length of psychiatric hospitalization for NGRI acquittees *after* reform was found to be 1404 days (nearly 47 months), compared with a median length of hospitalization of 1326 days (approximately 44 months) prior to legislative reform (p. 747).

❑ However, the investigators reported few differences between those who had invoked the NGRI defense before and after legislative reform in such characteristics as ethnicity, formal diagnosis, formal education, gender, marital status, previous history of psychiatric hospitalization, or target criminal offense.

⇨ *Successful Insanity Plea: Antecedents, Consequences*

In a study of factors associated with a successful insanity plea in one county in New York during a 10-year period, Steadman, Keitner, Braff & Arvanites (1983) reported that 83% of all such pleas were successful; but they discerned no significant relationships between acquittal and demographic factors, criminal history, severity of the current alleged offense, or history of psychiatric hospitalization. A similar study by Rogers, Cavanaugh, Seman & Harris (1984) found *convergence between clinical opinion and judicial determination* in 89% of the 112 cases they studied; curiously, convergence was observed at 100% in the case of female defendants. In an inventive study of the degree of congruence in clinical opinions based either on the M'Naghten or the American Law Institute standards for the insanity defense, Silver & Spodak (1983) retrospectively analyzed cases seen in one forensic psychiatric hospital, finding convergent conclusions in 95% of the cases.

In an intriguing follow-up study of all persons found not guilty by reason of insanity in New York state between 1971-76 and subsequently placed in state psychiatric institutions, Pasewark, Pantile & Steadman (1979) reported that, in comparison to other admittees, the "criminally insane" group tended to be proportionately more white and older, without a history of previous psychiatric hospitalizations, and with minimal or no prior records of criminal activity. They cited a discharge rate on the order of 35% over a five year period, with the period of hospitalization ranging from one to 1235 days.

Those data contrast markedly with the findings of Kahn & Raifman (1981), who undertook a 23-year follow-up study of accused offenders who invoked an insanity plea, with no significant difference in period of confinement between the third of their sample who pled successfully and were remanded to a state psychiatric hospital and the two-thirds whose pleas were rejected, were found guilty, and were imprisoned. Similar outcomes were reported for New Zealand by Medlicott (1976), who found in a 35-year follow-up that subjects found "not guilty on psychiatric grounds were likely to be held for longer periods than those [adjudicated] as criminals." Because the Federal Community Mental Health Act of 1963 produced a pervasive movement to de-institutionalize the mentally ill (Pallone, 1986), long-term hospitalization has virtually disappeared *except* among involuntary criminal committees.

Fein (1984) has contended that "the insanity acquittal may retard the treatment of mentally disordered and violent offenders [because] failure to assign responsibility to a mentally disordered offender may lessen his/her initiative and emotional opportunity to make needed changes in perceptions and functioning." He thus seems to argue in favor of the British system whereby an accused offender may be found "guilty, but with diminished responsibility," and subsequently, virtually at judicial discretion, be confined for treatment in a psychiatric hospital *or* incarcerated in a correctional facility (Dell, 1983; Dell & Smith, 1983; Beigel, 1983). Bush (1983) has observed that, even when the insanity plea is not successful (e.g., in 17% of the Steadman *et al.* sample), it is likely the case that some discernible psychopathological condition underlay the criminal behavior; in such instances, he recommends "treatment for the guilty" in prison settings.

By the mid-1980s, a standardized method for assessing whether the circumstances of an alleged offense and background factors associated with the accused offender met the M'Naghten standard, the American Law Institute standard, or the "guilty but mentally ill" standard had been developed and commercially marketed (Rogers, Seman & Wasyliw, 1983), and a second method designed to function as a gross screen for "false positives" against the M'Naghten standard was under development (Slobogin, Melton & Showalter, 1984).

⮞   *Release from NGRI Criminal Commitment: Pathways and Pitfalls in Assessing Dangerousness*

The process whereby confinement for treatment when a plea of "not guilty by reason of insanity" is terminated and the "patient" released poses some interesting questions about restriction of personal liberty. In some states, the decision to release can be made by the staff of the institution to which the defendant has been remanded for treatment; in others, it is made only by the judge but with the recommendation of the treatment staff in hand; in yet others, if the decision to confine for treatment has been made by jury, a similar jury must be involved in the decision to release; and in still other states, release is granted by a "dangerousness review board."

From the perspective of the mental health professional, the issue engages the question of the state of the art concerning the prediction of future dangerousness. From the perspective of the rights of the patient, the key issue is the rectitude of confining a person who has *not* been found guilty of a criminal act (*precisely because* the insanity plea has been successful) *beyond* the point at which those responsible for the treatment of his or her mental disorder believe he or she is either "cured" or sufficiently improved to return to the community. Is it ethically, and under the Fourteenth Amendment constitutionally, permissible to confine such an accused offender for a period greater than that for which a putatively "otherwise similar" mentally ill person who has not been accused of crime is customarily confined? And if, in the judgment of the mental health professionals, the accused offender found not guilty by reason of insanity has improved sufficiently to warrant release in the judgment of those responsible for his or her treatment, is it not likely that continued confinement violates the mental patient's right to treatment established in a series of U.S. Supreme Court decisions?

In the judgment of the American Psychiatric Association in its Statement on the Insanity Defense (1984, pp. 20-21), "the 'dangerousness' of insanity acquitees who have perpetrated violence has already been demonstrated. Their future dangerousness need not be inferred; it may be assumed." The sentiment hardly accords with the Association's (1974) stern warnings on the assessment of future violence. Nevertheless, *future dangerousness* or, at least, the judgment that the criminally committed patient is *no longer dangerous* to others or to himself or herself presumably represents the pivotal *criterion* governing release of those criminally committed to psychiatric hospitalization.

After lamenting that "the nature of in-hospital psychiatric intervention has changed over the last decade" so that "greater emphasis is now placed on psychopharmacological management of the hospitalized person" and warning that "such treatment, while clearly helpful in reducing the overt signs and symptoms of mental illness, does not necessarily mean that 'cure' has been achieved, nor that a patient's 'nondangerousness' is assured," the Association's Statement (1984, p. 21) rather pontifically declaims:

❑ The American Psychiatric Association is therefore quite skeptical about procedures now implemented in many states requiring periodic decision-making by mental health professionals (or by others) concerning a requirement that insanity acquittees who have committed previous violent offenses be repetitively adjudicated as "dangerous," thereby provoking their release once future dangerousness cannot be clearly demonstrated in accord with the standard of proof required.

Not quite consistently, the Statement then stipulates (1984, pp. 22-23) that "The American Psychiatric Association believes that the decision to release an insanity acquittee should not be made *solely* by psychiatrists or *solely* on the basis of psychiatric testimony about the patient's mental condition or predictions of future dangerousness." The Association thus recommends that "Confinement and release decisions should be made by a board constituted to include psychiatrists and other professionals representing the criminal justice system, akin to a parole board" and that "The board having jurisdiction over released insanity acquitees should have clear authority to reconfine."

Reinehr, Dudley & White (1985) studied the operation of "dangerousness review boards" composed in this fashion and empowered in Texas to make determinations concerning the prospective dangerousness of psychiatric patients prior to release both before and after expansion of the membership of such boards from psychiatrists exclusively to include social workers, psychologists, and attorneys as well, finding that the multidisciplinary boards certified *fewer* patients as not dangerous and thus eligible for release.

Forensic psychiatrists Seymour Halleck (1987, pp. 96- 100), Robert Simon (1987, pp. 339-358), and Norman Poythress (1990) discuss the matter of professional liability for "negligent release" when an accused offender found not guilty by reason of insanity commits a subsequent crime after release from mandatory treatment and when such release proceeds *without* judicial approbation. But it is *not* self-evident that *judicial* decisions to release an offender from criminal commitment *on the basis of professional recommendations* would exculpate the professionals who made the pivotal recommendations should future violence ensue.

defensible method of resolving conflict in the weighing of "aggravating" and "mitigating" factors. That position is strongly seconded by the Commission on Criminal Justice Mental Health Standards of the American Bar Association (1989, p. 389), which unequivocally holds that "Statutes which [permit] a verdict of guilty but mentally ill should *not* be enacted."

As if to explain so strong a reaction, distinguished forensic psychiatrist Seymour Halleck (1987, p. 77) believes that

> the guilty but mentally ill alternative offers no new advantages to offenders and can hardly be distinguished from an ordinary criminal conviction, unless it is accompanied by a firm commitment on the part of the state to expand its treatment resources and provide offenders with effective treatment. So far, no evidence shows that this is happening.

In some sharp contrast, Sir Gerhard Mueller compellingly distinguishes legal definitions of culpability from psychological and psychiatric constructs of normality in terms which pivot precisely on psychology's emphasis on typical and habitual patterns of behavior *vs.* the law's interest in single, specified acts which may or may not align with the behaver's customary patterns (Slobogin, Melton & Showalter, 1984).

Sequelae to a Successful Plea of Insanity: Institutionalization

In cases in which an insanity plea is upheld, the customary result is that the accused — who is *not* convicted and who therefore can*not* appropriately be denominated a criminal offender — is remanded to the care of an inpatient psychiatric facility for treatment. In some jurisdictions, discharge occurs upon decision of the treatment staff, without further contact with the court; in others, the staff decision to discharge must be ratified judicially by the sentencing judge or his or her successor; in yet others, where confinement for treatment is determined by jury deliberation, discharge similarly requires jury decision [*Note* 2]. For its part, the American Psychiatric Association (1984) statement proposed an alternate modality such that both confinement and release decisions in cases in which an accused has been found not guilty by reason of insanity would be made by a board of mental health professionals "representing the criminal justice system," thus effectively eliminating both the judicial discretion of presiding justices and juries *and* the professional discretion of those mental health professionals charged with providing treatment judicially mandated in lieu of incarceration.

As an alternate to inpatient hospitalization, some jurisdictions have begun to experiment with judicial commitment of an NGRI acquittee to *outpatient* mental health treatment (Wilk, 1988), a procedure that even further complicates issues such as liability for dangerous or violent behavior. One presumes that, in such cases in those jurisdictions, a plea of not guilty by reason of insanity rather regularly prevails in crimes that have not involved violence or personal victimization.

Extra-Judicial Exculpation

Beyond the formal exercise of an insanity plea to excuse the accused from culpability, however, it is our conviction that the practice of *plea-bargaining* operationalizes the notion of diminished responsibility much more pervasively and on a largely informal basis, often with minimal judicial oversight (Heberling, 1973, p. 462). In a plea-bargaining situation, an agreement is reached between the prosecutor and the defendant and his or her attorney that the charges on which the defendant has initially been indicted are to be reduced to charges (usually similar in character) that carry less severe sanctions. Data reviewed in the next chapter indicate that a very high proportion of all indicted offenders enter pleas of guilty, suggesting that it is reasonable to believe that plea bargains are involved in a large proportion of guilty pleas.

Though the rationale underlying the practice of plea-bargaining involves consideration of the costs associated with full-dress prosecution and jury trial as well as the complex issues associated with the development of convincing evidence and the credibility of witnesses, it is also reasonable to believe that some informal (and clearly extra-judicial) assessment of "extenuating circumstances" that diminish culpability or responsibility is among the variables considered by prosecutors in the decision whether to offer or to accept a bargained plea. As Berkley and his associates (1977, p. 245) put it, "The willingness of the prosecuting attorney to bargain in a particular case may be determined by the personal characteristics of the defendant — 'Does he deserve a break'?"

☐ *SUMMARY*

This chapter has addressed the boundaries in the conceptual domain that limit psychological research on criminal behavior. We contrasted psychology's interest in behavior which is psychogenic and recurrent with the interest of the enforcers of law and administrators of justice in behavior that specifically violates the law even in a single episode, whether psychogenic or not.

In the definition of criminal behavior, we have taken a conservative position, virtually dictated by a system of justice that presumes innocence until adjudication of guilt and which therefore holds that only that behavior which is judicially pronounced as criminal can appropriately be so denominated for purposes of psychological investigation.

We reviewed the philosophical concept of law as the institutionalization of social custom and distinguished between behaviors that are *mala in se* according to a variety of ethical codes and those that are *mala prohibita*, contending that the proper focus in the psychological study of criminal behavior is the latter, whatever the pristine moral character of such behavior. We also reviewed legal means for construing culpability for behavior that is *mala prohibita*, observing that the psychological condition of the accused offender represents a variable which operates both formally (through not-guilty-by-reason-of-insanity pleas or through arguments urging imposition of milder sanctions in consequence of "mitigating factors") and informally (through plea- bargaining) in the determination of culpability for behavior that violates the law.

In an optimal world, one might conceive a way to do otherwise, but the fact is that, in the real and non-optimal world, psychological research on formally criminal behavior necessarily proceeds with adjudicated offenders as its subjects. Hence, the results of that research must be understood against a complex conceptual and legal backdrop which (1) permits some accused offenders to avoid conviction through pleas of not guilty by reason of insanity and (2) informally makes adjustments in charges, very likely based on largely unguided estimates of culpability, through the mechanism of "plea-bargaining." In the first case, subjects are excluded from the pool upon which research is conducted; in the second, the offense-of-record for which a subject has been convicted may bear only faint resemblance to the offense he or she may actually have committed. This state of affairs clearly limits the generalizability of the results of psychological research on formally criminal behavior.

☐ NOTES & COMMENTARY

☐ 1. *Competence to Stand Trial*

The exception is the situation in which the mental health professional is asked to asses whether the defendant is *currently competent to stand trial*. In most jurisdictions, this legal construct has been defined either legislatively or judicially as indicative of whether a defendant understands the nature of the charges against him or her, understands the consequences that may result from conviction, and is able to participate with an attorney in the preparation of a defense. Insanity, mental retardation, and/or memory deficits are typically cited to support a claim of *incompetence* to stand trial. Should a defendant be so found, he or she is typically remanded to the state's forensic psychiatric hospital until such time as later assessments (if any) demonstrate that he or she is no longer incompetent to stand trial. In a major review of empirical studies related to the issue, Nicholson & Kugler (1991) reported that the principal characteristics of defendants who had been judicially declared incompetent were "(1) poor performance on psychological tests or interviews specifically designed to assess defandants' legally relevant functional [mental] abilities, (2) a psychotic diagnosis, and (3) psychiatric symptoms reflective of severe psychopathology." These investigators also reported that "traditional psychological tests" and "previous psychiatric hospitalization" were also related to such judicial declarations "to a lesser degree."

❏ *2. The Rights of Mental Patients*

Golann & Fremouw (1976) review in detail the series of cases involving the rights of mental patients, including those confined by judicial action following prosecution for criminal behavior. Among the work's many interesting features are "eyewitness" accounts by Stonewall B. Stickney, Alabama's commissioner of mental health (and therefore the chief executive officer for the state's public psychiatric hospitals) during the prosecution of the landmark cases that established, at the level of the U.S. Supreme Court, the rights of mental patients. Other fascinating eyewitness accounts of his personal role in shaping and prosecuting the landmark case (*Pugh v. Locke*, 406 Federal Supplement 318, 1976) that, also at the Supreme Court level, established the rights of prisoners to mental health care in prison settings are provided by Fowler (1976, 1988). Mayer (1990) reviews the current state of the right of prisoners to mental health treatment even in the absence of a judicial finding of insanity.

Chapter 3

Operational Constraints in Studying Criminal Behavior

WERE THIS A WELL-ORDERED WORLD, ONE MIGHT EXPECT TO FIND THAT most people who commit crimes are thereafter promptly apprehended, prosecuted, and punished in accordance with the law. The available facts belie that rosy expectation.

To survey the empirical domain transversed by the psychology of criminal behavior, we need to inspect data relative to the incidence of criminal behavior of various sorts and the sequelae thereto: arrest, indictment, conviction or acquittal, and the imposition of sanction. Data responsive to these concerns are found in a number of national, regional, and local statistical sources, among which the most valuable is the *Sourcebook of Criminal Justice Statistics*, a massive annual compendium of data relating to crime and the operation of the policing, judicial, and correctional systems in the U.S. compiled and edited at the Hindelang Criminal Justice Research Center (Albany) and published by the Federal Department of Justice's Bureau of Justice Statistics (Maguire & Flanagan, 1991).

The *Sourcebook* contains a wide range of information concerning reports of criminal activity from every law enforcement agency in the nation, along with data concerning police activity, judicial disposition in certain criminal cases, rates of incarceration in prisons and jails, probation and parole activity, and other indices of the size, complexity, and cost of criminal apprehension, adjudication, and sanction. At the outset, it might be observed that the data often prove dismaying to readers whose principal sources of information have theretofore been primarily journalistic.

❑ INCIDENCE OF CRIME AND APPREHENSION

Our first concern is the incidence of "serious" criminal activity reported to local, state, and Federal law enforcement agencies —

those offenses that are defined as *felonies punishable by imprison-*
ment rather than *misdemeanors punishable by fine* or relatively
short sentences to confinement in jail facilities rather than prisons.

Following conventions that have become standard, the offenses
are segregated into two principal categories: Those that do and do
not involve direct physical victimization of persons, with the former
denominated *crimes of violence* and the latter denominated *property*
crimes. DISPLAY 1 recapitulates data drawn from the *Sourcebook* on
(1) criminal activity reported to law enforcement authorities arrayed
by category of offense and on (2) the proportion of offenses in each
category and sub-category which are, in the terminology standard
in criminal justice statistics, "cleared" by arrest of a suspected

---

⇨ *Display 1: Annualized Incidence of Felony Crime*
Reported and "Cleared by Arrest"

Total number of crimes reported: *14,251,400*
Proportion of these crimes cleared by arrest: *21.1%*

CATEGORY/SUB-CATEGORY	% All Reported	% Cleared by Arrest
⇓ *CRIMES OF VIOLENCE*	11.6%	45.8%
❑ Murder, homicide	0.2%	68.3%
❑ Rape, sexual assault	0.7%	52.4%
❑ Robbery	4.6%	26.0%
❑ Aggravated assault	6.7%	56.7%
⇓ *PROPERTY CRIMES*	88.4%	18.0%
❑ Burglary	22.2%	13.8%
❑ Larceny/Theft	55.2%	20.2%
❑ Motor vehicle theft	11.0%	15.2%
TOTAL FOR ALL CRIMES	100.0%	21.1%

• *Sources:* Langan (1991, p. 1572); Maguire & Flanagan (1991, pp. 353, 445, 447).

offender, even though the arrest may not result in subsequent conviction.

Public opinion polls almost invariably report that typical citizens include the crime rate, or even rises in the crime rate, among their most pressing concerns. But few studies have focused on the matter of the accuracy of the typical citizen's perceptions about the rate of crime or about the sequelae to crime. One inquiry that addressed those issues directly was conducted by Kemp (1987) who found that most citizens of New Zealand represented in his sample *under*-estimate the aggregate volume of formal criminal activity but radically *over*-estimate the incidence of homicide and other crimes of violence. There is no particular reason to believe that we Americans are any better informed than Kemp's New Zealanders. Thus, data recapitulated in DISPLAY 1 are likely to provide some challenges to popular conceptions based on journalistic (or, worse, fictional) accounts. Among the inferences most pertinent to our concerns:

❑ Although more than 14 million crimes are reported annually, *only 21% of all reported episodes of criminal activity are cleared by arrest.*

❑ *Crimes that involve direct physical victimization of persons (crimes of violence) account for only 12% of all reported criminal activity,* a much smaller proportion than one would suppose on the basis of information from journalistic and entertainment media.

❑ In particular, *murder and (non-negligent) homicide account for only two-tenths of one percent of all reported criminal activity,* hardly what one might expect on the basis of the stock-in-trade of television drama. Indeed, it is very likely that there more murders are portrayed on network or cable television in a given year than are actually committed; that would require only 60 murders per day — likely not a difficult feat with as many as 35 channels operating in the "major media markets." Further, since (as we shall see in a later chapter) murder and homicide overwhelmingly involve close kinship relationships between offender and victim, these crimes are not nearly so random nor so unforeseeable as screaming headlines propose.

❑ *Property crimes are nearly eight times more frequent than crimes of violence,* a datum which alone proposes that profit motives very likely undergird what we have called "inclination" in the overwhelming preponderance of criminal activity.

❑ It may be disheartening to note that only 21% of all instances of criminal activity in a given year are cleared by arrest and, in particular, that *the most frequently reported types of crimes* (larceny, burglary) *are least frequently cleared by arrest* (20%

vs. 14%). That the arrest rates vary so substantially between crimes of violence (46%) and property crimes (18%) doubtless reflects our values as a society. Those values are reflected in at least an implicit focus on behavior that is universally regarded as *mala in se*, represented by the various sub-categories which comprise crimes of violence — even though it is clear that most property crimes would also be regarded as inherently wrong by most pristine moral codes. Taken together, these data hardly portray a well-functioning system of criminal detection and apprehension.

A Preoccupation with Biochemicals?

Not quite in passing, we might also observe that, during the same year as represented by the data in DISPLAY 1, police authorities reported a total of some 14,340,900 arrests (Maguire & Flanagan, 1991, p. 412). Of that total, only 21% correspond to the nearly 3,000,000 arrests for serious (i.e., felonious) crime reflected in DIS-PLAY 1, but fully 33% of all arrests reported relate *exclusively* to the use of chemical substances through such offenses as driving under the influence of alcohol, sale or possession of controlled dangerous substances, violation of liquor laws, public drunkenness, and disorderly conduct.

Were it not the case that so small a proportion of felony crime is cleared by arrest, these latter data might not prove disappointing. But, to the extent that they reflect our values as a society, they appear to suggest a major obsession with biochemicals that outweighs our attention to the detection and apprehension of those responsible for felonious crime. Such data seem to portray our policing authorities as overly committed to peace-keeping in rather too obvious ways (e.g., rounding up the town drunk). Whether positive law as enacted by legislatures *or* the record of actual police activity reflected in arrest data more accurately mirror operative societal values (Pallone, 1989) is a moot issue.

The point of these comments is not to deny the relationship between such "minor" (i.e., non-felonious) offenses as substance abuse and such major offenses as criminal violence, robbery, or burglary, though that relationship may not be so "causative" as it is usually portrayed (McGlothlin, 1985; Pallone, 1989, 1990-*a*, 1991, pp. 57-85), nor to propose that an understanding of the dynamics of criminal behavior in minor offenses will not illuminate the dynamics of behavior in major offenses. Rather, the data seem to us to reveal a peculiarly inverse set of preoccupations in a society that laments itself as crime-ridden.

Formal Adjudication of Behavior as Criminal

Following our insistence that only that behavior which has been formally declared to be criminal by a duly-empowered court represents the appropriate focus for the psychological study of criminal behavior, the sequelae to arrest are of major interest. Arrest of a suspect is but the first step in a long and complex process which may or may not result in the formal adjudication of behavior as criminal. There ensue, in serial order (Ferdico, 1985, pp. 27-36):

❏ *Indictment*, or the formal accusation of the suspect;

❏ The placing of a *plea to the indictment* by the accused and its acceptance by the court;

❏ A *trial* if the accused has pled not guilty (or sometimes a hearing to determine "extenuating circumstances" or aggravating or mitigating factors, if the accused has pled guilty);

❏ *Conviction* as a consequence of a guilty plea *or* a finding by trial *or acquittal* as a consequence of trial;

⇨ *Sidney Harring on Police Activity in the Nineteenth Century*

We may find it disturbing that only 21% of the arrests made in a year are made for felony crime *and/or* that one in every three arrests is made exclusively for offenses related exclusively to possession or sale of drugs, violation of liquor laws, or disorderly conduct. But our disturbance may reflect our own lack of historical perspective.

In his socio-history of the development of the police function in American cities during the nineteenth century, City University of New York legal scholar Sidney Harring (1983, pp. 224-225) makes it clear that these trends have long, long roots. In the last decade of the century:

❏ police were relatively unconcerned about *any* form of criminal activity, serious or otherwise — a fact hinted at when we note that the average police officer in the nineteenth century made less than one arrest per week, and then usually for "disorderly conduct" . . . felonies . . . account for a mere 15 percent of all criminal arrests (the remaining 85 percent being [for] misdemeanor offenses) . . . Most arrests during this period were related to drinking.

Clearly, then, the preoccupation with biochemicals is not a new phenomenon. Moreover, if we have progressed from a situation in the 1890s in which only 15% of all arrests reflected felony crime to a current picture in which 21% reflect felony crime, we might pronounce that a rate of improvement of 40% in the space of a century.

❑ Following conviction, *pronouncement of sentence* by the court that the accused who has pled guilty *or* has been found guilty either be placed in custody or on probation. In many jurisdictions, the sentence may be appealed either by the prosecutor or by the defendant as too lenient or too severe, even when guilt is not in question.

At any point after indictment, the prosecutor may elect to withdraw the charges, the defense may move for dismissal, or the presiding judge may dismiss the charges. For our purposes, it is important to stress that *formal adjudication of a given behavior as criminal occurs* only upon acceptance of a plea of guilty or *upon declaration of guilt* by the presiding judge subsequent to trial.

Following adjudication of guilt, the presiding judge (or, in Federal cases and as a result of the Kennedy-Thurmond Act of 1984 in reform of the Federal prison system, a sentencing board; and, in some state jurisdictions, a jury) *pronounces sentence.* The sentence may dictate

❑ *incarceration* for a fixed or indeterminate term, *or may alternately*

❑ place the offender on *probation* for a period generally corresponding to the length of incarceration for the offense prescribed by the legislative authority in the relevant criminal code,

❑ impose a *"community service" alternative* to incarceration,

❑ order *restitution,* or

❑ order some combination of restitution, probation, and community service.

In the typical circumstance, the decision on sentence is made by the presiding judge after receiving the report of a *probation office* responsible to the court concerning the *character* of the accused, his or her prior involvement with the criminal justice system, economic status, family obligations, and standing in the community, the likelihood of satisfactory completion of probation as an alternative to incarceration, and other factors likely to influence the court's decision in the matter of incarceration vs. probation (Frishtik, 1988).

❑ SUCCESSIVE FUNNELS FROM CRIME TO SANCTION

We have earlier insisted that only that behavior which has formally been declared to be criminal by a duly-empowered court — i.e., that behavior which has resulted in criminal conviction — constitutes the appropriate focus for the psychological study of criminal behavior. Consequently, the sequelae to reports of criminal activity

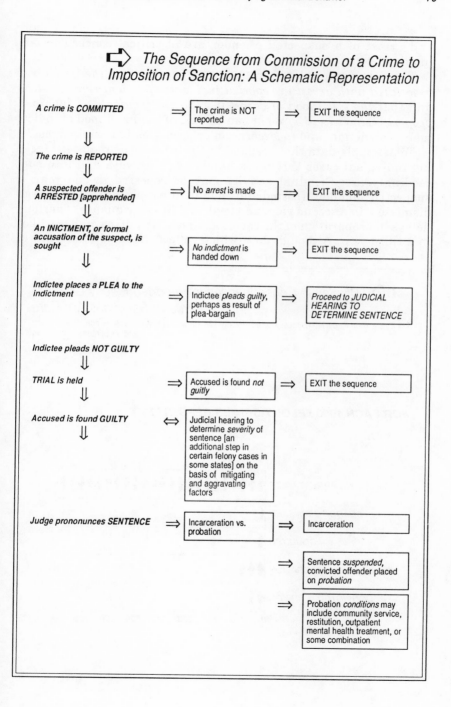

⇨ *The Sequence from Commission of a Crime to Imposition of Sanction: A Schematic Representation*

A crime is COMMITTED ⟹ The crime is NOT reported ⟹ EXIT the sequence

⇓

The crime is REPORTED

⇓

A suspected offender is ARRESTED [apprehended] ⟹ No *arrest* is made ⟹ EXIT the sequence

⇓

An INICTMENT, or formal accusation of the suspect, is sought ⟹ *No indictment* is handed down ⟹ EXIT the sequence

⇓

Indictee places a PLEA to the indictment ⟹ Indictee *pleads guilty*, perhaps as result of plea-bargain ⟹ Proceed to *JUDICIAL HEARING TO DETERMINE SENTENCE*

⇓

Indictee pleads NOT GUILTY

⇓

TRIAL is held ⟹ Accused is found *not guitly* ⟹ EXIT the sequence

⇓

Accused is found GUILTY ⟺ Judicial hearing to determine *severity* of sentence [an additional step in certain felony cases in some states] on the basis of mitigating and aggravating factors

⇓

Judge prononunces SENTENCE ⟹ Incarceration vs. probation ⟹ Incarceration

⟹ Sentence *suspended*, convicted offender placed on *probation*

⟹ Probation *conditions* may include community service, restitution, outpatient mental health treatment, or some combination

and arrest of a suspected offender are of critical concern to our inquiry.

The data recapitulated in DISPLAY 1 suggest that *the likelihood associated with arrest in reported incidents of violent crime is 46%* and that *the likelihood of arrest in reported incidents of felonious property crimes is 18%*. What can be said of the likelihood of indictment, conviction, and incarceration or probation following arrest?

To assemble data that respond to these concerns requires tracking individual cases through a number of pathways and into succeeding years: Criminal activity may be reported in one year, a suspected offender arrested and an indictment placed (or the charge dismissed) in a second year, and trial held (in consequence of various delays in preparation of the case, location of witnesses, and the like) in a third year. Although data which reflect the legal aftermath of

⇨ *Display 2: Consequences to Reported Felony Crime —*
Intrusive Sanctions Are Rare

For Every 1000 Reported Crimes, There Are Only 154 Convictions, with 95 Sentences to Probation and 59 Sentences to Prison

FOR EACH 1000 FELONY CRIMES REPORTED:

arrest on suspicion of criminal activity are clearly of interest to legislators and framers of public policy no less than to the enforcers of law and administrators of justice, the relevant data are fragmentary and must be pieced together from a variety of sources to form even the semblance of a coherent picture.

The most comprehensive estimates of national scope on the varied possible sequelae to arrest are to be found in the several editions of the *Sourcebook* through 1980, though these rest on a source that, in social science research terms, can only be regarded as quite dated — viz., the report of the President's Commission on Law Enforcement and Administration of Justice (1967), appointed by Mr. Johnson in the aftermath of the Kennedy and King assassinations. Since the data on which that report was based were themselves collected minimally five years earlier, those estimates now seem to belong to the distant past.

Though the *Sourcebook* annually enumerates the number of crimes reported to law enforcement agencies and recounts the proportion of these "cleared by arrest," comprehensive data on the proportion of those arrests that result in conviction and sanction are not available. As Flanagan & Jamieson (1988, p. 411) explain:

> Although the [Federal] Uniform Crime Reports and the National Prisoner Statistics programs provide nationwide data on specific law enforcement and correctional activities, no comparable uniform State and local judicial processing data exist.

Nonetheless, an earlier *Sourcebook* (Flanagan & Jamieson, 1988, pp. 412-413) reports results of a "pilot study" of the consequences to arrest for felony in eleven states selected to resemble the nation in important demographic and criminologic characteristics (Bureau of Justice Statistics, 1988); collectively, these states account for 38% of the national population and 37% of the episodes of *reported* crime (Flanagan & Jamieson, 1988, pp. 326-334).

When data from the study on consequences to arrest are juxtaposed in relation to data on episodes of criminal activity reported in a year in the same states, the picture that emerges is if anything even more dismal than that portrayed by the President's Commission nearly a quarter century ago. DISPLAY 2 arrays those data graphically to illustrate the rarity of intrusive sanctions following reported crime.

In DISPLAY 3, we have melded data from a variety of studies bearing upon the sequelae to arrest into a framework which rests on what the President's Commission initially identified as a series of "funneling effects" between reports of criminal activity and imprisonment of adjudicated offenders. But our framework takes as its

➡️ *Display 3: "Successive Funnels" with Ascending Probabilities — From Reports of Crime through Arrest, Indictment, Conviction, and Sentence*

⇓ *FUNNEL A } For every 1000 felonies reported . . .*   100.0%

- there are 207 *arrests*   20.7%
- there are 158 *indictments*   15.8%
- there are 154 *convictions*   15.4%
- there are 95 *sentences to probation*   9.5%
- there are 59 *sentences to prison*   5.9%
- but there are no arrests in 793 cases of reported felony   79.3%

⇓ *FUNNEL B } In every 1000 arrests for serious crimes . . .*   100.0%

- *indictments* result in 810 cases   81.0%
- *convictions* follow in 511 cases   51.1%
- *sentences to probation* follow in 317 cases   31.7%
- *sentences to prison* follow in 194 cases   19.4%
- and there is *no indictment* in 190 cases   19.0%

⇓ *FUNNEL C } In every 1000 indictments for felony crimes . . .*   100.0%

- *convictions* follow in 631 cases   63.1%
- and *acquittal* follows in 369 cases   36.9%

⇓ *FUNNEL D } In every 1000 convictions for felony crimes . . .*   100.0%

- *sentences to probation* follow in 620 cases   62.0%
- *sentences to prison* follow in 380 cases   38.0%

⇓ *FUNNEL E } Of every 1000 convictions for felony crimes . . .*   100.0%

- 860 likely result from *pleas of guilty*   86.0%
- 140 likely result from *trial verdict*   14.0%

• *Sources:* Langan (1991); Flanagan & Jamieson (1988, pp. 326-334, 412-413); Flanagan & McLeod (1983, pp. 292, 348, 376, 390); Parisi, Gottfredson, Hindelang & Flanagan, (1979, p. 545); President's Commission (1967, p. 67)

point of departure the relationship between the incidence of reported crime and the proportion of clearance through arrest, as reported in DISPLAY 1 and further incorporates data concerning the frequency with which pleas of guilty are entered by defendants to criminal charges (Parisi, Gottfredson, Hindelang & Flanagan, 1979, p. 545).

Inspection of the largely dispiriting statistics reflected in DISPLAY 3 reveals clearly a series of "funnels" between report of criminal activity and adjudication of behavior as criminal, followed by imposition of sanction.

- ❑ The ratio between conviction and reported felony crime is relatively small (at 15.4%, *Funnel A*),
- ❑ but increases more than three-fold (to 51.1%) once an arrest is made (*Funnel B*)
- ❑ and further increases (to 63.1%) if the presumptive evidence is sufficient to sustain an indictment (*Funnel C*),
- ❑ but very likely only as a function of the high rate at which those indicted plead guilty (*Funnel E*).
- ❑ Similarly, the ratio between imposition of imprisonment as a sanction following adjudication of behavior as criminal is small (5.9%) in relation to formal reports that a felony crime has been committed (*Funnel A*) but increases three-fold following indictment (to 19.4%, at *Funnel B*). In the aggregate, these data might be read to suggest that, whatever the impediments to efficient detection and apprehension, the evidence adduced at and after the point of arrest is sufficiently strong to support indictment in the overwhelming proportion of cases and to sustain conviction in a majority of arrests.

Intrusive Sanctions and the Expectation of Impunity

At close range, the most striking single datum reflected in DISPLAY 3 (at *Funnel A*) is that *there are only 154 convictions for every 1000 cases of felony crime reported*. In nearly 80% of the cases of serious crime reported, no arrest is ever made.

For every 1000 reported cases of felony crime, there are only 59 sentences to the intrusive sanction of prisons. Such a low rate of intrusive sanction (as distinct from probation, community service, or restitution) very likely serves to *reinforce the expectation of impunity* in the emission (or maintenance) of criminal behavior — whether observed directed or through what we have earlier labeled "long distance" vicarious conditioning. In the remaining 95 cases in which convictions occur (i.e., in some 62% of the cases in which the accused is found, or pleads, guilty), the adjudicated offender is placed on probation, assigned a community service alternative to incarceration, ordered to provide restitution, or otherwise escapes major inconvenience in consequence of his or her criminal behavior. We should not be surprised, then, to learn that on any given day the number of convicted offenders at liberty, with only the relatively mild intrusion of probation authorities as sanction for adjudicated criminal behavior exceeds by several times the number of convicted offenders who are serving sentences in state and Federal correctional institutions (Parisi, Gottfredson, Hindelang & Flanagan, 1979, pp. 594, 617, 619).

Add to this conceptual mix that the prisons are regularly filled to capacity, and that there is little reason to believe that judges who impose sentences are notably given to leniency. The data just reviewed might then seem to reflect operative social values more decisively than do formal criminal codes in their prescription of sanctions — viz., that it is preferable to permit adjudicated offenders to remain free than to provide the tax dollars that would be required to construct the physical facilities and provide the staffing to implement fully the sanction attached to adjudicated criminal behavior in the codes enacted by legislatures.

⇨ *"Just Deserts," Prison Overcrowding and Alternative Sanctions*

By the early 1990s, prison overcrowding had reached crisis proportions in many states. The variables at play included these:

❑ A social environment in which state correctional facilities operate at chronic levels of overcrowding — according to Flanagan & Jamieson, 1988, p. 501, nationally at 112% of capacity, with some states as high as 150% of capacity.

❑ Federal court orders affecting some three dozen states to improve prison conditions to Constitutionally acceptable levels, in accordance with the terms of the *Pugh v. Locke* decision of 1976.

❑ An electorate which chronically declines to support increased tax levies to support prison construction or prison staffing.

In such circumstances, even such prominent spokespersons for the "just deserts" perspective in corrections as Norval Morris and Michael Tonry (1990) joined in the appeal to divert a greater proportion of convicted offenders away from prison and into probation or other community-based alternatives as a matter of sheer economic necessity. In those circumstances, one might well expect the proportion of convicted offenders sentenced to the intrusive sanction of prison to *decline.*

Those given to the analysis of public policy questions might wonder whether it is not ultimately more effective simply to decriminalize many behaviors than to permit the *de facto* and sometimes random de-criminalization that ensues with the failure to implement legislatively-prescribed sanctions.

☐ GUILTY PLEAS: A FUNCTION OF PLEA-BARGAINS?

It is also germane to our purposes to inspect at close range the data presented at *Funnel E* relative to the high proportion of cases in which conviction eventuates from a plea of guilty. Data reported by Parisi, Gottfredson, Hindelang & Flanagan (1979, p. 545) from a major study of judicial practices in 1334 courts in 19 populous states indicate a *median rate of guilty pleas of 86% in all indictments for serious crime.* In the absence of comprehensive national data from all U.S. jurisdictions, there is no particularly strong reason to believe that this rate varies substantially, whether positively or negatively, in the courts and states not studied.

Similarly, data of national scope which speak to the extent to which the practice of plea-bargaining has preceded and produced so high a proportion of guilty pleas are not available. Indeed, empirical data on plea-bargaining have thus far been sparse and hardly revealing, a surprising state of affairs in view of what is assumed widely to be the universality of the practice. In some measure, the lack of responsive data may be explained by the finding that fully 69% of the criminal court judges responding to a nationwide survey of work styles in the courts reported that they were not aware of whether a plea bargain had been struck until the case actually came before them (Flanagan & McLeod, 1983, p. 110). But, in the absence of firm data, we observe the opinion of Mr. Justice Peters of California in *In re Tahl (1981 California Law Reporter,* 1 California 3d, 140, p. 577) that:

A substantial portion — probably the vast majority — of criminal cases are disposed of through the process of plea- bargaining. We also know that *most bargains do not appear on the record, and that defendants whose pleas have been obtained by promises of leniency are usually expected to deny the existence of such promises* in spite of the common knowledge of judge, prosecutor, and defense counsel to the contrary. *The result, in such cases, is that the entry of the plea is a ritual in which the recitations of the participants have little relation to reality.*

The available data, then, indicate that a plea of guilty represents the *modal* manner of disposition in criminal cases; judicial opinion supports the inference that some very large proportion of those pleas result from bargaining. In these circumstances, final disposition of those cases in which a guilty plea is *not* entered is also of interest.

Once again, responsive data prove fragmentary and incomplete but instructive nonetheless. Data concerning the final disposition in all criminal cases in a given year in two rather dissimilar states, Florida and Connecticut, are reported by the National Center for State Courts (1979, pp. 67-70) in a study of the operation of state courts. In all criminal indictments in which a final disposition was reached in the year under study and in which a plea of guilty was *not* entered, conviction after trial occurred in only 13.8% of the cases in Florida and in 8.5% of the cases in Connecticut; conversely,

➡ *Display 4: Sequential Frequencies between Reports of Crime "Cleared by Arrest," Prosecution, Conviction, and Imprisonment*

Category	% Arrested	% Prosecuted	% Convicted	% Imprisoned
⇓ CRIMES OF VIOLENCE	46	82	74	65
Murder, homicide	70	91	67	85
Rape, sexual assault	52	76	65	84
Robbery	25	84	66	76
Aggravated assault	58	79	70	52
⇓ PROPERTY CRIMES	18	86	77	60
Burglary	18	86	77	60
Larceny/Theft	20	90	77	53
Motor vehicle theft	15	66	78	74

• *Sources:* Flanagan & Jamieson (1988, pp. 326-334, 412-413); Bureau of Justice Statistics (1988)

charges were withdrawn or dismissed in 79% of the Florida cases and 86% of the Connecticut cases.

While extrapolations might prove interesting, the inescapable conclusions seem to be that *the overwhelming majority of criminal convictions almost certainly issue from pleas of guilty*, whether bargained or not, and that *proceeding to trial is far more likely to produce withdrawal or dismissal of charges than any other result*.

☐ *ESTIMATING THE PROBABILITY OF INTRUSIVE SANCTION*

Expressed in primitive terms, the standard statistical method for estimating the probability of the *sequential* occurrence of two or more events hinges on the multiplication of the probability associated with the occurrence of one event by the probability associated with the occurrence of each subsequent event.

In DISPLAY 4, we have recapitulated *Sourcebook* data on the rate at which specific crimes in each of the two major categories are "cleared by arrest" in juxtaposition to Bureau of Justice Statistics data from its pilot study on the sequelae to arrest. On that basis, we can proceed to consider what the data summarized in DISPLAY 4 might suggest in terms of the probability of imposition of the intrusive sanction of imprisonment in each of the principal subcategories of felony crime, particularly when read in juxtaposition to data on "clearance by arrest" recapitulated in DISPLAY 1. The arithmetic involved in the standard statistical formulae for combining probabilities works out this way:

☐ In the case of *criminal homicide, Sourcebook* data indicate that 70% of the *reported* episodes are cleared by arrest. According to Bureau of Justice statistics data, 91% of those arrested are prosecuted; by combing relative sequential frequencies (i.e., .70 x .91), we may say that it is likely that 63% of the homicides *reported* will result in prosecution. Of those arrestees for homicide on whom the decision is made to prosecute, 67% are convicted; by again combining relative sequential frequencies, we may say that it is likely that 43% (i.e., .70 x .91 x .67) will result in conviction. Of those convicted for homicide, 85% are sentenced to prison terms; by combining relative sequential frequencies yet again, we may say that it is likely that only 36% (i.e., .70 x .91 x .67 x .85) of the homicides *reported* will result in imprisonment. In assessing the import of these sequential frequencies, it is imperative to observe that criminal homicide is the felony most frequently (at 70%) cleared by arrest. Given so high a proportion of apprehension, that only

36% of the homicides *reported* are likely to result in imprisonment is the more alarming.

❑ In the case of *rape, Sourcebook* data indicate that 52% of the *reported* episodes are cleared by arrest. According to Bureau of Justice statistics data, 76% of those arrested are prosecuted; by combing relative sequential frequencies (i.e., .52 x .76), we may say that it is likely that 40% of the rapes *reported* will result in prosecution. Of those arrestees for rape on whom the decision is made to prosecute, 65% are convicted; by again combining relative sequential frequencies, we may say that it is likely that 26% (i.e., .52 x .76 x .65) will result in conviction. Of those convicted for rape, 84% are sentenced to prison terms; by combining relative sequential frequencies yet again, we may say that it is likely that only 36% (i.e., .52 x .76 x .65 x .84) of the rapes *reported* will result in imprisonment.

❑ In the case of *robbery, Sourcebook* data indicate that only 25% of the *reported* episodes are cleared by arrest. According to Bureau of Justice statistics data, 84% of those arrested are prosecuted; by combing relative sequential frequencies (i.e., .25 x .84), we may say that it is likely that 21% of the robberies *reported* will result in prosecution. Of those arrestees for robbery on whom the decision is made to prosecute, 66% are convicted; by again combining relative sequential frequencies, we may say that it is likely that 14% (i.e., .25 x .84 x .66) will result in conviction. Of those convicted for robbery, 76% are sentenced to prison terms; by combining relative sequential frequencies yet again, we may say that it is likely that only 11% (i.e., .25 x .84 x .66 x .76) of the robberies *reported* will result in imprisonment.

❑ In the case of *burglary, Sourcebook* data indicate that 18% of the *reported* episodes are cleared by arrest. According to Bureau of Justice statistics data, 86% of those arrested are prosecuted; by combing relative sequential frequencies (i.e., .18 x .86), we may say that it is likely that 15% of the burglaries *reported* will result in prosecution. Of those arrestees for burglary on whom the decision is made to prosecute, 77% are convicted; by again combining relative sequential frequencies, we may say that it is likely that 11% (i.e., .18 x .86 x .77) will result in conviction. Of those convicted for burglary, 60% are sentenced to prison terms; by combining relative sequential frequencies yet again, we may say that it is likely that only 7% (i.e., .18 x .86 x .77 x .60) of the burglaries *reported* will result in imprisonment.

❑ In the case of *larceny or theft* (as data recapitulated earlier in DISPLAY 1 indicate, the most frequently *reported* of the felonies, accounting for fully 55% of all episodes of crime *reported*), *Sourcebook* data indicate that only 20% of the *reported* episodes are cleared by arrest. According to Bureau of Justice statistics data, 90% of those arrested are prosecuted; by combing relative sequential frequencies (i.e., .20 x .90), we may say that it is likely that 18% of the larcenies *reported* will result in prosecution. Of those arrestees for larceny on whom the decision is made to prosecute, 67% are convicted; by again combining relative sequential frequencies, we may say that it is likely that 14% (i.e., .20 x .90 x .67) will result in conviction. Of those convicted for larceny, 53% are sentenced to prison terms; by combining relative sequential frequencies yet again, we may say that it is likely that only 7% (i.e., .20 x .90 x .67 x .53) of the larcenies *reported* will result in imprisonment.

❑ In the case of *motor vehicle theft, Sourcebook* data indicate that 15% of the *reported* episodes are cleared by arrest. According to Bureau of Justice statistics data, 66% of those arrested are prosecuted; by combining relative sequential frequencies (i.e., .15 x .66), we may say that it is likely that 10% of the motor vehicle thefts *reported* will result in prosecution. Of those arrestees for

---

⇨ *Prosecution vs. Restitution*

It is arguable that failure to apprehend, prosecute, and sanction not only vicariously reinforces predisposition toward criminal behavior among a relatively small segment of the population but also breeds contempt for the law and its visible enforcers among a substantially larger segment, thereby eliciting a variety of antisocial attitudes.

Nonetheless, for at least certain types of crimes, popular opinion seems to favor simple restitution rather than formal prosecution and sanctioning. Thus, Cutshall & McCold (1982), in an inventive study of failure to report episodes of cattle theft among Kraal tribesmen in Zambia, concluded that such failure issues from subjects' expectation that only mild sanctions would be imposed, if any at all. Far from wishing to "hang the rustlers high," however, tribesmen expected restitution; they regarded such presumably "civilized" sanctions as imprisonment as an inadequate substitute. However quaint we may find that attitude, it is replicated in the U.S. in regard both to "white collar" crimes of all sorts (Cullen, Link & Polanzi, 1982) and in regard to "corporate" crimes (Abel, 1985) — and may, indeed, be interpretable as illustrating that some members of society perceive the "transaction costs" associated with formal prosecution, at least for some crimes, not sufficiently offset by the benefits to accrue therefrom, especially when restitution is possible.

⇨ *Frank O'Connor on Punishment and Retribution: Formal vs. Community Sanctions in Ireland*

Frank O'Connor is sometimes accorded a place in the pantheon of Irish writers equal to that of James Joyce and John Millington Synge. In "Peasants," originally published in 1931, O'Connor (1982) aptly illustrates the sharp divergence between the sanctions to be applied for wrongdoing were the formal requirements of the law followed to the letter and the sanctions preferred by the members of a community. The case concerns the theft of funds from a sporting association:

❑ When Michael John Cronin stole the funds of the Carricknabreena Hurling, Football, and Temperance Association, commonly called the Club, everyone said: "Devil's cure to him!" "'Tis the price of him!" "Kind father for him!" "What did I tell you?" and the rest of the things people say when an acquaintance has got what is coming to him. And not only Michael John but the whole Cronin family, seed, breed, and generation, came in for it; there wasn't one of them for twenty miles round or a hundred years back but his deeds and sayings were remembered and examined by the light of this fresh scandal. Michael John's father (the heavens be his bed!) was a drunkard who beat his wife, and his father before him a land-grabber. Then there was an uncle or grand-uncle who had been a policeman and taken a hand in the bloody work at Mitchelstown long ago, and an unmarried sister of the same whose good name it would by all accounts have needed a regiment of husbands to restore. It was a grand shaking up the Cronins got altogether.

Indeed, in the view of the townspeople, that "shaking up" which permitted them to heap ridicule not only on Michael John but on the entire Cronin clan itself constituted the sole, proper, and appropriate sanction — and one far preferable to the formal penalties prescribed by law. But the parish priest insists and insists that Michael John be dealt with according to the requirements of the law. The townspeople retort that they will raise a collection to replace the stolen funds; yet the priest insists. The townspeople respond that they will raise a collection not only to replace the stolen funds but to run Michael John out of town, specifically by sending him to America; still the priest insists. In the event, Michael John is prosecuted, tried, convicted, and sentenced to a term of incarceration. Once he is imprisoned, the attitudes of the townspeople both toward Michael John and the members of his family change radically from gossiped opprobrium, replete with implicit self-inflation, to silent pity; eventually, Michael John is befriended by a "do-gooding" woman from a wealthy family, whom he weds upon parole. In his turn, the parish priest who had insisted that formal justice be served — and thereby robbed the townspeople of the opportunity to inflict the sanction they preferred — becomes a pariah. He had clearly mis-construed the "transaction costs" and the expected benefits of insistence upon formal justice:

❑ As for Father Crowley, till he was shifted twelve months later, he never did a day's good in the parish. The dues went down and the presents went down, and people with money to spend on Masses took it fifty miles away sooner than leave it to him. They said it broke his heart. He has left unpleasant memories behind him. Only for him, people say, Michael John . . . would never have married a girl with money, or had it to lend to poor people in the hard times, or ever sucked the blood of Christians. For, as an old man said to me of him: "A robber he is and was, and a grabber like his grandfather before him, and an enemy of the people like his uncle, the policeman . . ."

motor vehicle theft on whom the decision is made to prosecute, 78% are convicted; by again combining relative sequential frequencies, we may say that it is likely that 8% (i.e., .15 x .66 x .78) will result in conviction. Of those convicted for motor vehicle theft, 74% are sentenced to prison terms; by combining relative sequential frequencies yet again, we may say that it is likely that only 6% (i.e., .15 x .66 x .78 x .74) of the motor vehicle thefts *reported* will result in imprisonment.

We have already confessed to the speculative character of the method by which we have arrived at these probabilities, and we most assuredly do not take the position that the would-be offender calculates the statistical probabilities of apprehension and sanction associated with a prospective crime.

But we do contend that the would-be offender has available to him or to her ample evidence that there is linked to the emission of a criminal act a very low probability of apprehension leading to intrusive sanction — more particularly, since the number of offenses actually committed in each subcategory exceeds by several times the number reported. We hold that such evidence in the psychosocial environment serves to frame — directly, through one's personal past experience, or vicariously — the expectation of impunity.

It requires little in the way of willingness to take risks to "bet" on impunity when the probabilities associated with intrusive sanction are low, even in the case of crimes for which the rate of apprehension is relatively high.

☐ ATYPICAL OFFENDERS AS SUBJECTS FOR STUDY?

We have earlier insisted that only that behavior which has been formally adjudicated as such can properly be labeled as criminal and thus be included in the psychological study of specifically criminal behavior. Let us now consider how this conceptual demarcation interacts with empirical data reflecting the "real world" operations of the criminal justice system to limit rather severely the scientific study of criminal behavior.

We have observed that only a minor proportion of reported criminal activity results in arrest and an even smaller proportion in formal adjudication, whether through plea-bargaining — in which case, the offense-of-record may, in Mr. Justice Peters' phrase, "have little relation to reality" — or through conviction subsequent to trial. Consequently, the offenses for which adjudicated offenders have been convicted will in a significant proportion of cases very likely represent *legal euphemisms* for the criminal behavior actually emitted, so that there ensues a high probability for misleading conclusions, whether in data-gathering for administrative or policy purposes (e.g., head-counts of adjudicated offenders on probation or in custody for one or another type of offense) or in scientific research.

Further, there is the practical issue that a very minor proportion of those who emit criminal acts are likely to become subjects in psychological studies intended to illuminate the antecedents and dynamics of those acts, both in consequence of the low probabilities associated with formal reporting and with arrest, conviction, and sentence, and because those adjudicated offenders placed in the custody of correctional institutions are more likely than those placed on probation (or given another relatively non-intrusive sanction) to make themselves available as subjects in scientific studies. These considerations, based on the empirical data, suggest the likely *atypicality* of those adjudicated offenders who are accessible as subjects for the scientific investigation of criminal behavior.

But there is an even more fundamental issue: How does it happen, for example, that some burglars repetitively burgle without apprehension or sanction, while others are arrested or punished, particularly since the probabilities do indeed suggest impunity? Is it "luck," or perhaps *competence not merely in the craft of burglary but also in the manipulation of the criminal justice system?*

Certainly, that conjecture seems to accord with the "incidental" finding reported by Klein, Petersilia & Turner (1990) of the RAND Corporation in their study of nearly 15,000 sentencing decisions in California that a sentence to the intrusive sanction of incarceration (vs. probation) was potently associated with whether the defendant was represented in court proceedings by a private attorney *or* by a public defender or appeared *pro se.* In the normal course of events, one would expect that only those who had exhibited greater competence in something are likely to be able to afford the services of a private attorney.

That conjecture further seems congruent with the conclusion reached by Allen & Simonsen (1975) that, whatever the social, academic, or economic yardstick applied, prison inmates can appropriately be described as the "chronic losers" in a society. To that description may be added the observation by Wright (1991) that there is some reason to believe that, at least in some prisons in some states, a *majority* of inmates not only come from lower socioeconomic origins but indeed have been "state-raised" under the auspices of public child protective agencies, to which guardianship has been assigned as a result of abuse or neglect. With some frequency, such children have been the objects of neglect by substance-abusing parents or single mothers. Children under such protection are usually shunted from one foster home to another, with inadequate socialization as one of several deleterious long-term effects. That, surely, is a formula for a headstart toward becoming a "chronic loser." Thus, in his study of the characteristics of inmates who aggress against other inmates (i.e., the "violent vs. the victimized," Wright (1991, p. 5) observes:

> Prison populations are composed of predominantly poor, lower-class segments of society who differentiate themselves along ethnic lines and are generally hostile to one another . . . the worst of society's rejects . . . Many . . . lack commitment to public morality.

This more speculative question, then, reduces to whether the small proportion of offenders who are apprehended, convicted, and sentenced to imprisonment are simply atypically *less competent* than their counterparts who are neither apprehended, convicted, nor sentenced; and, virtually by definition, there are no responsive data on which to argue the question. But it may be that psychological research which self-consciously sets out to limit its inquiry to adjudicated offenders programs itself to atypicality, however necessary such limitations may be legally and morally.

Virtually alone among contemporary commentators, Yochelson & Samenow (1977) are fond of speaking of "the criminal personality," and they come very close to asserting that certain people are virtually "predestined" to crime. We hold, to the contrary, that Yochelson & Samenow have significantly misread the data, that (as we have earlier argued) the term "criminal personality" is devoid of meaning — and that, in a nation in which guilt can be pronounced only by a court of competent jurisdiction, the term *criminal* can properly be applied only to behavior, and then only after formal adjudication.

But, even were one to grant that Yochelson & Samenow and those similarly persuaded are correct in believing that there are some people who are, more or less, predestined to behave in ways that are contrary to the interests of society, the empirical portrait of the way in which our system of apprehension and prosecution actually operates very amply demonstrates that there is absolutely nothing "predestined" about whether even an act that is patently contrary to the interests of society will, in fact, be pronounced formally criminal. Indeed, we have seen that whether an act that is blatantly *mala in se* is ever formally pronounced criminal seems largely a function of vagaries and contingencies in the criminal justice system itself — and *not* a property inherent in the act.

☐ *SUMMARY*

This chapter has explored the "real world" domain transversed by the psychological study of criminal behavior.

We have reviewed the incidence of reports of serious (felonious) crime in the standard categories, the incidence of arrest for such alleged offenses, and the available data on the sequelae to arrest. We have seen that, with the exception of murder and aggravated assault, only small proportions of the reported incidents of criminal activity are cleared by arrest. In one of four cases, arrest is not followed by indictment, but conviction is a highly probable consequence to indictment — very likely as the result of plea-bargaining, since the majority of indictments are resolved by pleas of guilty.

We have seen that, in the aggregate, in only 5.0% of the cases of reported crime does conviction result and that in only 3.1% of the cases does imprisonment result. We have opined that would-be offenders, even though not knowledgeable about the precise probabilities, nonetheless have available to them a variety of indicators which suggest that a very low probability of apprehension and intrusive sanction is attached to the emission of a criminal act.

We have also reviewed the available data on the extent of plea-bargaining, concluding that, since the vast majority of criminal convictions result from pleas of guilty and are very likely themselves the result of plea-bargaining, the official offense-of-record is likely to prove misleading.

Finally, since so small a proportion of all those who commit crimes are apprehended, prosecuted, and punished, we have wondered whether the varied boundary conditions in the "real world" empirical domain converge to insure that psychological research on criminal behavior programs itself to study primarily the behavior of those who are *atypical* offenders.

Chapter 4

Methodological Constraints in Studying Criminal Behavior

SPECULATIONS ABOUT THE ENGINES THAT DRIVE HUMAN BEHAVIOR ARE as old as recorded human history. Certainly every enduring work of drama or fiction, from the *Oresteia* cycle of ancient Greece onward, can be interpreted as an account of the antecedents and/or consequences of a particular set of human behaviors on the part of particular persons, and it is likely that these works have endured precisely because the accounts they offer seem to hold some general applicability. There followed many centuries of more-and-less sophisticated speculation on the part of litterateurs, philosophers, theologians, and physicians.

But the more-or-less scientific study of human behavior by psychologists commenced no earlier than 150 or so years ago. Great drama and fiction typically concentrate on the global behavior of a single behaver (i.e., on the totality of his or her behavior across a wide variety of situations) and are generally conceded to flow from bursts of highly individualistic artistic insight. In sharp contrast, scientific psychology wants to know not about the global behavior of a single individual but about one or another particular behavior as it is emitted either universally or at least by a wide array of behavers. Hence, the aim of scientific psychology has been to identify — with some degree of pretension to precision, replicability, and public verifiability that is quite contrary to individualistic insights — either (or both) the *antecedents to* or the *correlates of* particular focal behaviors *and* in such a way that those antecedents or correlates can be predicated universally or at least across a reasonably wide array of particular behavers.

Hence, scientific psychology has proceeded by amassing empirical data, inferentially processing those data, and constructing what are usually called "conceptual models" of focal behaviors held to be either universally or at least generally predicatable. What methods of inquiry have been, and are now being, used in the psychological study of human behavior? Are these methods applicable to the study of specifically (and formally) criminal behavior? If not, why not?

☐ METHODS OF INQUIRY IN THE STUDY OF BEHAVIOR

Four principal methods of inquiry can be discerned in contemporary psychological studies, each keyed to a particular interpretive matrix, though it must be observed that, in any particular investigation, these methods are likely to be blended and mingled.

Clinical Case Study

Historically the first to emerge, and of utility both in differential and process psychology, *clinical case study* methodology arose as a method of investigation of the antecedents of a focal behavior largely as an adjunct to treatment processes applied to persons who have sought professional treatment for disordered behavior. But the methodology has also been adopted by developmentalists interested in "normal" behavior and has become the method-of-choice as well in psychohistorical studies. When it is employed by clinicians or by developmentalists, clinical case study typically proceeds contemporaneously with the unfolding of events in the life of the subject; when employed by psychohistorians, inquiry usually commences only well after the fact and without the personal cooperation of a subject typically long since deceased.

Clinical case study methods yield a great deal of information about a single subject, and, by their very nature, are not particularly concerned about whether this subject is representative of others or not. Modeled after modes of inquiry hallowed by centuries of use in medicine and dependent both on the subject's ability to recall and re-construct or re-construe (or, in the case of an historic subject, the adequacy of personal documents and records) and the inquirer's capacity to decipher and infer (or construe), clinical case study methodology was seized as the method-of-choice in the study of personality and behavior by Freud and other early members of the psychoanalytic school and by the early phenomenologists, and it very likely remains the modal method of inquiry among present day psychoanalysts. But this methodology has also been utilized by therapists of the behavioral school, who often also provide substantial detail about the psychophysiological processes activated in a single subject with respect to a focal behavior.

INHERENT IMPEDIMENTS AS A MODE OF INQUIRY

While clinical case study methodology doubtless yields much rich material probably not accessible in any other way, it presents virtually insuperable impediments as a modality for scientific inquiry:

❑ *First,* the material produced for inferential processing hinges almost inseparably on the clinical skill of a specific and particular investigator, so that *reproducibility* of specific steps in this method of inquiry as well as of results is tangential at best, thus calling into question the characteristic of *public verifiability* that is typically regarded as essential in scientific research.

❑ *Second,* studying single cases, or even many single cases in serial order, severely limits the generalizability of the results of such inquiry, the more so since it is unlikely that the behavior of the clinical investigator remains constant from case to case.

❑ *Third,* the self-selection process which leads some persons to seek psychotherapeutic assistance while others who may suffer the same disorders do not seek such assistance similarly serves to limit generalizability *even within* the domain of putatively disordered individuals.

❑ When employed in psychohistory, a fourth problem is engaged, since virtually by definition the subject chosen for historical analysis is by achievement or infamy held to be rather singular and atypical, rather than representative of members of a group, class, or population. Quite clearly, in this context case

---

⇨ *Hypnotic Stimululation of Criminal Behavior: Whom to Prosecute?*

In a paper on the hypnotic stimulation of antisocial behavior, DeYoub (1984) presents a case in which a 30-year-old man was "released" of his inhibitions by a non-professional hypnotist and, while in a trance-like state, told by the hypnotist that he could indeed commit bank robbery. The "patient" thereafter complied, post-hypnotically, with his "therapist's" suggestion.

DeYoub shouts alarum at this misuse of hypnosis but fails to record whether the robbery resulted in a judicial determination of criminal responsibility — on the part of the patient, the "therapist," or both.

study inquiry makes no pretense to more than accurate and perhaps insightful description of that singular subject.

Especially when fortified by the addition of instruments developed utilizing the techniques of psychometric methodology, clinical case study is unquestionably the method-of-choice for precise description of the individual client or patient preparatory to therapeutic intervention (i.e., in the task of constructing a conceptual model of psychological processes which may be active in a single patient across a variety of behaviors). But it is less useful than other methods in yielding data on many subjects in respect of a single focal behavior. Clinical case study methodology is capable of yielding a great variety of data about a single individual; in contrast, other methods of inquiry typically seek a more constricted range of data about many more subjects, who are usually selected so as to fairly represent a group or population.

CLASSIC EXEMPLARS

Clinical case study methodology is exemplified classically by a panoply of investigations by Freud and his early followers, on the basis of which important constructs in the formulation of psychoanalytic theory and the attendant theory of psychosexual development were elaborated. In the study of criminal behavior, the methodology is exemplified in the case studies reported both by such psychoanalytically-oriented investigators as Alexander and Staub (1956) and Lindner (1961) and by Eysenck (1977), unquestionably the leading behavior therapist to study criminal behavior (who, nonetheless, has made equally important contributions to the understanding of criminal behavior via psychometric methodology). Even Cattell (1985), the leading exponent of a mathematically based "calculus of behavior," has advanced a model that may be useful in clinical psychology for assessing both the probability of specific future behaviors and the change in behavior following psychotherapeutic intervention. In psychohistory, the methodology is exemplified in Erik Erikson's *Young Man Luther* and *Gandhi's Truth* and in Joan Erikson's work on Francis of Assisi.

THE PROBLEM OF RETROSPECTIVE ANALYSIS

The utility of clinical case study methodology in the study of criminal behavior is, however, severely constrained to the *retrospective analysis* of past criminal behavior by clinician and subject, or, in the case of psychohistory, the adequacy of surviving documents and/or contemporary eyewitness accounts. Even without legislative requirements that compel the clinician to take action to avert intended future behavior that violates the law, it is barely conceivable that a clinician or researcher could accept with equanimity the decision of the patient to behave in ways that are inimical to the patient's self-interest — as, surely, an act of formally criminal behavior is likely to prove.

When an intention to behave in ways that are anti-social, let alone formally criminal, is made known to the clinician, he or she is required to intervene so as to dissuade the patient from this course of action on the grounds of the psychological and social welfare of the client alone. And, of course, when such intervention is successful, the intended criminal behavior does *not* occur and cannot therefore be formally adjudicated as criminal. The same strictures would apply to any research investigator who employed clinical case study methodology even outside a therapeutic context.

Structured Observation

Next to develop historically, and more satisfactory as a method of inquiry, the *structured observation of behavior* introduces into a "naturally-occurring" behavioral situation a skilled observer (puta-

---

⇨ *Depression and Criminal Child Abuse: Cause or Consequence?*

Kinard (1982) has raised the problem of *post hoc* or retrospective analysis nicely in a paper on depression in relation to criminal child abuse. While a number of studies have concluded to a statistical link between verified episodes of criminal child abuse and a psychometric (or clinical) finding of depression in the abusing parent, "reading" of the parent's state has virtually invariably occurred only after the intervention of law enforcement or child protective services agency officials.

Thus, Kinard opines, it is not possible to conclude whether inventoried depression represents a *cause* or a *consequence* of criminal child abuse in the offender. It may further be the case that those characteristics which can be measured accurately through psychometric methodology at whatever point are simply not those implicated in criminal behavior.

In a review of the relevant scientific studies between 1950-75, Tennenbaum (1978) put the matter rather decisively: "Personality testing [i.e., psychometric methodology] has not differentiated between criminals and non-criminals. The data do not reveal any significant differences between criminal and non-criminal psychology."

tively unobtrusively) who is armed with an observation schedule, the reliability and validity of which have been determined in advance to assure public verifiability. The task of the observer is to record the target behavior, its observable antecedents and observable sequelae; pooling observations by many observers produces a sample of behavior among many behavers that is not so limited as to preclude generalizability. The methodology specific to structured observation is often fortified by incorporating psychometric methods in specific studies, as subjects whose behavior is to be "unobtrusively" observed undergo psychological tests of various sorts in advance of observation in order to identify certain typical characteristics antecedent to behavior in the situations under observation.

Structured observation methodology has the clear and obvious advantage of eliciting data from *in vivo* situations that are likely not accessible in any other way and on that account alone is much favored in process psychology. The intervention of the investigator, who is expected to affect the processes under investigation through personal participation, is direct in clinical case study; in structured observation, the investigator is at great caution *not* to participate in the behavior under investigation, so that he or she is instructed not to intervene. But the mere presence of an observer in a naturally-occurring behavioral situation may change the dynamics of the situation in many subtle and unintended ways. Even in the precise sciences, as von Heisenberg long ago argued in his "principle of uncertainty," the observed phenomenon may not be the same as the unobserved phenomenon, and, in the social sciences, as the "Hawthorne studies" on rates of industrial productivity in the 1920s seemed to argue, the subject's mere knowledge that he or she is being observed scientifically is likely to alter his or her customary behavior (Finlay, 1991).

CLASSIC EXEMPLARS

Structured observation techniques served well in the early days of empirical inquiry in social psychology and sociology in particular. The method is exemplified in general in the research of Sherif and his associates on leadership style (1954) and in the study of criminal behavior by such investigators as Thrasher (1936) and Yablonsky (1970) in their research on adolescent gangs. A more current example of the use of a quasi-structured observation methodology is the work of "reportage" (to use the term coined by Truman Capote to describe his "non-fiction novel" *In Cold Blood* of nearly 30 years ago) by journalist William Finnegan entitled "A Street Kid in the Drug Trade," which first appeared as a two-part series in the *New Yorker* (1990).

LEGAL OBLIGATIONS OF THE PARTICIPANT- OBSERVER

As is the case in clinical case study methodology, and for essentially the same reasons, the utility of structured observation techniques in the study of criminal behavior is severely limited. Though it might be argued that legislative requirements that bind the clinician in respect of the communication of criminal intent do not similarly bind the researcher in respect of the communication of similar intent among those whose behavior is under observation rather than under treatment, legal requirements which bind the ordinary citizen can hardly be said not to apply. Again, even in the absence of a formal obligation to intervene, it is barely conceivable that a researcher engaged in a structured observation study could fail to intervene so as to dissuade the emission of criminal behavior; and, again, when such intervention is successful, the intended behavior does *not* occur and cannot therefore be formally adjudicated as criminal. Thus, for example, *New Yorker* writer Finnegan (1990) recounts in some detail the several occasions on which he provided transportation for "Terry," the 16-year-old central figure in his vignette, on the way to meet the leaders of the "posse" (i.e., drug-distribution ring) of which he was a member — behavior that, if it did not directly aid and abet Terry's criminality, did little to dissuade

---

⇨ *Participant-Observers and Shop-Lifting*

In the United States, psychological researchers are constrained both by the ethical strictures of their professional organizations and by Federal law governing human subjects in experimentation. British researchers are not bound by many of the strictures that, by Federal law if not by ethical canon, constrain the conduct of psychological inquiry in the U.S. — apparently, including those that bind an ordinary citizen.

Thus, Buckle & Farrington (1984) had their research deputies "tail" some 503 customers of an English department store chain over a three-week period, observing — but not interfering with — thefts by shop-lifting among 3% of the male and 1.5% of the female customers. Among the investigators' focal concerns was the level of under-estimating of loss by theft and under-reporting of shop-lifting episodes. A wide array of ethical questions is engaged by such research, including the question of whether the "eyewitness" testimony of research observers is admissible, or even legally *compellable,* in an effort to convict.

it; yet it is curious that Terry's relatives perceived Finnegan as "the guy who's trying to keep Terry straight."

Psychometric Methods

Of greater empirical sophistication and the method of inquiry *par excellence* in differential psychology, *psychometric methodology* proceeds by determining statistically the relationship between performance on formal psychological measures (the reliability and validity of which can be determined empirically) and specific behavior, either directly measured, directly observed, or reconstructed from available records. Relatively larger numbers of subjects are typically investigated than is the case in clinical case studies or in structured observations, so that the issue of generalizability is directly addressed. Since the validity and reliability of the instruments employed can be determined with precision and since they are administered under standard conditions, the issue of public verifiability is similarly addressed.

Psychometric methodology makes it possible to conduct research on relatively large samples and to employ sophisticated statistical methodology in the analysis of results; both improve the likelihood of valid inferences and generalizations. Because psychometric methodology employs standard measuring instruments administered under standard conditions, and since the intervention of the investigator is as relatively covert as possible, the method is often considered "investigator-proof."

For these reasons, psychometric methodology is now very likely modal in research in most subfields of psychology that investigate human (as distinct from animal) subjects. But, to achieve that end, psychometric methodology sacrifices the direct contact with behavior implicit in both clinical case study, structured observation, and laboratory investigation and which is virtually essential in process psychology. Indeed, that much research rooted in the methodology of differential psychology proceeds by way of investigating the relationship between scores on psychometric instruments (representing, respectively, the so-called antecedent or independent variables on the one hand and the dependent or criterion variables on the other) *without* directly measuring behavior is a common criticism of the current state of psychological research in general.

CLASSIC AND CURRENT EXEMPLARS

The classic examples of psychometric methodology in large-scale psychological research on behavior of varying sorts are the longitudinal studies of Terman (1916, 1937, 1960) on subjects who scored at high levels on his test of intelligence and whose lives he and his associates followed for 50 years, grouped under the title *the genetic study of genius*; the developmental studies carried out over three decades on same-aged cohorts followed from birth at the Fels Research Institute (Kagan & Moss, 1962); and the nearly 10,000 studies utilizing the Minnesota Multiphasic Personality Inventory (MMPI) undertaken since the initial publication of that instrument some five decades ago (Graham, 1987).

Psychometric methodology is clearly the method-of-choice in research on criminal behavior from the perspective of differential psychology and has thus been employed in a panoply of investigations. The leading current exemplars, both of which are discussed in greater detail in Chapter 6, are:

❑ [1] the studies of Eysenck (1966, 1977, 1989) and his colleagues and collaborators on the extent to which psychoticism, neuroticism, and extraversion as measurable personality characteristics differentiate those who are formally adjudicated of criminal behavior; and

❑ [2] the investigations of Megargee (1977, 1984) and his colleagues and collaborators on the extent to which different *patterns* of personality characteristics as measured through the primary and derivative scales of the MMPI differentiate convicted and confined criminal offenders in respect of the types of crime of which they have been convicted.

PRACTICAL CONSTRAINTS

Constraints on the use of psychometric methodology in the study of criminal behavior issue largely from technical scientific considerations rather than from ethical or legislative impediments. Though it is possible to conceive a circumstance in which a large and undifferentiated subject pool were to be tested on a variety of psychological measures and then followed longitudinally to determine whether these *a priori* measures were related to later criminal behavior, in practice psychometric methodology is typically applied to convicted offenders *a posteriori* and thus can identify neither genuine antecedents nor correlates of criminal behavior. Instead, the more usual circumstance is, as we have seen in an earlier chapter, the classic post-diction situation.

Laboratory Analogue Experimentation

Laboratory analogue experimentation is the method of inquiry that is both the most powerful for, and best attuned to, research in *process* psychology. For very obvious reasons, it simply cannot be directly applied to research on criminal behavior. This modality

⇨ *Analogue Studies: Simulated Stealing, Tax Evasion,*
  Sexual Aggression, Jury Selection, Research Fraud

Despite the limitations in applicability, a remarkably large number of analogue studies relevant either to criminal behavior *or* to the administration of justice continue to be conducted.

❑ Thus, a series of investigations in Australia (Haines, 1982; Jackson & Haines, 1982; Haines, Jackson & Davidson, 1983; Jackson, 1984) focused on "simulated" stealing behavior among children and adolescents in an effort to devise and evaluate interventions capable of inducing "resistance to the temptation to steal."

❑ Similarly, Edney & Bell (1984) studied "stealing" among undergraduates engaged in a situation in which either theft or altruism were prospective behaviors, concluding that theft exceeded altruism at the ratio of five to one. In what appears an ethically questionable experiment however much "de-briefing" was accorded to subjects, Hosch & Cooper (1982) studied prior victimization as a determinant of eyewitness accuracy in a situation in which they caused calculators or watches to be "stolen" from undergraduate victims. In a study of tax evasion that spanned the Netherlands and the United Kingdom, Webley, Robben, Effers & Hessing (1991) claimed to have succesfully designed "experimental situations that engage the same psychological processes as the real world's counterparts."

❑ In studies which attempted to mimic violent crimes, Larrance & Twentyman (1983) investigated the responses of mothers with a history of child abuse, in relation to control subjects, in a photographic analogue that depicted their own children in the company of another child in a variety of interpersonal situations in which the "target" child was either transgressed upon or transgress upon others. Malamuth (1983) first collected data on attitudes on aggressiveness toward women and general response to rape among male subjects, then introduced them into a laboratory situation in which they could behave civilly or aggressively toward women; the results were as expected.

❑ At a time when several cases of fraud or deception in research on the part of previously well-respected biomedical scientists (including one Nobel Laureate) had stirred considerable public and official attention, Miceli, Dozier & Near (1991) created an analogue situation in which nearly 300 undergraduates witnessed "apparent wrongdoing" by a university researcher and were later given the opportunity to report such wrongdoing to a university administrator (a process known colloquially as "whistle blowing"). The investigators found that whistle blowing was more likely when the wrongdoing had been witnessed by more, rather than by fewer, observers. In this situation, there is evidence of the effect of lack of direct observation or deterrence on the wrongful behavior of another *and* upon one's own behavior, since student honor codes typically bind one to blow the whistle when they witness another's wrongful behavior. However valuable its findings, this study appears to verge quite close to systematic deception of subjects formally proscribed by Federal regulation.

❑ Other analogue studies have considered a variety of variables related to the criminal justice system. Thus, in an analogue that has some implications for jury selection, Kanekar, Pinto & Mazumdar (1985) studied the extent to which previous personal victimization affects the attribution of responsibility in cases of robbery and rape, while Leippe (1985) investigated whether the failure of an "eyewitness" to identify the accused as the perpetrator influenced decision about guilt among college students who comprised a mock jury. In another analogue which has implications for the study of victimization, Wakshlag, Vial & Tamborini (1983) demonstrated that heavy exposure to filmed violence triggers fear and apprehension leading to precautionary measures among undergraduate subjects.

proceeds by way of introducing subjects into behavioral situations that mimic "real life," but under controlled laboratory conditions (thus capitalizing on the strengths of structured observation methodology), often in which the antecedents to behavior on the part of subjects have been measured by psychological instrument (thus incorporating the strengths of psychometric research methodology) and/or by clinical interviews (thus incorporating the strengths of clinical case study).

One might wonder, for example, who will emerge as a leader in a task-oriented group whose members display varied levels of intelligence, varied orientations to authority, greater or lesser sensitivity to social cues, and the like. Each of these antecedent variables can be measured by a standard psychological instrument, and an investigator might assign a research associate to each of several subjects, to follow him or her in the daily round of activity, structured observation schedule in hand. But it is more efficient to bring prospective subjects into a laboratory situation in such a manner that a predetermined number display certain levels of each antecedent characteristic, then observe the emergence of leadership in respect of the accomplishment of a standard task in a reasonably close *in vitro analogue* to an *in vivo* situation.

CLASSIC EXEMPLARS

Though it preserves public verifiability and can assure generalizability through careful procedures for the selection of representative subjects, laboratory research methodology sacrifices the advantage of the *in vivo* situation standard in structured observations of naturally-occurring phenomena. But it permits the *in vitro* creation of experimental analogues by approximating naturally-occurring phenomena under controlled, albeit limited, conditions. Thus, Bandura (1963, 1973) could study the imitation of aggressive behavior among young children in a situation that approximated a kindergarten without the intrusive, artificial introduction of an observer into a naturally-occurring children's play group.

Moreover, certain processes regarded as "psychological" can also be studied in the laboratory by analogy, using infra-human species as subjects. Thus, much research on learning has proceeded with rats, doves, and monkeys as subjects (Skinner, 1938, 1957, 1974); conditions antecedent to the elicitation of behavior generally held to be indicative of neurotic anxiety have been studied using cats as subjects (Wolpe, 1969); conditions which elicit aggressive behavior have been studied using pigeons as subjects (Skinner, 1957; Azrin, Hutchinson & Dake, 1969); and willingness to aggress and to punish

⇨ *Research Evidence on the Prediction of Violence*

Not all mental health professionals are persuaded that the prediction of future dangerousness should be abandoned, whatever the position of their principal professional organizations (Bear, 1989; Gunn, 1982; Hall, 1982, 1984; Petrunik, 1982). But the weight of empirical evidence clearly supports the "official" view of the two APA's. In virtually all studies reported, the rate of "false positives" (i.e., those cases in which future violence is predicted, with restriction of liberty the likely consequence, but in which no future violence is observed) has been shown to be unacceptably high.

Thus, in a carefully planned and executed series of studies of post-parole violence among nearly 4200 subjects conducted at the National Council on Crime and Delinquency's Research Center, Wenk, Robison & Smith (1972) found that a complex and putatively sound method of prediction which utilized both psychometric or actuarial, clinical, life history, and criminal history variables produced a false positive rate of 86%. Similar studies (Kozol, 1972; Rubin, 1972; Cocozza & Steadman, 1974; Williams & Miller, 1977; Steadman & Cocozza, 1978; McDonald & Paitich, 1981; Rose & Bitter, 1982; Holland, Holt & Beckett, 1982; Holland, Beckett & Holt, 1982; Holland, Beckett, Holt & Levi, 1983; Mullen, 1984) reported false positive rates between 60% and 94%. In his review of relevant studies, Monahan (1976) found the highest the "true" positive rate reported at 46% (with, reciprocally, 54% as the false positive rate) in an unpublished manuscript prepared by Maryland correctional authorities but not subjected to the scrutiny of peer review customary in scientific journals and thus suspect in the scientific community; no other study he reviewed approached even this level of accuracy, and several reached false positive rates between 94% and 99.7%.

Hence, it is hardly surprising that both the American Psychiatric Association and the American Psychological Association have cautioned against predictions of future violence. An American Psychiatric Association Task Force (1974) on the assessment of violence warned: "The state of the art regarding predictions of violence is very unsatisfactory. The ability of psychiatrists or any other professionals to reliably predict future violence is unproved." For its part, the American Psychological Association (1978) similarly concluded: "The validity of psychological predictions of dangerous behavior, at least in the sentencing and release situations we are considering, is extremely poor, so poor that one could oppose their use on strictly empirical grounds."

Stone (1976), a prominent forensic psychiatrist at Harvard, trenchantly commented that, since "mental health professionals, whether or not they use [actuarial] devices, simply have no demonstrated capacity to generate even a cutting line that will confine more true than false positives" and concluded that "a lay person can predict dangerousness at least as well as a professional."

In a more recent review of the pertinent scientific literature, John Monahan (1981), a distinguished psychologist- attorney at the University of Virginia, concludes that "Psychiatrists and psychologists are accurate in no more than one out of three predictions of violent behavior over a several-year period among institutionalized populations that had committed violence in the past (and thus had a high base rate for it)," even though he observes that an unresolved, and perhaps insoluble, dilemma obtains between "the patient's right not to be a false positive and the victim's right not to be set upon by a false negative."

Fersch (1980), an attorney-psychologist, is even more acerbic: "The laws ought to be changed. All references to psychiatrists and psychologists as predictors of dangerousness ought to be eliminated. Courts ought to discontinue the practice of requiring or even asking psychiatrists and psychologists for predictions of dangerousness . . . any predictions of dangerousness which need to be made ought to be made by lay persons within the court or correctional systems using the best available evidence — the past acts of the individual in question."

As a countervailing force, however, there is the "duty to warn" a prospective victim if the latter stands in "clear and imminent danger," which duty has been *judicially* imposed on mental health professionals. The duty to warn has been held to apply even at the expense of sacrificing professional confidentiality which is otherwise protected by law. The key decisions arose in *Tarasoff v. Regents*, in which the Supreme Court of California affirmed in 1976 that the psychologist who had treated an emotionally disturbed student at the University of California (who communicated during treatment an intention to slay his former girl friend) had a duty to warn the prospective victim and that this duty extended to the psychiatrist who had supervised the treating psychologist and to the Regents of the University, in whose name both were acting; in a 1980 decision in *Thompson v. County of Alameda,* the same Court articulated "the requirement that there be a readily identifiable victim before a duty to warn can be imposed" (Simon, 1987, p. 309).

Litwack & Schlesinger (1987) have reviewed a number of court decisions that have placed upon mental health professionals at a minimum the *duty to warn* those they have reason to believe are in "imminent danger" of victimization on the basis of information revealed by patients. Such a duty requires that the clinician make a "prediction" of violence, albeit with the overt purpose of defeating that prediction (Hall, 1984).

Renowned legal scholar George Dix (1983) has underscored the capital distinction between an assessment of *clear and imminent* danger to a *particular* prospective victim, as explicated in the *Tarasoff* decision, and a more generalized opinion about the prospect that a particular person, at some future time and under some unspecified set of conditions, *might* perpetrate a violent crime.

As Dix puts it (p. 256): "there is little reliable evidence verifying claims made by some members of the [mental health] profession of predictive skill. Such research as is available concerns mostly long term predictions concerning the conduct of persons without traditional mental illness; this research suggests minimal predictive skill . . . psychiatrists' predictive ability is substantially greater when it is called into play concerning the short-term risk posed by persons whose assaultive tendencies are related to symptoms of identifiable serious mental illness. But claims of predictive skill even in these situations might be acknowledged to rest only upon intuition." Pallone (1991, pp. 115-117) has reviewed a number of other precedents and issues relating to predictive inefficiency vs. the duty to warn.

have been studied with human subjects by Milgram (1963, 1965) and Zimbardo & Ebbesen (1969).

LIMITATIONS IN STUDYING CRIMINAL BEHAVIOR

While such behavior as hostility, aggression, and even theft might be studied in the laboratory (presuming, in today's world, that such studies meet both the ethical guidelines of scholarly organizations and Federal regulations governing the human use of human subjects, which regulations themselves significantly limit laboratory investigations of behavior), the laboratory study of behavior that is *specifically and formally criminal* in the conservative way in which we have defined that term is obviously *not* possible. That conclusion is dictated by the virtual certainty that few prosecutors would choose to pursue to indictment an experimental *subject* whose otherwise criminal behavior had been deliberately elicited in the laboratory — though one cannot be sanguine that an experimenter who recurrently elicited from subjects behavior that violates the law (e.g., by inducing threats or provocations toward members of one gender or another, one ethnic group or another) would similarly escape sanction.

Laboratory studies may tell us a good deal about behavior that is anti-social, immoral, and/or unpleasant — and thus perhaps inform us about the likely antecedents of criminal behavior; but the very nature of laboratory experimentation precludes the official declaration of any behavior emitted under controlled experimental conditions as criminal. Thus, the method-of-choice in direct research on behavior from the perspective of process psychology is closed in investigations of specifically criminal behavior.

Nonetheless, both research on laboratory analogues to anti-social, aggressive, and self-aggrandizing behavior and process psychology research on the acquisition and maintenance of behavior in general may yield substantial conceptual material applicable *by analogy* to a process model of criminal behavior.

☐ CONSTRAINED METHODS OF INQUIRY & POST-DICTING CRIMINAL BEHAVIOR

If it be the aim of the psychological study of behavior to identify the *antecedents to* a particular focal behavior, it is clear that those antecedents should be identified, specified, or measured *in advance* of the emission of the behavior in question. If it be the aim of the psychological study of behavior to identify the *correlates of* a particular focal behavior, it is clear that those correlates must be

➪ *Unsettled Case Law on the Duty to Warn: Arizona vs. Pennsylvania*

While the duty to warn a *readily identifiable* prospective victim may seem to have been settled in *Tarasoff* and attendant cases, the precise limits of the obligations imposed thereby continue to be litigated — and the resultant decisions yield contradictory signals.

The Arizona Court of Appeals appears indeed to have broadened the "readily identifiable prospective victim" considerably by taking a loose-constructionist view of the duty to warn principle in its decision in *Tamsen v. Weber* (Arizona Appeals, 1991). The circumstances were these: Kevin Trahan was involuntarily committed to Arizona State Hospital on the grounds that he was dangerous to himself; while hospitalized, Trahan attempted suicide. Nonetheless, his psychiatrist permitted him to have "ground privileges," a status that meant that he could roam the hospital grounds unescorted. While so doing, he absconded. A day later, he abducted a woman previously unknown to him, beat her severely, and left her for dead.

Nonetheless, the victim recovered and subsequently sued the Hospital and the treating psychiatrist for damages attendant upon wrongful injury. In the court of first jurisdiction, the suit was dismissed. But the appeals court reversed, ruling that the evidence from case records at the hospital revealed "In blunt terms, Trahan was thinking about killing people," and that, in such circumstances, "The potential for grave physical harm mandates that a psychiatrist who undertakes to care for an involuntarily committed patient with known or reasonably discernible dangerous propensities must exercise due care or be held liable for the consequences."

But the Pennsylvania Superior Court took a very, very strict constructionist view in its decision in *Estate of Eyer v. Food Service East* (Pennsylvania Appeals, 1991). In that case, a student at Penn State University named Tindal strangled his live-in girl friend in the men's room of an emporium named the Cannery Store, "believing her to be a Russian agent." Tindal was under psychiatric care, was also being "treated" by a counselor at Penn State, and was taking Navane, a pharmacological preparation its manufacturer describes as a specific for "the chronic schizophrenic patient [that affects] the ability to concentrate and promote[s] a better attitude toward work and co-workers." The diagnosis was schizophreniform disorder.

The resulting liability case involved complex legal maneuvers. The estate of the victim sued the emporium, in essence charging that it had a duty to guarantee the safety of its customers, whether in the men's room or elsewhere. In its turn, the emporium petitioned the court that the University, the psychiatrist, and the counselor be "joined . . . as additional defendants."

In a wide-ranging decision, the Superior Court ruled that the University, the psychiatrist, and the counselor "did not owe a legal duty to [the victim] for failing to warn her of Tindal's propensity toward violence" because they "did not share with [the victim] the type of 'special relationship' that would justify the imposition of a duty to warn. Additionally, Tindal communicated no resolve, nor manifested any inclination to harm [the victim] prior to the date that he strangled her. Finally, the fact that Tindal lived with [the victim] did not automatically predispose her to abuse."

Quite clearly, these two decisions stand in diametric contrast: The Arizona decision extends the duty to warn to virtually any chance victim, while the Pennsylvania decision exempts the treating professional from the duty to warn even that person, who, on a statistical and actuarial basis (as the data reviewed in Chapter 5 indicate), is the most likely to become the victim of impulsive lethal violence.

identified, specified, or measured *contemporaneously with* the emission of that focal behavior.

By those standards, each of the customary avenues of investigation we have reviewed is seriously constrained in respect of the study of criminal behavior. Of the four principal methods of inquiry currently used in the psychological study of behavior, ethical considerations or legal constraints dictate that two (*clinical case study, structured observation*) cannot be employed *a priori*, in advance of the emission of formally criminal behavior, so that their use is limited to *retrospective analysis* only.

A third, powerful method (*laboratory analogue experimentation*) cannot be used either *a priori* or *a posteriori* in the direct study of formally criminal behavior.

Though it is possible to conceive a set of circumstances in which the fourth (*psychometric methodology*) might be employed *a priori* (e.g., in longitudinal studies that consider the emission of formally criminal behavior among a variety of other behaviors emitted by members of large subject pools), in practice even this method of inquiry is typically employed only after the formal adjudication of criminal behavior, and then more often in an effort to differentiate those who have already behaved criminally in one way from those who have behaved criminally in other ways (i.e., to differentiate those subjects, usually among a pool of convicted and incarcerated offenders, who have been found guilty of one sort of offense from those who have been found guilty of offenses of other sorts) — *rather than* to differentiate those who have behaved criminally from those who have not.

There can be little doubt, then, about the accuracy of Megargee's (1970) trenchant observation that "no method has yet been developed which will acceptably *post-dict,* let alone predict" criminal behavior. Indeed, the development of a method *or* a conceptual model which reasonably post-dicts the emission of criminal behavior might well constitute an achievement of considerable proportions in the face of the constraints implicitly or explicitly placed on the applicability of the principal methods of inquiry utilized in the psychological study of behavior to behavior that has been formally adjudicated as criminal — *especially when* that adjudication has occurred within a system of law enforcement and the administration of justice that itself yields a set of circumstances in which (because, as we have seen, most convictions likely occur as the result of "bargained" pleas of guilt) only a minor proportion of alleged offenders are convicted and sanctioned and in which the formal of-

⇨ *Predicting Violence in the Short Term*

Although they acknowledged the anomalous situation in which "courts and legislatures continue to require that mental health professionals assess and manage their patients' dangerousness, despite a large body of research suggesting that clinicians' ability to predict violence is severely limited," psychiatric researchers Dale McNeil & Renee Binder (1991) of the University of California's School of Medicine at San Francisco opined that, in the "real world" of risk management in a psychiatric hospital setting, mental health personnel nonetheless had a duty to make "short-term predictions [of violence] among acutely ill patients" (p. 1317) — for the protection not only of the prospective targets of potentially violent patients, but also for the protection of those patients themselves.

Thus, McNeil & Binder set out to determine the relative accuracy of predictions of violence made by experienced nurses and physicians at the time of a patient's admission to a "locked short- term psychiatric inpatient unit" at the University's Medical Center over a period of eleven consecutive months. During that period, 149 patients had been admitted to the unit, of whom 91% had entered on *involuntary* civil commitments "on the basis of grave disability and/or danger to the self or others," so that one might assume that the baseline probability for violence (as assessed, indeed, by the committing judge) was rather high. In the overall sample, 55% were male, 71% white, 86% were members of the "lowest two" social classes as determined by a standard measure of socioeconomic status; the mean age was 43. Some 28% had been diagnosed as schizophrenic, 16% as suffering from manic disorders, and 13% as suffering from psychotic conditions attributable to *organic* etiology.

Nurses and physicians were called upon to assess the probability of violence during the first seven days of hospitalization for each patient on an eleven-point continuum "ranging from 0% (definitely will not attack someone) to 100% (definitely will attack someone)." Assessing clinicians had available to them "clinical data from referring professionals, reports from family members, interview of the patient, and review of any available previous medical records." Among these 149 patients with a high baseline for prospective violence, 26 (17%) actually emitted physically aggressive behavior during the seven-day target of prediction. In contrast, ratings by nurses had placed 40% of the subjects in what McNeil & Binder called a "high risk" group (i.e., those assigned a probability for violence of 67% or higher), so that this group of clinicians *over*-predicted at a rate of 235%; ratings by physicians had placed 22% in the "high risk" group, so that they *over*- predicted at a rate of 129%.

McNeil & Binder (p. 1320) observe the prospect of a self-fulfilling prophecy "since the same staff members who assessed the risk of violence were responsible for managing the patients' behavior." That raises the specter of a two-edged sword: It may have been the case that clinicians who were particularly sensitized to prospective violence on the part of particular patients behaved clinically in ways calculated to defeat their own predictions. But it may be almost equally credible that such predictions caused some clinicians to behave apprehensively toward some patients — and that such behavior may actually have elicited aggressive violence on the part of those patients. The investigators leave open (p. 1321) "the issue of which interventions are warranted at a given level of assessed risk of violence [as] a matter of social policy, in which value judgments about the restrictiveness of the treatment environment, the potential damage to victims, etc., are important." So also, of course, are the rights of mental patients, prisoners, and all others confined against their will.

fense-of-record, in Mr. Justice Peters' (1981) phrase, "may have little relation to reality."

☐ EMPIRICAL DATA, INFERENCE, AND CONCEPTUAL MODELS

We have indicated that our goal is the inferential construction of a broad but empirically-anchored conceptual model which illuminates the psychological conditions antecedent to, and the processes activated in, the acquisition and maintenance of behavior that society, through its properly empowered agents, formally adjudicates as criminal. Can we discern the psychological processes activated in, and the psychological antecedents that interact together to yield, the emission of behavior that society, through its official agents, formally deems criminal? Under what conditions is formally criminal behavior emitted, and by whom?

The process model we offered, within a general framework of personal construct psychology, pivots on two inferentially-derived elements:

☐ (1) *that a formally criminal behavior is construed by the behaver as an acceptable behavioral option* and

☐ (2) *that the behaver construes the probability of detection and of the imposition of intrusive sanctions attached to formally criminal behavior as relatively low.*

The questions we thus need to ask of the empirical data are these: Are these inferences reasonable on the basis of current research evidence? If so, how do these personal constructs (i.e., of the acceptability of formally criminal behavior in relation to a given behavioral object *or* across varied behavioral objects; of the low probability of the imposition of intrusive sanction) arise within the personal behavioral repertoire of some persons but not in the repertoires of others? In relation to one object of behavior, or class of objects, but not in relation to others? If it be the case that such constructs appear to arise more frequently among members of certain sub-cultural groups than among those who belong to other sub-cultural groups, what variables either sensitize the members of those groups to particular objects of behavior and/or either encourage or tolerate formally criminal ways of behaving in relation to those objects?

Such conceptual constructions as those embodied in the process model proceed *inferentially* from the empirical to the conceptual levels. Before turning to the results of such inquiry, it may prove useful to review cursorily at least the character of conceptual models as inferential constructs.

Conceptual Models in the
Probabilistic Sciences

A distinguished philosopher of science, the late Sir Norman Campbell (1952, p. 105), regards it as the function of science "to make the world intelligible to us." Hence, it is generally held that the aim of scientific inquiry is to determine those conditions under which the phenomena of focal interest in a particular science are reliably observed to occur. In essence, then, scientific inquiry focuses on those phenomena which are publicly verifiable, seeking to render those phenomena intelligible in relation to antecedent, if not plainly causal, conditions.

The usual formulation to emerge from successful scientific inquiry into a given phenomenon has it: *Under Condition X (or Conditions X, Y, Z), if A, then B.* Homely illustrations can readily be drawn from elementary experiments in introductory chemistry (*Let two parts hydrogen and one part oxygen = A; electrical catalysis = X; then,* B = water), but only with full cognizance that the specification and weighting of the components in so complex a phenomenon as human behavior will rarely fall into so neat and well-packaged a formulation.

The *precise sciences* (most notably physics, chemistry, and, to a lesser extent, biology) seek to specify *antecedent conditions* which are both *necessary and sufficient* to yield the phenomenon under investigation, so that the formulation in the precise sciences can more typically be: *"If and only if* A, under Conditions X and Y but not under Conditions L and M, *then B."*

Such precision is rarely achieved in what are called the *probabilistic sciences,* among which psychology, sociology, anthropology, and economics are the chief exemplars. Rather, in these sciences, the relationship between antecedents and consequence is predicated in *probabilistic* terms, so that the typical formulation has it: "If A, under Condition X (or Conditions X, Y, and Z, but not L and M), *it is probable* that B will occur." In cases in which the relationship between antecedent conditions and consequence have been thoroughly explored empirically, it may possible to incorporate a statement of finite probability (e.g., 99%, 95%, 60%, 42%, etc.) into the formulation, which then is expressed in some formulation such as: *B is likely to occur in 65% of the cases,* etc.

For these reasons, probabilistic scientists very rarely express formulations which speak to "necessary and sufficient" conditions antecedent to a focal phenomenon — and even then at some peril, since it is widely held that the phenomena of their focal concerns are likely not amenable to specification in invariable and absolute terms. Instead, the probabilistic sciences are much more frequently content with the specification of the antecedent conditions *necessary* to a focal phenomenon, even when these conditions are *not* seen as *sufficient:* Granted that intelligence in the "bright-normal" range has been shown to be a necessary condition for the acquisition of a reading knowledge of Russian (at least among non-native speakers of Russian), for example, *what else* (e.g., exposure to competent language instruction) is necessary for such acquisition?

Philosophers of science like Sir Norman (1952, pp. 85-97) customarily make fine distinctions between *observations and experimentation,* which are said to inhere in the empirical level, and *elementary laws and theory,* which are said to inhere in the conceptual level. However intellectually intriguing, exploration of such distinctions, or even of their applicability to the probabilistic sciences of behavior, takes us well beyond the scope of this volume. Instead, we employ the simpler term *conceptual model* to denote the "If A, then B" formulation, with the understanding that such a model represents an empirically-anchored but conceptually abstract generalization about the conditions antecedent (understood as those which are *necessary,* but *not necessarily sufficient*) to a focal phenomenon, or, even more simply, a *conceptually abstract* model for B.

Conceptual Models as Inferential Abstractions

If a definition seems useful, it can be said that a conceptual model in the sciences of behavior is an *inferential abstraction* of the behavior in question that can be generally applied (or, more technically, "predicated"). Thus, a conceptual model is *inferential,* with the inferences derived from the empirical data adduced in the studies which have considered the focal phenomenon of which the conceptual formulation is a model (or close analogues thereto) in relation to a range of variables. Similarly, a conceptual model is an *abstract* statement whose validity or invalidity (or truth or falsity, if one prefers) clearly hinges on the available empirical evidence, so that a conceptual model which may be valid (or "true") at one point in time may become invalid as contrary empirical evidence is amassed and inferentially processed. In a very real sense, such models are "best guesses" based on an assessment of the currently available empirical evidence. The differentiating characteristic of *process models* is that they represent conceptual statements that *seek to describe the process or processes by which antecedent conditions interact with each other to yield a focal consequence.*

Though Sir Norman might shudder, we hold that conceptual modeling as a process of abstracting from the available empirical evidence can proceed relatively *atheoretically,* without particular anchorage in an undergirding theoretical matrix. In the development of empirically-derived conceptual models, it is absolutely necessary that one be attentive to the available empirical evidence bearing upon the focal consequence to be modeled; however intellectually gratifying the imposition of a theory (or, as Messick [1980] prefers, a "nomological network") on those observations may be, premature allegiance to such a theoretical system (or, worse, an ideology posing as a theoretical system) may not only *not* be required, but may prove counterproductive. The behaver-as-scientist tenets of personal construct psychology suggest that constructs are formed to give meaning to our empirical observations; it is only after the linking of many of these constructs that a theoretical system, or a nomological network, capable of giving meaning to many disparate observations, emerges. To follow Cronbach's (1972) distinctions, a conceptual model may be comprised of a series of psychological constructs that may or may not be woven together into an integrated "nomological net" that, for him, is determinative of scientific theory.

Rather, the validity of a conceptual model depends, in the first instance, on the validity of the empirical data from which it is derived and, in the second, on the validity of the inferential processing of those data, which inferences constitute the "constructs" for the model. Should an emergent conceptual model fit well within a theoretical matrix (as, indeed, we hold that the process model of criminal behavior blends congruently with *personal construct psychology* and, more generally, with social-cognitive theory, as general theoretical matrices), there is added an element that might be construed as intellectual elegance. But a conceptual model for a focal behavior should be judged on its own, largely empirical and pragmatic, merits and *not* on the merits of the theoretical substratum with which it does or does not meld.

Conceptual Models and Prediction in Clinical Practice

As an intellectual construction, the overarching purpose of a conceptual model in psychology is to render focal behavior comprehensible and intelligible. But, as a guide to clinical practice, a conceptual model is also called upon to fulfill quite a different purpose: to predict behavior. As intellectual structures, conceptual models in psychology might quite appropriately deal with behavior that has already happened in situations now past, seeking to render that behavior intelligible (i.e., to *post-dict* that behavior) within a matrix comprised of such antecedents as the developmental history, the pattern of learning experiences, the general personality characteristics, or the global phenomenology (or, more reasonably, some determinate mix of these antecedents) of the behaver understood as rather a prototypical abstraction.

But, as guides to clinical practice in the mental health professions, conceptual models in psychology are burdened with a more heroic task: not to explain what an abstract and prototypical behaver has done in the past, but to predict *with a degree of accuracy that improves upon chance* what a concrete, very particular behaver is likely to do in future situations in relation to a particular focal behavior in consequence of that litany of antecedents. It is in this clinical application — the prediction of behavior, though for very different purposes (the welfare, and, in the present context, the freedom of the individual client *vs.* the security and safety of society) — that the interests of psychology *appear* to coincide most closely with those of the enforcers of law and the administrators of justice. That appearance, however, masks some important distinctions, constraints, and limitations.

The Client as Predictor and Behaver

Perhaps the most important of these is that, at the optimal level of clinical practice in the mental health professions, the person who is both predictor and behaver is *the client* for clinical services *himself or herself*. Thus, in the optimal clinical alliance, the role of the psychoclinician is to assist the client to develop sufficient understanding of the engines of his or her own behavior to predict a future course of action with some degree of accuracy, but with very broad tolerances and *within a situation in which the goal is to change those patterns of behavior that are self-identified by the client as undesirable or inimical to his or her own welfare*:

❑ Is the client particularly sensitive to external stimuli of the class X? Is it the case that he or she typically or characteristically emits behavior Y in response to stimulus X? Does the emission of that behavior entail such adverse consequences that to continue to emit it represents an undesirable or self-defeating pattern?

❑ What corrective behaviors are accessible to the client — can he or she, for example, avoid X, and what are the consequences of such avoidance? Inhibit response Y, with whatever consequences ensue from such inhibition? Or can he or she learn to respond to X through behavior Z, which avoids the negative consequences, whether gauged in subjective or objective terms, which follow Y? What consequences follow for the integrity and economy of the client's total behavioral repertoire when behavior Z, in relation to stimulus X, is substituted for behavior Y?

❏ Alternately, can the emotional and psychological meanings attached to stimulus X be modified so that it no longer elicits an undesirable response?

Questions about how it came to pass that the client had developed particular sensitivity to stimulus X, why he or she had learned to respond to that stimulus (or amalgam of stimuli) in self-defeating or inappropriate ways, or what symbolic meanings either stimulus or habitual response might have for him or her are less important clinically than what can be done to rectify a situation the client finds undesirable.

Prediction, Risk, and the Tolerance of Error

That paradigmatic process is one in which the client learns to anticipate his/her characteristic psychological and behavioral responses to varying stimulus situations, chooses (or even, is led to choose) to undertake corrective action in relation to characteristic patterns of behavior which may be self-defined as inimical to his/her own welfare (including those patterns of behavior which are self-defined as inimical because they entail negative public or social consequences), and thus begins to exercise increasing control over his/her own behavior. The process differs in quite dramatic and obvious ways from one in which an external observer, no matter how clinically skilled, attempts to predict the behavior of a second party, the engines of whose behavior may have been studied minutely but who is, himself or herself, *not* a participant either in the act of prediction nor in the task of designing and implementing behavioral "course corrections" which avoid consequences which may be defined as adverse *only* by others *but not by the self.*

It is fair to say that these latter predictions, made without the behaver himself or herself as a participant in the process, more nearly approximate the aim and intent of those enforcers of law and administrators of justice who are concerned with the control, and therefore prediction, of criminal behavior at various stages in the process of administering justice — at the point of decision about release of an accused on bond, for example, or at the point of imposition of sentence, no less than in "primary prevention" measures to obviate crime.

However, as Tyler (1978) argues, the task of predicting the future behavior of a specific individual is of an order of difficulty not usually imposed even on the more precise of the physical sciences, and the level of difficulty can only be seen as the more intense when the stakes are, at one extreme, the safety of society and, at the other, the freedom of the individual. Borrowing Cronbach & Gleser's (1965)

⇨ *A Risk-of-Violence Scale: for Managing Dangerous Patients: Recapitulating vs. Post- Dicting Past Behavior*

A team of mental health specialists at Albert Einstein College of Medicine in New York City commenced in the mid-1980s a series of studies on the intrapersonal and demographic characteristics of psychiatric hospital patients who have committed violent offenses and those who have attempted suicide (Apter, Kotler, Sevy, Plutchik, Brown, Foster, Hillbrand, Korn & van Praag, 1991), in the process developing research scales to measure "risk of violence" and "risk of suicide."

Their "risk of violence" measure largely recapitulates the respondent's past behavioral history; the instrument (p. 884)

❑ consists of 12 items answered on a 3-point continuum of frequency. The patient is asked about acts of violence against others, the carrying and use of weapons, arrests, and loss of temper . . . results show clear discrimination among most of the groups on average level of expressed violence, with prisoners and self-referred violent patients scoring the highest and epileptic patients scoring the lowest . . . the scale significantly discriminates between patients reporting violent acts toward others and patients reporting neither suicidal nor violent acts.

In a recent study, the investigators compared "forensic patients [with] a long history of violence and assaultiveness" with a sample of "psychiatric inpatients hospitalized at a large general municipal hospital," who had neither a history of formally criminal behavior nor a history of violent behavior.

Somewhat tautologically, the investigators reported that scores on their "risk of violence" instrument significantly differentiated the two groups; but no significant differences were found on measures of impulsivity, anger, calmness, fear, sadness, instability, suspiciousness, rebelliousness, expectancy, happiness, trait anxiety, or state anxiety.

Those results indeed underscore empirically the conceptual issues activated in the *post-diction* of criminal behavior. Had it been the case that measures of personal or demographic characteristics *independent* of the "target" behavior itself had differentiated the two groups, the differentiating measures might be said to have *post-dicted* that behavior. But instead the only differentiating measure is an instrument that recapitulates (and perhaps thus more precisely codifies) the target behavior itself.

term, Peterson (1988) has spoken elegantly to "bandwidth-fidelity" in psychological assessment and prediction:

> Given constrained investments of time and effort, one can study phenomena within a narrow range precisely, or phenomena over a broad range inexactly, but the goal of precise measurement over a broad range is unattainable.

In our terms, we might readily be able to predict, in a "narrow bandwidth," that John Doe, who has taken a number of high school level courses in physics and mathematics, on a particular occasion when he is perfectly sober and subject to no discernible external stress, will be able to calculate, merely as a matter of intellectual interest, the force of a 3000-pound motor vehicle traveling at 40 miles per hour. In a broader bandwidth, we are less likely to be able to predict with accuracy the behavior of the same Mr. Doe while driving a 3000-pound motor vehicle on rain-slickened roads on the way home from a night of revelry while other members of the family traveling with him berate him for having imbibed rather too freely.

We are, moreover, rather more likely to tolerate errors in, say, meteorological forecasting when the penalty imposed upon us (as recipients of the prediction who alter our own behavior on that account) for an inaccurate forecast of light rain is that we have needlessly carted an umbrella about; but we are less tolerant when an un-forecast deluge causes massive flooding and consequent property damage or loss of life. Considerations bearing upon the low probability of accuracy in forecasting future violence prompted both the American Psychiatric Association (1974, 1984) and the American Psychological Association (1978) to caution their members against predictions of the future violent behavior — even of persons with whose past behavior they were intimately familiar (cf. Monahan, 1981; Stone, 1976, 1984; Simon, 1987).

Predicting Behavior vs. Predicting Conviction for That Behavior

Another set of constraints that distinguish the interests of psychologists as scientists and clinicians from those of the enforcers of law and administrators of justice in the prediction of future behavior issue primarily from the fundamental characteristic of criminal behavior — i.e., that such behavior is so denominated in consequence of its relation to a particular body of positive law at some given point in time, *rather than in consequence of a property inherent in that behavior.*

It may be the case that an amalgam of conceptual models may be called upon *formally and explicitly* to predict with reasonable ac-

⇨ *Display 5: What We Study vs. What We Do*

Sourcebook *Reports of Crime in a Year vs. Empirical Studies of Criminal Behavior, 1970-85 — The Correlation Approaches Zero*

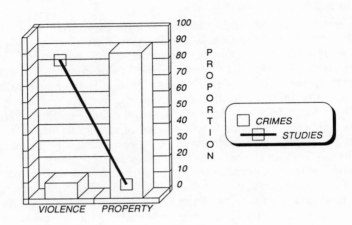

CATEGORY/SUB-CATEGORY	% Total Reported	% Total Studies
⇓ *CRIMES OF VIOLENCE*	11.6%	86.1%
❑ Murder, homicide	0.2%	18.0%
❑ Rape, sexual assault	0.7%	5.0%
❑ Robbery	4.6%	0.2%
❑ Aggravated assault	6.7%	4.0%
❑ Pedophilia, incest		6.0%
❑ Child abuse, neglect		18.0%
❑ Studies across categories, undifferentiated by kind		30.4%
⇓ *PROPERTY CRIMES*	88.4%	8.7%
❑ Burglary	22.2%	2.1%
❑ Larceny/Theft	55.3%	2.1%
❑ Motor vehicle theft	11.0%	2.1%
❑ Studies across categories, undifferentiated by kind		2.4%
⇓ *OTHER OFFENSES*		9.7%
❑ Juvenile delinquency		5.0%
❑ Status offense		0.7%
❑ Drug, alcohol offenses		4.0%
TOTAL FOR ALL CRIMES	100%	100%

curacy, in the paradigmatic clinical situation just described, particular behavior patterns that can be dependably and reliably described in mutually acceptable terms by the psychoclinician, the behaver himself or herself, and objective observers. But, given the data we have reviewed about the probabilities associated with apprehension and conviction, to call upon those same conceptual models to be able also to predict whether a particular, even patently contra-legal, behavior will result in a formal adjudication of criminality is to assign a task not merely of heroic, but of monumentally improbable, proportions. Thus, aggressive or self-aggrandizing or anti-social behavior can more readily be predicted than it can be predicted that aggressive or self- aggrandizing or anti-social behavior, *even when that behavior specifically violates positive law*, will be formally adjudicated as criminal, since such adjudication hinges on a variety of factors external to the self of the behaver. Hence, it may be considerably easier to predict, say, that X will behave aggressively toward some unspecified second person than that X will be *convicted* of aggravated assault against a specific second peron Y.

Post-diction and the Assessment of Responsibility

In a more limited arena of clinical practice, a forensic psychologist or psychiatrist may participate in a judicial proceeding intended to affix responsibility and therefore the appropriate sanction rather than guilt. In this case, a conceptual model may appropriately be called upon to *post-dict* criminal behavior — i.e., to explain how a certain behavior came about by identifying the antecedents to the specific criminal behavior on the part of a specific behaver on a specific occasion. Thus, the task becomes to explain why a particular person committed a particular criminal act, rather than to predict who is likely to commit a particular criminal act from among an array of prospective behavers *or* to predict which, from an array of prospective behaviors a particular behaver may be expected to emit, is likely to be formally adjudicated as criminal.

☐ WHAT WE STUDY VS. WHAT WE DO; THE CORRESPONDENCE APPROACHES ZERO

The construction of a process model for criminal behavior requires that empirical data from investigations utilizing the diverse research methodologies just described be integrated conceptually. The task before us, to which succeeding chapters are devoted, is to review current psychological research evidence bearing upon criminal behavior of very different sorts (viz., homicide *vs.* larceny) against the process model we have proposed.

Before we proceed to a detailed examination of that evidence, it may prove instructive to consider the body of current direct research on criminal behavior along general and gross dimensions, if only to understand fully the limitations therein. In DISPLAY 5, we contrast data from the 1991 *Sourcebook* (presented earlier in DISPLAY 1), which reflects the distribution of criminal activity reported in a year across the two major categories, *with* the distribution across the same categories of some 800 direct, empirical psychological studies of subjects whose behavior had been adjudicated as criminal; these studies, published between 1970 and 1985, are arrayed according to subcategories, and comparisons are presented both graphically and tabularly.

It is immediately apparent that *we do not study what we do* — i.e., that what psychologists study in respect of criminal behavior does *not* reflect the distribution of criminal behavior across categories of crime. Instead, the overwhelming preponderance of studies focus on crimes of violence, which constitute a relatively minor portion of all felonious crime reported; the sub-category of crime (larceny/theft) that is reported most frequently (accounting for 55% of all felony crime reported) is represented by a scant 2% of the current research studies.

Doubtless, the distribution of psychological research attention across categories and sub-categories of crime reflects both our system of criminal adjudication and our values as a society, which hold crimes of violence more detrimental to its structure than property offenses, whatever their relative incidence.

Given the imbalance between the crimes we commit and those we study, however, the extant body of research can at best be expected to yield a series of rather specific explanations for types of criminal behavior — and, very likely, retrospectively at that. If we are bound to search for "intelligibility" in the sense of a comprehensive conceptual model which seems applicable broadly across specific categories, we may have no choice but to enter the arena of analogy and inference.

☐ SUMMARY

This chapter has reviewed the process of the construction of conceptual models intended to render behavior, either in general or in the specific case, intelligible. We have reviewed the four principal methodologies employed in psychological research on behavior, noting in particular the applicability of each method to the study of criminal behavior. Three of these methodologies (*clinical case study, structured observation,* and *psychometric* modalities) are actively in use in research on criminal behavior; but, either for ethical and legislative or for practical reasons which inhere in how laws are enforced and criminal behavior adjudicated, these methods can, in practice, be applied only *a posteriori* and thus are useful only in the *retrospective analysis* of the engines for criminal behavior. The fourth, *laboratory analogue* methodology, the modality of choice in investigations in process psychology, is not directly applicable to research on behavior that has been officially adjudicated as criminal; but inferences arising from laboratory investigations of behavior *not* formally criminal may nonetheless prove instructive.

We also inspected the distribution of some 800 recent empirical studies across categories and sub-categories of serious crime in relation to the reported incidence of crime.

The imbalances are obvious, with principal research attention devoted to those crimes of violence which comprise a minor proportion of reported criminal activity. Since the construction of a conceptual model depends on the availability of sound empirical data concerning the behavior which is to be conceptually modeled, we can hardly expect the current research evidence to yield a single, comprehensive conceptual model capable of rendering criminal behavior intelligible across the spectrum of types of crime. Instead, the more realistic goal appears to be the inferential construction of a conceptual model with empirical anchors in research directly conducted on criminal behavior *but also drawing its inferences by analogy* from research on the processes activated in the acquisition and maintenance of behavior-in-general.

Chapter 5

Statistical Perspectives on Criminal Homicide: The Offense As It Is Committed

IN MOST NATIONS OF THE WORLD, A SINGLE CODE OF LAW, ENACTED BY what in the U.S. would be called a Federal legislature, applies equally throughout its borders. Within the United States, however, there are (in addition to a Federal code) as many distinct codes of law as there are states, each adopted by an independent legislature whose authority is limited only by the U.S. Constitution. In this situation, which some observers refer to as the "Balkanization" of the law, certain acts are defined as criminal only in the Federal code (e.g., air piracy), others only in state codes (e.g., the act of murder typically violates Federal law only when the victim is a Federal officer or when the crime is committed on Federal property), and still others violate both state and Federal codes. As we have earlier suggested in our brief discussion of morality and positive law, some acts are defined as criminal in the statutes of one state but not in those of other, even neighboring, states. Moreover, the specific empirical referents that define a particular crime vary considerably from one state to another, even when the codes of those states each designate behavior of a similar sort as criminal.

❏ THE LEGAL REFERENT AND ITS SEVERAL VARIANTS

For these reasons, even for the relatively primitive purpose of determining statistically the incidence of particular criminal behaviors, it has proved necessary to extract common descriptors from the codes of the several states and from Federal statutes in order to construct so basic a device as a common vocabulary for reporting episodes of crime reliably. Thus it happens that the stilted, if precise, bureaucratic lexicon of the Federal Bureau of Investigation's *Uniform Crime Reporting Handbook* (1978, pp. 5-6) contains these definitions of murder and its many variants:

❏ *Criminal homicide* . . . is the killing of one human being by another. This class consists of two parts: (a) killings due to willful acts (non-negligent), and (b) deaths due to negligent acts. These two subdivisions result from a careful study of the variations found in State statutes.

❏ *Murder and non-negligent manslaughter* (includes) any death due to a fight, argument, quarrel, assault, or commission of a crime (but excludes) suicides, accidental deaths, and attempted murders. Certain willful killings are classified as justifiable or excusable . . . on the basis of self-defense or the action of coroner, prosecutor, grand jury, or court. [Such] *justifiable homicides* are limited to: (1) killing of a felon by a peace officer in line of duty and (2) killing of a felon by a private citizen. . . .

❏ *Manslaughter by negligence* [denotes that] a person [has been] killed by the gross negligence of another . . .

❏ *Traffic fatalities* are excluded (and) attempted murders (are to be classified as) aggravated assaults.

If our process psychology model of criminal behavior pretends to validity, it should apply equally to crimes at diametric polarities. If we review the research evidence on criminal homicide, will we find confirmation of the process elements earlier described — i.e., will we find indicators that can be construed as representing predisposition, the opportunity to behave without direct deterrence, the expectation of reward, and the expectation of impunity?

☐ THE KNOWN PARAMETERS: MURDER AS IT IS COMMITTED

In Chapter 3, we reviewed *Sourcebook* data on the incidence of criminal homicide, along with data on the relative proportion of such homicides cleared by arrest. We observed that criminal homicide accounts for two-tenths of one percent of the more than 14 million felony crimes reported in a year. In whole numbers rather than as a proportion of the total number of felonies reported, some 28,500 homicides were revealed annually to police authorities. As earlier displays indicated, at the rate of 68%, it is likely that slightly more than 19,000 of these (in whole numbers) were cleared by arrest. It is worth observing, not quite parenthetically, that the *Sourcebook* (Maguire & Flanagan, 1991, pp. 251-269) provides a series of estimates (on the basis of victimization studies conducted by the

Bureau of the Census for the Bureau of Justice Statistics) of the number of episodes of criminal activity which are *not* reported to police authorities in every category of felonious crime *except* criminal homicide; the data reported for this crime and its variants, then, are apparently put forward as an *enumeration* of the total.

The *Sourcebook* provides a panoply of important information derived from accounts by police authorities about the episodes of criminal homicide which have been both reported and cleared by arrest. Other Federal sources — most notably reports the annual report on *Vital Statistics of the United States* from the National Center for Health Statistics and the *Statistical Abstracts of the United States* from the Bureau of the Census, periodic reports from the Violence Epidemiology Branch of the U.S. Department of Health and Human Services, the Bureau of the Census on prison inmates (including their self-assessments of the extent to which they were "under the influence" of alcohol or drugs or both at the time of the

---

⮕ *Display 6: Criminal Homicide in Relation to Other Causes of Death in the U.S. in a Typical Year*

Murder Is Frequent Neither as a Crime nor as a Cause of Death, Accounting for 1% of All Deaths and 14% of All "Preventable" Deaths (by Homicide, Suicide, Accident)

CAUSE OF DEATH	
⇓ *Physical/Medical Disorders*	*91.6%*
❑ Brain disorders	*8.9%*
❑ Cancer	*21.3%*
❑ Cardiac disorders	*50.0%*
❑ Liver disorders	*1.5%*
❑ Perinatal disorders	*1.9%*
❑ Pulmonary disorders	*2.9%*
❑ Respiratory disorders	*2.7%*
❑ All others	*2.8%*
⇓ *"PREVENTABLE" DEATHS*	*7.9%*
❑ Auto accident	*2.7%*
❑ Homicide	*1.1%*
❑ Household or industrial accident	*2.7%*
❑ Suicide	*1.4%*

instant offense), and such periodic recapitulative documents as the
Department of Justice's *Report to the Nation on Crime and Justice*
— provide a variety of data which, in the aggregate, can be construed
as situating the crime of homicide within a statistical context that
offers important perspectives on murder as a cause of death in this
country among victims of varying age, sex, and ethnic background
and on the known parameters of the crime as it is actually committed. We have condensed data from these sources into a series of
displays which, taken together, can be construed to represent the
known parameters which describe the crime of homicide *as it is
actually committed* in the United States:

❑ **Homicide is frequent neither as a crime nor as a cause
of death in the U.S.** As we have seen in DISPLAY 1, criminal
justice data indicate that homicides represent only 0.2% of all

---

⇨ *The Principle of Social Economy Applied to Causes of
Death*

From the radically different perspective of social economy, Gideon Vigderhous (1975) analyzed the *net addition to life expectancy* among the developing and developed nations of the world *were homicide and suicide to be
eliminated as causes of death.* Elimination of homicide would add 0. 07 years,
and elimination of suicide 0.76 years, to mean male life expectancy — but
elimination of arteriosclerotic and degenerative heart disease would add 2.71
years. If one applies the principle of social economy to these estimates, it
seems clear enough that the cost/benefit ratio to society would favor increased expenditures for research in cardiovascular medicine *rather than*
attention to measures to prevent or discourage *either or both* homicide or
suicide. But, were a choice to be made between the two, the species might
benefit more from the elimination of suicide than the elimination of homicide.
Deaths during war were not included in the Vigderhous analysis.

Vigderhous observed, virtually incidentally, that Hungary (at a point substantially before the collapse of the Soviet sphere of influence) typically
reported the highest suicide rate among the nations of the world, while
Colombia (even some while before its emergence as the mother lode for the
world's supply of cocaine and its derivatives) typically reported the highest
homicide rate. More than a decade later, the suicide rate in Hungary still led
the world, at a level that exceeded the nation in second place (Finland) by
50% and that of the nation with the lowest rate of suicide (Spain) by 1000%
(Bureau of the Census, 1989, p. 820).

➡️ *Display 7: Homicide from the Statistical Perspective*

MURDER IS NOT RANDOM: *In Cases in Which the Relationship between Victim and Slayer is Known (70% of All Cases Reported), Kinship or Friendship Predominates — In Only One in Five Homicides Are Victims and Slayers Strangers to Each Other*

⇓ *The Relationship between Victim and Slayer . . .*

- ❑ Boy friend, Girl friend — 5.9%
- ❑ Friend or acquaintance — 52.0%
- ❑ Neighbor — 2.0%
- ❑ Parent — 1.8%
- ❑ Relative other than spouse, child, sibling — 4.2%
- ❑ Sibling — 1.7%
- ❑ Son or daughter — 4.0%
- ❑ Spouse — 10.8%
- ❑ Stranger — 21.0%

CIRCUMSTANCES WHICH TRIGGER HOMICIDE: *In Cases in Which Triggers are Known (77% of All Cases), Nearly Three of Four Murders Occur as the Result of "Tinder Box" or Long Standing Disputes, with One of Four Committed During the Course of Other Felony Crimes*

⇓ *The "Triggering" Circumstance . . .*

- ❑ Argument over money, property, miscellaneous — 66.6%
- ❑ "Romantic triangle" — 3.1%
- ❑ During another felony crime — 27.5%

THE MEANS TO MURDER: *In Cases in Which the Means to Murder is Known (96% of All Cases), Firearms Overwhelmingly Represent the Weapon-of-Choice in Criminal Homicide — In More than Three of Five Murders, a Hand Gun or a Rifle Is the Instrument of Slaying*

⇓ *The Weapon Used in Slaying . . .*

- ❑ Arson — 1.2%
- ❑ Club or blunt instrument — 5.9%
- ❑ Fists or feet — 9.7%
- ❑ Firearm — 61.5%
- ❑ Knife — 21.3%
- ❑ Poison, explosives — 0.2%

ALCOHOL AND/OR DRUG USE/ABUSE LUBRICATES HOMICIDE: *According to Their Self-Reports, 52% of State Prisoners Confined for Criminal Homicide Were Actively under the Influence of Drugs and/or Acohol at the Time of Their Offense*

- ❑ Under the influence of alcohol only — 23.6%
- ❑ Under the influence of drugs only — 9.3%
- ❑ Under the influence of both alcohol and drugs — 19.0%
- ❑ Under the influence of either or both alcohol and/or drugs — 51.9%

MURDER RARELY CROSSES RACIAL BOUNDARIES: *In Cases in Which the Race of the Victim and Slayer is Known (99% of All Cases), Victim and Slayer Belong to the Same Group in 91% — But, in Relation to Their Membership in the U.S. Population, Blacks Are at Greater Risk for Homicide than Members of Other Groups*

⇓ *The Racial Pairing between Victim and Slayer. . . .*

- ❑ Both Black — 44.8%
- ❑ Both White — 44.5%
- ❑ Both Members of "Other" Races — 1.3%
- ❑ Cross-Race Pairing — 9.4%

• *Sources:* Flanagan & Jamieson (1988, pp. 337-341); Bureau of Justice Statistics (1988, p. 6)

felonious crimes reported in a year; Public Health Service data (Burreau of the Census, 1989, pp. 83-84) indicate that homicide accounts for only slightly over 1% of the nearly two million deaths that occur each year in the United States (DISPLAY 6).

Among the putatively relatively more "preventable" causes of death (i.e., suicide and auto or industrial and household accident) which in the aggregate account for approximately 8% of all deaths, the data indicate that two and a half times as many people die each year as the result of auto accidents as are murdered, two and a half times as many die as a result of other accidents as are murdered, and *25% more commit suicide than are murdered each year.*

❑ In those cases in which the relationship is known (70% of all reported cases), **in four of every five cases of criminal**

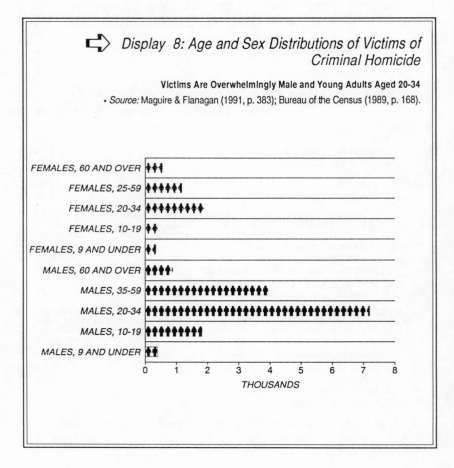

➪ *Display 8: Age and Sex Distributions of Victims of Criminal Homicide*

Victims Are Overwhelmingly Male and Young Adults Aged 20-34

• *Source:* Maguire & Flanagan (1991, p. 383); Bureau of the Census (1989, p. 168).

homicide, clearly identifiable kinship or friendship relationships had existed between victim and slayer prior to the crime (DISPLAY 7).

In only 20% of the cases were victim and slayer strangers to each other; 19% of the cases involved relatives and another 6% involved lovers, so that, in the aggregate, close kinship relationships account for more than 25% of all homicides; and the relationships of friend, neighbor, or acquaintance, in the aggregate, account for more than half of all homicide cases.

❑ Official **police accounts overwhelmingly cite arguments and disputes as the circumstances which precipitate murder,** whether of the "tinder box" variety or reflective of long- standing antagonisms, with two-thirds of all such cases so classified. It is also arguable that the 3% of the cases which are attributed to "romantic triangle" situations might be commingled with those cases which result from arguments and disputes.

Data on the relationship between victim and slayer suggest that such precipitating disputes are most likely to emerge between people who know each other well or at least are acquainted with each other. Thus, not surprisingly, nearly 90% of all homicides occur within the county in which the victim resides and nearly 70% occur on weekends (Public Health Service, 1984, pp. 3-4). Some 28% of all cases of criminal homicide, however, represent "felony murder" — i.e., murder which occurs during the commission of another crime, most often robbery or rape.

❑ **Firearms represent the weapon-of-choice in criminal homicide by an overwhelming margin**, accounting for 62% of the cases. Some 25% of victims are stabbed or clubbed to death; another 6% are beaten to death with hands, fists, or feet.

That firearms account for so large a proportion of these weapons would seem reason enough to oppose their sale and possession, especially when one considers that the approximately 12,000 victims of murder shot to death in a year are joined by another approximately 16,000 who take their own lives by means of firearms (i.e., half of all suicides) and approximately 2000 who die in a year as the result of accidents involving firearms (Public Health Service, 1984, pp. 298, 296; Wood & Mercy, 1990).

Yet, according to data reported in a national survey of hand gun ownership undertaken by the Center to Prevent Handgun Violence (Blumenthal, 1991), it is likely that at least one member in 50% of the nearly 80 million American household owns at least one hand gun — for a whopping total of nearly 40 million such weapons. Beyond that datum, there are an un-inventoried number of long guns. Thus, Zimring (1990) put the private ownership of firearms at 130 *million.*

However much we may find such widespread ownership of firearms personally abhorrent or uncivilized and however much we decry the deaths of nearly 30,000 citizens by means of firearms each year, extrapolation suggests that the total number of deaths by firearms — whether through homicide, suicide, or accident — corresponds to less than eight one-hundredths of one (0.075%) of the hand guns the ownership of which is acknowledged, to say nothing of the long guns. One must, however reluctantly, conclude that the supporters of the questionable "right to bear arms" apparently have the statistics on their side. Whether they also have the Second Amendment to the Constitution on their side is another matter. Although the "right to keep and bear arms" is indeed therein guaranteed, the preamble to that Amendment makes it crystal clear that such a right is framed within the context of a need to organize and maintain a formal military force to ensure the territorial integrity of a nation. That seems light years away from the view of the National Rifle Association that the fun-loving citizen has been guaranteed in perpetuity the right to own and maintain rapid-fire automatic weapons to pursue either blood sports or innocent target practice.

❑ According to the self-reports of prisoners confined in state correctional institutions for murder, **more than half the homicides are committed while the slayer is actively "under the influence" of alcohol, drugs, or a combination thereof.**

These data emerge from a survey conducted by the U.S. Bureau of the Census among convicted felons incarcerated in state prisons (Bureau of Justice Statistics, 1988), based on interviews with a stratified sample of 12,000 inmates (96% male; 49.7% white) carefully selected to represent accurately the total population of nearly 500,000 prisoners. These self-report data are largely consistent with the body of data drawn from such smaller scale studies as those of Holcomb & Adams (1985) and Welte & Miller (1987) on incarcerated violent and non-violent offenders and further accord with the observations of Lewis, Cloninger & Pais (1983) and Tuchfeld, Clayton & Logan (1982) on the interactive relationship between alcohol use, substance abuse, and felony crime (Pallone, 1989, 1990-*a*). While they may fail to reveal patterns of addiction among slayers, they surely speak to a powerful ingredient in the process which leads to murder in what may be more than half the cases.

Moreover, a study by Budd (1982), of the Los Angeles Coroner's office, reported that toxic levels of alcohol were found at autopsy in the blood samples of 61% of murder *victims* and, in a study which compared black women who committed homicide with their *victims* on a number of social characteristics, McClain (1982) concluded that the two groups "exhibit essentially similar behavior patterns that increase their probability of involvement in homicide," so that who becomes the victim and who the offender may be essentially a matter of the luck of the draw in a specific behavioral interaction, especially when alcohol or drugs lubricate emergent conflicts or strike a spark in the tinder-box of long-standing conflicts.

Nontheless, it is important to recall that, as we saw in Chapter 3 (DISPLAY 4), only 36% of all *reported* homicides result in the intrusive sanction of prison. That circumstance must clearly temper our judgment about the linkage berween alcohol or substance abuse and criminal homicide. In particular, we

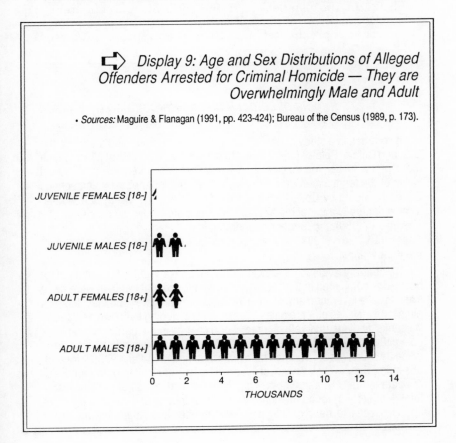

⟹ Display 9: Age and Sex Distributions of Alleged Offenders Arrested for Criminal Homicide — They are Overwhelmingly Male and Adult

• *Sources:* Maguire & Flanagan (1991, pp. 423-424); Bureau of the Census (1989, p. 173).

can conclude nothing about the state of intoxication or sobriety of those responsible for the 64% of reported murders which are *not* reflected among prisoners sentenced for this crim.

❏ **Criminal homicide is apparently tightly bound within racial groups.** Some 86% of all white victims are slain by other whites; 94% of all black victims are slain by other blacks; 57% of victims who are members of "other" racial or ethnic groups are slain by members of their respective groups. In view of data on the relationships between victim and slayer, these data on racial pairings are hardly surprising. Moreover, according to Klaus, Rand & Taylor (1983, p. 21), victim and offender are of the same race in 75% of all crimes of violence.

What is most striking in the data on homicide, however, is that *blacks and "others" are at substantially greater risk for murder than are whites.* Though whites currently outnumber blacks in the population at the ratio of approximately 5:1, blacks constitute 45% of all victims of murder — i.e., they are at risk at approximately four times their representation in the

---

⇨ *Targets of Lethal Violence Perpetrated by Women*

In contrast, in a study of gender differences in homicide and suicide in the U.S. and Britain, Palmer (1981) found that "females, if they kill at all, are much more prone to commit suicide than homicide." Moreover, the prototypical victim of the female murderer is her own child. The latter observation echoes the early finding by Cole, Fisher & Cole (1968) that the victim of a woman killer is generally another member of her immediate family, later confirmed by Steinmetz (1980) and further corroborated in a Canadian sample by Husain, Anasseril & Harris (1983), who enumerated children and spouses as the most frequent victims.

But contrary evidence is advanced by Wilbanks (1983), in a study of all homicides committed in the U.S. in 1980, who found that "women were more likely to kill a lover than any other victim/offender category" and that "females almost never killed other females," presumably including their own daughters. Wilbanks' findings may reflect a real-world change in the pattern of homicide committed by women, in consonance with the changing role of woman in crime as a function of liberation from male dominance (Adler, 1975). It is worth observing that, in their review of World Health Organization data on causes of death in the U.S. and 23 other highly developed industrial nations, Christofell & Liu (1983) found the homicide rates for infants and children aged 1-4 in this country to be atypically high, with mother as virtually the prototypic slayer.

population. Moreover, as Wood (1990) and O'Carroll (1990) have observed, homicide now represents a *leading* cause of death among black adolescents and young adults. These data may well mask the interactively confounded effects of race and socioeconomic status that have yielded a situation in which a substantial majority of blacks are entrapped in those strata of the society in which disputes erupt rather more easily and in which violence is readily construed as a means to resolve disputes, especially between young adult males. Fully 45% of all cases of criminal homicide involve victim and slayer pairs in which both are black; another 42% involve victim and slayer pairs in which both are white. *Only 11% of all cases involve victims and slayers of different races.*

❑ Further, **males are three times more likely to become victims of homicide** (DISPLAY 8); the disproportional levels of risk become even more dramatic when we add race as a dimension.

Criminal homicide claims, in a year, 65 of every 100,000 black males and 57 of every 100,000 males who belong to "other" races, but only 20 of every 100,000 white males; *black and "other" males are thus three times more likely than to become victims of murder than are whites.* Though murder claims only three of every 100,000 white females, it claims 13 black and 12 "other" females of each 100,000 of the population, respectively. As we have already observed, *95% of the time* the black males who are at greatest risk for murder are at risk *as the victims of other black males.*

❑ In the aggregate, **males are at substantially greater risk for criminal homicide than are females**.

Some 77% of all victims of criminal homicide are males (DISPLAY 8), and three of every five victims are males in late adolescence or early adulthood. Homicide claims almost equal numbers of male and female victims among children 14 and under — but women over the age of 60 are more likely to become victims than are women in other age groups. The explanations that suggest themselves are, respectively, that women constitute a higher proportion of the population in the over-60 age bracket than men and are thus likely to be living alone; older women living alone in urban areas have become quite vulnerable to episodes of "push-in" violence, particularly in connection with robbery.

❑ Similarly, **young adults between the ages of 20 and 34 are at substantially greater risk than are members of other age groups**; in the aggregate, 48% of all cases of criminal homicide claim men and women in the young adulthood age group (*Note* 1). Not surprisingly (DISPLAY 9), the alleged offenders are — at least as judged by data from arrest records —

⇨ *Intra-Caste Criminal Homicide and Suicide*

McClain (1982) examined the social characteristics of victims and offenders in 661 cases of black female homicide in the U.S., concluding to their essential similarity: "Victims and offenders are of low socioeconomic status backgrounds and exhibit essentially similar behavior patterns that increase their probability of involvement in homicide." In contrast, Lalli & Turner (1968) early observed that the rate of *suicide* among American blacks is only about half that among whites. Since the genesis of suicide is generally held to inhere in *anomie*, or a feeling of hopelessness and helplessness, that observation is striking when read in conjunction with data that demonstrate clearly that criminally murderous violence is largely directed *into* rather than *out from* the black community.

Poussaint (1983), a distinguished psychiatrist at Harvard, observing that "Black homicide rates are 7-8 times those of Whites [but] that Blacks have a rate of poverty only 4 to 5 times that of Whites," concludes that "Blacks — for both environmental and political reasons — are likely to reflect emotional predispositions that allow them to more readily become a homicide [than a suicide] statistic. Projected self-hatred facilitates blind rage and gives the perpetrator of a violent attack a sense of legitimacy and justification. In addition, Blacks have been indoctrinated by a criminal justice system that places higher value on a White life than on a Black life."

The observed encapsulation of criminal homicide largely within racial "castes" in the U.S. finds no consistent parallels in comparative data on an international scale — perhaps, indeed, because few nations are as ethnically diverse as ours. Thus, Hansmann & Quigley (1982) studied the relationship between homicide rate and measures of ethnic, religious, linguistic, and economic heterogeneity in some 40 nations of the world, concluding that heterogeneity is associated with higher rates of homicide — a finding that would indeed suggest that homicide rather readily crosses what we (following Dollard, 1937) have called "caste" lines. Moreover, in her study of those nations of the world which have traditionally reported the lowest rates of crime within their regions, Adler (1983) found *synomie* (the diametric contrary to anomie) an important determinant. To the extent to which synomie within a population is facilitated by racial similarity, there are implications for intra-caste vs. extra-cast homicide probabilities.

overwhelmingly adult males; *Sourcebook* data do not permit fine discrimination by age group, however.

Data from studies of less than national scope yield some indication of "trends" in criminal homicide which, when read in juxtaposition to enumerative *Sourcebook* data, tend to provide some detail to the statistical outline. Thus, criminal homicide has been linked to *climatological or weather conditions*, to a *pervasive regional subculture of violence*, and even, through quite complex neurochemical routes, to such variables as *the chemical composition of drinking water* and *annual national rates of consumption of corn and cigarettes* on a comparative basis among the nations of the world. These and similar variables are discussed as *environmental contingencies* in Chapter 7.

☐ AN EPIDEMIOLOGIC PERSPECTIVE ON THE PROSPECTIVE VICTIM

Expressed somewhat simplistically, the goal in medical epidemiology is to determine both the means by which physical disease (or illness) is transmitted and to identify those groups which are particularly at risk for a target disease. In the first case, medical epidemiology relies on the investigative methods of the biological sciences and, in the second, on those of the social sciences. These basic investigations are generally preparatory to the energizing of public health efforts to control the spread of illness or disease, through what is sometimes called "preventive medicine."

At the level of the control of illness or disease, the development of a statistical portrait of members of those groups empirically determined to be at particular risk (or, in the more familiar terminology associated with infectious medical disorders, "susceptible") is paramount. "Risk factors" may be found to inhere in genetic or constitutional predisposition, environmental influences (e.g., exposure to toxins), and/or "lifestyle" variables.

A current example that has engaged both medical epidemiologists and public health officials, no less than energized the public, is the control of acquired immune deficiency syndrome, *both* by stemming its spread in the population (largely through efforts to convince members of "at risk" groups to alter their behavior) *and* by developing pharmacologic agents that will alter the course of the disease once contracted. Analogously, the goal in *psychiatric epidemiology* has been to identify those groups statistically at greatest risk for mental and emotional disorders of various sorts (Srole *et al.*, 1962, 1986; Mechanic, 1980, pp. 54-72; Pallone, 1991, pp. 13-56) in relation to a variety of external stressors and/or predictive factors. A current example is the effort to identify those persons who are at risk inter-familially and/or intergenerationally for alcoholism and, again, the preventive measures pivot largely on efforts to convince "at risk" groups to alter their behavior.

On the basis of the data just reviewed, what sort of portrait of the person *"at risk" for criminal homicide* (Jason, 1984) might be drawn by an epidemiologist? We have seen that, "prototypically,"

- ❏ *the victim of murder in the U.S. is a young adult male* (DISPLAY 8)
- ❏ *who is shot to death* (DISPLAY 7) *by a friend, neighbor, or acquaintance*
- ❏ *during, or as a result of, an argument, dispute, or romantic triangle,*
- ❏ *with the behavioral interaction frequently lubricated by either or both alcohol and drugs.*
- ❏ *Such a prototypical victim is, in relation to the racial distribution in the general population, more likely to be black than to be a member of another racial or ethnic group* (DISPLAY 7).

Such a portrait, indeed, takes into account a variety of "risk factors" analogous to those studied by medical epidemiologists. Preventive medicine approaches to those at greatest risk for homicide might well proceed through attempts to convince prospective victims to alter their own behavior — e.g., to avoid disputes with intoxicated young men who have access to firearms, if anyone needs reminding; or, more succinctly, to make the choice to *avoid* those environments which tolerate risky behavior.

Though epidemiological methodology does much to illuminate the probability of victimization, it tells us little about the engines that drive the perpetrator. Why, for example, does the prospective killer have access to a firearm? What drives him or her into physical confrontation as a means to resolve disputes? What variables appear to be related to the readiness to construe the taking of a human life as an acceptable course of action in one's behavioral repertoire, even under the mood-altering circumstances of alcohol or drug intoxication?

Contemporary psychological research literature on the perpetrators of criminal homicide may provide some illumination. But, as we scan representative studies from that literature, we should be mindful of the epidemiologic portrait of murder — if only to reconcile whether the portrait of the typical murderer to emerge therefrom correlates with the portrait of the typical murder as it is reflected in data on homicide as it is actually committed.

☐ SUMMARY

This chapter has reviewed statistical data on the known parameters of criminal homicide as it is committed. On the basis of data collected by Federal agencies from each law enforcement agency in the nation and presented annually in the *Sourcebook of Criminal Justice Statistics,* we have sketched a portrait of the relationship between victim and slayer, the circumstances which trigger homicide, the means to murder, the racial similarity or dissimilarity between victim and slayer, and the age and sex of victims. From other sources, we have considered the relative frequency of homicide as a cause of death and the relative frequency with which convicted homicide offenders self-report that they were under the influence of alcohol or drugs or both at the time of the offense.

The picture of homicide as it is committed to emerge from these data suggests that murder is frequent neither as a crime (accounting for only 0.1% of the episodes of felonious crime in a year), as a cause of death (accounting for only 1% of all deaths), nor as a cause of "preventable" deaths (accounting for only 14% of all deaths by other then physical or medical disorders.

Homicide is seen not to be random, but instead a transaction between victims and slayers who, 70% of the time, are known to each other, with close kinship relationships accounting for 30% of all homicides. Arguments of a "tinder box" variety apparently trigger two-thirds of all homicides; victims are overwhelmingly young male adults and disproportionately non-white, even though murder rarely crosses racial boundaries. A firearm is overwhelming the weapon-of- choice, and more than half the convicted offenders report that they were under the influence either or alcohol or drugs or both at the time of the slaying.

☐ NOTES & COMMENTARY

☐ 1. *Rate of Death by Homicide Per 100,000 in the Population*

One could approach the data on the age and sex of homicide victims differently, by calculating the number of deaths by homicide per 100,000 of the population arrayed by those twin variables. In this configuration, the slope of the line on a graph depicting such an array would rise from the set representing males in their teens, peak at the set representing males between 20 and 35, and drop fairly rapidly thereafter.

In a cross-national study of the distribution of sex and age among victims of homicide, Lester (1986) reported that (as is the case in the U.S.) young adults were at greatest risk of victimization — but that in Europe, surprisingly and disturbingly, infants were at highest risk.

Chapter 6

Psychological Perspectives on Criminal Homicide: Variables Within the Offender

THOUGH THE SCIENTIFIC ANALYSIS OF CRIMINAL BEHAVIOR HAS OFTEN mistakenly been regarded as lodged primarily within the province of personality and abnormal psychology, research relevant to a process psychology model of criminal homicide issues not only from that quarter but from neuropsychology, social psychology, and the psychology of conditioning and learning as well. This chapter focuses on those intra-person variables that can be regarded as part of the "psychological baggage" we carry about from one behavioral situation to another.

That research on intra-person variables which would prove most valuable to a psychological understanding of homicide should not only *describe* homicide offenders in psychological terms but further provide an understanding of the ways (if any) in which those who have committed homicide differ from people-in-general *and* from those who commit other crimes — for it is only through such differentiation that we can infer whether such psychological characteristics function as *specific determinants of,* or merely as correlates of, the crime of murder. It should be conceded from the outset that we will find few investigations that meet these stringent criteria.

Following Megargee & Bohn's contention (1977, p. 32) that "there is clearly a consensus that all murderers are not alike," it will prove useful to group relevant studies into offender-victim categories, and, within each category, to examine generalizations that emerge from, or are supported by, the relevant empirical research. The broadest category includes studies of what we might call murder-across-the-board, not inflected by specific offender-victim relationships.

☐ NEUROPSYCHOLOGICAL VARIABLES RELATED TO LETHAL VIOLENCE

It is only within the relatively recent past that major technological advances in the neurosciences have made it possible to record brain activity and later to map that activity through technologically powerful imaging devices (Rosse, Owen & Morisha, 1987; Volkow & Tancredi, 1991). Concomitantly, an explosion of knowledge in psychopharmacology and psychoendocrinology has yielded new understandings of a panoply of interactions between brain morphology and functioning, neurochemistry, and emotional and behavioral disorder. According to distinguished neuropsychiatrist Joseph Coyle (1988, pp. 23-24) of Johns Hopkins, the "nearly logarithmic growth in neuroscience research over the last decade" has yielded a major paradigm shift in the mental health sciences, producing in the process "new methods for diagnosing psychiatric disorders, clarifying their pathophysiology, and developing more specific and effective therapies." The net effect, in the view of Herman Van Praag (1988) of Albert Einstein College of Medicine, has been to "enable psychiatry to be a medical rather than a social science," united (or, more properly, reunited) with biology as its governing discipline.

Because disordered brain and neurochemical processes often eventuate in violent behavior, and because subjects with a history of violence are to be found in great profusion in prison populations, many studies of the relationship between neurological disorder and violence have been conducted within correctional settings, with offenders convicted of violent crimes as subjects. These studies have contributed directly to the emerging picture of the neurogenesis of violence — though it must be added that only infrequently have these investigations segregated subjects according to the particular type of violent crime (e.g., homicide *vs.* assault) of which each had been convicted or which dominated his or her prior criminal record. However, because these studies have invariably involved either extensive laboratory equipment (e.g., technologically sophisticated equipment for computerized imaging) or surgical procedures (e.g., many studies of the metabolism of neural transmitting enzymes require samples of spinal fluid, available only through lumbar puncture), they have typically been limited to small groups of subjects.

Neurogenic Sources of Impulsive Violence

At the conceptual level, a persuasive (if not yet quite compelling) case can now be made linking dysfunction, anomaly, or abnormality

🖒 *Aggression as an Inevitable Consequence of Neurology*

Although his early work on the use of the phenothiazines (a group of powerful medications intended to combat the florid symptoms of psychosis) is internationally recognized, the conceptual formulations of French physician Henri-Marie Laborit on the biological bases of aggressive behavior remain accessible to the English world primarily through director Alain Resnais' remarkable 1980 film *Mon Oncle d'Amerique*, most accurately described as a richly illustrated lecture narrated by Laborit himself.

Much of Laborit's clinical experience in medicine came from service as a physician under combat conditions in the French Navy during World War II and included a dozen years as chief of the Naval Medical Corps from 1948 to 1960, a period that saw armed conflict in several French colonies in Africa and Asia seeking their independence. Such clinical experience surely provides unique vantage points from which to study aggression.

Laborit posits that aggression is endemic to any form of animal life. In order to survive, animals (including the human species) must move from place to place to procure by foraging the nutrients produced by plants; the alternative is death, so such a "need" is quite primordial. To make such movement possible, the process of evolution has yielded the brain and the central nervous system, along with a skeleton and the musculature. Endowed with a brain (in which memories of pleasure and pain can be recorded) and a central nervous system (capable of directing movement of the skeleton and musculature) and compelled to sustain life, any animal (no matter how primitive) inevitably seeks to establish dominance over a more-or-less defensible "territory" in which it can forage (or, where humans can cultivate).

To establish and to defend that dominance *requires* aggressive behavior — in the first instance, against the plant life (and, among many animal species and in the human species, against animal life as well) that must be consumed if even the simplest organism is to sustain its own life; and, in the second, against competitors who "covet" the same territory for the same life-sustaining purposes. In the human species, a variety of social controls, including both general societal norms and those role models which have been promulgated by the society in which one lives as generally positive and/or those which one has chosen ipsatively for emulation or imitation, may constrain and channel aggression in ways that are more *or less* socially acceptable. In infra-human species, the outer limits of aggression are set by competition with more powerful organisms; generally, those whose position in the evolutionary schema has yielded more highly developed central nervous systems are destined to "win" in such competition. Among humans, the sense of dominance may extend to include a variety of symbolic representations of "territoriality," both animate and inanimate (e.g., one's spouse, one's automobile).

Aggression itself is, in this conceptualization, construable as quite an inevitable consequence of life itself. The question, then, is not *whether* humans will behave aggressively in order to establish a sense of dominance or "territoriality" (a notion pioneered by anthropologist Desmond Morris [1969]), but rather whether such aggressive behavior as is an inevitable consequence of the sheer *fact* of neurology (the purpose of which is to permit motion and which therefore inevitably dictates aggression) will be sufficiently and appropriately socialized and channelized so as not to *unduly* impede the welfare of other humans.

Resnais' film begins with a sequence illustrating the mobility of simple marine organisms — and ends with a sequence of un-narrated, wide-angle shots of the devastation of one of America's abandoned inner-city ghettoes. The voyage between those extremes is populated by quite accurate laboratory demonstrations both of the conditions that elicit and sustain aggression and the prospective behavioral responses when an organism experiences frustration in the compulsion to behave aggressively — and by what can be construed as fictionalized case histories of three quite ordinary people.

in the neurological substratum to *impulsive* displays of violence and/or aggression. Because the statistical perspective on homicide as it is actually committed reveals a high incidence of what we have called "tinder box" slayings (in contrast to those slayings that are carefully deliberated and could hardly be denominated as "impulsive" events), such a linkage appears to hold promise for understanding variables at work in some large proportion of episodes of homicide.

CLINICAL EVIDENCE

The clinical literature in neuropsychology and neuropsychiatry especially is replete with dramatic examples of neurogenic violence. In his work on behavioral neurology, for example, Rhawn Joseph (1990, p. 102) summarizes the case of Charles Whitman, the "Texas Tower" sniper who killed 14 people and wounded 38 others on the University of Texas campus during a 90-minute shooting spree in 1966. Long before his murders, Whitman had consulted a psychiatrist with complaints of "periodic and uncontrollable violent impulses," achieving neither relief nor even an accurate diagnosis. But, at autopsy, there was revealed in Whitman's brain a "multiform tumor the size of a walnut compressing the amygdaloid nucleus." Joseph (*Ibid.,* pp. 96-103) thus attributes aggressivity to dysfunctions in limbic system structures in the brain, particularly the hypothalamus and the amygdala, citing experimental evidence on both animal and human subjects of the effects of electrical stimulation of these structures in producing violent behavior.

British neuropsychologist Rodger Llewellyn Wood (1987, pp. 21-22) attributes aggressiveness to injury to the frontal lobes of the brain, thought to be the seat of memory, concentration, abstraction, and judgment. Aggressive episodes are said to result from "some paroxysmal electrical event," so that "Once started, the patient seems to have little or no control over the course of behaviour." Moreover, "Diminished insight is an almost inevitable consequence of severe frontal lobe injury" (p. 25).

CATEGORICAL ATTRIBUTIONS

Neuropsychiatric researchers who have analyzed the cumulative evidence are united in the view that sudden-onset violent behavior (i.e., that which we would term "impulsive" violence) derives from neurologic dysfunction, although there obtains no consensus about whether the dysfunction(s) implicated are neurochemical, structural or morphological, or, as Wood intimates, bioelectrical.

Mount Sinai School of Medicine neuropsychiatrists Larry Siever and Kenneth Davis (1991, p. 1656) favor the neurochemical position.

They hold that "Impulsivity/aggression is a *genetically- transmitted* dimension associated with reductions in serotonergic activity" — that is, in an *inherited* incapacity to metabolize properly a powerful neurotransmitting fluid named serotonin. Substantial implications follow for treatment of impulsive aggression through neurochemical agents capable of "correcting" faulty metabolism of serotonin. Similarly, Siever & Davis attribute disorganization in cognition and perception — which may underlie the habitual mis-construing of costs, benefits, and risks associated with deviant behavior — to dysfunction in metabolizing the neurotransmitter *dopamine,* and, once again, there are implications for treatment by means of pharmacology.

Neuropsychiatrist David Bear of the Vanderbilt University School of Medicine (1989, p. 88) puts it categorically that repetitive aggression arises in neurologic dysfunction, which may be either morphological or neurochemical in character:

overly frequent or aimless aggression . . . in humans reflects structural or chemical dysfunction of . . . neuronal circuits [so that] unpredicted or even unpredictable aggressive acts . . . become understandable — and in an important sense, predictable — when viewed as a breakdown of specific neuronal systems regulating aggression at multiple levels within the human brain.

More expansively, Cornell Medical College neuropsychiatrist Kenneth Tardiff (1988, p. 1042) has summarized the accumulated evidence that links violent behavior with a burgeoning array of neuropsychological anomalies or dysfunctions:

A number of organic disorders are associated with violent behavior, including substance abuse, central nervous system disorders, systemic disorders, and seizure disorders. *Central nervous system disorders* which have been associated with violent behavior include traumatic brain injuries, including birth injury as well as trauma as an adult acutely and in the post- concussion syndrome; intracranial infections; cerebrovascular disorders; Alzheimer's disease [a degenerative brain disorder primarily affecting the cerebral cortex]; Wilson's disease [a disorder of liver functioning]; multiple sclerosis. *Systemic disorders* affecting the central nervous system include metabolic disorders such as hypoglycemia, vitamin deficiencies, electrolyte imbalances, hypoxia [a pulmonary disorder], uremia, Cushing's anemia [attributed to naturally-occurring excessive production of certain corticosteroids in the body], systemic infections . . . and industrial poisons such as lead.

⇨ *Schizophrenia Recast as a Brain Disease: Neurogenic vs. Psychosocial Origins*

Illustrative of current research which has revolutionized traditional conceptualizations of the genesis of mental and behavioral disorder are the studies of British researchers Brown, Colter, Corsellis, Crow *et al.* (1986), who found evidence at autopsy of structural brain changes particularly involving the temporal lobe among schizophrenic patients, and Harvard neuropsychiatrists Cohen, Buonanno, Keck, Finklestein & Benes (1988), who identified through computerized tomography (CT) scans and magnetic resonance imaging (MRI) techniques consistent *neuroanatomical* anomalies in depressive and schizophrenic patients, even though "standard" neurological examinations had failed to detect these abnormalities in nearly two-thirds of the cases. Similarly, at the Neurosciences Laboratory of the National Institute of Mental Health, Luxenberg, Swedo, Flament, Friedland, Rapoport & Rapoport (1988) identified through CT scans consistent neuroanatomical abnormality in patients diagnosed as obsessive-compulsive.

The evidence on the neurogenesis of schizophrenia, the most insidious and disabling of the mental disorders, is now so solid that many neuropsychiatrists regard schizophrenia as a brain disease. In a major review of that evidence, University of Maryland neuropsychiatrists Heinrichs & Buchanan (1988, pp. 16-17) conclude:

❑ In spite of some methodological limitations, the evidence for a higher rate of neurological abnormalities in schizophrenia is consistent and compelling. These signs are not random but are concentrated in the functional domains of sensory integration, coordination, and sequential motor acts. There is some suggestion that these functional systems are impaired at the level of subcortical structures such as the limbic system. Furthermore, there are indications that neurological signs are more prominent among those with thought disorder and cognitive impairments, as well as those with chronic forms of the illness. In addition, there is significant reason to believe that neurological abnormalities characterize a portion of the relatives of schizophrenic patients and *predate* the onset of the schizophrenic illness.

Though Heinrichs & Buchanan conclude *that* schizophrenia is neurogenic in origin, they do not specify which neurologic dysfunctions (chemical or anatomical) may constitute its sources. Other investigators have shown less reluctance.

Thus, in a detailed review of the studies published between 1963-1990 (and indeed including one report on the clinical effects of brain injury which appeared as early as 1868), Davis, Kahn, Ko & Davidson (1991) of the Mount Sinai School of Medicine in New York analyzed the research evidence linking dysfunctions in the metabolism of the neurotransmitter *dopamine* to the genesis of schizophrenia (Snyder, 1988), including studies done at autopsy and analyses of the contents of cerebrospinal fluid of schizophrenic and non-schizophrenic subjects focused on concentrations of dopamine and its successor metabolites.

Davis and his associates develop a complex and interactive model for dysfunctions in the metabolism of dopamine at several receptor sites in the brain, including the *frontal lobe*. Though they do not attribute schizophrenia to dopamine metabolism abnormalities as a sole cause, they conclude that "abnormal, although not necessarily excessive, dopamine activity is an important factor in schizophrenia."

In yet another major review completed at Albert Einstein College of Medicine, neuropsychiatrists Javitt & Zubin (1991) proposed that schizophrenia may result from a naturally-occurring *neurochemical* dysfunction at a specific binding site in the brain that serves as a receptor for a *particular* amino acid (NMDA, or, chemically, N-methyl-D-aspartate). These investigators observe that such dysfunction results in irregularities in the cognitive, emotional, and behavioral functions associated with the frontal lobes. Partially confirmatory evidence is provided in a study of the recovery of disorderd cognitive functions among former users of the street drug phencyclidine (PCP, or "Angel Dust"), the metabolites of which bind at the same frontal lobe site (Cosgrove & Newell, 1991). In addition, that receptor site "may play a key role in learning and memory . . . and has been implicated in neurodegeneration and stroke-related brain death" (Hoffman, 1991).

According to the U.S. Public Health Service edition of the *International Classification of Diseases* (1989, p. 1093), the principal symptomatology associated with *frontal lobe syndrome* includes "a general diminution of self-control, foresight, creativity, and spontaneity, which may be manifest as increased irritability, selfishness, restlessness, and lack of concern for others [although] measurable deterioration of intellect or memory is not necessarily present . . . particularly in persons previously energetic, restless, or aggressive, there may be a change toward impulsiveness, boastfulness, temper outbursts." Such a litany is not unfamiliar in a recitation of the antecedents to criminal violence; frontal lobe syndrome, in its turn, may constitute a precursor to the development of florid schizophrenia. Moreover, according to Feldman & Quenzer (1984, p. 248), *anatomical* irregularities in the frontal lobes have been linked in animal studies to lethal intra-species aggression. According to the conceptual model *either* of Davis, Kahn, Ko & Davidson *or* that of Javitt & Zukin, and although the specific mechanisms of neurotransmission responsible are held to differ, frontal lobe irregularities leading to impulsive violence may result from neurochemical brain anomaly. Further, a group of psychopharmacology researchers at Kyoto University in Japan announced in late 1991 that it had successfully "cloned" the NMDA receptor site; if that is so, it becomes possible to synthesize artificially successor metabolites, which may well become the basis for future medication not only in the treatment of schizophrenia but also in learning and memory disorders (Hoffman, 1991).

There is no consensus as yet on the specific neurochemical and/or anatomical brain anomalies that yield schizophrenia. But the terms of discussion in 1991 are radically different from those predating the explosion of knowledge in the neurosciences of the preceding three decades. Indeed, "back then," there abounded a variety of what can now only be regarded as rather fanciful (and generally psychodynamically-inclined) conceptual models about the origins of schizophrenia in faulty parent-child interaction during the early years of life. Gregory Bateson and his colleagues (Bateson *et al.,* 1956; Bateson, 1972, 1978), for example, attributed schizophrenia in adulthood to a pattern of communication between mother and child such that the mother consistently gave conflicting messages to the child, in which what might be termed cognitive content failed to replicate emotional content, within a pattern of interaction in which the "victim" is prohibited from "escaping," so that he or she has no option but to endure exposure to inherently indecipherable communications.

However conceptually elegant, intellectually engaging, and useful a contribution to understanding what social psychologists call "family systems" (Rieber, 1990), Bateson's "double-bind" theory is light years away from what is now known (and in "hard science," rather than social science, terms) about the neurogenesis of that package of disorders in perceiving, thinking, and feeling we group under the label "schizophrenia."

Head Trauma and Its Effects

Current leading scientific opinion in neuropsychiatry relates head trauma, often unreported and untreated, to a variety of consequent mental disorders, including "confusion, intellectual changes, affective lability, or psychosis . . . substance abuse, impulse disorders, and characterologic disorders, such as antisocial, borderline, and narcissistic personality disorders," although and very significantly, "the cognitive functions of the patient are preserved" (Silver, Yudofsky & Hales, 1987, p. 180).

Similarly, head trauma resultant in even subclinical epilepsy or epileptiform disorder (that is, disorders in brain bioelectrical activity that cannot be detected by electroencephalographic devices — some 15% of all cases), is said to perpetuate as *organic personality syndrome,* further differentiated into categories labeled "pseudo-psychopathic (characterized by emotional lability, impulsivity, socially inappropriate behavior, and hostility) and pseudo-depressive (characterized by apathy, indifference, and social disconnectedness)," with both syndromes "marked by indifference for the consequences of behavior and an inability to perceive appropriately the effects of such behavior on others" (Stoudemire, 1987, pp. 134-135). The latter characteristics (i.e., indifference to the consequences of behavior, disregard of the social impact of one's own behavior), indeed, are virtually the defining traits embedded in classic conceptions of psychopathy (Hare, 1985; Heilbrun & Heilbrun, 1985; Meloy, 1988).

In a study that provided further confirmation of Stoudemire's (1987) view that closed head injury perpetuates as organic personality disorder either of the "pseudo-depressive" or "pseudo-psychopathic" variety, Fletcher, Ewing-Cobbs, Miner, Levin & Eisenberg (1990) followed for a year a group of children aged between 3 and 15 who had sustained closed head injuries and had been treated in the children's pediatric neurosurgery service at the University of Texas' Houston medical campus. Data collected by means of structured checklists completed by parents (the Vineland Adaptive Behavior Scales, the Child Behavior Checklist) indicated that negative behavioral effects associated with the head injuries persisted throughout the follow-up period; those effects ranged from "quiet withdrawal to hyperactive, aggressive behavior" (p. 97).

Moreover, persons who have suffered past head trauma frequently fail to link such trauma to current disorders (Silver, Yudofsky & Hales, 1987, p. 180):

Prototypic examples of brain damage in which the patient, while providing a [psychiatric] history may fail to associate [current symptoms] with the traumatic event include the alcoholic who is amnestic for a fall that occurred while inebriated; the 10-year-old boy whose head was hit while falling from his bicycle, but who fails to inform his parents; or the wife who was beaten by her husband, but who is either fearful or ashamed to report the injury to her family physician. Such trauma may be associated with confusion, intellectual changes, affective lability, or psychosis; and the patient may first present [these latter symptoms] to the psychiatrist for evaluation and treatment.

Victims of head trauma, particularly that which has been un-detected, diagnosed imprecisely, or minimized, are "prone to the taking of risks," so that a vicious circle develops, since risk-takers are attracted to activities that entail a high probability for further

---

⇨ *Feldman & Quenzer: Neurogenic Aggression in Infra-Human Species*

Feldman & Quenzer (1984, pp. 248-252) have reviewed a number of studies on the neurogenesis of aggressive behavior among infra-human species. After observing that "one of the real problems in this research area . . . is the definition of aggressive behavior," they offer a several-fold clas-sification schema:

❑ *Predatory* aggression, exemplified by "an attack on an object of prey."
❑ *Intermale* aggression, typified by "fighting to establish dominance in mating functions."
❑ *Fear-induced* aggression, in reaction to threat or danger.
❑ *Irritable* aggression, induced by such stimuli as isolation, deprivation, or pain and "directed to any of a number of available objects."
❑ *Territorial defense,* represented by attacks on intruders.
❑ *Maternal aggression,* represented by defense of the young against predators.
❑ *Instrumental aggression,* represented by attacks on objects "associated with fear or injury."

Accumulated research evidence suggests that "each form of aggression has a *particular* anatomical and endocrine basis." As examples, Feldman & Quenzer cite evidence that:

❑ Stimulation of the *lateral* hypothalamus of the cat will cause it to ignore the experimenter and attack a rat, but stimulation of the *medial* hypothalamus will cause the cat to ignore the rat and attack the experimenter.
❑ *Frontal lobe* lesions induce mouse-killing in nonkiller rats, but the topography of the killing is different in that normal killers bite once or twice through the back of the neck of the victim, whereas killers with frontal lobe lesions are particularly vicious and ferocious, biting the mouse again and again even though the victim is dead.
❑ . . . testosterone is quite important in *intermale* aggression but of little importance in predatory aggression in rats . . . this aggression is irritable rather than predatory . . . castration reduces irritable aggression.

head trauma (*Ibid.,* pp. 180-181). Hence, victims of head trauma are at risk for risk-taking behavior which further increases the probability of future, additional head trauma, and which, in its turn, increases the likelihood of future risk-taking behavior. That circle indeed begins to sound very like the "tinder box" circumstances that surround a high proportion of the episodes of criminal homicide in this country.

Brain Function Anomalies Among Violent Offenders

An array of investigations has studied the incidence of brain and brain-bioelectrical anomalies among samples of incarcerated criminal offenders, usually by means of technologically sophisticated medical instruments but sometimes by means of complex neuropsychological test batteries that have been concurrently well validated against such "hands on" technology (Franzen & Lovell, 1987). Particularly in those cases in which data have been gathered through advanced imaging techniques, the samples in these studies tend to be rather small, so that the resultant conclusions can be generalized only with great caution. Nonetheless, the relevant studies suggest that:

❑ The incidence of epilepsy among prisoners incarcerated for criminal behavior of all sorts significantly exceeds that of control subjects matched for age (Wettstein, 1987, p. 458). In a study of all new adult male admissions to the Illinois state prisons utilizing comprehensive neurological examinations, including electroencephalograph (EEG) readings, Whitman, Coleman, Patmon, Desai, Cohen & King (1984) found the rate of epilepsy among prisoners to be four times higher than the incidence in a comparably aged group of non-prisoners and further opined on the basis of case history data that head trauma likely accounted for epilepsy in 45% of the cases detected. A variety of reports, many clinical in character, link epilepsy to homicidal violence (Hindler, 1989).

❑ The incidence of undetected and untreated closed head trauma, likely indicative of brain dysfunction of at least a subclinical level of severity, is substantially higher among members of lower socioeconomic status groups and among blacks, two groups among whom commission of crimes of violence also shows high prevalence (Bell, 1986).

❑ British neuropsychiatrist Denis Williams (1969) summarized data linking bioelectrial anomalies to aggressive crime in some 1250 prisoners he had examined over two decades. Among those whose criminal histories classified them as "habitual aggressives," he found that 65% had such anomalies, as

➪ *Schizophrenia, the Frontal Lobes, and Psychosurgery: Techniques from the Reliquary of Mental Healing*

The term *psychosurgery* applies to the aggregate of surgical procedures employed to ameliorate psychological disturbances by altering brain anatomy and/or biochemistry. Perhaps the most frequently performed of these procedures was the "prefrontal lobotomy," a technique developed in the mid-1930s by Egas Moniz, a Portuguese neurologist in collaboration with Almeida Lima, a surgeon (Bromberg, 1963, p. 259). and for which he was awarded the Nobel Prize in Medicine in 1949. According to distinguished psychiatric historian Walter Bromberg:

❏ Other brain surgeons followed Moniz cautiously . . . [But after] technics of surgical intervention were modified . . . neurosurgeons in Italy, Britain, Germany, and Switzerland repeated Moniz' experiences; in the United States, [two neuropsychiatrists single-handedly] performed the lion's share of pioneering in developing operative technics and diligently studying post-lobotomy patients . . . Although this type of brain surgery met with considerable opposition from psychiatrists dedicated predominantly to a psychogenic persuasion, it has gained adherents among observers who deal with chronic state-hospital material [i.e., long-term inmates of the "back wards," with characteristically low prospects for release].

Thus, this surgical procedure was utilized widely in Europe and the U.S. for the next two decades as a treatment for chronic schizophrenia and, less frequently, as a treatment for violent or aggressive behavior. According to Nathan & Harris (1980, pp. 72- 73), "This relatively crude operation involved using an instrument similar to an ice pick to destroy tissue in the frontal lobes by entering through the eye socket into the brain." Such surgery proved not particularly effective in relieving the symptomatology of schizophrenia, the disorder for which it had been proposed as a specific remedy, and was supplanted with less "invasive" procedures with the introduction of other techniques. As Black, Yates & Andreasen (1988, p. 388) put it:

❏ Initial reports were highly favorable, and many patients with varied diagnoses, including schizophrenia, received this therapy. It soon became clear that patients with chronic schizophrenia were rarely improved. In the largest study, 10,000 cases operated on in Great Britain between 1944 and 1955 were reviewed [with the finding that] 18% of patients with schizophrenia and 50% of those which affective disorder improved . . . With the introduction of ECT [electroconvulsive therapy, or "shock" treatment] and later anti-psychotic medication, the therapeutic situation changed dramatically and lobotomy fell into disuse.

Even though lobotomy has become something of a figure of fun in the history of mental healing, it is striking that the technique highlighted, albeit imprecisely and with the crude instrumentation available before the revolution in the neurosciences triggered by the introduction of highly sophisticated brain mapping technologies, what may be a critical role in frontal lobe dysfunction in the genesis of schizophrenia and impulsive violence.

Indeed, after properly decrying "serious and indiscriminate destruction of brain tissue [that] would render almost any offender so incapacitated as to be unable to think or act with sufficient efficiency to engage in many forms of criminal behavior," distinguished forensic psychiatrist Seymour Halleck (1987, p. 175) nonetheless opines that "Sophisticated psychosurgical techniques [can] be used to ablate tiny areas of the brain believed to regulate violent behavior" and that "such surgery need not interfere with other social capacities of [the] offenders and could . . . diminish their propensity for violent crimes."

measured by abnormal electroencephalograph (EEG) readings; among those who had committed a "solitary major crime" of an aggressive nature, only 12% had abnormal EEG readings. Moreover, "The areas of abnormality [i.e., those areas of the brain in which EEG findings indicated abnormality] were indeed the same as those most often involved in temporal lobe epilepsy" (p. 514). Clinical reports by Bonkalo (1967) and Gunn (1978-*a*) linked brain bioelectrical anomalies specifically to homicide.

❏ Howard (1984) took electroencephalograph (EEG) readings of consecutive admissions to a prison hospital in Britain, with the

---

⏩ *Robert Hare: On Cerebral Function and Psychopathy*

Robert Hare of the University of British Columbia, undoubtedly the leading authority worldwide on psychopathic deviation, is best known for construction, validation, and refinement of scales to measure psychopathy (Hare, Harpur, Hakstian & Forth, 1990; Hare, 1991). But he has also researched the relationship between psychopathy and cerebral function intensively (Hare, 1979, 1982), concluding to no particular relationship to dysfunction in the dominant hemisphere.

In a study which utilized an impressive array of neuropsychological rather than neurological measures, Hare (1984, p. 139) concluded that "psychopaths are less likely to display symptoms of neurological impairment or dysfunction than are individuals who exhibit some of the features of psychopathy but who fall short of fitting the complete clinical syndrome" (p. 139). That description sounds very like Stoudemire's (1987, pp. 135-135) characterization of *organic personality disorder, pseudopsychopathic type*.

In another study, Hare & McPherson (1984) administered a listening task that required activation of lateralized brain functions to inmates who had been classified as high or low in psychopathy and to control subjects who were presumably crime- free but whose level of psychopathy was not inventoried, finding that "psychopaths are characterized by asymmetric low left- hemisphere arousal." These results were replicated and amplified in studies by Jutai, Hare & Connolly (1987) and by Raine, O'Brien, Smiley & Scerbo (1990).

Whether brain lateralization (or any other brain anomaly, for that matter) represents a uniform characteristic of those who are properly classified as "fitting the complete clinical syndrome" of the psychopath or only of those who "exhibit some of the features of psychopathy," and should instead more properly be labeled as suffering the pseudopsychopathic variety of organic personality disorder, may be a more salient issue at the conceptual level than at the operational level of correctional management, law enforcement, or crime prevention.

finding that atypical brain activity was recorded in 60% of the cases. Howard further observed that particular anomalies in brain functioning were prevalent in subjects who had committed crimes of violence against strangers rather than against friends or acquaintances. His finding is clinically corroborated in a clinical study by Martinius (1983) of criminal homicide and partially corroborated among juvenile homicide offenders under the age of 13 examined at the NYU Medical Center by Lewis, Shanok, Grant & Ritvo (1983).

❑ Blackburn (1975, 1979) found electroencephalographic (EEG) evidence of abnormally high cortical arousal among prisoners diagnosed as "primary psychopaths." These subjects also scored significantly higher than controls on psychometric measures of "sensation seeking" and susceptibility to boredom, so that Blackburn's results support at a basic physiological level Hare's (1970) view that hyperarousability is a distinguishing characteristic of psychopaths.

❑ Similarly, Gorenstein (1982) found evidence among subjects classified as psychopaths on behavioral and psychometric criteria of dysfunction in the frontal lobe of the brain, thought to be associated with such psychological functions as foresight, planning, and the regulation of impulses. Parallel findings were reported by Krakowski, Convit, Jaeger & Lin (1989) in studies of schizophrenics with a history of criminal violence, verified by EEG readings, leading these investigators to conclude that "violence as well as neurological and neuropsychological deficits characterize a more severe form of schizophrenia." Raine & Venables (1988) similarly reported anomalies in parietal lobe functioning as measured by EEG among inmates diagnosed as psychopathic.

❑ In a rare instance in which evidence of brain dysfunction was available on a large birth cohort, Petersen, Matousek, Mednick *et al.* (1982) reported that "previous EEG abnormalities" detected in childhood or early adolescence were associated with later criminal behavior. Similarly, Virkkunen, Nuutila & Huusko (1976) followed a sample of brain-injured World War II veterans for nearly 30 years, concluding that the incidence of later criminality was associated with injury to the fronto-temporal region; importantly, they found that "the criminal acts very often happened only after several decades following the head injury."

❑ In a study that compared EEG readings, CT scans of the brain, and results of the Luria-Nebraska Neuropsychological test battery, Langevin, Ben-Aron, Wortzman & Dickey (1987), found "a consistent trend toward more neuropathology" in violent and assaultive offenders than in offenders who were guilty of property crimes; but, perhaps in a manner that explains weak statistical associations between inventoried personality traits and criminal violence, these differences in neuropathology were *not* matched by differences in subjects' psychometric profiles on the Minnesota Multiphasic Personality Inventory. Contrary data on the relationship between neuropathology as verified by advanced imaging techniques and MMPI scores were reported by Ball, Archer, Struve & Hunter (1987) of Eastern Virginia Medical College, who found that abnormal EEG patterns were matched on several MMPI scales, including that for psychopathic deviation, among adolescent psychiatric inpatients. Similarly, Cullum & Bigler (1988) reported that primary elevations on certain MMPI scales invariably followed head injury which had resulted in lateralized cerebral dysfunction (verified by CT scan) among patients who were treated at the Health Sciences Center of the University of California, San Diego. The question of whether

---

⇨ *Neurogenesis of Sexual Violence*

Pallone (1990, pp. 63-67) has elsewhere summarized the research evidence linking neuropsychological dysfunction with *crimes of sexual violence.*

Among the most telling studies are an extensive investigation that involved both administration of a comprehensive neuropsychological test battery, measures of penile tumescence in response to erotic stimuli of varying character (male/female, adult/child), and CT scans of the brain, Hucker, Langevin, Wortzman & Bain (1986) found a high incidence of neuropathology, particularly involving the left temporo-parietal region of the brain, among subjects whose criminal histories classified them as focused pedophiles.

Similarly, at the Kessler Institute for Rehabilitation Medicine, Galski, Thornton & Shumsky (1990) found evidence of significant neuropsychological dysfunction in 77% of the incarcerated criminal sexual psychopaths they examined on the Luria Nebraska Neuropsychological battery, discovering as well so strong an association between neuropsychological impairment and the degree of violence associated with the most recent sex offense that they were led to conclude that "violent sexual offenses seem to be linked with more severe neuropsychological dysfunction, specifically associated with left hemisphere functioning," thought to control (at least among those who are right handed) such functions as sequential and analytic processing of ideas and concepts (Taylor, Sierles & Abrams, 1987, pp. 4-5).

paper-and-pencil instruments like the MMPI can detect psychological *sequelae* to neuropathology thus remains moot.

❏ Most tellingly, Yeudall & Fromm-Auch (1979) found *evidence of neuropathology* through administration of a comprehensive neuropsychological battery *in 94% of the homicide offenders,* 96% of the sex offenders, 89% of the assaulters, and 86% of the juvenile offenders they examined, with these findings confirmed by subsequent EEG readings. Congruent findings were reported by Spellacy (1978), who also reported that neuropsychological assessment discriminated between violent and non-violent prisoners more effectively than did results of the MMPI. Similarly, though they employed only clinical neuropsychological test measures rather than medical neurological assessment devices, Bryant, Scott, Tori & Golden (1984) found consistent associations between neuropsychological deficit and a history of violent criminal behavior.

❏ In a retrospective analysis that eventuated in a new conceptualization of persistent criminal behavior as triggered by interaction between biological, social, and psychological contributors, Yeudall, Fedora & Fromm (1987) reviewed data on the *incidence of head injury among* alcoholic psychopaths *(77%), homicide offenders (75%),* rapists (21%), and offenders who had committed physical assault (25%). British psychologist Cedric Hart (1987) essentially confirmed these results in an investigation of neuropsychological impairment in two groups of homicide offenders, one of which was comprised of persistent violent offenders with previous convictions as well as a conviction for homicide and the other of which was comprised of "one-time aggressive" offenders without prior convictions. Hart's findings pointed toward greater impairment among persistent offenders.

Neurochemical Anomalies

At an even more fundamental level, the role of basic neuropharmacology and neuroendocrinology in violent behavior, whether such behavior be adjudicated as formally criminal or not, is only now beginning to be understood. A wide range of psychopharmacological and psychoendocrinologic research on offender groups has been reported and is underway, much of it in Scandinavian countries, and, because of the extensive laboratory protocols necessarily involved (e.g., studies of the metabolism of neural transmitting enzymes that require samples of spinal fluid), typically limited to small groups of subjects. Scattered studies yield fragmentary evidence that coalesces to produce a picture that may be indicative but is not yet definitive. Nonetheless, a number of studies point toward a prospective relationship between anomalies in neurochemistry and aggressive behavior:

☐ In studies of violent offenders across types of crime, Matti Virkkunen (1982-*a*, *b*, 1983-*a*, 1984, 1985, 1986, 1987, 1989) and his colleagues at the University of Helsinki have found evidence for the *abnormal metabolism of glucose,* an excess of which can produce "manic" states, especially among those diagnosed with anti-social personality disorder. Though their subjects had no particular history of criminal behavior, Gur, Resnick, Gur, Alavi *et al.* (1987) also found anomalies in the metabolism of cerebral glucose, especially in the left hemisphere of the brain, among schizophrenic patients (but not among non-schizophrenic controls) studied at the University of Pennsylvania using positron emission tomography (PET).

☐ Several investigators (Bradford & McLean, 1984; Dabbs, Frady, Carr & Besch, 1987; Rada & Kellner, 1976; Rada, Kellner, Stivastava & Peake, 1983; Virkkunen, 1985) have

---

⇨ *Anneliese Pontius: On Psychotic Trigger Reaction*

A neurological substratum for what Arboleda-Florez terms "post-homicidal psychotic reaction" has been proposed by Anneliese Pontius of the Harvard Medical School (1987, 1989). She attributes what she terms "psychotic trigger reaction" to a "seizure-like episodes" in the limbic system, which possibly occur "only once in a lifetime" because "A highly individualized external trigger stimulus has to be encountered within a specific context in which there is a vivid reactivation of memory for repetitive ... highly traumatic past experiences" (1987, p. 116).

According to Pontius, "in PTR, there is some interference with the usual settling down and forgetting, mediated by the hippocampus, of life's stressful experiences." Hence, "In the PTR, nondrive-motivated homicide is triggered by an individualized external stimulus that evokes a brief active reliving of past stressful, frequently repeated situations."

Pontius' descriptions, derived from case studies at Massachusetts General Hospital in which both psychological and neuropsychiatric factors in a number of homicide offenders were studied, certainly provide scientific corroboration for the homely account that "Something happened — and he 'snapped'."

reported *abnormally high concentrations of testosterone among inmates with a history of violent crime,* whether these were sexually focused or not. Pertinently to correctional treatment or control considerations, testosterone levels are amenable to biochemical manipulation through hormone-suppressing agents. There is fragmentary evidence that excess testosterone activates aggression even among mice (Gandelman, 1980). Among rats, according to Feldman & Quenzer (1984, p. 248), excess testosterone triggers aggression between males in order to establish dominance in mating functions but *not* aggression of other sorts.

❑ Boulton, Davis, Yu *et al.* (1983), Lidberg (1985), and Virkkunen, Nuutila, Goodwin & Linnoila (1987) have found evidence of the *abnormal metabolism of monoamine oxidase,* an important neural transmitter that regulates mood, the inhibition of which indeed constitutes the biochemical basis for many antidepressant psychotropic medications (Schatzberg & Cole, 1986, pp. 46-54), leading to the tentative conclusion of an enduring *relationship between impaired impulse control and naturally occurring anomalies in the body's regulation of neural transmission.*

❑ At Eastern Pennsylvania Psychiatric Institute, Coccaro, Siever, Klar & Maurer (1989) reported abnormal metabolism of serotonin, a powerful neurotransmitter directly related to the psychobiology of depression, among subjects with a history of impulsive aggression who had been independently diagnosed as psychopathic. Similar results were reported by Virkkunen & Narvanen (1987) in a more complex study that also traced the interactive effects between insulin, tryptophan, and serotonin. In animal studies, *abnormalities in the regulation of serotonin* have been linked to aggressive behavior (Feldman & Quenzer, 1984, p. 248).

❑ At a primitive molecular level, Virkkunen, Horrobin, Jenkins & Manku (1987), through analysis of cereberospinal fluid among violent offenders diagnosed with anti-social personality disorder, found anomalies in the production of prostacyclin, an ubiquitous metabolite of unsaturated fatty acids that in turn directly affects the metabolism of the powerful neurotransmitter norepinephrine and itself directly influences the perception of pain.

❑ In a multidimensional study that suggests the interaction of extrinsic forces and intrinsic neurochemical factors in the generation of violent behavior that extended Virkkunen's (1979) earlier work on the effects of alcohol on violence in subjects who had been diagnosed with anti-social personality disorder, Virkkunen, Nuutila, Goodwin & Linnoila (1987) observed a high rate of alcoholism among violent offenders in

⇨ Jan Volavka on Persistent Aggression and the EEG

Soon after the introduction of EEG into clinical practice, a dramatic case highlighted a relation between abnormal brain waves and violent criminal behavior . . . An apparently healthy man murdered his mother without any clear motive. However, EEG revealed abnormal discharges during hypoglycemia. This condition [is] associated with clouding of consciousness.

Many other studies were inspired by this original case report. Typical of these is an EEG study of murderers in Egyptian prisons and a mental hospital . . . that revealed the expected abundance of various abnormal findings in such a sample. *The incidence of EEG abnormality was particularly high among those offenders who murdered without apparent motive.*

In the best study of this type . . . 333 offenders who committed violent crimes underwent EEG. The principal and unique advantage of this study is the separation of the offender sample into two subgroups: Those who were habitually aggressive and those who had committed a single violent crime. Sixty-four percent of the habitually aggressive offenders had an abnormal EEG compared with only 24% of single [episode] offenders. When offenders with mental retardation, epilepsy, or a history of major head trauma were removed from analysis, EEG remained abnormal in 57% of the habitual aggressors but in only 12% of those who had committed a single violent crime. The pattern of EEG abnormalities remained similar to that observed for the complete sample. Thus, this study demonstrated that *it is persistent aggressivity that is associated with EEG abnormalities.* . . . relationships between violent crime and EEG findings sometimes emerge only after certain biochemical changes impinging on brain activity are introduced. Such changes may be elicited, for example, by administering certain drugs that activate EEG abnormalities to the violent offenders.

These findings, together with other neuropsychiatric abnormalities (such as psychomotor signs and symptoms, multiple neurologic soft signs, and impairments on [measures of neuropsychological functions]) . . . have raised the possibility that the degree of brain dysfunction (particularly epilepsy) in the violent offender has been seriously underestimated by most investigators, as well as by the criminal justice system.

Violent people are at risk for head injury, and such injuries may cause an EEG syndrome resembling immaturity. To distinguish the antecedents of violence from its consequences, one needs to perform longitudinal prospective studies that start with subjects who have not yet become violent . . . My colleagues and I performed two such studies . . . Both studies showed that a light slowing of the EEG frequency predicts later development of . . . crime.

• *Source:* Jan Volavka, Aggression, electroencephalography, and evoked potentials: A critical review. *Neuropsychiatry, Neuropsychology & Behavioral Neurology,* 1991, 3, 250-251, 257.

whom they had also observed anomalies in regulation of neural transmitters and opined that, because ingestion of alcohol represents a temporary corrective to abnormal metabolism of monoamine oxidase, *"alcohol abuse* in these individuals . . . *may represent an effort to self- medicate,"* even though "alcohol only makes the situation worse by further impairing impulse control." In other studies, Virkkunen and his colleagues have observed a relationship between habitual violence and abnormal metabolism of cholesterol (1983) and abnormal metabolism of glucose (1987) *under the influence of* alcohol. Nonetheless, it will patently be the case that, whether at the scene of a crime or in later studies which rely on social history variables, violent behavior will be attributed to alcohol ingestion; the issue of why it seems to a particular abuser of alcohol that he or she "feels better" when drinking (i.e., the issue of whether alcohol use or abuse is itself an effort to self-medicate and thus *secondary* to a naturally occurring neurologic anomaly) will scarcely be raised.

❑ Results from clinical rather than experimental investigations suggest yet other neurochemical contributions to violence. Hall (1989) found evidence at autopsy both of cadmium and lead, powerful *neurotoxins,* in a mass murderer who killed himself but who had previously been a rather quiet and law-abiding citizen, leading to the conclusion that "immunotoxic biochemical pathology due to heavy metal poisoning affected inhibitory control mechanisms." Similarly, at the Medical College of Ohio, Lesco (1989) attributed a murder-suicide by a 67-year-old male with no history of mental illness, violent behavior, or substance abuse to rapid-onset paroxysms in brain-bioelectrical activity associated with *Alzheimer's disease.* Conacher & Workman (1989) and Pope & Katz (1990) have reported cases of homicide in which the use of *anabolic steroids* by the young adult perpetrators "played a necessary, if not primary, role in the etiology of the violent behavior" *(Ibid.,* p. 28). In all cases, there was no history of criminal violence, nor of anti-social personality disorder; the crimes were committed impulsively. Until Spring 1991, anabolic steroids were freely available at health food stores as dietary supplements to stimulate weight gain and had become especially popular among gymnasts concerned with "body building." These substances also have legitimate medical uses in the treatment of underweight children. But these substances achieve their effect precisely by altering naturally-occurring endocrinological processes, so that whatever propensity for violence is unleashed by their use is to be attributed to deliberately-induced (though perhaps unintended) neurochemical anomaly. Anabolic steroids have now been placed on the roster of "controlled substances" by the Federal Food and Drug Administration.

The Matter of Physique

Based perhaps on the commonplace observation that "bullies" tend to be tall in stature, muscular, often laconic and perhaps slow in thought, and frequently bordering on corpulence, early conceptualization linked body type to violent and/or criminal behavior (Hall & Lindzey, 1970, pp. 338-377; Wilson & Herrnstein, 1985, pp. 72-103). In criminology, the leading advocate for a perspective that in fact attributed criminal violence causally to body type was the 19th century Italian physician, penal reformer, and prison superintendent Cesare Lombroso; in psychology, the principal spokesperson has been the late William Sheldon of Harvard.

Both Sheldon (1949) and Sheldon and Eleanor Glueck (1956) carried out extensive studies of juvenile delinquents, finding the *mesomorphic* physique prevalent in their samples, with that body type described as "strong, tough, resistant to injury, and generally equipped for strenuous and exacting physical demands." Associated psychological characteristics were said to include aggressiveness, assertiveness, a need for dominance, high energy, a taste for risk, and particular reactivity to alcohol (Sheldon, 1942). As Herrnstein (1990, p. 12) has observed, "just such a combination of personality traits has been directly associated with criminal tendencies."

Later investigators linked the mesomorphic physique to the presence of an additional "male" chromosome in the genetic endowment, so that it was hypothesized that a propensity for violent and/or criminal behavior is indeed transmitted genetically. But detailed cytogenic analyses of a large sample of imprisoned offenders have revealed a "double" male chromosome in fewer than 1% of the cases (Finley, McDanal, Finley & Rosecrans, 1973). Thus, as Herrnstein (1990, p. 12) has put it:

> The extra Y chromosome turns up unpredictably in any social class or ethnic group or family setting. Such men are taller than average and have other minor physical characteristics [in common]. They also have a 10 to 20 times greater tendency to break the law than do genetically normal men from comparable populations. Even with their elevated criminal tendencies [however], there are too few XYY men to affect overall crime rates much.

It is a reasonable assessment to say that there remains little interest in the pursuit of a genetic-physiological substratum for criminal violence, but the "why" of that situation is rather more difficult to discern. Surely the state of the evidence, though fragmentary, suggests the utility of continued investigation (Mednick & Christiansen, 1977).

In view of the massive explosion in research in the neurosciences on the substratum for violence, it may be that an interest in physique has been subsumed into a focus on neuropsychological functioning. Or, considering the prospective political and cultural consequences to inquiry into genetic determinants and limitations, self-censorship on the part of researchers may be as valid an explanation as any.

Yet it remains the commonplace observation that "bullies" do tend to cluster in a certain shape and size, while others who may be *internally* disposed toward bullying but who lack the requisite physique *either* opt for other ways to assert themselves into dominance (e.g., verbal cajolery, intimidation) — *or* perhaps opt for the use of weapons that equalize differences in physique.

Cause, Correlative, or Consequence?

Though the evidence of a statistical association (technically, no more than a correlative relationship) between bioelectrical or neurochemical anomalies and violent criminal behavior is relatively strong, the state of the evidence does not yet permit determination of precedent and antecedent (much less, of "cause and effect") relationships. Such determination would require, as Heinrichs & Buchanan (1988) have observed in regard to the evidence on the neurogenesis of schizophrenia, clear indication that neurophysiological dysfunction "predates" criminal violence. As Robert Wettstein (1988, p. 1066), a leading forensic psychiatrist at the University of Pittsburgh, has put the matter aptly in respect of the prospective relationships between epilepsy and criminal violence, but his reasoning applies more generally to the relationships between neurological anomaly and violent behavior as well:

> several relationships between antisocial conduct and epilepsy can be inferred: a) antisocial act caused by a seizure; b) cerebral malfunction causing both epilepsy and antisocial behavior; c) antisocial behavior resulting in low self-esteem and social rejection suffered by patients with epilepsy; d) antisocial behavior symptomatic of a mental disorder as a result of epilepsy; e) psychosocial environmental deprivations causing both epilepsy and antisocial behavior; and f) antisocial behavior which produces accidental brain trauma.

The *directionality* of the relationship is complicated by the relative insensitivity of even highly sophisticated measuring devices to the *time of onset* of brain dysfunction, except perhaps in cases of very recent head trauma, typically independently verifiable from physical evidence of concussion. Though most knowledgeable commentators would regard neurochemical anomalies as constitutional or congenital rather than acquired through accident or injury, the regulation of neurotransmitting fluids may be affected by brain dysfunctions consequent to injury sustained during violent behavior; thus, the issue of directionality may apply as well to anomalies in neurochemical processing.

There is also the issue of the interaction between brain dysfunction, substance abuse, and violence, as Virkkunen, Nuutila, Goodwin & Linnoila (1987) have suggested. Hence, people who over-imbibe alcohol (or use psychotomimetic drugs) tend to find themselves in violence-prone situations; people in violence-prone situations are susceptible to head injury, whether from fights with others also intoxicated or from injuries attendant upon arrest; alternately, simple intoxication may lead to falls that engender head injury or compound pre-existing dysfunctions.

NEUROGENIC VIOLENCE AND CRIMINAL CULPABILITY

The scientific picture on the neurogenesis (as distinct from the biogenesis, at least in the sense of inherited constitutional predispositions, as Herrnstein [1990] uses the term) of violence is currently richly suggestive but not yet definitive. Given what is currently either known or hypothesized about brain and neurochemical anomalies thought to "control" impulsivity and aggression, and in light of at least fragmentary evidence about the incidence of anomalies in brain and neurochemical functioning among violent offenders, it may well be the case that future research will demonstrate conclusively that criminally aggressive behavior is "triggered" by very primitive neurophysiological or neurochemical processes over which the individual can be expected to exert little *volitional* control.

Some rather silly academic debates about antecedent and consequent conditions — concerning whether, for example, such personality traits as are measurable through psychometric or clinical instruments result from disordered neuropsychological processes or whether such traits (presumably acquired as the remnants of disordered developmental or learning processes) dictate disordered neuropsychological processes — might then be expected.

But the more salient debates will concern the implications of revolutionized understandings of the genesis of violent behavior that is formally criminal for societal and legislative notions of culpability, as Wilson & Herrnstein (1985, pp. 504-505) have somewhat satirically foreseen:

If society should not punish acts that science has shown to have been caused by antecedent conditions, then every advance in knowledge about why people behave as they do may shrink the scope of criminal law. If, for example, it is shown that [violent] offenders suffer from abnormal hormones combined with certain atypical relations with their parents, then, by the existing standards of responsibility, why should their attorneys not demand acquittal on grounds of bad hormones combined with a particular family history?

The matter of directionality may not be particularly pertinent in fixing culpability for a specific offense, unless it be the case that the putatively "triggering" brain or neurochemical anomaly can be demonstrated to have arisen *consequent* to that offense. Consider a situation, for example, in which earlier, documented episodes of criminal violence have yielded neuropsychological anomalies of such character that the emission of violent behavior is virtually beyond the control of the individual, and in which there is also documented evidence that the individual in question was free of such anomalies prior to those earlier episodes.

In an *instant* case of criminal violence *subsequent* to the onset of such anomalies, what degree of culpability should attach to that individual? In that situation, whether earlier episodes of violent

---

⇨ *Causation, Logic, Epistemology, and the Undistributed Middle*

Correlation implies neither causation or exculpation. Busch & Cavanaugh (1986), of Rush-Presbyterian Medical Center in Chicago, recast the issue as a problem in epistemology. The data do not begin to suggest that most people with diagnosable psychiatric illness commit homicide — or any other crime, for that matter. Indeed, to so assert would be to embrace what Aristotle's *Logic* terms the fallacy of the "undistributed middle term" — as in the pseudo-syllogism: *Fidel Castro is a red-eyed Marxist, and he believes in child labor laws. George Bush is a red-eyed Capitalist, and he believes in child labor laws. Ergo, Bush is a Marxist; or Castro is a Capitalist.* What is missing, of course, is the proposition (to which few would assent) that *All those who believe in child labor laws are either red-eyed Capitalists or red-eyed Marxists.*

Yet it may nonetheless and simultaneously be the case that most homicides are committed by people with diagnosable psychiatric illness. Given the vast imbalance between the incidence of diagnosable psychiatric illness in the general population and the incidence of criminal homicide, it is clear that such illness cannot independently constitute an explanatory condition; instead, we must again inquire *what else is required?* to provide a comprehensible explanation.

behavior that "caused" such anomalies themselves constituted "willful misconduct" may be quite irrelevant to the determination of *current* culpability.

IMPLICATIONS FOR THE M'NAGHTEN STANDARD

A formal diagnosis of "organic psychosis" as the perpetuation of neurogenic disorder would seem to fit within legislatively established criteria for nonculpability. Yet most current formulations of the criteria for culpability and exculpation as reflected in the M'-Naghten Standard and its variants do not explicitly recognize cases in which criminal behavior is triggered by brain or neurochemical dysfunction.

Quite clearly, advances in knowledge about the neurogenesis of violence will inevitably "shrink the scope of criminal law" — indeed, as effectively as the scope of the law underwent shrinkage a century and a half ago when then-current scientific knowledge led to the initial formulation of the M'Naghten Standard. In particular, the exclusion of psychopathic deviation (i.e., that "the terms 'mental disease or defect' do not include an abnormality manifested only by repeated antisocial conduct") in the American Law Institute's formulation needs substantial discerning reconsideration in the light of evidence that links, even correlatively, criminal violence with neurophysiological and neurochemical dysfunction.

→ *INFERENCES, SPECULATIONS, CONJECTURES*

The present state of knowledge supports a cautiously-framed generalization:

There is sound evidence linking neuropsychological dysfunction with impulsive violence. Because so large a proportion of homicides each year occur under "tinder box" circumstances, there is reason to believe that disordered neurology represents a *contributing* factor in many such cases.

☐ *DIAGNOSABLE FORMAL PSYCHIATRIC DISORDER*

Reports of the proportion of those *convicted* of murder (and thus excluding those accused but acquitted by reason of insanity) who exhibit clear symptoms of "severe" diagnosable psychiatric disorder (whether diagnosed through clinical or actuarial methods) range from a high of 100% to a low of 60%. These proportions exclude offenders diagnosed as suffering those "adjustment disorders" that, while included in current diagnostic lexicography, might be construed as artifacts of correctional confinement. In general, these

⇨ *Case Studies of Convicted Killers*

Among a large cadre of essentially clinical studies of psychiatrically disordered killers are those of

❏ Kahn (1967), on the Rorschach responses of 43 accused murderers, with the finding that lack of "adherence to reality" represents a significant impairment.

❏ Turns & Gruenberg (1973), on a mental patient who murdered a ward attendant and the impact of that crime on other patients.

❏ Blackman, Lum & VanderPearl (1974), on the role of denial and projection leading to "sudden murder.

❏ Newman (1974), on self-esteem in 46 prisoners sentenced for murder, assault, and/or armed robbery.

❏ Rascovsky (1974), on filicide in relation to the projection of aggression in war.

❏ Harris & Pontius (1975) on a murderer who dismembered his victim, following the pattern of an Aztec sacrificial ritual.

❏ Thornton & Pray (1975), on a paranoid schizophrenic who succumbed to violent impulses.

❏ Brown (1977), the medical director of Utah State Prison, on the case of Gary Gilmore, who petitioned for the execution of his own death sentence, an episode in recent social history memorialized by Norman Mailer in *The Executioner's Song*.

❏ Humphrey (1977), on the "psychological autopsies" of 62 homicide offenders in North Carolina.

❏ Dallas (1978), on a father who brutally murdered his 23- year-old son on a school playground in full view of 50 elementary pupils.

❏ Lancaster (1978), on a 23-year-old Briton of extraordinarily high intelligence convicted of murder and necrophilia.

❏ McKee (1978), on the fantasies of mutiny and murder among members of the U.S. Navy between 1798 and 1815.

❏ Scott (1978), on the treatment through hypnosis of a 31- year-old alcoholic who committed murder during a "fugue" (black- out) state.

❏ Arnold, Fleming & Bell (1979), on an "over-controlled" Canadian who shot his wife.

❏ Keltikangas-Jarvinen (1980), on identical 24-year-old male twins, each convicted of murder.

❏ Benezech, Bourgeois, Boukhabza & Yeasavage (1981), on a French case of murder, cannibalism, and vampirism by a paranoid schizophrenic.

❏ Grant & Combs (1983), on a Vietnam combat veteran suffering severe post-traumatic stress disorder who was nonetheless convicted of murder.

❏ Martinius (1983), on an aggressive fourteen year old boy with a circumscribed lesion in the right temporal lobe of the brain who killed an eight-year-old.

❏ Milliken (1983), on three trans-sexuals, one of whom committed murder, one of whom attempted murder, and the third of whom experienced frequent homicidal impulses.

❏ Vaisanen & Vaisanen (1983), on an abused daughter who slew her mother after suffering abuse and incest and witnessing the victim's murder of her step-father.

❏ and Master (1984), on a 17-year-old boy who murdered his high school psychology teacher.

studies are entirely *descriptive* rather than comparative — i.e., they do not essay to compare the rate of such disorder *either* between convicted murderers and those convicted of other crimes *or* between convicted murderers and the general population. Moreover, the methodologies used in these studies have varied from highly sophisticated actuarial assessment to clinical impression. But, for purposes of comparison, we might note that a review of the relevant epidemiological studies of psychiatric disorder in the general population in the U.S. and Canada suggests a rate of diagnosable disorder that ranges from 11% to 81% and that the rate among *imprisoned* offenders not inflected by offense-of-record may be as high as 76% (Pallone, 1991, pp. 13-56, 117-137).

Incidence among Convicted Offenders

The upper limit of 100% was reached in a study of convicted homicide offenders in the prisons of Finland by Keltikangas-Jarvinen (1978), with 71% diagnosed as psychopathically deviate, 21% as neurotic, and 7% as schizophrenic. Some 92% of similar offenders in the prisons of Scotland were diagnosed as dysthymic (depressed), neurotic, or delusional (Heather, 1977). Among murderers convicted in Contra Costa County, California over a three-year period (Wilcox, 1985), 69% were diagnosed as psychotic (including those suffering from the drug-induced psychoses), brain-injured, addicted, or psychopathically deviate. In one study in Poland (Szymusik, 1972),

---

⇨ *Clinical Studies of Homicide Defendants*

❑ Kahn (1971) studied 43 accused murderers in Arizona who entered insanity pleas, with 51% diagnosed as psychopathically deviate in the classic M'Naghten formulation of an inability to tell right from wrong but essentially free of other severe mental disorder and only 14% diagnosed as psychotic.

❑ Bluestone & Travin (1984) reported on five accused offenders acquitted on the grounds of insanity, asserting that "In each case, subjects were seen to have underlying conflicts with psychodynamic determinants," which conflicts erupted into murderous violence "when the ego state is weakened due to ... variable intrapsychic or external stresses, neurophysiological phenomena such as epilepsy, [or] altered states of consciousness induced by fugues or drug or alcohol intoxication."

❑ In France, Benezech (1984) studied 109 accused killers found not guilty by reason of insanity, with 63% diagnosed as schizophrenic and 37% as paranoid, with the former more likely to have murdered parents and the latter more likely to have murdered relatives or friends.

60%— and in another (Sila, 1977), 64%— of convicted murders were diagnosed as psychotic, alcohol-addicted, or suffering from degenerative brain disease. And, in a retrospective analysis of all known homicides in Iceland between 1900 and 1979, 66% of the offenders were post-diagnosed as psychotic, mentally retarded, neurotic, alcohol-dependent, drug-dependent, or suffering from personality pattern disturbances (Petursonn & Gundjonsson, 1981).

Incidence among Homicide Defendants

These reports are augmented by a vast array of *clinical* case studies, usually of a single murderer, that amply demonstrate severe psychiatric disorder in the instant case, and by studies of those acquitted by reason of insanity, in which case severe mental disorder has been judicially determined. In virtually the only *comparative* study reported within a 15-year period, however, Langevin and his associates (1982) at Clarke Institute of Psychiatry, Toronto, compared the rates of psychiatric disorder observed among homicide offenders, offenders who had committed non-violent crimes, and members of the community not accused or convicted of any crime. These investigators found no significant differences in the rate of psychiatric disorder among or between the three groups.

Studies of convicted murderers are further amplified by reports on psychiatric disorder among those *accused* of homicide. Thus, Daniel & Harris (1982) found "at least one primary psychiatric disorder," identified as schizophrenia, personality pattern disturbance, alcoholism, or organic psychosis, in 85% of the women charged with homicide who were examined at the University of Missouri College of Medicine. But these investigators found a *higher* rate of such disorder (i.e., 93%) among the women they examined who were charged with crimes *other than* homicide.

Data from the United Kingdom on either side of the point at which the death penalty was abolished by Parliament in 1965 provide remarkable contrasts — and perhaps some suggestion that the diagnostic process is not untainted by consideration of the consequences that flow from formal categorization. Thus, distinguished Oxford criminologist Nigel Walker (1968) reported that, in the eight-year period immediately preceding abolition of capital punishment, an astoundingly high aggregate total of 46% of accused homicide offenders were adjudicated to be *either* not guilty by reason of insanity, incompetent to stand trial, *or* guilty but with diminished responsibility by virtue of mental condition. That proportion speaks only to those psychiatric disorders which are severe enough to reach the M'Naghten tests for insanity, incompetence, or diminished responsibility (according to Walker, at pp. 27-28, generally schizophrenia or *grand mal* epilepsy) and is thus less than exhaustive as a catalog of all mental disorders which these defendants might have been suffering.

In rather sharp contrast, Gillies (1976) reported that psychiatric abnormality of any sort was found in only 10% of 367 defendants accused of murder in Glasgow and examined at Stobhill General Hospital at the request of the *prosecution*. Yet Heather (1977) reported a rate of formal psychiatric disorder more than nine times greater (i.e., at 92%) among *convicted* murderers in all of Scotland. When Gillies' rate of diagnosable psychiatric disorder of 10% among *accused* murderers examined at the request of the prosecution (which presumably has an interest in finding that the defendant is free of mental illness, particularly in a situation in which both "insanity" and "diminished responsibility" are available as defenses) is juxtaposed to Heather's 92% rate among inmates convicted of homicide who were examined at the request of *prison authorities,* the difference is no less than incredible. Perhaps some explanation is to be found in the formulations of psychiatrist Julio Arboleda-Florez (1981) on the *post-homicidal induction of mental illness* immediately following arrest and while awaiting prosecution, in which the stressors associated with the experience of apprehension and detention are paramount. It may be arguable that the very high rates of diagnosable psychiatric disorder among convicted and imprisoned murderers reported in the several studies reviewed reflect disorders induced, or at least led from incipient to florid states, *following, and perhaps as a result of,* conviction and imprisonment. Or, for the jaundiced, it may more simply be the case that the interests of the party requesting or authorizing the diagnosis influence its content.

Cautions against Attributing Causation

With a discrepancy on the order of two-or three-fold between the rates of psychiatric disorder in studies of the general population and those reported in studies of criminal offenders, Langevin aside, it is tempting to attribute criminal homicide to severe psychiatric disorder, even in causal fashion. Before we yield to that temptation, however, we need to observe that, virtually uniformly, the diagnoses reflected in the gross data were made *after* the homicide occurred, and in this connection we should at least nod to Arboleda- Florez and his views on post-homicidal mental illness. But there are other important caveats to be borne in mind as we interpret the data:

❑ A very large proportion of the diagnoses reflected in the gross data are diagnoses of *psychopathic deviation,* one empirical referent for which is criminal behavior itself, so that (as we observed in Chapter 2) a tautology of impressive proportions emerges.

❑ Among the studies we have reviewed, only one (Wilcox, 1985) is set in the U.S., and that is limited to a single county whose racial composition (in consequence of substantially larger Hispanic and Oriental populations than is the case nationally) is itself atypical. Finland, Scotland, and Poland are clearly racially homogeneous societies; though Canada and Iceland

---

⇨ *Revitch & Schlesinger: On the Post-Diction of Homicide by Means of Rorschach Responses*

Not all clinicians are as persuaded of the superiority of actuarial to clinical assessment as we have confessed ourselves to be. In counterpoint to our gloomy conclusions about the usefulness of projective testing, for example, psychiatrist Eugene Revitch and psychologist Louis Schlesinger (1981, pp. 29-30) are markedly more positive:

❑ Psychodynamic inferences on the Rorschach come from analysis of content with special regard to the specific stimulus pull of the various inkblots. Certain Rorschach cards are thought to tap different areas of conflict (e.g., father, mother, sex, etc.); thus, responses to these cards have obvious significance . . . this type of analysis is heavily imbued with psychoanalytic theory . . . Empirical research on the Rorschach with cases of homicide has been very limited [but] one of our cases . . . was administered the Rorschach after killing his girlfriend as the direct result of paranoid delusions. We had the opportunity of examining a Rorschach given to this man ten years prior to the murder. On Card VII, the "mother" card, the patient perceived a "crude ax," which suggests that destructive impulses toward women were present but controlled at that time.

Alternately, another clinician might construe a subject's projection of a "crude ax" onto Card VII, which indeed is frequently regarded as eliciting perceptions of the mother figure, as revealing *castration anxiety.* Even in this case, one might infer — in an abreactive and circuitous way — hostility toward women other than the mother. From a process psychology perspective, however, the more germane issue is how a *latent* hostility toward women came to be *potentiated* in such fashion that homicide resulted.

are racially heterogeneous, the racial distribution of their populations differs in very dramatic ways from ours.

The U.S. is not only a racially heterogeneous society — but one in which, as we have seen, the members of one racial minority group are vastly overrepresented both among the victims and the offenders in cases of homicide. Is there any particular reason to believe that the rates of severe psychiatric disorder among convicted homicide offenders observed in those racially homogeneous societies apply to our own? Alternately, since the data from the Wilcox study not only do not differ from, but instead closely parallel, those to emerge from studies in racially dissimilar societies, is there any reason to *doubt* that the rates of severe psychiatric disorder among convicted homicide offenders observed in racially homogeneous societies apply to our own?

→ *INFERENCES, SPECULATIONS, CONJECTURES*

The data at hand can support only an inference worded with very great restraint:

❑ The relevant studies, many of them undertaken outside the U.S., suggest an incidence of severe psychiatric disorder among convicted homicide offenders two to three times greater than that observed in epidemiological studies of the general population in this country and Canada. Because the diagnoses reflected in these studies were made after conviction for criminal behavior, whether the disorders observed pre-existed the criminal act or whether they were induced after the commission of the crime, apprehension, prosecution, and, in most cases, imprisonment, must remain indeterminate. Because the racial composition of the societies in which the majority of relevant studies were undertaken differ from that of the U.S. in marked ways, conclusions to emerge therefrom can be predicated of the U.S. only with substantial caution.

❑ **MEASURABLE PSYCHOLOGICAL CHARACTERISTICS**

Psychiatric diagnoses are made on the basis of a variety of types of evidence, including both past behavior (as we have repeatedly observed with respect to psychopathic deviation), clinical observations, the subjective expressions of the person being diagnosed, and those personal characteristics that are measurable through psychological instruments, whether of the "projective" or "actuarial" variety. A rather large group of studies has considered the psychological characteristics of convicted homicide offenders measurable through psychometric means — without, however, progressing beyond the measurement of particular characteristics to the construction of diagnoses.

Data from Projective Instruments

The so-called "projective" psychometric instruments are devices of markedly low internal stimulus structure, so designed as to elicit highly variable interpretations or "projections" of their meaning from an examinee. It is believed that these interpretations or projections of meaning reveal the examinee's perceptions, beliefs, attitudes, and/or values.

Chief among the several devices of this sort are the *Rorschach Psychodiagnostic Plates,* a series of essentially symmetric inkblots devised by Swiss psychiatrist Herman Rorschach in 1921, and the *Thematic Apperception Test,* a series of reproductions of drawings showing one or more persons about whom the subject is to invent a story, devised in 1938 by Harvard psychologist Henry A. Murray. Though a variety of "scoring" systems has been developed for each, the interpretation of the examinee's responses depends essentially on the examiner's acuity and experience, and, as one might expect, is extraordinarily variable between examiners; one still, in fact, hears murmurs about something called "clinical intuition" in the interpretation of projective test data.

Doubtless reflecting the current state of practice in psychology and psychiatry, only a relative handful of contemporary studies have relied exclusively on projective test data to describe or distinguish convicted or accused homicide offenders. Thus:

❑ In a descriptive study of the Rorschach responses of 43 *accused* murderers, Kahn (1967) concluded that a variable he called "reality adherence level" and described as "extensively related to measures of primary process thought and impulse" represented an important characteristic in his subjects.

❑ Perdue & Lester (1974) concluded to the essential similarity of the Rorschach responses of 33 black and 33 white *convicted* murderers but did not essay to distinguish their subjects from other offenders or from the general population.

❑ After administering the Thematic Apperception Test to 115 condemned killers awaiting execution in Uttar Pradesh, Srivastava (1976) reported high levels of depression and obsession with religious issues. Another observer might have intuited similar conclusions without projective data.

❑ In a comparative study of the Rorschach responses of 20 male homicide offenders in contrast with those of 20 non- offenders in Brazil, Bukowski & Gehrke (1979) contended that the homicide offenders' projections more frequently revealed sadism, while comparison subjects more frequently evinced insight and "the capacity for atonement."

❑ Utilizing the Thematic Apperception Test, Kundu & Bhaumik (1982) contrasted the projections of 30 male murderers with those of 30 male property offenders, concluding that murders "were more depressed, anxious, frustrated, and aggressive" than the property offenders in the comparison group.

→ *INFERENCES, SPECULATIONS, CONJECTURES*

❑ Clearly, *both the paucity of studies and the instability of the interpretations preclude any valid generalizations based on projective test data.*

Data from Actuarial Measures

In contrast, "actuarial" instruments are devices of markedly high internal stimulus structure, so designed as to severely restrict an examinee's responses — generally, to responding *yes / no* to a series of questions. The examinee's responses (or pattern of responses) to the items which comprise the instrument are then compared to those of subjects in a "norm group" of known dimensions whose contemporaneous or subsequent behavior has been recorded, so that many such instruments claim "predictive" validity in addition to their capacity to compare and contrast an examinee with "otherwise similar" subjects.

Because these instruments are objectively scored (today, often by computer) and because scores are expressed in terms of norms,

---

⇨ *MMPI Scales to Identify Potential Child Abusers*

MMPI scales to identify "potential child abusers" independently by gender (i.e., abusive mother *vs.* abusive father) have been derived by Paulson (1974, 1975) and Milner (1979, 1980). Indeed, in one study, Paulston *et al.* (1975) identified 13 MMPI *items* that correctly and post-dictively identified 100% of their sample of abusing fathers, even though no single MMPI *scale* did so. Sociological investigators like Strauss (1979) in the United States and Baldwin & Oliver (1975) in Britain have identified epidemiological factors related to child abuse. On the basis of such indicia, intervention programs for "families at risk of poor parenting" have been developed by child care agencies in various constituencies (Ayoub & Jacewitz, 1982; Otto, 1990).

To the contrary, in their review of the *post-* dictive validity of nine different MMPI-derived scales to identify prospective child abusers, Furlong & Leton (1977) concluded that "Attempts to develop such scales are based on a psychopathological model of child abuse which assumes that there is one dominant, unique personality which predisposes the abusers' actions and that this personality type can be identified through the use of conventional psychometric instruments. There is little evidence to support these assumptions."

derivation of scores from the examinee's responses is invariant between examiners. Further, since many actuarial instruments contain multiple scales to measure several traits simultaneously, it is possible to compare an examinee's *score profile* on these several scales to those of others in a norm group.

The classic exemplar of devices of this sort is the *Minnesota Multiphasic Personality Inventory,* an instrument developed in 1943 at the University of Minnesota's School of Medicine by psychologist Starke Hathaway and psychiatrist Charnley McKinley which has been the subject of not fewer than 9000 published scientific research studies in the interim and is doubtless the most widely used psychometric instrument in the world (Graham, 1987; Parker, Hanson & Hunsley, 1988). Few contemporary psychoclinicians would quarrel with Meehl's (1954, p. 138) conclusion about the superiority of actuarial over projective instruments: "Always, the actuary will have the last word."

Some investigations utilizing actuarial measures of psychological characteristics attend to individual traits, relying on absolute scores on the individual scales of the actuarial instrument employed, while other studies focus more on *profiles,* or aggregate patterns of scores on individual trait scales. Whatever the focus, such investigations frequently seek to differentiate convicted murderers from offenders convicted of other crimes; since such instruments are scored on the basis of norms, comparisons to members of the general population who are putatively non-offenders are relatively easy to make, though the statistical significance (i.e., probability that the observed difference does not arise by chance) of such comparative differences is rarely calculated with precision.

Personality Measures: The Minnesota Multiphasic Inventory

Structurally, the MMPI consists of some 566 statements, with a fourth grade reading level, which subjects endorse as True or False in relation to themselves. Through a sophisticated psychometric process called "criterion referencing," the *pattern* of responses given by each subject can be compared to those of members of the standardization sample whose psychiatric diagnoses were established through exhaustive formal diagnostic procedures conducted by mental health professionals *not* including results of the instrument under development, so that the resulting "scores" reflect the degree of congruence between a given subject's self-reports and those of members of distinct diagnostic groups whose differential diagnoses had been firmly established by customary intensive professional examination (Anastasi, 1988, pp. 526-530; Graham, 1987, pp. 4-5). In an inventive study in which he administered the instrument once again to subjects after an interval of 40 years, Greene (1990) found remarkable stability in scores over this substantial time span. That situation sits at a diametric contrast with the customary instability over even short periods of time characteristic of projective assessment methods. Indeed, some who are as persuaded on the projective side of the ledger as we are on the actuarial might argue that it is by design that projective devices tend to be sensitive to nuances that distinguish the psychological state of *this* moment from that of the next moment.

To that argument, the actuarialist will respond that only knowledge of relatively *enduring* intra-person characteristics — as distinct from momentary and evanescent conditions — will permit even the post-diction of behavior (criminal or otherwise) at a reasonable level of accuracy. Whatever the terms of the conceptual debate, the sort of longitudinal stability in those intra-person characteristics measured by the MMPI, as demonstrated by Greene, suggests that such characteristics may indeed constitute enduring aspects of personality and behavior; and that, in turn, may even prompt reconsideration of the pre/post-diction issue. If certain intra-person characteristics remain stable over a period of four decades that have seen major societal changes on a global scale no less than the usual intra-personal changes expected over the better part of a life span of an individual, it might may be that the measurement of a characteristic taken *post-hoc* on the MMPI can *under some conditions* nonetheless be interpreted *pre*dictively.

The MMPI yields scores on three measures of what has been called "test-taking attitude," including dissimulation, and on ten "primary clinical" scales. The measures of "attitude" (often collectively called the "validity" scales) are:

❑ *L,* a measure of the extent to which the subject answers certain questions so as to portray himself or herself in a favorable light, and thus considered a "social desirability" index;

❑ *F* a measure of the extent to which a subject endorses a variety of test items rarely endorsed by subjects in the standardization sample found on other grounds to be free of disabling psychiatric symptomatology;

❑ *K,* a measure of defensiveness and consistency in responding to test items.

The ten primary clinical scales are denominated:

❑ *Hypochondriasis (Hs),* or abnormal preoccupation with physical complaints;

❏ *Depression (D)*;

❏ *Hysteria (Hy)*, or the tendency to translate emotional problems into physical symptoms;

❏ *Psychopathic deviation (Pd)*, or the tendency toward disregard of customary social mores;

❏ *Masculinity-femininity (Mf)*, or the tendency to endorse traditionally opposite-gender-linked interests and attitudes;

❏ *Paranoia (Pa)*, or fearful hypervigilance against external psychological, social, or physical threat;

❏ *Psychasthenia (Pt)*, or obsessive rumination coupled with compulsive behavior;

❏ *Schizophrenia (Sc)*, or disorientation, apathy, emotional constraint and/or coldness, sometimes coupled with delusion or hallucination (Colligan *et al.*, 1989, p. 17);

❏ *Mania (Ma)*, or elevated mood and accelerated speech and motor activity; and

❏ *Social introversion*, or the tendency to withdraw from social contacts and responsibilities.

Over the course of the years, some 132 additional or "derivative" scales have been developed (Graham, 1987, pp. 116-194), in the main also on a criterion-referenced basis (e.g., the MacAndrew Alcoholism Scale, the Harris-Lingoes Inhibition of Aggression Scale, the Wiggins Authority Conflict Scale).

A score equivalent to the 97th percentile (represented by a value of 70 on the normalized "T" distribution on which scores are reported) constitutes the customary threshold level for assessment of serious disorder in professional mental health diagnosis; this point is usually called the "threshold of clinical significance." In the early days of the instrument's use, index codes representing the two or three highest scales (and often the lowest one or two as well) were employed to describe configural patterns for subjects (Hathaway & Meehl, 1956), but this practice has more recently yielded to computerized scoring and profile interpretation. Essentially a self-administering, paper-and-pencil device, the MMPI is incapable of directly detecting neuropsychiatric disorder, brain syndromes, or mental deficiency except at the most profound (non-reader) level. Nonetheless, the MMPI is sensitive to a number of characteristics (e.g., psychopathic deviation, mania, schizophrenia, psychasthenia, social introversion) which *may*, in given cases, represent behavioral manifestations secondary to underlying neuropsychiatric disorder amenable to psychometric inventory.

In addition to its ubiquity in clinical practice, the MMPI is very likely the most widely researched diagnostic instrument in history

(*Note* 1); by Anastasi's (1988, p. 526) count, it had been the subject of some 8000 investigations in the half-century following its publication, with additional studies accumulating at the rate of 250 per year (Maloney & Ward, 1979, p. 312). A decade ago, a major restandardization study was undertaken at the Mayo Clinic to provide contemporary norms inflected by age and sex (Colligan, Osborne, Swenson & Offord, 1989).

STUDIES AMONG HOMICIDE OFFENDERS

Again reflecting the current state of practice, the *Minnesota Multiphasic Personality Inventory* (MMPI) has become the actuarial measure-of-choice in current psychological studies of homicide offenders, whether of individual traits or of profiles. Among contemporary studies which have focussed on traits rather than profiles or patterns and which have relied on what are called the instrument's "primary" or "clinical" scales:

- ❑ Sutker, Allain & Geyer (1978) compared 22 convicted women homicide offenders to 40 non-violent women offenders, finding that the *non-violent* group scored significantly higher on *Pd* and *Mf* and on a "validity" (rather than clinical) scale which measures denial of psychopathology (*K*).

- ❑ Panton (1976, 1978) found *no* significant difference on any scale between North Carolina death row inmates who had been convicted of murder vs. those convicted of rape.

- ❑ Among an array of characteristics investigated, Langevin (1982) reported that only significantly higher scores on the MMPI scale which measures the tendency to "convert" psychological problems into physical symptoms (*Hy*) distinguished the murderers in his sample from non-violent offenders and from comparison subjects not implicated in crime.

- ❑ An increasingly sophisticated series of investigations has been reported by Holcomb and his associates. Holcomb & Adams (1982) reported that their sample of black convicted homicide offenders scored significantly higher than white convicted homicide offenders on an MMPI scale which measures the tendency toward manic behavior (*Ma*) but lower on the scale measuring social introversion (*Si*).

- ❑ These results were partially replicated in a second study of racial differences (Holcomb, Adams & Ponder, 1984-b), in which a sample of black *accused* murderers scored significantly higher on *Ma* and on a scale which measures deviant ways of responding to the instrument's questions (*F*). And the results of the latter investigation, in turn, were also partially replicated in a study of accused murders not inflected by race, in which abnormally high scores were observed in a scale (F) which measures test-taking attitude and deviant response set.

❏ Holcomb & Adams (1985) also compared convicted males who had committed murder while alcohol-intoxicated with other convicted offenders who committed murder not in a state of intoxication, with a comparison group of non-violent offenders with no history of significant alcohol problems, and with alcoholics who were not implicated in crime. The investigators reported that the intoxicated offenders had higher scores than the non-intoxicated killers on an MMPI scale which measures the tendency of the examinee to present the self in a favorable light (L) but lower scores on the Mf and Pd scales. As a group, the homicide offenders in the sample, intoxicated or not, had higher scores on the MMPI scale which measures suspiciousness and hypervigilance (Pa) but lower scores on Ma than did the non-violent offenders or the alcoholic non-offenders.

❏ In an effort to detect "malingered amnesia" for the offense among men accused of murder, Parwatikar, Holcomb & Menninger (1985) reported that the putative amnesiacs had higher scores on Hy and on MMPI scales which measure subjective depression (D) and hypochondriasis, or an obsessive concern with physical health (Hs). In yet a more ambitious investigation, Anderson & Holcomb (1983) employed an advanced statistical procedure called "cluster analysis" to identify five "types" of capital murderers on the basis of MMPI scores.

❏ Similarly, in a study of convicted homicide offenders in Britain reported by McGurk (1978), cluster analysis of MMPI scores revealed two broad categories of characteristics — labeled respectively the over-controlled and the under-controlled; but whether these two personality "types" are unique to murderers or may be reflected in the broader offender population remained indeterminate.

❏ In a three-way contrast, Kalichman (1988) compared the MMPI profiles of adult women who had murdered their husbands (or male partners), adult men who had murdered their wives, and adult men who had murdered strangers during the course of another crime. Women scored higher on Pa and on Si than men in either group; men who had committed felony murder scored higher on Ma than men who had committed spousal homicide.

❏ Cornell, Miller & Benedek (1988) compared the MMPI profiles of *adolescent* homicide offenders with those of a comparison group of adolescents charged with larceny; the homicide cases were further subgrouped into those who committed homicide secondary to robbery or rape and those who acted in the context of interpersonal conflict with the victim [roughly corresponding to what we have earlier labeled "tinder box" homicides]. No significant differences were found between the homicide and larceny groups; but the "felony crime" killers differed from the "conflict" killers on *F, Hs, Hy,* and *Sc.*

In addition to its use in studying offenders, the MMPI has also been employed extensively to study law enforcement officers and corrections personnel and is used with some frequency as a pre-employment selection device in some jurisdictions (Bartol, 1991; Pallone, 1992).

THE MEGARGEE-BOHN TYPOLOGY STUDY

Without question, the most extensive body of MMPI data about convicted criminal offenders has eventuated from the Megargee-Bohn Typology Study, undertaken in the mid-1970's to develop an actuarially-anchored system on which to base decisions about level of correctional supervision required, determine treatment needs (if any), and assign subjects to rehabilitative regimens while incarcerated.

In that ambitious undertaking, Edwin Megargee of Florida State University (who had earlier made important contributions to the understanding of criminally assaultive behavior that eventuated in the development of an MMPI scale to measure "over-controlled hostility," as described by Megargee in 1966, Megargee, Cook & Mendelsohn in 1967, and Megargee & Cook in 1975) and Martin Bohn of the Federal prison system analyzed in detail MMPI data on 6350 inmates of the Federal prison, including 1350 who were followed throughout the period of their incarceration and subsequent to release. Extensive analysis yielded a typology of ten distinct offender groups with characteristic MMPI profiles (assigned colorful names derived from military nomenclature, like "Easy" and "Foxtrot"), with which specific patterns of criminal behavior and distinct social history variables were found to be statistically associated (Megargee, 1977; Megargee & Bohn, 1977; Megargee, 1986).

Megargee & Bohn (1979) described both their method of cluster analysis of the MMPI and the derivation of their forensic scales in a seminal monograph. That work reviews varying taxonomic systems for classification of offenders and describes in detail studies undertaken in the Federal prison system with the MMPI over a seven year period, beginning with 2500 youthful offenders in Tallahassee. From the psychometric profiles of these inmates, classificatory rules were devised for 9 profile clusters; further revision yielded 10 groups, and decision rules for classification were computerized. The final revision resulted in the capacity to computer-assign 96% of sample, so that an actuarial method could be employed in the classification

⇨ *Display 10: Clinically High Elevations on the Primary MMPI Scales and Characteristic Offense Patterns among Offender Groups in the Megargee-Bohn Typology Study*

⇓ GROUP NAME	% Total Sample	*Scales Above 70*	*Offense Pattern*
☐ Able	17	*Pd*	Moderate, median violence, heavy use of marijuana
☐ Baker	4	*Pd*	Violent, extensive; heavy alcohol, little drug use
☐ Charlie	9	*F, Pd, Pa, Pt, Sc, Ma*	Extensive, violent, heavy drug use
☐ Delta	10	*Pd*	Violent, often for excitement; Heavy use of amphetamines
☐ Easy	7	*None*	Non-violent
☐ Foxtrot	8	*F, Pd, Sc, Ma*	Violent; Heavy use of drugs with antagonistic biochemical properties (i.e., *both* CNS stimulants *and* depressants)
☐ George	7	*D, Pd*	Drug, liquor offenses
☐ How	13	*F, Hs, D, Hy, Pd, Pa, Pt, Sc*	Mixed; More often victim rather than perpetrator in violent crime; Heavy use of LSD
☐ Item	19	*None*	Non-violent, draft, drug, liquor
☐ Jupiter	3	*Pt, Sc, Ma*	Property offenses

• *Source:* Megargee & Bohn, 1979, pp. 107-234

of prisoners. An array of attitude, ability, achievement, demographic, family history, and criminal history data were analyzed to determine the defining characteristics of members of the final ten groups. Detailed statistical analysis found differences in behavior, social history, lifestyle, personality pattern, and offense histories.

The Megargee-Bohn typology has been cross-validated in a number of studies, including those by Edinger (1979) on a large sample of prisoners (1291 males, 146 females) in state correctional facilities; by McGurk (1981) on homicide offenders in Britain; by Edinger, Reuterfors & Logue (1982) on adult males in a forensic mental health unit; by Henderson (1983) on non-violent offenders; by Smith, Silber & Karp (1988) on women inmates; by Veneziano & Veneziano (1986) on juvenile offenders; by Walters (1986) on offenders in the armed forces; by Dahlstrom, Panton, Bain & Dahlstrom (1986) on death row inmates; by Mrad, Kabacoff & Duckro (1983) on paroled offenders in halfway houses; by Megargee (1986) on prisoners who had threatened to assassinate the president; and by Greene (1987), who investigated the stability of the ten offender types in relation to ethnic variation. In a review of the accumulated research evidence, Zager (1988) concluded that "the reliability, validity, and practical utility of the system have been demonstrated." Similarly, Villanueva, Roman & Tuley (1988) reported that the typology accurately *post*-dicted rehabilitation outcome among offenders in a residential treatment facility.

Nonetheless, some investigators have questioned the universal applicability of the Megargee-Bohn typology to offender populations in such specialized settings as halfway houses (Motiuk, Bonta & Andrews, 1986) and medium security facilities like prison camps (Baum, Hosford & Moss, 1984), or for *post*-dicting lifetime criminal violence (Moss, Johnson & Hosford, 1984). Megargee himself has questioned the predictive validity of several derivative scales concerning prison adjustment constructed from the initial typological data (Megargee & Carbonell, 1985); Louscher, Hosford & Scott (1983) and Kennedy (1986) have similarly questioned the effectiveness of the typology in predicting inmate aggression; and Johnson, Simmons & Gordon (1983) have questioned the stability of the typology over time.

It is important to emphasize that the Megargee-Bohn typology study was *not* undertaken to link psychological characteristics to type of criminal offense for which an inmate had been sentenced, but instead to provide a sound actuarial basis for decisions for security classification and program assignment. Nonetheless, because their principal monograph is rich in its presentation of source material (Megargee & Bohn, 1979, pp. 107-234) it is possible to *reassemble* the source data so as to trace such linkages with some degree of precision. DISPLAY 10 represents such a reassembly.

REASSEMBLING THE MEGARGEE-BOHN SOURCE DATA

Because the seminal study reflected the distribution of offenses in a *Federal* as distinct from a state prison, only a minor proportion of subjects had been convicted of crimes of violence and/or of crimes against persons. It is a corollary to the Balkanization of the criminal law that, for example, homicide is a Federal crime only when committed against a Federal officer or on Federal property (like an Indian reservation or the lobby of a post office) or in a Federal "territory" over which the Federal criminal courts have jurisdiction, like the District of Columbia, the U.S. Virgin Islands, and the Mariana Islands in the Pacific. With respect to the latter political units, the Federal prisons function in lieu of what would otherwise be correctional institutions indistinguishable from state prisons. Hence, the distribution of offenses between the two principal categories varies substantially between state and Federal institutions; violent offenders comprise 55% of the inmates of state but only 23% of the inmates of Federal prisons; indeed, there are fully 50% more inmates confined for violation of immigration laws than are confined for homicide in the Federal prisons (Flanagan & Jamieson, 1988, pp. 495, 518).

Accordingly, it is not surprising that only some 31% (though a higher proportion than among Federal prisoners generally) of the initial Megargee-Bohn sample evinced criminal records characterized by crimes of violence — those assigned to the groups denominated *Baker, Charlie, Delta,* and *Foxtrot.* Among this segment of their sample, clinically significant mean elevations were observed for all four groups on the *Pd* scale. In addition, clinically significant mean elevations were observed on the *Pa* scale and on the *Pt* (obsessive-compulsive) for Group Charlie (comprising 9% of the total sample, and approximately 39% of those offenders with records of crimes of violence); on the *Sc and Ma* scales for Groups Delta and Foxtrot, collectively comprising 18% of the total sample and 58% of those with records of violent crimes (Megargee & Bohn, 1979, pp. 139-234).

While these traits may *describe* violent offenders in the Federal prison population, they do not uniformly *differentiate* such offenders from their non-violent counterparts. Though a clinically significant mean elevation on the *Pd* scale was found for each of the four groups whose offense records reflected crimes of violence (representing in the aggregate 31% of the total sample), a similar mean elevation was found for non-violent offenders in Groups Able, George, and How, representing in the aggregate 37% of the total sample; hence, that trait cannot be held to differentiate violent from non-violent offenders among the Megargee-Bohn subjects.

Similarly, for only one group of violent offenders (Charlie, representing 9% of the total sample and 29% of the subsample of violent offenders) was the mean elevation on *Pa* above the threshold of clinical significance, while a similar mean was observed among members of a group of non-violent offenders (How) representing 13%

⇨ *Frank Farley: On Thrill-Seeking as a Function of Age*

Distinguished psychologist Frank Farley of the University of Wisconsin has long been concerned with a dimension of behavior he has termed "thrill-seeking." Farley (1986, pp. 45-46) distinguishes those who "are risk-takers and adventurers [and] seek excitement and stimulation wherever they can find or create it" from those who "cling to certainty and predictability, avoiding risks and the unfamiliar," labeling those in the first group as *T*-types (i.e., the *capital T* types) and those in the second as *t*-types (i.e., the *lower-case t* types). Moreover, "thrill-seeking can lead . . . to outstanding creativity . . . but it can [also] lead to extremely destructive, even criminal, behavior." Farley holds that the genesis of thrill-seeking or thrill-avoidance is likely physiological, but is both mediated by, and mediates, social factors:

❑ . . . we all seek unconsciously to maintain an optimal level of "arousal" or activity in the central nervous system . . . If arousal is too high or too low, we try to adjust it to some middle ground, often by choosing environments and experiences that are either soothing or stimulating . . . Some of our research and that of others implicate such physiological arousability as the basis for stimulation-seeking, while other research suggests a role for biochemistry (such as monamine oxidase or testosterone). These interpretations may not be incompatible, but the precise biological bases are not certain at present . . . Experiences around the time of birth or perhaps early nutrition may also play a role.

Whatever its source, thrill-seeking appears to fluctuate inversely with age:

❑ [thrill-seeking] is most often found among those in the 16-to-24 age range. From then it drops off gradually, as my colleagues and I found in two large studies of people from approximately 10 to 75 years old . . . most people reach their strongest expression of [thrill-seeking behavior] in their late teens to early 20s, with a decline into old age.

Farley's data, then, are highly congruent with those of Colligan and his associates (1989) on age-related decline in scores on the *mania* and *psychopathic deviation* scales of the MMPI and of Hare and his colleagues (1988) on the age-related decline in criminal behavior among offenders categorized as psychopaths.

of the total sample (and 19% of all non-violent offenders in the sample). On the *Pt* scale, for only Group Charlie (9% of all offenders represented) was the mean at a clinically elevated level, while two groups of non-violent offenders (How, Jupiter) collectively comprising 16% of the total sample (and 21% of all non-violent offenders) had a mean elevation at that level.

THE Ma SCALE AS A DIFFERENTIAL IDENTIFIER OF VIOLENT OFFENDERS

The *Ma* scale rather clearly serves to differentiate, however; and the picture with respect to scores on the *Sc* scale raises some interesting speculations.

On the *Ma* scale, two groups of violent offenders (Charlie, Foxtrot, comprising 17% of the total sample and 55% of the subsample of violent offenders) have mean scores at or above T = 70; however, only Group Jupiter (representing 3% of the total sample and 4% of all non-violent offenders) scored at or above the clinical threshold. To put the matter slightly differently: *Clinically significant levels of mania were found fourteen times as often* among violent as among non-violent offenders in this sample. This trait thus bids fair to differentiate violent from non-violent offenders — especially in a situation in which there is essentially no difference between the two groups in level of psychopathic deviation.

On the *Sc* scale, two groups of violent offenders (Charlie, Foxtrot), collectively comprising 18% of the sample (and 58% of all violent offenders) had a clinically significant mean elevation, while two groups of non-violent offenders (How, Jupiter) representing 16% of the total sample and 23% of all non-violent offenders had a mean elevation beyond that threshold. That appears to suggest that schizophrenic symptomatology was found two and a half time more frequently among violent offenders as among non-violent offenders.

Or, to speculate about the matter from yet another perspective: Might it be the case that the readiness to engage in impulsive violence of the character that leaders in neuropsychiatry now attribute to neurogenic influence *perpetuates itself* in such fashion that it is reflected in clinically elevated scores on the MMPI's mania scale — and that its expression is aided and abetted by impairments in the capacity to assess "reality" correctly (perhaps most particularly, in the realistic assessment of costs, benefits, and risks associated with prospective lines of behavior), as reflected in clinically elevated scores on the MMPI's schizophrenia scale? If in fact some identifiable proportion of criminal homicide falls precisely into what we have described as "tinder box" circumstances, should we expect that those who perpetrate such impulsive violence will display *actuarial-*

⇨ **The California Psychological Inventory: Dimensions of "Normal" Personality That Differentiate Criminal Offenders**

From its inception, the MMPI was intended to function as a diagnostic instrument, identifying those persons suffering from emotional disorders of one or another sort who were presumably in need of professional mental health treatment. To that extent, the instrument sought to differentiate the "abnormal" from the "normal" — and to differentiate those who are "abnormal" in *this* way from those who are abnormal in *that* way.

But the MMPI has never claimed to be able to differentiate particularly efficiently among persons who are not disordered in some way. Instead, the task of differentiating the various aspects of "normal" personality has been ceded to instruments designed for that purposes, including Cattell's *Sixteen Personality Factor Questionnaire*, a "factor-pure" instrument described briefly in Chapter 1.

Among the best-known and most widely used of the instruments intended for what is called the "multidimensional assessment of normal persons" is the *California Psychological Inventory* (CPI) developed by Harrison G. Gough of the University of California at Berkeley and available commercially since 1956. Intended for use with subjects as young as 13, the instrument measures such dimensions of *normal* personality as dominance, flexibility, intellectual efficiency, (need to) achieve by means of conformance or by means of independence, responsibility, sense of well-being, tolerance, sociability.

Not surprisingly, the CPI has been employed with some frequency in studies of criminal offenders in situations in which no assumption has been made that such investigations require instruments that focus on psychopathology. Because its lower limit encompasses a significant proportion of juvenile offenders who are adjudicated through the courts (rather than "handled" through the state's child protective agency without formal court intervention), the CPI is especially popular in both clinical and research applications with young offenders. Moreover, though it is difficult to document such a generalization, one suspects that the wide use of the CPI with offender populations is at least in part an abreaction to the failure of the MMPI to post-dict criminal behavior with unquestioned efficiency. Thus, for the differentialist, if the multidimensional assessment of abnormal personalities fails, perhaps the multidimensional assessment of normal personalities will succeed.

In the view of Laufer, Skoog & Day (1982, p. 562), who reviewed some 62 studies of offender groups with the CPI, that is precisely the case: "Scales from the [CPI] inventory . . . have proven to be moderately predictive of parole success, assault proneness, prisoner's grades in educational courses, probationer/parolee employment stability, and recidivism ".

Moreover, the profiles that emerge from these studies show considerable similarity. In particular, mean scores for samples of offender subjects on the *responsibility* and *socialization* scales are typically quite low, often equivalent to the second percentile. Since the purpose of the instrument is to assess "normal" personalities, the most cautious interpretation of such findings is that, in comparison with persons who are considered to be psychologically normal rather than abnormal, criminal offenders are markedly less responsible and less positively socialized. That is, of course, precisely what one would expect of people who, as a group, tend to score high on the *Mania* and *Psychopathic deviation* scales of the MMPI.

ly measurable personal characteristics *other than* psychopathic deviation, impulsivity, and impaired contact with reality?

THE MAYO CLINIC RESTANDARDIZATION AND AGE-RELATED DECLINE IN Pd SCORES

A decade ago, a major restandardization study was undertaken at the Mayo Clinic to provide contemporary norms inflected by age and sex (Colligan, Osborne, Swenson & Offord, 1989). Particularly since scores on the *Pd* scale have rather consistently differentiated correctional populations from general populations, it is germane to consider an "incidental" finding reported by Colligan and his associates (p. 44) that scores on the *Pd* scale were significantly *negatively* correlated with age among both male and female subjects in their restandardization sample (at $r = -.30$ and $-.22$, respectively); the same phenomenon was also observed on the scales that measure *paranoia* (at $-.19$ and $-.16$), *mania* (at $-.38$ and $-.25$), and, among males only, *schizophrenia* (at $-.20$).

It is important to underscore that these findings emerged from a restandardization study whose subject pool represented the general population, putatively free of criminal offenders. But these findings are remarkably congruent with the general direction of research in career criminality (as reviewed in Chapter 1), so much so that one cannot help but wonder whether a naturally-occurring psychological phenomenon (which might, as Pallone & Tirman [1978] suggested, be termed "symptom abandonment" as a function of age) is not also reflected in decreases in overt criminal behavior.

More pointedly, Hare, McPherson & Forth (1988) analyzed the criminal careers over a 25 year period of Canadian offenders who had been identified in Hare's earlier studies as psychopaths or as nonpsychopaths, reporting that "the criminal activities of non-psychopaths were relatively constant over the years, whereas those of psychopaths remained high until around age 40, after which they declined dramatically," adding that "The results are consistent with clinical impressions that some psychopaths tend to 'burn out' in middle age." If decline in impulsivity and psychopathic deviation be accepted as reasonable operational approximations to "burn out," those clinical impressions seem to be *psychometrically verified* through the Mayo Clinic data base.

A NEUROGENIC ETIOLOGY FOR PSYCHOPATHIC DEVIATION?

As we have already observed, there is at least fragmentary evidence for the proposition that the "characteristic" or "syndrome" variously labeled *psychopathic deviation* or "anti-social personality disorder" may arise from a neurogenic etiology, whether that characteristic is measured by the familiar *Pd* scale, by Hare's scales of psychopathy (1970), or through clinical devices.

We have noted that Blackburn (1975, 1979) found evidence of abnormally high cortical arousal, as measured through electroencephalograph (EEG) readings, among prisoners diagnosed as psychopathic, findings that support Hare's (1970) view that hyperarousability is a distinguishing characteristic of psychopaths. Gorenstein (1982) reported evidence of dysfunction in the frontal lobe of the brain, held to govern such functions as foresight, planning, and the regulation of impulses among subjects otherwise diagnosed as psychopathic. Investigations by Hare & McPherson (1984) and by Jutai, Hare & Connolly (1987) similarly found "asymmetric left-hemisphere arousal" patterns among subjects who had been identified through Hare's methodology as psychopathic.

PSYCHOPATHY: TRAIT OR PATTERN OF BEHAVIOR?

In three sequential studies on a total of 663 Federal prisoners, Hare & McPherson (1984) found that those who scored high on Hare's measure of psychopathic deviation also had more convictions for violent crimes and provided interview histories of more frequent violent and aggressive behavior. From these data, they seem to conclude to psychopathic deviation as a psychological characteristic which the more violent and aggressive of their subjects cart about from one behavioral situation to another (cf. Howard, Bailey & Newman, 1984).

But there may be alternate interpretations. First, the level of psychopathic deviation in their subjects was measured *a posteriori,* long after the emission of the violent crimes for which they had been incarcerated, so that it is not in evidence that the putative "characteristic" obtained in these subjects *prior to* the criminal behavior for which they were serving sentences. Second, precisely because the measure of psychopathy is retrospectively validated through an offense record which recounts episodes of violent criminal behavior (cf. Elion & Megargee, 1975), is it not a reasonable interpretation that the psychological measure is merely redundant of the record of behavior?

Nor are we alone in our preference for an assessment of behavior over the psychometric measurement of psychopathic deviation understood as an enduring and "portable" personality characteristics, especially when such measures are redundant with recorded behavior. Thus, Bursten (1985) has decried the practice of "predicting" criminal child abuse through the psychometric assessment of parents on such dimensions as psychopathy *prior to* the emergence of behavioral evidence. Similarly, Rachlin, Halpern & Portnow

(1984) have argued that psychopathic deviation should be equated with socially deviant behavior rather than mental illness: "There is a tremendous difference between . . . acts that are truly irresistible and those that are merely not resisted."

In another variation, Heilbrun (1979) found that psychopathic deviation as measured by the Minnesota Multiphasic Personality Inventory was indeed related to violent crime — but only when mediated by low levels of intelligence, so that "psychopaths with limited intelligence evidenced the greatest *impulsivity* in the commission of their crimes," a formulation which responds to the question of *What else is required?* in our statement of the process model. Heilbrun (1990) has more recently reported data that link criminal homicide to the *interaction* between low levels of intelligence and highly anti-social attitudes. And Wheeler (1976) has argued from a sociological perspective that the so-called psychopathic deviate "is an individual whose behavior conforms to the standards of his subculture but not to 'normal' social standards [who] often does not show any significant abnormality in behavior outside adherence to non-normative standards and values." Similarly, after an extensive four-way comparison between convicted homicide offenders, offenders guilty of assault, offenders guilty of armed robbery, and non-violent control subjects, Lang, Holden, Langevin & Pugh (1987) concluded that personality indices of any sort were inefficient differentiators; in what reduces to a redundancy of the first magnitude, only the past criminal history of the subject differentiated efficiently.

Withal, it is not unreasonable to believe that neurogenic factors underlie what has typically been identified as psychopathic deviation *and* that the term itself is largely redudant with, and recapitulative of, behavioral history.

Personality Measures: The Maudsley/Eysenck Inventory

In the first edition of his landmark work *Crime and Personality,* the distinguished British psychologist Hans Eysenck (1966) of the University of London set forth the proposition that criminal behavior is a function of three personality characteristics — *psychoticism, neuroticism, extraversion* — and that a fourth dimension, roughly encapsulated as the extent to which an individual seeks to appear "normal" either to all others or to selected others, contributes to certain types of criminal behavior. What has been called the Eysenck theory of criminality has been further elaborated in the second edition (1977) and by Eysenck & Gundjonsson (1989) in *Causes and Cures of Criminality.*

Each of the three personality dimensions is measurable through an instrument initially named the Maudsley Personality Inventory (after the teaching hospital in London where Eysenck held his faculty appointment and where he pioneered in the development of behavior therapy) or the Eysenck Personality Inventory (EPI), the successor instrument. The theoretical rationale that underlies the instrument holds both that these characteristics of personality exist because they are measurable (a somewhat tautological argument that nonetheless conforms to the principal tenets of logical positivism as a guiding force in empirical behavioral science) and that they represent in adulthood the product not only of psychosocial developmental experiences but also of typical patterns of neuropsychological organization. Thus, neuroticism as a characteristic of the adult personality is held to reflect lability in the autonomic nervous system, while extraversion reflects cortical inhibition (Jensen, 1965). A number of contemporary studies, often conducted by Eysenck and his colleagues at the Maudsley, have focused on the psychological characteristics of violent offenders in general or of homicide offenders in particular, with results not always supportive of the original conceptual formulation:

❑ In a study that provided further confirmation for the conceptual model but did not seek to differentiate offenders by type of crime, Eysenck & Eysenck (1977) reported by-age comparison of scores on the EPI for 2070 British prisoners and 2442 non-offender control subjects. Prisoners score significantly higher on the *P* (Psychoticism) and *N* (Neuroticism) scales in all age groups, ranging from 16 to 69; on the *E* (Extraversion) scale, score differences proved not significant until age 30-39, when they fell in the predicted directions. Some 22% of the prisoners and 15% of controls, however, scored at clinically significant thresholds on all three scales, while 5% and 13% respectively scored low. Scores on all three scales were found to decline with increasing age among both prisoners and controls. Up to age 30, prisoners had higher *L* (essentially, social desirability) scores than controls, but the reverse situation obtained at higher age levels. Correlations between *L, E, P,* and *N* scores were low both among prisoners and among controls, a finding which contributed evidence to the proposition that these are independent traits of personality; thus, scores in combination with each other should provide a sounder basis for a prediction of criminal deviance. Not incidentally, there is remarkable congruence between the findings in this study on age-related decline in EPI scores held to be related to criminal deviance and the similarly age-related decline in scores on the

MMPI *Pd* scale reported by Colligan and his associates (1989) in the Mayo Clinic restandardization study.

❑ Similarly, studies by McGurk & McDougall (1981) and by McGurk & Bolton (1981) on delinquents aged 17-20 in comparison to similarly-aged control subjects and by Putnins (1982) on delinquents aged 15-18 and comparable controls established the applicability of the conceptual model to juvenile offenders, but without providing evidence that EPI scales successfully discriminated according to type of offense. In a cluster analysis of the EPI scores of delinquents aged 14-17, McEwan (1983) was able to post-dict the number of offenses in subjects' prior criminal records but not to discriminate between types of offenses. Gossop & Eysenck (1983) successfully discriminated incarcerated felony offenders from (non-incarcerated) drug addicts, but without differentiation as to type of offense among felons.

❑ Data which supported the contention that violent and nonviolent offenders can be differentiated on the basis of EPI scores were reported by Eysenck, Rust & Eysenck (1977), however, in a study of adult prisoners in England, and by Singh (1980) in a study of convicted homicide offenders in the Punjab, among whom members of the family had most frequently been the victims. Barack & Widom (1978) similarly demonstrated the utility of the instrument and the applicability of the conceptual model to American women awaiting trial on varied felony charges. In a study which contrasted murderers in India from criminal recidivists who had not been convicted of homicide, Ram (1987) found higher levels of psychoticism in the homicide offenders but higher levels of extraversion and neuroticism among the non-homicidal recidivists.

Several investigations have proposed methodological refinements or modifications to the instrument as a device for offender populations. Thus:

❑ In an investigation of the validity of the *P* scale on a sample of patients in a hospital for abnormal offenders who completed both the EPI and the MMPI, Davis (1974) proposed that the EPI psychoticism scale measures a dimension he denominated *emotionality* — a construct that bears a striking resembles to *mania* as measured by the MMPI's *Ma* scale.

❑ Similarly, Saklofske, McKerracher & [Sybil] Eysenck (1978) extracted from the *E, N,* and *P* scales those items which had most robustly differentiated adult offenders from control subjects to construct a "second order" scale they denominated *criminal propensity,* cross-validated on samples of adjudicated delinquents vs. non-delinquent adolescents.

❑ Blackburn & Maybury (1985) employed the EPI to determine correlates of the particular reactivity to environmental stimuli, lack of affect, and lack of behavioral control considered by many to constitute the defining characteristics of the psychopathic personality.

→ *INFERENCES, SPECULATIONS, CONJECTURES*

In consequence of our epidemiologic portrait of the prototypical murder as it is committed, what *traits* might one expect to find among those who *commit* that prototypical murder? It seems reasonable to expect that, in contrast to members of the general population, they would:

❑ Seek competitive situations, evince a variety of problems in impulse control, and arouse resentment and hostility in others — as might be suggested by scores that are *low* on MMPI Scale *Si* (Graham, 1987, p. 70) — and that expectation is supported, at least tangentially, by Holcomb & Adams (1982) and by Megargee & Bohn (1979);

❑ Evince high energy, prefer action to thought, display restlessness and an inability to tolerate frustration, and have an exaggerated sense of self-importance — as might be suggested by scores that are *high* on MMPI Scale *Ma* (Graham, 1987, p. 67) — and that expectation is supported, also tangentially, by Megargee & Bohn (1979), Holcomb & Adams (1982), and Holcomb, Adams & Ponder (1984-b) and further buttressed by Davis' (1974) conclusions on the *P* scale of the EPI as a measure of emotionality;

❑ Be excessively suspicious of others and hypersensitive to criticism — as might be suggested by scores that are *high* on MMPI Scale *Pa* (Graham, 1987, pp. 54- 55) — and, once again, the expectation is supported tangentially by Holcomb & Adams (1985);

❑ Tend to act without consideration of the consequences of their behavior — as might be suggested by scores that are *high* on MMPI scale *Pd* (Graham, 1987, pp. 46- 49). That expectation is not quite supported in these studies; instead, it appears to be countered by Megargee & Bohn (1979), Sutker, Allain & Geyer (1978) and Holcomb & Adams (1985). It may be the case that the offender in the prototypical murder is indeed positively rather than negatively socialized, albeit positively socialized to a subculture of violence; or it may be the case that a clinically significant level of psychopathy represents a uniform characteristic that is relatively invariable among offenders across specific categories of offenses. However, demographic data on the age distribution of victims of homicide and statistical data on the age, sex, and race similarity of victims and offenders seem entirely congruent with Mayo Clinic data on an age-related decline in *Pd* scores (Colligan *et al.*, 1989) as well as with the Eysenck & Eysenck data on age- related decline in extraversion, neuroticism, and psychoticism among both offenders and non-offenders.

In sum, it appears that *at least tangential evidence from studies of personality traits among homicide offenders as measured by actuarial instruments tends to corroborate the expectations derived from an epidemiologic portrait of murder as it is committed.* Some investigations have found offenders convicted of homicide or of violent crimes involving assaultive behavior to be more competitive, impulsive, manic, and suspicious than people-in- general; and there is some suggestion that they more frequently display impairment in reality contact. Contrary to expectation, however, they have been found to be neither more nor less psychopathically deviant than offenders convicted of other crimes.

It may be, however, that an elevated level of psychopathic deviation represents an intra-person threshold for the emission of criminal behavior, that the character of that behavior is contingent upon other intra-person variables interacting with stimulus determinants — and that impaired contact with reality and impulsivity as intra- person variables are likely to incline toward impulsive violence of the character reflected in a majority of the cases of criminal homicide reported statistically in the United States.

Measures of Intelligence

If one accepts Wechsler's (1958) classic definition of intelligence as "the global capacity to act purposefully, to think rationally, and to deal effectively with the environment," one might hypothesize a difference in intelligence between members of the general population and those who become embroiled in the sorts of tinder-box disputes that seem to be implicated in our epidemiologic portrait of murder — that is, one would expect that higher levels of the capacity to "think rationally" and to deal effectively with the environment, even an environment which reflects a "culture of violence," might incline one to avoid such conflicts or to find resolutions thereto which do not involve the risk of emerging as a homicide statistic, whether as offender or as victim.

Contemporary studies quite frequently measure intelligence among their subjects but rarely focus on this variable; instead, measured intelligence is used to "equate" groups that are to be compared to each other (so that prospective subjects at extreme ends of the intelligence spectrum are likely to be excluded) *or* reported merely descriptively. Data on intelligence must thus be culled from

⮕ *Significant Mental Retardation and Exculpation*

Significant mental retardation of such character as to render the person unable to appreciate the nature of his or her behavior is a prime empirical determinant for exculpation for the responsibility for criminal behavior under the M'Naghten Standard (West & Walk, 1977) for insanity prevalent in the criminal codes of the various states. In most jurisdictions, although rarely legistlatively defined, that level is generally taken to be an IQ of 55 or below, congruent with the American Psychiatric Association's definitions in the *Diagnostic and Statistical Manual of Mental and Emotional Disorders*, a statement itself drawn in concert with the American Association for Mental Deficiency. Nonetheless, it is not infrequent that a "mental retardation" defense is raised on behalf of a defendant whose inventoried IQ falls into the "low-normal to borderline range" (i.e., between 65-75), to which Herrnstein (1990) attributes a majority of "impulsive violent and opportunistic property crimes."

In a well-ordered world, in which criminal defendants availed themselves of the defenses open to them, one would expect to find few mental retardates among the prison population; instead, one would expect such offenders to be confined in forensic psychiatric institutions. Few empirical studies are responsive to these issues. However, Daniel & Harris (1982) found that 32% of their sample of women *accused* of homicide, but only 2% of the women accused of non-violent crimes, were mentally retarded. Yet, in a survey among prison administrators in 48 states, Denkowski & Denkowski (1985) reported that mentally retarded inmates constituted 2% of the prison population. Their operational definition for assessment of mental retardation was set as an IQ below 70 on the Wechsler Adult Intelligence Scale, Revised, the standard threshold on the psychometric measure of intelligence standard in clinical practice but significantly higher than that typically accepted as evidence of exculpatory retardation.

In consequence of the psychometric specificities of the Wechsler instrument in relation to the normal probability distribution, one would anticipate finding some 2.27% of the general population below an IQ level of 70 (Anastasi, 1988, pp. 90, 252), so that the prevalence rate for prisoners reported by Denkowski & Denkowski is slightly (and, very likely, not significantly) *lower* than chance expectancy for the general population. That may, indeed, argue that those who are significantly retarded (IQ below 55) and who have committed crimes have been remanded to psychiatric rather than correctional institutions.

Persons who are severely mentally retarded (some 0.13% of the general population, with IQs below 55 on the Wechsler) continue to be confined in institutions for the care of retardates (Landesman & Butterfield, 1987). Perhaps for this reason, few epidemiological studies of mental health and illness in the general population have assayed the prevalence of mental retardation. Pasamanick (1962) fixed the ratio at 1.5% on the basis of detailed examination of his subjects at Johns Hopkins Hospital and further observed that the incidence was greater among nonwhites than among whites at a ratio of 161%. In Epidemiological Catchment Area studies carried out under the auspices of the National Institute of Mental Health and based on the Diagnostic Interview Schedule, Burke & Regier (1988) report the rate of "severe cognitive impairment" at 1.3%.

According to the Denkowski & Denkowski data, *the prevalence of psychometrically-inventoried mental retardation in the prison population exceeds that found in the general population*, whether by Pasamanick's psychometric methods (at a ratio of 133%) or through nonclinician interviews (in the NIMH studies, at a ratio of 154%). While these ratios are not astronomical, they are the more surprising since mental retardation itself constitutes the grounds for exculpation under the M'Naghten Standard.

among the focal variables in such studies, despite easy generalizations that turn on largely impressionistic evidence (Lowenstein, 1989). With these caveats, current studies lend little support to such a hypothesized relationship between intelligence and murder. In studies of *convicted* homicide offenders:

❑ Langevin (1982) reported lower levels of intelligence as measured by the Clark Vocabulary Scale and the Raven Progressive Matrices among those subjects convicted of homicide than among non-violent offenders or comparison subjects not implicated in criminal activity in his sample; it may be important to note that he also found a higher frequency of neurological dysfunction, long held to be significant in intellectual functioning, among homicide offenders. Similarly, Hays, Solway & Schreiner (1978) found significantly lower scores on the Wechsler Intelligence Scale for Children among juveniles who had been convicted of homicide than among juveniles who had been convicted of "status" offenses.

❑ But Panton (1976) found no significant differences in intelligence between a group of capital offenders convicted of murder *or* of rape and the entire non-capital offender population of North Carolina. In a study in Greece, Kokkevi & Agathonos (1988) found significantly lower levels of intelligence among mothers convicted of child-battering than among control subjects; but the same effect did not obtain among battering fathers.

❑ In contrast, Heilbrun (1978) concluded that intelligence is a *moderating* variable in criminal violence, so that higher levels of intelligence may serve to *inhibit* violence even when violence cannot be attributed to low intelligence. Essentially similar findings were reported by Kandel, Mednick, Kirkegard-Sorensen & Hutchings (1988) in a methodologically advanced study of a large birth cohort in Denmark, which concluded that high intelligence constituted a "protective factor for subjects at high risk for antisocial behavior."

These studies are augmented by reports on subjects *accused* of murder:

❑ Kahn (1971) reported that the 43 subjects he studied who had pled insanity to charges of murder evinced essentially normal levels of intelligence as measured by the Wechsler scales; since he also reported that electroencephalographic [EEG] examination had revealed no gross anomalies in brain functioning, his finding may be particularly pertinent.

❑ Holcomb & Adams (1982) and Holcomb, Adams & Ponder (1984-a) reported significant differences between black and white men *accused* of murder, and Holcomb, Adams & Ponder

(1984-b) reported findings of low mean intelligence across races among males *accused* of murder.

It is instructive to observe that the laws of most states include significant mental retardation (operationally, as evidenced by an inventoried IQ of 55 or below) among the criteria for demonstration of insanity according to the M'Naghten standard. For this reason, it may well be that very low intelligence is implicated in homicide-as-committed more frequently than will appear to be the case if one bases inferences solely or primarily on studies of *convicted* offenders. Indeed, it might be observed that distinguished psychologist Richard Herrnstein (1990, p. 12) holds that certain types of offenses clearly issue from low levels of intelligence: "the impulsive violent crimes and the opportunistic property crimes are most often committed by people in the low normal and borderline retarded range" of intellectual functioning. The "low normal and borderline range" is generally taken to be in the range 65-75, substantially higher than that required to sustain an exculpability pleading on the basis of retardation.

However that may be with respect to other crimes and however appealing the logic that would attribute violent confrontation as an avenue to settling conflicts between *pairs* of actors to a mutual deficit in the conceptual ability to attempt resolution by verbal or other non-violent means (or, for that matter, to assess costs, risks, and benefits associated with criminal behavior realistically), studies of the intelligence of homicide offenders support no such easy general linkage.

→ *INFERENCES, SPECULATIONS, CONJECTURES*

Thus, *current studies of convicted offenders yield little evidence of a relationship between level of measured intelligence and murder.* Because mental retardation constitutes an appropriate basis for an insanity defense in many states, it may be that very low intelligence is implicated in homicide as it is committed more often than can be discerned in studies of convicted offenders.

☐ STUDIES OF ATYPICAL HOMICIDE OFFENDERS

Close Kinship Murder: Filicide

Without question, those episodes of criminal homicide that energize us most strongly involve the murder of children — and, most particularly, when the victims are slain by their own parents (or by a parent surrogate, as in the case of Lisa Steinberg, the New York

⇨ *Infanticide in London and Miami*

British psychiatrist P.D. Scott (1973) of the Maudsley Hospital studied 29 cases in which the father had beaten a child under the age of 5 to death. Some 65% of these offenders had criminal convictions as adults. They were prototypically semi-skilled or unskilled workers who had themselves come from families "in which the incidence of frank psychiatric disorder does not seem especially high." On the basis of EEG readings after arrest, none of the offenders were found to have neurological disorder. Even though Scott found that subjects were massively impaired in their capacity to cope with ordinary stress, "In no case was the father considered mentally ill at the time of the offence, nor whilst under observation [and] none was significantly intoxicated with alcohol or drugs at the material time."

Even with so little evidence of mitigating factors (i.e., absence of pre-existing formal mental illness, no neurogenic etiology for violence) and with evidence of an aggravating factor (prior criminal convictions in nearly two-thirds of the cases), the *modal* sentence (imposed on 41%) was three to six years; another 14% received sentence of under four years *or* probation, respectively; 10% were sentenced to ten years; 20% were given life senten-ces, by then Britain's most severe punishment.

In a description that reflects the level of ironic understatement charac-teristic of the United Kingdom, Scott catalogs the events that triggered the actions of these fathers in beating their infant children to death (p. 199):

❑ There is always an *immediate precipitating stimulus* from the child . . . the refusal of food, vomiting, sucking the tongue, crying, screaming (especially at night or when the television is on), 'swearing,' looking scared or blank, staring, refusing to smile, disobedient, refusal to learn, knocked over pot, spilling things, getting in the way, wet, dirty. Many of these factors, it will be appreciated, are inseparable from infancy.

Quite similar results were reported by Crittenden & Craig (1990) in an analysis of all recorded homicides of children under the age of 12 over a 30-year period in Dade County (Miami), Florida. The investigators concluded that "deaths of infants, toddlers, and preschoolers were usually the result of parental attempts to control child behavior [and are] unintended and related to the child's physical vulnerability." And, to distinguish the "intended" from the "unintended" murder of a child, Korbin (1989) has proposed the aggravat-ingly euphemistic term "fatal maltreatment."

City child brutally beaten to death by her attorney-stepfather, while her surrogate stepmother stood helplessly by). A number of investigations, many relying on clinical data extracted retrospectively from case and court records as the basis for their conclusions, have studied such crimes, the characteristics of which differ markedly from the portrait of the prototypical adult homicide drawn from statistical perspectives.

In an early and classic study on the "slaughter of the innocents," forensic pathologist Lester Adelson (1961) of the School of Medicine at Western Reserve University analyzed 46 child murders which had taken place over 17 years in Cuyahoga County (Cleveland), Ohio. Some 41 assailants were responsible for these 46 deaths; of these, 17 (42%) were the fathers of the victims, 11 (27%) the mothers, 6 (15%) were parent-surrogates (grandparents, aunts, uncles), and 8 (19%) were unrelated to the victims. *Asphyxiation* was the means of slaying for 16 victims; another 17 were beaten or kicked to death; 8 were shot. Adelson's (p. 1346) description of the circumstances, both intra-person and extra-psychic, which precipitated the deaths:

> Frank psychosis in the assailant was the single most common factor in precipitating the fatal incident. Seventeen persons were patently mentally ill when they unleashed their show of violence. Included in this number are 7 fathers who attempted to, or succeeded, in wiping out their entire families, and 8 mothers who killed 10 children . . . 5 husbands killed their wives incident to fatal attacks on their child . . . Three children died when parents attempted suicide and wanted to "take the children with them." One mentally ill mother killed her 2 children and tried to kill herself by inhaling carbon monoxide from automobile exhaust. She was saved . . . Nine children were killed by their fathers during an emotional outburst triggered by frustration and aggravation. Prolonged and repeated crying episodes, defecation in their clothing, persistent harassment, and other temper-abrading activities goaded the fathers . . . No mother killed with such provocation . . . Four girls and 1 boy were killed during sexual assaults . . . Three children, all less than one year of age, died of starvation resulting from home situations where vicious and thoughtless neglect or downright stupidity or both were the dominant factors . . . One six-year-old girl was burned to death when her father, divorced from her mother, threw an inflammable liquid on the bed in which mother and child were sleeping and set it afire . . .

Of the 41 alleged offenders, 40 were apprehended; eight committed suicide before criminal justice proceedings could be initiated. Of the remaining 32, eight were committed to psychiatric hospitals *before* trial; six were convicted of murder, three of manslaughter; the grand jury declined to indict in another case; apparently none were acquitted on the basis of insanity, despite the "frank psychosis" said to be the "single most common" precipitating factor in these cases (*Ibid.*, p. 1347). It is a matter of extreme interest to underscore that *only 9 convictions resulted from these 41 filicides,* so that the ratio between crime and conviction is only 22% — particularly when, as we have seen (DISPLAY 4, Chapter 3), the rate of conviction for all criminal homicides on a national basis is 67%.

⇨ *When Innocents Slaughter Innocents: A Juvenile Mother Attempts to Murder Her Newborn Son*

Good girls go to school every day, as everyone knows who reads storybooks. Pigtails bobbing as they skip along clean sidewalks to gather with friends at the big front door, laughing.

Though her life in a New York City ghetto was an ugly parody of that storybook version, a certain 12-year-old girl [whose name, because of her age, will not be revealed by authorities] last week clung fiercely to the ritual.

After giving birth in the early hours of the morning in her bedroom, after cradling the 6-lb., 10-oz. boy until dawn, after carrying him into the hallway, stuffing him inside a plastic bag and throwing him down a garbage chute, the little girl did the only thing that made sense in her life. She went to school. [The infant was rescued, after landing at the bottom of the chute, by an alert custodian — but only moments before a refuse container was to undergo pulverization.]

[At school] she slumped forward on her desk. When the teacher asked what was wrong, she said, "I'm sick." The story of this little girl is about an illness, but of a different kind . . .

With the fatalism of big-city survivors, her neighbors have already declared that this 12-year-old never had, and never will have, a chance: "Most of us don't expect her to recover from this. She has gone through too much too young."

At four, the girl lost her parents in a fire. She moved in with her aunt in the Brownsville section of Brooklyn, a moonscape of brick towers, security fences, dusty playgrounds, scrawny trees, and empty lots. The housing project was the turf of local gangs with names like the Co-ops and the Young Guns, who settle their drug disputes with automatic weapons. When [Black] Muslim security guards were hired three years ago, the tribal warfare did not go away. It just changed, pitting the Muslims against the gangs.

The world inside her adoptive family's home was a quiet nightmare. Drugs and alcohol infiltrated the fourth-floor apartment. On at least two occasions, her 21-year-old cousin [had] had sex with the girl. Last week, neighbors woke up to discover the [cousin] threatening to jump off the rooftop. The police pulled him down, arrested him, and charged him with statutory rape.

For the girl, what mattered after delivering the baby was cloaking her latest humiliation in a thin veil of dignity . . . Her teachers didn't help; though she had faithfully attended classes [during her pregnancy], they say they never realized she was pregnant.

• *Source:* Priscilla Painton, Miracle in Brooklyn: The rescue of a desperate 12-year-old girl's abandoned baby shows that hope can survive on even the meanest streets. *Time,* April 8, 1991, 31.

Both congruent and contrasting findings have been reported in a number of similar studies:

❑ Myers (1967, 1970) reported a *post hoc* analysis of cases of child murder between 1948 and 1965 in the city of Detroit. Only 71 convictions (53%) issued from 134 cases; in 38% of the cases, charges were dismissed before trial. Among those convicted, psychosis was found in 54% and "impulsive rage" in another 32%. Demographically, the prototypical offender was a young mother, under age 30; asphyxiation was the most common means of killing.

❑ In a retrospective analysis of 112 cases of child homicide in New York City, Kaplun & Reich (1976) found a "pattern" of long-term maltreatment in the families of victims that extended to the victim's siblings *and that continued* after the murders. In this study, the victims were prototypically illegitimate and of pre- school age; the killers were prototypically their mothers or their paramours, whose social histories were replete with episodes of assaultiveness and social deviance. According to these investigators, the offender killed in an episode of impulsive rage; few offenders displayed evidence of psychosis.

❑ Relatively congruent findings were reported by Bourget & Bradford (1990) in a study of filicide in the province of Quebec; in addition, these investigators found a history of suicidal behavior among their subjects, indicative of severe episodes of depression both before and after the murders.

❑ After reviewing 131 cases of filicide, Resnick (1969) proposed a classification scheme by imputed motive and circumstance: The altruistic ("for the child's own good," as in a case of life-threatening illness) cases, said to account for fully 49% of such murders; the acutely psychotic cases, accounting for 21%; the unwanted child cases, accounting for 14%; accidental cases, accounting for 12%; and spouse revenge cases, accounting for 4%. Of the total, 67% of the victims had been slain by their mothers, most of whom were under the age of 35. According to Resnick, 95% of the mothers and 86% of the fathers who had slain their children were suffering from diagnosable psychiatric disorder.

❑ A roughly parallel set of *motives* was set forth in a study by Lukianowicz (1972) of attempted infanticide as revealed clinically through out-patient treatment in Irish hospitals, with the cases generally *not* prosecuted; clinically significant depression was diagnosed in 60% of cases and personality disorder in 25%. Campion, Cravens & Covan (1988) similarly found "chronic psychiatric impairment" among the dozen paternal filicide offenders they studied at New York's Mount Sinai

Medical Center, even though they attributed the "filicidal acts" to "isolated explosive behavior."

❑ On the basis of clinical data from only nine cases of maternal filicide, Korbin (1989) proposed a sequential process model that progresses through four stages: Negative parent-child interaction, a signal that help is needed, denial followed by continued abuse, yielding to the murder. Alternately, after reviewing data on all homicides committed by women in Canada over a 22-year period and comparing spousal homicides with filicides, Silverman & Kennedy (1988) warned against easy generalizations, cautioning that "female perpetrators of homicide should not be treated as a homogeneous group."

→ *INFERENCES, SPECULATIONS, CONJECTURES*

Because studies of filicide use a wide array of methodologies, often (and virtually necessarily) relying on date collected retrospectively, few valid inferences can be drawn. Nonetheless, there are some trends that might be underscored: *There is some fragmentary evidence that the rate of formal psychiatric disorder among filicide offenders is visibly high. There is some tangential evidence that some filicide offenders are notably deficient in their ability to cope with the customary stresses of daily living. Unlike other cases of homicide, the suicide of the offender even before the initiation of criminal justice processing is a noticeable phenomenon, with rather clear implications for the concept of remorse.* Clearly, as Milner and his coworkers (Ellis & Milner, 1981; Milner & Ayoub, 1980; Milner & Wimberly, 1979, 1980) have stressed, lack of coping skills on the part of violence-prone parents is a relatively remediable deficit which may be addressed directly so as to preclude criminal behavior.

Women Homicide Offenders

Sourcebook data we reviewed in Chapter 5 indicate that both victim and offender in homicide are overwhelmingly male. When women kill, 80% of the time the victim is a family member (D'Orban, 1990). Moreover, in cases of spouse murder committed by women, the killer almost invariably kills in self-defense (Goetting, 1989-*b*, 1989-*c*), whether as the result of an instant attack or as the consequence of a long-standing pattern of abuse.

Based on an investigation of homicides committed by women in Detroit over a two-year period, Goetting (1988) has sketched what she calls a "statistical profile" of the prototypical offender: "a locally born black female in her early 30s who is Protestant, married, and living with her family. She is an undereducated, under-employed welfare recipient with an arrest record." Goetting (1988) also inspected at closer range homicides in which women killed other members of their own gender, primarily their own children. Goetting's "statistical profile" again portrays offenders who "were predominantly minority mothers who were unemployed, undereducated welfare recipients with an arrest record." In Britain, D'Orban (1990) reported that formal mental disorder is frequently a factor in homicides committed by women, so that the probability of a finding of diminished responsibility is far greater for women than for men who commit homicide. Similarly, D'Orban & O'Connor (1989) studied British women who had killed their parents. In this sample, nearly 60% were found to be psychotic, with 35% diagnosed as schizophrenic and 29% as suffering from psychotic depression; another 18% were diagnosed as suffering personality disorder and 6% were diagnosed as addicted to alcohol.

→ *INFERENCES, SPECULATIONS, CONJECTURES*

Women are relatively infrequently the perpetrators of homicide; when they are, their victims are likely to be their children or their spouses. There is some indication that pre-existing formal mental disorder, perhaps itself the result of a pattern of abuse by a spouse (or a parent), contributes to homicide as it is committed by women.

Juvenile Homicide Offenders

As Cornell (1989) has observed, early (and largely clinical) studies had led to a portrait of the juvenile homicide offender as one who usually kills members of his or her own family, often in retaliation for physical or psychological abuse, and/or who acts from deep psychiatric disorder, usually psychotic in nature. More recent data challenge that picture. Indeed, Goetting (1989) has called attention to the "changing patterns of homicide among juvenile offenders," fueled to some large extent by the involvement of juveniles in the marketing and distribution of controlled dangerous substances. Thus:

- ❏ In a clinical study of juvenile homicide offenders over an 18 month period in one California country, for example, Sorrells (1977) reported that nearly 70% of the episodes resulted from circumstances similar to those we have described as "tinder box" in character and that 80% exhibited indicia of mild to severe mental disorder.

- ❏ Similarly, at the University of Pittsburgh's Western Psychiatric Clinic, Petti & Davidman (1981) studied a group of children aged *11 and under* who had committed homicide, attributing their "murderous aggression" to a phenomenology of repressive external control that, in fact, approximated the reality.

❏ Essentially similar dynamics were cited in a study by Fiddes (1981) of adolescents convicted of homicide during the 1970s in Scotland, though alcohol lubricated the offense in some 43% of these cases.

❏ In a study of nearly 800 killings by juveniles, Rowley, Ewing & Singer (1987) reported that intrafamilial killings represent a

---

⇨ *The Appropriate Sanction for a Juvenile Homicide Offender*

Every nation which subscribes to the International Covenant on Civil and Political Rights (Amnesty International, 1987, pp. 221-226) sponsored by United Nations Economic and Social Council (UNESCO) — and most states of the union, even those which have retained or re-instituted the death penalty for adult offenders — impose sanctions less severe than capital punishment for even quite deliberate murder when committed by a juvenile offender (Ogloff, 1987). If tried as a juvenile, in most jurisdictions the offender will be "held" in correctional custody only until the age of 21; if tried as an adult (a legal maneuver available in many U.S. jurisdictions), he or she may, however, face whatever constitutes the ultimate penalty for adult offenders.

The distinction between a strapping 16-year-old armed with an automatic weapon whose aggressivity has been fueled biochemically and an adult may be more metaphysical than real; therein, indeed, lies society's dilemma in determining the appropriate handling and disposition of homicide and other violent offenses committed by offenders who are, technically, "juveniles" — but who are frequently also those whom life circumstances have denied any semblance of normal childhood or adolescence.

But it would be erroneous to limit one's perception of the juvenile homicide offender to that strapping 16-year-old. Thus, at the Rigshospitalet in Copenhagen, Mouridsen & Tolstrup (1988) detailed the evaluation and treatment of a 9-year-old boy who had intentionally killed his mother. No severe family conflicts or other psychogenic factors that could explain the action were found. Apart from some indications of subclinical epilepsy in the EEG record, no somatic pathology was verified. But, during a year in a child psychiatric department after the homicide, the boy became actively psychotic and was diagnosed as suffering from a schizophrenic disorder that is presumed to have developed in the years preceding the matricide but had remained "latent" until some unidentifiable emotional crisis that directly precipitated the murder.

❏ In an investigation which seems to recapitulate earlier findings, distinguished forensic psychiatrist Carl Malmquist
(1990) of the University of Minnesota studied 30 male and 14
female homicidal adolescents by means of the MMPI, the Beck
Depression Inventory, and clinical assessment data. Malmquist concluded univocally that "In all subjects, the symptom
picture of a major affective disorder was present that often
included some of the attentional, motoric, impulsive, and conduct disturbances seen in conduct and affective disorders" (p.
23). Though substantiating data were not reported, the presumption is that the principal elements in that "symptom
picture" pre-existed the homicide.

❏ In some sharp contrast, at the NYU School of Medicine, Lewis,
Lovely, Yeager & Ferguson (1988) studied differences in an
array of biopsychosocial characteristics between two groups of
juvenile murderers between the ages of 12 and 17 (one group
evaluated *after* and the other *before* the homicide) and two
groups of incarcerated delinquents, one guilty of nonviolent
offenses and the other of violent but nonhomicidal offenses.
Juvenile murderers were found *not* to not differ significantly
from their violent but nonhomicidal counterparts; but a constellation of neuropsychiatric and family characteristics differentiated them (and, since there were no differences between
them and the violent nonhomicidal offenders, this group as
well) from their *nonviolent* counterparts.

Psychiatrist Elissa Benedek and psychologist Dewey Cornell and
their colleagues at the University of Michigan's Center for Forensic
Psychiatry have reported a series of progressively more sophisti-
cated studies of juvenile homicide offenders and their offenses
(Benedek & Cornell, 1989; Benedek, Cornell & Staresina, 1989;
Cornell, Benedek & Benedek, 1987-*a*, 1987-*b*, 1989; Cornell, Miller
& Benedek, 1988; Cornell, Staresina & Benedek, 1989). The direc-
tion of their findings seems relatively more congruent with those of
Lewis and her colleagues at NYU than with those of Malmquist.
Thus:

❏ Relatively few offenders had a verifiable history of mental
health treatment prior to the killing: only 7% were diagnosed
as psychotic at the time of the offense (Cornell, Benedek &
Benedek, 1987-*a*).

❏ After constructing an instrument based on an array of 52
background variables concerning such issues as family dysfunction, school adjustment, childhood problems, violence history, delinquent behavior, substance abuse, psychiatric problems, and stressful life events prior to the offense, the investigators found that juveniles charged with *larceny* evinced
higher scores (i.e., displayed more indicia of social and psy-

chosocial disorganization and dysfunction) than did juveniles charged with murder (Cornell, Benedek & Benedek, 1987-*b*, 1989).

❏ Similarly, in a study that utilized highly sophisticated methods of data analysis, Busch, Zagar, Hughes & Arbit (1990) found no evidence of psychiatric abnormality as a differentiator between juveniles who had been convicted of homicide and a matched sample convicted of nonviolent offenses. Instead, they found four cluster of variables that differentiated the two groups — viz., juvenile homicide offenders came from families that included other members with documented records of criminal violence, tended to be members of gangs, had experienced severe educational difficulties earlier in life (often leading to withdrawal from school), and evinced a history of early-onset alcohol abuse.

→ *INFERENCES, SPECULATIONS, CONJECTURES*

Earlier studies had depicted the juvenile homicide offender as prototypically slaying a member of his or her own family as a result of his or her own victimization in abuse and as suffering from relatively severe mental disorder.

Contemporary studies challenge such a picture. Instead, the current research tends to suggest that murder committed by juveniles is very likely to flow outside the family and to be committed during the course of another felony. The relationship between the readiness to engage in extrafamilial violence and personal victimization, however, is not satisfactorily addressed in these studies. But the relative paucity of data permits only speculation, not generalization.

Serial and Mass Murderers

According to one Federal estimate, serial murders — i.e., sequential homicides committed by the same person — account for less than four-tenths of one percent of the aggregate slayings in a year (Paretsky, 1991). Nonetheless, serial murder occupies a central place in fictional treatments of homicide.

Something more than a century elapsed between the publication of Robert Lewis Stevenson's *Dr. Jekyll and Mr. Hyde* and Thomas Harris' *The Silence of the Lambs,* both tales of serial murder and mutilation focusing on a physician in whom "the dark side" rather inexplicably triumphs. Within the past quarter century, from John Wayne Gacey in Illinois to Jeffrey Dahmer in Milwaukee, the real-world cases of the Los Angeles Hillside Strangler, the Atlanta Child Slayer (Wilson, 1987), and the Gainesville Slasher in our country and the Yorkshire Ripper in England have claimed major press attention and spawned documentary and semi-documentary "enter-tainments."

From the fictional terminal points alone, we might conclude that cleverly planned and brutally executed sequential homicides hold an endless fascination for English-speaking audiences. Yet, for reasons that may be quite apparent, there have been remarkably few studies of serial murderers that meet reasonable methodological standards.

On the basis only of "long distance" clinical evidence, Bailey (1985) undertook what he terms a "paleopsychological analysis" of mass murderer Ted Bundy, who sexually brutalized and killed at least 36 victims and was executed in the state of Florida. From those data, Bailey concludes that "a major contributor was the breakdown of neuropsychological inhibitions, which allowed extreme phyloge-netic regression to occur."

In a review of the relative handful of methodologically sound studies of serial murderers, Holmes & deBurger (1985) offered what they termed a "general typology" of such offenders as "visionary, mission-oriented, hedonistic, power and control-oriented . . . Some general characteristics of serial killers include being white, intelli-gent, charming psychopathic, and highly mobile, and having a his-tory of physical or sexual abuse as children." Similarly, Leibman (1990) analyzed four case histories of serial murderers (at long distance), concluding to patterns of parental rejection, abuse, and violence.

By definition, *mass* murder denotes that situation in which a single slayer, on the same occasion rather than sequential occasions, kills more than one victim — with suicide (or being killed by police) a frequent consequence; there is no comparable estimate of what proportion of homicide cases reported in a year represent mass slaying situations.

The case of the "mad Chinese physicist" at the University of Iowa in Fall 1991 is virtually prototypical:

A distraught graduate student went on a shooting rampage in two buildings on the University of Iowa campus in Iowa City yester-day, killing four people and critically wounding two others before fatally shooting himself in the head . . . Gang Lu, a doctoral candidate in physics from China, methodically searched out his victims. He had been disgruntled over his failure to receive an academic award for his doctoral dissertation . . . police said the gunman burst into a meeting of students in the physics department's building, and killed the four men without saying a word. He then stalked out of the building and ran two blocks to [the building where] he injured [two victims] in the Office of Academic Affairs (Myers, 1991).

Among the slayer's victims were distinguished psychologist T. Anne Cleary, an administrator in the Office of Academic Affairs, who died a day after the rampage; his other victims were slain in a building named for James Van Allen, a University of Iowa professor emeritus who had achieved the Nobel Laureate, and who was himself at his office in the building at the time of the slayings.

The bloody episode in Iowa occurred less than a month after a wealthy recluse named George Hennard had driven his truck through the window of a cafeteria in a small Texas town, killed 23 patrons by shooting, and then committed suicide. Press accounts portrayed Lu as extraordinarily bright and competent though socially isolated from his fellow students from China, Hennard as surly and uniformly abrasive to the few contacts (primarily with storekeepers) his reclusive lifestyle permitted; but neither had a history of violent behavior directed toward others *or* toward himself. In both cases, however, whether a psychotic episode of sudden onset represented a precipitating factor or not, the availability of weapons (in Texas, with automatic loading and rapid firing capabilities) appeared to potentiate whatever intra-person variables inclined toward lethal violence.

Perhaps because mass murder is characteristically interpreted as the result of a sudden and acute psychosis that befalls the perpetrator and ends in his or her own death, it is less frequently the stuff of entertainment. There are notable exceptions in cases in which mass murder is not immediately followed by suicide or police slaying, among which perhaps the leading exemplar is Truman Capote's tour de force of three decades ago *In Cold Blood,* tracing the developmental history of two "state-raised" slayers who killed the members of a prosperous Kansas farm family during an attempt at robbery. A more current member of the genre is the book-*cum*- television mini-series *Fatal Vision*, concerning the murder of his wife and children by an Army dentist, by Joseph McGinniss. In each case, the authors had been granted virtually unlimited access by their subjects and apparently quite willing cooperation of a variety not likely to be gained by a scientific researcher committed to objectivity. In the McGinniss case, the author admitted freely that he had pledged to his subject to take an advocacy position, so that there was little effort at objectivity in reporting or analysis.

Clearly, there are virtually insuperable impediments to scientific study either of mass or serial murder. At best, one can hope for case study data, with all its inherent limitations; at worst, one sees groundless speculations made at long distance and prototypically long after the fact. Generalizations made from such a severely constrained data base will be speculative at best, downright fanciful at worst. As a result, it may be that the soundest insights concerning either or both mass and serial murder indeed emanate from literary accounts.

→ *INFERENCES, SPECULATIONS, CONJECTURES*

The paucity of evidence permits few reasonable speculations. Because *serial* murders as they are committed differ so substantially from the prototypical "tinder box" homicide, however, it is reasonable to conjecture that — precisely because the data necessarily emanate from studies of "atypical" rather than prototypical offenders — psychological characteristics found to differentiate the typical homicide offender will *not* be similarly found to differentiate the serial murderer.

Alternately, however, one recurrent characteristic in mass murder is the frequency with which such homicide end in suicide. For that reason, there is credence to the general impression that these killings may result from a acute psychotic episode. Whether such sudden-onset psychosis is, in fact, determinable through case study technique remains speculative. As we have seen earlier in this chapter, neuropsychologist Rhawn Joseph (1990, p. 102) holds that competent *neurological* examination of Charles Whitman, the "Texas Tower" sniper responsible for 14 deaths in a mass murder spree, would have *post-dictively* revealed the brain tumor he cites as responsible for (or contributory to) Whitman's lethal violence.

☐ SUMMARY

This chapter has reviewed psychological perspectives on criminal homicide from the particular vantage point of variables *within* the offender that can be regarded as part of the "psychological baggage" carried from one behavioral situation to the next. Such baggage is comprised of neuropsychological variables, psychological characteristics (or personality traits), and intelligence. We have also reviewed data on formally diagnosable psychological disorder among homicide offenders and from (largely clinical) studies of filicide offenders, women who commit homicide, juvenile homicide offenders, and serial and mass murderers.

On the basis of the relevant data, we have seen that it is reasonable to infer and/or speculate that:

  ❑ There is sound evidence linking neuropsychological dysfunction with impulsive violence, particularly that violence that is not predictable on the basis of psychosocial history. Because so large a proportion of homicides each year occur under "tinder box" circumstances, there is reason to believe that disordered neurology represents a contributing factor in such cases.

❑ The relevant studies, many of them undertaken outside the U.S., suggest an incidence of severe psychiatric disorder among convicted homicide offenders two to three times greater than that observed in epidemiological studies of the general population in this country and Canada. Because the diagnoses reflected in these studies were made after conviction, whether the disorders observed preexisted the criminal act or whether they were induced after the commission of the crime, apprehension, prosecution, and, in most cases, imprisonment, must remain indeterminate. Because the racial composition of the societies in which the majority of relevant studies were undertaken differs from that of the U.S. in marked ways, conclusions to emerge therefrom can be predicated of the U.S. only with substantial caution.

❑ Both the paucity of studies and the instability of the interpretations preclude valid generalizations concerning homicice based on projective test data alone.

❑ At least tangential evidence from studies of personality traits among homicide offenders as measured by actuarial instruments tends to corroborate the expectations derived from an epidemiologic portrait of murder as it is committed. Some investigations have found offenders of homicide or of violent crimes involving assaultive behavior to be more competitive, impulsive, manic, and suspicious than people-in-general; and there is some suggestion that they more frequently display impairment in reality contact. Contrary to expectation, however, they have been found to be neither more nor less psychopathically deviant than offenders convicted of other crimes. It may be, however, that an elevated level of psychopathic deviation represents an intrapsychic threshold for the emission of criminal behavior, that the character of that behavior is contingent upon other intra-person variables interacting with stimulus determinants — and that impaired contact with reality and impulsivity as intrapsychic variables are likely to incline toward impulsive violence of the character reflected in a majority of the cases of criminal homicide reported statistically in the United States (i.e., those with a "tinder box" flavor).

❑ Current studies of convicted offenders yield little evidence of a relationship between level of measured intelligence and homicide. Because mental retardation constitutes an appropriate basis for an insanity defense in many states, it may be that very low intelligence is implicated in homicide as it is committed more often than can be discerned in studies of convicted offenders.

❑ There is some fragmentary evidence that the rate of formal psychiatric disorder among filicide offenders is visibly high. There is some tangential evidence that some filicide offenders are notably deficient in their ability to cope with the customary stresses of daily living. Unlike other cases of homicide, the suicide of the offender even before the initiation of criminal justice processing is a noticeable phenomenon in cases of filicide.

❑ Women are relatively infrequently the perpetrators of homicide; when they are, their victims are likely to be their children or their spouses. There is some indication that pre-existing formal mental disorder, perhaps itself the result of a pattern of abuse by a spouse (or a parent), contributes to homicide as it is committed by women.

❑ Fragmentary evidence suggests that juvenile homicide offenders may not differ significantly in psychological and psychosocial characteristics from juveniles who commit violent but nonhomicidal offenses; but there is the indication that both these groups differ from juveniles who commit property offenses. Later we shall argue that such data may reflect a pervasive "culture of violence" among young people.

❑ The paucity of evidence on serial murderers permits no reasonable speculations. Because serial murders as they are committed differ so substantially from the prototypical "tinder box" homicide, however, it is reasonable to conjecture that psychological characteristics found to differentiate the typical homicide offender will *not* be similarly found to differentiate the serial murderer. But mass murder frequently ends in suicide; for that reason, the general impression that these killings may result from a precipitate psychotic episode is not unreasonable.

❑ **NOTES & COMMENTARY**

❑ 1. *The MMPI-2*

In 1989, a major revision of the MMPI was published as the *MMPI-2*. Though producing similar score patterns, this version utilizes contemporary language and terminology that, *inter alia*, "eliminated sexist wording and outmoded content" and has been normed on a larger and more demographically representative national sample. As of this writing, few studies have appeared in the literature either of clinical or of correctional psychology utilizing the MMPI-2 or contrasting offender groups on the new version.

Chapter 7

Psychological Perspectives on Homicide: Social Learning and Stimulus Determinants

WHAT THE PERSON BRINGS TO THE BEHAVIORAL SITUATION IN THE WAY of what we have called "psychological baggage" represents but one set of variables in the process equation. The characteristics of the situation itself and the reinforcing properties of the elements in the situation represent other sets. These sets of variables interact with each other in processes which yield — or, in some cases, inhibit — a behavioral outcome.

❑ *PARADIGMS FOR LEARNING THROUGH SOCIAL IMITATION*

In general, conceptual models for the process of learning among humans or in infra-human species from Tolman to Guthrie to Skinner have focused on how learning occurs in an individual, typically in a one-to-one situation in which an individual learner stands in a singular relationship with an individual instructor or experimenter. Yet it is patently the case that most learning occurs not in one-to-one situations in which an individual learner is socially isolated from other learners. Rather, from the time a child enters a classroom (in today's world and as a function of extraordinarily high rates of participation in the labor force on the part of mothers, perhaps modally at the age of 3) until he or she leaves school, learning occurs in a social context and much of what is learned is acquired through methods of instruction that quite deliberately capitalize on social factors. Outside school and throughout post- school life, we continually are the targets of communications through the media, from neighbors and co-workers, from the pulpits, that more or less consciously rely on the process of social learning to achieve effect. Yet so universal and so ubiquitous a process as social learning has been studied formally for no more than half a century.

Following Miller & Dollard (1950), Bandura and his associates established with scientific precision that learning frequently occurs not through immediate and direct reinforcement of Learner *A*'s behavior but because Learner *A* has observed Learner *B* behave and has observed *and vicariously experienced* the reinforcement (positive or aversive) that follows *B*'s behavior, so that *A* learns to behave through *social imitation* and is *reinforced vicariously* (Bandura, 1962, 1965; Bandura & McDonald, 1963; Bandura & Rosenthal, 1966; Bandura, Ross & Ross, 1963). Reciprocally, that Learner *A*'s behavior can be *extinguished vicariously* — whether through observation and vicarious experiencing of lack of positive reinforcement or of directly aversive (punitive) reinforcement — has also been amply demonstrated (Bandura, Grusec & Menlove, 1967).

The case can readily be made that, at some pre-scientific level, the pivots for the process which has guided the construction of the heroic myths and the transmission of the normative values in every society designed to elicit and maintain pro-social behavior are to be found in the principles of social learning by means of vicarious conditioning. Thus, we tell children the fable of George Washington, the cherry tree, and the inability to tell a lie, while simultaneously conveying the high regard in which Washington is held, in order to persuade the young to conform their behavior to that of an idealized behavioral model.

In their rich array of investigations, Bandura and his colleagues utilized principally *laboratory analogue* methodology; indeed, it is fair to say that their studies are the exemplars nonpareil of such methodology. Some flavor of their experimental approach can be obtained by inspecting at closer range a well-known experiment on the vicarious extinction of phobic behavior, in which young children who feared dogs were "de-conditioned" through the influence of a behavioral model (Bandura, Grusec & Menlove, 1967). The subjects were children from 3 to 5 who attended nursery schools. First, their parents were asked to describe the extent of the child's fearful and avoidant behavior toward dogs. Next, behavioral measures of the same variable were taken in a laboratory analogue situation (*Ibid.*, pp. 17-18):

> The strength of avoidance responses was measured by means of a graded sequence of 14 performance tasks in which the children were required to engage in increasingly intimate interactions with the dog. A female experimenter brought the children individually to the test room, which contained a brown cocker spaniel confined in a modified playpen. In the initial task, the children

were asked, in the following order, to walk up to the playpen and look down at the dog, to touch her fur, and to pet her . . . to open a hinged door on the side of the playpen, to walk the dog on a leash to a throw rug, to remove the leash, and to turn the dog over and scratch her stomach. The strength of the children's avoidant tendencies was reflected not only in the [tasks] completed, but also in the degree of vacillation, reluctance, and fearfulness that preceded and accompanied each task.

On subsequent occasions, subjects were exposed to one of several experimental "treatments." In what the investigators termed the "modeling-positive" treatment:

Children . . . observed a fearless peer model display approach responses toward a cocker spaniel within the context of a highly enjoyable party atmosphere. There were eight 10-minute treatment sessions conducted on 4 consecutive days. Each session, which was attended by a group of four children, commenced with a jovial party. The children were furnished with brightly colored hats, cookie treats, and given small prizes. In addition, the experimenter read stories, blew large plastic balloons for the children to play with, and engaged in other party activities . . . After the party was well underway, a second experimenter entered the room carrying the dog, followed by a 4-year-old male model . . . The dog was placed in a playpen located across the room from a large table at which the children were seated. The model, who had been chosen because of his complete lack of fear of dogs, then performed pre-arranged sequences of interactions with the dog for approximately 3 minutes during each session . . . The fear-provoking properties of the modeled displays were gradually increased from session to session by varying simultaneously the physical restraints on the dog, the directness and intimacy of the modeled approach responses, and the duration of interaction between the model and his canine companion.

On the day following the final experimental treatment session, the "performance test consisting of the graded sequence of interaction tasks with the dog" with which the subjects had begun their participation in the study was re-administered, except that for half the children the interaction was with an unfamiliar animal. A month following completion of the experiment, a follow-up session was held, in which the sequence of approach tasks was repeated for the third time.

Bandura and his colleagues focused their inquiries on behavior that was aggressive in nature — but without particular regard as to whether such behavior had been formally adjudicated as criminal or, indeed, whether such behavior could reasonably be considered formally contrary to the law. Nonetheless, since his work is pivotal

⇨ Transformation of Primitive Reinforcers into Symbolic Substitutes

Few would dispute that even very simple organisms experience what we might, with conscious anthropocentrism, describe as "pleasure" or as "pain." At the most primitive level, consumption and elimination are held to be pleasurable, while pressure and confinement are held to be painful. That even the most primitive organism behaves so as to sustain pleasurable sensations and to avoid painful ones is foundational to every conceptual schemata for the process of learning. Not only in the human species but among a wide array of infra-human species as well, a variety of symbols come to elicit the responses associated with pleasure-giving or pain-provoking stimuli; not only the human infant but also the family's pet dog responds to mother's verbal injunction "It's dinner time" and/or to the rattling of food boxes. So much might be explained through the mechanism called *associative* learning, whereby the pairing of a neutral stimulus (e.g., mother's voice intoning certain words) with a "natural" or "unconditioned" stimulus (e.g., a bowl of porridge) yields a "conditioned response" (whereby the child comes to respond to mother's voice *alone* with great whoops of glee, salivation, or what have you).

But, in the normal course of events, it might be anticipated that the so-called "neutral" stimuli to which natural responses are conditioned might be highly variable from learner to learner: In addressing Fido, for example, one pet owner intones "Chow down," another "Feeding time," a third *Mangere,* while a fourth whistles in imitation of a canary. Indeed, one of Skinner's more dramatic contributions to the psychology of learning consisted in demonstrating that the *accidental temporal* pairing of a neutral with a natural stimulus results in the learning of what he termed "superstitious behavior." In such circumstances, those symbolic, indirect reinforcers which come to substitute for primitive, direct reinforcers in eliciting and maintaining behavior vary substantially between the learning repertoires of individual behavers.

Quite in contrast, however, *social learning* situations depend to some very large measure on the extent to which the meanings of identical symbolic reinforcers are *shared* between individual learners. In social learning, *A* learns behavior *X* not because *A* behaves in way *X* and is reinforced (positively or aversively) therefor, but rather because *A* observes *B* behave in way *X* and obtain reinforcement therefor; so also, observers *C*, *D*, and *E* may learn behavior *X* in the same way, and at the same time, as *A*.

For learning to occur in that manner, it is minimally necessary that *A* (and *C*, *D*, *E* as well) in some way identify with *B*, or have been previously socialized to the extent that he or she finds the same symbolic mechanisms of reinforcement (praise, punishment, scolding, candy, food, etc., etc.) to have a similar effect on him or her as on *B*. But, in the face of what is likely quite different learning histories, how does it happen that rather primitive and elemental forms of physical punishment or means of physical gratification come to be experienced symbolically in much the same way through such mechanisms as a teacher's praise or scolding?

Sociologists interested in the genesis of criminal behavior frequently speak of "identification with a deviant subculture." Were such identification pervasive throughout the learning history of the individual behaver, we should expect that widely-shared social learning stimuli would have little impact on individual behavior; but the data on long-distance vicarious conditioning argue otherwise. Similarly, sheer *social imitation* seems an inadequate account. Thus, the process by which elemental forms of reinforcement are transformed into symbolic substitutes — a process that antecedes and underlies the process of social learning — itself constitutes a fascinating exercise in the psychology of socialization.

to the process psychology paradigm for criminal behavior, it is imperative to observe that Bandura attributes the genesis of aggressive behavior to a varity of antecedents, functioning alone or in interaction with each other.

Long Distance Vicarious Conditioning and Criminal Behavior

We have earlier opined that vicarious conditioning and extinction need not be limited only to those situations in which a behaver is physically present while another is conditioned, but instead that social learning can occur through what we have called "long-distance" vicarious conditioning, as the individual interacts with

---

⇨ *Albert Bandura — A Social Learning Perspective on Aggression*

Social learning theory holds that . . . the [sources] of aggression are found in structural determinants, observational learning and reinforced performance. Mechanisms that give rise to acts of aggression include the following:

❑ aversive instigators (physical assaults, verbal threats and insults, adverse reductions in conditions of life, thwarting of goal-directed behavior);

❑ incentive instigators (the expectation that aggressive behavior will bring benefits);

❑ modeling instigators (the disinhibitory, facilitative, arousing, or stimulus-enhancing influence of other people's behavior);

❑ instructional instigators (aggression as obedience);

❑ and delusional instigators (the influence of bizarre beliefs, e.g., a divine mandate to assassinate the president) . . .

The following conditions sustain or regulate aggressive responses:

❑ external reinforcement (tangible rewards, social and status rewards, expressions of injury, alleviation of aversive treatment);

❑ punishment (inhibitory or informative);

❑ vicarious reinforcement through observed reward and observed punishment;

❑ and self-reinforcement, including self-reward, self-punishment, and strategies for neutralizing self-punishment (moral justification, palliative comparison, euphemistic labeling, displacement of responsibility, diffusion of responsibility, dehumanization of victims, attribution of blame to victims, misrepresentation of consequences).

• *Source:* Albert J. Bandura, Mechanisms of aggression from the social learning perspective. In Hans Toch (editor), *Psychology of Crime and Criminal Justice.* New York: Holt, Rinehart, 1979.

those sources that inform (or appear to inform) him of the world beyond his immediate psychosocial environment. Thus, the journalistic and the entertainment media are characteristic vehicles for long-distance vicarious conditioning.

Moreover, it may be the case that, when those media *confirm* a behavior, belief, attitude, or value that the individual already holds (technically, has already acquired), the tenacity with which that behavior (or belief or attitude or value) will be held in the future increases in a geometric progression (Stern & Pallone, 1971).

Or, to put the matter more technically: Behaviors that are maintained through random or intermittent schedules of reinforcement become highly resistant to extinction (Holland & Skinner, 1961, pp. 117-136). Long-distance vicarious conditioning provides either random or intermittent reinforcement. When such reinforcement supports a previously acquired behavior, that behavior (or belief or attitude or value) becomes enormously difficult to change.

A number of investigators, many of them from the fields of communication and information sciences, have studied what we have called such long-distance conditioning in eliciting or extinguishing the emission of *criminal behavior.* Among studies that focused directly on the influence of the journalistic or entertainment media on the emission of criminal behavior, positive findings were reported by:

❑ Lester (1981) in a study homicide rates in nations with a free press vs. those with a controlled or censored press;

❑ Phillips (1983), in an investigation of the impact of heavily publicized prize fights in relation to subsequent homicides, measured through a sophisticated time-series regression analysis;

❑ Harry (1983), in a study of changes in the rate of assaultive episodes among patients in a maximum security hospital for mentally disordered offenders following the exhibition of excitatory or pacifying motion pictures;

❑ Hennigan (1982), in an assessment of the impact of the introduction of regular television broadcasting into previously television-less cities on crime rates;

❑ Wass, Raup, Cerullo & Martel (1989) on the effects of a preference for music celebrating themes of homicide, Satanism, and suicide on dispositions toward murder and suicide among adolescents;

❑ Zillman & Bryant (1983) and Linz, Donnerstein & Penrod (1984), in studies of the effect of exposure to filmed or televised violence against women in relation to sex offenses;

❑ Wahl & Lefkowits (1989) on the effects of a television film about a psychotic killer, as judged by the attitudinal reactions of college students in a laboratory analogue situation;

❑ White (1989) on the relative incidence of homicides in standard metropolitan statistical areas whose professional football teams were participating in televised NFL playoffs, with the finding that a greater number of killings was reported in cities with losing than with winning teams consistently over a six-year period.

❑ Stack (1989), in an assessment of the effect of the publicizing of mass murders and murder-suicides by means of network television news reports on suicide and homicide rates over a 12-year period, with a particularly strong effect observed for "gangland" mass murders.

❑ In a major review of the research evidence on the extent to which violence in the media elicit or contribute to aggressive behavior among viewers, Wood, Yong & Chachere (1991) concluded that the effect was particularly strong among children and stronger yet among children previously diagnosed as emotionally disturbed.

Other investigators have considered how more pervasive social and cultural beliefs and norms influence criminal behavior. Thus:

❑ Davidovich (1990, pp. 28-30) has illustrated how injunctions in the Koran on the relationship between men and their wives "have perpetuated violence against women in many of the Middle Eastern countries."

❑ Similarly, Hull & Burke (1991) have identified supports for the tolerance of sexual abuse in the attitudes toward women fostered by the "religious right" in the U.S.

❑ A wide and impressive array of studies has confirmed *exposure to violence and/or violent pornography* (Comstock, 1986; Donnerstein & Linz, 1986; Goleman, 1985; Heath, Kruttschnitt & Ward, 1986; Linz, Donnerstein & Penrod, 1984; Malamuth & Briere, 1986; Malamuth & Ceniti, 1986; Sommers & Check, 1987; Smeaton & Byrne, 1987), often in laboratory analogue situations, as a determinant *either* of increasingly negative attitudes toward women *or* of prospective sexual violence. Indeed, that effect is now so well established that criminal sexual aggression is held to result from the acceptability of violent male behavior toward women, supported by frequent depictions of their victimization in the mass and entertainment media (Briere, Malamuth & Check, 1985; Malamuth, 1986, 1988; Malamuth & Check, 1985; Marolla & Scully, 1986; Scully & Marolla, 1985).

Moreover, there is evidence of a long distance vicarious condition effect even on the behavior of prosecutors in criminal proceedings.

⇨ *Racial and Ethnic Stereotypes in the Media*

Sociologists and social psychologists demonstrated nearly half a century ago that *racial and ethnic stereotypes* are at the least reinforced through media for mass information and entertainment; it may well be that the images of one or another ethnic group that one derives from newspapers, magazines, motion pictures, and television in fact shape one's perceptions and expectations of that group at least as effectively a personal encounters with members of that group; and it may be *either* that the images derived from the media precede and thus shape personal encounters *or* that personal encounters are reinforced via the images contained in the media. In turn, those perceptions and expectations lead one to "assign" members of that group to certain roles, but not to others. Such role "assignments" function as behavioral prescriptions, in the sense that they define and constrain the sort of behavior members of the majority anticipate — *and/or will tolerate* — from members of a minority group. Since the group in question is subjected to the same stereotypical images of itself from the same sources of mass communication, the affected group tends to internalize the popular image of itself. That, surely, is an ample paradigm for long-distance vicarious conditioning.

In what is probably the landmark inquiry, Berelson & Salter (1946) studied the manner in which members of the white majority (and most particularly, those of Anglo-Saxon or Nordic ancestry) and members of several other racial and ethnic minority groups were portrayed in magazine fiction — at a time when weekly magazines like *Collier's* and the *Saturday Evening Post* constituted a principal means of recreation. Both in this study and in a panoply of successors, the results were as anticipated: Members of the majority were typically portrayed in the roles of hero and heroine, as good-looking, bright, courageous, trustworthy, successful, well-employed, etc., etc.

But members of minority groups were portrayed (if at all) in minor and clearly stereotypic roles, with Italians as gangsters, blacks as shoe shine "boys" or servants, Jews as aggressively money- grabbing, the Irish as jovially dim-witted, American Indians as treacherous and prone to alcoholism. Frequently, derogatory "nicknames" were used to describe minority characters; even so sensitive a writer as Graham Greene, in a 1939 short story, speaks of "a Dago in a purple suit" oggling the wares on display in a shop window on the "forever tawdry" Tottenham Court Road in London. Those stereotypes were largely transferred — at least until the civil rights explosion socially and legislatively during the 1960s — to motion pictures and television, as reflected in the portrayal of such characters as Amos 'n Andy, Mrs. Goldberg, and Frank Nitti of "The Untouchables."

After nearly three decades of such research, Berelson & Steiner (1964, pp. 502-505) concluded to a clearly interactive and mutually reinforcing set of stereotypes which, if not directly elicited, were strongly reinforced through the mechanism we have called long-distance vicarious conditioning, with mass communications media as the principal channels:

❏ The common stereotypes of the society tend to be copied . . . in the mass media of communication . . . People prejudiced against one ethnic group tend to be prejudiced against others . . . The stereotyping of ethnic groups tends to be quite similar across the society, among various social groups, and *often within the stereotyped group itself.*

Jean Genet's *The Blacks: A Clown Show* illustrates with ultimate irony both that art "copies" stereotypes from the larger society and that the stereotype is often internalized by members of the minority group in question. The play centers around a rag-tag company of black actors and actresses who are called upon (for reasons Genet never fully explicates) to entertain an audience of affluent whites. After considerable discussion about what the audience will find pleasing, the company decides to enact that which whites will find most credible — the violent rape of an elderly white woman by a young black man.

So much for the entertainment media. We might expect that the information media, whose avowed role is merely to report facts, might be less tainted by stereotypes. Nonetheless, in a remarkable decision for a court whose membership by that time had been assessed as strongly conservative, the U.S. Supreme Court in essence affirmed the effect of information media on the eliciting and reinforcing of racial stereotypes in October 1991 in a decision in a case against the nation's leading daily newspaper that focused on the content of its *advertising* pages.

In a suit brought by civil rights groups, plaintiffs charged that the *New York Times* had violated those provisions of the Federal Civil Rights Act of 1964 concerning non-discrim-ination in housing because it had *not,* over a period of 20 years, insisted that those firms that placed real estate advertising in its pages consciously and deliberately portray racial and ethnic mixtures among the frolicking and gamboling families depicted in photographs of the house and apartment developments placed on offer. Over the course of that period, a disproportionately small number of models — in comparison to the racial composition of society at large — had been members of minority groups.

Hence, plaintiffs asserted, the net effect of those advertisements had been to communicate to members of the white majority that the residences offered were intended for "people like us," while members of minority groups had by the same set of tokens been led to feel that such residences were *not* intended for "people like us," despite disclaimers in small print that the developer adhered rigidly to Federal equal opportunity and/or affirmative action guidelines.

The Court found no merit in the *Times'* argument that it merely printed advertising copy as submitted by its paying customers. Instead, the court seemed to say, the *Times,* as the closest we have to a national journal of record and as a principal influence on public opinion, has a positive obligation break the interactive chain.

Thus, in a remarkable inquiry conducted at the School of Journalism at Indiana University, Pritchard (1986) found that the level of press attention to murder cases. as determined by average length of newspaper reports, emerged as the most potent single predictor of whether *prosecutors* offered plea-bargains in subsequent cases.

The agency of conditioning in these investigations appears to be behavioral modeling. But there are other variations, in which the agency for influence is not modeling but rather the relatively more indirect transmission of norms and values.

Thus, Williams (1985) found that "extralegal factors inhering in the social context" were potent influencers of substance abuse, and Gomme (1985) provided strong evidence that peer group norms were potent predictors of both status and criminal offenses among Canadian youth. And, in a charming study of perceptions of crime and criminality among gold miners in Western Australia, O'Connor (1984) found, not surprisingly, that his subjects viewed violent criminal offenders with hostility and opprobrium but regarded the swindler as an eccentric and lovable character. That indeed is precisely how those who commit criminal fraud are depicted in the entertainment media — witness the portrayal of Academy Award winner George C. Scott in the title role of *The Flim-Flam Man* or that of Steve McQueen in the film version of William Faulkner's *The Rievers.*

Understandably enough, the entertainment media have periodically launched counter-attacks on the scientific community. Thus, Milavsky (1990), a researcher at the National Broadcasting Company, contended that "the scientific evidence does not support such definite conclusions" about the linkage between television violence and crime — indeed, in a study financed by the Federal National Institute of Justice during a period in which a media star sat in the White House. Milavsky, *inter alia*, criticized the massive experimental evidence on the social learning of aggression among children by complaining that "Most of the experiments deal with mild forms of aggressive behavior directed at toys . . . Serious interpersonal aggression [has not been] studied because the constraints of research ethics do not allow placing people in real jeopardy." Indeed so — but apparently no such ethical constraints guide the entertainment industry, despite what comes close to incontrovertible evidence. And, in richly detailed counterpoint, the distinguished forensic psychiatrist Carl Malmquist and his University of Minnesota colleague Paul Meehl (1978), perhaps the leading international authority in actuarial assessment, recount the clinical dynamics through which a film portrayal of Barrabbas (the "bad thief" of the

⇨ Thomas W. Milburn: A Military Psychologist's View of the Character of Deterrence

Deterrence can be considered to cover the *processes* through which one influences the choices, the alternatives and their nature, that decision makers [or behavers] perceive as available to them. Usually deterrents are considered negative incentives employed to dissuade [a behaver] from aggression or violence. The idea of deterrence does not rule out the coordinate application of positive incentives to persuade the [behaver who is the object of the effort to deter] to act, behave, or operate in other directions or with other means (conceivably specific ones) than dangerous, violent means . . .

Deterrence is a *process* in that its success is related to several conditions that change over time. It is an *influence* process in that one seeks, through employing various combinations of incentives, to induce conformity to some code of action or avoidance of some specific classes of behavior . . .

Deterrence is assumed to involve the choice matrices (and thus the conscious, purposeful choice behaviors) of [behavers] who seldom choose so few as two paths to their goals without considering expecting costs and gains and their estimates of the likelihood of success of pursuing each path.

Thus, to *deter* means to dissuade from some actions or classes of actions. One may deter another not only by threat but also in other ways, as when one gets the other to choose behavior incompatible with the deterred behavior. One can consider "rewarding" another for going in directions that are not only not dangerous . . . but also in harmony with positive goals and preferred means.

Employing some expectation of gain ("reward") for some behaviors or for an expanding class of behaviors that are notdangerous [*or* not criminal, *or* even pro- social] at the same time that one employs clear, contingent threats for some to-be-deterred alternative behaviors can offer advantages.

The contrast between *promising* and *discouraging* classes of actions can, perhaps, increase the perceived salience of each; each may, depending on the circumstances, act perceptually as a figure for which the other serves as ground; each may serve as context to heighten the perceived significance of the other.

• *Source:* Thomas W. Milburn, Design for the study of deterrence. In S.B. Sells (ed.), *Stimulus Determinants of Behavior.* New York: Ronald, 1963. Pp. 224-225.

New Testament, whom the crowds urged that Pilate free even as the Christ was led to crucifixion) stimulated one viewer to homicidal rage.

Deterrence as the Conditioning of Avoidance Behavior

Constructs like learning, conditioning, aversive reinforcement, and extinction are ubiquitous in the lexicon of learning and social learning. Among those concerned with the prevention of crime especially, the construct *deterrence* conveys powerful meaning. What psychological realities (if any) might that term denote?

"Deterrence" seems to suggest a situation in which a criminal behavior has *not* been emitted — or, interpreted psychologically, a situation in which a criminal behavior has not been acquired. That is not quite the same thing as *extinction*, which conveys the notion of "unlearning," or the extirpation from the actor's repertoire of a behavior which has already been learned. Similarly, *inhibition* suggests that a behavior that is an element in the repertoire is *not* emitted (perhaps because of strongly aversive situational contingencies, to be sure), but there is no suggestion that the behavior that is inhibited is thereby removed from the repertoire.

Perhaps the notion in the lexicon of social learning theory that most nearly equates to deterrence is rather more complex — viz., the *learning of avoidance behavior*. The psychology of learning is replete with ample evidence that subjects, both animal and human, learn to avoid emitting behaviors that are associated with noxious or aversive reinforcements. In experiments with children, Bandura, Grusec & Menlove (1967) demonstrated conclusively that avoidance behavior can be learned (and extinguished) vicariously as well as directly; and Church (1959) holds that the phenomenon can be observed even among rats, so long as the aversive reinforcers produce a sufficiently powerful (indeed, painful) effect on those subjects to whom they are directly applied. From a criminal justice perspective, it may be that "extinction" of a criminal behavior already acquired is a construct that properly belongs within the realm of corrections, while "deterrence," in the sense of learning to avoid criminal behavior in the first instance, is a construct that properly belongs within the realm of crime prevention.

Evidence for Long-Distance Vicarious Deterrence

The research evidence on what we might call "vicarious deterrence" tends to be somewhat tangential. Nonetheless, a study

⇨ *Florida, Georgia, Texas: A Trio of States That Accounts for 14% of the Population — and 63% of the Executions*

In its ruling in *Furman v. Georgia* in 1972, the U.S. Supreme Court that the death penalty — as then applied — constituted cruel and unusual punishment in violation of the Eighth and Fourteenth Amendments. The Court's rulings in this and related cases imposed, in effect, a moratorium on executions that lasted four years, while legislatures in "retentionist" states enacted legislation that met the Court's standards for conformance with the Constitution.

Executions under the revised statutes resumed in 1976. According to Amnesty International (1987, pp. 192-193), three states — Texas, Florida, and Georgia — collectively carried out 63% of all the executions in the nation in the decade following restoration of the death penalty. In the aggregate, those three states account for only 14% of the nation's population (Bureau of the Census, 1989, pp. 22-23).

by Phillips & Hensley (1984) seems to provide support for the proposition that knowledge of sanctions imposed on others through long-distance vicarious conditioning *either* elicits *or* deters similar criminal behavior. After reviewing all relevant studies, they conclude that attention given in the information media to "stories in which violence is rewarded or unpunished" is followed by "imitative increases in fatal violence," including homicides, suicides, and deaths by auto. Alternately, "the number of homicides significantly decreases [after] the broadcasting of a punishment story."

In a carefully designed study at the University of Michigan's Institute for Social Research, Kessler, and their associates (1988) studied the rate of teenage suicides subsequent to televisions newscasts concerning suicide over an eleven-year period. During the period between 1973-80, the rate of suicides increased after such broadcasts. Following substantial attention to the problem of adolescent suicide by major political and entertainment figures resulting in a (short-lived, it must be admitted) anti-suicide campaign at the break of the decade, adolescent suicides were found to *decrease* after newscasts about suicide. Though the investigators are skeptical about applying the constructs of imitative learning to either phenomenon, less cautious commentators might point to the putative effects of behavioral models presented *negatively* in contrast to those presented positively or even neutrally.

In a related context, however, in her study of crime rates in cities which previously had no access to television following the introduction of TV broadcasting in those locales in the 1950s, Henigan (1982) found that "the introduction of television was consistently associated with increases in larceny," but not with increases in violent crime. Attributing this finding to the content of television programming in that era, during which "the advertising of consumption goods was high, upper- and middle-class lifestyles were overwhelmingly portrayed, and larceny was portrayed much less often than crimes of violence," Henigan concluded that the observed increases in larceny were *not* associated with "the social learning of larceny through viewing it on TV," but rather with "viewing high levels of consumption, relative deprivation, and frustration."

CONTROVERSIAL STUDIES ON THE DETERRENT EFFECT OF CAPITAL PUNISHMENT

The classic (and surely most controversial) studies that have considered what we here term vicarious deterrence are those which have focused on the deterrent effects of the death penalty, with sharp and adamant positions taken by "abolitionists" and "retentionists" respectively — often at the expense of adopting an "advocacy scholarship" that was never dispassionate and hardly clothed in objectivity. These studies were undertaken principally during that period in the mid-1970s in which the matter of capital punishment was Constitutionally in limbo [*Note* 1].

Pioneer criminologist Thorstin Sellin (1959) fired the opening salvo in a study which compared homicide rates between 1920 and 1974 in neighboring U.S. states with similar social and demographic characteristics that were said to differ only in whether they did or did not have death penalty statutes in effect. Sellin concluded that *either* there were no differences in rates of homicide between neighboring "abolitionist" and "retentionist" states *or*, where such differences obtained, the rates were lower in "abolitionist" jurisdictions. Utilizing a quite different research methodology (viz., time-series analyses) over a 50-year period in one state, Decker & Kohfeld (1984) concluded that "the death penalty had no deterrent effect on homicides."

Put into terms from the lexicon of the psychology of learning: There is little support in the Sellin or Decker & Kohfeld studies for the notion of vicarious deterrence of homicide attached to the death penalty; instead, there is the suggestion in Sellin's study that retention of the death penalty produces a mild but discernibly paradoxical effect — by eliciting rather than extinguishing criminal homicide.

Sellin's position was countered by Isaac Ehrlich (1975-*a*, 1975-*b*), a specialist in econometrics, in a study of homicide rates between 1933 and 1967 in neighboring states. Utilizing the methods of economic cost-benefit analysis, Ehrlich reached the conclusion that each death penalty that was *not* imposed had resulted in the murder

---

⇨ *Zimring & Hawkins: A Blood Bath of Legalized Killing —*
and a Surfeit of Aversive Reactions

Legal scholars Franklin Zimring & Gordon Hawkins (1986) imply a sort of aversive conditioning in the arithmetic they use to depict the degree of *escalation in annual executions* necessary if (1) U.S. courts continue to impose the death penalty at the recent rate and (2) the nation is to reduce the current log-jam phenomenon on death row so as to avoid future court contests claiming that prolonged anticipation of execution in itself constitutes cruel and unusual punishment.

To follow their formula: To reduce, even within a ten year period, the current death row population of approximately 1800 to a stable group of no more than 300, and assuming continuation of the current rate of imposition of the death penalty, would require something like 450 to 500 executions annually — an increase on the order of 3000% over the current rate. Thereafter, assuming a constant rate of homicide and of imposition of the death penalty in a burgeoning population, we would need to execute in excess of 350 per year. That, they quite properly contend, would constitute a blood bath of proportions unprecedented in peacetime in any nation at any time in the history of the human species that is likely to prove totally unacceptable to the American public — to say nothing of our relative physical incapacity to execute at that rate even if we wanted to.

Clinically, we can attest that most people we know who enjoy rousing violence in the entertainment media are simultaneously aware of the make-believe character thereof — the actor who is drawn and quartered in tonight's offering will be up-and-at-'em tomorrow. Though the research evidence is far from clear, we suspect that what most citizens want is the *threat* of the death penalty rather than its implementation through executions — just as the television viewer's thirst for make- believe blood reduces to what is no more than a make-believe thirst. If we are correct in that surmise, executions at the rate of two or more for every working day in the calendar year will very likely produce a massively adverse reaction on the part of the citizenry.

of eight victims — or, alternately, that imposition of the death penalty on one offender in one homicide deters other homicides by other offenders at the ratio of 1:8. That is powerful support for vicarious deterrence indeed. Similar, but not quite so powerful, conclusions were reached by Lester (1989) in an analysis of data on the number of executions and murders in California over a ten-year period and by Archer, Gartner & Beittel (1983) in a study of the extent to which homicide rates had *declined* in 14 nations following abolition of the death penalty.

In his turn, Ehrlich was answered (often with criticism of his methodology, admittedly more at home in the field of economics than in criminology) by such luminaries as Daniel Glaser (1979) and William Bailey (1975, 1976-*a*, 1976-*b*, 1980, 1989, 1990). In what it may have conceived as an ultimate effort to resolve the matter at the level of public policy, the National Academy of Sciences commissioned seasoned researchers Lawrence Klein, Brian Forst, and Victor Filatov (1978) to review and distill the empirical evidence. They concluded (p. 351) that "the deterrent effect of capital punishment is definitely not a settled matter, and this is the strongest social scientific conclusion that can be reached at the present time." In an independent review, Arnold Barnett of the Sloan School of Management at MIT (1978, p. 291) concluded that "no specific evidence has been presented that indicates with any conclusiveness whether executions deter murders," a conclusion repeated by Bailey (1990). Clearly, such findings please partisans of neither the abolitionist nor the retentionist camp, however much they suggest that, with respect to capital punishment and subsequent homicides, there is as much reason to support as to reject the notion of vicarious deterrence. Hence, the debate continues — at both the empirical and conceptual levels, with McFarland (1983) reporting no pattern of deterrence either nationally nor locally following four well publicized executions in the U.S. and with Archer *et al.* (1983) reporting a *reduction* in the homicide rate in some 14 nations of the world following abolition, and with such data variously interpreted (Bailey, 1983-*a*; Bowers, 1983; Forst, 1983; Yang & Lester, 1988).

CAPITAL PUNISHMENT AS AN INFREQUENTLY- IMPLEMENTED SANCTION

Yet what has been omitted in these analyses is consideration of the real-world context in which capital punishment is, and has historically been, administered in "retentionist" jurisdictions. When the rates at which the death penalty is, and has been, implemented (i.e., legislatively prescribed, judicially imposed, and, after the inevitable or in some state mandatory appeals have been exhausted, actually carried out) at any time in this century are added to the picture, the question of whether homicide rates are higher or lower in "retentionist" or "abolitionist" jurisdictions reduces largely to a straw-man issue.

According to the U.S. Department of Justice's (1983) *Report to the Nation on Crime and Justice,* the number of homicides reported

> ⇨ *Lenient Penalties for Juveniles: Stimulus Determinants for Criminal Violence in Adulthood?*
>
> Statutes that specify the penalties to be assigned to offenders who are legally minors below the age of 18 typically prescribe sanctions that are far more lenient than those statutorily prescribed for the same crimes when committed by adults. In most states, offenders who are aged 14 or under can be held at maximum until they reach legal majority or, in some cases, the age of 21; in others, incarceration for three years constitutes the maximum penalty for these offenders. In some states, the same strictures apply to offenders between the ages of 15 and 18, while in others an accused offender in this age group may be tried as an adult (and assigned an "adult" penalty if convicted) following a judicial proceeding that accounts the accused's prior history. Nearly invariably, the death penalty cannot be imposed on an offender below the age of 18.
>
> Some commentators hold the view that laws that prescribe lenient sentences constitute part of the environmental fabric that, in essence, conveys a message that lethal violence is easily tolerated. The *Washington Post's* account of a 14-year-old killer:
>
> ❑ "Serve the man and take his car!" That order from his drug dealer sent D.J., a 4-foot, 9-inch, 140-pound, 14-year-old drug runner, to the car of Marvin Alston with a $20 rock of crack cocaine. When Mr. Alston, a regular drug customer, refused the order to leave his late model Maxima and tried to defend himself, D.J. shot him in the head and then in the face with a .32-caliber pistol. A few hours later, D.J. got into an altercation with another man — and shot him dead . . . Last Thursday, the dealer for whom D.J. worked — 27-year-old Daryl Smith — was convicted in District of Columbia Superior Court of felony murder for ordering Mr. Alston's death. D.J. was in that courtroom last Thursday also — as a spectator. For committing those two cold-blooded murders exactly three years ago in Northeast D.C., D.J. paid his debt to society by spending a total of 26 months in the District's Oak Hill youth facility. Now nearly 17, D.J. reportedly has been seen at neighborhood crime scenes, sometimes taunting the police.
>
> ❑ What makes this so frightening and sickening is that there are more "D.J.s" on District streets, and, say prosecutors, their numbers are growing. In part it's explained by something older drug dealers know that most law-abiding citizens don't suspect: Some 14- and 15-year-old kids can be easily recruited and paid to deal drugs and commit murders, because when they are caught and "adjudicated" in the District as juveniles their sentences tend to be relatively light. These dealer/mentors also know what the juvenile justice system is starting to learn: that in the minds of some youths, the power and reputation they gain from own and using a gun outweigh the risks of getting caught.
>
> • *Source:* D.J., *Washington Post,* July 31, 1991, A-20. [Unsigned editorial]

⇨ *Vicarious Conditioning and the Expectation of Impunity*

There is a substantial body of research evidence that *novel* modes of aggressive behavior are readily acquired through observation of aggressive models. Findings of these controlled investigations lend support to field studies demonstration the crucial role of modeling in the genesis of antisocial aggressive behavior and in the cultural transmission of aggressive response patterns. Modeling influences continue to regulate aggressive responsiveness to some extent even after the behavior has been acquired. The behavior of models continually exerts selective control over the types of responses exhibited by others in any given situation. Moreover, seeing individuals behaving aggressively without adverse consequences reduces restraints in observers, thereby increasing both the frequent with which they engage in aggressive activities and the harshness with which they treat others.

• *Source:* Albert Bandura, *Principles of Behavior Modification.* New York: Holt, Rinehart, Winston, 1969. P. 379.

---

nationwide annually between 1930 and 1935 varied between 10,200 and 12,000.

The "peak" year for *executions* (i.e., not for the imposition of the death penalty at trial, but for its actually being implemented) nationwide was 1935, when 199 offenders were executed. If 199 executions in 1935 represents the peak, it seems clear that *the death penalty has never been carried out in this country in this century at a ratio greater than 2% of the known cases of murder.* In full and appropriate context, the question of deterrence thus becomes whether homicide rates are higher or lower in those states in which the death penalty has *not* been imposed and implemented in something on the order of 98% of the murders for which it has been the legislatively prescribed sanction, even during a period many would regard as the most bloodthirsty in our recent history.

There are very many reasons indeed to be found in the psychology of learning to support the hypothesis that a sanction that is *infrequently-implemented sanction* will have at best a marginal effect on behavior despite its severity. That proposition is substantively related to the well-demonstrated resistance to change of a behavior that is maintained on either a random or intermittent schedule of reinforcement. A more objective analysis of the evidence might conclude that: *Because the death penalty is and has been an infre-*

*quently-implemented sanction in the U.S. even in those jurisdictions
in which it is prescribed by law, no statement can be made about its
deterrent effect with any pretense to scientific validity.*

To settle the question of deterrent effect would seem to require
either cross-national comparisons with societies (if any such exist)
in which the death penalty is virtually universally imposed and
carried out as a sanction for capital crime, with all sorts of adjustments for endemic differences — or a radical and unthinkable
change in the imposition and implementation of the capital sanction
in "retentionist" U.S. states. That such investigations have not been
undertaken may be as it should be, however — for, as Zimring &
Hawkins (1986) and Lowenstein (1988) seem to argue, the *moral*
issue of whether to retain or abolish capital punishment may be
simply too important a policy decision to be left to empirical behavioral science.

→ *INFERENCES, SPECULATIONS, CONJECTURES*

The research evidence from studies in social learning for
vicarious conditioning and extinction is incontrovertible. The research evidence for *long-distance vicarious conditioning* in the sense
of elicitation of criminal behavior is rather more fragmentary, but
the direction is relatively clear, whether the agency of influence is
the behavioral model or the relatively less direct transmission of
normative attitudes and values. Similarly, there is evidence that
supports the notion of *long-distance vicarious deterrence,* although
the evidence on long-distance deterrence of homicide through the
ultimate sanction of capital punishment is mixed; there is, by judgment of a blue-ribbon jury of social scientists empaneled by the
National Academy of Sciences, as much evidence in favor of the effect
as in opposition to it. It may be the case that the relative infrequency
of the actual carrying out of death sentences even during those
periods in which such sentences were rather freely legislatively
prescribed and judicially imposed clouds the situation in such a way
as to preclude dispassionate conclusions. Certainly, there is strong
reason to believe, on the basis of evidence from studies of learning
and social learning, that a negative sanction that is infrequently
imposed has little aversive value.

☐ *STIMULUS DETERMINANTS: ELICITING OR POTENTIATING VIOLENCE*

Most members of a society undergo relatively similar social learning experiences. Most of us have heard the same pious tales of
Washington, Abraham Lincoln, Betsy Ross, Molly Pitcher, Crispus

Attucks, or Sojourner Truth. For that matter, most of us view the same televised football games or prize fights or crime drama — or witness in "real-time" mass destruction in the Arabian desert, on a scale unprecedented in the annals of destroying *or* of witnessing.

Some behavioral scientists hold the view that disparate elements in the social learning process congeal (rather than "blend") so as to constitute a relatively pervasive social-cultural environment that delivers relatively homogeneous messages about what is good or bad, acceptable or unacceptable, in ourselves, in others, and in our relations with each other. Once congealed, that environment is itself recycled through the process of social learning, so that mutual reinforcement occurs circularly and constantly. We are likely to regard that circular process as inevitable — and indeed to applaud

---

⇨ *External Stress, War, Domestic Homicide*

Though the effect of war on domestic homicide rates has been demonstrated in a number of investigations, there may be explanations that are not rectilinear. Thus, legal scholar Simha Landau (1988) of the Hebrew University examined the relationship between *external* sources of stress and the rates of both homicide and robbery over an 18-year-period in the history of Israel punctuated by threats to that nation's survival. Both offenses were found to vary *inversely* in relation to the extent of external threat. At a micro-psychological level, it may well be the case that a realistic threat to the survival of one's nation serves to disinhibit one's antisocial behavior.

In a congruent study that focused on economic threat rather than threat to one's very survival, Brenner & Swank (1986) of the Johns Hopkins School of Medicine reported a strong relationship between homicide rate and economic recession. And, in a more expansive investigation, Humphrey & Palmer (1987) analyzed the "stressful life events" experienced, respectively, by large samples of homicide and property offenders. Their principal findings (p. 299):"[homicide offenders] experienced [stressful life events] in greater number and more consistently than nonviolent felons. [Homicide offenders whose victims had been members of their own families or close friends] tended to suffer more [stressful life experiences] involving loss . . . Results suggest that homicide offenders are responding to chronic stress."

it when it serves *either* those ends that we endorse *or* those values we hold to be required for the maintenance of civilized society, such as a respect for the truth, diligence, honesty, compassion. Indeed, whenever we approach a traffic intersection, we rather trust that social learning and stimulus determinants (such as the color of the light signal) will control the behavior of others in pro-social ways — that is, that we can proceed confidently when we face the green signal, with reasonable assurance that the behavior of others is being determined by the stimulus value of the red signal.

But the case can also be made that the very process of large-scale social learning and teaching that holds forth the positive behavioral models of which society-at-large approves must perforce portray the reciprocal — that is, in order to depict what is right and proper, it is also necessary to portray what is wrong and improper (Pallone, 1986, pp. 64-69), so that implicitly or explicitly every positive behavioral model conjures a reciprocal negative model. And that process occurs even when the intent is to convey positive behavioral images, let alone when the intent is what Wilson & O'Leary (1980, p. 210) have called "unhealthy persuasion."

There is some empirical evidence that such reciprocal negative models sometimes exert their own attraction, elicit among some the learning of *negative* social behavior; and that our societal preoccupation with violence — whether conveyed through crime drama, professional sports events, or acid rock — serves to further *legitimate* violence as an acceptable feature of our society (Daly & Wilson, 1989). Some commentators, indeed, believe that the process by which violence as a means of resolving conflicts or presumably intractable problems is perceived as an acceptable behavioral option for the individual has its genesis in formal public policy that governs the ways in which a society or a nation deals with its citizens and with other societies or nations — and that popular culture merely reflects formal public policy on the acceptability of violence. Thus, King (1978) described the "brutalization effect" that follows publicity about executions and, in his judgment, actually elicits violent behavior in its wake. Or, as Wilkes (1986, p. 26) put it after reviewing data from some 110 nations, "when a nation does violence to human beings by conducting wars or executing criminals, it incites its citizens to . . . criminal violence" precisely because that nation has itself legitimated violence. One might expect that it *also* "incites" the creators of television entertainments and the arbiters of what is portrayed in the news media.

⇨ *The "Victimization Quotient" — Application of Psychometric Scaling Methods to the Assessment of Subcultures of Violence*

Customarily, sociologists, criminologists, and social statisticians have compiled data reflecting the frequency of crimes of various sorts; less frequently, these data have been examined in relation to other variables that speak to the social characteristics of locales, cities, regions, or sub-cultural and even ethnic envelopes. By and large, these efforts have been primarily descriptive, with little effort to examine, determine, or assess the extent to which these data covary. For example, during "scare" campaigns, local law enforcement agencies may sponsor public service announcements which proclaim that "The crime of assault [*or* rape *or* burglary] occurs every X minutes in this jurisdiction."

What is left out in such an approach, of course, is the *relative ratio* between the actual occurrences and the *opportunities* for crime to occur. In a city of 200,000, for example, there may occur annually 300 robberies — so that 0.15% of that city's population is victimized by robbery (providing, of course, that no citizen is victimized twice in the same year). Those figures suggest that one robbery occurs each 29 hours. But, in a city of 1,000,000, there may occur annually 900 robberies. In this case, only 0.09% of the population is victimized, even though the *absolute* number of robberies is three time greater than in our city of 200,000 *and* even though a robbery occurs ever 9.7 hours. The comparisons grow even more tenuous when very large cities, such as New York or Los Angeles, are compared with such municipalities as, say, Colorado Springs or San Jose.

In an inventive analysis of these phenomena which avoids inconsistencies and misleading conclusions, Hennessy & Kepecs-Schlussel (1992) applied a psychometric methodology used widely in intelligence test scaling to data from the 1989 *Uniform Crime Reports* compiled by the FBI concerning the number of crimes reported in each of the several subcategories for the 76 largest cities in the US — in effect, all cities whose populations exceeded 200,000.

In order to better understand the relative incidence of reported crime in jurisdictions whose populations vary substantially, these investigators devised a scale that effectively reduces disparate numbers to comparable units of measurement. Such a "transformation" procedure has routinely been employed in test development, particularly in aptitude and achievement measures, and is perhaps best exemplified by the several Wechsler scales. In the first step, Hennessy & Kepecs-Schlussel computed the *ratios* between *crimes reported* in each major category (i.e., *crimes of violence,* further syllabicated as murder, rape, assault, robbery, arson, and *property crimes,* further syllabicated as larceny, burglary, motor vehicle theft) and *population* within the reporting jurisdiction. Ratios were also computed both between the FBI's *crime index — total* and population.

Those ratios — one for each city for each category of crime and one for the total crime index for each city — were then converted to standard z score transformations, values which indicate the deviation of each ratio from the *mean* value for its category. By their nature, z distributions have a mean of zero and a standard deviation of +/-1.0. Thus, the transformation of each ratio to a z distribution allows for direct calculations of the relative differences and/or similarities in reported incidences *across* categories of crime *and between* cities.

While virtually all statistical analyses operate at the level of z score analysis, these values may be difficult to interpret because of negative signs. Hence, it has become customary to further transform z scores to more "user-friendly" integers, typically through addition or multiplication by a constant.

Hennessy & Kepecs-Schlussel transformed the z scores for each of their ratios into a scale score system comparable to that used to report subtest performance on the Weschler intelligence measures — that is, scales that have means of 10 and standard deviation of 3. They also computed "quotients" for aggregated scale scores for crimes of violence, for property crimes, and for total crimes.

The substantive findings reported by Hennessy & Kepecs-Schlussel lend little support to an attribution of the engines for a subculture of violence to region of the country; instead, the racial composition of the 76 cities they studied emerged as a potent indicator of the confluence of violence.

In their analysis, the highest "quotients" for crimes of violence were earned by Atlanta, Detroit, Dallas, Kansas City (Missouri), St. Louis, Cleveland, and Miami (in that order). Four of these cities properly fall within the orbit of "Southern-ness." On the other hand, the lowest "quotients" for crimes of violence were earned by Virginia Beach, Mesa (Arizona), Honolulu, Colorado Springs, Arlington (Texas), and Anchorage; two of these cities fall within the orbit of Southern-ness. From these data, region does not emerge as a strongly determining factor in the incidence of crimes of violence.

Alternately, according to Bureau of the Census data, among the eight "most dangerous" cities, the median proportion of racial minority population is 48%, while among the five "safest" cities, the median proportion of racial minority population is 10%. Read in juxtaposition to the consistent finding that crimes of violence rarely cross racial lines, these data are no less than devastating.

These investigators also reported that the highest quotients for property crime were earned by Atlanta, Dallas, Miami, Fort Worth (Texas), and Tampa (in that order), while the lowest quotients for property crime were earned by Virginia Beach, Anchorage, San Jose (California), Lexington (Kentucky), and Honolulu. Quotients for crimes of violence and for property crimes correlated at $r = +.64$ over the 65 largest standard metropolitan statistical areas (SMSAs) in the nation.

Beyond the substantive findings concerning the confluence of crimes of violence, the investigators propose development of "norms" based on an enumeration of census tract areas to aid in policy development and program planning , particularly for crime prevention efforts.

A Subculture of Violence

Political and cultural historians have long attributed a major role in the shaping of the American ethos to the myths and realities of the taming of the frontier. Though they may have held Royal patents, the European-born colonists who settled New England and the mid- Atlantic in essence purchased their land from Native Americans; in contrast, the Spanish *conquistadores* who invaded what is now Florida and the southwest and those primarily American-born pioneers who tamed the ever-shifting western frontier from Kentucky to Colorado merely seized their lands from Native Americans by force of arms. Though the older settlements of the East sought to emulate the lawfully ordered life of European cities,

---

⇨ *David Lester on Lethal Violence and Traditionalist*
Social Values

Prolific researcher in suicidology David Lester and his colleagues have conducted a series of inquiries that link lethal violence to what can be construed as a variety of traditionalist social values. Thus:

❑ Lester (1987-*b*) reported that the rate of both suicide and homicide in the various U.S. states varied inversely with the extent of regular church attendance and with marital status (1987-c).

❑ In a cross-national study of 18 industrialized nations, Lester (1988-*b*) corroborated the relationship between homicide rate and the participation of women in the labor force.

❑ In an investigation of homicides and suicides in 1970 in the 48 coterminous U.S. states, Lester (1986-*a*) had reported that varied directly with the divorce rate, certainly an index to abrogation of traditionalist values.

❑ Similarly, in a study of the 48 coterminous U.S. state, Baker & Lester (1986-*b*) reported the larger the number of births in a state between May and November, "the better the performance of its high school students and the lower its homicide rate."

Children born in May should ordinarily have been conceived in August; those born in November should ordinarily have been conceived in February. Whether the time of conception is related *either* to church attendance, the extent to which women enact the traditionalist role of stay-at-home wife and mother, *or* to other traditionalist values is not explored by Baker & Lester.

On the other hand, in a cross-national study of 17 countries, Lester (1987-*a*) also found that the suicide (but not the homicide) rate was lower in those nations with a higher proportion of citizens with Type O blood — and that surely seems to be a matter quite independent of church attendance or other traditionalist values — but perhaps not to time of conception.

the settlements of the frontier were governed principally by threat of violence.

Commentators from Edwin Lawrence Godkin (1898, pp. 25-31) and Frederick Jackson Turner to Vernon Louis Parrington (1930, pp. 159- 165) hold that, in forcing individuals to rely on themselves rather than on a social order controlled by a monied elite (witness the early limitation that the privilege of voting in elections extended only to those who owned property), the taming of the frontier immeasurably catalyzed the development of true participative democracy in this country. That may be the positive side.

On the negative, there is no question that the process of Western expansion left in its wake the popular image of the frontiersman and his successor, the two-fisted gunman, ready to risk all in pursuit of his wants or needs, celebrated in legends ranging from Daniel Boone to Billy the Kid. Quite clearly, the ethos of the frontier embodied the normative expectation of violence; we should not be surprised, then, to find empirical evidence from the behavioral sciences that confirms that the normative expectation of violence represents a central thrust in a variety of American subcultures — a situation the historians seem to have unearthed nearly a century ago.

REGIONAL CULTURES OF VIOLENCE

After investigating the confluence of suicide, homicide, and violent crime in the several regions of the nation, Gastil (1971) had early proposed what he termed "a subculture of violence" situated primarily in the American South. Largely confirmatory data were adduced by Loftin & Hill (1974), Doerner (1975), Bailey (1976- a), Franke, Thomas & Queenen (1977), Humphrey & Kupferer (1977), Huff-Corzine, Corzine & Moore (1986), and Lester (1988-a), while O'Carroll & Mercy (1989) claimed that the American West rather than the South constitutes the pre-eminent subculture of violence. If one adds to the litany of distinguishing regional characteristics the matter of judicially-ordered executions, however, there is simply no question that the American South far and away leads the nation (Amnesty International, 1987, pp. 54-64).

In more discerning analyses of nearly 500 "standard metropolitan statistical areas" (SMSAs) in the U.S., Messner (1982, 1983-a, 1983-b) studied the rates of death by violence of all sorts (i.e., homicide, suicide, traffic fatalities, household accidents, industrial accidents) per 100,000 of the population, finding that these were highest in the South. While racial composition of the SMSA and proportion of the population below the poverty level were related to homicide rate *outside* the South, no such relationships obtained *within* that region, so it is concluded that the propensity for violent death appears to pervade the region, regardless of race or economic deprivation. Nonetheless, Lalli & Turner (1968) and Hawkins (1989) hold that social class constitutes a pivotally important mediator in the confluence between suicide and homicide, whatever the region of the country. Similarly, Williams (1984) adduced evidence that poverty and racial inequality are potent predictors of homicide rate across a sample of 125 SMSAs across the nation. In a slight variation, McDowall (1986) used time-series analyses to study the link between the proportion of families at or below the poverty level in a single city (Detroit) over the period of half a century and the rate of criminal homicide, finding that the two varied together. McGahey (1990) has opined that poverty level, as measured by joblessness at least, may differentially affect crime rates in accordance with offense category — e.g., minor drug offenses might actually increase in incidence during times of general economic affluence. Nonetheless, in a "macrodynamic time series analysis," Rattner (1990) found consistent positive relationships between level of unemployment and rate of homicide; the intervening variable may be the abiding sense of frustration and futility generally experienced in times of economic hardship, termed *anomie* and often invoked as a principal pivot for both criminal violence and political revolution in sociological accounts.

CONFLUENCE OF DEATHS BY VIOLENCE

A significant and growing body of research, both in the United States and cross-nationally, seems to confirm that a relatively high coincidence of deaths by violence (homicide, suicide, traffic fatalities, and other accidents) comprise the indicia either of a culture of violence or at least of general societal acceptance of violence. Thus:

❑ Hirsch, Rushforth, Ford & Adelson (1973) early observed a confluence in the rate of homicide and suicide in single midwestern county in the U.S. Similarly, Day (1984) found a high correlation between homicide and suicide over a 30-year period in some 40 nations.

❑ In a study of the 50 states and the District of Columbia, Sivak (1983) reported a high congruence between the homicide rate and the rate of traffic fatalities in a single year. Those findings were largely replicated by Lester (1988), who underscored in particular the confluence between homicides and traffic fatalities.

❑ Similarly, Wilbanks (1980) found both a high congruence between suicide rate and accident rate and a positive correlation between suicide and homicide rates in a sample of 181 regions in the U.S., again in a single year, though in a later study (1982) he concluded that these relationships varied "among subgroups of the population [in] so complex a pattern of correlations" that no unilinear theoretical explanation seemed applicable. Hollinger (1980) confirmed Wilbanks' initial findings on the confluence of death by violent means, with particular emphasis on mortality among young adults; and Hollinger & Klemen (1982), in a study which analyzed mortality rates from suicide, homicide, and accident throughout the nation between 1900 and 1975 found that these rates "tend to be parallel over time," a finding they interpreted as "reflecting self-destructive tendencies."

☐ Yang & Lester (1988-*b*) confirmed the relationship between suicide and homicide in the various states of the union, finding as well a higher rate of homicide in states in which a greater proportion of women were employed outside the home on a full-time basis — a factor they interpreted as indicative of the disintegration of traditionalist social values. But rather sharply contrasting findings have been reported (Straus, 1979, 1890; Straus & Gelles, 1990) from a major series of studies at the Family Violence Research Institute of the University of New Hampshire, however. Thus, Gelles & Hargreaves (1990) found no significant differences in prevalence of episodes of child abuse between mothers who were employed full-time, those employed part-time, and those not employed outside the home; but they reported a significantly lower rate of family violence in those families in which the mother was employed full-time. In this detailed investigation, prevalence of episodes was found to vary according to the age of the child-victim and according to the interaction between the child's age and the mother's employment status. In a companion investigation, Kalmuss & Straus (1990) measured both "subjective" and "objective" dependency among married women and related these measures to episodes of wife abuse. Their unequivocal conclusions: "The rate of severe violence is almost three times higher among women high than among those very low in objective dependency. The increment in severe violence between the parallel levels of subjective dependency is only two-fold."

PREVALENCE OF VIOLENT DEATH INFLECTED BY AGE

Hollinger, Offer & Ostrov (1987) analyzed suicide and homicide rates over five decade in the United States in relation to the *age* of those who kill themselves or others. Their results show significant positive correlations between suicide and homicide rates *among those who are between 15 and 24 years old* over the entire 50-year period — as well as significant *negative* correlations between those rates among adults aged from 35 to 64.

On the basis of the findings of Hollinger and his colleagues on the confluence of deaths by violent means among young adults, one might reasonably conclude that the confluence in violent deaths is a phenomenon inflected largely by the age of the person responsible — a conclusion quite in conformance both with the data we examined in Chapter 5 on homicide as it is committed and with data we examined in Chapter 6 on age-related decline in the propensity to behave antisocially.

→ *INFERENCES, SPECULATIONS, CONJECTURES*

To the extent that there is high correlative incidence of death by one or another violent means in the psychosocial environment, we might expect such a phenomenon to function in such a way as to lead the individual behaver to believe that violence constitutes an acceptable feature of social interaction. To that extent, *we might expect a culture or subculture of violence to potentiate other variables inclining a behaver toward violence.*

However, *individuals in our society are relatively free to self-select their own sociocultural environments.* Hence, we might expect that those persons who are internally disposed toward violence will, with some degree of deliberation, elect to place themselves into sociocultural situations in which violence is an acceptable feature of social interaction. In turn, their presence within such a sociocultural situation serves further to reinforce the normative expectation governing the acceptability of violent behavior.

Intergenerational Transmission of Patterns of Violence

We should expect those sociocultural factors that accept, favor, or tolerate violence to be reflected, modeled, and learned intra-familially. In particular, we should expect something approaching a pattern of the intergenerational transmission of propensity toward violent behavior as parents function as pervasive role models for their children. There is a rather rich literature that suggests that such is precisely the case, though the question of the specific mechanisms of transmission and the relationships through which such propensities are transmitted (e.g., whether transmission occurs more potently between parents and children of the same gender) remains unsettled. Thus:

❑ Feldman, Mallouh & Lewis (1986) conducted detailed clinical interviews with close relatives of adults who had been convicted of murder, with evidence that 87% of them had suffered extreme physical and/or sexual abuse as children and that 53% had been the victims of attempted filicide. Data from interviews with relatives were supplemented by psychiatric evaluations and Army, prison, school, and juvenile court records on assailants. According to these investigators, "The mechanisms whereby such abuse and parental behavior may contribute to subsequent violence include modeling, organic consequences of abuse, lack of parental attachment, and displaced rage." Similar results linking childhood victimization with later criminal behavior were reported by Shoham, Rahav, Markowski & Chard (1987) in an investigation of violent vs. non-violent adult offenders. But Pollock, Briere, Schneider & Knop (1990) found no significant differences in anti-social behavior among young adult males aged 18-21 as a function either of *paternal* alcoholism or of victimization in child abuse perpetrated by their fathers.

❑ In a study of *juveniles* who had been charged with homicide or attempted homicide over an 18-month period in California, Sorrells (1977) found clear evidence of intergenerational transmission of violence. Despite family histories that were prototypically violent and chaotic and despite the records of crime, violence, and substance abuse characteristic of their parents, however, these accused juvenile homicide offenders "were not seen as more *psychiatrically* disturbed than other delinquents." That rather surprising finding was further elaborated in a study by Cornell, Benedek & Benedek (1987), who examined case records over an eight-year period for 72 adolescents between 12 and 18 who had been charged with homicide and for a control group of 35 adolescents who had been charged with larceny. These investigators garnered information on some 52 variables reflecting family dysfunction, school adjustment, childhood problems, history of violence, delinquent behavior, substance abuse, psychiatric problems, and stressful life events of sources. Their gloomy conclusion: "Subjects charged with larceny scored higher [i.e., had more problems] on composite measures of school adjustment, childhood symptoms, criminal activity, and psychiatric history" than did those charged with homicide. Such conclusions as those of Sorrells and of Cornell and his colleagues seem to argue for a larger role for variables that are extra-psychic than for those what are intra-person in the behavioral mix that results in criminal homicide.

❑ To the extent to which Cloninger, Reich & Guze (1975) were correct in proposing that *psychopathy* is intergenerationally transmitted and further compounded by a process they identify as "associative mating" (whereby individuals choose spouses not very different from themselves), it may be that harsh child rearing practices in a subculture that condones violence (Erlanger, 1974; Laybourn, 1986) constitutes an important intervening biopsychosocial variable.

❑ Further, one would expect that child rearing practices in such a subculture would favor (or at least condone) physical punishment as a means of behavior control; and, indeed, Wauchope & Straus (1990, p. 142) reported that the incidence of physical violence directed against children in "blue collar" families was nearly twice that in "white collar" families. Especially in light of Bell's (1986) findings on the incidence of head trauma in relation to social class, the prospect that such class-linked child rearing practices may yield a higher incidence of "accidental" head injury (and thus also of consequent neuropsychological dysfunction) cannot be dismissed out of hand.

❑ Some support for such an interpretation emerges from studies by Tarter, Hegedus, Winsten & Alterman (1984) on neuropsychological impairment among juvenile delinquents who had themselves been the victims of parental physical abuse; by Wolfe, Fairbank, Kelly & Bradlyn (1983) on autonomic arousal levels in relation to videotaped depictions of even non-stressful interactions between parents and children on the part of physically abusive mothers; and by Rohrbeck & Twentyman (1986) on neuropsychological deficits among abusive mothers.

One might naively expect that, if a child has suffered violence at the hands of a parent, he or she would undertake ever greater controls over his or her own behavior as an adult so as *not* to inflict similar experiences upon others. Yet there remains little debate about *whether* an inclination toward violence is transmitted from one generation to another. Rather, there remain questions only about the *how* of transmission. The psychoanalytically-inclined may appeal to the notion of "identification with the aggressor" as an explanatory mechanism; and that may be as useful a piece of intel-

---

⇨ *Intergenerational Perpetuation of Sexual Violence*

There is substantial evidence that *personal sexual victimization* in childhood, often at the hands of a parent or sibling, is frequently linked to criminal sexual psychopathy in adult life (Burgess, Hartman & McCormick, 1987; Davis & Leitenberg, 1987; Pallone, 1990; Pierce & Pierce, 1987). There is every reason to believe that victimization not of a sexual nature similarly perpetuates — perhaps through the psychological mechanism termed "identification with the aggressor." The evidence amassed by Straus & Gelles (1990) on the intergenerational transmission of patterns of intrafamilial physical abuse surely argue in that direction.

lectual shorthand as any. Thus, after reviewing a wide array of investigations essentially from a social learning perspective, Kaufman & Zigler (1987) concluded that:

> The best estimates of the rate of intergenerational transmission suggest that approximately 30% of all individuals who were physically or sexually abused or extremely neglected will subject their offspring to one of these forms of maltreatment. Being maltreated as a child puts one at risk for becoming abusive (Owens & Straus, 1975), but the path between these points is far from direct or inevitable.

Such results were confirmed by Dembo, Dertke, LaVoie & Borders (1987) with particular attention to risk for drug abuse. And, in a substantial review of a wide array of empirical studies, Widom (1989) concluded to the dependability of intergenerational transmission but attributed the phenomenon to complex interaction among psychosocial variables. DiLalla & Gottesman (1991) amplified Widom's conclusions by underscoring the role of biogenetic and other physiological variables: "There is clear evidence for a genetic role in criminality and for a physiological basis for violent behavior. The inclusion of such genetic and biological evidence is necessary for an . . . understanding of the transmission of violence from one generation to another."

→ *INFERENCES, SPECULATIONS, CONJECTURES*

Whatever the relative contribution of psychosocial, cultural, genetic, and biological factors, there appears to be no dispute as to the *fact* of the transmission of patterns of violence between generations. Further, the interaction between a culture of violence, violent role models in the family, and the *elicitation* of violent behavior seems clear.

The Availability of Weapons

If indeed either the general society or segments thereof implicitly foster *or* tolerate a culture of violence, one would expect to find also a high tolerance for the possession of lethal weapons. The data we have reviewed in Chapter 5 concerning the means to murder point with absolute clarity to firearms as the weapon most frequently used in killings; moreover, as we have seen, firearms are also the most frequent means of self-destruction (Wood & Mercy, 1990). We have opined that these reasons alone might argue in favor of strict control over the possession of such weapons — even though death by firearms, whether through homicide or suicide, represents only a tiny fraction in relation to the known ownership of handguns and long guns. Distinguished legal scholar Franklin Zimring (1990) has

⇨ *On the Availability of Assault Weapons by Mail Order*

In the late 1950s, a young investigator for a Committee of the U.S. Senate named Michael James McInerney was assigned the task of gathering evidence on the availability of firearms by means of *mail order.* One of McInerney's classmates in high school had been Joseph A. Bruno, later a member of Lyndon Johnson's White House Staff. Bruno owned a dog, whom he had named (without particular originality) Fido. McInerney began to order by mail weapons of all sorts in the name of Fido Bruno; if required by terms of the coupon clipped from a sportsmen's magazine, he listed the dog's age correctly — at 7.

The rather dramatic result was the gathering of a small arsenal of weapons of all sorts, ranging from single-shot Derringer pistols to rapid-fire, automatic-loading long guns capable of decimating a 200-year-old oak more effectively, and faster, than a chain saw. On the basis of such evidence, the Federal Congress adopted legislation sponsored by Senator Thomas Dodd to regulate (though only in some mild fashion) the sale and purchase of deadly firearms.

Then as now, substantial opposition was raised by the National Rifle Association and other membership groups composed of those committed either to blood sports or to "recreational" shooting by means of target practice (or both). Virtually invariably, opposition is rooted in what is held to be a right to bear arms guaranteed by the Constitution — but prototypically quoted well out of context. In fact, the full text of the Second Amendment reads:

❑   A well-regulated militia being necessary to the security of a free state, the right of the people to keep and bear arms shall not be infringed.

The conditional clause which opens the text is surely susceptible to the interpretation that "the right . . . to keep and bear arms" *arises within and is limited to* those circumstances under which an organized governmental authority finds it necessary to establish and to equip an armed force — thus, the Armed Forces of the United States and the militia (or, as they are termed today, National Guard units) of the various states. More particularly, the Amendment surely contains no language that suggests that it is the right of every citizen to own an automatic weapon capable of delivering tens, or hundreds, of rounds per minute, especially since such "assault" weapons are barred from use in blood sports in most states.

In October 1991, only a day after recluse George Hennard drove his van through the window of a cafeteria in a small suburban Texas town and killed 23 patrons with rapid-fire automatic weapons, the Federal Congress acted on a set of measures to further control the sale of weapons.

The legislation, termed the "Brady bill" after the press aide who had taken some of the bullets John Hinckley had intended for President Reagan and suffered subsequent paralysis, was nonetheless defeated. In some large measure, the opposition based its case on the perception that, between a pastiche of current Federal regulations and state gun control legislation, there was no need for further Federal intervention. And it is indeed the case that current Federal regulations constrain the sale of some weapons to some people — at least by mail order. In 1991, McInerney could not possibly pull off the stunt of 30 and more years ago. Or could he?

If one visits one of those "sporting goods-*cum*- gun shop" establishments that line America's highways, one will typically not be able to purchase an automatic weapon — and surely not without a Federal Firearms Permit. But one can purchase a copy of a weekly newspaper called *The Shooter's News.*

If one turns toward the back pages of that publication, one begins to encounter advertisements offering the sale of what are called "model kits," each denominated as suitable for "display only." One ad will offer, for example, a do-it-yourself kit with which one can construct a stock and a barrel for a weapon remarkably like an Uzi submachine gun (a "look-alike"); the ad will stress that the resultant model will *not* fire — and that no Federal Firearms Permit is required for its purchase. The reader is instructed to send his or her check to a company located, say, in *Suite 14,* 100 Cupertino Boulevard, Ventura, California. On the opposite page, there appears a similar advertisement, this one offering a do-it- yourself kit with which one can construct the operating mechanisms for a "work- alike" model resembling an Uzi submachine gun; the ad stresses that no firing pin is included, that the resultant model will not fire, and that no permit is required; the reader will be instructed to send his or her check to a company located in *Suite 15* at 100 Cupertino Boulevard, etc. With those two components, all one needs in order to assemble an operative weapon is a firing pin. And where will that be found? *Turn the next page of The Shooter's News.*

The data are rather clear on the relationship between gun owndership and death by firearm of all sorts — murder, suicide, accident — in a typical year. Were legislation to be adopted which simply banned the private ownership of firearms *because* a firearm might be used to wrongfully terminate a human life, the resultant rate of *false positives* would be outrageously and unacceptably high. Yet, with the relative ease of obtaining powerful assault weapons, one might be led to wonder why so *few* murders, suicides, and accidental deaths are attributable in any year to firearms.

put the private ownership of firearms at some 130 million; as we saw in Chapter 5, the number of deaths by firearm of any sort — homicide, suicide, accident — aggregate to no more than 30,000 annually. If Zimring's estimate is accurate, the ratio between firearms *acknowledged* to be owned and death by such a weapon is of the order of 4333:1. If one assumes a 1:1 correspondence between a single firearm and a single death by firearm and further assumes that each of the 30,000 or so firearms represented in an annual enumeration of death by firearms is also represented in the aggregated acknowledged ownership (both statistically questionable assumptions), legislation which banned the private ownership of firearms altogether would yield a *false positive* rate on the order of 99.9998%.

The relationship between gun ownership and control policies and the rate of violent crime has been studied and debated among social scientists as avidly as in the popular press and in legislative chambers. Yet the empirical data yield few unclouded conclusions:

❑ King (1973) underscored a paradox early on by analyzing the extraordinarily liberal gun control legislation and very low rate of violent crime in Switzerland *vs.* the strict gun control legislation, tradition of unarmed constabulary, but burgeoning rate of violent crime in Britain. Menninger (1984) offered similar contrasts between the high rate of homicide by firearm in the U.S. with the low rate in Japan, contending that gun ownership in this country is tied to our "pioneer, frontier-conquering heritage."

❑ After studying both homicide and suicide cases in a single American city, Danto (1971) concluded that "murderers and suicidal persons are prone to misuse the firearm as they would misuse any potential instrument of destruction" — that is, were a firearm not available, another instrument would be selected to accomplish the lethal task, a view echoed by Lester (1987-*d*). But it is at some variance with Clarke's (1987) data about the role of opportunity in criminal behavior in general and of the availability of the means to suicide in particular. Indeed, Klein, Reizen, Van Amburg & Walker (1977), in an analysis of all fatalities (whether homicide or suicide) in one U.S. state over a five-year period, found that the weapons employed had been acquired primarily for "self protection," rather than for recreational *or* criminal purposes.

❑ More discerning analyses have studied the *effects of tightening or loosening extant gun control legislation* on homicide and suicide. Thus, Lester (1982) concluded that states in the U.S. that had enacted tight handgun control laws evinced lower rates of suicide by firearm two years after the introduction of such legislation, but with no sharp decrease in overall suicide rate, so that other means were apparently found once the weapon-of-choice became relatively less accessible; but no similar effect was observed on the rate of mortality by homicide through handgun. The same investigator (1987) demonstrated that police officers were murdered at higher rate in jurisdictions with lax gun control legislation. In a later study, however, Lester (1988-c, p. 176) found that "Gun ownership, rather than the strictness of gun control laws, was . . . the strongest correlate of the rates of suicide and homicide."

❑ Several investigators have considered the *deterrent effect of strict gun control legislation*. Loftin & McDowall (1984) amassed data from Florida during a period in which possession of an unlicensed firearm carried a mandatory three-year prison sentence. They concluded that implementation of that legislation "did not have a measurable effect on violent crime." In a similar study in Michigan, Loftin, Heumann & McDowall (1983) concluded that the introduction of similarly strict legislation, which carried a mandatory two-year sentence, produced no significant deterrent effects on violent crime. Perhaps such findings led to the very loose Florida legislation of the late 1980s (adopted after a publicity campaign on the part of conservative legislators whose rallying cry was "Law-abiding citizens are armed and dangerous"), whereby firearms permits could be issued virtually without examination of such characteristics as psychiatric stability of the applicant or prior criminal history.

❑ But, in an investigation of neighboring cities in the U.S. and Canada with very different local legislation on handgun ownership, Sloan, Kellerman, Reay & Ferris (1989, p. 1256) unearthed an interesting network of relationships: "Despite similar overall rates of criminal activity and assault, the relative risk of death from homicide, adjusted for age and sex, was significantly higher in Seattle than in Vancouver. Virtually all of this excess risk was explained by a 4.8-fold higher risk of being murdered with a handgun in Seattle. Rates of homicide by means other than guns were not substantially different in the communities studied."

→ *INFERENCES, SPECULATIONS, CONJECTURES*

The central thrust of these studies surely veers in the direction of a linkage between the availability of firearms and criminal violence. But the linkage may not be rectilinear. Two non-rectilinear propositions compete with each other:

❑ [1] Those who commit homicide, suicide, or aggravated assault short of homicide by means of firearms do so *because* firearms are rather freely and widely available *vs*.

⇨ *Self-Assessed Alcohol and Drug Use Prior to the Offense of Record among Convicted Offenders Serving Sentences in State Prisons*

Under the influence of alcohol during instant offense

Crimes of violence	*20%*
Property crimes	*18%*
Drug offenses	*6%*
Public order offenses	*28%*
All other offenses	*12%*
All offenses combined	*19%*

Under the influence of drugs during instant offense

Crimes of violence	*13%*
Property crimes	*21%*
Drug offenses	*32%*
Public order offenses	*13%*
All other offenses	*13%*
All offenses combined	*17%*

Under the influence of both alcohol and drugs during instant offense

Crimes of violence	*20%*
Property crimes	*18%*
Drug offenses	*11%*
Public order offenses	*12%*
All other offenses	*14%*
All offenses combined	*18%*

Under the influence of either or both alcohol and/or drugs during instant offense

Crimes of violence	*54%*
Property crimes	*57%*
Drug offenses	*48%*
Public order offenses	*53%*
All other offenses	*39%*
All offenses combined	*54%*

• *Source:* Bureau of Justice Statistics, 1988.

❑ [2] Because firearms are more readily available than alternate means, those inclined toward lethal violence are likely to commit (or attempt) such violence by means of firearms rather than search out those alternate means.

The second proposition seems to us a sounder conjecture than the first — that is, *it seems likely that the availability of firearms potentiates, rather than elicits, a disposition toward lethal violence.* But, if that proposition approximates the reality, Danto (1971) may well be correct in predicting that, in the *absence* of a readily available firearm, those inclined (whether intrapsychically, by means of social learning, through eliciting stimuli, or through some combination of such variables) toward lethal violence will soon enough either deliberately search out or otherwise happen upon a substitute weapon. Moreover, we would expect those who are disposed toward violence to self-select those environments in which firearms or other weapons are relatively readily available.

Biochemical Lubricants of Criminal Violence

Intoxication and habituation to mood-altering substances of a variety of sorts (not limited to alcohol and those illicit drugs that have been legislatively declared "controlled dangerous substances" but including medicants available by prescription as well) biochemically trigger psychological states that are relatively substance-specific, each with predictable behavioral consequences. Some substances trigger (or perhaps potentiate — or both) aggressivity and impulsivity that find expression in behavior that is formally criminal. It should not be surprising, then, to find a linkage between substance abuse and criminal violence.

VARIANT METHODS OF INQUIRY

Variant approaches have been used to study the intersection between criminal behavior and alcohol or substance abuse, each encumbered by specific (and largely intrinsic) constraints (Pallone, 1990- *a*; 1991, pp. 57-86):

❑ Some investigators have addressed *criminal activity among known alcoholics or substance abusers.* Data have been collected either through retrospective interviews or, in more elaborate designs, from longitudinal studies of persons who have undergone rehabilitative treatment in mental health clinics and who have been followed thereafter (Gordon, 1983). Some studies, particularly those that rely on retrospective self-reports by known abusers, have produced such astounding data — e.g., Ball, Rosen, Flueck & Nurco (1982) report that their sample of 243 known abusers had been responsible for 473,000 serious felony crimes over a period of eleven years, or 1946 crimes per person, or one crime every two days — that distinguished criminologist James Inciardi (1982) has denominated certain research designs as likely conducive to eliciting fraudulent data. While that may be too harsh a reading, even if one presumes their *willingness* to reveal the truth, there is ample reason to question the *accuracy* of memory of subjects who are either self-identified or who have been otherwise officially designated as addicted to substances known to affect memory.

❑ Other investigators have utilized sophisticated *laboratory assay methodologies* to detect the presence of alcohol or drugs in the physical systems of *arrestees* for crimes of one or another sort (Richardson, Morein & Phin, 1978; Toborg & Bellassai, 1987; Wish, Brady & Cuadrado, 1986; Wish & O'Neil, 1989; Wish, 1990). These studies have generally found alcohol-positive and/or drug-positive rates vastly in excess of those found by self-report methodology, whether in studies of known abusers or of known offenders. While the scientific evidence for the presence or absence of mood-altering substances of various sorts is incontrovertible at the point of apprehension, for reasons we have explored in Chapter 3, it is fallacious to equate *arrest* with conviction. Moreover, except for the rare situation in which an alleged offender is apprehended almost immediately after a criminal act as a result of "hot pursuit," that a suspect is under the influence of a mood-altering substance at the time of arrest tells us little about his or her condition at the time the criminal event occurred.

❑ Yet other investigators have utilized self-report data from persons who have been *convicted* of crimes of one or another sort in studies of alcohol and substance abuse among subjects known to be criminal offenders (Bureau of Justice Statistics, 1980, 1988; Bennett & Wright, 1984; Holcomb & Adams, 1985; Welte & Miller, 1987). This methodology shares the problem of the accuracy of retrospective self-reports encountered in studies of criminal activity among known substance abusers.

ALCOHOL AND CONTROLLED DANGEROUS SUBSTANCES

As we observed in an earlier chapter, tn a typical year, the aggregate total of arrests made for offenses *exclusively* related to sale and possession of "controlled dangerous substances" (opium, cocaine, marijuana, or synthetics) *or* to alcohol (driving under the influence, public drunkenness, and other violations of liquor laws, such as sale to minors) and *not* related to felony crime exceeds the aggregate total of arrests made in all jurisdictions for *all* felony crimes *combined* (McGarrell & Flanagan, 1985, pp. 451-461) by a ratio of 175%. Offenses in which alcohol or drugs are implicated can be categorized as those which are legislatively defined as *criminal in themselves* (e.g., driving under the influence, possession of a controlled dangerous substance, whether for personal use or in sufficient quantity to suggest an intent to distribute) and those which are *criminogenic,* in the sense that alcohol or drugs contribute to felony offenses beyond the mere fact of substance misuse. Conceptually, the use or abuse of alcohol and other psychoactive substances, whether "controlled" and "dangerous" or not and whether obtained illegally or through medical prescription, might be associated with felony crime in one or more of these ways:

❑ As *engine,* functioning so as to induce a person "under the influence" to commit a criminal act of which he/she might otherwise seem incapable when not actively intoxicated.

❑ As *lubricant,* functioning so as to facilitate what, at least *post-hoc,* appears to be a predisposition to criminal behavior, with the felony committed either "under the influence" or not.

❑ As *motive,* functioning as the goal to which criminal activity is directed, with the felony committed typically while the offender is *not* "under the influence."

The *engine* and *lubricant* functions correspond to what the late William McGlothlin (1985, p. 155) of UCLA has called the "direct pharmacological effects" of drug or alcohol use, among which he catalogs "drug-induced disinhibition resulting in impulsive actions, crimes of negligence such as those resulting from driver-impaired performance, and the occasionally reported use of drugs . . . as a means of fortifying [oneself] to engage in criminal activities."

To be useful to a conceptual model of the genesis of crime, research on alcohol and drug use or abuse should first establish *whether* substance use functions as *engine, lubricant,* or *motive,* and, optimally, *in relation to what crimes.*

Self-reports among convicted offenders may be the only viable route to determining whether substance use was perceived to function biochemically as "engine" or "lubricant" in criminal behavior; and that situation may be even further exacerbated by the availability of "designer drugs" relatively less detectable by even sophisticated laboratory assay. Studies of *arrestees* may not be particularly relevant, since there is no particularly strong reason to believe that even those arrestees who will later be formally adjudicated as guilty and who were found to be alcohol-positive or drug-positive at arrest were actively "under the influence" when the instant offense was committed.

When we reviewed statistical data on homicide as it is committed in Chapter 5, we observed that 52% of all prisoners convicted of, and confined for, criminal homicide in state correctional institutions

reported that they were actively under the influence *either* of drugs
or alcohol *or both* at the time of their offenses [DISPLAY 7, p. 107].
Similar findings were reported by Gottlieb, Gabrielsen & Kramp
(1988) in a study of homicide offenders in Denmark over a 25-year-
period. We shall shortly inspect data on the extent of drug and
alcohol use among homicide *victims*. The bald data would seem to
suggest that these substances at least "lubricate" the interaction
between intra-person variables that incline one toward becoming a
homicide offender (or, indeed, a homicide victim) and stimulus
determinants that either elicit or at least tolerate violent behavior.

FOODSTUFFS AND ADDITIVES

Beyond alcohol and those drugs which have been formally denominated "controlled dangerous substances," a number of other ingest-
ibles have been linked to the emission of violent behavior, or, in some
cases, to the inhibition of violent behavior.

❑ *Lithium* is a naturally-occurring (rather than synthesized)
chemical "element" whose psychoactive properties have been
known since the 1870s (Olfson, 1987). Lithium produces a
variety of effects which tend to calm or tranquilize manic or
impulsive behavior; in precise chemical interaction with car-
bon dioxide, it has become (as the compound lithium carbonate)
the medication-of-choice in the treatment of manic-depressive
schizophrenia (Feldman & Quenzer, 1984, pp. 395-397). Since
lithium is a natural substance, it is transportable through
natural means, such as wind and rain. Thus, Dawson, Moore
& McGanity (1972) studied the level of lithium in the water
supplies of 200 Texas counties (induced "naturally" through
rainfall, rather than added artificially in the manner of fluori-
dation) in relation to state psychiatric hospital admissions,
suicides, and homicides. They found that the higher the rate of
naturally-transported lithium in the water supply, the lower
the rate of homicide as well as of suicide and psychiatric
hospital admissions; and, in what must surely be interpreted
as an Orwellian proposal, recommended that "any community
should derive prophylactic benefit from lithium ingestion with
respect to . . . homicidal tendencies." That their proposal was
apparently not adopted is likely salutary, for later research has
demonstrated that heavy concentrations of lithium (or what
might be called "overdoses") induce a variety of organically-
based psychiatric disorders (Dubovsky, 1987; Perry, 1987;
Hartman, 1988, pp. 210-211).

❑ *Tryptophan* is an amino acid that affects the metabolism of
brain serontinin, a powerful neurotransmitter and neural reg-
ulator; one current hypothesis on the genesis of disorders of
affect attributes their source to functional deficiencies in the

metabolism of a tryptophan by-product (Martin, Owen & Morisha, 1987). Tryptophan ingestion affects the body's production of dietary niacin; niacin deficiency produces such behavioral sequelae as "malaise, poor concentration, nervousness, irritability, emotional lability, and depression" (Gross, 1987). The substance is found in corn, so that "dietary niacin deficiency is common in areas of the world where corn is a dietary staple." Thus, Mawson & Jacobs (1978) studied the relationship between annual consumption of corn, measured in bushels per capita, and homicide rates across 45 nations of the world; consumption and homicide were found to vary inversely. Kitahara (1986) replicated the Mawson & Jacobs study, with essentially similarly findings of linkages between low levels of tryptophan consumption and high homicide rates when socioeconomic variables were used to equate a sample of 18 nations in Western and Southern Europe. As if to provide a clinical extension, Morand, Young & Ervin (1983) administered oral tryptophan (or a placebo) to a sample of male schizophrenics

---

⇨ Walker Percy: The Thanatos Syndrome

A scenario in which lithium (or a substance very like it) is introduced into the water supply without the knowledge or consent of the citizenry became the nub of the late psychiatrist- novelist Walker Percy's 1987 *The Thanatos Syndrome*, a marvel of irony and comic genius that takes as its theme no less than the conflict between the heavily biological means of mood alteration and behavior control emphasized in the mental health professions today and yesterday's emphasis on the gentle art of "the talking cure."

In Percy's rendition, those responsible are high-level Federal scientists — acting quite beyond their warrants, however. Moreover, though the substance produces the anticipated decrease in aggressive behavior, it also elicits retrogressive tendencies — with macabrely picaresque consequences, including the wholesale sexual molestation of children. Into this morass to save the day and restore the community to its usual, aggressive, but relatively more predictable, self returns Percy's hero — an alcoholic psychiatrist recently released from prison after serving a term for defrauding health insurance companies.

who had been convicted of violent crimes — with the expected tranquilizing results, but without inquiry into the etiology of the violent behavior of which their subjects had been convicted. Even in infra-human studies (Feldman & Quenzer, 1984, p. 249), a metabolite of tryptophan has been linked to intra-species aggression. Until Summer 1990, when its sale came under the control of the Federal Food & Drug Administration, tryptophan was freely available as a dietary substance in health food stores, where it was billed as "nature's tranquilizer."

❑ *Nicotine* has been found to facilitate concentration and memory in human subjects but to interfere with learning; there is some, but not definitive, evidence that it stimulates central nervous system arousal ("readiness to fight"?) states (Feldman & Quenzer, 1984, pp. 146-148). In a short paper that does not essay the neuropsychopharmacology implicated, Lester (1977) found that, among a wide array of variables investigated in a multivariate analysis, per capita cigarette consumption was the most potent predictor of homicide rate among *women* (but not among men) in a sample of 18 industrialized nations.

❑ Schoenthaler (1982, 1983-*a-d*) has rather convincingly demonstrated that aggressive behavior can be reduced among institutionalized juvenile delinquents, including repetitive violent offenders, as a direct result of the simple dietary manipulation of *reducing intake in refined sugar* — primarily by substituting unsweetened orange juice for sugar-laden soda and/or fruit for heavily processed snack foods. If such results occur under confinement or under highly controlled conditions, it may be the case that violent behavior can be *deterred* through dietary manipulation. In a study that examined the obverse hypothesis, Rosen, Booth, Bender, McGrath, Sorrell & Drabman (1988) added small amounts of sugar to the diet of preschool and elementary children, reporting "small increases in the children's activity level" (and decrements in cognitive performance among girls) among experimental subjects in relation to controls fed a sugar substitute. Similarly, Kruesi, Rapoport, Cummings & Berg (1987) reported that "duration of aggression against property" was significantly associated with ingestion of sugar, but not of a sugar substitute, among preschool children.

❑ The clinical literature contains many reports of impulsive rage leading to murder attributable either to freely available over-the-counter substances the sales of which are not regulated *or* to combinations of controlled and uncontrolled substances. Thus, Pope & Katz (1990) recounted three cases examined at Boston's McLean Hospital "who impulsively committed violent crimes, including murder, while taking *anabolic steroids,*" substances then freely available at health food stores as "body-building" dietary supplements much favored by weight lifters. According to the investigators, all had "benign premorbid psychiatric histories, no evidence of antisocial personality disorder, and no history of violence." The Federal Food & Drug Administration began to regulate the sale of steroids in Spring 1991.

□ Similarly, Strauss (1989) reported the case of a man aged 27 who had "used both cocaine and an *over-the-counter cold preparation.* The combination of drugs resulted in a psychosis that led to the homicide of a close friend . . . [the offender] had no psychiatric history and only minor legal difficulties." Such a case presents many interesting legal challenges, particularly in relation to the "pathological intoxication" laws we reviewed in Chapter 2. Moreover, doubtless the psychological state induced by drug interaction constituted a *brief psychotic reaction,* rather than the induction of psychosis itself.

DIFFERENTIALLY CREDIBLE BIOCHEMICAL CONTRIBUTIONS TO CRIMINOGENESIS

Biochemically-determined neuropsychological sequelae follow the use or abuse of psychoactive substances of various sorts. As cataloged in a variety of standard sources on psychopharmacology (Hofmann & Hofmann, 1975; Schatzberg & Cole, 1986; Frances & Franklin, 1988, pp. 313-355), each of the major classes of "abusable" substances possesses specific biochemical properties that produce predictable neuropsychological consequence. These range from euphoria, aggressivity, and overwhelming impulsivity (as in the case of psychotomimetic central nervous system stimulants, such as cocaine and the amphetamines) through disinhibition of customary methods of behavior control (alcohol) to persistent passivity and withdrawal (as in the case of narcoleptic central nervous system sedatives and depressants). Substances with variant biochemical properties may be *differentially criminogenic* in relation to criminal behavior of one sort, but not of other sorts — i.e., the use or abuse of substances with particular biochemical properties which produce predictable, but very particular, neuropsychological effects accelerates or contributes to particular types of criminal activity, but not to other types.

Hence, it is *biochemically credible* to suppose that the use or abuse of *central nervous system stimulants* and perhaps of hallucinogens accelerates *crimes of violence and personal victimization.* Among the property crimes, it seems likely that *burglary* alone might be accelerated by stimulants. Conversely, it is likely that the *central nervous system depressants retard violent behavior* of all sorts. These speculations, however, do not necessarily point to substance use or abuse as the primary *engine* for crime; instead, such use or abuse might more convincingly be regarded as a *lubricant* that potentiates other predisposing factors, both intra-person and extra-psychic. And almost certainly it is the *"profit crimes"* of burglary and robbery that are implicated when the acquisition of abusable substances functions as *motive*.

Alcohol is something of a special case because of the paradoxical effects typically observed at low and at high levels of consumption and early and late in the process of metabolism. At high levels of consumption, alcohol produces the pattern of psychomotor retardation associated with central nervous system depressants. But at low levels of consumption and early in the process of metabolism (during what many experienced drinkers call the "rush" at first ingestion), alcohol produces what is commonly referred to as disinhibition of impulse control accompanied by a sense of exhilaration, a state of affairs conducive to aggressivity and assaultiveness (Frances & Franklin, 1987, pp. 141-143). Biochemically, it thus seems more likely that alcohol will prove criminogenic during the early or "rush" phases of ingestion than after prolonged ingestion. As Levin (1987, p. 19) has described the process:

> The sedative-hypnotics, including alcohol, initially depress the inhibitory synapses of the brain. Since the negation of a negative is a positive, the depression of the inhibitory synapses is excitatory. It is for this reason that alcohol is sometimes misclassified as a stimulant, although it is a depressant. Behaviorally, this disinhibition may manifest itself in high spirits and a devil-may-care attitude which may subjectively be experienced as euphoria. Anxiety is concomitantly reduced . . . Excitatory synapses are soon also depressed, however, and the behavioral and experiential effects of alcohol catch up with its pharmacological effect, which has been depressive all along.

From the pioneering studies of premier criminologist Marvin Wolfgang (1958) onward, a considerable body of research evidence, much of it summarized by Collins (1981), Roizen (1981), and Gottlieb, Gabrielsen & Kramp (1988) has pointed toward a consistent link between alcohol and violent crime, with considerable evidence that a similar link obtains cross-nationally (Lindqvist, 1986); because of ubiquity and ease of access (at least since repeal of the Volstead Act), alcohol is apparently infrequently implicated as motive in profit crimes. After reviewing a number of studies, however, Blum (1981, pp. 115-116) proposed that the criminogenic character of alcohol consumption in relation to criminal violence is modulated by a number of impinging variables — or, in our terms, that alcohol potentiates other variables inclining the behaver toward criminally violent behavior:

> Under no circumstances will alcohol be a sole "cause" of violence. Alcohol may alter perceptions, cognitive performance, moods and emotions, and response capabilities and preferences. Less adaptive solutions, such as violence . . . occur with decrements in judgment. Violence may also be adaptive, or perceived as such . . . . One expects that violence will occur when both preexisting and situational factors stimulate, facilitate, or permit it. Violence in association with alcohol may vary with dosage and, in turn, with pharmacologically specific effects including arousal levels, cognitive deficits, and psychological reactions to such changes (e.g., anxiety).

Hence, in McGlothlin's (1985, pp. 154-155) comprehensive formulation of the biochemically credible linkages between alcohol and substance use and criminogenesis:

> drug use contributes to crime directly by potentiating impulsive and violent behavior . . . Alcohol is the only drug for which there is sufficient statistical data to establish a causal connection: the evidence clearly shows a relationship between acute effects and crimes of both violence and negligence [and] barbiturates have been found to potentiate assaultiveness . . . amphetamines and

---

⇨ *Hypoglycemia, Alcohol, Violence*

An alternate explanation incorporates hypoglycemia (a rapid decrease in blood glucose level) as a modulator in the link between alcohol and violence. As Pernanen (1981, p. 19) puts it: "Hypoglycemia has been [reported] as a factor responsible for violent behavior. Alcohol is known to cause hypoglycemia in individuals who are under-nourished. Since much excessive alcohol use is associated with poor nutritional habits, this condition could be a factor in explaining the association between prolonged alcohol use and violent crime."

According to Berkow & Fletcher (1987, p. 1084), alcohol-induced hypoglycemia results both from nutritional deficiency and impairment in the capacity of the liver to metabolize glucose, with the impairment itself perhaps due to heavy alcohol usage (p. 870). A reasonably large body of research suggests a relationship between hypoglycemia and non-criminal aggression even in the absence of alcohol ingestion (Messer, Morris & Gross, 1990).

cocaine in high doses can produce paranoid reactions resulting in violence . . . Marijuana and the stronger hallucinogens are also capable of producing psychotic reactions, and there are occasional references [in the research literature] to violent behavior during these episodes [but] marijuana typically decreases both expressed and experienced hostility . . . there is growing evidence that the pseudohallucinogen, phencyclidine [i.e., PCP], has a fairly high potential for producing combative and violent behavior . . . Opiates produce a reliable sedating reaction without the increased emotional lability and aggressiveness accompanying alcohol and barbiturate use. Thus, the pharmacological properties of opiates would be expected to decrease rather than potentiate criminal behavior, and this is generally consistent with the available evidence . . . Finally, and perhaps this is the issue of major concern, there is the question of income-generating crime among individuals with expensive drug habits [and] commission of acquisitive crimes during a period of withdrawal.

→ *INFERENCES, SPECULATIONS, CONJECTURES*

Surely, there is more than ample evidence of linkages between the use or abuse of alcohol and other mood-altering substances and crime. Acute effects of some powerful psychotomimetic substances are linked in the clinical literature, indeed, to the *elicitation* of lethal violence by some behavers for whom such violence was out of character and otherwise unpredictable.

A vast array of empirical data suggests a potentiating effect even in cases in which elicitation is not in question. In particular, more than half the convicted offenders confined in state prisons for criminal homicide self-report that they were under the influence *either* of alcohol *or* of drugs *or both* at the time of their lethal offenses.

Given such data, the continuing wide availability of alcohol quite legally (Dull & Giacopassi, 1988) and of controlled dangerous substances despite more than half a century of recurrent "wars on drugs" itself constitutes an element of the social environment that appears to favor violence.

☐ ENVIRONMENTAL CONTINGENCIES AS CONTRIBUTORY VARIABLES

A small but growing body of research has considered the relationship between rates of criminal homicide and weather conditions, lunar phase, and air pollution. Since indicia of effect arise *not* from studies of individual cases, but rather from studies of whole populations, these investigations speak more to the matter of *environmen-*

tal contingencies that favor criminal violence than to particular motives or peculiarities.

❑ Several investigators have considered the relationship between *climatological or weather conditions* and criminal homicide. Thus, Michael & Zumpe (1983-*a*, *b*) studied the role of temperature in relation to murder, rape, assault, and robbery in 16 cities, finding seasonal, temperature-related variations for rate of rape, assault, and robbery but not for murder. Confining their investigation to the summer months and to two cities only, Anderson & Anderson (1984), however, observed a linear progression between temperature increase and violent crime, a finding they interpret as indicative of the relationship between "negative affect and aggression." Deuser, DeNeve, Anderson & Wood (1991) hold that such relationships are modulated by "comfort level," a variable that mediates between ambient temperature and readiness to aggress. The point is made artistically in *Dog Day Afternoon*, a semi-fictional motion picture account of a bank robbery with hostage-taking in the 1960s, in which the motive was the financing of a sex-change operation. In a study of a wide range of variables in relation to rate of criminal homicide in 18 industrialized nations, Lester (1977) reported that the number of thunderstorm-days per year emerged as the second most potent predictor (after per-capita cigarette consumption) in a multivariate equation.

❑ Rotton & Frey (1985) studied *air pollution* as a stimulus determinant of violent crime over a two year period. They found that "high temperatures and low winds preceded violent episodes, which occurred more often on dry than humid days" and concluded that "atmospheric conditions and violent episodes are not only correlated but also appear to be linked in a causal fashion."

❑ Perry & Simpson (1987) examined, in a longitudinal study, relationships between monthly rates of murder, rape, and aggravated assault over a ten-year period in one American city in relation to weather, population, and unemployment. They reported that "environmental variables were found to have significant influence on rape and aggravated assault but less effect on murder. Unemployment rates had negative effects on monthly rates of rape and aggravated assault. Murder and aggravated assault were negatively associated with population expansion." Ellen Cohn (1990) of the Institute for Criminology at Cambridge University chided Perry & Simpson as too cautious, contending that "the literature of the last three decades on weather, seasons, and crime" had indeed established "the relationship between violent crimes, temperature, and precipitation."

⇨ *Interaction between Intra-person, Intra-familial, and Stimulus Determinants in Juvenile Homicide*

In an essentially clinical study, psychologist James Sorrells examined 31 juvenile homicide offenders in one California county over a period of 18 months:

About one-third of the homicides occurred during the commission of a robbery. In about one-fourth of the homicides, the assailant was intoxicated. About two-thirds of the assailants were carrying the weapon used, suggesting that a predisposition to kill or injure may be present without necessary premeditation. Almost all the assailants were males, and half were sixteen or younger. Two thirds had prior correctional involvement; the others had never demonstrated antisocial behavior

In general, this group of juveniles would not be seen as more disturbed than any other delinquent sample . . . A youngster may desire to steal the shiny new car with the keys in the ignition because it will bring him esteem among his peers. His desire to steal the car may be intense or only slight. His judgment concerning the likelihood of getting caught and the consequences of getting caught may be poor or good. *Regardless of his judgment of the situation he may be the sort of person who must have what he wants when he wants it . . .*

If a youngster has little impulse control and his current life is miserable and gives little hope of anything better in the future, he is susceptible to the most fleeting of impulses and seldom stops to exercise judgment . . . Every young person learns or fails to learn impulse control from the combined influence of the peer group, the media, and the family. Many of [these] youngsters had parents who were unable to control their own violence . . . Children undoubtedly learn more from what they observe than from what they are told. These children observed their parents get drunk, assault each other, and, in general, operate from impulse rather than from purposeful direction. They learned from their parents that *to feel is to act* and that *being out of control is the expected state of affairs.* If a child fails to get models of integrity and nonviolence in his home, he is certainly unlikely to get them from the media . . . violence on television is portrayed as both romantic and exciting and the victims die cleanly. One youngster who had stabbed a man to death commented that he didn't expect his victim to writhe and gasp while dying — people don't die like that on TV . . .

Violence is a cheap form of excitement, and excitement is a cheap form of gratification. For these youngsters, the adults in their families and the adults in popular entrainment usually chose violence over long-term gratification. So did they.

• *Source:* James M. Sorrells, Kids who Kill. *Crime & Delinquency,* 1977, 312-320.

❏ Mixed findings have been reported concerning the relationship between *lunar phase* and homicide (Lieber & Sherin, 1972; Pokorny & Jachimczyk, 1974). In a review of the published scientific studies on the relationship between phases of the moon and homicides, suicides, and psychiatric hospital admissions, Campbell & Beets (1978) concluded that "lunar phase is not related to human behavior." But Lieber (1978), in an independent review of the same studies, arguing that "gravity directly influences the human nervous system," concludes that lunar phases are related to "social tension, disharmony, and bizarre behavior" and that, based on data from police authorities, "homicides appear to be directly correlated with the appearance of the full moon." In an early study, Lester (1973) found that age-adjusted homicide rates in the U.S. vary by latitude and longitude; in a later study, Lester (1980) reported a similar variation both for homicide and for suicide.

→ *INFERENCES, SPECULATIONS, CONJECTURES*

The relationships reported earlier between homicide rate and such quasi-environmental contingencies as level of lithium in the water supply or cultural variations in the consumption of corn (and therefore of tryptophan) seem straight forward enough. That between homicide and such variables as weather conditions elicit conjectures easily enough, as W. Somerset Maugham anticipated in *Rain*. Since nicotine is a central nervous system stimulant, the relationship between cigarette consumption and rate of criminal violence may be mediated by level of neural arousal.

But the relationship between violence and gravity or the frequency of thunderstorms is more difficult to decipher. It may be that the nexus is once again neurochemical — that these variables also contribute to the level of neural arousal, yielding to a "readiness to fight" through biological pathways that are presently only imprecisely understood. Thunderstorms, for instance, are believed to release vast quantities of nitrogen into the atmosphere; it is not unreasonable to conjecture that such rapid infusion may well trigger episodes of nitrogen narcosis, "a condition resembling alcohol intoxication" (Berkow & Fletcher, 1987, p. 2380); and, about the relationship between alcohol intoxication and criminal violence, there is little mystery.

☐ *INTERACTION: A TASTE FOR RISK AND THE SELF- SELECTION OF RISKY ENVIRONMENTS*

Thus far, we have concentrated primarily on the psychological components — very nearly at an atomistic level — rather than on the ways in which the elements blend, then congeal as ways of construing situations and possibly ways of behaving before entering the behavioral repertoire of an individual behaver.

We have insisted that criminal behavior in general (and criminal violence in particular) results not from single factors but from

---

⇨ *Dorothy Otnow Lewis — The Biopsychosocial Constellation Underlying Criminal Violence*

In our follow-up study of formerly incarcerated delinquents . . . we found that . . . a constellation of neurological, psychiatric, cognitive, and experiential variables was associated with increasing degrees of adult violence. Subjects with . . . evidence of serious neuropsychiatric impairment and a history of growing up in violent, abusive families tended to become violent criminals.

The biopsychosocial constellation we have described [is comprised of] recurrent aggressive behaviors in the context of neurological impairment, cognitive dysfunction, episodic psychotic symptoms, and abusive family violence . . .

How might these biopsychosocial variables interact to engender violence? First, the effects of central nervous system injury are usually diffuse, affecting the frontal lobes, the limbic system, and, in essence, all parts of the brain concerned with adaptation. These kinds of injuries impair judgment and reality testing and increase impulsivity. The cognitive impairment that is often a consequence of diffuse brain injury diminishes the ability to appreciate the subtle meanings of human interactions, to pick up cues, to plan logically, and to anticipate the consequences of behaviors. Injury to the limbic system may contribute further to the intensity of emotions, including rage. Paranoid misperceptions and misinterpretations, whether caused genetically, psychodynamically, or as a result of brain injury, contribute further to the tendency to lash out in response to real or imagined provocations.

When children with these kinds of neuropsychiatric and cognitive vulnerabilities are raised in violent abusive households, adding, as it were, insult to injury, violent behaviors are generated in the following ways. First, physical abuse itself often injures the brain, thus increasing emotional lability, impairing cognition, and diminishing impulse control. Second, violent irrational parental behaviors engender rage in the helpless child, a rage more often than not displaced onto individuals other than the abusers. Finally, parental violence and abusiveness act as models for behavior.

• *Source:* Dorothy Otnow Lewis, Neuropsychiatric and experiential correlates of violent juvenile delinquency. *Neuropsychology Review,* 1990, 1, 132-133.

interactive sets of variables that inhere both in the psyche of the behaver, in his or her learning and social learning history, and in the characteristics of the environment which either elicit behavior directly or potentiate pre-existing dispositions.

Concentrating on criminal homicide, we have for example observed that, in the prototypical homicide as it is actually committed, most victims and offenders are known to each other and that that prototypical homicide occurs under "tinder box" circumstances in which arguments or disputes erupt into lethal violence, under a powerful set of stimulus determinants that at least potentiate intra-person variables that dispose a behaver toward violence — and that certainly dispose him or her toward self-selecting those psychosocial environments which indeed resemble tinder boxes.

We have also observed that impulsivity as psychometrically inventoried appears to reliably differentiate violent offenders both from non-violent offenders and from non-offenders; that impulsivity is a frequent consequence of even relatively minor neurologic injury; that patterns of violence can be learned intra-familially and inter-generationally and can be reinforced or extinguished by long- distance vicarious learning and conditioning.

But so far we have not essayed to convey the flavor of how these elements blend with, reinforce, and potentiate each other so that the habit of construing criminal violence as desirable, acceptable, tolerable, or "normal" — or perhaps normal in response to certain stimuli in certain psychosocial environments which themselves seem either to evoke, expect, or tolerate violent behavior — enters the behavioral repertoire of an individual actor.

We have reproduced portions both of Sorrells' clinical description of the juvenile homicide offenders he studied, even to the level of their television viewing habits, as a sample of a blend of one kind, and of Lewis' description of the constellation of neurological, cognitive, psychological, and social learning elements associated with criminal violence. Other blends are suggested by considering empirical data concerning *similarities* between victims and offenders in certain types of criminal homicide.

Young Males, the Choreography of the Dare & Character Contests

In contrast to the emphasis Gastil and his successors placed on geographic region, Wolfgang & Ferracutti (1967) identified a "sub-culture of violence" as linked to chronological age. Congruently, Hollinger (1979) identified "fatal violence" (through homicide, suicide, or accident) as the *leading* cause of death among victims from the age of 19-34 in the U.S. Marohn, Locke, Rosenthal & Curtiss (1982) observed a similar, very strong confluence between homicide, suicide, and accidental death among adolescents.

Such propensity toward fatal violence has been interpreted by Wilson & Daly (1985) as indicative of a "young male syndrome," in which "status competition, 'taste for risk,' dare-devilry and gambling" are said to be principal features. Observing that the data from some 700 homicides in Detroit demonstrate that "victim and offender populations were almost identical, with unemployed, un-married young men greatly over-represented," these investigators propose that the "taste for risk" is "primarily a masculine attribute and is socially facilitated by the presence of peers in pursuit of the same goals."

As if to underscore the impact of the normative expectations held by one's peers, both Felson (1982) and Steadman (1982) confirmed that the presence of third parties in a conflict situation tends to potentiate the probability of violence, with that finding corroborated by Henderson & Hewstone (1984); Felson, Ribner & Siegel (1984) found the degree of potentiation particularly powerful among youn-ger combatants. In a joint analysis, Felson & Steadman (1983) indeed identified what they described as a "systematic pattern" in a study of such episodes:

> They began with identity attacks, followed by attempts and fail-ures to influence the antagonists. Threats were made, and finally the verbal conflict ended in physical attack . . . retaliation is a key principle in the escalation of these incidents in that aggressive actions by the victim were associated with aggressive actions by the offender and the likelihood that the victim would be killed.

Following Goffman (1967), Luckenbill (1977) has termed this phenomenon a "character contest," in which *both the prospective victim and the prospective offender stipulate to violence as a means of conflict resolution.* In such circumstances, whether one emerges from the contest as one sort of homicide statistic or another — or, for that matter, whether the contest ends in a charge of aggravated assault short of homicide, or indeed ends without formal criminal charges — may represent no more than the luck of the draw, abetted to be sure by physical agility; or perhaps even, if the contest is held outdoors, by an unexpected thunderstorm.

Conceptually, the notion of the character contest has much in common with what Redl & Wineman (1957) had, in a somewhat different context, termed "the choreography of the dare" and with Farley's (1986) empirically-derived description of the thrill-seeking personality. It is, moreover, quite congruent with the description that Feldman & Quenzer (1984, pp. 248-252) provide of what is termed "intermale aggression" among members of infra-human species, as we saw in Chapter 6 and, of course, quintessentially illustrates the legacy of the ethos of the frontier.

Among literary observers, prison psychologist Robert Lindner's case study *Rebel Without a Cause* (later to become a celebrated motion picture of the mid-1950s) hinges upon precisely such a character contest, to which both participants readily agree and which ends in lethal violence, albeit technically by accident. Similarly, novelist Aldous Huxley proffers in *The Genius and the Goddess* a description of a "game" once popular among young men in this country, in which two contestants drive automobiles at each other, head-on, at high speed; whomsoever first applies the brakes is declared to be "Chicken." Among young men in the 1990s, a new version of that game is played with four-wheel drive trucks with oversized tires spinning in mud flats.

Similar scenes are memorialized cinematically in literally hundreds of Hollywood films and television productions featuring "shoot- outs" between gunmen of the Old West, a depiction of a character contest enacted precisely according to the ethos of the frontier. Indeed, a film such as *High Noon* (derived loosely from Stephen Crane's magnificent short story "The Bride Comes to Yellow

---

⇨ *Tinder Box Circumstances in Non-Homicidal Violence*

Elsewhere, Pallone (1990, pp. 29-67) has identified "tinder box" circumstances in a large proportion of the cases of rape and sexual assault. Some 83% of the cases of rape estimated to have been *committed* in a year (only half of all cases which actually occur are reported to law enforcement authorities) are committed by a lone offender; the remainder are "gang" rapes, of which the press is particularly fond. Of the lone offender cases, 56% are committed by friends, relatives, or acquaintances — and, by and large, in the victim's own home, into which she (or he, especially in the case of homosexual child rape) has quite willingly admitted the offender. Those circumstances seem to portray a set of "tinder box" conditions not unlike those surrounding a majority of the cases of homicide.

Though comparably detailed data of national scope are not readily available, it seems likely that similar "tinder box" conditions attend episodes of *aggravated assault* (i.e., assault involving the use of a weapon) — and, indeed, it may be the case that essentially chance factors preclude these episodes from becoming cases of homicide.

Sky") remains memorable 40 years after its release precisely because it depicts the process through which one member of the dyad in a character contest of long standing refuses to further engage in a recurrently choreographed dare because he has now encumbered himself with the adult social responsibility of marriage; nor is it accidental that the new wife is a mail-order bride from a lawfully ordered city of the East. It is not difficult to see in such a process a graduation from the mores of a violent subculture to embrace those of the larger, less violent society — or perhaps both the very "burn out" in violent behavior empirically identified by Hare, McPherson & Forth (1988) *and* one of the developmental pivots therefor.

Strong empirical validation for the suppositions which undergird the notion of the character contest is found in a study by Fishbain, Fletcher, Aldrich & Davis (1987) which contrasted some 20 subjects who had died while playing Russian roulette with 95 who had committed suicide. The former were distinguished from the latter by a history of drug and alcohol abuse, and the investigators opined that they "were trying to treat their depression through risk taking behavior." Similarly, in a study which compared black women who committed homicide with their victims on a number of social characteristics, McClain (1982) concluded that the two groups "exhibit essentially similar behavior patterns that increase their probability of involvement in homicide," so that who became the victim and who the offender was indeed essentially a matter of the luck of the draw in a specific behavioral interaction. Similar findings were reported by Mann (1990): "Black female homicide offenders . . . kill those closest to them in homicides that are intraracial and intrafamilial."

Those results seem to echo the findings of Jarvinen (1977) in a study in Finland of violent offenders vs. psychiatric patients who had attempted suicide, in which she reported essentially similar personality structures and characteristics between the two, as well as those of Daradkeh (1988) on motives for murder in Jordan. As a matter of course, potentially homicidal disputes arise primarily between persons who share similar social and economic backgrounds. Such findings are, moreover, entirely consistent with results of studies by Stewart & Helmsley (1979, 1984) on risk-taking in prospective criminal behavior situations among convicted offenders. These investigators found that offenders who were more willing to take risks typically also exhibited signs of psychoticism as measured by the Eysenck Personality Inventory and further harbored unrealistic "expectancy of gain" — that is, that risk- takers characteristically misconstrued costs and benefits in a stimulus situation in which criminal behavior was construed as normative.

Emerging as Victim Rather than Offender: The Luck of the Draw?

Support for the hypothesis that the person who emerges from the contest as victim has consented to violence in the resolution of conflict is found in a study by Budd (1982), of the Los Angeles Coroner's office, who reported that toxic levels of alcohol were found at autopsy in the blood samples of 61% of murder *victims*. Similar findings were reported by Abel (1986, 1987) in an investigation of homicide victims in Erie County, New York over a 12-year period. Toxic alcohol levels were found in 45% of these victims, with drugs detected in another 4.2%. Abel (1988) further reported that the victims of homicide by means of stabbing more frequently displayed such toxic levels than did those who had died as a result of gunshot wounds. In a more detailed investigation utilizing the same data set, Welte & Abel (1989) found significant correlates between the victim's blood alcohol level and other variables, so that higher levels were found in young male adults, among victims killed in warmer months,

---

⟹ *Stephen Crane: A Poet's View of the Self-Fulfilling Prophecy*

Tinder box situations peopled by impulsive risk-takers who engage in character contests within social environments that aid, abet, and otherwise approbate and reinforce both impulsivity and risk-taking quintessentially illustrate what has come to be called the *self-fulfilling prophecy.*

As is so frequently the case, the poet has led where the behavioral scientist has followed. Stephen Crane's "Two youth, in apparel that glittered," from *War Is Kind,* his 1897 collection of poetry, is often cited to illustrate the proposition that, as a consequence of how we construe ourselves, each of us writes our own script precisely through such a mutually interactive process of construing what is possible and what is normative and then behaving in accordance with those constructions:

Two youth, in apparel that glittered,
Went to walk in a grim forest.
One was an assassin, the other a victim.
They chanced to meet.
"I," said the assassin, "am an assassin."
"And I," said the victim, "am a victim.
And, believe me, sir, I am enchanted
To die thus, in the best medieval fashion."
Then took he the wound, gladly, and died, smiling.

⇨ *Anti-social, Pro-social, and Adventurous (A-Social)*
Risk-Takers: From the Same Mold?

In a marvelously inventive study, psychologist Michael Levenson (1990) compared and contrasted *anti-social, pro-social* and *adventurous* risk-takers in relation to emotional arousability, conformity, moral reasoning, psychopathy, proclivity to use or abuse of mood-altering substances, and sensation-seeking. His sample of *pro-social risk-takers* consisted of police and fire officers who had been decorated for bravery in the line of duty; his *adventurous risk-takers* consisted of skilled mountain climbers; and his *anti-social risk-takers* were habitual drug offenders.

Levenson found no differences between the three groups on three of the variables he investigated: moral development, empathy, and independence vs. conformity. Indeed, one might well expect heroes to differ from villains on each of these three dimensions; yet such was not the case. But significant differences were found between the groups on each of the ten other variables Levenson studied: substance abuse proclivity, emotionality (impulsivity), depression, psychopathy, disinhibition, susceptibility to boredom, and three measures of sensation-seeking behavior.

Hence, Levenson concluded (pp. 1073, 1079) that the three groups "appear to represent *both* different psychological types and different forms of risk taking . . . different types of risk taking have very different antecedents and consequences . . . [pro-social risk takers] literally risk their lives in the performance of their duties [but] the reasons for pro-social risk taking may be very different from those for risk or sensation-seeking. It is important to distinguish doing harm to others for personal gratification (anti-social behavior) from the antistructural violation of social norms in the service of positive social change."

Levenson's findings complement those of distinguished University of Wisconsin psychologist Frank Farley. In summarizing a decade of research on what he has termed the "thrill-seeking" or *Type-T personality,* using a variety of measures (some patterned after scales from the Eysenck Personality Inventory), Farley (1986, p. 46) has identified four sub-types among thrill-seekers:

❑ *Constructive T (or T +) — Mental,* a group that encompasses "people who seek stimulation mainly in the mental domain, such as artists, scientists, entertainers."

❑ *Constructive T (or T +) — Physical,* a group that includes "people who seek stimulation mainly in the physical domain, such as adventurers physical risk-takers.

❑ *Destructive T (or T -) — Mental,* a group that encompasses "people who seek stimulation mainly in the mental domain, such as criminal masterminds, schemers, and con artists."

❑ *Destructive T (or T -) — Physical,* a group that includes "people who seek stimulation mainly in the physical domain, such as violent delinquents and criminals."

Farley's *Constructive T+ — Physical* group seems to correspond *either or both* to Levenson's prosocial risk-takers (fire and police officers decorated for bravery) *or* his asocial risk-takers (mountain climbers), while both Farley's *Destructive T-* groups are peopled by antisocial risk-takers. Farley's schemata has, however, the additional advantage of categorizing both what he calls the "criminal mastermind" and those who behave in particularly violent and brutal ways.

But the personal testimony of two young men who would be classified as "adventurous" risk-takers under Levenson's model or as *T +* thrill-seekers under Farley's model suggests that the categories may not be *experienced phenomenologically* as quite so distinct as the conceptual schemata suggest.

In New York City, the practice of riding about *on the tops* of subway cars has developed into a sport called "subway surfing." At times, its practitioners are not content merely to ride along (whether in a standing, sitting, or reclining position), but instead engage in a wild array of acrobatic stunts — with the train hurtling through an underground tunnel at 70 miles per hour or on elevated tracks several stories above street level at somewhat slower speeds. Quite clearly, this is a dangerous sport, and many deaths have resulted from its practice.

According either to the Farley or the Levenson schematizations, there should be little correspondence between thrill-seeking behavior in this unusual and risky "sport" and other risk-taking behavior. Not so, according to interviews with two of its practitioners, as reported in the Parkchester Journal (1991) of the *New York Times:*

❏ Elliott Ortiz, at 22 years old, is an old-timer at the dangerous stunt that he and other young people perform on the roofs of trains across the city, particularly along the elevated tracks in the Bronx. It is called "surfing" or "hang on," and the transit authorities say it is the most perilous of the many games that threaten and occasionally kill young people on New York City's subways . . . . *The risk is the lure,* Mr. Ortiz, who is unemployed, said . . . . "I've got to learn not to be afraid of nothing; rats, cockroaches, a gang from one block to the other," he said. "It's like . . . you are escaping from hell."

Another expert subway surfer echoed those sentiments — and conveyed clear and explicit perceptions both of the "character contest" and the "choreography of the dare" implicated in the activity in his description:

❏ Joseph Araujo, a 17-year-old senior at Harry S. Truman High School in the Bronx, said that he and a few friends surf every day . . . "It's mostly like a dare to see who is who, what you can do, he said. "Some people just do it to see how far they can go — how close they can get to death without really dying." He compared [subway] surfing to proving yourself on the street, where being tough and fearless is often more important than safety. "Sometimes it's scary," he said. "That's what the street is all about."

And it may well be the case that, among those whose phenomenological world is constrained by rats, cockroaches, and gangs and punctuated only by the risk of lure, the process of *response generalization* occurs rather more readily than among those affluent enough to mountain-climbing as a preferential sport.

among victims killed at night, among black victims, and among victims killed on weekends.

Some evidence that the "character contest" may not be limited to young males emerges in a review by Hotaling & Sugarman (1986) of a wide array of studies on spouse abuse perpetrated by husbands. Among some 97 variables they assessed, they found that "Only witnessing violence in the wife's family of origin was consistently associated with being victimized by violence," since exposure to such violence as a child and adolescent apparently produces either or both an expectation of and tolerance for such behavior in adulthood — and, to the extent to which the victimized spouse regards spousal violence as "normal," he or she has acquiesced therein. Similarly, Heath, Kruttschnitt & Ward (1986) reported that an interactive effect between exposure to violence by means of television in childhood *plus* victimization in child abuse was succeeded by an expectation of violence as normal in adult life.

In his remarkable study of the characteristics of inmates who aggress against other inmates in contrast to those who become the victims of aggression while incarcerated (i.e., the "violent vs. the victimized" in state prison populations), Wright (1991) found that the "most deviant personality types" (those with the most significant psycho- pathology) found among his subjects (that is, those whose profiles matched those of Groups Charlie and How in the Megargee-Bohn Typology Study, as detailed in DISPLAY 10, Chapter 6) "are clearly *over*-represented among the *victimized.*" Accordingly, Wright concluded (pp. 3, 6) that, in "the exploitive environment found in today's prisons . . . a world in which the prospect and often the reality of violence are facts of everyday life . . . *victims . . . may be aggressors who lose in contests of wills.*"

A Tinder Box Peopled by Risk-Takers

A behavioral situation in which *both* participants agree to violence and in which both lubricate themselves for that violence by means of alcohol or drugs surely sounds like "tinder box" circumstances writ large and peopled by the "risk takers" described by Silver, Yudofsky & Hales (1987), whose propensities for violence were said to inhere in brain dysfunction.

Indeed, a major study conducted at the medical faculty of Semmelweiss University of Budapest produced strongly congruent cross-national evidence not of toxic levels of alcohol or illicit drugs but rather of a neurogenic impairment in the capacity to inhibit violent behavioral responses. Demeter, Tekes, Majorossy & Palkovitz (1988, 1989) conducted postmortem examinations of the brains of homicide victims and of control subjects; they found among homicide victims consistent morphological anomalies in brain structures involved in the metabolism of serotonin, so that the inhibiting effect of that substance was compromised in the brain of the victim. Surely it is not difficult to understand the process by which *both* participants construe violence as normal and normative, with such construing indeed mutually reinforcing. Moreover, to the extent that one participant construes violence as normal and normative, he or she is likely to search out and to self- select those psychosocial environments peopled by like-minded others.

Age-Related Decline in the Taste for Risk

Clarke (1985) and other commentators have opined that such a "taste for risk" likely declines with advancing age. Such an interpretation seems consistent with the findings of Loeber (1982), Ageton (1983), Holland & McGarvey (1984), Blumstein & Cohen (1987), and Hare, McPherson & Forth (1988) on the age-related decline in the emission of violent behavior; with those of Colligan, Osborne, Swenson & Offord (1988) on the age-related decline in psychopathic deviation to emanate from the Mayo Clinic restandardization of the MMPI; and with those of Farley (1986) on thrill-seeking as a function of age.

From an alternate perspective that does not, however, require the inferential invention of an internal trait/state like "taste for risk," it might be argued in respect of homicide that most males who are likely to kill have already done so by age 35 and, in consequence of the high ratio of apprehension and prosecution for homicide (in contrast to that for other felony crimes), are serving prison sentences thereafter; and all those "essentially similar" risk-takers who are likely to become victims are already dead.

→ *INFERENCES, SPECULATIONS, CONJECTURES*

In our initial statement of the process model of criminal behavior, we set forth the propositions both that criminal behavior results from interaction between intra-person and extra-psychic variables and that these sets of variables potentiate each other. But we also suggested that the specific weights attached to each variable and set of variables vary from one "otherwise similar" behaver to another, from one behavioral situation to another, and even within the same behaver from one situation to another.

Nonetheless, consideration of data that address an array of variables provides some flavor of some blends through which variables reinforce and potentiate each other. In particular, the interplay between family dysfunction, substance abuse, negative behavioral modeling in the family, and the reinforcing effect of long-distance vicarious modeling by means of entertainment media is highlighted by Sorrells' analysis of juvenile homicide offenders.

Data from several investigations suggest the interaction between an age-related "taste for risk," the self-selection of environments peopled by like-minded persons, the willingness to agree to violence as a "character contest" to resolve interpersonal disputes, in a devastating portrayal of a set of "tinder box" circumstances in which the question of which of two willing participants emerges as the slayer and which as the slain may be merely the luck of the draw.

☐ SUMMARY

This chapter has focused on extra-psychic variables in criminal homicide, with special emphasis on paradigms for learning through social imitation. We have considered the growing body of evidence for the long-distance vicarious conditioning of criminal behavior, on deterrence as the conditioning of avoidance behavior, and on the deterrent effect of the death penalty. We next considered a variety of stimulus characteristics that may either elicit or potentiate violence (including characteristics that inhere in subcultures), the intergenerational transmission of patterns of violence, the availability of weapons, biochemicals which lubricate violence, and environmental contingencies of several sorts. We essayed portrayals of several interactive "blends" in which neuropsychological, personality, social learning, and stimulus determinants interact so that an individual behaver construes violence as an acceptable, tolerable, or "normal" way to behave and that violence thus enters that individual's behavioral repertoire. On the basis of the evidence we have reviewed, we believe it is reasonable to speculate or conjecture that:

❑ The research evidence from studies in social learning for vicarious conditioning and extinction is incontrovertible. The research evidence for long-distance vicarious conditioning in the sense of elicitation of criminal behavior is rather more fragmentary, but the direction is relatively clear, whether the agency of influence is the behavioral model or the relatively less direct transmission of normative attitudes and values. Similarly, there is evidence that supports the notion of long-distance vicarious deterrence, although the evidence on long-distance deterrence of homicide through the ultimate sanction of capital punishment is mixed; there is, by judgment of a blue-ribbon jury of social scientists empaneled by the National

Academy of Sciences, as much evidence in favor of the effect as in opposition to it. It may be the case that the relative infrequency of the actual carrying out of death sentences even during those periods in which such sentences were rather freely legislatively prescribed clouds the situation in such a way as to preclude dispassionate conclusions. Certainly, there is strong reason to believe, on the basis of evidence from studies of learning and social learning, that a negative sanction that is infrequently actually implemented has little aversive value.

❑ To the extent that there is high correlative incidence of death by one or another violent means in the psychosocial environment, we might expect such a phenomenon to function in such a way as to lead the individual behaver to believe that violence constitutes an acceptable feature of social interaction. To that extent, *we might expect a culture or subculture of violence to potentiate other variables inclining a behaver toward violence.* However, individuals in our society are relatively free to self-select their own sociocultural environments. Hence, we might expect that those persons who are internally disposed toward violence will, with some degree of deliberation, elect to place themselves into sociocultural situations in which violence is an acceptable feature of social interaction. In turn, their presence within such a sociocultural situation serves further to reinforce the normative expectation governing the acceptability of violent behavior.

❑ Whatever the relative contribution of psychosocial, cultural, genetic, and biological factors, there appears to be no dispute as to the *fact* of the transmission of patterns of violence between generations. Further, the interaction between a culture of violence, violent role models in the family, and the *elicitation* of violent behavior seems clear.

❑ The central thrust of the relevant studies veers in the direction of a linkage between the availability of firearms and criminal violence. But the linkage may not be rectilinear. Two competing non-rectilinear propositions suggest themselves: (1) Those who commit homicide, suicide, or aggravated assault short of homicide by means of firearms do so *because* firearms are rather freely and widely available *vs.* (2) Because firearms are more readily available than alternate means, those inclined toward lethal violence are likely to commit (or attempt) such violence by means of firearms rather than search out those alternate means. The second proposition seems to us a sounder conjecture than the first — that is, *it seems likely that the availability of firearms potentiates, rather than elicits, a disposition toward lethal violence.* But, if that proposition approximates the reality, Danto (1971) may well be correct in predicting that, in the *absence* of a readily available firearm, those inclined (whether intrapsychically, by means of social learning, through eliciting stimuli, or through some combination of such variables) toward lethal violence will soon enough either deliberately search out or otherwise happen upon a substitute weapon. Moreover, we would expect those who are disposed toward violence to self-select those environments in which firearms or other weapons would be relatively readily available.

❑ There is more than ample evidence of linkages between the use or abuse of alcohol and other mood-altering substances and crime. Acute effects of some powerful psychotomimetic substances are linked in the clinical literature, indeed, to the *elicitation* of lethal violence by some behavers for whom such violence was out of character and otherwise unpredictable.

❑ A vast array of empirical data suggests a potentiating effect even in cases in which elicitation is not in question. In particular, more than half the convicted offenders confined in state prisons for criminal homicide self-report that they were under the influence *either* of alcohol *or* of drugs *or both* at the time of their lethal offenses. Given such data, the universal availability of alcohol quite legally (whatever a prospective purchaser's age) and the nearly-universal availability of controlled dangerous substances despite more than half a century of recurrent "wars on drugs" itself constitutes an element of the social environment that appears to favor violence.

❑ Fragmentary evidence suggest a linkage between criminal violence and a wide array of environmental contingencies, including weather conditions, gravity, the frequency of thunderstorms. It may be that nexus is neurochemical — that these variables contribute to the level of neural arousal, yielding to a "readiness to fight" through biological pathways that are presently only imprecisely understood.

❑ Consideration of data which address an array of variables provides some flavor of some blends through which variables reinforce and potentiate each other. In particular, the interplay between family dysfunction, substance abuse, negative behavioral modeling in the family, and the reinforcing effect of long- distance vicarious modeling by means of entertainment media is highlighted by analysis of juvenile homicide offenders.

❑ Data from several investigations suggest the interaction between an age-related "taste for risk," the self-selection of environments peopled by like-minded persons, the willingness to agree to violence as a "character contest" to resolve interpersonal disputes, in a devastating portrayal of a set of "tinder box" circumstances in which the question of which of two *willing* participants emerges as the slayer and which as the slain may be merely the luck of the draw.

☐ NOTES & COMMENTARY

☐ 1. *"Advocacy Scholarship" on the Death Penalty*

Pallone (1988) has reviewed both legal and social science developments during the period that evoked the most impassioned of the "advocacy scholarship" studies of the death penalty. Thus, Zimring & Hawkins (1986) declared that they had divined a "stunningly simple" pattern in the social history of those nations which have abolished the death penalty: First, that executions cease, and then laws are changed, so that formal abolition follows informal abolition; second, that public opinion favoring capital punishment changes diametrically soon after formal abolition, since most citizens adhere to the societal norms embodied in formal law.

Yet neither the empirical data nor recent legislative history confirm that Zimring & Hawkins intuit. The Supreme Court seemed to accomplish judicially what we lacked the courage to accomplish legislatively by invalidating the death penalty statutes of the 40 states with such laws on the books in its *Furman v. Georgia* decision of 1972. But that surcease was to endure only four years. The legislatures of some 37 states re-wrote their laws to correct the deficiencies the Court had pointed to in *Furman* (perhaps, as Zimring & Hawkins believe, in response to a Federal judicial challenge to a traditional state legislative right), by and large limiting the death penalty to pre-meditated murder, separating the determination of guilt from the imposition of sentence in independent trial "phases," providing for automatic judicial and sometimes gubernatorial review of death sentences once imposed, and according the accused all manner of counsel and assistance in the preparation of the defense in both the "guilt" and "penalty" phases of trial. With those changes, the Court found (in *Gregg v. Georgia*, 1976) that the newly-revised state statutes *no longer* constituted that "cruel and unusual" punishment against which the Eighth and Fourteenth Amendments protect us. Most recently, the Congress has added large-scale drug distribution (or "king-pinning") to the litany of Federal offenses for which the death penalty can be imposed, with court challenges sure to follow.

In the nearly two decades since *Furman*, the Court has ruled that mandatory death sentences are unconstitutional (*Woodson*, 1976); that death is "grossly disproportionate and excessive" as a penalty for rape (*Coker*, 1977) or for kidnapping which does not result in murder (*Eberheart*, 1977) or when imposed upon accomplices who are not direct participants in a slaying (*Edmund*, 1982); that the accused has a right of access at public expense to mental health expertise in the preparation of his/her defense (*Ake*, 1985); that prosecutors may not peremptorily challenge prospective jurors in a capital case solely on the grounds of race (*Batson*, 1986); and that states may not execute a person who has become insane since conviction (*Ford*, 1986). Those decisions seem to fall distinctly on one side of the Zimring & Hawkins equation.

But the same Court has also ruled that prosecutors may challenge for cause prospective jurors who oppose the death penalty in principle (*Lockhart*, 1983); that a Federal judge need not stay an order to execute in order to permit a condemned prisoner to prepare an appeal to the Federal courts (*Barefoot*, 1983); that a presiding judge may in effect overrule a jury when it imposes a sanction less than death during the "penalty" phase of a capital trial (*Spaziano*, 1983); that the right to counsel earlier enunciated in *Gideon* (1963) does not extend to a right to *competent* or effective counsel (*Strickland*, 1984); that it is not necessary that any but very local standards be applied in review of the "proportionality" of the death sentence against non-capital sentences imposed in the same state for similar crimes under similar circumstances (*Pulley*, 1984); that, although the Federal Food & Drug Administration patently has the authority to determine the safety of drugs used in experiments on human subjects, many of whom are volunteers in the prisons, and on animals, it is justified in declining similar review of the toxins used to execute by lethal injection, since these pose "no threat to public health" (*Clancy*, 1985); and that, while conceding that the death penalty is more often imposed when the victim is white than when the victim is a member of another race, the "mind set" of the community from which jurors are drawn does not in itself deprive an accused of his/her rights (*McClesky*, 1987). Those decisions would seem to fall on the other side of the equation.

In the world beyond the courts, the number of executions has risen steadily year by year, and every public opinion poll since *Furman* to raise the question has revealed strong and sometimes overwhelming support for the death penalty among the electorate. Yet a political figure like New York's Mario Cuomo openly opposes capital punishment, threatens to veto such legislation if enacted, and still virtually walks away with gubernatorial elections. More ominously, some observers point to an increase in what might be regarded as the "extra-judicial" execution of murder suspects killed by police *not* under circumstances of "hot pursuit." Consider the 1985 case of Alex Mengel, accused of murdering both a police officer and a woman IBM executive. Mengel was arrested in Canada while wearing the scalp and hair of his female victim. He was fatally shot "in self defense" when, though manacled, he attempted to disarm one of two state police investigators transporting him from court to a jail facility after arraignment. A grand jury investigation cleared both officers, and state police authorities vowed to "review and upgrade the procedures used when transporting prisoners." The generally liberal press of New York raised no significant cry of police brutality.

From quite a different perspective, the staff of Amnesty International (1987) asserted that, by 1985, the *mean* cost of appeals following imposition of the death sentence stood in excess ooof $1.8 million per case (paid principally from public funds), surely a sum that exceeds the aggregate cost of imprisoning a convicted murderer for 50 years, far beyond the 30 years that is customarily taken to be the equivalent of "life." In contrast, the imposition of a life sentence confers few parallel rights to automatic appeals on this scale, nor does it provoke sustained and polarized public campaigns aimed at the granting of clemency, often, as Zimring & Hawkins observe, at the expense of irrationally romanticizing the convicted murderer and, by implication, denigrating his/her victim. That point is amply if tragically illustrated in the celebrated case of Jack Henry Abbott, convicted of murdering a fellow inmate in Utah State Prison in 1965, who became Norman Mailer's literary "find," briefly the toast of literary New York in the early 1980's, and published first-person accounts in *In the Belly of the Beast* and *My Return*. Without Mailer's romanticizing intervention, it is not probable but absolutely certain that Richard Adam would not have been murdered by Abbott; Adam was a customer in the Greenwich Village restaurant where Abbott worked who was stabbed to death six weeks after Abbott's release on parole over a relatively trivial dispute.

Chapter 8

Criminal Homicide: Extended Clinical Case Illustrations

IN CHAPTER 4, WE OUTLINED THE LIMITATIONS AND CONSTRAINTS EN-demic to clinical case study as a method of *inquiry* in the sciences of behavior. While clinical case study is not a very satisfactory means of uncovering new knowledge, it remains unsurpassed as a means to *illustrate* how the engines of behavior actually operate in real-world terms and in real-world people. Thus, the quintessential way to illustrate the manner in which intra-person and extra-psychic variables intersect (or perhaps even, collide with) each other so as to eventuate in criminal violence is by means of detailed examination of a single case, the parameters of which have been reasonably well documented.

❏ SQUIRE'S STORY

Squire's is such a case; though it is factual in all significant particulars, consistent with Federal guidelines and current ethical canons we here render it as a fictionalized account.

Squire is "state-raised" and no stranger to the insides of prisons. His story involves victimization in incestuous homosexual child abuse, anti-social explosiveness in adolescence, neurological injury, and the murder of one prison inmate by another. Ultimately, it may not be an unusual tale.

The Path to Sexual Victimization

Squire was born to a non-commissioned officer in the U.S. Army and his wife (whom we shall call Kay) during that brief lull between the end of World War II and the beginning of the Korean conflict (we never got around to calling it a war) in 1951. Because his father's unit was dispatched to Korea early in that first of America's Asian adventures, Kay moved herself and her son back to her family's farm in a northeastern state to await the return of her husband.

But neither fate nor the military forces of North Korea, widely regarded as a puppet state of a virulently Maoist People's Republic of China, would have it so. The husband-father was killed in action in the early days of the armed conflict, when his son was barely a year old. In accordance with U.S. military custom, the news of the death was borne in person by another non-commissioned officer, whom we shall call Art.

So far as we know or have been able to determine, Kay and Art had not known each other until that morbid occasion. Thereafter, however, they began to "keep company" — as one did in the 1950s, if not thereafter — and a marriage ensued in due course. The happy bridegroom left the Army after his enlistment terminated, ending some 12 years of service, and repaired to Kay's family's farm; in view of a service-connected injury, Art was entitled to a small monthly pension as a disabled veteran. In the succeeding years, two children were born of the new union.

After a time, as death claimed his in-laws, Art and his bride found themselves the sole owners of the farm property, which by now had become relatively valuable as the cities and the suburbs of the northeast began to expand under the pressure of the "baby boom" of that era.

Because land prices had begun to escalate, Art found that the proceeds from the sale of parcels of property, when combined with his small disability pension, made it unnecessary for him either to hold a job outside the farm or even to work the farm assiduously. Instead, he had both the leisure and the income to indulge a taste for beverage alcohol. He had certainly stumbled upon someone's notion of an approximation to the lifestyle of the country gentleman.

Revelation of Victimization — and Its Aftermath

There the story might have ended (and reasonably idyllically at that) had it not been the case that, at the break of the decade, the child welfare agency in the state in which the family lived launched an early and vigorous campaign to promote awareness of child sexual abuse. Then as now, such campaigns often began with "awareness" sessions in the public schools conducted by social workers from the state's official child welfare agency, who urge their hearers not only to sensitize themselves to unwarranted advances from adults or from older children but to report such episodes and their sequelae to their teachers or other adults in positions of formal authority.

Thus it was that Squire revealed that, for some three years past, his stepfather had treated him as a love object. The response of the school, child welfare, and law enforcement authorities was electric. In short order, Squire was removed from the home to be placed under the guardianship of the child welfare agency, while Art was indicted.

Art was represented by a skillful attorney, who advised him immediately upon release on bail to enter into sustained psychotherapy. He also advised Art to plead guilty, thus obviating a jury trial and reducing the single court proceeding to the imposition of sentence. During that session, the attorney was able to bring forward for the perusal of the sentencing judge Art's relatively distinguished service record and the reports of the treating psychotherapist, with the outcome that Art was given a 10-year suspended sentence and placed on probation, with the strict condition that he continue outpatient psychotherapy.

These events convey some flavor, in real life terms, of the origins of the data on the relative infrequency of intrusive sanction for felonious crime recounted in DISPLAYS 1 and 2 in Chapter 3. There is no evidence, by the way, that Art ever complied with that condition of probation.

The sentence satisfied almost everybody — except the child welfare agency.

There was then, as there is now, in the state in question an ironclad regulation that an offender who has been convicted of child abuse is not to be permitted to share a domicile with his or her victim. Clearly, the agency told Kay, Art would have to leave the family home. Indeed, since the laws governing divorce in that state, then as now, listed conviction of a spouse for a sexual offense as a ground for the immediate dissolution of the marital union, it would not have been untoward to expect Kay to divorce Art.

Removal from the Family: What Is Reinforced?

But Kay was not so minded. Instead, she surrendered custody of her son to the child welfare agency. Because his biological father was deceased and because Art had never formally adopted him, only Kay enjoyed parietal rights over the child. Thus, Squire was removed from the temporary shelter into which he had been placed and put instead into the first of a series of foster homes.

Now we have a pretty picture: Society, through one of its recognized agents (the child welfare agency), operating in conjunction with another of its agents (the schools), urges one of its small citizens to reveal wrongdoing. He does; and for his trouble he is, to borrow the Bard's phrase, untimely ripped from the bosom of his family. He was deposited, as it developed, into totally unfamiliar school and social environments in an inner-city neighborhood. Because Art had been given a 10-year sentence, and because Squire was at that point already 11 years old, the decision to seek foster-care placement meant, in essence, that he would never live with his family again — at least not before he attained adulthood. What a marvelous set of messages concerning our values, our system of justice, and the rights and obligations of our citizens was thereby conveyed.

It was, of course, many decades after these events that we were able to interview Squire — who, incidentally, acquired his nickname in that first inner-city foster home. What he remembers and what he is willing to reveal about what he remembers may be quite different. But, in any event, it certainly seemed to us that, even at a remove of more than a quarter century, there was more than a tinge of regret as he recounted the decision to reveal Art's wrongdoing.

That regret, which the accumulated research evidence indicates is by no means uncommon among victims of incestuous child abuse (Pallone, 1990-*b*, pp. 46-49), appears to pivot largely on lack of awareness of the likely consequences: On one day, life is normal, even comfortable, with the abused child (albeit all unawares) even enjoying the "special" relationship he or she shares with a parent or sibling; on what appears to be only the next day, life is a shambles, the *non*-abusing parent is tearful and even accusatory, and the world appears to have turned upside down.

In such circumstances, especially when siblings also lay the burden for disruption in their lives upon the victim in one variation of the "blame the victim" scenario that has become a popular international pastime (*Ibid.*, pp. 41-44), there is little mystery in the *retrospective* assessment by victims that, if they had it to do over again, they would continue to endure the abuse (and, perhaps, also enjoy the benefits of that "special relationship" with an abusing parent or sibling) rather than undergo the tumult that ensues upon its revelation.

Hostility and Impulsivity Enter the Behavioral Repertoire

The records we have been able to obtain from that era reveal not regret, but rather anger in great abundance. Further, the anger was omni-directional, emitted in explosive and disruptive behavior both in school and in the foster home; the behavior in school was quite in contrast to that observed by his former teachers. Within short order, these first foster parents gave up the ghost and, at their request, the child welfare agency transferred Squire to another placement.

This pattern was to repeat itself over the course of the next several years, with greater and greater vehemence exhibited in the pattern of explosive and disruptive behavior. That behavior became most virulent whenever an adult male — whether teacher, police officer, or Boy Scout Troop Leader — attempted to assert his quite legitimate authority over Squire. We need not long detain ourselves with discussions of stimulus generalization and discrimination to underscore the source of such razor-edge hostility.

There finally came a day in 1967 when Squire came before the same juvenile judge before whom he had appeared many times in the past. Squire was at that point 17 years old, nominally still enrolled in high school, and generally considered uncontrollable by the child welfare agency. Despite an escalating record of juvenile acts, he had not served time in a reformatory — very probably because sentencing judges regarded his background as *explanatory if not exculpatory* of whatever had been his instant delinquent behavior. On this occasion, however, the judge gave Squire a *choice* of the sort popular in an era in which the nation was at war (Viet Nam), universal military conscription was the order of the day, and the possession of a high school diploma was not yet a prerequisite to enlistment. The choice: *Tomorrow, you will either be in the uniform of one of the armed services, or I will sentence you to a maximum term in a juvenile reformatory.*

Acute Neurological Toxicity
Potentiates Criminal Behavior

It was to the Navy that Squire presented himself and, after a series of tests of cognitive ability and vocational aptitude, the Navy accepted his enlistment. Photographs taken then for identification purposes show Squire much as he looks today: tall (6' 4"), thin virtually to the point of emaciation, a narrowing of the eyes that would be interpreted by most people as an unspoken challenge, a positioning of jaw and lips that most would interpret as a smirk rather than a smile.

Not incidentally, it was apparently at this point that Squire first *heard* an adult who told him that he was more intelligent than average; doubtless, that message had been conveyed repeatedly by school officials but ignored. Now, however, intellectual standing had real meaning, for it qualified Squire to undergo training in a specialized Navy school.

We have not been able to obtain access to Squire's scores to that series of examinations given at the time of enlistment. However, we administered the *Hartford-Shipley Institute for Living Scale* (Suinn, 1960; Wiens & Banaka, 1960; Zachary, 1990), a measure of intelligence developed at the Hartford Retreat (the oldest psychiatric hospital in the United States) and derived from the original Wechsler-Bellevue Scales. On this instrument, Squire's intelligence quotient was estimated to be 114, a figure that would place him on the border between the "bright normal" and "superior" groups among adults. We have no particular reason to believe that Squire has become either more or less intellectually able in the years intervening between examination by the Navy and our administration of the Hartford-Shipley.

From among the choices the Navy presented to him, he elected training as a ship-to-shore radio operator. Service records indicate a relatively large number of relatively minor disciplinary infractions, primarily involving insubordination to military superiors, during training; but Squire graduated, only a few weeks late, and was assigned to an aircraft carrier shortly to embark for Southeast Asia.

For the next three years, punctuated by appropriate "rest and relaxation" rotations, Squire served aboard that carrier, whose principal mission was the fueling and refueling of Navy and Marine planes and helicopters with Dioxin, an herbicide better known as Agent Orange which has since become notorious for its acute neurological and physiologic toxicity (Roberts, 1991). Like everyone else aboard the carrier, Squire ingested Agent Orange through respiration and through dermal contact on a daily basis. According to neuropsychologist David Hartman (1988, p. 238) of the University of Illinois Medical Center:

> Over 100 million pounds of this potent herbicide were applied by the United States as a defoliant in Viet Nam. Agent Orange has been linked to a variety of toxic effects, including cloracne, porphyria cutanea tarda, liver disorders and immune system abnormalities... Veterans who had been exposed reported significantly more subjective psychological difficulties both on the MMPI and self-report inventories. Problems reported included depression, anxiety, rage attacks, and irritability.

Squire's account of his time aboard ship suggests a great frequency of hostile encounters with military superiors, including physical confrontations, brawls, fist fights; such a pattern is surely in conformance with the record of his earlier behavior during adolescence — and it is simultaneously consistent with *potentiation* of that earlier pattern as a consequence of acute Dioxin toxicity. Nonetheless, few formal disciplinary actions are recorded in Squire's military records during this period. It may, of course, be the case that Squire's memory has romanticized the past, that he was really mild as a lamb aboard ship; or it may be that, since acute Dioxin toxicity was surely prevalent among the crew, the military had no choice but to overlook episodes of hostile insubordination it might in other times and at other places have prosecuted.

Opting for a Criminal Lifestyle

Among the several friends Squire made while aboard the carrier was a young, devil-may-care pilot whom we shall call Mike, who apparently became a hero to disaffected enlisted men because of his own negative attitudes toward authority. Those attitudes, however, were offset by what were in Squire's account spectacular successes in fearless combat missions. Such fearlessness, according to Squire (and here his account finds some corroboration in published accounts of the war in Viet Nam), was in part attributable to central nervous system stimulants ingested by combatants precisely to enhance their fighting capacity.

We have been able to confirm little about this officer and virtually nothing about his history prior to entering the Navy; but we are nonetheless struck by certain similarities between Squire's description and the portrait of the neurogenic risk-taker drawn by Silver, Yudofsky & Hales (1987), right down to the biochemical lubrication of the disposition to take risks. Here, surely, we have mutual reinforcement in risk-taking behaviors on the part of the pilot, who alternately risks his life in combat and risks his career through little-disguised contempt for his superiors. Nor is there any serious question as to why Squire found Mike an attractive behavioral model.

Mike's tour, and his enlistment, ended about three months before Squire's. The two had already planned to return to the West Coast city which had been Mike's home and there to pursue auto theft as a career. Mike had engaged in such activity on a part-time basis while in high school and college and, after training and experience as a Navy pilot, had perfected a variety of skills required to coax an engine into life in the absence of an ignition key; Mike also averred that he still had many contacts with operators of "chop shops" and dealers in stolen autos and auto parts. Squire had little such experience, but he had amply demonstrated his mechanical aptitude while on tour; moreover, he had become highly skilled in electronic communication devices, and these figured prominently into Mike's planning.

The two partners planned to devote the proceeds from these activities to the pursuit of a luxuriant lifestyle, itself lubricated with plentiful supplies of central nervous system stimulants. That such plans were made while the two were actively Dioxin-toxic is surely congruent with Stoudemire's (1987) description of the "pseudopsychopathic" variety of organic personality disorder. That they were made aboard a military ship in the territorial waters of a foreign nation by American servicemen who had been rendered neurologically toxic as a direct result of their pursuit of their nation's objectives simply boggles the mind.

In the event, the reality proved more satisfying than the planning. Mike and Squire found, within six months or so, that they needed three additional members in their firm; these they recruited from among their former shipmates. In Squire's account, which may romanticize the past, the group was able to acquire up to eight to ten automobiles per day, typically ordered to specification (a maroon Audi, a gold Mark IV, and the like). In the main, the vehicles were "ordered" by "chop shop" operators who planned to cannibalize them for parts, rather than to re-sell the entire unit.

However exaggerated the figure may be, what is certain is that, after three and a half years of successful operation and on an occasion on which Squire's electronic communication network had failed them, Squire, Mike, and their confreres were arrested and charged with 60 counts of auto theft.

Mike was nothing if not meticulous; thus, he had kept extraordinarily accurate records of all his business transactions. Since these were highly congruent with the records of the organizations to which the group had sold the stolen vehicles, there seemed little point in denial. Accordingly, Squire pled guilty, and, in a plea- bargain predicated to some large extent on the fact that he had no prior criminal convictions in any state as an *adult,* he was given a relatively light sentence, of three to five years.

In light of the legislative and administrative regulations governing parole in the state in which he was sentenced, we might have expected Squire to serve only a year, or roughly 33% of the minimum sentence that had been handed down. But that outcome would have required some degree of cooperation of his part, or at least a willingness to hold his impulsive hostility in check; instead, disciplinary infractions and altercations while in prison extended his stay by something over a year beyond his first parole eligibility, with the result that he actually served some 26 months of this sentence.

An Attempt to Diversify Leads to Federal Prison

Upon parole, Squire lost little time in absconding from the jurisdiction of that state and its parole officers. Gathering what valuables he could and exchanging them for drugs and cash, he set off cross-country in a rather vague plan to return to the northeast.

Since he had by now perfected the skills of auto theft, it seemed a simple enough matter to steal a car in one city, drive it some 150 to 200 miles or so, abandon it, steal another, repeat the process — the while, selling whatever of value had been left it the vehicle by its owner (camera, portable radio, briefcase, etc.) for cash as he traveled.

Thus it came to pass that, on a Saturday afternoon during May, Squire found himself in a public park in a small city in a southern state. He was, in point of fact, scouting a likely prospect for transportation — when, miracle of miracles, there came into view an *unattended* armored truck. Never in his wildest dreams had Squire even conceived such a possibility.

Years later, he recounts a jumble of thoughts about Southerners and hick towns and the like when he contemplates stumbling upon that armored truck. Squire recollects that he had the vehicle hot-wired and moving within 90 seconds. Later events demonstrated that the driver and guard were no more than 200 feet away, in a coffee shop, and that one caught a glimpse of Squire sufficient to provide a reasonable description.

Since an armored truck is relatively more identifiable even than a maroon Audi, Squire determined to abandon the vehicle at the earliest opportunity; therefore, he bore south, crossed the boundary between one state and another, and headed directly into the Gulf of Mexico, along the way stuffing his duffel bag with bundles of dollars. In his account, within 45 minutes of first spotting the truck, the vehicle was submerged in the Gulf along with about $500,000 in cash, while he, his duffel bag, and another 200,000 U.S. dollars were hitch-hiking eastward.

We have earlier observed that crime specialization rather than graduation from one sort of offense to another is likely characteristic of the offender who successfully eludes apprehension. Squire had specialized in auto theft and had been successful for a reasonably long period. He should have left armored trucks alone, for he had no notion of the operations of the financial industry, of serial number registration, and the like; nor had he considered that, because of various contingencies like propinquity to the border between one state and another, the armored truck that presented itself as a powerful stimulus determinant might itself be engaged in interstate transportation of bank funds — and that, therefore, its theft might represent a Federal offense, no less than transporting across state lines a stolen vehicle of any sort.

Only 23 days elapsed between the theft and Squire's apprehension by Federal officials. When arrested, he had with him nearly $185,000 of the $200,000 he had taken. The balance had been used to purchase an automobile and clothes and for incidental expenses; every dollar he had spent had become a signpost pointing to his whereabouts.

Once again, Squire entered a guilty plea; but, because he now had a prior adult conviction, his sentence was not so lenient. It was to be served in a Federal penitentiary.

Re-traumatization Potentiates Disposition Toward Violence

It is beyond the scope of this volume to delve in detail into the ethos of prison life. Instead, the reader is referred to the comprehensive work of Toch & Adams (1989) and of Wright (1991). For our purposes, it will suffice to observe that virtually each prison has its rites of initiation.

And, in common with many other institutions and despite the best efforts of prison staff, the Ritual of 'Hood was in full flower when Squire arrived at the penitentiary to which he was assigned. The Ritual of 'Hood is a ceremony in which a new inmate is "robbed of his manhood" through anal rape. In some institutions, as in that in which Squire was incarcerated, those longer-term inmates who have established themselves in leadership positions may cast lots to determine which new inmate constitutes whose legitimate prey.

Thus it was that Samb drew Squire. As the court papers later verified, Samb (apparently, short for "Sambo") was a mid-40s, often-convicted dealer in drugs, weapons, and other contraband. Among those of Squire's fellow inmates we were able to interview, there was general agreement that Samb had established himself within the institution in part because he was able to trade favors and merchandise on the inside for favors and merchandise on the outside, since he maintained active contact with his compatriots still at liberty.

Because of what follows, it is important to observe that, while Samb appeared phenotypically to be an American black, his accent immediately marked him as other than a native American. A native of a Francophone Caribbean island republic, Samb was certainly heterosexual by choice; but, like many in the Caribbean culture, he did not regard sexual relations between men in situations in which women were not available as constituting homosexuality.

There was even some indication among some inmates that we interviewed that Samb indeed had interest in the Ritual of the 'Hood only to the extent that his participation was required in order to maintain his position of authority within the inmate community.

Some three months after he had entered the institution, Squire became the object the Ritual of the 'Hood. The locale was a common shower room on the inmate wing where he, but not Samb, resided. Samb was to be assisted by two other inmates over whom he exerted virtually dictatorial influence. These two held Squire, spread-eagle style, facing a wall while Samb prepared himself for penetration.

It happened, however, that a disturbance elsewhere on the wing brought a contingent of guards to the entrance. The attempt was quickly abandoned — and never repeated. Squire had neither cried out in terror during the attempt, nor did he report it to prison authorities — though, if he had, Samb would doubtless have responded with an ironclad alibi.

Nonetheless, word quickly spread of an attempt that had been foiled and of the fearlessness with which it had been greeted by its intended victim. Other inmates regarded it as the mark of one who fully understood and accepted the rite of initiation for what it was that Squire dealt with the incident stoically.

Word of this episode, combined with a distorted version of his background, stimulated in the inmate community a portrait of Squire as a genuine tough guy; when commingled with tales about his military experiences in Viet Nam, Squire was regarded as an ace jungle fighter who had personally accounted for the demise of thousands of the enemy.

For his part, Squire returned to his work in the prison's electronics workshop and kept his counsel for the next six months. When we question him about his immediate response to this incident or ask him about his feelings during the attack itself, Squire will only tell us: "I knew what I had to do." It seems to us self-evident that Squire had re-lived during the attack the trauma he had experienced years earlier with Art. But even that self-evidence may lie only in our interpretation. What the record shows is that, six months after the attack just described, Samb was found dead in his cell in a very different wing of the prison. He had been strangled with a set of fine, very strong, razor-sharp wires which had sliced skin, flesh, and muscle. On the dead man's chest had been placed a sign that read *Goodbye, Gook*; it was signed "Squire."

Construing Lethal Violence as an Acceptable Behavior

Even some years after our first acquaintance with Squire, we cannot be sure of whether he is being candid with us when he insists that the thought *I know what I have to do* came to him whole and entire during the attempted rape. Squire affirms, and later events surely confirm, that the thought — even upon first thinking —

⇨ Edward Opton: On Brutalization as Normative

In 1968 in the remote village of My Lai in south Viet Nam, William Calley, a junior officer in the U.S. Army, directed and participated in the wholesale massacre of non-combatant women and children. Following a substantial public outcry engendered by press coverage during television's first "live" war, Calley was later court-martialed and convicted — an outcome that considerably troubled many then serving in the military as well as some large segment of U.S. citizens who failed to discriminate between what is the "legitimate" killing of an armed enemy and what is an unjustified atrocity perpetrated on a non-combatant.

In a remarkable analysis entitled "It Never Happened — and Besides, They Deserved It," Edward M. Opton (1971, pp. 52-56), a senior research psychologist at the Wright Institute in Berkeley, reconstructed the psychological forces that had led to the construing of lethal violence as normative, desirable, and/or to be applauded:

❑ The My Lai massacre was only a minor step beyond the standard, official, routine United States policy in Vietnam. This official policy is to obliterate not just whole villages but whole districts and virtually whole provinces. This policy has been eulogized in polished academic prose by [a distinguished] professor of government at Harvard [as an effort to promote] massive migration from countryside to city [so as to undercut] the basic assumptions underlying the Maoist doctrine of [agrarian] rural revolution. This description of the most massive bombing and scorched-earth operation in the history of the world as an "American-sponsored urban revolution" must be one of the most panglossian rationalizations of the murder of civilians since Adolph Eichmann described himself as a coordinator of railroad timetables . . . The genocidal policy is carried out in other ways as well. I have personally accompanied a routine operation in which Cobra helicopters fired twenty-millimeter cannons into the houses of a typical village in territory controlled by the National Liberation Front. They also shot the villagers who ran out of the houses. This action was termed *prepping the area* by the American lieutenant colonel who directed the operation . . . he added by way of reassurance that this treatment was perfectly routine . . . These small- scale war crimes have become so common that our reporters seldom report them; they are no longer news. They have become routine to many of our soldiers [who] have developed the classical psychological methods of justifying what they see happening. They come to think of the Vietnamese not as humans like themselves or even, as the Army indictment for the My Lai massacre put it, as "Oriental human beings," but as something less than human. It is only a small further step to the conclusion that "the only good dink is a dead dink" . . . The furor over the My Lai massacre must have seemed grimly illogical to the troops in the field . . . The best way to kill civilians is with bombs, rockets, artillery shells, and napalm. Those who kill women and children in these ways are called heroes. How is it that to kill women and children at less than 500 paces is an atrocity, but at more than 500 paces an act of heroism?

conveyed that *I must kill Samb*, so that the behavioral *goal* was simultaneously construed and adopted, even though it was some time later that Squire construed the *means* by which to achieve that goal in specific steps.

How it came to be that Squire came to construe the killing of Samb as a *desirable* behavior is perfectly *post*-dictable. We have already observed that Squire's hostility, impulsivity, and explosiveness in late childhood and adolescence emerged in the aftermath of his removal from the family home following revelation of homosexual child abuse. Our psychoanalytic colleagues will comment that the principal dynamic at play was *displacement* of anger and aggression from Art (an inaccessible target) primarily to adult males in positions of authority, who were relatively more accessible as targets.

But it is also worth observing that the very act of removal weakened whatever inclination Squire may have had to embrace pro-social beliefs and values; and that, despite his many appearances in juvenile court, no strongly intrusive sanctions had been imposed on Squire. We should not be surprised to find, then, that the prospect or threat of punishment had little deterrent effect on his behavior, then or later; as we noted in our discussion of the apparent lack of deterrent effect associated with the death penalty, an infrequently- imposed sanction has little effect on behavior. Moreover, intrusive sanction had merely been threatened but not imposed on Art, so that the *expectation of impunity* had been elicited early and was subsequently reinforced by Squire's own experiences in juvenile court. Finally, his single adult conviction for auto theft had resulted in a relatively lenient sentence. If one of the characteristics of the so- called psychopathic personality is an absence of fear of punishment, Squire's case surely illustrates the *social learning* processes that result in such a condition.

But Art was by no means Squire's only behavioral model for the acceptability of violent behavior. He was succeeded, first, by a wide array of foster-siblings in the succession of homes in which Squire was placed and, second, by the heroic figure of Mike.

We have suggested something of the hero worship in which Squire held Mike and of Mike's reputation as an obstreperous but fearless combat pilot. Our psychoanalytic colleagues may see in this hero worship something like a latent homosexual attachment, as to an older brother — and perhaps reminiscent of an attachment to Art, through the process they would label as "identification with the aggressor." We would not be disposed to quarrel overlong, but we would point out that, if there was homosexual content to the attachment, it remained quite latent.

According to Squire, Mike flew a minimum of two combat missions daily in a fighter-bomber; each of those missions presumably resulted in death for the enemy. In light of Squire's message on Samb's body, it is worth observing that, in Viet Nam, the enemy was indeed a citizen of a former French colony that has been Francophone for most of its existence — and that the enemy was routinely referred to as "Gook."

It is also worth observing that, so far as we know, criminal violence had played little part in Mike's life before the war or since. Many journalistic accounts of the Viet Nam war, however, have detailed the extent to which American military leadership fostered the view of the north Viet Namese as an inferior people, expressed in the slogan: "The only good Gook is a dead Gook." There was, in that process, a peculiar twist to familiar themes of racism; for, in this case, it was not racial difference but nationality purely and simply on which the judgment of superiority vs. inferiority was to pivot — that is, since a message that merely portrayed whites as superior to non-whites might have yielded disturbances between the races *within* the American military, it was necessary to transmit a message that combined Americans of different races into a phenomenological *us* perceived as superior to *them*. That certainly is racism in a new key.

Racism of the traditional sort was apparently a problem neither for Mike nor for Squire; two of the three former shipmates they invited to become members of their auto theft "firm" were black Americans themselves.

Whether these two new recruits shared Squire's notions about Gooks is not known. Our psychoanalytic colleagues may be interested to know that Art's military decorations emanated from the campaign in the Pacific during World War II, so that the enemy was the Japanese. To the extent that Squire admits to a negative view of Asians which pre-existed his entrance into the Navy, there may be an element that our colleagues will surely term "identification with the aggressor" that rendered Squire rather fertile ground for racism in a new key.

So: Let us start with that remote anti-Asian seedbed. Blend in the effects of an active anti-Gook campaign undertaken by the American military *as personally filtered* through Squire's relationship with Mike. Flavor with long-standing hostility and impulsivity.

Stir in a disregard of consequence, born of an expectation of impunity itself resting on the observation that intrusive sanctions are rarely applied — whether to Squire or to Art.

Add, finally and just before the cauldron overflows, what may be the ultimate stimulus determinant that is most likely to elicit an extreme response — an attempt by a Francophone Gook to do to Squire by force what Art had done so often in the past by cajolery. That Squire then construes lethal violence as an acceptable, desirable behavior is not surprising; *nor* is it surprising that, for him, the thought seems to spring whole and entire — surely, it had been germinating long enough.

But the conviction *that* Samb must die is quite different from planning *how* he is to die. While Squire is willing enough to discuss with us how he fashioned the garrote he used from parts readily available to him in the prison's electronic workshop (where he repaired a variety of radio and video transmitting devices), he has been no more forthcoming with us about how he traveled from his cell to Samb's in another wing (and back) than he was during the subsequent investigation or at court.

Almost certainly, the subornation of prison staff was involved; and we certainly admire Squire's unwillingness to involve others in criminal charges. Further, in consequence of extensive prison "grapevines," it is difficult for us to believe that other inmates did not know of Squire's plans; but we are unlikely ever to have the answers to these questions. They are important to us only to the extent that they would establish (or disconfirm) that a large segment of the prison community had in fact acquiesced to violence — that is to say, agreed to a "character contest" — as an acceptable way of resolving the long-standing grievance Squire held toward Samb.

Because Squire had in essence confessed to the slaying of Samb in the message he placed on the latter's chest, there was little question of entering any plea but "guilty." During the sentencing process, Squire's attorney (from the Office of the Federal Public Defender) adduced evidence of the widespread knowledge within the prison that Samb had attempted to perpetrate the Ritual of the 'Hood on Squire and of Squire's service during the Viet Nam war, with a small mention of Dioxin exposure. The sentence was 18 years, on a charge reduced to manslaughter, to be served *subsequently* to Squire's then-current sentence for theft of the armored truck.

In our interview years after these events, we asked the attorney why she did not present as an argument the details of Squire's background, his removal from the home, and the like; by then, professional knowledge of the "new" psychiatric disease called "post-traumatic stress disorder" had burgeoned, and it was widely believed to be the case that the re-living of one component of a trauma was likely to re-instill whatever feelings the patient had experienced during the original trauma. Thus, if Squire had experienced rage as a child victimized by Art, it is likely that he experienced rage during the attempt by Samb.

Perhaps good and true, replied the attorney, but still explanatory and not exculpatory; after all, six months had elapsed between the attempt and Samb's killing, and that is a very long time for rage to continue unabated. Moreover, she said, in a prison population the fact of child abuse, however brutal and demeaning, is not in the least unusual — a clinical observation later confirmed empirically by Wright (1991).

Squire's MMPI Profile and the Post-Diction of Violence

During the course of our many contacts with Squire, we became interested in pursuing a clinical "hunch" of our own. Between the time of Samb's murder and our work with Squire, the Megargee-Bohn Typology Study had been published and cross-validated, as detailed in Chapter 6. Though the typology was not yet in use in the facility in which Squire was confined, we wanted to know to which of the Megargee-Bohn offender groups Squire would be assigned on an actuarial basis alone — and whether that assignment comported with his actual offense record.

Accordingly, Squire agreed to complete the MMPI. Both our clinical sorting and computerized actuarial sorting — by means of a technologically sophisticated program called the Weathers Report [*Note* 1] — indicated that the best "fit" occurs between Squire's profile and that of *Group Charlie* in the Megargee- Bohn Typology. Both sets of scores are reported in DISPLAY 11.

A narrative "interpretation" accompanies the Weathers Report exercise in determining best fit between profiles. The narrative merely reports statements that have been found to be empirically associated with membership in the group of best fit; it is clear that the narration deals with what *has been*, and thus quite obviously post-dicts rather than predicts — and does so entirely on an actuarial basis.

For Squire, the computer-generated, actuarially-based narrative reads, in part:

The client is a member of Group Charley with a fit of medium accuracy . . . This is a bitter, hostile, antisocial person who is sensitive to perceived insults and lashes out readily. Acting-out and aggressive behavior is common. This individual has some proclivity for crimes against persons, fraud, and possession of contraband other than drugs. This person is likely to have come from a stressful, deviant, inadequate family of origin. Discipline is likely to have been inadequate, possibly because of lack of contact with the father, and as a result, [persons in this group] tend to be estranged from their family. A paranoid, suspicious resentment haunts life . . . There is an antagonistic, aggressive style that tends to alienate others. There tends to be an extensive criminal history . . . There is usually substantial authority conflict [and] significant emotional difficulties as well as social constric-

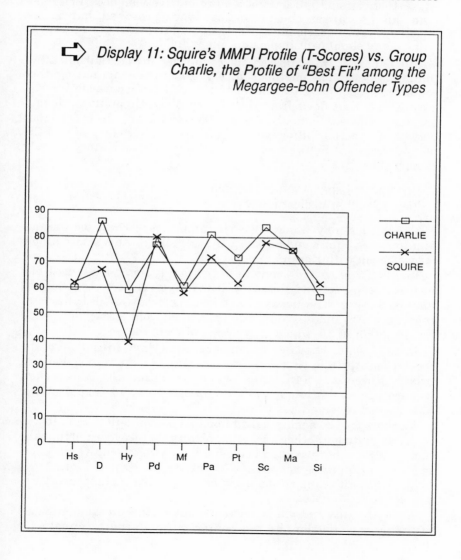

Display 11: Squire's MMPI Profile (T-Scores) vs. Group Charlie, the Profile of "Best Fit" among the Megargee-Bohn Offender Types

tion, poor sociability, [which may] result in difficulty adapting to incarceration. This is a hostile loner who is socially withdrawn and aggressive. There is considerable inner turmoil with high levels of state and trait anxiety, poor adjustment, deviant value system . . . Other people are seen as a potential threats, instead of as avenues for emotional support. Relationships with others tend to be acrimonious and exploitive . . . This individual has not been able to either internalize or live by ordinary cultural values . . . Institutional infractions tend to involve violence. [Prisoners in this group] respond to hostility when provoked, but do not actively seek out trouble . . . Institutional treatment is unlikely to have any significant impact on this individual.

In Chapter 4, we confessed our commitment to actuarial rather than purely clinical methods of assessment, denominating that commitment not merely a matter of personal preference but instead a conviction that flows from rigorous consideration of the relevant evidence (Dawes, Faust & Meehl, 1989). Even so, the congruence between the actuarially-generated description here quoted and the factual record of Squire's psychosocial and offense history is truly remarkable.

Postscript: Expectation of Impunity Yields Another Victim of Incest

The reader may wonder how it came to pass that we became familiar with Squire and his story. In truth, the route was circuitous, for we began with Karen.

In 1963, Squire had been out of the family home for some time; he was a teen-ager and already well on his way to perfecting hostile, impulsive, aggressive behavior as a leading feature of his behavioral repertoire. Art and Kay were still reasonably young; they decided to have another child, whom they named Karen.

In 1977, Squire had been in and out of the Navy, in and out of the West Coast prison, and convicted of manslaughter in a Federal prison; Karen was 14. It was in that year that the state's child welfare agency initiated a new campaign on child sexual abuse. History had repeated itself.

Workers for the agency called upon us to evaluate Karen. It was in delving into her father's criminal history that we learned that she had a half-brother who had been similarly victimized; Karen knew nothing of Squire — not even of his existence; Kay had long since lost contact with him, so she knew nothing of his current incarceration for manslaughter.

Art pled guilty and was convicted — but, on this occasion, because of the prior conviction, he was sentenced to an indeterminate 15-

year sentence, to be served in his state's special prison for repetitive sex offenders. Art believed the sentence harsh and engaged repeated appeals, all of which were denied; his belief was certainly justified on the basis of his earlier experience, which had led him to expect impunity.

With Art's departure for prison, Kay became more and more morose. She intensified those feelings with alcohol. Shortly, she began openly to blame Karen for the loss of Art. For her part, Karen entered a psychiatric hospital some months after Art's incarceration and Kay's embrace of alcohol; there have been seven subsequent admissions.

Neither Art, nor Kay, nor the sentencing judge, nor the probation officer who prepared the recommendation concerning disposition, nor the social worker for the child welfare agency to whom Karen reported her victimization, seem in the least concerned or even curious about Squire — and even less, about a "Gook" who was murdered in his cell in a Federal prison.

A TINDER BOX IGNITES ON CHRISTMAS NIGHT

The account of Samb's demise deviates in many important respects from the statistical parameters of the prototypical homicide as we reviewed them in Chapter 5. Though a character contest had been engaged between Samb and Squire in the Ritual of 'Hood, no tinder box was thereby explosively ignited. Instead, Samb's killing involved careful, cool, and deliberate planning on Squire's part. The case of Ben and Paco more closely illustrates the tinder box conditions that surround a major proportion of homicides, including social learning variables which dictate the taste for risk, the self-selection of risky environments, and the role of mood-altering substances in the lubrication of lethal violence. Moreover, its consequences in criminal justice terms illustrate how, and perhaps why, plea-bargains are struck.

"If My Wife Calls, Tell Her I Ain't Here"

Seaport cities in the northeastern states tend to have long and colorful histories, commencing from the days when they provided hospice to the first colonists. In the succeeding generations, as the first arrivals became the landed gentry, those cities continued — even as their zenith passed and gave way to urban decay — to welcome newcomers.

So it was in the city in which there is located a watering hole that is at least a century old and that has been called, since the end of Prohibition, "If My Wife Calls, Tell Her I Ain't Here." Once a haven for the Germans and the Irish, and later for the Italians and the Portuguese, who labored as stevedores on the city's docks, today its clientele is largely Central American.

As for the city itself, the docks are still there but largely disused, having yielded to new sites capable of accommodating the cranes and overhead railways required for the containerized modes of shipping that have replaced the hand-and-back labor of yesterday. Its once splendid warehouses are still there, some crumbling, others converted to warrens that house dozens of small manufactories that deserve to be called "sweat shops." These are establishments typically operated by bilingual native-born Americans, who make it their business to hire only non-English-speaking new arrivals — preferably, those who have entered the country illegally and who, therefore, have little choice but to accept employment for sub-standard wages and under sub-standard working conditions.

Sweat Shops and Counterfeit Merchandise

The range of products fabricated there is quite wide, with women's handbags and blue jeans at the diametric poles. In the main, these products are frank — and quite illegal — copies of so-called "designer" merchandise replete with intricate symbols and fancy labels meticulously copied from the original, constructed to be sold in the dozens of "indoor flea markets" that dot the eastern seaboard. That the products they manufacture are themselves the result of deliberate criminal fraud represents another source of entrapment for those workers who, in the parlance of the Federal Immigration and Naturalization Service, would be termed "illegal aliens."

It was in a clothing manufactory — a shop that specializes in imitating jeans and similar accoutrements that carry the names and symbols of Calvin Klein, Ralph Lauren, Guess, Members Only — that Paco and his sister Carmelita found employment soon after their arrival from Guatemala (via a circuitous and personally denigrating route to be sure, not unlike that depicted in the film *El Norte*). Lita (as the sister preferred to be called) soon became quite expert in accomplishing the decorative back-pocket stitching that had become the "signature" of each major designer whose designs were being pirated. Because her employer paid on a piecework basis and because she had mastered both speed and accuracy in her task,

Lita was soon earning what seemed, within the frame of reference from which she had sought refuge, an enormous weekly sum.

Paco had no skill whatever in the needle trades, but he had a good eye for the judging of shapes and sizes and displayed what was universally described as "a good head for figures," capitalizing on skills he had perfected in the Jesuit high school he had attended before leaving his home country. He was hired on as a packer in the shipping department; but, within a work environment in which seniority has no meaning and in which advancement is entirely a matter of preferment by one's superordinate in return for God-knows-whatever the superordinate finds valuable in one's performance, his good eye for judging shapes and sizes (so that he seemed, invariably, to know what sort of container was required for each order as if instinctively) and his good head for figures quickly won him advancement. Within a matter of weeks, Paco was second in command within the shipping department.

Romance Enters Paco's Life

During this period, Lita and Paco had shared a furnished room in the sort of "no questions asked" boarding house not uncommon in seaport cities. But Paco became attracted to a co-worker of Lita's named Ramona, who had been employed at their mutual place of work for some years and who had earned a strong reputation as the very epitome of skill, accuracy, and speed in a wide variety of needle trade tasks. Ramona reciprocated; and soon enough, Lita and Paco moved into an apartment Ramona shared with her brother Benavides, known universally as Ben.

To all who knew them during that period, it seemed clear that Ramona, Lita, and Paco were cut from the same cloth; each seemed bright, ambitious, devoted to work, determined to get ahead. Ben seemed clearly the "odd person out." But that had been Ben's role for a very long time.

Ben was only 14 and Ramona 19 when they arrived in the United States. Ramona and their mother immediately sought employment; Ben was to attend school. But Ben, everyone agreed, had always been "a little slow"; school records showed him at that point barely literate in Spanish and quite clearly illiterate in English. What he learned best during the handful of days he attended school over the next two years in the local school district's version of bicultural and/or bilingual education was a healthy taste for *cannabis sativa,* known to him as "sinsemella" and to the rest of us as marijuana.

At this point in his life, even were we to grant strong positive motivation, Ben's daily school experience had become predominantly one of frustration. Biochemically, marijuana represented a perfectly adequate choice to combat that experience. As a central nervous system depressant, the substance will assuredly not remove the source of frustration but will instead blunt its effect substantially, so that the user is said to "mellow out" or even to "chill out" (Seymour & Smith, 1987, pp. 91-95; Hartman, 1988, pp. 224-228). The sources of frustration remain untouched, but the user, in his or her newly "mellow" mood, seems no longer concerned. That is surely a formula for the blunting of ambition, devotion to work, determination to get ahead.

The Role of Odd Man Out

Ben thus fell into a pattern of life quite unlike Ramona's. His lethargy contrasted sharply with her energy and enthusiasm; his lack of interest in gainful employment with her singular devotion to get ahead, to "make something of herself." Nonetheless, after their mother's death, Ramona dutifully took upon herself the responsibility for providing food and shelter for Ben. He limited his own gainful employment to odd and/or temporary jobs sufficient to keep himself reasonably supplied with cannabis, which (in keeping with the custom in his social circle) he sometimes combined with liberal amounts of beverage alcohol. Biochemically, since both are central nervous system depressants, one substance potentiates the effects of the other.

It was into this peculiarly polarized social unit that Lita and Paco moved in early Spring. Structurally, the dwelling consisted of a railroad-style flat on the second floor of a Brownstone building within easy walk of the recycled warehouses where the three wage-earners labored and where Ben occasionally found the odd job. Of the two bedrooms, Ramona and Paco were to share the larger; Lita was to bed down on the couch in the living room; Ben was to retain his small bedroom toward the rear of the house, converted from what had once been a rear-facing sun room.

During the ensuing weeks, Lita was observed frequently in hushed conversation with Ben, and scolded and warned thereof by Ramona and Paco. Later reports indicate that they told her that Ben was "bad news," that she should keep herself away from him; they offered to find her "a real man." But, as every writer of fiction since the dawn of time has known, there is no greater appeal for a woman than the prospect of redemption for a man fallen from grace. Thus, the conversations continued; and, by midsummer, Lita was no longer sleeping in the living room.

Ben Meets "Savage Henry"

For his part, it must be said that Ben had made some efforts at reform. He had taken to looking for work, though not assiduously; finally, he sought Paco's help in finding stable employment. One of the shops in an adjacent building produced pornographic comic books to titillate both heterosexual and homosexual readers; "Savage Henry" was its best-selling series, and the entries therein were regularly translated into several languages for maximum sales potential. Paco had come to know the warehouse supervisor rather well from sessions at the "If My Wife Calls" and through other social contacts; he used his influence to obtain employment for Ben in a position he correctly judged to involve light duties and to require less than full-time attendance.

Autumn passed quietly enough, at least at surface level. Ramona, Lita, and Paco continued to work apace, welcomed the overtime hours that came with the Christmas rush, and silently thanked their God for having led them to the Promised Land. For his part, Ben apparently spent on average about 30 hours per week at his place of employment, though later inspection of payroll records indicated that he was typically compensated for only 20 of those hours; the remainder he apparently spent, to the amusement of not a few of the shop's employees, reading (or otherwise ogling) the Spanish edition of the Savage Henry series.

Drug-Induced Impairment in Sexual Performance

In retrospect, it seems entirely clear that it was Savage Henry's limitless sexual prowess that attracted Ben, rather than the gender preference displayed therein.

For, in truth, Ben had a problem in sexual performance — one which was clearly related to his continuing ingestion of cannabis punctuated by alcohol. In terms of sexual behavior, habitual use either or both of cannabis and alcohol typically yields rapid psychological arousal accompanied by notably decelerated physical arousal; the spirit, veritably, is willing but the flesh is weak — so weak that the sexual partner may be required to devote considerable energy to eliciting and/or maintaining physical arousal. But, since cannabis use also sharply alters one's phenomenological experience of time, the user may report a sublime sexual experience — sometimes even complaining that it ended too abruptly — quite in contradiction to fact in respect both of duration and quality. Neither Ben nor Lita associated impaired sexual performance with cannabis use, however; nor did Ramona and Paco, who heard the overlong sounds of sexual arousing drone on hour after hour on many and many an occasion.

Lita later reported that Paco had often urged her, quietly and in brotherly fashion, to rid herself of the "sissy" with whom she had become involved, who spent so much time reading Savage Henry comics and who couldn't maintain an erection; he offered to find Lita a "real man" from among his widening circle of friends. In Lita's account, confirmed by Ramona, Paco never confronted Ben directly with these accusations until the fatal night. Though Lita remained silent when questioned later, it is highly likely that such abortive and/or prolonged sexual encounters with Ben produced massive sexual frustration within her. In turn, even though she had spurned Paco's direct offers to find a replacement for Ben, it seems quite likely that certain self-doubts were inevitably raised — for example, *Am I able only to attract pot-heads who don't really want to work, who like to read gay porn comics but who can't maintain an erection?* In their turn, such doubts may indeed have influenced her choice of costume on the fatal night.

Those of our colleagues who hew to the psychoanalytic perspective will doubtless see in Paco's behavior some trace elements of incestuous ideation, however well disguised. In our own interviews with Lita and Ramona, it was surely evident that Paco regarded himself as the head of the household; hence, an Oedipal or an Electra interpretation might also be in order. While we regard such speculations as intriguing, they seem to us to require unwarranted levels of inference which move further and further away from the base of empirical data.

Duardo Announces a Party

Christmas fell on a Wednesday that year. In keeping with long-standing custom, the sweat shops closed at 3:00 on Tuesday afternoon. Those among the workforce so minded had the rest of the day to prepare a traditional Christmas Eve repast preparatory to Midnight Mass; those not so minded were enabled to begin their version of partying that much earlier. Within the community, it was accepted that the daylight hours on Christmas Day were to be spent with the members of the family; but the evening hours, for both the traditionally religious and the irreligious, were to be spent at a highly secularized Christmas Party at "If My Wife Calls," presided over by Duardo, who by age and wisdom had long since emerged as the acknowledged leader of the Central American community.

In appearance, Duardo is a striking figure: Obviously a septuagenarian, of medium height, thin, agile, triangular face punctuated by starkly white handle bar moustache atop a black string bow tie, bony hand wrapped around a brass-headed cane — an aging Ricardo Montalban role-cast as a Mediterranean dandy. He has not worked for many years but is said to have substantial means. A confidante of the local pastor and known deferentially to members of the largely Anglo police force at all ranks, he is widely regarded as a man who "knows how to get things done."

For that reason, members of the community bring their problems to him; in his turn, he refers to the appropriate official source for resolution, invariably with success. Members of the community say that Duardo was married long ago but that his wife died in Central America. A number of middle-aged men who bear some physical resemblance to Duardo call him *tio*, but no one in the community is prepared to discuss the matter of illegitimacy. Duardo's "office" is a corner table at "If My Wife Calls." When he announces a party — on Christmas Day, on the Cinco de Mayo, on the Fourth of July — everybody comes.

The Gift of Love and Bouts of Love-Making

Because none of the four were minded toward a religious obser-vance, Ramona, Paco, Lita, and Ben exchanged gifts by mid-after-noon on Christmas Eve. To Lita's specification, Ben had purchased for her a lace blouse adorned with swans; she was ecstatic at the reality. Drinks and good cheer were passed around among the four and, at dusk, the two couples repaired to their respective bedrooms to welcome Christmas with the gift of love.

Ramona was later to say that, several times during the evening and the night, she had heard what she took to be angry voices from the rear bedroom. On several occasions, she had heard Lita go from the bedroom into the dining room; once, when she heard sobbing, she joined Lita, but Lita declined to discuss whatever was troubling her. At the same time, Ramona recalls the aroma of sinsemilla.

So also went the next morning, until around noon. At that point, Ben emerged from the bedroom, announced to the world that he had just had just concluded the best sexual encounter since the begin-ning of recorded human history, opined (according to Ramona) that Lita would be unable to walk for a week, availed himself of the toilet facilities, returned to the bedroom, and fell into a deep and apparent-ly untroubled sleep.

For their part, according to Ramona, she and Paco had mutually achieved orgasm half a dozen times between evening and morning.

Lita Chooses a Costume

Near dusk, Ramona, Lita, and Paco began to dress themselves for Duardo's Christmas Night gala. Ramona chose her best going-out dress and adorned it with a large *mantilla*, to be worn over the shoulders. In accordance with custom, Paco clothed himself in the "full dress" outfit that had become standard in the community: a white shirt of a silken material, tight-fitting black breeches, knee-height black boots, an ensemble highly reminiscent of the Flamenco dancer. Into the sheath provided for it in the right purpose-built black boot, Paco stuffed the final element in this *machismo* costume: a horn-handled, seven-inch switchblade knife.

For her part, Lita dressed in a tight-fitting black skirt under the new blouse Ben had given her; though she wore a low-cut slip, she did not avail herself of a brassiere. All in all, those who saw her that night agree, she was quite an eyeful — and her appearance was quite out of character for the serious, hard-working young woman they had all known for several months.

Ben initially seemed impervious to the trio's efforts to wake him; indeed, at one point (according to Ramona), they were prepared to leave without him. But he finally roused sufficiently to dress — in garb and accouterments identical to Paco's, down to a similar switchblade. Bleary-eyed and apparently somewhat disoriented, he accompanied them to Duardo's party.

Ben Claims His Woman

Ben appears to have remained in this stupefied state until well after the foursome's arrival at "If My Wife Calls." Once there, Ben began nursing a pint of Mexican beer, while the other three table-hopped, danced, and generally joined in the merriment for which they had come.

While Lita was engaged in a particularly spirited and sinuous dance, Ben appears to have awakened fully — and, with the greatest alacrity, moved to claim Lita as his own.

Eyewitness accounts differ, but they can be pieced together in relatively coherent fashion. Ben apparently strode to the small clearing that served as a dance floor. wrenched Lita by the shoulder away from the young man with whom she was dancing, announced to her and the world that she looked like a lady of easy virtue and that she was going home with him on the instant — apparently to face a beating for her behavior.

Paco, who had also been on the dance floor, sought immediately to intervene on his sister's behalf. Again, eyewitness accounts differ, but they agree that no accusations of homosexuality were hurled during this encounter. Apparently, Paco contented himself with statements like *Let my sister alone* and *She's only having fun.*

An Ancient Dance

It was at this point that Duardo intervened, with exhortations to both parties to simmer down, chill out, etc., etc. Duardo produced a number of hand-rolled "cigarettes," urging the would-be combatants to "have some smoke," to which each agreed.

By this time, there was a general mill-in centered about Ben and Paco on the dance floor. Hand-rolled cigarettes were passed from one to the other and back again among several members of the group. Ben later said that he believed he was smoking cannabis; very likely, so did Paco. Subsequent chemical analysis showed they were mistaken.

From a tense and somber mood, the emotional atmosphere seemed to change almost instantly to euphoria and good feeling. From among the crowd on the dance floor, someone shouted "Kiss and make up." An ancient dance, predicated indeed on the "choreography of the dare," was about to commence.

By that time Paco and Ben were standing about a dozen feet away from each other, each enjoying deep draughts of Duardo's cigarettes. In what seemed to be a display of magnanimity, Paco beamed at Ben, opened his arms wide, strode toward him, and — in an ancient gesture recognizable universally in Latin and Mediterranean cultures and interpretable only as an accusation of homosexuality by one male against another — kissed Ben on the mouth.

Ben immediately broke away; the circle widened; hands flew to sheaths; switchblades crackled open. One eyewitness believed she recalls that Paco shouted something like *My sister needs a real man, not a sissy like you — you can't make any woman happy.* Other eyewitnesses recall even stronger words, including the threat of castration. Paco and Ben flew at each other.

When they disengaged, Ben was bleeding profusely from a deep gash in his right upper arm. His own blade had punctured the chest cavity to find the right ventricle of Paco's heart.

The Call to 911

It was Ben himself who called for emergency help by dialing 911. Because the state that is the site of our case is composed of many small municipalities with but few major cities, to achieve economies of scale it is an operator employed by the telephone company who responds to a call to 911, not an employee of a municipal agency that will provide assistance. All incoming and outgoing calls through 911 are automatically tape recorded.

The recording for that night indicates that a male speaking broken English called at 10:17 p.m. to say that there had been a stabbing. The operator asks where; the caller responds with a barely decipherable version of the name of the tavern — *If my wife calls, tell her I ain't here* — but it is clear that the operator believes she has a crank caller on her hands. The operator asks the location again, with the same result; she then inquires of the street address; Ben excuses himself (sort of) from the phone, returns — and gives an incorrect street address. A call (also recorded) is then made by the operator to the police department of an adjacent town, who inform her there is no such address in either municipality.

At 10:31, another call is made to 911; again, it is clearly Ben's voice. This time, the operator insists upon knowing both the address and the name of the town; very quickly, both police and emergency medical vehicles are dispatched.

But thirteen minutes had been lost between the first call for help and the transmission of that call to the appropriate authorities. During that period, partygoers had moved Paco into what they believed to be a more comfortable position and had attempted to staunch the flow of blood with whatever fibrous material of whatever level of sterility came to hand.

We can only guess at whether those minutes were crucial to Paco's life. Paco was taken to a local hospital, where he was pronounced dead, with both the wound and sepsis apparently emanating from efforts to staunch the flow of blood implicated in the cause of death.

Chemical Structure and Behavioral Effects of a "Designer Drug"

Ben was also taken to hospital, in police custody, where he was treated for the wound to his arm. Because it appeared that a transfusion might be necessary, a sample of Ben's blood was taken both for typing and for chemical analysis. As is routinely the case in homicide, a sample of the victim's blood was also taken for analysis.

That the blood samples of both victim and offender contained toxic levels of beverage alcohol was not surprising, nor was the finding of a high level of a metabolite of cannabis in Ben. But quite an unusual substance was found in both victim and offender — aldehyde dehydroxegenase, a metabolite of formaldehyde, a common disinfectant that is sometimes also used as a pesticide. How in the world did trace elements of a substance that is not generally ingested knowingly come to be present in the physical systems of the combatants?

If one is interested in the changing fashions in substance abuse, the era before 1975 can properly be characterized as the time of ascendance of the narcoleptics, when central nervous system depressants were the drugs-of-choice; the decade between 1975-85 can be characterized as the time of ascendance of central nervous system stimulants. Quite clearly, the period since 1985 has become the epoch of the "designer drugs." These are substances constructed from readily, and most typically *legally*, available ingredients that, when combined with the skill required to pass a sophomore-level course in organic chemistry, "mimic" the effect of one or another of controlled dangerous substances, the possession or sale of which constitutes criminal behavior. In terms borrowed from the computer cloning industry, designer drugs are sometimes called "look alikes" or "work alikes" to denote their resemblance in appearance or effect to controlled dangerous substances (Seymour & Smith, 1987, p. 131). Because they are usually considerably less expensive to bring to the point of sale than the substances they mimic, designer drugs have a particularly strong appeal to those abusers with limited financial resources. Thus, one may confidently expect that such designer drugs, replete with the contaminants and impurities that come with back-street manufactories, will be found in abundant supply in lower socioeconomic status communities.

Aided by a psychopharmacologist from a nearby university, investigators for the Office of the Public Defender learned that a designer drug named "Love Boat" had appeared on the scene in a major metropolitan area not far from the seaport that housed "If My Wife Calls." In the regional formulary, "Love Boat" is constructed by obtaining ordinary cigarette tobacco quite legally from a tobacconist and formaldehyde from a hardware store, also quite legally, then soaking the tobacco in the formaldehyde for a period of 24 hours, drying it, and finally rolling the formaldehyde-impregnated substance into a cigarette.

Once ingested by smoking, "Love Boat" produces intense and immediate central nervous system stimulation, akin to the "rush" produced by cocaine, including ideation and/or fantasy that mimic psychosis. While these reactions are extraordinarily intense, they last for a very brief period; these reactions are strongly potentiated when the substance interacts with toxic levels of alcohol *or* of cannabis. Far from aiding in the process of "chilling out," the substance would almost surely ignite a tinder box, particularly following ingestion of alcohol or marijuana. Biochemically, once ingested, the substance follows the route of aldehyde metabolism, so that the usual laboratory assays for controlled dangerous substances would typically *not* detect the residue of "Love Boat."

Analysis of the residue of the half-smoked "cigarettes" passed around immediately prior to the fatal engagement provided confirmation that the substance around which they were constructed was not marijuana, but indeed tobacco which had been soaked in formaldehyde.

When he was questioned about the cigarettes he had supplied on the fatal night, Duardo claimed to be unaware that they were other than the customary marijuana-filled "reefer." He claimed to have won a cache of these cigarettes in a poker game the night before with several of his "nephews" and various of their relatives who were visiting for Christmas. Neither Duardo nor any of his fellow gamblers, however, was willing or able to remember who had ventured these peculiar stakes.

Virtually no one found Duardo's account credible. Instead, police authorities offered private opinions about the "test marketing" of emergent designer drugs. Neither, however, did anyone believe Duardo knew, or could have known, that the designer drug he was test marketing was likely to ignite a tinder box of lethal violence.

The Issue of Pathological Intoxication

Both Ben and Paco had ingested, in the thirty-six hours prior to the homicide, a vast quantity of alcohol; and both had, however knowingly or unknowingly, taken a "hit" of "Love Boat." In addition, Ben had consumed a large quantity of marijuana. The case was certainly arguable that neither Ben nor Paco was in full control of himself when the two struck at each other; and, equally clearly, who emerged as victim and who as offender was virtually a matter of the luck of the draw.

Before the law, however, the question turned more precisely: Was the survivor sufficiently out of control that he should be exculpated — for example, by reason of temporary insanity? Yet, was his lack of control not palpably the result of the *voluntary* ingestion of a combination of mood-altering substances?

The state's legislature had only recently enacted an amendment to the insanity defense which incorporated the exception concerning mood-altering substances proposed by the American Law Institute and endorsed by the American Bar Association which we discussed in Chapter 2 — to the effect that "temporary" states of insanity attributable to the ingestion of drugs the effects of which the defendant had reason to know in advance shall *not* be held to be exculpatory. The legal question then became whether Ben knew, or could have been expected to know, that the substance he and Paco had smoked to "chill out" after their initial confrontation was in fact a highly potent psychotomimetic likely to provoke further violence that was, in fact, virtually a brand-new entry on the drug scene.

Were a jury to respond in the negative to that question, an important precedent would have been lodged against newly enacted "pathological intoxication" legislation. The defense attorney who successfully argued in favor of such a precedent would have thereby ensured his reputation; the prosecutor who argued unsuccessfully would have ensured a reputation of quite another sort. In the event, the prosecutor proved unwilling to risk the precedent.

Aggravating Factors Minus Mitigating Factors = Plea Bargain?

Beyond the question of pathological intoxication lay an array of both aggravating and mitigating factors. From their dynamic calculus emerged a plea bargain.

Among the litany of aggravating factors: That Ben had armed himself with a lethal weapon before leaving home; that the weapon had been concealed; that mere possession of a weapon of that character, whatever its use, itself constituted a felony; that, quite apart from the designer drug, he had voluntarily intoxicated himself by means of alcohol, a perfectly legal substance, and marijuana, an illegal substance. Yet Paco was similarly armed, and many members of the community were prepared to testify that what the police called a weapon was no more than a decoration to a native costume; and Paco, too, had ingested a toxic level of alcohol.

In mitigation: That it was simply not possible to prove who had unsheathed a lethal weapon first, so that it was similarly not possible to argue either way in respect of self-defense; that the victim had in any case provoked violence by the accusation he acted out against the assailant via the kiss; that, by so doing, the victim either solicited or participated in the violence that led to his death; that the assailant had neither arrests nor convictions for felony offenses on his record, though he had twice before been arrested (and released) for possession of small quantities of marijuana; finally, that the assailant himself had twice pleaded for emergency assistance for the victim, nor had he fled the scene of the homicide.

When all was said and done, prosecutor and public defender agreed to a bargain that involved a plea of *guilty* to a charge of *voluntary manslaughter,* a felony that carries a sentence of 12 to 15 years' incarceration. State parole policy requires that 25% of the sentence be served before first parole consideration. Under a program jovially termed the "good time policy," the prison system awards 1.33 days of credit toward parole eligibility for each 1.0 day an inmate *avoids* disciplinary infractions or institutional charges. Under those rubrics, Ben would become eligible for parole after serving 27 months in prison. But some nine months elapsed between Ben's arrest and his appearance at court to enter formally the negotiated plea to the reduced charges; this period is automatically deducted from the minimum number of months of incarceration required before parole consideration. All tolled, then, in return for Paco's life, Ben will serve some 18 months in a penitentiary in addition to the nine months he spent in county jail awaiting trial.

Voluntary manslaughter is the offense with which I might be charged if, after learning that the brakes on my automobile needed expert attention but having willfully declined to have the required repairs accomplished, I ran you down and you died of of your injuries. Any resemblance between that offense and the events of Christmas night at "If My Wife Calls, Tell Her I Ain't Here" is virtually coincidental. Moreover, in view of the substantial discrepancy between the criminal event itself and the offense-of- record, if some future researcher sought to involve Ben as a subject in an empirical investigation, Ben would likely be mis-classified without the most meticulous review of the police account of Paco's death antecedent even to the court record.

☐ SUMMARY

This chapter has presented two extended case illustrations that portray the intersection of intra-person variables with stimulus determinants and environmental contingencies to yield situations in which an individual actor construes lethal violence as an acceptable, or even desirable, behavior. Squire's story depicts stages in the devlopment of a criminal lifestyle by a "state raised" victim of child sexual abuse, the intergenerational transmission of patterns of violence, the role of social conditioning and vicarious reinforcement, and the effects of acute neurologic toxicity in yielding a homicide. The case of Ben represents a classic character context and the choreography of the date, lubricated by the ingestion of a psychotomimetic mood-altering substance.

◻ NOTES & COMMENTARY

◻ 1. *The Weathers Report*

Several technologically sophisticated programs are now available to administer, score, and interpret the MMPI by computer (Butcher, Keller & Bacon, 1985). Some programs merely replace clerical work in providing scores for the various scales, but others offer interpretive summaries as well. The latter programs, as Fowler (1985) put it, attempt to "simulate the expert test interpreter." In his review of available programs, Fowler (1985) assessed his own system, developed at the University of Alabama in the early 1960s, along with others developed at the Mayo Clinic, at the University of Minnesota, at the University of Kentucky, and those developed for more or less commercial purposes.

The *Weathers Report* program was developed by Dr. Lawrence Weathers, 227 West 24th Avenue, Spokane, Washington, 99210. As of this writing, it is usable only with the original MMPI, not with the revised MMPI-2. Indeed, despite an avalance of commerical promotion that has confessed the willingness of its publishers to sacrifice an enormous body of research on the MMPI, "there is little evidence that the MMPI-2 will replace the original MMPI and its extensive empirical foundation anytime soon" (Bartol, 1991, p. 127).

The *Weathers Reports* program both (1) yields scores on the MMPI's three validity and ten primary clinical scales, on some 132 secondary or derivative scales, and on 20 "forensic scales" derived from the massive typology study of Federal prisoners by Megargee & Bohn (1979) and from Megargee & Carbonell's (1985) validation studies of correctional scales developed by other researchers; and (2) provides an "interpretive summary" of current mental health or illness patterns on the basis of comparison of subject's scores on all scales in relation to norms developed in 1983 at the Mayo Clinic (Colligan *et al.*, 1989), along with proposed diagnoses from the current American Psychiatric Association lexicon and indications of probable receptivity to psychotherapeutic and psychopharmacologic treatment of various sorts. Along with other programs of its type, the *Weathers Reports* variation proceeds along the lines of "best fit" in relating presumably clinically relevant statements to configural codetype profiles.

Chapter 9

Larceny: Statistical and Psychological Perspectives

OF ALL THE FELONY CRIMES CONTAINED IN THE USUAL LITANY OF INDEX offenses, we have observed that criminal homicide is the least-frequently committed (DISPLAY 1, Chapter 3) but most frequently studied (DISPLAY 5, Chapter 4). In contrast, larceny is the most frequently committed but one of the least frequently studied. For those who derive pleasure from such indices: For every homicide *reported* in a year, nearly 350 episodes of larceny are reported. However, though they intimate that 100% of the acts of homicide are reported or otherwise uncovered, Federal agencies estimate that only 27% of the acts of larceny actually committed are reported to law enforcement authorities in a year (Flanagan & Jamieson, 1988, p. 215; Bureau of Justice Statistics, 1986, p. 9), so that the ratio between the episodes of larceny and homicide *committed* may be more nearly on the order of 1400:1.

That larceny is one of the least-studied crimes is likely congruent with our societal assessment that those crimes that involve violence and personal victimization — homicide, rape, assault, armed robbery — deserve the major share of our attention, whatever their relative frequency. But that relative infrequency in scientific attention also reflects a widespread perception-*cum*- attitude that larceny is thievery, pure and simple, unadorned and unromantic, not spiced by the charm of the confidence trickster, the titillation of threatened violence that accompanies armed robbery, or even the aerial artist agility of cat burglary; it is not the stuff of high drama, but instead seems prosaic, ordinary, humdrum.

In addition to a sharply reduced frequency, there is a considerably greater breadth in the behavioral science studies focused on larceny. While the bulk of studies concerned with homicide center on variables within the offender, those focused on larceny much more frequently consider issues like stimulus determinants, deterrence, and fairly precise preventive measures.

☐ THE LEGAL REFERENT: LARCENY IN ITS MYRIAD FORMS

The Federal Bureau of Investigation's *Uniform Crime Reporting Handbook* (1984, pp. 1-5) extracts the following definition from the criminal codes of the several states and the Federal Congress:

> *Larceny — theft* (except motor vehicle theft): The unlawful taking, carrying, leading, or riding away of property from the possession or constructive possession of another. Examples are thefts of bicycles or automobile accessories, shoplifting, pocket-picking, or the stealing of any property or article which is *not* taken by force and violence or by fraud. Attempted larcenies are included. Embezzlement, "con" games, forgery, worthless checks, etc., are excluded.

☐ STATISTICAL PERSPECTIVES: LARCENY AS IT IS COMMITTED

In DISPLAYS 12, 13, and 14, we have assembled data from the *Sourcebook of Criminal Justice Statistics* (Maguire & Flanagan, 1991) on the crime of larceny as it is committed. In contrast to comparable data on criminal homicide, these data reveal much more about the circumstances of the offense than they do about either the offender or the victim. Thus:

☐ Larceny is our most frequent crime, accounting for 55% of all episodes of felonious crime reported to law enforcement agencies in a year.

☐ But victimizations studies conducted by the Bureau of Justice Statistics indicate that larceny tends to be significantly *under*-reported and that three times as many episodes may be committed as are reported (DISPLAY 12).

☐ The most frequent reason cited by victims who did not report the offense was that an attempt at larceny failed or that the object of larceny was returned, so that restitution was made. Only 10% of these victims believed that law enforcement authorities would decline or otherwise fail to pursue a formal report of the occurrence of a crime. That is in some sharp contrast to the 18% of victims of *rape* who endorsed the same reasons for not reporting that offense (Flanagan & Jamieson, 1988, p. 219). The *rate* of under-reporting might be construed as a powerful stimulus determinant which facilitates the be-

☞ **Display 12: Larceny As It Is Committed — Frequency of Committing and of Reporting**

LARCENY IS OUR MOST FREQUENT CRIME: Larceny Accounts for 55% of All Episodes of Felonious Crime Reported to Law Enforcement Agencies, Although It Is Estimated That Nearly Three Times As Many Episodes Are Committed As Are Reported

⇓ *Estimated Number of Episodes Committed Annually* 22,241,980
- ❏ Episodes reported to law enforcement agencies 7,872,400
- ❏ Proportion of committed cases reported to law enforcement agencies 35.30%
- ❏ Proportion of reported cases "cleared by arrest" 20.2%
- ❏ Proportion of committed cases "cleared by arrest" 0.6%
- ❏ Proportion of arrested cases prosecuted 90.0%
- ❏ Proportion of committed cases prosecuted 0.8%
- ❏ Proportion of prosecuted cases convicted 69.0%
- ❏ Proportion of committed cases convicted 0.6%
- ❏ Proportion of convicted cases incarcerated 37.0%
- ❏ Proportion of committed cases incarcerated 0.2%

VICTIMIZATION STUDIES INDICATE THAT 73% OF THE EPISODES COMMITTED ARE NOT REPORTED: Respondents Cite a Variety of Reasons for Not Reporting to Law Enforcement Authorities, With Recovery the Most Prevalent

⇓ *Reasons cited by respondents in national victimizations studies for not reporting . . .*
- ❏ Object recovered, offender unsuccessful 26.8%
- ❏ "Not important enough" 2.0%
- ❏ "A private or personal matter" 2.8%
- ❏ Reported episode to someone else, not law enforcement authorities 17.1%
- ❏ Not aware that a crime had occurred until later 5.8%
- ❏ Unable to recover property — no identifying marks 8.5%
- ❏ Lack of proof 10.7%
- ❏ "Police would not want to be bothered" 7.9%
- ❏ "Police would be inefficient, ineffective, insensitive" 2.6%
- ❏ Fear of reprisal 0.3%
- ❏ Reporting would be too inconvenient or time consuming 3.9%
- ❏ All other reasons cited 11.6%

• *Sources:* Maguire & Flanagan (1991, pp. 251-259, 353-355); Bureau of the Census (1989, pp. 169-173); Flanagan & Jamieson (1988, pp. 215, 218-219, 315, 325).

havior of theft; the *reasons* for not reporting point toward a pathway toward extra-legal exculpation of offenders.

❏ Once an episode of larceny is reported, there is only a 20% probability that an arrest will be made. Though the ratios that follow for prosecution, conviction, and incarceration after an arrest has been made suggest a due diligence in the application of sanction, quite a different picture emerges (one that reminds us of the "successive funnels" depicted in DISPLAY 3, Chapter 3) if we consider those apprehended, prosecuted, and convicted as a proportion of the number of episodes estimated to be committed in a year.

❏ From that perspective, conviction follows the commission of larceny in only 0.60% of the cases and incarceration follows in only 0.20%. In whole numbers, the ratio between larcenies committed and prison sentences imposed for larceny is 500:1. That, surely, represents an infrequently-imposed sanction unlikely to deter behavior. Moreover, with so small a proportion of committed offenses followed by prison sentences, we encounter a severe problem in regard to the generalizability of whatever results emerge of psychological studies of convicted larceny offenders.

❏ Larceny appears to be demographically anchored in the nation's metropolitan areas (DISPLAY 13). These regions account for 77% of our population but for 86% of the episodes of larceny reported.

❏ Economic loss from *reported* cases of larceny aggregates to some $2,800,000,000 annually. When the figure for mean dollar loss per reported case is applied to *estimated* cases, the figure aggregates to more than $10,000,000,000.

❏ Some 38% of all known cases involve thefts *from* motor vehicles (e.g., of merchandise carried in an unlocked trunk) or *of* motor vehicle accessories (e.g., hub caps, wheel rims, radios).

❏ Data concerning the age, sex, and race of "victims" are not available; nor, since the victim is often a corporate entity, would they be likely to be meaningful.

❏ However, data concerning the age and sex of persons *arrested for* larceny (DISPLAY 14) indicate that, of the approximately 1,150,000 annual arrestees, 29% are juveniles aged 17 and under and 30% are women or girls. Whether arrestees adequately represent those who commit the crime of larceny — or, instead, reflect only those who are (as we suggested in Chapter 4) incompetent at eluding detection — constitutes a matter for conjecture.

❏ Among state prisoners confined for larceny (DISPLAY 14), alcohol and/or drug use or abuse is extensive. Their self-reports indicate that nearly 55% were actively "under the influence" of

⇨ *Display 13: Larceny As It Is Committed — The Statistical Perspective on Reported Cases*

LARCENY IS PREDOMINANTLY AN URBAN CRIME: 86% of All Reported Episodes Are Reported to Law Enforcement Agencies in the Nation's 282 Standard Metropolitan Statistical Areas (SMSAs) Which Account for 77% of the U.S. Population

⇩ *Location of Law Enforcement Agency to Which Reported*
- ❑ Standard Metropolitan Statistical Area   *86.0%*
- ❑ Other Cities + Rural Areas   *14.0%*

ECONOMIC LOSS THROUGH LARCENY VARIES BY METHOD: Economic Loss Attributable to Reported Cases Tops $2,800,000,000 Annually *and,* at the Same Rate of Loss, May Aggregate to More than $10,000,000,000 for Known and Estimated Cases Combined — 38% of All Reported Cases Involve Thefts from Motor Vehicles or of Motor Vehicle Accessories

⇩ *The Method/Location*

	% of Cases	*$ Loss*
❑ Pick-pocketing	1	*248*
❑ Shoplifting	15	*86*
❑ Purse-snatching	1	*208*
❑ From motor vehicles	21	*428*
❑ Of motor vehicle accessories	17	*282*
❑ From buildings	15	*648*
❑ From/of coin machines	1	*129*
❑ All other methods/locations	22	*606*
❑ All methods/locations combined	100	*400*

ALCOHOL AND/OR DRUG USE/ABUSE IS EXTENSIVE AMONG IMPRISONED LARCENY OFFENDERS: According to Their Self-Reports, 55% of State Prisoners Confined for Larceny Were Actively under the Influence of Drugs and/or Acohol at the Time of Their Offense

- ❑ Under the influence of alcohol only   *15.7%*
- ❑ Under the influence of drugs only   *23.6%*
- ❑ Under the influence of both alcohol and drugs   *15.5%*
- ❑ Under the influence of either or both alcohol and/or drugs   *54.8%*

• *Sources:* Flanagan & Jamieson (1988), pp. 215, 315, 319, 325, 344-348, 392, 395, 412, 413, 494-496, 497; Bureau of the Census (1989), pp. 27, 169.

either or both alcohol or drugs at the time of the offense for which they were apprehended and prosecuted. It seems more reasonable to conjecture that "being under the influence" is more credible as a causative factor linked to detection and apprehension than that it constitutes a driving force for the crime itself.

❏ Particularly since it may be the case that only one in 500 who commit larceny are imprisoned, whether so high a proportion characterizes those offenders who are *not* apprehended, prosecuted, or incarcerated must remain a matter of the sheerest speculation. To the extent that competence in eluding apprehension would seem to be negatively associated with intoxication, the proposition seems unlikely.

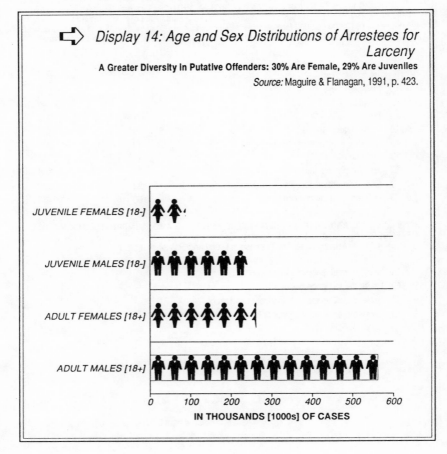

➩ *Display 14: Age and Sex Distributions of Arrestees for Larceny*

A Greater Diversity In Putative Offenders: 30% Are Female, 29% Are Juveniles

Source: Maguire & Flanagan, 1991, p. 423.

JUVENILE FEMALES [18-]

JUVENILE MALES [18-]

ADULT FEMALES [18+]

ADULT MALES [18+]

0   100   200   300   400   500   600

IN THOUSANDS [1000s] OF CASES

☐ PSYCHOLOGICAL PERSPECTIVES ON THE OFFENSE AND THE OFFENDER

Psychological studies of larceny cover an array of topics, from clinical concentration on intra-psychic variables to relatively extensive treatment of stimulus determinants and methods of deterrence.

Clinical Studies

Several reports have essayed to detail the dynamics underlying larceny on the basis of clinical data obtained from patients in treatment, some of whom were referred specifically for therapy for larceny and some of whom committed larceny during the course of treatment for other mental disorders. Given the radical discrepancy between the number of episodes committed, the number reported, and the number of offenders convicted, the matter of the generalizability of data extracted from clinical treatment arises with a great vengeance — for, in addition to the criminal justice filters operative in the successive funnels between commission of a crime and the sanctioning of a criminal behavior, other filters operate to bring what is undoubtedly a very small and highly selective group of larceny offenders into contact with mental health clinicians.

A small-scale study by Norton, Crisp & Bhat (1985) illustrates the issues clearly. These investigators analyzed the motives for theft among a sub-sample of psychiatric patients who were under treatment for *anorexia nervosa,* a psychosomatic ailment in which the principal features are "a disturbed sense of body image and morbid fear of obesity, manifested by abnormal patterns of handling food, self-induced marked weight loss, and amenorrhea in women" (Berkow & Fletcher, 1987, p. 2124). In a population of 102 anorexic patients, evidence of theft was confirmed in the case records of only 13. These authors claim that theft is triggered by the level of pre-morbid sexual activity in these patients — and are not in the least bashful about generalizing from this very small, highly filtered sample to that doubtless very large group of people who commit the most frequently reported felonious crime.

Similarly, British psychiatrist Jeremy Coid (1984) reported a case study in which a woman of 54 "alleviated feelings of profound depression and anxiety by shoplifting." Since the feelings the patient sought to alleviate were associated with withdrawal from diazepam (in this country, better known under its trade name as Valium), a tranquilizing agent available by prescription which she had taken for a period of 25 years, and since Coid came to conclude that "the motive for the subject's behavior was to relieve withdrawal symp-

⇨ *On Kleptomania and Compulsion*

In contrast to most other criminal behaviors (with the notable exception of child sexual abuse, but not other types of sexual crimes), *kleptomania* is identified in the American Psychiatric Association's *Diagnostic and Statistical Manual of Emotional Disorders* as a mental illness in its own right. To follow the logic for the inclusion of this behavior in the roster of mental disorders, it would seem to be the case that the APA regards other criminal behaviors to be *neither* mental disorders in their own right *nor* the result of other, independent mental disorders. That surely strikes a responsive chord.

The *DSM* defines kleptomania as "the recurrent failure to resist impulses to steal objects not needed for personal use or [for] their monetary value," accompanied by "pleasure or relief at the time of committing the theft" and in a situation in which "the stealing is not committed to express anger or vengeance." That definition itself seems to covey the pivotal perception that renders kleptomania a mental disorder — i.e., that the behavior of theft is senseless and purposeless and therefore quite irrational.

According to the current edition of *DSM* (at p. 323), "because shoplifting is more common among females, kleptomania is probably more common in females than in males," even though "fewer than 5% of arrested shoplifters give a history that is consistent" with a diagnosis of kleptomania.

Within such a context, even so acute a psychiatric observer as Julio Arboleda-Florez (1977) classified a sample of Ottawa arrestees for shoplifting into three diagnostic categories, each distinguished by identifiable psychological abnormality — a procedure that argues, in effect, that theft results from psychopathology. Simillarly, a team of Harvard psychiatrists undertook a clinical study of a sample of kleptomaniacs to determine the prevalence of *compulsive disorders* therein — or, in the stilted language research psychiatrists use when they remember they are physicians as well as social scientists, the "comorbidity" of kleptomania and compulsive disorders (McElroy, Pope, Hudson, Keck & White, 1991). They also reasoned that, if kleptomania is indeed a form of compulsive disorder, it should be susceptible to treatment by pharmacological agents used to treat compulsions effectively.

After a sample selection procedure that would barely stand muster at the sophomore level, the investigators wound up with 20 subjects: "Patients with apparent kleptomania were recruited by asking clinicians at our hospital to refer to us all inpatients and outpatients with possible kleptomania." In the final sample thus recruited, 60% were women. The sampling procedure stands virtually as a model of the deficits of clinical case study methodology, about which we spoke with vigor in Chapter 4.

Various data about these subjects were collected by questionnaire and interview. Curiously, only one of the 20 subjects indicated that he (or she) had simply discarded the item or items stolen; the other 19 told researchers that they had used or given away the items they stole. A strict constructionist might quibble that only that solitary subject who *behaviorally demonstrated* that his (or her) theft was genuinely purposeless meets the appropriately stringent *DSM* criteria for a diagnosis of kleptomania. For that single subject, not quite incidentally, treatment with lithium led to cessation in kleptomaniac stealing for a period of 11 months.

For the other 19 (some of whom claimed to have stolen as often as 120 times a month), results were not so positive. A regimen of treatment involving both verbal psychotherapy and psychoactive medication produced *no* diminution in kleptomaniac behavior in 12 of the 19 (63%). For the remaining seven subjects, remission in the symptomatic behavior ranged from periods of three to 15 months.

Formal diagnostic procedures categorized seven of the 20 subjects with signs or symptoms of obsessive-compulsive disorder (35%), a weak basis for regarding one as a sub-species of the other. But 13 of the 20 were diagnosed as suffering mood disorders (65%). That high proportion might lead some to rush to judgment — were it not the case that these subjects were "recruited" from among the active case rosters in a distinguished psychiatric hospital, where one would expect rather a high baseline for mental disturbances of all kinds. And thus the investigators conclude: "The most striking finding of this study was that all patients demonstrated substantial psychopathology in addition to kleptomania — most notably major mood disorder (in particular, bipolar [i.e., manic-depressive] disorder)."

Slightly variant conclusions were reached, however, by their Harvard colleague Marcus Goldman (1991) in a review of the published research on kleptomania over roughly a 30-year period. Goldman (p. 994) concluded that "individuals with kleptomania appear to suffer from many abuses — in childhood, marriage, and relationships. This may give us some clues as to the origins of the *compulsive, addictive* symptoms."

One can only speculate what the results of the investigation by McElroy *et al.* might have been if, say, the researchers had forsaken their laboratories in suburban Belmont for the precinct house in Roxbury and there "recruited" as their sample 20 sequential arrestees for shoplifting. They might have found substantial "comorbidity" between theft and wrenching poverty *or* uncontrollable substance abuse *or* any one of a number of other, equally devastating *social* disorders. And the behavior called shoplifting might not have seemed so senseless, purposeless, and irrational an act.

toms through the excitement of stealing," a happy ending was found
by resumption of the regimen of medication.

In what is perhaps a quintessential illustration of the long-standing romance between clinical case study methodology and the habit
of over-generalization, Ornstein, Gropper & Bogner (1983) report on
the psychoanalytic treatment of *four* patients referred after their
arrest on charges of shoplifting. With pontifical abandon, these
investigators declare (p. 311);

> The precipitating experience was either some form of narcissistic
> injury or an actual or threatened loss of self-object . . . childhood
> humiliations had to be endured passively. Shoplifting represented
> an active mastery of these childhood experiences. Turning passive
> into active is a mental mechanism frequently employed to ward
> off the threat of fragmentation that may follow narcissistic injury.
> Thus, shoplifting is often accompanied by a sense of triumph and
> entitlement, and it may be used as an emergency psychological
> measure to establish a sense of cohesion in a fragmentation-prone
> self.

In DISPLAY 12, we have seen that the activity of shoplifting
accounts for 15% of the more than 7,250,000 episodes of larceny
reported annually, or for a total of approximately 1,100,000 crimes,
and aggregates to an economic loss on the order of $95 million. Not
only is the offense ubiquitous; apparently so are the offenders. In a
survey of some 1200 high school students, Klemke (1982) found that
63% self-reported that they had committed one or more episodes of
shoplifting.

"Fragmentation-prone selves" who in adulthood remain fixated
on narcissistic injuries they suffered during childhood humiliations
sound to us as if they would prove relatively incompetent *either* at
shoplifting *or* at eluding apprehension thereafter. Try as we might,
we cannot convince ourselves that crimes of such frequency result
from the efforts of such persons to transform "childhood humiliations that had to be endured passively" into an active "sense of
triumph and entitlement." But that is not at all to say that such
dynamics indeed describe the overwhelming proportion of shoplifters competent enough in the operation of the criminal justice system
to escape apprehension and avoid prosecution.

→ *INFERENCES, SPECULATIONS, CONJECTURES*

The paucity of clinical studies, and most particularly their limited
generalizability, render even attempts to draw conjectures based
thereupon inappropriate.

Psychometric Studies

Psychometric investigations typically report on substantially larger samples of subjects selected randomly or in other ways so as to reflect populations accurately and thus obviate problems of generalizability. But, like clinical studies, psychometric studies of larceny offenders are meager in number. Thus:

❑ Eysenck, Rust & Eysenck (1977) found substantially less evidence of psychopathology, as measured by the Eysenck Personality Inventory, among prisoners convicted of fraud than among those convicted of crimes of violence *or* than among prisoners whose prior criminal histories revealed a pattern of shuttling between crimes of violence and property crimes. Similar findings were reported by Henderson (1983) in studies of scores and profiles on the Minnesota Multiphasic Personality Inventory which differentiated violent from nonviolent offenders.

❑ Ray, Solomon, Doncaster & Mellina (1983) administered the MMPI to a sample of first-offender shoplifters in Texas. *Relative to themselves,* subjects' highest scores were on the *Pd* and *Sc* scales. But the *absolute* levels of these elevations did *not* meet or exceed the threshold of clinical significance on these (or on any other) scales. Thus, it is to be concluded that subjects in this sample were free of psychometrically-inventoriable psychopathology.

❑ Similarly, Cupchik & Atcheson (1983) studied a sample of what might be called "rapid onset" shoplifters who had never (or seldom) stolen previously. These investigators found that 67% of the women in their sample and 50% of the men had scores on the MMPI *Pd* scale above the threshold of clinical significance, with no other score at that level. They also concluded, on the basis of clinical data, that nearly 100% of their subjects had experienced at least moderate situational depression *preceding* the shoplifting episode. Thus, for a large portion of this sample, it might be concluded that *both* a habitual disregard of social mores, as reflected in psychometrically-inventoriable psychopathic deviation, *and* a precipitating stressor were required to trigger criminal behavior. The conjecture concerning the role of stress as a precipitating factor finds support in a study by Bradford & Balmaceda (1983) which compared shoplifters with psychiatric patients and with subjects referred for forensic psychiatric examinations for other offenses.

❑ Moore (1984) conducted a large-scale study of shoplifters referred by the court. Subjects ranged in age from 16 to 73; 68% reported that they shoplifted on a weekly basis or more often; among adults, 57% were women. Personality disorders rather than psychoneuroses or psychoses represented the modal psychiatric diagnoses. Financial benefit was the motive for criminal behavior cited most frequently (by 68% of the sample). Although Moore found that the incidence of psychological stress to be high among women shoplifters, he concluded that *"Most shoplifting is premeditated, purposeful, habitual, and conscious, goal-directed behavior."*

❑ In another investigation, Moore (1983) found "little evidence that pathology or maladjustment were significant contributing factors" to criminal behavior among a sample of fulltime college students who had been convicted of shoplifting; moreover, he found "no meaningful personality differences on the California Psychological Inventory between . . . shoplifters [and] a sample of undergraduates who denied ever shoplifting." Hence, Moore concluded, "these subjects are not delinquent [or] criminal personalities [or] psychopaths . . . They stole for a variety of reasons, including the acquisition of personally attractive goods while saving money for other purposes."

❑ Such results are congruent with the findings of Holzman (1982) in a study of nearly 30,000 adult males who had been convicted and incarcerated at least twice for robbery, burglary, or both. Holzman reported that 78% of these subjects had been employed full-time in *non-criminal occupations* at the time of their arrest for the instant conviction, so that he concluded that "it seems reasonable to view the present subjects' *involvement in property crime as secondary employment of an entrepreneurial kind"* and characterized "the serious habitual property offender as a moonlighter," in much the same way as any law-abiding citizen with a part-time, income-producing occupation might be categorized.

One is hard-pressed to conclude from these studies that larceny is driven by murky intra-person variables; instead, following Moore and Holzman, it seems more reasonable to believe that larceny as a criminal behavior is governed primarily by economic variables and perpetrated largely by non-pathological, reasonably intelligent, and well-organized people competent enough to avoid detection, apprehension, and conviction.

→ *INFERENCES, SPECULATIONS, CONJECTURES*

The relatively meager psychometric studies of larceny offenders permit few broad-gauged inferences. Nonetheless, in the absence of psychometric evidence to the contrary and in light of statistical data concerning the ubiquity of the offense and the infrequency of apprehension, it seems reasonable to believe that the Ray *et al.* (1983) results may indeed apply to that vast cadre of larceny offenders competent enough to elude apprehension and to hold, with Moore (1983), that larceny is an offense characterized by premeditated, purposeful, conscious, goal-directed behavior. Moreover, precisely because of the relative infrequency of apprehension and conviction, we must presume that the majority of larceny offenses are committed by persons skilled in evading detection for criminal behavior.

Social Learning Variables

Investigations which have considered social learning variables in larceny and its aftermath can be categorized into studies of pro-social beliefs and attitudes, the expectation of impunity, and extra-legal exculpation, including what might be construed as a "just deserts" attitude toward those persons or organizations which are the victims of economic loss. Because the prevention of such loss constitutes a major issue for corporations which operate large factories, warehouses, and retail establishments, a significant portion of this body of research has been conducted by psychologists who specialize in personnel and industrial applications and are likely to identify themselves with management consulting functions rather than with the study of criminal behavior.

PRO-SOCIAL BELIEFS AND ATTITUDES

Larceny includes theft from business establishments by employees. Considerable research attention has been devoted to methods of identifying attitudes toward theft on the part of *prospective* employees as a means of reducing what is typically called "inventory shrinkage." Though these studies have usually been sharply focused and conducted by psychologists whose primary concern lies in organizational and personnel psychology rather than in criminal behavior, they are in essence studies of the internalization and operation of pro-social beliefs and attitudes. Hence:

❑ Hawkins (1984) investigated the extent of theft *by* restaurant employees *from* the establishment itself, from customers, and from co-workers. Remarkably, 77% of a relatively sizable sample indicated that they had discussed *methods* of theft with co-workers, and 60% has discussed with their co-workers "which patrons deserved to be stolen from."

❑ Terris & Jones (1982) determined that, in the opinion of clerks and managers of "convenience" stores, the most common techniques for theft among employees was removal of cash from registers. The investigators also reported a high correlation between scores on sections of a psychometric instrument called the *Personnel Selection Inventory* were correlated with theft on the job. Pre-hiring use of the instrument over a 19-month period in a convenience chain with 30 stores was more effective in deterring "inventory shrinkage" than the use of a pre-employment polygraph ("lie detector") procedure, a practice since

---

⇨ Trustworthiness Tests in Employment Screening: A Statement from APA

Quite clearly, the ability to identify those candidates for employment who are likely to steal merchandise from their employers — or, for that matter, conspire with others to under- charge for merchandise purchased by their cohorts — would represent a considerable boon for commercial establishments of various sorts. Accordingly, many efforts have been launched to create and validate measures of "trustworthiness" that can be utilized as employment screening devices.

But the judicial and legislative context for employment screening has changed markedly over the past quarter-century. It is a fair assessment to say that, through roughly the mid-1960s, a *laissez-faire* attitude prevailed in personnel testing — virtually in the literal sense of "anything goes." Employers, abetted by psychologists or psychometrically-trained personnel administrators, were fond of utilizing batteries of instruments, some of which had no conceivable relationship to the character of the work to be performed.

As a result of massive social changes in the wake of the Federal Civil Rights Act of 1964, and including several key decisions of the U.S. Supreme Court (most notably, *Griggs v. Duke Power Co.,* adjudicated in 1974) that led the Federal Equal Opportunity Commission to formulate a set of administrative regulations that have the force of law, that picture is today much changed. No longer, for example, can an arbitrary height requirement be activated to deny otherwise qualified applicants appointment to a police force — a practice that once severely, and artificially, limited the number of Hispanic law enforcement officers. Instead, employment decisions must be based on criteria that have been *demonstrated* to be relevant to job performance to a reasonable degree of scientific certainty. When applied to psychological tests, that stricture means that an instrument utilized in personnel selection must demonstrate a level of *predictive validity* that is scientifically acceptable and that, further, is predictive with respect to the *specific* job for which a vacancy exists.

That is, indeed, quite a heavy, and an unusual, burden for a psychological instrument, as our earlier discussion about the prediction of violence has demonstrated.

With particular focus on employee theft, in order to demonstrate true *pre*dictive validity for a trustworthiness instrument, it would be necessary to employ — and thus to give the *opportunity to behave criminally* — *both* to applicants whose pre-employment scores were indicative of the "readiness" to steal and those whose pre-employment scores were quite otherwise. Needless to say, such a procedure can rarely be practicably followed.

After reviewing both the instruments available from commercial publishers which claim to predict trustworthiness among employees and the research base on which they rest, the American Psychological Association released in Summer 1991 *A Report on Questionnaires Used in the Pre-employment Selection Decision* produced by a blue-ribbon Task Force on Prediction of Dishonesty and Theft in Employment Settings with a membership of measurement, industrial, personnel, and social psychologists, including the eminent Lee Sechrest.

Though critical that most instruments fail to "provide a clear and detailed account of the development of each measure and a summary of the evidence for its reliability and validity," the Task Force found in general "adequate levels of validity for these tests" and concluded that "honesty tests, when used appropriately and in conjunction with additional selection procedures, have demonstrated useful levels of validity as selection procedures."

To that extent, and despite the fact that most such instruments have been validated *post*-dictively rather than *pre*-dictively, the use of trustworthiness instruments in employee selection appears to have earned the APA's stamp of approval.

Whether the use of such instruments — which, in essence, would deny employment to an applicant on the basis of an inferred "predisposition" and perhaps even in the absence of any evidence of past wrongdoing — will survive legal challenge is quite another matter. Indeed, on the heels of release of the APA Report, legislation was introduced in New York State that would ban the use of such trustworthiness tests altogether.

Though the dimensions may be less dramatic, at base the crux of the issue mirrors Monahan's (1981) dilemma in the prediction of violence — viz., the prospective employee's right not to be denied employment because he/she is identified as a false positive on a post-dictively validated trustworthiness test *and* the prospective employer's right not to be the victim of theft or chicanery perpetrated by a false negative.

precluded by Federal law — and further did not unfairly disadvantage minority applicants. Similarly, Jones & Terris (1983) inquired whether attitudes toward and beliefs about theft, as measured by the Personnel Selection Inventory administered to employees in "do it yourself" home improvement centers prior to hiring, correlated with future theft. Results indicated significant relationships both with loss by theft and with general employee productivity as assessed by managers.

❏ Brown & Pardue (1985) screened some 700 newly hired employees of a chain of retail drug stores on the Personnel Selection Inventory. Over a three-year period, there ensued both a significant increase in the proportion of employees who "passed" a polygraph examination annually administered to employees *and* a decrease in "shrinkage losses" of some $1,000,000.

❏ Though less dramatic, similar results were reported by McDaniel & Jones (1986) in their meta-analysis of the validity of scales for the prediction of theft on an instrument titled the *Employee Attitude Inventory,* with the added benefit that coefficients of predictive validity were found to be relatively invariant across organizations and occupations.

❏ In a strictly psychometric (rather than behavioral) study, Kochkin (1987) compared results of Cattell's *16 Personality Factor Questionnaire* with those of a personnel selection instrument called the *Reid Report* designed to predict proneness to theft among a large group of job applicants. Those applicants who scored positively (i.e., were categorized as *not* theft-prone) on the Reid instrument were found on the 16PF "to have high ego strength and to be less anxious, more apt to behave in socially desirable ways, less driven by id impulses, and less inhibited" than those who were categorized as theft-prone.

❏ In a study of an array of variables related to the decision *not* to purchase goods known to be stolen, Sheley & Bailey (1985) found that only "moral belief" about whether such a purchase was proper or not predicted such a decision with accuracy. Hence, these investigators concluded, only "moral belief... has practical policy implications to [reduce] theft as a market-oriented offence that can be influenced by changes in consumers' willingness to make black-market purchases."

❏ Similarly, George (1991) reported that what she termed "positive mood at work," essentially localized to the work environment and the employing body, was more potent in "role- prescribed pro-social behavior" than a more generalized set of pro-social attitudes not specifically tied to the work setting.

EXTRA-LEGAL EXCULPATION

There is some evidence that we are far from single-minded concerning what sanction should follow adjudication for larceny — or even whether larceny should be prosecuted as a crime.

The data we reviewed on the rate of under-reporting and the reasons for not reporting (DISPLAY 12) suggest that *restitution* rather than *retribution* is the principal goal to which many of us subscribe. In that respect, we appear to be much like members of the Ila tribe in Zambia in their response to cattle theft. According to Cutshall & McCold (1982), Zambian victims rarely report these episodes to law enforcement authorities but instead are disposed to seek restitution; they are not particularly interested in whether the perpetrators are formally sanctioned. Moreover, given the incredibly small ratio between sentences for larceny and the number of episodes actually committed annually, a strong preference for restitution seems not in the least irrational. Since the probability of recovery of the stolen object is quite low, the very act of formal reporting may represent what Stenross (1984) called a"negative rite of cleansing" that benefits the victim emotionally more than an crucial step in detection and apprehension.

⇨ *Pre-Employment Screening via Polygraph*

McCauley & Forman (1988), Raskin (1989), Rogers (1986, pp. 197-200), and Patrick & Iacono (1991) discuss the reliability and validity of polygraph measurement, a form of integrated biofeedback, with particular emphasis on admissibility of polygraph evidence in court proceedings, along with legal regulations in many states concerning the qualifications of those admissible in trial proceedings as "polygraph experts."

Quite apart from these issues, however, is the rectitude of the use of such evidence to determine *suitability for employment.* The Employee Polygraph Protection Act adopted by the Federal Congress in 1988 prohibits the use of lie detector tests for pre-employment screening *except* in the case of "certain prospective employees of security service firms (armored car, alarm, and guard) and of pharmaceutical manufacturers, distributors, and dispensers" (Employment Standards Administration, 1988). Doubtless, the guarantees against unreasonable search and seizure as well as the due process guarantees contained in the Fourth, Fifth, and Fourteenth Amendments to the U.S. Constitution strongly influenced legislative intent.

Our unsettled views apparently begin early and extend even into the ranks of those formally charged with the enforcement of the law. Thus:

- [ ] Dodson & Evans (1985) studied the incidence of theft by class-mates from school premises among subjects in the fourth, eighth, and tenth grades, inquiring as well into the penalties their respondents believed should be assigned. While their results suggest that in-school theft by classmates is a wide-spread problem, there emerged little in the way of consensus about the sort of penalty that should be meted out.

- [ ] Certainly, the same theme underscores the results of a study by Feuerverger & Shearing (1982) on variables related to the decision to prosecute for shoplifting on the part of a sample of store detectives. In general, the characteristics of the *offender* rather than of the offense were found to be potent contributors to the decision to prosecute.

Of course, every decision *not* to prosecute both constitutes an extra-legal act of exculpation of criminal behavior and either engenders or reinforces an expectation of impunity. At quite a different level of discourse, we might wonder whether we have already begun to construe larceny as merely *mala prohibita* rather than as *mala in se;* such a conjecture is surely consistent with a preference for retribution *rather than* formal sanction. If that conjecture is accu-rate, can we expect serious efforts to decriminalize larceny — or at least such larceny as is directed at objects of theft under a certain dollar value — with restitution and fine replacing currently pre-scribed sanctions?

THE EXPECTATION OF IMPUNITY

Hollinger & Clark (1983) surveyed nearly 10,000 employees of industrial firms concerning their own involvement in theft of prop-erty from their employers or co-workers in relation to their percep-tions of the probability of severity of the organizational sanctions likely to be applied. They found that the most effective deterrent to theft was a *combined* perception of a *high certainty of detection* (so that there could be no reasonable expectation that one's behavior would escape surveillance) and an expectation that a *severe penalty* would be exacted (so that there could be no reasonable expectation of impunity). But these twin perceptions were *negatively* correlated with age, so that the investigators concluded that "younger employ-ees are not as deterrable as their older peers." One might speculate about whether that conclusion represents an outcropping of the age-related decline in anti-social behavior *or* whether societal norms have in fact changed so that the experiential base of older workers includes a relatively greater assurance that misdeeds would be punished while that of younger workers includes a relatively greater assurance of impunity for misdeeds — *or* whether it is simply a situation in which experience has proved an excellent teacher.

In an investigation that underscored the relative punitiveness of *stigmatization* vs. formal sanction like probation or prison, Grasmick & Scott (1982) informed their subjects of the minimum and maximum sanctions for three types of theft behavior. Then they asked their sample of adults whether they had, in fact, committed certain criminal acts in the past and whether they intended to do so in the future. Some 25% revealed that they had evaded payment of taxes in the past, and 31% predicted they would do so again; 23% had committed grand theft, but only 8% predicted they would do so again; and 53% had committed petty theft, but only 17% planned to do so again. These subjects apparently felt that no stigma attaches

---

⇨ *Opportunity + Expectation of Impunity as Process Variables in Tax Evasion*

In a remarkable study conducted by the American Bar Foundation, Stalans, Kinsey & Smith (1991) examined the prospective effects of varied means to dissuade tax evasion among subjects whose "income sources provide an opportunity to avoid official detection," as is the case in those occupations (e.g., taxi driver, shopkeeper, even some professions) in which cash rather than other forms of currency is typically exchanged.

In a sample of more than 1000, these investigators found that communication with co-workers actually *accelerated* subjects' expectation of impunity, minimized their perception of the fairness of tax laws, and weakened personal or internal disposition to comply with the laws. Alternately, however, communications from family members were found to reinforce perceptions of fairness and personal disposition toward compliance. There is ample demonstration in this study of the role of the opportunity to behave without direct observation or deterrence, the impact of both positive and negative social learning, and the interaction between and among these variables and intra-person characteristics in yielding pro-social *vs.* anti-social behavior.

to conviction for tax evasion, while a palpable stigma attaches to grand theft. Certainly, one can conceive sanctions in which stigmatization is the principal mechanism — public labeling, for example, through publication of an offender's biography in the local newspaper — and which may serve to deter far more effectively than other, infrequently imposed, sanctions. In a later investigation, Grasmick Bursik & Kinsey (1991) reported that shame and embarrassment function as more potent deterrents than fear of formal legal sanction (in this case, a fine) to dissuade adults from littering the streets.

Moreover, there is some evidence that both offenders and some observers not only exculpate offenders but *decriminalize* the act itself when economic loss from larceny is to be borne by large corporations rather than individuals (Fedler & Pryor, 1984; Solomon & Ray, 1984). Sacco (1985), for example, found that most citizens have little empathy or concern for the victim of shoplifting when that victim is a major retail chain. This phenomenon virtually represents a "just deserts" mode of construing the crime of larceny, predicated neither on the characteristics of the offense nor of the offender, but rather on those of the *offended.* That the aggregate costs not only of rectifying "inventory shrinkage" but of insuring against theft are ultimately passed on to consumers, so that the impersonal commercial giant is in fact little inconvenienced, is a matter conveniently not accounted in this way of construing things.

Similarly, Greenberg (1990) studied rates of theft among employees in an industrial plant during a period of economic recession in which their wages had been "temporarily" reduced in relation both to pre- and post-reduction theft rates for the same employees and to theft rates among employees whose incomes had not been affected. Greenberg concluded that the "temporary" increases in employee theft were attributable to feelings of equity vs. inequity and labeled economic loss by employee theft "the hidden cost of pay cuts."

→ *INFERENCES, SPECULATIONS, CONJECTURES*

Once again, the evidence is fragmentary rather than definitive. Nonetheless, it is reasonable to speculate that pro-social beliefs and attitudes deter larceny, that a widespread preference for restitution rather than sanction may give rise to an expectation of impunity, and that stigmatization may serve as an effective deterrent than the legislatively prescribed sanctions that follow prosecution and adjudication.

Stimulus Determinants

Since so few episodes of larceny are detected and prosecuted, it is likely that most occur under conditions in which the offender can act unobserved. Research on stimulus determinants tends to focus on contingent conditions that emphasize or minimize isolation and lack of surveillance. Thus:

❑ Brown & Altman (1983) underscored "cues of openness and unoccupied appearance," and Griswold (1984) demonstrated the impact of increased illumination in street lighting, on the reduction in thefts.

❑ More pertinently, Mayhew (1990) demonstrated the role of a set of variables she termed "vehicle accessibility" in both thefts *of* automobiles (in the U.S. lexicon, the crimes of motor vehicle theft) and thefts *from* automobiles (in the U.S. lexicon, larceny) in England and Wales over a 16-year period.

❑ But Sheley & Bailey (1985) explored quite a different sort of stimulus determinants by investigating methods through which to discourage the *purchase* of stolen goods. They surveyed high school and college students concerning their attitudes toward stolen property, finding that "only one predictor, moral belief, has practical policy implications." The results quite clearly underscore the importance of the transmission of pro-social attitudes.

❑ Reason & Lucas (1984) studied a phenomenon they called "absent-mindedness while shopping" among British citizens who felt themselves to have been wrongly accused of shoplifting. They found that "poor supermarket practices" in customer surveillance interacted with intra-person variables to produce petty larceny.

❑ In a direct effort to assess the effectiveness of a relatively non-intrusive method of theft deterrence, Geller, Koltuniak & Schilling (1983) placed messages discouraging the theft of newspapers from indoor and outdoor racks that were not controlled, with the messages varying between a polite appeal to conscience and a threat of dire consequences. Each sign was found to reduce theft by some 15% from baseline figures; nor did the aversively-worded sign produce a negative reaction among patrons.

❑ Similarly, after an extensive and methodologically sophisticated analysis of a variety of methods intended to deter shoplifting by consumers, Kallis & Vanier (1985) concluded that "retailers desiring to curb shoplifting should [rely] on messages designed to appeal to the shoplifter's innate sense of individuality."

→ *INFERENCES, SPECULATIONS, CONJECTURES*

Yet again, the evidence is fragmentary and indicative, rather than definitive. Accessibility, openness, and freedom from surveillance may accelerate larceny, and the willingness of the public to purchase stolen property may represent another stimulus determinant. Manipulation of these variables appear to be associated with modest reductions in the rate of theft.

☐ JULIO-THE-MICK: CASE STUDY OF A SPECIALIST IN VICTIMLESS THEFT

Once again, we turn to an extended case description to illustrate the interplay between intra-person and extra-psychic variables.

When we first met Julio — who has red hair, a freckled face, and a last name that is very, very Irish — we assumed that the first name was a nickname. Not so; he is the son of an Irish father and a Mexican mother, parents of a large and religiously devout family. By the time of our meeting, Julio was 37, married to a full-blooded Irish woman named Kathleen, and the father of five. Julio told us that his mother had given him his grandfather's first name; because of the incongruity between his prototypically Castilian first name and his prototypically Irish last name, he was dubbed "Julio the Mick" at some point in grade school.

A Prosaic Childhood

There was little remarkable in Julio's childhood, adolescence, or young adulthood. He was a slightly below average student academically and had little in the way of athletic ability or interest to distinguish himself from his classmates.

As the middle of nine children, however, he began to work after school in various retail establishments in order to contribute to the family coffers. The habits of thrift and industry were well modeled for him by his father, who drove a refuse truck for the city, and his mother, who worked as a clerk in a small supermarket.

So far as Julio was later able to recall, he had no personal vocational ambitions in those years, but his parents apparently pointed him in the direction of entry into one of the uniformed civil service occupations — fire department, police department, or sanitation service.

Though, in his senior year of high school, Julio underwent the respective entrance examinations, his scores were mediocre, placing him below the median, so that the prospect of his selection for employment was slight. Accordingly, at his parents' advice, because the practice of awarding "veterans' preference" bonus points to civil service examination scores had not yet been judicially suppressed as evidence of sexism, and even though the nation no longer conscripted for military service, Julio joined the Army. He spent three years driving Jeeps uneventfully on state-side Army bases.

While he was in the Army, Julio had been given a vocational interest (or perhaps preference — we were not able to verify which) test and was told (perhaps among other things) that "he would make a good locksmith." That description of the event does not accord with what we know of the practice of vocational psychology, particularly in view of the sharp distinction that its practitioners make between interest and aptitude; but it does, in any event, conform to Julio's memory. There was, apparently, no further consideration of pursuing civil service entrance; perhaps Julio had had enough of uniformed service occupations.

Choice of an Occupation

It was during one of a series of pre-discharge meetings that Julio learned that his GI Bill benefits would cover the costs of attending one or another trade school, including a school of locksmithing. Recalling his interview concerning results of the vocational interest test, Julio wrote to several such schools in and near his hometown. Some eleven months later, he graduated from a school of locksmithing and subsequently underwent successfully the steps necessary to obtain designation as a registered locksmith.

Through the placement service at his alma mater, Julio obtained employment in what had been a one-person shop. Its owner and operator was a 60-year-old named Brendan, who was later to become Julio's father-in-law. At that time, Brendan was suffering both from eye and from joint disorders; he was clearly looking for a successor. Anti-theft devices and home security systems had only recently become reasonably popular and salable consumer items; it was to the installation of these that Brendan assigned Julio.

Years later, Julio genuinely seemed not to remember how his relationship with Kathleen began; his description is that "It just happened." In any event, at the age of 25, Julio married Kathleen, then 21 and fresh out of nursing school with a license as an LPN. Their first child was born eleven months after their wedding and, with a dependable regularity, a child was born to the couple at intervals of 16 to 18 months thereafter. The couple moved into a house of their own during the third year of their marriage, located quite near a church and a religiously-operated school, for such a nexus was important to both Kathleen and Julio; Brendan had advanced the funds for the down payment.

Brendan died in the seventh year of Julio's marriage. As his only heir, Kathleen inherited ownership of the business; Julio became its operator. Virtually from the beginning of their new arrangement, the couple began to experience financial difficulties; though Julio had become quite expert at his craft, he apparently had little skill or inclination in the management of a business, in the matter of collection of delinquent accounts, or in short-time cash-flow financing.

Mercado Becomes a Client

But, by then, Mercado had become a client of Julio's. Julio had fitted several personal and business vehicles owned by Mercado with numerous anti-theft alarm systems and had installed integrated security and surveillance systems in three business locations operated by Mercado.

Two of those locations seemed to be essentially warehouses, stocked with electronic audio and video equipment — compact disc players, videocassette recorders, and the like. It was during a business call to one of those locations that Julio overheard a conversation between Mercado and two others that led him to conclude that Mercado was in fact engaged in the business of buying and selling stolen merchandise. As events developed, the buying and selling of stolen merchandise was but one of Mercado's enterprises, a source of ready cash; the purpose to which that cash was put was to finance a medium-sized drug trafficking operation, but Julio did not know that at the time of which we speak. Instead, he was impressed by the scope of the operation.

Like most whose acquaintance with "fencing" had been gained through a Hollywood filter, Julio had expected such an operation to deal largely in individual units, not in truck loads. On subsequent visits, he observed that Mercado apparently sold merchandise in case lots and truck loads to discount retailers. When we later questioned Julio about his cognitive and emotional reactions to such revelations, he focused largely on the legerdemain in business matters displayed by Mercado and his associates, in some sharp contrast to his own showing.

"For Once Do Something Bad And You'll Survive"

Another year or so passed. Julio's business continued at a hectic pace of activity, but its — and the family's — financial position worsened. Some six years before we met him, an event occurred that Julio afterward construed as the product of "chance," but that was readily post-dictable. He was called to the parking lot of a busy suburban shopping center to rescue a hapless motorist who had locked his keys in his car. While Julio extracted that motorist from his predicament, he observed what appeared to be a father and son emerge from the mall, each carrying three Panasonic boxes, deposit them in the back seat of a Cadillac Sedan de Ville, turn on their heel and retreat once again into the mall — without locking their vehicle. As events would later reveal, each box contained a videocassette recorder that the father and son had purchased at a "close out" sale at a department store in the mall for re-sale at their booth in a local "flea market." They had returned to the store to pick up six more units.

Once his own customer had departed, Julio moved his truck to a parking place next to the Cadillac and transferred the Panasonic boxes from that vehicle to his. When asked years later to recall his feelings during this episode, Julio describes the massive anxiety that assaults him as soon as he opens the door of the Cadillac — and that continues for the better part of a week. He recalls that, if he had been able to figure out how to return the stolen merchandise to its owners without revealing his own identity and thereby courting arrest, he would have done so. Though he had never been more than a "light social drinker," Julio availed himself liberally of spirits that week; alcohol, a central nervous system depressant, indeed neuro-chemically relieves anxiety.

Finally, Julio told Mercado that he had available six Panasonic VCRs, unopened and in original boxes, that he wished to sell. Mercado offered Julio $300 for the lot — at then-current prices, approximately 10% of their retail value, but also, at then-current rates, approximately 75% of the weekly wages to which Julio would be entitled if the finances of his business had permitted him to pay himself what he earned.

In the Blitzstein version of *Threepenny Opera,* Captain Mac-Heath, by way of *apologia* for his criminal lifestyle, urges his listeners: "How does a man survive? — He feeds on others . . . For once do something bad — and you'll survive."

So it was with Julio. The first episode of larceny had taught him that some five minutes of observation and theft — coupled, to be sure, with a week's worth of anxious guilt thereafter — had yielded him income equal to four days' worth of honest labor. The first episode had been fraught with guilt, anxiety, tension, fear of apprehension and its consequences; in succeeding episodes, the strength of those emotions faded, until all that was left was a lingering mild fear of the aftermath of apprehension.

Construing Theft as Possible

Julio did not sally forth on the night of that first theft in search of a target. Yet it seems clear that, in the very few minutes' worth of observation preceding the first act of larceny, Julio construed theft as an act that was both possible and desirable. Given his upbringing in a law-abiding family replete with pro-social role models, how could such construing arise — or are we dealing with an aberration in cognition and behavior?

Even though his role models had been strongly pro-social and his own life exemplary to that point, Julio had also been exposed to Mercado, who wore his disregard for the law elegantly, and who, not incidentally, might be expected to know how to dispose of stolen goods profitably. Moreover, in his usual occupational activities, Julio was daily concerned with the *prevention* of theft. Indeed, in order to persuade his clients to the purchase of various anti-theft devices, Julio distributed a wide array of promotional literature that, at least *inter alia*, well illustrated the incredible range of means of thievery that fertile imaginations can devise.

But it is very pertinent that, on the occasion of that first larceny, two additional factors collided with each other and with the several intrapsychic variables which had become part of Julio's psychological baggage — viz., particular financial need and specific opportunity to act unobserved. Finally, because *both* his principal means of livelihood *and* (because it provided a credible "cover" for his presence in parking lots) his supplemental income from thievery depended on maintenance of his status as a registered locksmith, it was eminently necessary that Julio avoid detection and apprehension.

An Episode Becomes a Pattern

A pattern emerged after only a few weeks, in which Julio posted himself in his locksmith's truck — "You know, nobody ever questions what a locksmith is doing in a parking lot" — observed someone emerge from the mall with some item of audio or video equipment (or, later, computer gear), place it inside the passenger cabin (*not* the trunk) of a late model luxury automobile (Jaguar, Mercedes, BMW, Cadillac, Lincoln, occasionally Audi or Chrysler), fail to lock the vehicle, depart.

In later years, as the American Express Company began vigorously to promote its credit card by advertising that it would guarantee merchandise purchased therewith against theft or damage for the first 30 days of ownership, Julio began to be even more selective in the identification of target vehicles by searching for tags that signaled that the vehicle's owner belonged to the American Express

Motor Club, a motorist aid organization whose membership is open only to cardholders. In that way, Julio reasoned, he could be absolutely sure that the vehicle and its contents were protected against loss; indeed, he (erroneously) believed, if the motorist maintained the usual auto policy *and* had made the purchase using the American Express Card, he or she might be doubly compensated for the loss of merchandise.

In formulating these "guidelines" for his criminal behavior, Julio had much in common with the so-called kleptomaniacs studied by McElroy and her associates at Harvard (1991, p. 654): "Several patients developed rules for their stealing behavior — for instance, stealing only from work or from certain types of stores (e.g., drug stores but not department stores), or stealing certain items but not others (e.g., jewelry but not clothing.)"

Further, and Julio is quite adamant on this point, though it would have been easy enough for a trained locksmith to do so, he never forced a lock or entered a locked vehicle; moreover, he regarded any vehicle equipped with an anti-theft device off-limits as a target.

There are some elements in his behavior — limitation of his activity to expensive, late model vehicles; preference for vehicles logically linked to drivers who were protected financially against loss from theft; avoidance of vehicles that had mechanical or electronic barriers to theft — that suggest that, at some level, Julio construed his targets and victims from the "just deserts" perspective that Sacco (1985) has identified.

Declaring the Proceeds as Taxable Income

Mercado was always accommodating. Julio was able to increase his income on average from $200 to $400 per week, though the net figure should be reduced by the cost of the alcohol required to relieve anxious guilt; he preferred Bushmill's, and he permitted himself a quart per week, at a cost ranging toward $25. Unlike the subjects studied by Grasmick & Scott (1982), Julio apparently feared the consequences of tax evasion, so he meticulously recorded weekly cash payments from Mercado (receipted as "for services rendered") and declared that income when he filed tax returns for his business.

The records indicate income from Mercado in amounts ranging from $15,000 to $20,000 for each of six years. If the ratio of approximately 10% of retail value holds, the aggregate value of the merchandise Julio stole over that period may be as high as $1,000,000. Moreover, Julio was quite forthcoming to Kathleen, by telling her that Mercado had many small jobs that required doing, that these would occupy him two or three nights per week, but that the family's financial troubles would thereby be sharply curtailed. Not without some justification, Mercado became a revered figure in the household.

Despite our earnest pledges of confidentiality and anonymity, Mercado has steadfastly refused our entreaties that he permit us an interview. Even in the absence of direct confirmation, however, it seems likely that, in his eyes, Mercado was "doing a guy a favor" by purchasing the merchandise Julio stole; in terms of what we have learned about his operation from sources other than Julio, Mercado is accustomed to dealing only in wholesale quantities. In the midst of a transportation hub in a heavily populated region — and in an ethos, we are told, in which the disappearance due to "breakage" of 3% of a total load being shipped by truck, railroad flatbed, or ocean-bound container (including medicinal preparations from the area's many pharmaceutical plants) is accepted as "normal" — such an attribution is entirely credible.

A Surfeit of Prospective Targets

During the entire period of his criminal activity, Julio claims, he never "hit" the same mall or shopping center twice. Further, he not only evaded detection but was never seriously threatened. On some occasions, he told us, he was approached by a police car and some conversation of a stereotypically sexist type might ensue: *Some silly dame locked herself outa the car again, huh?* Yeah, and then she musta found her keys, 'cause the car ain't here now. *Figures, doesn't it?* And off Julio would drive.

To understand how this level of activity could be sustained for so long, it is necessary to appreciate the mammoth size of the New York megalopolis — or, in the nomenclature now preferred by the Bureau of the Census (1989, p. 30) the "New York-Northern New Jersey-Long Island-Southern Connecticut *Consolidated* Metropolitan Statistical Area." The aggregate population is listed at something over eighteen and a half million people, a total that exceeds that of most nations of the world and that accounts for approximately 8% of the U.S. population. If one of every 12 people in the country live in that Consolidated Metropolitan Statistical Area, it is reasonable to believe that at least one of every 12 shopping centers or malls in the country is also located in the same CMSA. According to Census data (*Ibid.,* p. 757), there are nearly 31,000 shopping centers nationwide. If 8% are located in the New York megapolitan CMSA, there should be nearly 2500 such units therein. It is to be noted that, although many of the larger "indoor" malls in the megapolis employ private security firms to patrol interior corridors, most rely on local municipal police to patrol their capacious parking lots.

If Julio "hit" a different unit on each of two days during each week, he had struck at some 100 different centers or malls per year — or at a total of some 600 during the course of his six-year criminal career. He could have continued that pattern of activity for a total of something on the order of 24 years *without* the sort of replication that might court detection and apprehension. During the course of our contacts with him, he sometimes reminded us of that; and not without a hint of regret over what might have been.

Young Brendan, a Gift of Marijuana, and a Father's Rage

But Julio's six-year pattern of criminal behavior came to light in a very different way and for very different reasons.

Kathleen and Julio had named their first-born son after her father and their benefactor. Young Brendan seemed to have the best qualities of each of his parents; he did well enough at school, played on the usual Little League and Pop Warner teams, became a mainstay in the Scouts, performed admirably as an acolyte.

In addition, though he and his parents thought of him as college-bound, he exhibited considerable interest in his father's work, particularly when Julio expanded to the installation and servicing of cellular telephones, and occasionally accompanied him on Saturday calls. It was in this way that Brendan came to know Mercado personally and to meet a number of the men who appeared to be Mercado's employees. One of them was Ty, a nattily-attired young man of 25 or so who drove a flaming red Corvette that Julio had fitted with a telephone.

Brendan's upbringing sounds quite prosaic in the telling. But the fact is that, in late 20th century America, a prosaic upbringing almost by definition includes experimentation with drugs. Much more as a follower than as a leader, Brendan had thus experienced marijuana and various mood-altering pharmaceutical preparations (principally Valium, Librium, Elavil), largely during parties — indeed, organized around the televiewing of an athletic contest — hosted by one or another of his friends. Supplies were ordered by telephone (a "900" number), in quite a transparent code that designated one or more pre-packaged assortments in quantities for a specified number of users (e.g., "suitable for a party for between 10 an 12 guests"), and delivered either by mail or express delivery service — or, for those end-users who enjoyed a bit of cloak-and-dagger excitement, by courier in some clandestine location.

Thus it happened that Brendan accompanied his friend Dick to a rendezvous in the grotto outside Our Lady of Fatima church one Saturday afternoon. There they were joined by none other than Ty — who greeted Brendan as an old friend and (quite to Dick's delight, for that matter) grew quite adamant that neither he nor Mercado would dream of accepting payment from the son of a business associate of long standing.

Perhaps because he had been relieved of paying for the order, or perhaps because he now saw Brendan in a new light, Dick was quite strong in insisting that Brendan should take custody of their small

---

⇨ *Prevalence of Drug Experimentation among Adolescents*

To acknowledge widespread experimentation, particularly with so-called "soft" drugs, among youth of high school age is not to condone such experimentation, however (Oetting & Beauvais, 1990).

For many years, the Institute for Social Research at the University of Michigan has surveyed a national, stratified sample of high school seniors concerning their attitudes toward drugs and drug use. By the late 1980s, fully 85% of respondents indicated that marijuana was readily *available* to them, while amphetamines were identified as readily available by 64% and tranquilizers by 51% (Johnston, O'Malley & Bachman, 1987, p. 152).

Similarly, the *National Household Survey on Drug Abuse* conducted by the National Institute on Drug Abuse (1987, pp. 10-24, 30-33, 46-49), based on a stratified sample of households representative of those in the nation, 33% of these largely adult respondents admitted to at least occasional use of marijuana, 12% to the use of cocaine, 7% to the use of hallucinogens, 9% to the use of stimulants, and 86% to the use of alcohol, with these categories not mutually exclusive. There is even some evidence that experimentation with alcohol begins *modally* in seventh grade (Graham, Marks & Hansen, 1991).

With pervasive behavioral role models among adults within their own households favoring the consumption of mood-altering biochemicals and with the so-called "soft" drugs (no less than alcohol) widely available for illegal purchase, there is little mystery as to why drug experimentation may well have become a majority experience among American adolescents, whatever their particular socioeconomic circumstances.

package (about the size of a single packet of cigarettes) and then make a triumphal entry into the party at Dick's the following day. Thus, it was that Brendan — who, though a not inexperienced drug user, had no experience whatever in covering his tracks when in the possession of patent contraband — carried away from this encounter a quantity of controlled dangerous substances and, upon arriving home, placed the package neatly atop his dresser. In the reconstruction of the events of that day, the time was approximately half past five in the afternoon.

The audiotape log at "hot line" headquarters for the state's child protective agency indicated 8:14 p.m. as the time a call was received from a neighbor two doors away from the family home to the effect that severe child abuse was at that very moment being perpetrated by Julio against Brendan. Following standard protocol, the hot line operator dispatched the social worker on duty at the agency office closest to the scene, then notified police.

Since there was some blood from a split lip but no major injuries, the police were willing to confiscate the drugs and write the matter off, without even much attention to Ty — particularly since, in everyone's account, the drugs had *not* been sold and purchased. Not so the social worker; for reasons she latter attributed to that marvelously fictive *deus ex machina* called "clinical intuition," she decided to (in the agency's parlance) "open a file" on the family. That meant, *inter alia,* psychological evaluations of the principal actors in the conflict, perhaps preparatory to invocation by the agency of its emergency powers to temporarily suspend parental rights and place Brendan in foster care.

The MMPI Turns Detective?

And thus it was that Julio, Kathleen, and Brendan found themselves in our clinical offices. Following our customary procedure, we asked each to complete the MMPI; again following our customary procedure, we submitted their scores to the Weathers Report interpretive program derived from the Megargee-Bohn Typology Study — even though no formal criminal charges were pending against anyone for anything.

For Kathleen and for Brendan, their scores on none of the primary clinical scales met or exceeded the threshold of significance and, further, the resultant print-outs told us that their profiles fit well with those of none of the Megargee-Bohn Offender Types.

For Julio, it was similarly the case that his scores on the clinical scales failed of significance; those scores are arrayed in DISPLAY 15.

But the Weathers Report print-out told us that, in comparison to subjects in the Megargee-Bohn data base:

> The client is a member of Group Baker with a fit of medium accuracy . . . This individual may appear anxious under stress and somewhat neurotic. [Members of Group Baker] are. . . likely to be involved in interstate stolen cars and possession of contraband, other than drugs. There is a tendency to be an academic under-achiever, possibly because anxiety interfered with intellectual functioning. Interpersonal relations and adjustment are poor. Though their juvenile criminal records are likely to be about average, their adult records may be considerably more serious. Drugs tend to be avoided, while alcohol is likely to be used in excess. Authority conflicts and poor adaptation to the environ-ment are characteristic. Affect is constricted, and socially they are withdrawn, passive, and unassertive. Authority conflicts tend to be of a passive-aggressive nature, rather than overt confrontation and defiance. Anxiety,both state and trait, is high, and social maturity is low . . . Unconscious needs for punishment may drive this person's criminal behavior and underachievement . . . Attitudes towards mothers and to some extent fathers tend to be good . . . [Group Baker members] usually make a very positive impression upon the [institutional] staff who work with them. They tend to be rewarding clients because staff perceive that their efforts have a positive impact.

An idealized scenario might have it that, after hearing about the computer's actuarial match between his scores and those of a group of known offenders, Julio demanded a police stenographer, recited *Miranda* warnings by rote, unburdened his conscience, and en-treated punishment.

That didn't happen. In fact, and it is somewhat shamefacedly told, we did not place particular store in the Weathers Report print-out. We were, after all, dealing with a person who had been charged with no offense; police had become involved because a perfectly under-standable paternal act of discipline had gone rather too far, but not even the child welfare agency was contemplating charges of abuse.

Even on technical grounds, we were justified in discounting much of what the Weathers Report had to say. Julio had been charged with nothing, let alone convicted of anything. To compare him with a sample of adjudicated offenders through a process that is intended only to sort offenders into groups so as to facilitate their manage-ment and/or correctional rehabilitation — and decidedly *not* to post-dict guilt for anything, let alone to post-dict guilt for particular offenses — is certainly to compare horseshoes with apples, peaches, pears, and grapefruit. Rather serious psychometric issues are thereby raised, not to mention questions of equity. As it developed, we might have been well advised to be somewhat more adventurous in our reaction to the Weathers Report print-out.

Search for Hidden Meanings: Mercado, Booze, the Frizzle

In our clinical work with Julio, it was not the scientifically-anchored, actuarial MMPI interpretation that we found troubling; quite to the contrary (and here our psychoanalytic colleagues might applaud), what we found disturbing was Julio's relationship with Mercado. The account given to the police, to the child welfare agency, and to us had it that an employee of a client of Julio's (viz., Ty, but

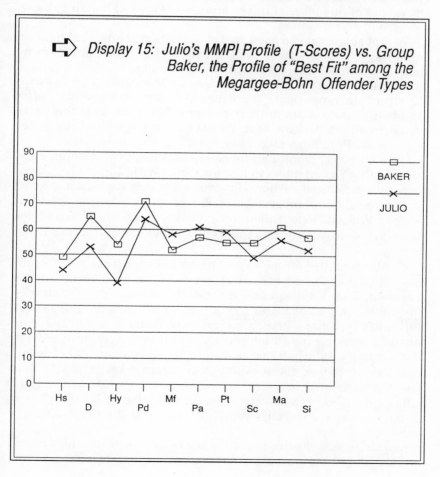

Display 15: Julio's MMPI Profile (T-Scores) vs. Group Baker, the Profile of "Best Fit" among the Megargee-Bohn Offender Types

unnamed) had, as a gesture of kindness, given a cache of marijuana to Brendan. When we probed this account, few further details emerged. Yet Julio seemed to display some anger, not toward the employee but toward his employer — as if Mercado had set out, through Ty as his minion, to suborn Brendan into an active dependence on drugs. When we attempted to probe that anger further, Julio became morosely sullen and secretive. Now that is a sure sign that one is nearing the mother lode.

Thus, on we probed. Candidly, and here we must admit to an undue influence from our psychoanalytic counterparts, we began to suspect a homosexual relationship of some sort, overt, latent, or symbolic, between Julio and Mercado — the more so, since the emergence of any piece of information was followed instantly by an increase in secretiveness.

We probably wasted a good deal of time approaching that topic on one pussy-foot or another. Yet the bald fact is that there is some element of a shared secret in Julio's revelation of his first theft and a powerful element of control exercised by Mercado in Julio's virtually ritualistic repetitions. There may also be some flavor of an *alter ego* identification Julio projected toward Mercado, as if the latter embodied Julio's darkest, most sinister, most uncivilized yearnings — or, as the Freudians might say, his *id*.

Piece by piece, small details emerged; then, one evening, Julio said simply, "You might as well know it all." With that, he began the recitation recounted earlier. However cleansing confession proved for his soul, we were now possessed of quite a burden of what Stephen Vincent Benet called "inconvenient knowledge" — and, for reasons that will shortly be explicated, were essentially immobilized thereby.

We also searched for a clearer linkage between alcohol and criminal activity in Julio's case. But every source of information we consulted, from Kathleen onward, confirmed that Julio drank only Bushmill's, only at home, and rarely to excess. It is quite true that Bushmill's is rather a luxury, typically not found in what used to be called "a working man's house," except on very special occasions. Biochemically, Julio had chosen the proper substance to "wind down" from the tension of those evenings of larceny. Yet to assert that alcohol was related to larceny in any remotely "causative" way in Julio's case is akin to asserting that one develops a headache as a consequence of a naturally-occurring surplus in the supply of aspirin.

And there was the matter of the tension of those evenings itself. Many malefactors we have known over the course of the years, within and without correctional institutions, have spoken of the exhilaration they have experienced, particularly when they have eluded detection under "close call" conditions; a large proportion of them have referred to that exhilaration as "the Frizzle," that special feeling that arises when one knows he or she has "gotten over" on another — and preferably, on someone in a position of formal authority. Certainly, few who have so described that exhilaration have troubled to trace the term etymologically, so that they are unlikely to know that in an earlier time it denoted "that which has been fried." Though the specific referent is substance abuse, the description given by medical pharmacologist Renata Bluhm of Vanderbilt (Roueche, 1991, p. 73) is quite apt: "Adrenalin is turned on by more than the drug itself. [Users] know there is a risk — anything might happen — and *that risk is part of the experience*. There is an excitement in a jump into the unknown." Surely, that should have been a component of what Julio found reinforcing for all those years. Yet, we could find no confirmation anywhere; instead, Kathleen described Julio as fatigued and morose when he returned from what he called his "night calls."

Try as we might, then, and despite Julio's secretiveness, we were unable to uncover buried pathologies. Instead, Julio's criminal behavior became comprehensible as what it was — to borrow Moore's (1984) phrasing, "premeditated, purposeful, conscious, goal-directed behavior" that might have gone on for years had he not lost his temper with his son.

Frontier Justice — Imposed by Vigilantes Under a Mask of Benevolence

But he had indeed lost his temper with his son, an agency of social control (i.e., the child welfare agency) other than the police had "opened a file" on him that in his view had nothing to do with his pattern of criminal behavior — and, after pursuing several veins of what turned out to be fool's gold, we had uncovered a mother lode of "guilty knowledge," in the appropriate use of which we now found ourselves immobilized.

From their reaction to the physical violence between Julio and his son, we intuited that the local police were unlikely to pursue with diligence information about past criminal activity over a very long time in a wide array of jurisdictions other than their own, even if we were disposed to make such a report — or able to convince Julio that he should voluntarily incriminate himself. Since Mercado's places of operation were also outside the local jurisdiction, we anticipated that local police would only be slightly more interested in him, though there might be kudos enough if an ensuing investigation resulted in the uncovering both of a "fencing" and a medium-sized drug distribution operation. But, though Julio had seen only a kindly side of Mercado, surely there was an unkindly side that was no stranger to retaliatory violence — and both Julio and Brendan seemed likely targets. Moreover, if it developed that information from Julio proved pivotal in the prosecution of Mercado, it might well have been the case that a resulting plea-bargain would convict Julio of a misdemeanor, with a sanction that would hardly constitute a motive for changing one's behavior, though it might jeopardize his standing as a registered locksmith. Finally, given a vast array of target vehicles in a large number of jurisdictions, restitution seemed patently impossible.

And our sense of immobility had another source as well. We have seen, from our discussion of the *Tarasoff* case in Chapter 4, that when a person who stands in the relationship of patient reveals to a psychologist (or psychiatrist) that he or she intends to do violence to himself or herself or to another, the mental health professional incurs a positive obligation to inform law enforcement authorities. But it is not so clear that such an obligation ensues if the patient tells the clinician that he or she intends, at some future and unspecified time and from some victim yet to be determined, to steal a set of tires, or commit some other property crime which does not involve violence or even personal victimization (Berlin, Malin & Dean, 1991). It is even arguable that the message that the patient has many times stolen *in the past* must, under prevailing ethical canons, be treated as archival information only, subject to all the usual guarantees of confidentiality, perhaps even activating Fifth Amendment protections against self-incrimination (Myers & Caterine, 1990).

On the other hand, we had obtained (or, perhaps more accurately, fumbled upon) information about his past crimes from a father whose fitness to parent we were called upon to evaluate. It is *not* clear that information about past crimes ferreted out during the course of an evaluation to determine appropriateness as a role model for an adolescent (who had shown some inclination to disregard the law in the matter of controlled dangerous substances at least) does *not* constitute fair game. That position is at least arguable.

So, we determined to present to Julio a schematic based on an aversive response-cost paradigm; others might say that we resorted to blackmail. We proposed to Julio that, in return for a most solemn promise to forsake criminal behavior, we would not make a negative recommendation to the child welfare agency. In addition, we expected Julio to devise an equitable equivalent to a "community service alternative" that would simultaneously provide Brendan (and his friends, for that matter) pro-social role models and in some way compensate for the substantial economic losses attributable to his criminal activity. The alternative, we intimated, might be a prosecution which, even if it resulted in acquittal, might still cost him his status as a registered locksmith and thus loss of his means of livelihood. Julio had little choice but to accept.

The community service project he has undertaken has been to equip churches of all denominations in his community with anti-theft devices. Most of those churches had, because of economic loss from theft and vandalism, adopted policies that limited the hours of church opening to times when a monitor could be present to serve, in effect, as a watchman. Installation of electronic security devices has meant that some of them can remain open unattended, thereby increasing community access for spiritual purposes.

About Mercado and Ty, we have taken no action. Julio claims he no longer services Mercado's account, predicated on an explanation that he wishes to confine his routine business activity to a smaller geographic area; we have no reason to disbelieve him. To compensate for the loss of family income from criminal activity, Kathleen has returned to work for the first time in a dozen years. She claims that she has never felt better.

No police, no prosecutor, no jury, no judge were involved in determining what constitutes justice in Julio's case — only social workers and psychologists. Patently, we exercised social control far beyond our societal warrant.

Anytime anyone, however benevolently motivated he or she believes himself or herself to be, decides that he or she need not bother with the formal process of criminal adjudication *and most particularly when the decision not to bother pivots in some measure on an expectation that wrong-doing will remain unsanctioned*, respect for the rule of law is weakened — and, following the lead of benevolent vigilantes, we have taken another step in the direction of the jungle.

☐ SUMMARY

This chapter has considered larceny, the most frequently committed and one of the least frequently studied of the felony crimes, from both statistical and psychological perspectives. On the basis of data from the *Sourcebook,* we have sketched larceny in its known parameters: the frequency of commission, the ratio between commission and reporting and the reasons cited by victims for not reporting, average and aggregate economic loss engendered by theft by various methods and in various locations, the probable influence of alcohol and drugs in episodes of larceny, age and sex distributions of larceny arrestees, and the relatively infrequency of intrusive sanction.

On the basis of pertinent behavioral science research, we have concluded or conjectured that:

❑ No clear directions emerge from the relatively meager psychometric studies of larceny offenders. But, in the absence of psychometric evidence to the contrary and in light of statistical data concerning the ubiquity of the offense and the infrequency of apprehension, it seems reasonable to hold, with Moore (1983), that *larceny is an offense characterized by premeditated, purposeful, conscious, goal-directed behavior.*

❑ The evidence on the role of social learning variables is fragmentary rather than definitive. Nonetheless, it is reasonable to speculate that pro-social beliefs and attitudes deter larceny, that a widespread preference for restitution rather than sanction may give rise to an expectation of impunity (at least in the sense of immunity from intrusive sanction), *but* that stigmatization may serve as an effective deterrent.

❑ Similarly, the evidence on stimulus determinants is fragmentary and indicative, rather than definitive. Accessibility, openness, and freedom from surveillance may accelerate larceny, and the willingness of the public to purchase stolen property may represent another stimulus determinant. Manipulation of these variables appears to be associated with at least modest reductions in the rate of theft.

❏ *Chapter 10*

Refinements, Implications, Applications

IN CHAPTER 1, WE OUTLINED A PSYCHOLOGICAL MODEL OF CRIMINAL behavior with anchors *not* in abnormal psychology but instead in the process psychology of Raymond B. Cattell, the personal construct psychology of George A. Kelly, and the psychology of social learning of Albert Bandura.

❏ THE PROCESS PSYCHOLOGY PARADIGM REVISITED

We were quite insistent that a process psychology approach to understanding criminal behavior does not make the assumption that psychopathology triggers criminality. Instead, we identified as the psychological engines for formally criminal behavior four process elements that interact with, and indeed potentiate, each other in a behavioral situation:

❏ *Inclination* (or predisposition) to behave in ways that are construed by the behaver (or held by the society, or both) to be formally and legally criminal, although we opined that such inclination is limited to specific criminal behaviors or classes of behavior and does not generalize across a wide spectrum of criminal acts;

❏ *opportunity* to behave without direct deterrence or observation;

❏ *expectation of reward,* either tangible or symbolic; and

❏ *expectation of impunity.*

We also proposed that the interaction between these process elements is regulated and confined by a series of complex, but nonetheless discernible, boundary conditions — viz., that:

❏ *In a specific criminal offense, the weights attached to each of the four process elements vary, but in no case is the weight attached to any element zero — that is, each process element influences the behavior emitted during a specific criminal offense and in no case is any single element inoperative.*

❑ *In any criminal act, there obtains a relation between "predisposition" and "opportunity" such that opportunity potentiates predisposition in what is likely an exponential manner.*

❑ *Expectation of reward likely varies in inverse relation to the other three elements.*

❑ *Expectation of impunity is likely geometrically potentiated by what the prospective behaver observes in the psychosocial environment as others who emit criminal behavior of whatever sort remain undetected and unpunished. A specific act of criminal behavior may thus be vicariously reinforced by an act of criminal behavior of the same (or even of a different sort) not emitted but merely observed by the behaver directly or indirectly (e.g., through the journalistic or entertainment media) which either actually remains undetected or unpunished or is so construed.*

In subsequent chapters, we explored conceptual, methodological, and operational constraints on the psychological study of behavior that has been formally adjudicated as criminal, then turned to a detailed examination of statistical and behavioral science data bearing upon homicide and larceny, two crimes at diametric extremes.

Homicide is the least frequently committed of the felony offenses but is very frequently studied, while larceny is the most frequently committed but is very infrequently studied; and the two contrast sharply with each other in terms of what we might call social gravity. We reasoned that, if the process psychology paradigm outlined in Chapter 1 proves broad, elastic, and sensitive enough to accommodate statistical and psychological data on these offenses at diametric poles and on the people who have formally been declared guilty of committing them, then the process paradigm should be robust enough to stand as a general model for understanding criminal behavior across specific offense categories.

Throughout our excursions, we searched for those psychological variables that, singly and in interaction with each other, render comprehensible the process whereby formally criminal acts are construed as possible and desirable by individual actors — and the attendant process by which an actor who construes a formally criminal act as possible and desirable self-selects those psychosocial environments that either structurally enable, or at least do not impede, such acts.

We found an array of intra-person variables and of stimulus determinants related in one way or another to the two specific categories of formally criminal behavior we examined. In general, we found considerable evidence of perfectly "normal" — as distinct from abnormal, pathological, or otherwise recondite — processes of *personal construing* and *social learning* that, in certain combinations with each other, rather dependably yield criminally deviant behavior. In some offenses, we found some reason to believe that neurogenic violence — in some cases, even technically classifiable as organically-based psychopathology — constitutes an *interactive* contributing factor, particularly inclining some actors to seek psychosocial environments with high tolerance for normatively violent behavior. In contrast, we found little evidence to support the proposition that criminal behavior springs from psychological illness, that it is to be attributed to functional (i.e., non-organically-based) psychopathology as its source in any but a minor proportion of cases.

☐ RECAPITULATION: PROCESS ELEMENTS SINGLY AND IN INTERACTION

Our excursions into the empirical literature have yielded support for each of the elements proposed as integral to the process psychology paradigm of criminal behavior.

Inclination: Intra-Person Variables

It is reasonable to believe that what we have called *inclination* to behave in formally criminal ways is comprised of an amalgam of intra-person variables. These include certain personality characteristics, neuropsychological anomalies, level of intelligence, and whether the would-be actor is behaving under the direct pharmacological influence of alcohol or drugs — or perhaps whether the acquisition of illicit drugs through profit from crime is functioning as motive.

We have seen that clinically significant *impulsivity* as a relatively enduring characteristic of personality (i.e., as a habit of behaving) fairly reliably differentiates people who commit crimes of violence from those who commit crimes of other sorts, as well as from presumably non-offending subjects in the general population.

In contrast, larceny offenders in the aggregate evince *no* clinically significant traits of personality, but instead display those personal characteristics that render them capable of purposeful, conscious, goal-directed behavior.

There is a burgeoning body of evidence that suggests a *neurogenic basis for violent behavior,* including criminal violence, but no such etiology has been proposed to underlay larceny. There is sound basis for the view that neurological and/or neuropsychological dysfunctions themselves represent the physiological substratum for impulsivity as a habit of behavior and further predispose toward abuse of certain mood-altering substances; in turn, those who abuse alcohol and/or other mood-altering substances place themselves at greater risk for sustaining future neurological injury. Hence, it is a proposition of "best fit" with current data that neurological anomalies interact with personality characteristics and with substance abuse in primitive and circular ways, such that only very detail historical data may be able to resolve the cause vs. effect question in particular cases.

There is evidence that level of *intelligence* may function interactively with other variables to *inhibit* criminal violence — that is, that would-be actors with higher levels of intelligence *avoid* violence in the same circumstances that elicit violence among those of lower intelligence.

The specific dynamic guiding such inhibition has not yet been identified, but it may be that higher levels of intelligence yield more realistic estimates of the costs, benefits, and risks attached to criminal behavior. In contrast, and especially in light of the vast imbalance between the number of larcenies estimated to be committed annually and the number of arrests made therefor in a year, there is some reason to believe that higher levels of intelligence facilitate theft, or at least that theft that does not result in apprehension.

In a very real sense, a would-be actor's *social learning history* also constitutes part of the "psychological baggage" he or she carries from one behavioral situation to another. Whether one has learned, through direct or vicarious conditioning at close hand or by long distance, to behave pro-socially or anti-socially and whether he or she has learned, in a general way, to expect approbation and reward for pro-social behavior vs. disapprobation and negative sanction for anti-social behavior most assuredly represents facets of the readiness-to-behave.

These variables are not independent of one another but instead interact among themselves. Thus, a person in whom impulsivity is an enduring personality characteristic is more likely to be under the biochemical influence of a central nervous system stimulant than is one in whom impulsivity is at a normal or relatively low level. Similarly, a person who has suffered severe neurological damage is likely *both* to exhibit a lower level of intelligence *and* to exhibit greater impulsivity as a behavioral characteristic; and so on, across other specific interactions even among intra-person variables.

Opportunity to Behave without Deterrence

We have emphasized repeatedly that people are relatively free to self-select their own psychosocial environments. Those who construe violent behavior as normal or ordinary are likely to search out and elect to implant themselves in environments that either hold a normative expectation for, or display a high tolerance of, violent behavior — such as are to be found in regional or age-related subcultures that foster "character contests," especially between young males. Such environments are not likely to deter — but rather to elicit or foster — violent behavior. Because a large proportion of homicides in the United States occur precisely under such "tinder box" circumstances and in view of the growing evidence on the neurogenesis of impulsive violence, we have wondered whether impaired neurology undergirds subcultures of violence that constitute tinder boxes writ large.

Because both criminal homicide and most other crimes of violence are relatively tightly confined intra-racially, because young males are the prototypical perpetrators and victims of criminal homicide (so that young black males are, relative to their representation in the population, at substantially greater risk for homicide victimization *and* for homicide offending than members of other racial groups), and because certain neurological disorders are more prevalent among blacks than among members of other racial minority groups (at least in a society organized around a caste system that links race with economic status), there is reason to worry that neurological injuries suffered disproportionately — as Bell (1986, 1990) and other medical investigators have shown — by minority group members may yield impulsivity leading to character contests played out in a subculture of violence in ways that directly and massively place young black men at life-threatening risk.

Opportunity to behave without deterrence appears to contribute to larceny as well, but in quite different ways. In contrast to impulsive violence emitted within the social context of a subculture which construes violence as normative, the thief more typically seeks environments which are a-social and in which the physical objects which constitute the targets of his or her criminal behavior are in fact quite devoid of human companionship. In an impulsive character contest, both combatants typically seek, at least *inter alia,* the accolades of their peers — but within a context in which an attempt to intervene so as to forestall or terminate the contest is quite alien both to the combatants and to their like-minded audience. Quite in

⇨ *Process Elements in Rape and Sexual Assault*

After reviewing an array of nearly 500 research investigations on offenders and victims in the crimes of rape and sexual assault and on the circumstances surrounding those crimes, Pallone (1990-*b*) identified the operative *process elements.*

On the basis of data contained in the 1988 *Sourcebook* and similar sources, with regard to the *crime as it is committed* (pp. 30-34):

❏ Five and a half times as many episodes of rape and attempted rape as of criminal homicide occur during a typical year, of which 50% are *not* reported to law enforcement authorities; somewhat curiously, a larger proportion of *completed* (61%) than of *attempted* rapes (47%) are formally reported. Some 83% of the cases estimated to have been committed, whether reported or not, involve a *single offender,* the remaining 17% are cases of *gang rape.*

❏ Some 56% of the rape offenses involving a *lone* offender were committed by *friends, relatives, or acquaintances* and 44% by strangers; in contrast, in gang rape only 16% of the offenses involving *multiple* offenders were committed by friends, relatives, or acquaintances. Only 27% of *completed* rapes but fully 63% of *attempted* rapes are perpetrated by strangers. Such data may well explain the sharp differentiation in the rates at which attempted and completed rapes are reported to police. *Only 52% of all cases of rape reported to police are "cleared" by arrest* ; *the ratio between the estimated number of rape victimizations and arrests is thus on the order of 4:1.*

❏ Some 51% of all rapes occur in the victim's own home or in the home of a neighbor or friend; only 22% occur in such accessible open spaces as streets, parks, or parking lots; 36% occur between 6 p.m. and midnight, 24% between midnight and 6 a.m.

❏ The most comprehensive data available on the consequences of felony arrest suggest that only 52% of the *reported* cases of rape are *cleared by arrest;* among those arrested for rape, 76% are prosecuted and 50% convicted; among those convicted, 84% are sentenced to incarceration, 16% to probation or some other non-custodial sanction; among those sentenced to incarceration, 69% are given sentences greater than one year. *Thus, the ratio between crimes committed and convictions is on the order of 11:1* and *the ratio between crimes committed and the intrusive sanction of imprisonment is on the order of 13:1.* As an outrageous apostrophe as well as a judgment on the efficacy of the criminal justice system, only 17% of victims who had indeed reported victimization in completed rapes and 11% of the victims in attempted rapes expected the offender to be punished.

❏ Some 77% of the victims are white, 23% non-white, so that *the rate of victimization varies from the distribution of races in the national population* in such fashion that non-whites (who constitute only 16% of the total population) are vastly "over- represented" among victims in relation to their proportion of the overall population. The estimated *rate of rape victimization* of persons over the age of 12 is 10 per 100,000 among *white males* and 20 per 100,00 of *black males,* 110 per 100,000 among *white females* and 200 per 100,000 among *black females.* Thus, *there is no question that blacks, whether male or female, are at significantly greater "risk" than are whites.* Estimated rate of victimization also varies substantially by socioeconomic class, such that the rate is 150 per 100,000 of the population among families whose annual income is less than $7500 but only 10 per 100,000 of the population among families whose annual incomes is more than $50,000; the confounds between race and social class are well documented.

❏ *Rape perpetrated by a single offender against a single victim crosses racial lines relatively infrequently.* In such lone offender/single victim cases, 79% of the white victims in *attempted* rape cases and 82% in *completed* cases were attacked by white offenders; 82% of the black victims in cases of attempted rape and 87% in completed rapes were attacked by black offenders. *Data on gang rape contrast sharply.* In cases involving multiple offenders and either single or multiple victims, 25% were committed by groups of offenders who were homogeneously white, 22% by groups of offenders who were homogeneously black, and 42% by groups of offenders of mixed races.

❏ In only 23% of the cases of rape or attempted rape were perpetrators perceived by victims to be armed with a weapon, with knives (53%) and guns (25%) as the typical instruments. Since weapons were not used in over three-quarters of the cases, it would appear that intimidation and/or threat of physical force is the modal instrumentality used by the offender to gain compliance.

Concerning *intra-person* variables within the offender, sexual criminality has been found to be empirically related to (pp. 55-68):

❏ Deficiencies in *heterosocial skill development* likely to result in feelings of heterosocial inadequacy and lack of assertive capacity in heterosocial situations; deficiencies in the offender's sense of *psychosexual identity; impulsivity;* personal *sexual victimization earlier in life;* pre-existing *formal psychiatric disorder,* a generalized *tendency toward aggression and/or hostility,* a generalized tendency to view women as inferior; a generalized tendency to deny or minimize personal psychological dysfunction; *neuropathology* of various sorts, including neurochemical anomalies, abnormal bioelectirical activity, and morphological or structural brain anomalies; *psychophysiologic reactivity to aberrant sexual stimuli,* typically as measured by penile circumference changes in response to *in vitro* exposure of convicted offenders to aberrant stimuli of various sorts. Indeed, Quinsey, Chaplin & Upfold (1984, pp. 656), utilizing penile tumescence as the dependent measure, found strong evidence that rapists are so sensitized to aberrant stimuli that they differ markedly from offenders convicted of non-sex crimes not only in their responses to sexual stimuli but also to stimuli which depict *non*-sexual violence, such that "[the sexual responses of] non-sex-offenders are inhibited by descriptions of violence and victim injury, whereas [those of] rapists are not."

Among *stimulus determinants* (pp. 55-77) were identified:

❏ Abuse of alcohol and/or other psychoactive substances as *biochemical lubricants;* exposure to violence and/or violent pornography, activating the typical mechanisms for *social imitation and long-distance vicarious conditioning;* dysfunctional family life, activating very tangible role models in the offender's immediate psychosocial environment; and even seasonal variations in atmospheric temperature as an environmental contingency.

Through analysis of studies of the reactions of third party observers (including prospective jurors) of depictions of rape scenarios, the *blame the victim effect* was identified both as an "international pastime" and as an element in the general social environment which supports the systematic degradation of girls and women.

The "blame the victim" effect, with male-female gender differences between respondents (such that males are more likely than female respondents to attribute blame toward the female victim), is said to obtain whether the respondents cast in the role of third-party observers were college and university undergraduates in the United States; or undergraduates in Canada, Germany, India, or Sicily; or non-student citizens of Britain or Canada; or, more disturbingly, nursing or medical students in the United States, who might be expected to serve at some future point on the staff of crisis intervention centers; and even among spouses whose partners have been victimized. This effect is especially strong when the experimental depictions suggest that the victim failed to take appropriate precautions or had herself consumed alcohol prior to, or during, the interaction that led to the rape attempt. In one particularly troubling finding, "subjects responded least favorably to an unattractive rape victim, particularly when she resisted the rape by fighting with her attacker."

Apparently, not even behavioral science researchers are immune from the tendency to blame the victim. Thus a study that must surely have warmed the hearts of National Association for Man-Boy Love [NAMBLA] stalwarts attributed responsibility for victimization in homosexual child abuse to "deprivation and family disturbance" and opined that "the children were none the worse off" because they had been criminally assaulted by adult gays; another attributed the "seductive behavior" of the victim of child sexual abuse to "pseudomaturity" on the victim's part; and yet another concluded that "rape vulnerability" was a product of psychosocial incompetence on the part of the victim. Even more disturbingly, an analysis of the decisions of British appellate courts in cases in which the penalty for incest was at issue found that "where the daughter was not a virgin, the court all but held her responsible." The underlying sexism is so rampant that it requires no interpretation. As one might expect, of course, the same effect has been observed among rapists themselves, so that it might be concluded that offenders and the general public equally enjoy "blame the victim" as a pastime.

contrast, the last thing the perpetrator of larceny seeks is an audience of any kind.

Symbolic or Tangible Reward

For the larceny offender, especially for the larceny offender who eludes detection and apprehension, tangible reward is sought, expected, and achieved. For some larceny offenders, there may be the additional benefit of a symbolic reward through what we have called "the Frizzle," which is, at bottom, a sort of savoring of the fact that one has beaten the system — for the first time, or again. To the extent that "the Frizzle" is particularly indicative of psychopathic deviation and may in fact constitute a reinforcer therefor, it is germane to underscore again the substantial body of evidence that points to a neurogenic basis for that pattern of behavior that is usually labeled by the aggregate term "psychopathic deviation."

In the case of those homicide offenders who kill during the course of tinder box-ignited character contests within a subculture of violence, the anticipated rewards are almost surely symbolic. Such is likely also the case in the balance of tinder box homicides that occur when instant arguments or long-standing disputes between friends, neighbors, or acquaintances erupt into violence. For the killer who slays a victim during the course of another felony, however, the reward expected is quite tangible — i.e., eluding detection for felony crime.

Expectation of Impunity

A substantial body of research evidence on social learning, no less than the actual data on the relative infrequency of imposition of intrusive sanction for felony crime of any sort and most particularly for property crimes, suggests that impunity may well constitute a normative expectation in a society which enacts penal laws with abandon but imprisons far less frequently than would be expected if the sanctions spelled out in those statutes were to be uniformly imposed on all parties declared guilty. Nonetheless, we believe that the generalized tendency to *under*-estimate costs and to misconstrue the benefits and risks that attach to criminal behavior is pervasive among many who behave criminally — and may, in fact, represent one operational facet of psychopathic deviation; but that tendency to under-estimate and to thus mis-construe in its turn may arise from neurogenic sources and eventuate in impulsivity as an enduring feature of behavior.

As a case in point, we focused in some detail on the research evidence on the deterrent effect of the death penalty. The most dispassionate, scientific conclusion to be drawn therefrom would appear to be that the matter remains moot. But that conclusion masks utterly the relative *in*frequency with which the death penalty has been imposed at any time in the nation's history, including during those periods when it represented the legislatively- prescribed sanction for many, many offenses short of premeditated murder in many, many states. We argued that we should not be surprised to find that the threat of the death penalty wields little deterrent effect — any more than we are surprised that the infrequency of intrusive sanction for felony crime of any sort breeds and supports a wholesale expectation of impunity on the part of would-be felons.

The expectation of impunity is in part an intra-person variable, to the extent that it reflects a generalized expectation that the actor carries about from one situation to another. But it is in part also a property of the stimulus situation, both in the specific (e.g., the opportunity to behave unobserved) and in a more generalized sense (e.g., a generalized expectation, perhaps normatively shared in certain subcultures, that criminal acts of various sorts are rarely sanctioned intrusively). Virtually the same line of reasoning applies to the stimulus value of real or imagined sanctions.

Stimulus Determinants and Potentiation of Process Variables

Among stimulus determinants, we include such characteristics as the relative accessibility of prospective targets for aggression or for theft, characteristics of the largely self-selected psychosocial environments into which the prospective actor elects to implant himself or herself, which may include environmental cues approving or disapproving criminal behavior of various sorts (e.g., violence, substance abuse, sexual offending), and contingent features of the physical environment.

These may either evoke, facilitate, or inhibit criminal behavior — and thus serve to *potentiate* other variables just as effectively as interaction among and between the principal sets of variables potentiates those sets.

☐ *REPRISE: TINDER BOX CRIMINAL VIOLENCE*

We have characterized some rather large proportion of criminal homicides as occurring under what we have termed "tinder box" circumstances — that is, circumstances in which offender and victim are *not* strangers to each other (as we have seen in Chapter 5, 79%

of all cases in which relationships can be ascertained) and in which disputes or arguments (rather than instrumental means to perpetrating another felony crime) are reported as triggering lethal violence (70% of all cases). It is likely that a large proportion of other crimes of violence take place under similar "tinder box" circumstances. To assess one dimension only: Large-scale victimization studies suggest that offender and victim are known to each other in well over half the rapes, aggravated assaults (i.e., those in which a weapon is used), and simple assaults committed annually, whether these are formally reported to law enforcement officials or not (Flanagan & Jamieson, 1988, p. 235).

We have speculated that the essential components in such tinder box circumstances are *two* actors, known to each other, *each of whom has a taste for risk,* and an *environment* that regards the taking of risks as normal or normative, so that the social milieu which envelopes both actors reinforces risky behavior. We have also opined that some (perhaps quite large) proportion of episodes may have their remote origins in disordered neurology that inclines toward impulsivity.

Neurogenesis vs. Social Learning: An Analogy

In a review of the research evidence that links alcoholism with "biological markers and precursors," the prestigious Group for the Advancement of Psychiatry (1991) observed that it has now been clearly established that, in some people, alcoholism is virtually an inherited disease and that "efforts to map the gene or genes that convey a vulnerability to alcoholism are underway." Moreover, what may be congenital, if not hereditary, dysfunctions in the neurohormonal system have also been firmly linked to alcoholism.

Suppose, for the sake of analogy, that Person X has indeed inherited the gene that yields that vulnerability to alcoholism and that he or she also suffers those neurohormonal dysfunctions that predispose to alcoholism — but that he or she has been raised in a traditionally strict Moslem culture, in which neither role models for the ingestion of beverage alcohol nor purchasable beverage alcohol are available. Would we expect that person to become an alcoholic? Or is it not more reasonable to suppose that the biological precursors are, at best, *necessary but not sufficient* conditions for the development of alcoholism? If that is so, Person X may remain forever *prone* to alcoholism — but, in the absence of socially conditioned role models and the availability of the substance itself, forever free of that addiction.

Analogically, that situation may not be very different from the linkage between neuropathology and what we have called "tinder box" criminal violence.

Neurogenesis, Socialization, Channelization

The present state of the evidence in the neurosciences inclines us strongly to the *belief* that such a taste for risk may have its origins in brain function anomalies of one or another sort, whether structural, neurochemical, or bioelectrical. For us, the case is attractively persuasive, but not yet compelling. The evidence is not so clear that it can as yet be posited axiomatically that such anomalies lead invariably to violent behavior — for it may be the case that some very large proportion of the cases of tinder box violence have their origin in brain dysfunction; but it may *not* be the case that nearly all instances of brain dysfunction lead to such violence.

What intervenes, of course, is the complex process of socialization; and that process incorporates such elements as the influence of role models within and outside the family, the intergenerational transmission of patterns of behaving, long distance vicarious influences, social imitation, *in vivo* exposure to environments that elicit and/or constrain behaviors of various sorts.

In the course of development, some people are socialized into quite peaceable and pro-social environments, so that whatever proclivities one may feel toward the emission of anti-social, aggressive, or violent behavior is quickly either suppressed or channelized into pathways the sociocultural envelope deems positive (Zaleski, 1984). Others are socialized into anti-social, or at least a-social environments, in which anti-social, aggressive, and violent behavior is readily modeled and easily learned by social imitation. To judge by the enormous popularity of motion pictures in which even "good guy" heroes, ranging from "Dirty Harry" Callahan to "The Terminator," behave in incredibly violent ways (and often in direct violation of constraints laid down for them by their acknowledged superordinates) in order to achieve purposes that are presented and widely perceived as essentially *not* anti-social, one can only conclude that the central thrust of the society at large is toward the image of the frontiersman who defines the law for himself. That image, as American cultural historians have said for a century (as we saw in Chapter 7), conveys the portrait of the invincible hero who constitutes himself the sole arbiter of the good, the true, and the just, who sets himself beyond the formal requirements of the law — and who may well, as Farley (1986) intimates, thrive on thrill-seeking for its own sake. Shorn of its romanticism, of course, that portrait reveals a set of beliefs and behaviors deeply corrosive to societal order through the rule of law.

Some interpreters will assert that diametric sociocultural milieux are sufficient in and of themselves to account for diametric differences in behavior. We assert, not quite to the contrary, that the *interaction* between a sociocultural environment of the anti-social or a-social sort and a neurogenic proclivity toward impulsivity yields a geometric progression in which one potentiates the other; moreover, we assert that a sufficiently compelling neurogenic proclivity will propel one to self-select an environment that one construes as encouraging the discharge of impulse into behavior. Nonetheless, it is patently not the case that all, or perhaps not even the majority, of those persons who suffer neurologic dysfunction will eventually behave in violently criminal ways; and, quite clearly, *socialization* and *channelization* are key constructs in understanding why they do not.

The Experience of Restlessness

But, proceeding from what we have clearly labeled as a belief, there appears to us a characteristic developmental sequence flowing from neurologic dysfunction that yields in its path psychological and social consequences of substantial import.

It is reasonable to believe that the person who suffers brain function anomaly — especially at a sub-clinical level of severity that is *not* the subject of medical attention — experiences that anomaly merely as "restlessness," as an inability to concentrate on a particular or single topic for an appreciable length of time; as a result, he or she is propelled constantly to seek serial sources of stimulation and excitement. Inevitably, the constant search for serial stimulation in order to relieve restlessness in the here-and-now rivets the person to the present, precluding consideration of the future. But he or she construes such restlessness not as something alien to how he or she construes the self, but rather as part and parcel of the self — as what our psychodynamicist colleagues would term *ego-syntonic*, rather than *ego-alien* characteristics of the self. Indeed, the prototypical person here described may be volubly proud that he/she "can't sit still — have to be up and doing," etc., etc., with little or no awareness of how distant such a pattern of behavior is from that of most members of the relevant age cohort. In its turn, an inability to concentrate impedes the capacity to construe long-term goals and objectives and the capacity to construe the means to achieve those goals and objectives; these very capacities are generally conceded to form the foundation for that *planfulness* that characterizes self-sufficient, responsible adults who are able to postpone gratification of momentary impulses in favor of achieving long-term goals.

Observers will say that the subject of our exemplary sequence has a short attention span; because of that limited capacity to concentrate coupled with the propulsion toward constant craving for sources of stimulation, he or she is likely to experience school learning problems, often formally diagnosed as "attention deficit disorder" (Bellak, 1979, 1992; Curtiss, Feczko & Marohn, 1979). Differential psychologists might want to group the composite of anomalous brain function and its sequelae under the trait-label "impulsivity," believing that, once such a trait has been named, it acquires some metaphysical reality apart from the *aggregate behaviors* for which it is a label. In its turn, that behavior which results from impulsivity rather than from planfulness is typically described as "violent," whether criminally or not.

The Continual Search for Stimulation

Phenomenologically, the person we have described will experience "boredom" with great regularity; and, to combat boredom, will constantly and serially seek new sources of stimulation, either or both in the form of novel activities or new people with whom to engage in those activities. Indeed, a quarter century ago Quay (1965) saw in the need for constant stimulation the seeds of psychopathy. By early adolescence, those efforts will almost surely lead to experimentation with mood-altering substances, particularly the central nervous system stimulants. In using such substances, he or she may actually be choosing a form of self-medication for an undiagnosed neurological disorder. But, as we have seen, people who use mood-altering substances, whether central nervous system stimulants or depressants, are at risk for both closed and open head injury, the result of which will almost certainly be an exacerbation of an underlying neurological disorder. Attempts to change the behavior of the person thus described, especially through aversive means, typically fail to produce positive results. Instead, it seems to be the case that such aversive treatment may in itself be greeted as a novel form of stimulation.

Substantial empirical evidence links such early learning problems as "attention deficit disorder" to the later emission of criminal behavior; early learning problems are held, in turn, to be precursors to the development of psychopathic deviation in adolescence (Lilienfeld & Waldman, 1990); impulsivity and psychopathic deviation are highly correlated, as are impulsivity, psychopathic deviation, habituation to mood-altering substances, and certain forms of neurological anomaly; those who score high on measures of psychopathy customarily have few friendships (and these are often quite shallow) and are typically described as "unable to profit from experience," so that even the aversive treatment of penal incarceration appears to affect their behavior minimally.

Perhaps because those of us who are not impulsive and/or do not experience a strong taste for risk tend to shun the company of those who are and who do, the latter soon enough encounter others like themselves, even if they have not been socialized in environments that reflect a culture of violence and/or a taste for risk. That conjugation is certain to produce a social environment in which impulsive behavior is construed as normal or perhaps even as desirable — an environment in which the satiation of one's taste for risk through impulsive and violent behavior is a normative expectation, especially when biochemical lubricants are added and weapons are available. Such environments, with their high tolerance for risky behavior, present unprecedented *opportunity* to behave *without* deterrence and with the full expectation of *impunity;* they systematically reinforce the mis-construing of costs, risks, and benefits associated with behavior.

The Like-Minded Playmate Who Becomes a Victim

Interpersonal disputes are inevitable in any social environment, and perhaps more so in the environments peopled by the neurogenic risk-takers we have just described. Such disputes may, in fact, be kept alive by mutual agreement between the protagonists rather than reconciled, *precisely because* they provide the rationale for a fine bout of "mixing it up" with one's "playmates" — that is to say, they may be kept at a "simmering" point by relatively conscious and deliberate decision on the part of *both* disputants. Such an interpretation conforms to the observations of Farrington, Berkowitz & West (1982) on situational characteristics that differentiate individual from group conflicts.

But those deliberately-simmering disputes add the final element to the tinder box which what observers may construe as merely a "chance spark" may ignite into criminal violence; since an analogy to sheer internal combustion implies only one actor rather than two or several, it seems inapplicable here. Yet only a subset of those disputes between contending actors are in fact ignited into lethal violence — or even into such aggravated assault as comes to the attention of law enforcement authorities. Why? Given a behavioral situation in which the elements for conflagration have been aggregated into a tinder box, what accounts for an episode of lethal violence at *this* moment, but not at some prior moment?

The intellectual shorthand, of course, is *acute potentiation*, typically of one or more intra-person variables, typically by the introduction of a new and powerful stimulus determinant or environmental contingency *or* because the salience of one or more determinant or contingency has rapidly escalated, perhaps because new observers have been added to the audience to a long- enacted "dance of the dare" — with such potentiation sufficient to interactively transform those intra-person variables Cattell would call "traits" into a "state" of readiness-to-act. Though that process is in fact quite orderly, at least at the point of post-diction reconstruing, phenomenologically it is frequently not experienced as the product of conscious deliberation or what most of us would regard as "decision."

Indeed — and here we must stress the speculative nature of our conjecture — it seems likely that the denizens of such risky environments regard each other not as "enemies," but in fact (and consistent with what the psychodynamicists would term "fixation" at a preadult level of psychosocial development) rather as "playmates." Now, one surely wants to "mix it up" with one's playmates, often in very stimulating rough-and-tumble ways, but not to harm them in any significant, much less life-threatening, way. Indeed, if our conjectures to this point are not woefully off the mark, to resolve a long-standing dispute (whether murderously or not) would be, for the risk-taker, quite counter-productive — for a long-standing dispute, with recurrent violent exchanges between the disputants, is in itself precisely the source of stimulation risk-takers seek when they self-select what we have termed "risky environments."

A conceptual model that invokes acute potentiation of one or another intra-person variable or a rapid increase in the salience of one or another stimulus determinant and/or environmental contingency is amply illustrated by Paco's death. The long-standing hostile interaction between Paco and Ben reduces to lethal violence during a very particular moment on a very particular day; mutual ingestion of a powerful psychotomimetic substance clearly potentiates whatever latent disposition toward violence lay within either antagonist — but so also does the structure of a social tradition that mandates the donning of "machismo" costumes replete with lethal weapons. In that light, we no longer see the kiss on the mouth as quite so "chance" a spark. Such an interpretation is also consistent with Farley's research on thrill-seeking behavior, with psychologist's Robert

Lindner's theme in the case study *Rebel without a Cause,* and with novelist Aldous Huxley's account of the game of "Chicken."

Hence, in the final irony, the person who, driven by disordered neurology and spurred by impulsivity and the self-selection of risky environments, has committed lethal tinder box criminal violence will characteristically denominate his or her behavior as unintentional, as an "accident." Phenomenologically, he or she may be offering us quite an accurate interpretation of how he or she has construed the situation. And, as we have seen, in such tinder box circumstances who emerges as victim and who as offender may turn on the luck of the draw; again, Paco and Ben epitomize the matter.

Our conjectural schematic linking disordered neurology to tinder box criminal violence is portrayed graphically in DISPLAY 16.

The Phenomenology of Risk

Central to our explanation of tinder box criminal violence is the notion that those prone to the taking of risks *self-select* those environments in which risky behavior is not unusual, but quite normative — those environments in which, in Wright's (1991) description, "the prospect and often the reality of violence are facts of everyday life." Now, how in the world does such a choice, patently irrational to you and to me, come to be construed as normative or desirable?

We have earlier argued that, at bottom, the pivot that guides the behavior of those persons who are labeled, on the basis of psychometric tests, as psychopathically deviate is essentially the *mis-construing* of the costs, benefits, and risks associated with behavior — invariably in the direction of *under-* estimating costs and risks and of *over*-estimating benefits. What requires further elaboration is the matter of how risks are construed and particularly how risks are *experienced.*

I do not know you, but I would wager a guess that you and I would not behave terribly differently from each other in some situations. At 3:00 a.m. and fully sober, I daresay both of us would be willing to risk breaking the law by running a red light in a non-residential area. The process of construing that stimulus situation would for each of us doubtless include consideration of the sanction attached to the behavior — i.e., breaking a law that speaks to a behavior that is *mala prohibita* rather than *mala in se,* with a sanction that is typically limited to a fine, but with no prospect (given the hour and some small vigilance on our part) of instant deterrence and but little probability of detection thereafter. Neither of us is likely to construe our *physical* safety as in jeopardy. To the extent that we construe the prospect of arrest and prosecution as unlikely *and* construe our physical safety as not likely to be compromised, we are behaving rather like the "reasonable adventurer" described by Harvey (1962) or the "eternally optimistic gambler" described by Atlas & Peterson (1990), who in essence is willing to place bets only when losing seems to have a markedly low probability and winning seems to have, on objective and publicly verifiable criteria, a substantially better than even probability.

Our belief is that the habitual risk-takers we have described, especially when their risk-taking habits have a neurogenic etiology, are quite *unreasonable* adventurers.

Were you and I to wander into the sort of environment we have denominated as part of the tinder box circumstance — say, a dingy bar whose denizens appear at least alcohol-inebriated if not drug-intoxicated as well, with many of them brandishing weapons, and with loud arguments on the periphery — I daresay that each of us would experience a threat to our physical safety. That experience will doubtless involve the classic physiological indicators of apprehension, stress, anxiety — clammy palms, lowering of peripheral body temperature (a combination that many, quite accurately, describe as "breaking out into a cold sweat"), increased heart rate, the elements indeed of "The Frizzle" as we described it (with help from Vanderbilt pharmacologist Renata Bluhm) in the last chapter. For most, that experience is quite unpleasant; your behavioral response and mine is likely to be *flight,* as we seek to distance ourselves from those fear-provoking stimuli and circumstances. On the other hand, and usually only long after we have fled from those noxious stimuli and achieved sufficient physical safety to permit rumination, if we are genuinely honest with ourselves we may admit that, for a moment back there, The Frizzle felt kind of good — but only for a moment, mind you.

Our contention is that, for the *unreasonable* adventurer, the habitual risk-taker, the phenomenology of The Frizzle is assuredly *not* as (at best) momentarily positive but quickly to be terminated, but rather as pleasurable in and of itself — and therefore to be prolonged. Perhaps anticipating the work of Farley on thrill-seeking behavior, novelist Aldous Huxley aptly described such phenomenology in his 1955 *The Genius and the Goddess;* "You want some special kind of thrill, and you deliberately work away at yourself until you get it — a green or bruise-colored lump of fear; for fear, of course, is a thrill like any other, fear is a hideous kind of fun."

Moreover, for the unreasonable adventurer for whom risk-taking issues from a neurogenic etiology, it may be that the *threshold* for the phenomenology of The Frizzle (in a very real sense, and as a result of neurological anomaly) is substantially higher than for you and me; the findings of Farley & Sewell (1976) on thrill-seeking and sensation-seeking among juvenile delinquents certainly seem to argue in that direction. If that conjecture is anywhere near the mark, then we might expect *both* that the habitual risk-taker not only does not perceive danger to physical safety in situations that would provoke apprehension followed by flight in you and me *but also* that, once he or she has penetrated the risky environment sufficiently to step over his or her own ipsative threshold for apprehensive anxiety, he or she construes the adrenalin-pumping experience of stress as pleasurable — and thus behaves in ways so as to continue or increase the sense of risk.

Unreasonable Adventurers Seeking the Frizzle

Just as one might become habituated to the normal dosages in prescription medication and thus require ever escalating dosages in order to achieve the medically therapeutic effect, so it may also be the case that the threshold for the apprehension of risk escalates for habitual risk-takers, who will in turn require ever greater and more palpable threat to physical safety before the pleasurable experience of The Frizzle is engaged. One attractive competing hypothesis might argue that, among at least some unreasonable adventurers whose habitual risk-taking behavior has a neurogenic etiology, the experience of stress, tension, anxiety, or fear is *neurochemically inhibited* in very direct ways as a consequence of neurologic anomaly or dysfunction; another might argue that those responses are inhibited in consequence of *social imitation* of fearless "macho" figures.

To the extent that he or she is successful in avoiding painful physical or social consequences even as the threshold escalates, at some extreme point a third-party observer might be tempted to characterize the *successful* unreasonable adventurer as feeling immune to the negative consequences of risky behavior; and, in common with such usage in the behavioral sciences, to attribute such a feeling of immunity to *grandiosity*, understood as an internal quality or characteristic of personality. For us, such a feeling or immunity (or indeed of grandiosity, if one prefers) *results from* behavior that has been positively reinforced; and, even though in a kind of intellectual shorthand, one might describe that immunity or grandiosity as a driving force for ever greater escalation in future risky behavior, to assert that the "trait" pre-exists behavior in any meaningful way (as a "potentiality" to behave that pre-exists behavior) is simply to

➡️ *Display 16: From Neurogenic Impulsivity to Tinder Box Criminal Violence — A Stepwise Progression*

→ NEUROLOGICAL OR NEUROPSYCHOLOGICAL ANOMALY OR DYSFUNCTION

→ RESTLESSNESS, INABILITY TO CONCENTRATE, NEED FOR SERIAL STIMULATION AND EXCITEMENT [AN AGGREGATE DIFFERENTIALISTS WILL CALL IMPULSIVITY]

→ LEARNING PROBLEMS IN SCHOOL

→ AN INCREASING TASTE FOR RISK

→ EXPERIMENTATION WITH MOOD ALTERING SUBSTANCES

→ SENSITIZATION TO, AND SELF-SELECTION OF, ENVIRONMENTS WITH HIGH TOLERANCE FOR RISK

→ HABITUAL MIS-CONSTRUING OF COSTS, BENEFITS, RISKS ASSOCIATED WITH IMPULSIVE BEHAVIOR, SUPPORTED BY VICARIOUS CONDITIONING

→ DISPUTES [OR "CHARACTER CONTESTS"] WITH "PLAYMATES" IN SUCH A TINDER BOX, BUT USUALLY OF LONG DURATION

→ ACUTE POTENTIATION OF INTRA-PERSON VARIABLE[S], USUALLY THROUGH INTRODUCTION OF A NOVEL STIMULUS DETERMINANT OR ENVIORNMENTAL CONTINGENCY, TYPICALLY CONSTRUED BY OBSERVERS AS A "CHANCE" SPARK

→ IGNITES *LETHAL VIOLENCE*

mis-construe the interactive calculus that is the very focus of process psychology.

Risk Experienced as Visceral

Thus far, we have described the phenomenology of risk-taking as largely *visceral and emotional* for the unreasonable adventurers, but as essentially *cognitive* for you and me.

No wonder, then, that we found no evidence of the pursuit of The Frizzle in the classic sense in Julio's case. True enough, on the occasion of his first theft, there were classic signs of apprehension as Julio contemplated the prospect of detection, arrest, and prosecution. But at no time, either or that first occasion nor afterward, did Julio construe himself to be in *physical* danger. Hence, though on each occasion he engaged the risk of detection and prosecution (at a low level of probability), at no point did he experience himself as in physical danger; neither the victims of theft from automobiles nor police who happen upon, or are called to, the scene are likely to assault an unarmed perpetrator. Thus, Julio's experience of risk-taking was largely cognitive, not emotional; to that extent, Julio seems more like you and me than, say, like Samb, Paco, or Ben.

Yet, toward what proved the end of his criminal career, there were surely discernible in Julio some behavioral indicia that could be construed to suggest that he believed himself to be immune from formal negative sanction — and into such immunity could be read the sense of grandiosity, as least as it applied to his criminal behavior.

Now, if that conjecture is not woefully inadequate, we may have reached a nexus that connects the person who *habitually or persistently* commits crimes of violence with little regard for the consequences of that behavior and the person who repeatedly commits crimes against property but has *successfully eluded sanction.* In the first case, sanctions will have little deterrent value, since what might be called motivation is largely visceral and emotional; in the second case, sanctions will have major deterrent value, since motivation is largely cognitive, not visceral and emotional.

And, to understand that both the former and the latter might appropriately be denominated by the differentialist (or even the psychodynamicist) as exhibiting a personality characteristic called "grandiosity" while *simultaneously* understanding that the former and the latter have arrived at what appears to be the same point by means of very different pathways, involving very different sequences of positively and negatively reinforced behavior, is to have understood the cognitive operations that quintessentially characterize process psychology.

Neurogenesis: Neither a Necessary Nor a Sufficient Condition?

Neuropathology (or, at least, neurologic anomaly) is very likely a contributory factor in a very large proportion of cases of tinder box criminal violence (and, indeed, were transitory states of organic dementia consequent upon the ingestion of mood-altering drugs to be added to the grouping, perhaps in very nearly all such cases). But it is not our contention that neuropathology alone is either a "necessary" nor a " sufficient" antecedent condition to criminal violence, or even to criminal violence of the tinder box variety.

Nor do we hold that social imitation alone constitutes either a necessary or a sufficient condition for violence, whether criminal or pro-social. Not every citizen who applauds Clint Eastwood's celebrated "Go ahead, kid; make my day" statement in the film *Sudden Impact* is, by virtue of the force of social imitation and vicarious conditioning alone, destined to arm himself or herself with an appropriately menacing Smith & Wesson revolver and walk the San Francisco waterfront (or its analogue elsewhere) in search of societal predators worthy of execution by a rogue cop who has become by self-warrant the singular arbiter of the good, the true, and the just.

Instead, the issue turns on the *interaction* between significant neuropathology (perhaps indeed experienced as restlessness, but construed as fearlessness in the face of societal predators) and an attractively violent role model (perhaps presented via a popular entertainment medium) on the one hand, and, on the other, the availability of a weapon in a sociocultural atmosphere that invites or tolerates violence. That *interactive* mix may indeed yield a *sufficient* condition for lethal violence — undertaken for what the actor construes as society's betterment when the role model is positive and pro-social, so that the actor construes himself or herself among the "good guys," but undertaken for quite contrary purposes when the actor construes himself or herself and his or her role model in diametrically different ways.

☐ THE PROCESS MODEL AND CORRECTIONAL REHABILITATION

Psychological intervention into criminal behavior most typically occurs only *post hoc,* after a crime has been committed and the offender apprehended and sentenced either to incarceration or to probation. With an assumption that criminal behavior issues from psychopathology lingering at some deeply recondite level, it is not surprising that much psychological intervention with individual offenders takes the form of individual psychotherapy. "Therapy," we all recognize, is that which is done to rid a "patient" of a "disease." Why we should be prepared to undertake a process of treatment for disease when the evidence does *not* suggest that criminal behavior is a function of disease remains quite mysterious.

Correctional rehabilitation consonant with a process psychology understanding of criminal behavior would proceed quite differently. Since there is no assumption of psychopathology as a universal trigger for criminality, professional intervention rooted in a process psychology paradigm would scarcely resemble traditional "talking cure" approaches. Since the process psychology model derives in some major part from social learning paradigms, and since social learning theory and behavior therapy are conceptually birth mates, it is to be expected that psychological intervention consistent with the process model would strongly resemble the educative and/or re-educative processes that lie at the core of behavior therapy techniques. Since the process paradigm takes full cognizance of the prospective neurogenic base for criminal behavior, we should expect that intervention based thereupon would fully utilize remedies available to correct or compensate for neurological anomalies. Thus:

- ❏ We have seen that impulsivity is consistently associated with criminal violence. A wide variety of psychological intervention strategems, *from* progressive relaxation and reciprocal inhibition *through* what Kendall & Braswell (1985) identify as "self-instructional training" for behavior control and Daniel (1992) calls "stress inoculation" *to* biofeedback techniques, have demonstrated their efficacy in curbing impulsivity. While those strategems certainly constitute psychological interventions, they most assuredly do not resemble traditional "talking cure" psychotherapy.

- ❏ At least some cases of criminal violence have a neurogenic base. An array of psychopharmacological preparations are available to curb or control neurogenic violence. Their use constitutes professional intervention, but not of the "talking cure" variety typical of traditional psychotherapy.

- ❏ We have seen that some considerable portion of criminal violence occurs under "tinder box" and "character contest" situations, in which both demography and subcultural characteristics seem to elicit behavior that, in essence, *conforms* to normative expectations embedded in a subculture of violence. A variety of behavioral intervention techniques are useful in promoting self-reliance and firm, but non-violent, self-assertion. Once again, their use constitutes effective professional intervention, but not of a character recognizable as standard psychotherapy.

❑ We have seen that a tendency to underestimate costs and to misconstrue risks and benefits is widespread among offenders. An array of educative techniques have demonstrated their utility in engendering or improving skills required for reality assessment and effective decision-making. Once again, these do not resemble standard psychotherapy.

So much for what we might do differently, in light of the process paradigm, *after* a crime has been committed and the offender apprehended. That process is analogous to treating a case of whooping cough once it has been contracted. What can or should be done to prevent infection by the pathogens that cause whooping cough, or to prevent criminal offending? Does the process paradigm point toward specific measures?

❑ THE PROCESS MODEL AND PREVENTIVE MEASURES

Once the sources of an illness are known, it is possible to undertake what have come to be called preventive medicine approaches. These customarily follow two principal avenues:

❑ Identification and elimination of pathogens that "cause" disease — as, for example, impurities in supplies of drinking water;

❑ Identification through epidemiologic measures of those persons who are particularly "at risk" to contract disorders of particular sorts (e.g., those who do not routinely have access to purified drinking water), followed by efforts to persuade such "at risk" persons to change their behavior so as to obviate the risk of disease (e.g., to find other sources of drinking water).

What are the analogues for criminal offending, and how are the means of prevention illuminated by the process paradigm?

Antecedent and Consequent Conditions and Levels of Probability

When we considered the nature of the probabilistic sciences in Chapter 4, we observed that their overarching goal is to specify a set of antecedent conditions *following which* a focal phenomenon can be expected to occur *at a particular level of probability*.

In our terms, the goal is therefore to be able to make a scientifically valid statement such as: *The multiple correlation is +0.75 between the theft of automobiles and these conditions:*

❏ *Whether* [1] the vehicle is a *late model* machine

❏ [2] that has been *left unattended,*

❏ [3] with the *key in the ignition*

❏ [4] and the *motor running,*

❏ [5] *at dusk,*

❏ [6] in a place where it *cannot be seen* by its owner or anyone else

❏ [7] when a *physically agile*

❏ [8] *adult male* with

❏ [9] a touch of *impulsivity* and

❏ [10] a *lack of due regard* for societal mores

❏ [11] *happens* on the scene.

That formulation speaks to certain antecedent conditions, both of an intra-psychic character (viz., that the prospective thief has in his or her "psychological baggage" two variables likely to dispose one toward criminal behavior) and those emanating from what we have called stimulus determinants (viz., the unattended condition of the vehicle, the opportunity to act unobserved); and the statement offers a prediction (or post-diction) at a level of association that is strong enough to energize us to want to take some preventive action.

But preventive action of what sort? Ought we to ferret out all adult males with "a touch of impulsivity and lack of due regard for societal mores" (as might be inferred from high scores on the *Ma* and *Pd* scales of the MMPI) and seek to constrain their behavior in some way? Should we discourage motorists from leaving their cars unattended so long as the motors are running and the keys are in the ignition? Or should we increase police patrols (or the extent of artificial illumination, for that matter; or insist upon the installation of remote surveillance devices utilizing closed-circuit television) in locations (like parking lots and garages near workplaces within cities) where autos might be left outside the surveillance of owners or other observers and especially at certain times (like immediately after normal working hours, roughly corresponding to dusk)?

Individual Rights and Empirical Certainty

The responses we give to those questions turn in some large measure on what we might do preventively that does *not* violate the respect for the rights of the individual that is the hallmark of a democratic society. But, in some measure, the responses turn as well on purely empirical factors. In the contemporary world, Constitutional guarantees against unreasonable intrusion and/or extra-judicial restriction of liberty surely extend to protect an individual against *assault by means of regression equations* derived from multiple correlations that are, virtually by definition, capable of revealing only non-causal associations.

Suppose, for example, that we were able to make a scientifically valid statement that conveyed a high probability of theft quite apart from considerations about the intra-psychic characteristics of prospective behavers — e.g., *The coefficient of multiple correlation is +0.75 between the theft of an automobile and these conditions: The vehicle is a late model machine that has been left unattended, with the key in the ignition and the motor running, at dusk, in a place where it cannot be seen by its owner or anyone else.* That formulation has very, very different implications for the task of prevention — implications that will not even tempt us to want to intrude upon the privacy of individuals.

We could, for purposes of illustration, vary the formulation in dozens of other ways. For example, we could predicate a strong association between theft and purely intra-psychic variables; in that circumstance, we might be tempted to urge upon our legislators changes in Constitutional guarantees so as to permit the imposition of constraints on prospective thieves. Or: we might leave our formulation precisely as it is, but attach to that set of antecedent conditions an association with theft of only +0.20. In that case, we would likely not be anxious to undertake more than cursory and non-intrusive methods of prevention.

Predicting Probability of Occurrence

In our excursions into the research literature of the probabilistic sciences of behavior bearing upon homicide and larceny respectively, we found evidence of relationships of one or another sort between criminal behavior and a wide array of psychological variables.

In general, however, the relationships were "weak" rather than "robust" — that is, the relationships exceeded chance associations but were not nearly strong enough so that knowledge of a set of antecedent variables would permit a probabilistic statement of the occurrence of an episode of criminal behavior at high levels of likelihood. Moreover, few studies dealt with multivariate antecedent conditions, and fewer still attempted to attach relative weights to the variables that comprise an antecedent set. That state of affairs yields a knowledge base that is not mired at ground zero; but neither has the knowledge base progressed very far beyond.

Correlation is a typical, if not indeed the preferred, method for assessing strength of association in the sciences of behavior; and multiple correlation has emerged as the clearly preferred method for discerning multivariate relationships between a criterion and sets of antecedent variables. In the illustration we just offered, we cited a correlation level of +0.75 between certain antecedent conditions and a criminal consequence. Were such a (multiple) level actually to emerge from an empirical expedition in search of the antecedent conditions to any felony crime rather than from a fanciful excursion such as this, there would ensue the scientific equivalent of dancing in the streets.

Uncertainty of Prediction

But it is important to bear in mind precisely what even a coefficient of this strength will *and will not permit* us to predicate. We can calculate with precision the proportion of variance in the criterion for which a coefficient of correlation of this magnitude accounts; the standard formula tells us to square the coefficient. Thus, a coefficient of +0.75 accounts for 56% of the variance in the criterion; the remaining 44%, quite clearly a proportion not to be brushed casually aside, remains unexplained by the variables compressed into even our strong coefficient and is customarily termed the variance which is "residual" in the criterion.

If we are able to predict (or, more typically, post-dict) with very great precision 56% of the variance in criminal behavior, then most certainly we have progressed beyond ground zero. But if we are able to predict *only* 56% and must attribute the remaining 44% to factors that have not yet been identified, or perhaps are unidentifiable through the customary methods of psychological research, we have clearly not progressed very far beyond ground zero.

Indeed, in any particular prediction we might make on the basis of a strong coefficient of correlation like the one we have fantasized at +0.75, in the individual case we have very nearly as high a probability of being wrong as we have of being right. That is certainly an insufficient basis for mucking about — quite in contravention of guarantees contained in the Fourth, Fifth, and Fourteenth Amendments to the Constitution — with the restriction of the liberty of those persons who might exhibit whatever intra-person characteristics load into our coefficient.

From Social Learning to Social Engineering

On the other hand, little is to be lost (at least in terms of respect for individual rights) by focusing on stimulus characteristics that elicit criminal behavior by providing the opportunity to act unobserved — in our example, perhaps by increasing illumination and visibility or increasing the frequency of police or guard patrols or requiring that vehicles be equipped with alarms or installing movement-sensing electronic security devices in or near parking lots; and those measures are equally consistent with our multivariate approach.

So: Does it all reduce to saying that, if in fact the process paradigm is robust enough to hold as a general conceptualization of criminal behavior, the only points at which we can intervene in a preventive way have to do with openness and surveillance at or near likely places of occurrence of one crime or another (Garofalo & McLeod, 1990)? Or, in crimes of violence, does it seem likely that society will not be able to control inclination or predisposition, however much control may be exerted over opportunity and the availability of weapons and/or biochemical lubricants?

Surely not at the conceptual level. Instead, on the basis of a process paradigm that has strong anchors in social learning, we can readily construe a program of *social engineering* designed not merely to prevent crime, but indeed to extirpate "inclination" and perhaps "opportunity" altogether. Thus:

❑ We have seen that social learning occurs by means of vicarious conditioning, and frequently at long-distance, so that a would-be felon comes to construe criminal behavior as possible for him or her in some large measure from the observation of role models. An ambitious program of social engineering would exert control over the journalistic and entertainment media and other means of cultural information exchange to insure the exclusive presentation and lionization of pro-social behavioral models, perhaps even to the exclusion of those negative behavioral models that purvey what Wilson & O'Leary (1980) have called "unhealthy persuasion."

❑ We have seen that infrequency of apprehension and particularly of imposition of intrusive sanction very likely functions so as to engender or reinforce an expectation of impunity. An ambitious program of social engineering would seek to redress that situation, simultaneously revamping criminal codes so that sanctions are proportionate to offenses — perhaps thereby also obviating the practice of plea-bargaining, which itself functions to evoke the expectation that no one is really expected to abide by the letter of the formal law.

❑ We have seen that alcohol and/or drug use or abuse is frequently implicated in criminal behavior, whether as engine, lubricant, or motive. An ambitious program of social engineering would perforce seek to extirpate both the motive for, and the possibility of, substance abuse.

❑ We have seen that neurological dysfunction frequently underlies impulsive violence. An ambitious program of social engineering would provide massive resources for both remedial and
preventive medicine to address the matter of neurogenic violence, with a particular focus on the disproportionately high
incidence observed in minority communities.

That agenda is indeed utopian. It likely goes without saying that
we do not anticipate its adoption and implementation. The imposition of controls over the point of opportunity is admittedly a distant
second- best step; but it is a step.

Epidemiology, At-Risk Profiling, and Self-Fulfilling Prophecies

In Chapter 5, we ventured into the arena of epidemiology, observing that, from the statistical data alone, we may be able to derive a
portrait of those who are at particularly high risk for homicide
offending. When we add even the scant evidence on personality
characteristics dependably associated with criminal homicide and
the stronger evidence on social learning, subcultural influences, and
stimulus determinants, there emerges an even clearer "at-risk"
profile.

In that case, might not preventive measures flow along epidemiological lines, following pathways charted by public health campaigns, for example, against the use of tobacco products or those
personal habits of behavior associated with contracting acquired
immune deficiency syndrome (AIDS)?

Were we to mount such a campaign in respect of criminal homicide, we might target that group at greatest risk both for victimization and for offending — viz., young black males. We might make
particular efforts to search out those among the target group with
known neuropsychological deficits, who have perhaps already exhibited impulsivity as a characteristic of personality and behavior.

And, barring massive social and economic engineering to change
the realities of life, what is our message to be? *That you are members
of the group in our society at highest risk both for homicide offending
and for homicide victimization — so much so that some sizable
proportion of you will be dead by violent means before the age of 30.*
And to *defeat* that prediction, what inducement or intervention
might we offer, short of that massive social and economic restructur-
ing? Indeed, if we have but substituted the CAT scan of today for
Lombroso's phrenology, we have not traveled far in the space of a
century.

It is at that point, of course, that there rises to the fore our
helplessness as a society to affect those conditions that are anteced-

ent to that dismal prediction. Indeed, one need not even be much of a Marxist camp follower to wonder whether a situation in which homicide, sexual assault (Pallone, 1990, pp. 34-36), and other crimes of violence (O'Brien, 1987) remain largely intra-racial — so that non-whites kill, injure, maim, and rape other non-whites out of all proportion to their representation in the society *and* that fewer whites are so victimized than would be expected as a function of their representation in the society — is not perfectly acceptable in a society that still divides itself largely into racial castes.

TINGED REBELLIOUSNESS

One needs no re-reading of Frantz Fanon's *The Wretched of the Earth*, nor even of Anthony Burgess' *A Clockwork Orange*, to be convinced that the majority is far safer when aggressive propensities reinforced by a subculture of violence remain directed inward — rather than flow outward. Indeed, Toch & Adams (1988, pp. 189-193) have used the term "tinged rebelliousness" to describe situations in which aggressivity is directed primarily toward persons perceived as occupying positions of authority. In a caste-riven society, the task of maintaining the *status quo* is surely facilitated by conditions that contain criminal violence intra-racially.

But, if we are left with a bald prediction followed by no means of effective intervention — whether through attention to remediation of neurological injury and disorder in the minority community (Bell, 1986), of pervasive poverty and social disorganization (Hawkins, 1989), or of subcultural influences that elicit "character contests" as a routine feature of life (Thomas, 1987) — our exercise in epidemiological alerting will perhaps reduce itself to the pronouncement of a self-fulfilling prophecy.

In that circumstance, we might want to distribute arm patches inscribed with slogans like "Born to Kill" (*or*, to borrow Nick Romano's celebrated shibboleth in the 1948 film *Knock on Any Door,* "Live fast, die young, and have a good looking corpse") along with our campaign literature — for we shall certainly have applied a *label* that creates its own self-fulfilling prophecy (Goffman, 1963; Newman, 1974, 1975). As Scheff (1964) has it, the very act of labeling formulates a role to be played by the person who is being labeled — indeed, essentially with the *permission* of whoever is doing the labeling. Thus:

> Labeling . . . creates a pattern of "symptomatic" behavior in conformity with the stereotyped expectations of others. To the extent that the role [implied in the label] becomes a part of the self- conception, a person's ability to control his own behavior may actually become impaired.

There is every reason to believe that applying a *predictive* label like *at high risk for criminal violence* may in fact potentiate whatever intra-person and external determinants are at play in the person to whom that label is applied in such fashion as to elicit a self-fulfilling prophecy.

POSITIVE PRESCRIPTIVE LABELS: THE ROSENTHAL EFFECT

A substantial body of research over a long period (Scheff, 1966; Mechanic, 1900, pp. 94-106; Pallone, 1986, pp. 39-40) has demon-

---

▭⟩ *Choreography of the Dare: A Math Teacher Challenges a Juvenile Delinquent*

In earlier chapters, we have referred to several investigations conducted by Carl Bell of the University of Chicago medical faculty and published in the *Journal* of the *National* (as distinct from the American) Medical Association. Bell's career itself traces the remarkable effects of a "dare" choreographed into precisely the appropriate moment in the life of a young delinquent who seemed well on his way to becoming a homicide statistic:

☐ Psychiatrist Carl Bell is a man with a mission: to stem the tide of violence destroying the black community from within . . . A former gang member, Bell transformed himself into a physician and decided to commit his own time and the resources of the mental health center [he directs in Chicago] to fighting black-on-black violence. He knows that by age 11, four of every five urban black children will have witnessed a beating, stabbing, or shooting. And as a community psychiatrist, he wants them to know that there is a better way. . . . "If you see one child with a rat bite, as a physician you carefully treat the rat bite and hope that it never happens again; but if you see two children from the same neighborhood with rat bites . . . you set up a program in that neighborhood to exterminate the rat population." Carl Bell knows what an inner city young man's aggressiveness can accomplish, both bad and good; he's been there. "I was pretty much a juvenile delinquent until I met Milton Bins, my geometry teacher, who is black . . . When I was 15 or so, I messed up something in his class, and he embarrassed me by asking, 'Are you going to use your brains or are you going to be a jerk for the rest of your life?' I was furious, and I decided to get him, but on his own terms. Suddenly I learned how to learn, and I was on my way . . . I think that the reason I studied as hard as I did was negative — I wanted to prove that blacks are not academically inferior."

That decision led to Bell's own remarkable upward climb. In the best of all worlds, it should have been a path suddenly filled with light, air, hope, happiness — but, in Bell's own words:

☐ My brother Bill had gone from the gangs to the Army and then to being a Chicago cop. There was a robbery one night, and Bill, who was off duty and out of uniform, joined two uniformed white officers in chasing the robbers . . . Bill had trapped one of the robbers. Well, two other policemen had joined the chase and they apparently weren't aware of who Bill was. When they saw him — a black man with a gun in his hand — they killed him. I was told that he had six bullets in the back.

• *Source:* Meharry Medical College. 1991. *Psychiatrist Carl Bell.* Nashville: The College.

strated rather conclusively that the pronouncement of labels that convey *deviance* dependably enable, elicit, or otherwise engender behavior that deteriorates after application of, and in congruence with, the application of the label — that is, that deviates *negatively* from a norm. That effect is particularly strong when the application of a label (like "mentally ill") is accompanied by some action on the part of those applying the label to segregate those to whom the label is applied (for example, through placement in a psychiatric hospital).

That is certainly the "downside." But there is also evidence that *positive* self-fulfilling prophecies can also be pronounced and induced to fulfillment through the attachment of label which convey positive rather than negative behavioral expectations and thus enable, elicit, or otherwise engender behavior that deviates in positive directions from a norm.

Nearly 25 years ago, Harvard psychologist Robert Rosenthal and educator Leonore Jacobsen (1968) published a study entitled *Pygmalion in the Classroom*, destined for fame and controversy [Note 1]. To test whether a prophecy could be induced to self-fulfillment, these investigators told teachers that certain children who were to be in their classes the following school year had scored at high levels on a fictitious measure of "late intellectual blooming" (termed the "Harvard Test of Inflected Acquisition") administered during the summer *and* that the teacher could therefore well expect a major *and positive* change in the child's intellectual behavior during the subsequent year. In actuality, the children had merely been selected at random; and, it is imperative to note, in this study the children themselves were *not* told that they had been included among the mythical group of "late bloomers." Yet communicating positive information about the expectation of improved intellectual performance of "late blooming school children" to the teachers of these children indeed led to higher grades for the "bloomers" group than for a control group about whom no expectation statements were made.

What appears to have happened constitutes a classical paradigm for the self-fulfilling prophecy. Communicating *positive* expectations about the cognitive development of school children seemed dependably to be followed by several positive effects:

❑ Teachers apparently expected more positive behavior from the "late blooming" children and communicated these expectations in many subtle ways.

❑ The children responded by behaving in ways that corresponded to their teachers' expectations.

❑ Once they had experienced (with the appropriate feedback and reinforcement) that they were able to behave in positive ways that elicited appropriate, positive reinforcements, *the children came to expect themselves to behave in these more positive ways* — and, for aught we know, to perceive themselves in very much more positive ways on that account.

And these effects appear to have occurred *in the absence of* any basis whatever for expecting a change in the behavior of the children; instead, the children targeted for this *positive but baseless* self-fulfilling prophecy had simply been selected at random. Indeed, it is a matter of some irony that, because it involved systematic deception (of the teachers), the Rosenthal/Jacobsen study could not be conducted under Federal guidelines and ethical canons concerning human subjects that prevail today.

More recently, Rosenthal (1987) has reported results of a large scale meta-analysis of over 400 studies of "expectancy effect" that demonstrate conclusively that individuals who are targeted for *positive but baseless* expectations are found to have experienced a *positive* self-fulfilling prophecy — i.e., they behave in accordance with the expectation.

It is a macabre observation that Charles Thomas (1987) of the University of California at San Diego proposed — in an article published in the *Journal* of the *National* Medical Association, the remnant of a "separate but equal" organization for nonwhite physicians that traces its origins to those days (not long ago) when membership in other medical organizations was closed to people of color — that "the best antidote to Black homicidal violence comes from a pro-social effort based on a self-image that gives a feeling of positive accomplishment." The methodology of Rosenthal & Jacobsen might suggest a means and a pathway to eliciting accomplishment and to the subsequent construction of a positive self-image predicated on genuine accomplishment.

❑ **ENSURING CONDITIONS THAT ELICIT PRO-SOCIAL BEHAVIOR**

In our illustration, we set forth a prediction that, at a particular level of probability, an automobile would be stolen. We did not prognosticate about what would happen thereafter, nor did we sketch alternate scenarios that might unfold under the reciprocal probability that the vehicle would *not* be stolen.

Thief *A* might take the vehicle for a joy-ride but abandon it sometime later essentially undamaged. But *B* heads immediately for a "chop shop," where he can dispose of the vehicle for cash and where it will subsequently be cannibalized. With some confidence, we can predict that the A's motives differ substantially from B's.

These two do not exhaust the possibilities, however. There is also C, who takes the car for a joy-ride, then yanks the stereo system from the dashboard in unseemly manner, slashes the leather seats, punctures the tires, and cracks the windshield into the bargain. We might suspect that C's motives differ both from those of A and from those of B. And we might extend the permutations and combinations almost endlessly. Suffice it, however, to underscore that the same anti-social behavior, even in the face of the same stimulus characteristics and opportunity structure, may pivot on very different intra-person characteristics.

But our tale is not finished, for here comes Person D, who sees the vehicle, notes its accessible condition, shrugs or shakes his head (perhaps as if to say to himself, "People should be more careful"), and walks blithely on. Finally, there is E, who similarly notes the condition of the vehicle, takes it upon himself to remove the keys from the ignition, and searches out the owner.

To make the tale complete, let's have E say something to the owner rather more like "I think you must have forgotten your keys" than like "Look, you dumb SOB, you're damn lucky an honest citizen like me found these keys. Anybody stupid enough to leave the keys in the ignition doesn't deserve a nice car like that."

The problem for our society and our world is to learn how to breed more people like E. We might confidently expect that a world filled with Es might look very different in terms of crime and justice.

Distinguished psychologist George Albee (1959) has long insisted that the only effective means to impede mental disorder is through what he calls "primary prevention," by which he means the construction of a set of conditions that reliably and dependably elicit and reinforce positive development and pro-social attitudes and behavior. In more operational terms, for Albert Bandura the task might be the "design of those social conditions under which persons will emulate high standards of self-reward," even in the absence of third-party observation, in a "self-monitoring reinforcement system" oriented pro-socially (Bandura, Grusec & Menlove, 1967-a, 449).

That sounds indeed like a formula for the propagation of E — and we seem to have come to the point at which the primary interests of process psychology and of criminal justice coincide precisely.

☐ EPILOGUE: EXCULPATION VS. EXPLANATION — ON THE INTERSECTION OF CRIMINAL AND PSYCHOLOGICAL DEVIANCE

LIKE MOST OTHER PSYCHOLOGISTS WHOSE WORK HAS INCLUDED FORENSIC and correctional applications, our initial contacts with persons involved in the criminal justice system came through those adjudicated as guilty of criminal behavior *or* who were awaiting trial on criminal charges. In those days, now quite long past, mental health professionals who had contact with the criminal justice system primarily through direct service to adjudicated offenders sentenced to incarceration whose behavior within the institution had suggested to someone in authority that psychological intervention might be required *or,* in outpatient settings, when the question of the mental health or illness of a defendant was at issue in a pleading or at time of sentencing.

Hence, our clinical experience with offenders or alleged offenders came through a subset in whom our clinical judgment told us psychological and criminal deviance existed side-by-side. It is little wonder, then, that the prevailing view among those of us whose experience is limited to contact with offenders or alleged offenders belonging to that subset tends to congeal around the proposition that psychological and criminal deviance are intimately, and possibly causally, related.

By the same set of tokens, those observers, analysts, and commentators whose experience with offenders has been limited primarily to those belonging to other subsets — in whom, for example, criminal behavior coexists with socially pathological family circumstances *or* with mental retardation *or* with economic entrapment in poverty-ridden communities *or* with consistent exposure to negative role models which lionize crime and delinquency *or* with habituation to mood-altering biochemical substances *or* with colossal indifference to religion, for that matter — will understandably enough want to attribute the "causes" of criminal behavior to those co-extant factors they themselves have been sensitized to observe, analyze, and comment upon.

Indeed, after reviewing the data on the epidemiology of mental disorder among imprisoned offenders, Pallone (1990, pp. 123-127) has argued with some conviction *both* (1) that the rate of such disorder diagnosable according to formally recognized criteria such as are contained in the American Psychiatric Association's *Diagnostic & Statistical Manual of Mental Disorders* is very likely nearly 60%, or roughly three times as high as among the general population; *and* (2) that, against the M'Naghten Standard and its variants, only a tiny proportion of such disorders are *exculpatory* of criminal behavior.

At best, then, formal mental disorder may be *explanatory but not exculpatory*. But: explanatory in what sense — that is, "causative," or merely "correlated with"?

For reasons we have reviewed in some detail in earlier chapters, the view that criminal behavior issues from, or is "caused" by, mental illness proves quite really rather naive about the process by which behavior comes to be formally labeled as criminal. Instead, it seems to be the case that some (but by no means all) psychologically disordered persons commit formally criminal offenses — and that some (but by no means all) formally criminal offenses are committed by persons who are psychologically disordered. Once we expand our limited clinical experience by turning to the empirical data of the sciences of behavior, it becomes quite unnecessary to appeal conceptually to psychological disorder as a *pivotal* generative construct in order to understand the psychological dynamics which undergird the emission and maintenance of criminal behavior.

INSTEAD, THE PROCESSES BY WHICH A BEHAVIOR — even one known to be contrary to the provisions of law, let alone pristine morality — comes to be construed as possible and desirable for the self, by which that behavior is incorporated into an actor's personal repertoire for recurrent or habitual emission, by which behavior is learned through social imitation and maintained through cultural reinforcement — essentially processes within the domain of the "normal" rather than the "abnormal" — account adequately for the dynamics of that behavior which, given the vagaries and contingencies of our system of criminal justice, may *or may not* come to be formally adjudicated as criminal. For those reasons, the process psychology paradigm *explains*, but does *not* exculpate criminal behavior.

Moreover, if we think as deeply about these issues as have Erikson (1966) and Wiggins (1973), we recognize that, even *a priori*, there is no particularly strong reason to equate criminal deviance and psychopathological deviance.

IT IS AROUND THE INTERACTIVE BIOPSYCHOSOCIAL PROCESSES that yield criminal behavior that the process psychology paradigm has been constructed — as a general framework through which the psychological dynamics antecedent to formally criminal behavior can be comprehended and through which emerging empirical data can be ordered. And that paradigm, moreover, is also capable of incorporating data bearing on socially pathological family circumstances, mental retardation, economic entrapment in poverty-ridden communities, consistent exposure to negative role models which lionize crime and delinquency, habituation to mood-altering biochemical substances — and even colossal indifference to religion, for that matter.

YET AND STILL, YET AND STILL— there is something deeply troubling about the disjunction, something many of us find not quite right or proper. It may be more difficult for us to accept a junction between psychological and criminal deviance that is "merely" explanatory — but not exculpatory.

Most of us are unlikely to raise major objections to the proposition that property crimes (particularly those which we can delude ourselves into believing are "victimless," at least in the sense that loss is compensable through casualty insurance) are quite understandable as the product of perfectly "normal" and not pathological psychological processes. But there is something residually disturbing about the proposition that the cruel and deliberate aggression of one human being against another is *not* the product of pathological psychological processes.

Have we, perhaps, become so inured to "forgiving," to simply writing off, to exculpating in a very real sense those acts of cruelty which are patently the product of disordered minds that some of us would much prefer it to be the case that all such acts of criminal violence could be construed as arising from mental disorder?

And is that a way of saying that, among those who have been reasonably well socialized in concert with prevailing social norms and values, psychological deviance is more *understandable* — and, to that extent, more "acceptable" — than is criminal deviance, or at least that criminal deviance that involves deliberate or premeditated violence?

BUT: "UNDERSTANDABLE" IN WHAT SENSE? Axiomatically, if not really by definition, the actions of a madman are unpredictable. But not so unpredictable are those of an actor following an orderly progression dictated by the dynamic calculus between intra-psychic and extra-psychic variables, each of which is discoverable and, once discovered, susceptible to positive control by one means or another.

Well, then: Perhaps "acceptable," because we can accept that the mentally deranged might (all unwittingly, of course) behave in cruel, vicious, destructive ways — for they are, indeed by definition, abnormal, quite unlike you and me. *We* behave in accordance with the "normal," and we do not behave criminally. How then can it be that criminal behavior is the product of "normal" psychological processes?

❏ *Well, then, Julio, me lad: You had the best of it, you know. Married the boss's daughter and inherited the business into the bargain. Needed a few extra bob — and simply reached out for it. And got away with it for donkey's years, so don't be complainin'. A good job of it if you'd been nipped proper by the coppers, and you'd have had to pay the price.*

❏ *Sad, sad, sad, Ben. You certainly should have stayed at home. Had you never tasted marijuana, might you and Paco have celebrated many a Christmas night together?*

❏ *Alas, Squire! Did you ever have much of a chance? A victim you were, and over and over, and we should all hang our heads in shame. Who belongs behind bars — you or us?*

IF JULIO LACKED THE WIT AND CHARM of the confidence trickster celebrated in the entertainment media, so that he failed to elicit our sympathy, neither did he evoke our strong enmity. Most of us were content that Julio had belatedly been forced to "go straight," and few of us would have preferred that he be convicted and given an intrusive penalty. But few of us doubted that Julio behaved with calm deliberation, nor were we tempted to attribute his motivation or his behavior to pathological psychological factors.

Squire is patently a different story. To be sure, Squire was a victim, and he never had much of a chance; there's little to debate in that. Nor is there much to debate about his embrace of lethal violence — and *not* during the heat of battle, not under tinder box conditions, but instead with considerable foresight, planning, and patience. Those are certainly not the characteristics of a madman.

That Squire construed taking the life of another human being as an acceptable and even desirable behavior, and surely as infinitely preferable to invoking the mechanisms of formal social control by reporting to prison authorities an attempt at aggravated assault (a way of behaving that, however civilized it may seem to us, would have marked him as unmanly within prison society), that he drew from his repertoire precisely those behaviors needed to construe a clever and well-conceived plan, and that he implemented that construction in lethal violence, is itself a measure of the extent to which he had *not* been socialized in concert with the social norms and values we like to believe prevail in the society at large. And that is perhaps as sound an operational definition of criminal behavior as one can propose.

Understanding that Squire was indeed victimized over and over again (first by his father, then by the child protection agencies and the courts, finally by the American military) and that he surely never had much of a chance helps to *explain* his homicidal behavior — but does not exculpate that behavior.

WE ARE LED INEVITABLY BACK to Kai Erikson (1966, p. 6): "Deviance is not a property *inherent in* any particular kind of behavior; it is a property *conferred upon* that behavior by those people [who] consider [it] so dangerous or embarrassing or irritating that they bring special sanctions to bear against the persons who exhibit it."

YOU AND I HAVE BEEN SOCIALIZED to apply one set of sanctions, which we identify as more-or-less punitive, to those whose behavior is so dangerous or embarrassing or irritating that society has defined it as criminally deviant. We apply quite another set of sanctions, which we are likely to identify as more-or-less therapeutic, to those whose behavior is so dangerous or embarrassing or irritating that society has defined it as psychologically deviant.

Consistent with the way we construe ourselves, perhaps we prefer the therapeutic over the punitive perhaps because that way of construing things *retrospectively* justifies a mask of benevolence. To that extent, a junction between criminal and psychological deviance that is exculpatory may be infinitely more congruent with how we construe ourselves than a junction that is merely explanatory. But, however much it may reveal about how we would like to perceive the world as an orderly place where only mad people do bad things, an exculpatory junction has very little to do with the reality of criminal behavior.

☐ SUMMARY

This chapter has summarized the process psychology paradigm for criminal behavior, offered some refinements thereof, and discussed its application, principally through correctional rehabilitation and through alternate preventive regimens. In addition, we reviewed an elaborated schemata for tinder box criminal violence, anchored in the process psychology paradigm.

Tinder box circumstances surround a large proportion of criminal homicides in this country and may also further characterize other crimes of violence. Quintessentially, tinder box circumstances involve disputes, often long-standing, between actors who are related to or known to each other. We have offered a reprise of our notions on the progression from neurologic or neuropsychological anomaly or dysfunction to lethal criminal violence under tinder box circumstances.

After sketching an ambitious program of social engineering based on the process paradigm, we urged that such measures be directed primarily at stimulus characteristics that convey a sense of opportunity to prospective actors rather than to the characteristics of

those persons we might perceive to be prospective malefactors themselves. The springs for such urgings lie not only in the safeguarding
of individual liberty that constitutes the bedrock for any democratic
society, but also in the very real limitations of empirical behavioral
science.

Finally, we touched briefly on Albee's conception of "primary
prevention" and on Bandura's conception of positively-oriented "self-
monitoring reinforcement systems" in relation to the elicitation and
reinforcement of pro-social attitudes and behavior — and perhaps
arrived at the point at which the interests of process psychology and
of criminal justice intersect.

☐ NOTES & COMMENTARY

☐ 1. *Sharp Criticism of the Rosenthal Effect*

Not all commentators agree with our sanguine view of the Rosenthal &
Jacobsen methodology. Indeed, quite sharp criticisms were offered contemporaneously by the eminent psychologist Robert L. Thorndike (1968) and more
recently by Samuel Wineburg (1987). These criticisms have both been anticipated (1966) and countered (1987) by Rosenthal.

Glossary

ADJUDICATION According to Simon (1988, p. 147), the formal pronouncement of a decision in a legal case by a duly authorized judge. The decision in a criminal case will speak to the guilt of the defendant and in a civil case to the merits of the claims of each litigating party. *See also* JURISDICTION.

ADDICTION According to Feldman & Quenzer (1984, p. 435), "compulsive drug use, characterized by overwhelming involvement with the use of the drug, the securing of its supply, and a high probability of relapse after withdrawal."

ALEXITHYMIA In the *Glossary* of the American Psychiatric Association (Stone, 1988, p. 10), "difficulty in describing or recognizing one's own emotions, with a limited fantasy life and general constriction in the affective life." Persons who display this symptom are often said "not to have an inner life." As a result, their behavior seems to be governed by external stimuli, with little or no concern for the consequences of their actions.

ALCOHOLISM [Alcohol dependence syndrome] In the U.S. Public Health Service edition of the *International Classification of Diseases* (1989, p. 1080), a psychological and physical state "resulting from taking alcohol and characterized by behavioral and other responses that always include a compulsion to take alcohol on a continuous or periodic basis in order to experience its psychic effects, and sometimes to avoid the discomfort of its absence; [physical] tolerance may or may not be present. A person may be independent on alcohol and other drugs . . . alcohol dependence is associated with alcoholic psychosis or with physical complications." In its turn, *alcohol psychosis* is described as an "organic state due mainly to excessive consumption of alcohol" in which "defects of nutrition are thought to play an important role." Among the principal manifestations of alcohol psychosis are *alcohol amnestic syndrome,* which appears to affect memory for recent events in particular, and *alcoholic dementia.*

ANOMIE In the *Glossary* of the American Psychiatric Association (Stone, 1988, p. 15), "apathy, alienation, and personal distress resulting from the loss of goals previously valued." The term derives from the work of EMILE DURKHEIM on the triggers for suicide. Anomie is often cited as a principal pivot for criminal beavior in sociological accounts of criminogenesis (Cohen, 1988).

BIOFEEDBACK In the *Glossary* of the American Psychiatric Association (Stone, 1988, p. 23), "the use of instrumentation [e.g., to measure the psychophysiological correlates of stress, anxiety, tension] to provide information about variation in one or more of the subject's own physiologic processes not ordinarily perceived, e.g., brain wave activity, muscle tension, or blood pressure." Biofeedback instruments are frequently used in *clinical behavior therapy* to help clients or patients gain control over their emotional states (or at least over the physiological correlates thereof) and are sometimes used in psychological assessment to validate emotional states depicted in the results of projective or actuarial measuring devices.

BIVARIATE ANALYSIS *See* MULTIVARIATE ANALYSIS.

BRAIN STRUCTURES [Brain Morphology] A term that refers collectively to the principal anatomical structures of the brain. In what she calls "the modal brain," according to Liederman (1988, pp. 375-376), the *right hemisphere* "is more important for the synthesis of stimuli over space and time into configurational gestalts," so that the "perception of three- dimensional space, visuospatial patterns, and musical chords is mediated primarily by the right hemisphere," while the *left hemisphere* "is more important for the analysis of stimuli as discrete, finely timed events," so that "behaviors such as speech, speech-sound discrimination . . . and syntactic comprehension are mediated primarily by the left hemisphere." The *frontal lobes* are generally held to be the "seat" of such mental functions as cognition; the *parietal lobes,* of such functions as the integration of sensory signals and of motor activity; the *temporal lobes,* of such functions as memory, pattern recognition, and visual-motor coordination; and the *occipital lobes,* of vision. The various lobes are linked through complex networks of neural pathways, across the synapses or junctions of which signals are transmitted bioelectrically and biochemically, via a wide array of neurotransmitting enzymes and agents. According to the U.S. Public Health Service edition of the *International Classification of Diseases* (1989, p. 1093), *frontal lobe syndrome* is a condition characterized by "Changes in behavior following damage to the frontal areas of the brain," including "a general diminution of self-control, foresight, creativity, and spontaneity, which may be manifest as increased irritability, selfishness, restlessness, and lack of concern for others . . . measurable deterioration of intellect or memory is not necessarily present . . . particularly in persons previously energetic, restless, or aggressive, there may be a change toward impulsiveness, boastfulness, temper outbursts."

COMPETENCE to stand trial Legal concept, indicative of whether a defendant in a criminal proceeding understands the nature of the charges against him or her, understands the consequences that may result from conviction, and is able to participate with an attorney in the preparation of a defense. Insanity, mental retardation, and/or memory deficits are typically cited to support a claim of *incompetence* to stand trial. According to the *Glossary* of the American Psychiatric Association (Stone, 1988, p. 196), "The test for competency to stand criminal trial applies to the defendant's state of mind *at the time of the trial*" and is thus to be distinguished from his or her state of mind at the time of the allegedly criminal behavior; the latter may determine whether or not an *insanity* defense may be responsibly raised but is quite independent of the competence issue. *See* Chapter 2.

CONDUCT DISORDER A diagnostic category *and / or* a common-usage description frequently applied to juveniles who engage in aggressive, wanton, or seemingly senseless delinquent acts. In the U.S. Public Health Service edition of the *International Classification of Diseases* (1989, p. 1085), *conduct disorders* are described as "mainly involving aggressive and destructive behavior and . . . delinquency . . . used [to describe] abnormal behavior in individuals of any age which gives rise to social disapproval but which is *not* part of any other psychiatric condition [although] Minor emotional disturbances may also be present. To be included [in this diagnostic category], the behavior, as judged by its frequency, severity, and type of associations with other symptoms, must be *abnormal in its context.*" According to this source, *conduct disorders* differ from *adjustment reactions* by virtue of "a longer duration and a lack of close relationship in time and content to some source of stress." Conduct disorders differ from *personality disorders* "by the absence of deeply ingrained maladaptive patterns of behavior present from adolescence or earlier." Among the conduct disorders of particular interest to the student of the engines for criminal behavior is *impulse control disorder,* described as a "failure to resist an impulse, drive, or temptation to perform some action which is harmful to the individual or to others." Another important category, especially for those interested in the behavior of delinquent youth gangs, is *socialized conduct disorder,* described (p. 1086) as a "conduct disorder in individuals who have acquired the values of behavior of a delinquent peer group to whom they are loyal and with whom they characteristically steal, play truant, and stay out late at night. There may also be sexual promiscuity."

CONSTRUCT According to Wiggins (1972, p. 398- 399), "some postulated attribute of people, assumed to be reflected in test performance." More generally, however, *that which is construed;* therefore, an idea, conceptualization, or conceptualized plan of behavior or action which has been developed after reasonably detailed thought.

CONTINGENCY According to O'Leary & Wilson (1975, p. 481), the extent to which the occurrence of one event is dependent on the occurrence of another event.

CRIME, Taxonomy of A *crime* is any behavior prohibited by a code of *criminal law* for which a *punitive sanction* (whether by fine or incarceration) is legislatively prescribed. A crime is usually further categorized as a *felony* or as a *misdemeanor* [q.v.]. The two major groupings that have come to be recognized for data-gathering purposes are *crimes of violence* and *property crimes.* Among the *crimes of violence* (sometimes, virtually interchangeably, called *crimes against the person* or *crimes of personal victimization*). the following are typically included: *Homicide, forcible rape, robbery* (taking something of value from another *by force* or threat of force), and *aggravated assault* (an attack upon the person of another, usually with the use of a weapon). Among the *property crimes*, these offenses are typically included: *Burglary* (unlawful entry of a structure to commit a theft or other felony), *larceny, motor vehicle theft,* and *arson* (purposeful fire-setting). Other criminal offenses generally not included in the two major categories (though clearly classifiable into one of those clusters) are *buying, selling, or receiving stolen property; counterfeiting; disorderly conduct; drug law violations,* including those related to operating a motor vehicle while intoxicated; *embezzlement; family law offenses,* including neglect, abuse, non-support, and desertion of family and/or children; *forgery; gambling law violations; liquor law violations; prostitution; sex offenses other than forcible rape; simple assault; vagrancy; vandalism;* and *weapons laws violation.*

CRIMINOGENESIS Collectively, those variables from which crime arises; thus, the causes, correlates, and/or antecedents of criminal behavior.

CULPABILITY A legal term, indicative of whether an actor is *formally* guilty of an act of criminal behavior and is thus liable to punishment therefor. Culpability is established only upon *adjudication.* An actor may emit a behavior that is patently contrary to the provisions of law but may elude detection *or* an actor may be found to lack the intent to break the law or to harm another (i.e., to have acted without *mens rea*). In either case, he or she has escaped culpability.

DECRIMINALIZATION Term used to describe a situation in which a behavior which has previously been defined legislatively as a *felony* punishable by a term of imprisonment is re-defined *either* as a *misdemeanor* punishable by imposition of a fine *or* by a term of incarceration for a relatively short period in a jail rather than prison facility *or* as no longer contrary to law and thus does not merit punishment. In the first category fall situations in which, in some states the possession of so-called "soft drugs" in quantities small enough to suggest that the intent is for personal use rather than for trafficking has been re-defined legislatively as a misdemeanor, for which the prescribed sanction (at least upon first conviction) is a fine. In the second category fall situations in which the so-called "Sunday blue laws" which prevented the conduct of business on the Christian Sabbath have been repealed, so that opening or patronizing stores of all sorts no longer carry any penalty. In yet another situation falls the impact of the U.S. Supreme Court's decision in the historic *Roe v. Wade* abortion rights case, so that, subsequent to that decision, the seeking or performing of an abortion was *judicially* rather than legislatively re- defined as a non-criminal behavior.

DETERMINANT In mathematics, a term which refers to a member of that collectivity that determines a function — for example, the points *A* and *B* are said to be the determinants of the straight line which connects them (on a plane surface). In the behavioral sciences, the term is used analogically to refer to each of the variables which determines (or even more loosely, contributes to) a behavior. In process psychology, behavior is seen as a function of the interaction betwen two sets of determinants: those which are categorized as *intra-person,* to refer to relatively enduring characteristics of the behaver, and those categorized as *stimulus determinants,* to refer to the characteristics of an ambient stimulus situation which evoke or elicit certain types of behavior. Some process theorists would also include in the dynamic calculus that produces behavior other extra-psychic characteristic such as the general political structure of the health of the general economy, while others hold that these variables acquire potency only as they are incarnated either in the person or in the impinging stimulus situation. *See* CHAPTER 1.

DEVIANT *See* NORMAL.

DRUG ABUSE   In the U.S. Public Health Service edition of the *International Classification of Diseases* (1989, pp. 1089-1090), a medical diagnostic category that "includes cases where an individual . . . has come under medical care because of the maladaptive effect of a drug on which he is *not* dependent and that he has taken on his own initiative to the detriment of his health or social functioning." In the same source (p. 1090), *drug dependence* is described as a psychological and physical state "resulting from taking a drug, characterized by behavioral and other responses that always include a compulsion to take the drug on a continuous or periodic basis in order to experience its effects [or] to avoid the discomfort of its absence." Drug dependence gives rise with some frequency to such *concomitant* conditions as **drug-induced psychosis, drug-induced hallucinosis,** and/or **drug-induced organic delusional syndrome** and may perpetuate as **organic personality disorder.**

ECONETICS   According to Cattell (1980, pp. 220-221), "that branch of psychology concerned with laws *relating ecometric to psychometric* properties . . . classifying and measuring the social, physical and ideational world around us efficiently." Econetic properties are the physico-socio-ideational- historical characteristics of the external environment. Cattell asserts that "the psychologist would have only half a science, and indeed, a 'private world' if he were content to continue simply to describe and measure situations solely in psychological terms, unattached to an outer taxonomy" which taxonomy the ecometric properties are found.

EMPIRICAL   A term of art in the sciences and especially the sciences of behavior, employed in contrast to the term *conceptual.* An *empirical* approach proceeds from the *measurement,* through more or less sophisticated means, of a phenomenon of interest. The means of measurement may be no more than the observation, verified by many observers simultaneously, *that* a phenomenon has occurred, or that a phenomenon regularly occurs under certain conditions, which conditions are also dependably observed and validated among many observers; or the means of observation may involve highly developed measurement through psychometric or other instruments, along with the manipulation of certain variables (typically termed "experimental" variables) in order to determine their effect(s) on the phenomenon under investigation. An empirical approach thus invariably proceeds *inductively,* from empirical data at the level of observation and measurement, to the level of conceptualization, at which a number of different instances of observation and measurement of the same phenomenon (or highly similar phenomena) may be cognitively integrated to yield a *conceptual model.*

ENZYME   In the *Glossary* of the American Psychiatric Association (Stone, 1988, p. 62), "An organic compound that interacts with a biologic substrate to form a new chemical, either . . . through the process of synthesis or through degradation. For example, the enzyme *monoamine oxidase* degrades *biogenic amines,"* *including dopamine,* through the process of **metabolism** (q.v.) As indicated in Chapter 6, there is some evidence that dopamine irregularities may account for symptoms of schizophrenia.

ERRORS IN PREDICTION Two types of errors or incorrect decisions can be made in any prediction. In the first instance, called a *Type-I* or a ***False Positive*** error, a chance difference is accepted as being a meaningful one. In this instance, a treatment may be initiated, or some recommendation for admission, discharge, or initiation of service that has a risk attached, may be made. For example, a Parole Board releases a prisoner because the prisoner's composite rating on a "Good Prospects for Successful Parole" scale is high; upon release, the former prisoner reverts to criminal behavior and is re-incarcerated within a short time. In the second instance, called a *Type II* or ***False Negative*** error, some treatment is withheld, or an applicant who is otherwise qualified or likely to benefit or succeed, is denied treatment, release, or admittance. Following the earlier example, a second prisoner, whose composite rating is below the cut-off score on the illustrative scale, is denied parole; yet, once he serves his full sentence and is released, he never again violates any laws. Each kind of error has its own costs; utility models have been developed to estimate and compare these costs as guides for decision-makers. *See* Chapter 4 for a discussion of the prediction of future violence, including policy statements by both the American Psychiatric Association and the American Psychological Association.

EXTINCTION The cessation of a behavior as the result of its absolute non-reinforcement by positive reinforcing agents *or* because, whenever that behavior is emitted by the organism, it is greeted with negative reinforcing agents. In the experimental analysis of behavior, the application of negative reinforcing agents is often termed *punishment.*

FELONY According to Cromwell, Killinger, Kerper & Walker (1985, p. 388), an offense for which the prescribed maximum sanction is sentence to incarceration in a *penitentiary* (i.e., a prison rather than a jail or reformatory) for a term of *more than* one year. Includes those offenses for which the prescribed maximum sanction is death.

FORENSIC PSYCHOLOGY The application of scientific psychology to problems and issues in the law, including both civil and criminal law. A similar meaning attaches to such terms as forensic *psychiatry,* forensic *toxicology,* etc.

FRIZZLE According to *Webster's New Universal Unabridged Dictionary,* 2nd edition (1979, p. 175), as a *verb transitive,* "to make or cause a sputtering, hissing noise, as in frying; to sizzle." As a noun, "the steel upright part of a flintlock gun, against which the flint strikes to produce sparks." From the verb form, now archaic, derives the meaning *that which has been sizzled,* or, by extension, *the experience of sizzling.* The term may be etymologically related to the Old French gerund *frisson,* which translates roughly as "apprehensive excitement." *See* Chapters 9 and 10 for its "street" usage.

HALFWAY HOUSE According to Amnesty International (1987, p. 82), "A halfway house is a hostel where offenders are placed under supervision as an alternative to prison. They may do outside work but must report back to the hostel each night. In some states, prisoners on parole are placed in halfway houses before their proper release." The placement (or proposed placement) of a halfway house for prisoners (or even for those recovering from alcohol or substance abuse) within a residential community typically raises the ire of local citizens, with attendant protests and publicity.

HYPOTHALAMUS In the *Glossary* of the American Psychiatric Association (Stone, 1988, p. 80), "the principal center in the forebrain for integration of visceral functions involving the autonomic nervous system." According to Berkow & Fletcher (1987, pp. 1017-1020), the hypothalamus is thus "the master gland . . . the final common pathway directing input [which] receives input from virtually all other areas of the central nervous system." Among the neurohormones modulated by the hypothalamus are *dopamine,* a ubiquitous and powerful neurotransmitter in the brain which is also a precursor to the equally powerful neurotransmitter norepinephrine, and a hormone labeled TSH, which stimulates the activity of the thyroid gland, itself a modulator of hormonal activity throughout the endocrine system.

IMPULSIVITY As used in this volume, the habit of acting upon urges *without* due consideration to the costs, risks, and benefits associated with behavior. According to the conceptual model for tinder box violence described in Chapters 7 and 10, such urges may well have their origins in neurogenic dysfunctions or anomalies that either or both create the experience of restlessness in the prospective actor and/or sensitize him or her to particular targets of behavior. In rather an archaic fashion, the *Glossary* of the American Psychiatric Association (Stone, 1988, p. 82) defines *impulse as "a psychic striving; usually refers to an instinctual urge,"* then goes on, equally archaically, to define an *"instinct" (p. 85)* as *"an inborn drive,"* identifying *"the primary human instincts [as] self-preservation, sexuality, and, according to some proponents, aggression."* But impulse *[control] disorders* are appropriately identified (p. 83) as "A varied group of *non-psychotic* disorders in which impulse control is weak [such that] The impulsive behavior is usually pleasurable, irresistible, and *ego-syntonic."* When a prospective actor is simultaneously subject to a variety of impulsive urges to behave, he or she may be said to be in a state of *mania,* a condition identified by the *Glossary* (p. 95) as "A mood disorder characterized by excessive elation, hyperactivity, agitation, and accelerated thinking and speaking. Sometimes manifested as *flight of ideas.* Mania is seen in *mood disorders and in certain organic mental disorders"* and is further a dependable consequence of central nervous system stimulants. Mania (or some aspects thereof) is measurable through the *Ma* scale of the Minnesota Multiphasic Personality Inventory, which may also represent a rough gauge to the respondent's typical level of impulsivity. In the interactionist paradigm, impulsivity is the antonym of *planfulness,* which in its turn is an essential ingredient to mature judgment. *See* Chapter 6.

INTER ALIA Legal and literary term. From the Latin. Literally translates as "in between others." Most appropriate English rendering is probably *among other things.*

IPSATIVE Term used principally in psychometrics, which denotes a form of measurement in which the *subject himself or herself is his or her own yardstick,* as is frequently the case when a teacher assesses how much a particular student has learned during a course of instruction from his or her base of knowledge at the beginning of the program of instruction. At a diametric pole stands *normative* measurement, in which the performance of the individual is *not* compared with a self-baseline but is instead gauged according to norms derived from analysis of the performance of similar persons. In this example, an aggregation of ipsative measurements among the members of an instructional group may also constitute an assessment of the effectiveness of instruction. When "normative" measurement is employed, there is frequently a more-or-less absolute standard that functions as a threshold — as is the case in licensure examinations in the medical and legal professions. The term *idiographic* is conceptually related to "ipsative" and is used by social psychologists who study the behavior of complex organizations, but with the meaning that the welfare of the individual rather than that of the organization (or the capacity of the organization to fulfill its mission, for that matter) becomes the paramount focus. To that term, however, they oppose the term *nomothetic,* which denotes a perspective that places primary focus on the welfare of the organization and/or its capacity to fulfill its mission.

JURISDICTION Legal term, designating which of several courts has the "right to pronounce the law" in cases of various sorts. Thus, *state criminal courts* have jurisdiction over cases involving criminal laws enacted by that state's legislature; Federal courts have jurisdiction over cases involving criminal laws enacted by the U.S. Congress; state domestic relations courts have jurisdiction over divorce, child custody, and the like under the laws enacted by that state's legislature. Whatever the court of original jurisdiction, however, decisions can customarily be appealed to *appellate* courts in the state or Federal court systems. Ordinarily, a decision of a state court can be appealed through the Federal appellate system only when plaintiff argues that his or her rights under the U.S. Constitution have been violated through the state system.

JUST DESERTS A school of thought in penology that holds, in essence, that the punishment should fit the characteristics of the crime *rather than* the characteristics of the offender, or, in cases of violent crime, those of the victim. The just deserts approach would limit rather sharply a sentencing judge's discretion in considering a convicted offender's prior criminal history, so that anyone convicted of Crime Y would be given the same sentence, in contrast to the situation in which a first-time offender convicted of that crime is sentenced to probation while a repeat offender convicted of that crime is sentenced to incarceration. Moreover, thorough implementation of a just deserts approach would also rather severely limit the joint and sequential practice of inflating charges so that the accused offender appears to be faced with sharply intrusive sanctions, with these inflated charges largely intended to be sharply reduced during plea-bargaining, yielding a situation in which neither the inflated charges *nor* the offense-of- record upon which the accused is sentenced after a bargained plea bear more than a passing resemblance to the actual character of the criminal behavior in question. In some interpretations, extension of the just deserts perspective would also abolish parole or other early release programs, so that the sentence as prescribed legislatively and imposed judicially would in fact be served in full. Some advocates of the just deserts perspective also propose a substantial overhaul of that legislation that prescribes the sanctions attached to various offenses, so that (in contrast to the situation in which an artificially long sentence is imposed, but an offender serves only, say, 25% thereof before being paroled for reasons that have largely to do with his/her behavior within the correctional institution *rather than* with the character of the criminal behavior *on account of which* he/she has been institutionalized) legislatively prescribed sanctions conform more closely to sentences as they are actually served for the various offenses. Perhaps the most comprehensive (and most balanced) statements of the just deserts perspective have been provided by ANDREW VON HIRSCH in *Doing Justice: The Choice of Punishments* (1976) and *Past or Future Crimes: Deservedness and Dangerousness in the Sentencing of Criminals* (1985). Philosophically, the just deserts position shares substantial common ground (though not often recognized as such) with iconoclastic psychiatric reformer THOMAS SZASZ, who has railed for three decades against what he calls the "psychiatricization" of criminal behavior. As Szasz (1987, pp. 14, 268) puts it in *Insanity: The Idea and Its Consequences,* "Modern man welcomes the idea of insanity — of mental illness as a disease — as a supposedly scientific explanation of murder and mayhem: this is why, despite its nonsensical character, the view that 'only crazy people commit crazy crimes' enjoys a large measure of intellectual respectability . . . Largely because of the effect the idea of mental illness has exercised, for more than 200 years, on the Western mind, and especially on the concept of responsibility, many people are now profoundly confused about who is, or ought to be, held responsible for certain actions and consequences." Within a social context such as that described by Szasz, focus would per force shift from the character of the allegedly criminal behavior to the character of the person who allegedly behaved criminally; accordingly, sanctions would be predicated not on what the offender had done (a posture congruent with a just deserts approach) but on why he or she had behaved in such a manner (a posture congruent with an erasing of the lines of demarcation between psychological and criminal deviance).

MANIA *See* IMPULSIVITY.

M'NAGHTEN STANDARD In nations following British legal precedents, the touchstone legal test for the inability to comport one's conduct to the requirements of the law. Pronounced by the House of Lords formally in 1843, but with many precedents in the English legal tradition. *See* Chapter 2.

MENS REA In the *Glossary* of the American Psychiatric Association (Stone, 1988, p. 198), an intent to do harm. Formal guilt cannot be pronounced in the absence of *mens rea*.

MENTAL DISORDER In the *Glossary* of the American Psychiatric Association (Stone, 1988, p. 99), "an illness with psychologic or behavioral manifestations and/or impairment in functioning due to a social, psychologic, genetic, physical/chemical, [and/] or biologic disturbance. The disorder is not limited to relations between the person and society." There are two principal taxonomic sources for mental disorders of various sorts — the *International Classification of Diseases* issued by the World Health Organization and the *Diagnostic & Statistical Manual of Mental Disorders* issued by the American Psychiatric Association. These sources are largely congruent, except for the classification of sexual preference (e.g., homosexuality) and appetitive (e.g., nicotinism) disorders.

MENTAL RETARDATION In the U.S. Public Health Service edition of the *International Classification of Diseases* (1989, p. 1098), "A condition of arrested or incomplete development which is especially characterized by subnormality of intelligence . . . Mental retardation often involves psychiatric disturbances and may develop as a result of some physical disease or injury." Mental retardation at a moderate (i.e., an IQ roughly in the range of 55) or at a severe (IQ below 50; or, in some states, a mental age below 7) constitutes a basis for a pleading of *Not guilty by reasoning of insanity*, inability to understand the right to remain silent during a police investigation as guaranteed under the *Miranda* decision, and *incompetence to stand trial*.

METABOLISM According to Hinsie & Campbell (1970, p. 468), "The bio-physiological processes by which the living cells and tissue systems of an organism undergo continuous chemical changes in order to build up new living matter and to supply the energy necessary for the life of an individual." Thus, the process by which material ingested by an organism is transformed by that organism (through the action of enzymes produced by the endocrine system) and hence rendered usable by that organism. Within the present context, particularly applicable to those substances the ingestion of which is related to the process of **neurotransmission**. The transformed substance usable by the organism that emerge from such a process of metabolism is termed a **metabolite**. According to Rafuls, Extein, Gold & Goggans (1987, p. 323), dysfunctions in metabolism (which are typically attributable to the body's over- or under-production of the enzymes principally involved in neural regulation, called **neuroendocrines**) may account for mental disturbances of various sorts, including delirium, dementia, anxiety, apathy, depression, irritability, euphoria, aggressivity, and psychosis.

MISCEGENATION Marriage between persons of different races. Miscegenation was typically prohibited by law in Southern and "border" states until well into this century.

MISDEMEANOR According to Cromwell, Killinger, Kerper & Walker (1985, p. 289), an offense for which the prescribed maximum sanction is sentence to incarceration in a confinement facility *other than* a penitentiary — hence, a jail or similar institution, including a reformatory — for a term of one year or less.

MOOD *See* State.

MOTIVATION According to Cattell & Child (1975, pp. 10-15), motivation is the strength of interest in a course of action, or a tendency to a course of action in response to a stimulus. Cattell & Child hold that no fewer than seven independently varying components are needed to account for this complex psychological construct, including a component that signifies determination in the quest to satisfy personal desires, comparable to the Freudian notion of the "id"; a second, which signifies a mature interest in and contact which reality, resembling the Freudian notion of "ego"; a component approximating the Freudian "superego" that reflects an interest in displaying restraint and inhibition as a product of social forces.

MULTIVARIATE ANALYSIS According to Tatsuoka (1988, p. 1), "that branch of statistics which is devoted to the study of multivariate (or multidimensional) distributions and samples from those distributions . . . In applied contexts [such as psychological research] multivariate analysis is concerned with a group (or several groups) of individuals each of whom possesses values or scores on two or more variables, such as tests or other measures." In general, multivariate analyses consider two or more sets, or *vectors,* of variables, where set or more may be considered "independent" or "predictor" variables and the other set(s) considered "dependent" or "criterion" variables. These sets are analyzed simultaneously to determine relationships between them. The major multivariate methods include *canonical correlation analysis,* in which the relations between two sets of continuously measured variables are calculated; *discriminant analysis,* in which predictions about membership in two or more groups are estimated from a set of continuously measured and/or categorical variables; and *multivariate analysis of variance,* in which the significance of mean differences between two or more groups on a set or vector of continuously measured variables is determined. The term *bivariate analysis* generally is used to refer to the determination of the direction (positive or negative sign) and magnitude (the size of the correlation, which can range between +/- 1.00) of relation between two variables, or between one variable and two or more other variables (multiple correlation analysis) where no cause and effect or temporal relations are implied. The *Pearson product-moment correlation coefficient* is the most widely used bivariate statistic. The term *univariate analysis* generally refers to those analyses that seek to determine the effect or influence of one or more variables (usually referred to as "independent" or "predictor" variable) on a single other variable (usually designated as the "dependent" or "criterion" variable). Methods such as the *t*-test, analysis of variance (ANOVA) or covariance (ANCOVA), and multiple regression analysis fall under the rubric of *univariate* methods. All statistical methods are sub-cases or derivatives of the general multivariate conceptualization.

NARCISSISM In the *Glossary* of the American Psychiatric Association (Stone, 1988, p. 105), "self-love, as opposed to object love (love of another person). To be distinguished from *egotism*, which carries the connotation of self- centeredness, selfishness, and conceit. Egotism is but one expression of narcissism."

NARCOTIC/NARCOLEPTIC According to Feldman & Quenzer (1984, p. 443), "any analgesic drug of the opiate class that reduces pain and induces sleep."

NERVOUS SYSTEM, CENTRAL In the *Glossary* of the American Psychiatric Association (Stone, 1988, p. 31), "the brain in the spinal cord." Usually distinguished from the *autonomic nervous system* (p. 20), "the part of the nervous system that innervates [activates] the cardiovascular, digestive, reproductive, and respiratory organs. It operates outside of consciousness and controls basic life-sustaining functions such as heart rate, digestion, and breathing. It includes the *sympathetic nervous system* and the *parasympathetic nervous system.*" In turn, the *sympathetic nervous system* (p. 163) is identified as "The part of the *autonomic nervous system* that responds to dangerous or threatening situations by preparing a person physiologically for fight or flight," while the *parasympathetic nervous system* is identified as "The part of the autonomic nervous system that controls the life-sustaining organs of the body under normal, danger-free conditions."

NEUROHORMONE In the *Glossary* of the American Psychiatric Association (Stone, 1988, p. 107), "A chemical messenger usually produced within the *hypothalamus,* carried to the pituary and then to other cells within the central nervous system. Neurohomones are similar to neurotransmitter, except that they interact with a variety of cells, whereas neurotransmitters interact only with other neurons."

NEUROPSYCHOLOGY According to Hartlage (1987, p. 4), "a body of scientific knowledge related to brain-behavior relationships that uses measurement procedures developed on the basis of psychological research for the description and diagnosis of behaviors mediated by the central nervous system." Clinical neuropsychology, according to Hartlage, "involves the professional application of psychological tests, modified neurological assessment procedures, clinical observation, and anamnestic data toward the formulation of diagnostic and treatment conclusions related to the functional status of the central nervous system" (p. 9).

NEUROHORMONE In the *Glossary* of the American Psychiatric Association (Stone, 1988, p. 107), "A chemical messenger usually produced within the *hypothalamus,* carried to the pituary and then to other cells within the central nervous system. Neurohomones are similar to neurotransmitters, except that they interact with a variety of cells, whereas neurotransmitters interact only with other neurons."

NEURORECEPTOR According to Berkow & Fletcher (1987, p. 2475), "a small binding or recognition site (possessing a specific molecular configuration) on a cell surface that causes a physiological response upon stimulation by a neurotransmitter or other chemical, such as a drug or toxin. Some receptors cause inhibitory (e.g., relaxation of a muscle) or excitatory (e.g., contraction of a muscle) physiological responses."

NEUROTRANSMITTER According to Feldman & Quenzer (1984, p. 444), "a chemical substance that is released [within the central nervous system] and stimulates or inhibits adjacent neurons or stimulates effector organs such as muscles and glands." According to Berkow & Fletcher (1987, pp. 2472-2475), the process of *neurotransmission* follows four sequential steps: Synthesis (chemically, usually from chemical substances that are metabolized by the action of *enzymes* from what are typically called "precursor" substances to yield the neurotransmitting substance) and storage of the neurotransmitter in a nerve structure that is "prejunctional" (or chemically adjacent) to the nerve terminal at which transmission will occur; release of the neurotransmitter from the nerve terminal; interaction of the neurotransmitter with the receptor nerve; and rapid termination of the interaction between the neurotransmitter and the receptor nerve. Among the *major neurotransmitters* (sometimes called the "ubiquitous" neurotransmitters because they act at a variety of receptor sites), Berkow & Fletcher include acetycholine, dopamine, norepinephrine, serotonin, *gamma*-Aminobutyric acid (termed "the major *inhibitory* neurotransmitter in the central nervous system"), *Beta*-Endorphin, and vasopresin. *Dopamine* is frequently cited in accounts of the neurogenesis of severe mental disorder. Both dopamine and *serotonin* interact with the enzyme *monoamine oxidase,* the chemical inhibition of which is pivotal to the action of a variety of *anti-depressant* pharmaceutical agents. Berkow & Fletcher (p. 2477) apply the term *pathology of neurotransmission* to the aggregate "defects in the process of neurotransmitter storage, release, synthesis, degradation [chemical decomposition] and changes in receptor activity . . . that lead to faulty transmission resulting in clinical disorders." Such defects might occur as the consequence of neurochemical dysfunctions or of damage to (or destruction of) brain morphological structures that function as transmitter or receptor sites. *See also* Metabolism.

NOMOLOGICAL NETWORK According to Wiggins (1973, p. 399), an interlocking system of laws which relate constructs to one another and to observable properties of the environment; synonymous with "theory" or "conceptual model" in some usages of those more widely, and more imprecisely used, terms.

NORMAL In its strictest sense, *normal is a statistical concept* with a meaning that derives from a precise mathematical formula. What is normal in that strict sense is whatever is true of the middle 68% of a population (or group); those technically-minded will recognize that the reference points are the mathematical *mean* plus and minus a *standard deviation* on either side of the mean, with each such unit accounting (in the "normal" or Gaussian distribution) for 34% of the cases. Hence, cases in the lowest 16% and the highest 16% are, by definition, said to be *deviant* cases. The person who thus differs from the normal is sometimes termed a *deviate.* But these technical meanings take on variant shades when applied to particular groups, subgroups, or subcultures which differ from the larger population. In particular, as a term which is relative rather than absolute, *normal* is to be sharply distinguished from *healthy.* It may, for example, be the case that 68% of the population consume between one and six ounces of beverage alcohol per week (the equivalent of one to three 12-oz. bottles of beer); those in the upper 16% consume six or more ounces per week, ranging perhaps to highs of 168 ounces per week, while those in the lower 16% consume zero ounces per week. In a statistical sense, both the excessive drinker and the tee-totaler are *equally* deviant, but there is no question that, in health terms, abstinence is preferable. Similarly, in the society at large, most people (at least the middle 68%) do not resolve dispute by reaching for baseball bats or tire irons. But, in some subcultures or groups within the larger society, it may be the norm that disputes are resolved precisely through armed conflict — and he or she who declines to engage in such conflict (but prefers instead to attempt resolution through discussion, negotiation, or recourse to the civil courts) may be perceived as deviant with respect to that subculture or group — even though his or her behavior conforms to the norm of the larger society. Those behaviors which are true of the middle 68% of a group or subculture thus constitute *normative expectations* for the behavior of the members of that subculture or group. Indeed, those criminologists who are wedded to a Marxist perspective in social analysis often attribute the character of criminal behavior to a clash in cultures which produces a conflict in normative expectations between, for example, those who control the means of production and those who labor to produce.

OFFENSE OF RECORD A term of art, designating the "leading" offense under which a convicted offender has been sentenced most recently. As a result of plea-bargaining, the offense as recorded may differ from the offense as committed — e.g., an offender who rapes a 12-year-old, with force, may plead guilty to an offense such as "impairing the morals of a minor," with the latter carrying only a three (3) year sentence in contrast to a 30 year sentence for rape and/or statutory rape. When convicted offenders are selected as subjects in behavioral science research, they are classified according to the offense as recorded in sentencing documents rather than according to the offense as committed — a practice quite consistent with criminal law procedures which nonetheless is likely to yield rather misleading conclusions.

PARADIGM According to Mahoney (1976, p. 19), following Kuhn in *The Structure of Scientific Revolution*, a "set of generally accepted assumptions and rules regarding the nature of problems in a given discipline and the appropriate means for addressing them (e.g., 'where' to look, with what instruments, and so on)." Customarily used to denote a relatively complex *conceptual model* which seeks to identify the principal variables antecedent to a phenomenon of interest — as in such phrases as a *paradigm for altruism, a paradigm for aggression,* etc.

PAROLE According to Cromwell, Killinger, Kerper & Walker (1985, p. 390), the conditional release from incarceration of a convicted offender, usually after serving a proportion of the original sentence to confinement. The offender thus released is typically required to fulfill certain conditions, including regular meetings with a parole officer. Failure to meet these conditions results in a return to confinement to serve the balance of the sentence.

PARADIGM According to Mahoney (1976, p. 19), following Kuhn in *The Structure of Scientific Revolution*, a "set of generally accepted assumptions and rules regarding the nature of problems in a given discipline and the appropriate means for addressing them (e.g., 'where' to look, with what instruments, and so on)." Customarily used to denote a relatively complex *conceptual model* which seeks to identify the principal variables antecedent to a phenomenon of interest — as in such phrases as a *paradigm for altruism, a paradigm for aggression,* etc.

PEDOPHILIA In the U.S. Public Health Service edition of the *International Classification of Diseases* (1989, p. 1105), "sexual deviations in which an adult engages in sexual activity with a child of the same or opposite sex."

PENROSE EFFECT The observation, initially made half a century ago by British psychologist Lionel Penrose (1939), that a neatly inverse relationship obtained between the number of prison beds and the number of mental hospital beds across the nations of Europe in the 1930s. There is some evidence that the "Penrose Effect" is alive and well in the United States (Adler, 1986; Brown & Smith, 1988; Conacher, 1988; Kramer, 1977; Lamb, 1988; Lamb & Grant, 1982; Pallone & Hennessy, 1977). According to data from the National Institutes of Health, the number of beds in public and private mental hospitals declined nationally from 451,000 in 1965 to 177,000 in 1985. According to Bureau of Justice Statistics data, during roughly the same period the number of convicted offenders confined in state and Federal prisons increased from 210,000 in 1965 to 420,000 in 1983, not including in either case those confined in jails or on probation or parole. In an exhaustive review of the then-current research literature, Teplin (1983), although complaining about methodological flaws (perhaps inevitable, because research in this domain does not readily lend itself to the random assignment of "otherwise similar" subjects to such categories as offender vs. non- offender), concluded that "the research literature offers . . . support for the contention that the mentally ill are being processed through the criminal justice system."

PERSONALITY DISORDER In the U.S. Public Health Service edition of the *International Classification of Diseases* (1989, p. 1106), *personality disorders* are a group of mental disorders characterized "by deeply ingrained maladaptive patterns of behavior generally recognizable by the time of adolescence or earlier and continuing throughout most of adult life, although often becoming less obvious in middle or old age." Among the disorders included in this cluster which are of particular relevance to the study of criminal behavior are *anti-social personality disorder* and *explosive personality disorder*. According to the same source, *anti-social personality disorder* is "characterized by disregard for social obligations, lack of feeling for others, and impetuous violence or callous unconcern. There is a gross disparity between behavior and the prevailing social norms. Behavior is not readily modifiable by experience, including punishment. People with this personality [disorder] are often affectively cold, and may be abnormally aggressive or irresponsible. Their frustration tolerance is low; they blame others or offer plausible rationalizations for the behavior which brings them into contact with society." *Explosive personality disorder* (pp. 1107-1108) is described as "characterized by instability of mood, with liability to intemperate outbursts of anger, hate, violence, or affection. Aggression may be expressed in words or in physical violence. The outbursts cannot be readily controlled by the affected persons, *who are not otherwise prone to anti-social behavior.*"

PHENOMENOLOGY A school of theory in psychology which traces its remote origins to the 18th-century philosophers IMMANUEL KANT and GEORGE BERKELEY and its more proximate origins in the 19th century to such thinkers as FRANZ BRENTANO and MAX SCHELER, is associated in this century variously with the formulations of KURT LEWIN, ROLLO MAY, DONALD SNYGG, and ARTHUR COMBS, and serves as the foundation for the form of psychotherapeutic practice introduced by CARL R. ROGERS. Its basic tenet is that behavior is a function of how the person *perceives* things to be rather than how they "really" are. The correspondence between a person's perceptions and how things "really" are is held to be an important index to that person's mental health. Since behavior is held to follow and to flow from perceptions, it is necessary to change perceptions if behavior is to change. In phenomenologically-rooted psychotherapy, the therapist subtly offers "correctives" to the impaired perceptions of the client, with the hope and expectation that such a process will result in more "accurate" perceptions on the latter's part and thus eventuate in more positive (*or* self-advancing, *or,* in some formulations, "integrative," *or,* in the present context, more socially acceptable) behavior. Some phenomenologists, following Kant, hold that the way a thing "really" is (termed the *noumenon*) is, at its core, essentially unknowable and that only the way a thing "appears" to be (termed the *phenomenon*) is knowable. From a process psychology perspective, the matter of *why* a person perceives things as he or she does represents an important issue.

PHENOTYPE In the *Glossary* of the American Psychiatric Association (Stone, 1988, p. 124), "The observable attributes of an individual," and hence the *appearance* of the individual. Typically contrasted with *genotype,* a term which refers to the attributes customarily observable among all members of the same *genus* in a species; hence, what is characteristic of the group rather than of the individual. In general usage, the term *phenotype* is used to designate how the appearance of a particular person differs from the genotype of his or her group.

PLEADING According to Schwitzgebel & Schwitzgebel (1980, p. 300), "the process in which alternate and opposing written statements are presented [in a court *or* before a jury *or* to a judge] by the contesting parties" to stimulate adjudication of an issue under dispute in criminal or civil litigation.

POST-CONCUSSION SYNDROME In the U.S. Public Health Service edition of the *International Classification of Diseases* (1989, p. 1110), a "state occurring after generalized contusion of the brain, in which the symptom picture may resemble that of frontal lobe syndrome or that of any of the neurotic disorders, but in which in addition headache, giddiness, fatigue, insomnia, and a subjective feeling of impaired intellectual ability are usually prominent. Mood may fluctuate, and quite ordinary stress may produce exaggerated fear or apprehension. There may be marked intolerance for mental or physical exertion, undue sensitivity to noise, and hypochondriacal preoccupation . . . This syndrome is particularly associated with the closed type of head injury [i.e., without skull fracture] when signs of localized brain damage are slight or absent."

PROBATION According to Cromwell, Killinger, Kerper & Walker (1985, p. 391), a form of sanction that may be imposed by a *criminal* court following conviction for felony or misdemeanor *in lieu of* incarceration. In such situations, the sentence to incarceration is *suspended*. The court may impose certain conditions upon the defendant to be fulfilled during probation, including restitution, community service, outpatient mental health treatment, etc. The probationer may be "supervised" intensively (e.g., ordered to report to his or her probation officer on a weekly basis or even more freely) or relatively lightly and may "graduate" from more to less intensive levels of probation supervision as he or she fulfills the conditions of probation satisfactorily. Violation of the terms of probation may result in incarceration to serve the previously-suspended sentence.

PROCESS According to Cattell (1979, p. 31), "States and associated behaviors (that) follow a certain sequence . . . Such a process may be unique, never again repeated; but actually a great deal of our behavior and our developmental patterns repeat some characteristic sequence and constitute common processes. Thus the sequence of yielding to some particular temptation and experiencing remorse afterward may repeat itself in some clinical cases . . . " and in instances of recidivistic behaviors often observed in the criminal justice system.

PSYCHIATRY In the *Glossary* of the American Psychiatric Association (Stone, 1988, p. 134), a branch of medicine "that deals with the origin, diagnosis, prevention, and treatment of mental disorders." *Psychiatrists* are *physicians* who specialize in psychiatry, whether through the "talking cure" of psychotherapy or through *pharmacotherapy* or other forms of *somatotherapy,* such as electroconvulsive treatment.

PSYCHOANALYSIS A school of theory and practice in the mental health disciplines issuing largely from the contributions of SIGMUND FREUD and his disciples and imitators. At the conceptual level, behavior is held to issue from a "dynamic exchange" between the three elements which in the aggregate comprise the so-called "mental apparatus" — viz., the *id,* or the locus of unconscious and instinctual desires and strivings; the *superego,* the locus of the categorical moral imperatives the person has internalized; and the *ego,* the seat of conscious processing and decision-making. Both the id and the superego are typically held to be quite blind and uncivilized; only the ego, in its role as assessor of the demands of reality on the one hand and of the id and superego on the other, is conscious, aware, and controlling; for that reason, a sub-school emphasizes EGO PSYCHOLOGY. In classical psychoanalysis, mental illness is seen as the result of faulty conflict resolution by or within the ego between the demands of the id and superego, largely attributable to deficits in *psychosexual development* in childhood and adolescence. In *psychoanalytic treatment,* the goal is to "raise" conflicts from the unconscious to the conscious level, where they can be dealt with more or less rationally by the ego; thus, it is necessary to penetrate the unconscious by means of such techniques as the analysis of dreams, free association, and analyses of paraphraxes (slips of the tongue). The landmark works in the psychology of criminal behavior from the psychoanalytic perspective are *The Criminal, the Judge, and the Public,* originally published in the German in 1931 and in an English edition 25 years later (Alexander & Staub, 1956); and the works of American psychologist ROBERT LINDER, including *Handbook of Correctional Psychology, Rebel Without a Cause,* and *The Fifty-Minute Hour.*

PSYCHOENDOCRINOLOGY The study of the effects of the functioning of the endocrine system upon behavior and emotion, as mediated by the central nervous system. According to Rafuls, Extein, Gold & Goggans (1987, p. 308), "Psychiatric disorders are often seen in patients with primary disorders of the neuroendocrine system . . . Of those endocrine disorders causing psychiatric symptoms, hypothyroidism has been found to be responsible for a large percentage . . . The next most frequent are disorders of glucose regulation, with the most common being diabetes mellitus."

PSYCHOLOGY In the *Glossary* of the American Psychiatric Association (Stone, 1988, p. 136), psychology is simultaneously "an academic discipline, a profession, and a science dealing with the study of mental processes and behavior of people and animals." The term "psychologist" applies equally to those who are engaged in the science *or* in the practice of psychology, but a *professional psychologist* applies the principles of psychological science to the clinical amelioration of problems in learning and adjustment. *Scientific* psychology is typically said to have been born in the laboratories of Wilhelm Wundt in Leipzig in the 1870s; *clinical* psychology is typically dated to the establishment of a "psychoeducational clinic" for the identification and amelioration of learning problems experienced by children under the direction of Lightner Witmer at the University of Pennsylvania in 1896 (Korchin, 1976, p. 42); because of the focus of Witmer's clinic (no less, for that matter, than the purpose of Binet's work in France in the decade following), the date is also sometimes claimed as the birth of *school* psychology. *Counseling psychology,* which dates from the research and clinical work of sociologist Frank Parsons at Boston's Workingman's College (a forerunner to today's Northeastern University) in the first decade of this century, emerged as a distinct specialty only in the 1950's and is distinguished by one of its founders as concerned with the application of scientific psychology to "normal problems of normal personalities" *and* to "normal problems of abnormal personalities" (Super, 1956), such as adjustment to work, family living, social interaction (including emission of pro-social and anti-social behavior), and use and abuse of mood-altering substances. Because they are not physicians, the practice of professional psychologists does not include pharmacotherapy but is instead limited to psychotherapy and/or various forms of behavior therapy.

PSYCHOPATHOLOGY In the *Glossary* of the American Psychiatric Association (Stone, 1988, p. 137), "the study of the significant causes and processes in the development of *mental disorders.* Also the manifestation of mental disorders."

PSYCHOSIS In the U.S. Public Health Service edition of the *International Classification of Diseases* (1989, p. 137), a mental disorder in which "impairment of mental function has developed to a degree that interferes grossly with insight, ability to meet some ordinary demands of life, or to maintain adequate contact with reality." The latter characteristic is generally conceded to be that which differentiates the psychoses from other forms of mental disorder (e.g., the neuroses, personality disorders, organic mental disorders, substance-induced disorders). This category of mental illness includes the *organic psychotic conditions* (attributable to organic sources), the several varieties of *schizophrenia,* disorders of affect such as *manic-depressive* illness, and *paranoid* states. Ordinarily, only mental disorders that qualify as psychoses can serve to exculpate a defendant under the M'Naghten Standard.

PSYCHOPATHIC DEVIATION An early term used to denote a pattern of anti-social behavior, now often considered either synonymous with, or a precursor to, the formal diagnostic category ***anti-social personality disorder.*** According to Hare (1970, p. 5), the leading international authority, the psychopathic deviate is unable to show empathy or concern for others, manipulates and uses others, and displays extreme egocentricity, inability to experience warm emotional relationships with other, aggressiveness, inability to profit from experience (including punishment), and a high degree of impulsivity. The scale which measures psychopathic deviation on the Minnesota Multiphasic Personality Inventory has relatively consistently differentiated adjudicated criminal offenders who have committed crimes of violence. *See* Chapter 6.

RECIDIVISM The act or condition of committing another criminal offense subsequent to conviction for a prior offense. A person who is thus categorized as a "repeat offender" is said to have *recidivated.*

REINFORCER Any event whose occurrence in a temporal contiguity with a particular response increases the probability that that response will be repeated when the organism is confronted with the same (or similar) stimulus conditions at some point in the proximate or remote future.

RELIQUARY In ecclesiastical law and custom, a place (or a container) in which sacred relics are kept when not on display; hence, by extension, a repository for the valuable, quaint, or antique.

RESPONSE The behavior (internal *or* external) of an organism as a consequence of stimulation.

SCHIZOPHRENIA In the U.S. Public Health Service edition of the *International Classification of Diseases* (1989, p. 1117), "a group of *psychoses* in where there is a fundamental disturbance of personality, a characteristic distortion of thinking, often a sense of being controlled by alien forces, delusions which may be bizarre, disturbed perception, abnormal affect out of keeping with the real situation, and autism . . . The disturbance of personality involves its most basic functions which give the normal person his feeling of individuality, uniqueness, and self-direction. The most intimate thoughts, feelings, and acts are often felt to be known to or shared by others and explanatory delusions may develop, to the effect that natural or supernatural forces are at work to influence the schizophrenic person's thoughts and actions in ways that are often bizarre. He may see himself as the pivot of all that happens. Hallucinations, especially of hearing, are common and may comment on the patient or address him. Perception is frequently disturbed in other ways: there may be perplexity, irrelevant features may become all-important and accompanied by passivity feelings, may lead the patient to believe that everyday objects and situations possess a special, usually sinister, meaning intended for him. In the characteristic schizophrenic disturbance of thinking, peripheral and irrelevant features of a total concept, which are inhibited in normal directed mental activity, are brought to the forefront and utilized in place of the elements relevant and appropriate to the situation. Thus, thinking becomes vague, elliptical, and obscure, and its expression in speech [is] sometimes incomprehensible. Breaks and interpolations in the flow of consecutive thought are frequent, and the patient may be convinced that his thoughts are being withdrawn by some outside agency. Mood may be shallow, capricious, or incongruous. Ambivalence and disturbance of volition may appear as inertia, negativism, or stupor." For students of criminal behavior, an important subcategory is *pseudopsychopathic schizophrenia,* which the same source (p. 1119) equates with latent schizophrenia.

SEXUAL DEVIATION In the U.S. Public Health edition of the *International Classification of Diseases* (1989, p. 1121), an "abnormal sexual inclination or behavior [in which] the sexual activity of affected persons is directed primarily either towards people not of the opposite sex, or toward sexual acts not associated with coitus normally, or towards coitus performed under abnormal circumstances." The several sub-categories include *exhibitionism, fetishism, homosexuality, nymphomania, pedophilia, satyriasis, sexual masochism, sexual sadism, transvestism, voyeurism,* and *zoophilia.* Many of these behaviors are defined legislatively as criminal, even between consenting adult partners; homosexuality is no longer considered a sexual deviation by the American Psychiatric Association (Pallone, 1990, pp. 19-21).

SOCIAL WORK   Rather too cavalierly defined in the American Psychiatric Association's *Glossary* (Stone, 1988, p. 157) as "the use of community resources and the conscious adaptive capacities of individuals and groups to better their adjustment to their environment." *Social work* is a somewhat imprecise term that applies to a cluster of human service professions. Some historians would trace the remote origins of what has become modern social work to the almshouses for the poor and disabled of the late Middle Ages and early Renaissance. Others would trace its founding to the 19th century, associated with the establishment of the "Docklands ministries" in London for immigrants from Eastern Europe by Divinity students from Oxford and Cambridge and with Hull House in Chicago and similar so-called "settlement houses" in other U.S. cities; as practiced in these institutions, social work derived from the application of the then-new science of sociology (often, especially in Britain, with a heavy grounding in formal religion) to a variety of problems encountered by families newly arrived in the then-burgeoning industrial cities, among which were child rearing, family financial planning, securing medical assistance, and the control of alcohol consumption. Contemporary social work, however, draws equally from psychology and economics as from sociology; its practitioners may specialize in fields as diverse and wide ranging as family planning, marriage counseling, parent-child or family systems interaction, community organization, or addiction treatment and relapse prevention. Social workers typically staff the child protective agencies in the various states and form the largest professional cadre among probation and parole officers. *Clinical social workers* are licensed in many states and provide counseling and psychotherapy services to the general public, usually focussed on family interaction and sometimes in cooperation with a psychiatrist or a psychologist. Because they are not physicians, the practice of clinical social workers does not include pharmacotherapy but is instead limited to psychotherapy and/or various forms of behavior therapy.

STATE   According to Cattell (1979, p. 14) "the result of the effect of a situation upon a state liability" or condition of deficiency (or *need*) within an organism. With somewhat less complexity, Smith (1988, p. 722) defines state as "a temporary condition resulting from the interaction of an external situation and an internal . . . proneness." The definition clearly reflects the principal tenet in Cattell's formulation of process psychology, which holds that an understanding of an individual's behavior requires identification of those traits, states, and environmental factors which contribute to the sequence of actions taken by an organism in response to a stimulus situation.

STIMULUS   An object, event, or situation that elicits a response from an organism.

SYNAPSE   According to Feldman & Quenzer (1984, p. 448), "the junction usually between the axon terminals of one neuron and the dendrites or soma of an adjacent neuron. Nerve impulses in the axon cause a release of neurotransmitters at the synapse that act upon the adjacent neuron either to excite or inhibit it."

TRAIT   According to Cattell (1979, p. 14), "that which defines what a person will do when faced with a defined situation." A trait is a relatively stable and enduring personality disposition that can be observed in the correlations of behaviors or responses to specific environmental influences. Traits observed at this level of measurement are called *surface* traits. The factor analysis of a matrix of surface traits yields *source* traits, which according to Cattell are more truly unitary components.

References

Abel, Charles F. 1985. Corporate crime and restitution. *Journal of Offender Reha-bilitation,* 8, 71-94.

Abel, Ernest L. 1986. Guns and blood alcohol levels among homicide victims. *Drug & Alcohol Dependence,* 18, 253-257.

Abel, Ernest L. 1987. Drugs and homicide in Erie County, New York. *International Journal of the Addictions,* 22, 195-200.

Abel, Ernest L. 1988. Guns and blood alcohol levels among homicide victims. *Drug & Alcohol Dependence,* 18, 253-257.

Adelson, Lester. 1961. Slaughter of the innocents: A study of forty-six homicides in which the victims were children. *New England Journal of Medicine,* 246, 1345-1349.

Adler, Freda. 1975. *Sisters in Crime: The Rise of the New Female Criminal.* New York: McGraw-Hill.

Adler, Freda. 1983. *Nations Not Obsessed With Crime.* Littleton, CO: Rothman.

Adler, Freda. 1986. Jails as a repository for former mental patients. *International Journal of Offender Therapy & Comparative Criminology,* 30, 225-236.

Ageton, Suzanne S. 1983. The dynamics of female delinquency, 1976- 1980. *Criminology,* 21, 555-584.

Albee, George W. 1959. *Mental Health Manpower Needs.* New York: Basic.

Alexander, Franz, & Frederick Staub. 1956. *The Criminal, the Judge, and the Public.* Glencoe, IL: Free Press. *Originally published in Berlin, 1931 (German).*

Allen, H.E., & C.C. Simonsen. 1975. *Corrections in America.* New York: Benziger, Bruce.

American Bar Association. 1989. *ABA Criminal Justice Mental Health Standards.* Washington, DC: The Association.

American Psychiatric Association. 1954. *Diagnostic and Statistical Manual of Mental Disorders.* Washington: The Association.

American Psychiatric Association. 1968. *Diagnostic and Statistical Manual of Mental Disorders, Second edition.* Washington: The Association.

American Psychiatric Association. 1974. *Clinical Aspects of the Violent Individual.* Washington, DC: The Association.

American Psychiatric Association. 1980. *Diagnostic and Statistical Manual of Mental Disorders, Third edition.* Washington: The Association.

American Psychiatric Association. 1984. *Issues in Forensic Psychiatry.* Washington, DC: American Psychiatric Press.

American Psychiatric Association. 1987. *Diagnostic and Statistical Manual of Mental and Emotional Disorders, Third edition, Revised.* Washington, DC: The Association.

American Psychological Association. 1978. Report of the task force on the role of psychology in the criminal justice system. *American Psychologist,* 33, 633-638.

American Psychological Association. 1991. *A Report on Questionnaires Used in the Pre-employment Selection Decision: A Report of the Task Force on the Prediction of Dishonesty and Theft in Employment Settings.* Washington, DC: The Association.

398   *Criminal Behavior: A Process Psychology Analysis*

Amnesty International. 1987. *United States of America: The Death Penalty.* London: Amnesty International.

Anastasi, Anne. 1988. *Psychological Testing,* 6th ed. New York: Macmillan.

Anderson, Craig A., & Donna C. Anderson. 1984. Ambient temperature and violent crime: Tests of the linear and curvilinear hypotheses. *Journal of Personality & Social Psychology,* 46, 91-97.

Anderson, Wayne P., & William R. Holcomb. 1983. Accused murderers: Five MMPI personality types. *Journal of Clinical Psychology,* 39, 761-768.

Appelbaum, Paul S. 1987. *Allen v. Illinois:* The Fifth Amendment and the sexually dangerous person. *Hospital & Community Psychiatry,* 38, 25-26.

Apter, Alan, Moshe Kotler, Serge Sevy, Robert Plutchik, Serena-Lynn Brown, Hilliard Foster, Marc Hillbrand, Martin Korn & Herman M. van Praag. 1991. Correlates of suicide in violent and nonviolent psychiatric patients. *American Journal of Psychiatry,* 148, 883-887.

Arboleda-Florez, Julio. 1977. Shoplifting: An ordinary crime. *International Journal of Offender Therapy & Comparative Criminology,* 21, 201-297.

Arboleda-Florez, Julio. 1981. Post-homicide psychotic reaction. *International Journal of Offender Therapy & Comparative Criminology,* 25, 47-52.

Archer, Dane, Rosemary Gartner & Marc Beittel. 1983. Homicide and the death penalty: A cross-national test of a deterrence hypothesis. *Journal of Criminal Law & Criminology,* 74. 991-1013.

Arizona appeals court says state hospital psychiatrist owed duty to protect victim from violent acts of his patient. 1991. *Register Report: Newsletter for Psychologist Health Service Providers,* 17 (1), 19.

Arnold, Larry, Russell Fleming & Valerie Bell. 1979. The man who became angry once: A study of overcontrolled hostility. *Canadian Journal of Psychiatry,* 24, 762-766.

Atlas, Gordon D., & Christopher Peterson. 1990. Explanatory style and gambling: How pessimists respond to losing wagers. *Behaviour Research & Therapy,* 28, 523-529.

Ayoub, Catherine, & Marion Jacewitz. 1982. Families at risk for poor parenting: A model for service delivery, assessment, and intervention. *Child Abuse & Neglect,* 6, 351-358.

Azrin, N.H., R.R. Hutchinson & D.F. Hake. 1969. Extinction-induced aggression. In Leonard Berkowitz (ed.), *Roots of Aggression.* New York: Atherton. Pp. 35-60.

Bailey, Kent G. 1985. Ted Bundy: A paleopsychological analysis of a mass murderer. *New Trends in Experimental & Clinical Psychiatry,* 1, 41-62.

Bailey, William C. 1975. Murder and capital punishment: Some further evidence. *American Journal of Orthopsychiatry,* 45, 669-688.

Bailey, William C. 1976-*a.* Some further evidence on homicide and a regional culture of violence. *Omega: Journal of Death & Dying,* 7, 145-170.

Bailey, William C. 1976-*b.* Use of the death penalty v. outrage at murder: Some additional evidence and considerations. *Crime & Delinquency,* 22, 31-39.

Bailey, William C. 1980. Deterrent effect of the death penalty: An extended time series analysis. *Omega: Journal of Death & Dying,* 10, 234-259.

Bailey, William C. 1983. The deterrent effect of capital punishment during the 1950's. *Suicide & Life-Threatening Behavior,* 13, 95-107.

Bailey, William C. 1985. Disaggregation in deterrence and death penalty research: The case of murder in Chicago. *Journal of Criminal Law & Criminology,* 74, 827-859.

Bailey, William C. 1990. Murder, capital punishment, and television: Execution publicity and homicide rates. *American Sociological Review,* 55, 628-633.

Bailey, William C., & Ruth D. Peterson. 1989. Murder and capital punishment: A monthly time-series analysis of execution publicity. *American Sociological Review,* 54, 722-743.

Baker, Gerald, & David Lester. 1986. Seasonal births, academic achievement and psychopathology (suicide and homicide): A regional analysis. *Psychological Reports,* 59, 742.

Baldwin, J.A., & J.E. Oliver. 1975. Epidemiology and family characteristics of severely-abused children. *British Journal of Preventive & Social Medicine,* 29, 205-221.

Ball, John C., & David N. Nurco. 1984. Criminality during the life course of heroin addiction. *National Institute on Drug Abuse, Research Monograph Series, 49.* Pp. 305-312.

Ball, John C., Lawrence Rosen, John A. Flueck & David N. Nurco. 1982. Lifetime criminality of heroin addicts in the United States. *Journal of Drug Issues,* 12, 225-239.

Ball, John D., Robert P. Archer, Frederick A. Struve & John A. Hunter. 1987. MMPI correlates of a controversial EEG pattern among adolescent psychiatric patients. *Journal of Clinical Psychology,* 43, 708-714.

Bandura, Albert. 1962. Social learning through imitation. In Marshall R. Jones (ed.), *Nebraska Symposium on Motivation.* Lincoln: University of Nebraska Press. Pp. 211-274.

Bandura, Albert. 1965. Influence of models' reinforcement contingencies on the acquisition of imitative responses. *Journal of Personality & Social Psychology,* 1, 589-595.

Bandura, Albert. 1969. *Principles of Behavior Modification.* New York: Holt Rinehart Winston.

Bandura, Albert. 1973. *Aggression: A Social Learning Analysis.* Englewood Cliffs, NJ: Prentice Hall.

Bandura, Albert. 1977. Self-efficacy: Toward a unifying theory of behavioral change. *Psychological Review,* 84, 191-215.

Bandura, Albert. 1978. The self-system in reciprocal determinism. *American Psychologist,* 33, 344-358.

Bandura, Albert. 1985. Catecholamine secretion as a function of perceived coping self-efficacy. *Journal of Consulting & Clinical Psychology,* 53, 406-414.

Bandura, Albert. 1986-*a.* Fearful expectations and avoidant actions as coeffects of perceived self inefficacy. *American Psychologist,* 41, 1389-1391.

Bandura, Albert. 1986-*b.* From thought to action: Mechanisms of personal agency. *New Zealand Journal of Psychology,* 15, 1-17.

Bandura, Albert. 1986-*c. Social Foundations of Thought and Action: A Social Cognitive Theory.* Englewood Cliffs: Prentice-Hall.

Bandura, Albert. 1986-*d.* The explanatory and predictive scope of self-efficacy theory. *Journal of Social & Clinical Psychology,* 4, 359-373.

Bandura, Albert. 1989-*a.* Human agency in social cognitive theory. *American Psychologist,* 44, 1175-1184.

Bandura, Albert. 1989-*b.* Regulation of cognitive processes through perceived self-efficacy. *Developmental Psychology,* 625, 729-735.

Bandura, Albert, & Carol J. Kupers. 1964. Transmission of patterns of self-reinforcement through modeling. *Journal of Abnormal & Social Psychology,* 69, 1-9.

Bandura, Albert, & Frederick J. McDonald, 1963. Influence of social reinforcement and the behavior of models in shaping children's moral judgments. *Journal of Abnormal & Social Psychology,* 67, 274-281.

Bandura, Albert, & Theodore L. Rosenthal. 1966. Vicarious classical conditioning as a function of arousal level. *Journal of Personality & Social Psychology,* 3, 54-62.

Bandura, Albert, & Richard H. Walters. 1963. *Social Learning and Personality Development.* New York: Holt Rinehart Winston.

Bandura, Albert, Joan E. Grusec & Frances L. Menlove. 1967- *a.* Some social determinants of self-monitoring reinforcement systems. *Journal of Personality & Social Psychology,* 5, 449-455.

Bandura, Albert, Joan E. Grusec & Frances L. Menlove. 1967-*b.* Vicarious extinction of avoidance behavior. *Journal of Personality & Social Psychology,* 5, 16-23.

Bandura, Albert, Joan E. Grusec & Frances L. Menlove. 1967. Some social determinants of self-monitoring reinforcement systems. *Journal of Personality and Psychology,* 5, 449-455.

Bandura, Albert, Dorothea Ross & Sheila A. Ross. 1963. Vicarious reinforcement and imitative learning. *Journal of Abnormal & Social Psychology,* 67, 601-607.

Bannister, Donald, & Fay Fransella. 1971. *Inquiring Man: The Theory of Personal Constructs.* Harmondsworth, UK: Penguin.

Bannister, Donald, & J.M.M. Mair. 1968. *The Evaluation of Personal Constructs.* London: Academic.

Barack, Leonard I., & Cathy S. Widom. 1978. Eysenck's theory of criminality applied to women awaiting trial. *British Journal of Psychiatry,* 133, 452-456.

Barnett, Arnold. 1978. Crime and capital punishment: Some recent studies. *Journal of Criminal Justice,* 6, 291-303.

Bartol, Curt R. 1991. Predictive validation of the MMPI for small- town police officers. *Professional Psychology,* 22, 127-132.

Bateson, Gregory. 1972. *Steps to an Ecology of Mind.* New York: Ballantine.

Bateson, Gregory. 1978. The birth of a matrix, or double bind and epistemology. In Milton M. Berger (ed.), *Beyond the Double Bind: Communication and Family Systems, Theories, and Techniques with Schizophrenics.* New York: Brunner/Mazel.

Bateson, Gregory, Don D. Jackson, Jay Healey & John Weakland. 1956. Toward a theory of schizophrenia. *Behavioral Science,* 1, 251-264.

Baum, Maureen S., Ray E. Hosford & C. Scott Moss. 1984. Predicting violent behavior within a medium security correctional setting. *International Journal of Eclectic Psychotherapy,* 3, 18-24.

Bear, David. 1987. "Psychotic Trigger Reaction:" Neuro-psychiatric and neuro-biological (limbic?) aspects of homicide, reflecting on normal action. *Integrative Psychiatry,* 5, 125-127

Beigel, Herbert. 1983. In defense of the insanity defense. *Hillside Journal of Clinical Psychiatry,* 5, 73-90.

Bell, Carl C. 1986. Coma and the etiology of violence. *Journal of the National Medical Association,* 78, 1167-1176.

Bell, Carl C. 1990. Neuropsychiatry and gun safety. *Journal of Neuropsychiatry & Clinical Neurosciences,* 2, 145-148.

Bellak, Leopold. 1979. *Psychiatric Aspects of Minimal Brain Dysfunction in Adults.* New York: Grune & Stratton.

Bellak, Leopold. 1992. Comorbidity of attenion deficit hyperactivity disorder and other disorders. *Ameican Journal of Psychiatry,,* 149, 147-148.

Benedek, Elissa, & Dewey Cornell (eds.). 1989. *Juvenile Homicide.* Washington, D.C.: American Psychiatric Press.

Benedek, Elissa, Dewey Cornell & Lois Staresina. 1989. Treatment of the homicidal adolescent. In Elissa Benedek & Dewey Cornell (eds.), *Juvenile Homicide.* Washington: American Psychiatric Press. Pp. 219-247.

Benezech, Michel M. 1984. Homicide by psychotics in France: A five- year study. *Journal of Clinical Psychiatry,* 45, 85-85.

Benezech, Michel M. Bourgeois, D. Boukhabza & Jerome Yesavage. 1981. Cannibalism and vampirism in paranoid schizophrenia. *Journal of Clinical Psychiatry,* 42, 290.

Benezech, Michel, Jacques de Witte, Jean J. Etcheparre & Marc Bourgeois. 1989. A lycanthropic murderer. *American Journal of Psychiatry* 146, 942.

Bennett, Trevor, & Richard Wright. 1984. The relationship between alcohol use and burglary. *British Journal of Addiction,* 79, 431-437.

Berelson, Bernard, & Patrician J. Salter. 1946. Majority and minority American: An analysis of magazine fiction. *Public Opinion Quarterly,* 10, 168=190.

Berelson, Bernard, & Gary A. Steiner. 1964. *Human Behavior: An Inventory of Scientific Findings.* New York: Harcourt, Brace & World.

Berkley, George E., Michael W. Giles, Jerry F. Hackett & Norman C. Kassoff. 1977. *Criminal Justice: Police, Courts, Corrections.* Boston: Holbrook.

Berkow, Robert J., & Andrew J. Fletcher. 1987. *The Merck Manual of Diagnosis and Therapy,* 15th ed. Rahway, NJ: Merck, Sharp & Dohme Research Laboratories.

Berlin, Fred S., H. Martin Malin & Sharon Dean. 1991. Effects of statutes requiring psychiatrists to report suspected sexual abuse of children. *American Journal of Psychiatry,* 148, 449-453.

Black, Donald W., William R. Yates & Nancy C. Andreasen. 1988. Schizophrenia, schizophreniform disorder, and delusional (paranoid) disorders. In John A. Talbott, Robert E. Hales & Stuart C. Yudofsky (eds.), *American Psychiatric Press Textbook of Psychiatry*. Washington, DC: American Psychiatric Press. Pp. 357-402.

Blackburn, Ronald. 1975-*a*. Aggression and the EEG: A quantitative analysis. *Journal of Abnormal Psychology*, 84, 359-365.

Blackburn, Ronald. 1975-*b*. An empirical classification of psychopathic personality. *British Journal of Psychiatry*, 127, 456-460.

Blackburn, Ronald. 1979. Cortical and autonomic arousal in primary and secondary psychopaths. *Psychophysiology*, 16, 143- 150.

Blackburn, Ronald, & Clive Maybury. 1985. Identifying the psychopath: The relation of Cleckey's criteria to the interpersonal domain. *Personality & Individual Differences*, 6, 375-386.

Blackman, Nathan, John T. Lum & Robert J. VanderPearl. 1974. Disturbed communications: A contributing factor in sudden murder. *Mental Health & Society*, 11, 345-355.

Bluestone, Harvey, & Sheldon Travin. 1984. Murder: The ultimate conflict. *American Journal of Psychoanalysis*, 44, 147-167.

Blum, Richard H. 1981. Violence, alcohol, and setting: An unexplored nexus. In James J. Collins, Jr. (ed.), *Drinking and Crime*. New York: Guilford. Pp. 110-142.

Blumenthal, Deborah. 1991. How to keep guns safely. *New York Times*, 30 March, 36.

Blumstein, Alfred, & Jacqueline Cohen. 1987. Characterizing criminal careers. *Science*, 237, 985-991.

Blumstein, Alfred, & S. Moitra. 1980. Identification of "career criminals" from "chronic offenders" in a cohort. *Law & Policy Quarterly*, 2, 321-334.

Bonkalo, A. Electroencephalograpy in criminology. *Canadian Psychiatric Association Journal*, 12, 281-286.

Boulton, Alan A., Bruce A. Davis, Peter H. Yu, Stephen Wormith, & Donald Addington. 1983. Trace acid levels in the plasma and MAO activity in the platelets of violent offenders. *Psychiatry Research*, 8, 19-23.

Bourget, Dominique, & John M. Bradford. 1990. Homicidal parents. *Canadian Journal of Psychiatry*, 35, 233-238.

Bowers, William J. 1983. *Executions in America, 1864-1982: A Study of Death as Punishment*. Boston: Northeastern University Press.

Bowers, William J., Glenn L. Pierce & John F. McDevitt. 1983. *Legal Homicide: Death as Punishment in America, 1864-1982*. Boston: Northeastern University Press.

Bradford, John M., & Rufino Balmaceda. 1983. Shoplifting: Is there a specific psychiatric syndrome? *Canadian Journal of Psychiatry*, 28, 248-254.

Bradford, John M., & D. McLean. 1984. Sexual offenders, violence, and testosterone: A clinical study. *Canadian Journal of Psychiatry*, 29, 335-343.

Brenner, M. Harvey, & Robert T. Swank, 1986. Homicide & economic change: Recent analyses of the Joint Economic Committee Report of 1984. *Journal of Quantitative Criminology*, 2, 81-103.

Briere, John, Neil Malamuth & James V. Check. 1985. Sexuality & rape-supportive beliefs. *International Journal of Women's Studies*, 8, 398-403.

Brody, Baruch. 1980. *Mental Illness: Law and Public Policy*. Boston: D Reidel.

Brody, Nathan. 1988. *Personality: In Search of Individuality*. San Diego, CA: Academic.

Bromberg, Walter. 1963. *The Mind of Man: A History of Psychotherapy and Psychoanalysis*. New York: Harper & Row.

Brown, Barbara B., & Irwin Altman. 1983. Territoriality, defensible space, and residential burglary: An environmental analysis. *Journal of Environmental Psychology*, 3, 203-220.

Brown, Phil, & Christopher J. Smith. 1988. Mental patients' rights: An empirical study of variation across the United States. *International Journal of Law & Psychiatry*, 11, 157-165.

Brown, Rosemary, Nigel Colter, Nicholas Corsellis, Timothy J. Crow, Christopher D. Frith, Roger Jagoe, Eve C. Johnstone & Laura Marsh. 1986. Postmortem evidence of structural brain changes in schizophrenia: Differences in brain weight, temporal horn area, and parahippocampal gyrus compared with affective disorder. *Archives of General Psychiatry,* 43, 36-42.

Brown, Thomas S., & Jerry Pardue. 1985. Effectiveness of the Personnel Selection Inventory in reducing drug store theft. *Psychological Reports,* 56, 875-881.

Bryant, Ernest T., Monte L. Scott, Christopher D. Tori & Charles J. Golden. 1984. Neuropsychological deficits, learning disability, and violent behavior. *Journal of Consulting & Clinical Psychology,* 52, 323-324.

Buckle, Abigail, & David P. Farrington. 1984. An observational study of shoplifting. *British Journal of Criminology,* 24, 63-73.

Budd, Robert D. 1982. The incidence of alcohol use in Los Angeles county homicide victims. *American Journal of Drug & Alcohol Abuse,* 9, 105-111.

Buikhuisen, Wouter. 1982. Aggressive behavior and cognitive disorders. *International Journal of Law & Psychiatry,* 5, 205-217.

Buikhuisen, Wouter, & B.W.G.P. Mejs. 1983. Psychosocial approach to recidivism. In Katherin T. van Dusen & Sarnoff A. Mednick (eds.), *Prospective Studies of Crime and Delinquency.* Boston: Kluwer-Nijhoff. Pp. 99-115.

Bukowski, Nilzete T., & Roselane Gehrke. 1979. O Rorschach em homicidas. *Psico,* 16, 5-27.

Bulkley, Josephine. 1981. Other relevant child sexual abuse statutes: Domestic violence and sexual psychopath laws. In Josephine Bulkley (ed.), *Child Sexual Abuse and the Law.* Washington, DC: National Legal Resource Center for Child Advocacy and Protection, American Bar Association. Pp. 89-102.

Bureau of the Census, U.S. Department of Commerce. 1988. *Profile of State Prison Inmates.* Washington, DC: Bureau of Justice Statistics, U.S. Department of Justice. Report NCJ-109926.

Bureau of the Census, U.S. Department of Commerce. 1989. *Statistical Abstract of the United States.* Washington, DC: U.S. Government Printing Office.

Bureau of Justice Statistics, U.S. Department of Justice. 1980. *Profile of Jail Inmates: National Prisoner Statistics Report* SD NPS J-6, NCJ-65412. Washington, DC: The Bureau.

Bureau of Justice Statistics, U.S. Deparment of Justice. 1983. *Report to the Nation on Crime and Justice: The Data.* Washington: The Bureau. NCJ-87068.

Bureau of Justice Statistics. 1988. *Criminal Victimization in the United States: Trends.* Washington, DC: U.S. Department of Justice.

Bureau of Justice Statistics. 1990. *Population Density in Local Jails.* Washington, DC: U.S. Department of Justice.

Bureau of Justice Statistics. 1991. *Prisoners in 1990.* Washington, DC: U.S. Department of Justice.

Burgess, Ann W., Carol R. Hartman & Arlene McCormack. 1987. Abused to abuser: Antecedents of socially deviant behaviors. *American Journal of Psychiatry,* 144, 1431-1436.

Burke, Jack D., & Darrel A. Regier. 1988. Epidemiology of mental disorders. In John A. Talbott, Robert E. Hales & Stuart C. Yudofsky (eds.), *American Psychiatric Press Textbook of Psychiatry.* Washington, DC: American Psychiatric Press. Pp. 67-90.

Bursten, Ben. 1985. Detecting child abuse by studying the parents. *Bulletin of the American Academy of Psychiatry & the Law,* 13, 273-281.

Busch, Katie A., & James L. Cavanaugh. 1986. The study of multiple murder: Preliminary examination of the interface between epistemology and methodology. *Journal of Interpersonal Violence,* 1, 5-23.

Busch, Kenneth G., Robert Zagar, John R. Hughes & Jack Arbit. 1990. Adolescents who kill. *Journal of Clinical Psychology,* 46, 472-485.

Bush, John M. 1983. Criminality and psychopathology: Treatment for the guilty. *Federal Probation,* 47, 44-49.

Butcher, James N., Laura S. Keller & Steven F. Bacon. 1985. Current developments and future directions in computerized personality assessment. *Journal of Consulting & Clinical Psychology,* 1985, 53, 803-815.

Campbell, David E., & John L. Beets. 1978. Lunacy and the moon. *Psychological Bulletin, 85, 1123-1129.*

Campbell, Norman. 1952. *What Is Science?* New York: Dover.

Campion, John F., James M. Cravens & Fred Covan. 1988. A study of filicidal men. *American Journal of Psychiatry,* 145, 1141- 1144.

Carbonell, Joyce L. 1983. Inmate classification: A cross-tabulation of two methods. *Criminal Justice & Behavior,* 10, 285-292.

Carbonell, Joyce L., Karen M. Moorhead & Edwin I. Megargee. 1984. Predicting prison adjustment with structured personality inventories. *Journal of Consulting & Clinical Psychology,* 52, 280-294.

Cattell, Raymond B. 1963. Formulating the environmental situation and its perception in behavior theory. In S.B. Sells (ed.), *Stimulus Determinants of Behavior.* New York: Ronald. Pp. 46-75.

Cattell, Raymond B. 1980. *Personality and Learning Theory: The Structure of Personality in Its Environment.* New York: Springer.

Cattell, Raymond B. 1985. *Psychotherapy by Structured Learning Theory.* New York: Springer.

Cattell, Raymond B., & Dennis Child. 1975. *Motivation and Dynamic Structure.* New York: Hold, Rinehart, Winston.

Cavanaugh, James L., & Oriest E. Wasyliw. 1985. Treating the not guilty by reason of insanity outpatient: A two year study. *Bulletin of the American Academy of Psychiatry & the Law,* 13, 407-415.

Chakraborty, Ranajit, & Kenneth K. Kidd. 1991. The utility of DNA typing in forensic work. *Science,* 254, 1735-1739.

Christoffel, Katherine K., & Kiang Liu. 1983. Homicide death rates in childhood in 23 developed countries: U.S. rates atypically high. *Child Abuse & Neglect,* 7, 339-345.

Church, R.M. 1959. Emotional reactions of rats to the pain of others. *Journal of Comparative & Physiological Psychology,* 52, 132-134.

Clarke, Ronald V. 1980. "Situational" crime prevention. *British Journal of Criminology,* 20, 136-147.

Clarke, Ronald V. 1984. Opportunity-based crime rates: The difficulties of further refinement. *British Journal of Criminology,* 75, 77-85.

Clarke, Ronald V. 1985. Delinquency, environment, and intervention. *Child Psychology & Psychiatry,* 26, 505-523.

Clarke, Ronald V. 1987. Practicalities of prevent car theft: A criminological analysis. In *Car Theft.* Sydney: National Roads & Motorists Association.

Clarke, Ronald V., & David L. Weisburd. 1990. On the distribution of deviance. In Don M. Gottfredson & Ronald V. Clarke (eds.), *Policy and Theory in Criminal Justice.* Avebury, UK: Gower. Pp. 10-27.

Clarke, Ronald V., & David B. Cornish. 1985. Modeling offenders' decisions: A framework for research and policy. *Crime & Justice,* 6, 147-185.

Clarkin, John F., & Stephen W. Hurt. 1988. Psychological assessment: Tests and rating scales. In In John A. Talbott, Robert E. Hales & Stuart C. Yudofsky (eds.), *American Psychiatric Press Textbook of Psychiatry.* Washington, DC: American Psychiatric Press. Pp. 225-246.

Cloninger, C. Robert, Theodore Reich & Samuel B. Guze. 1975. The multifactorial model of disease transmission: Sex differences in the familial transmission of sociopathy(antisocial personality). *British Journal of Psychiatry,* 127, 11-22.

Coccarro, Emil F., Larry J. Siever, Howard M. Klar & Gail Mauer. 1989. Serotonergic studies in patients with affective and personality disorders: Correlates with suicidal and impulsive aggressive behavior. *Archives of General Psychiatry,* 46, 587-599.

Cocozza, Joseph J., & Henry J. Steadman. 1974. Some refinements in the measurement and prediction of dangerous behavior. *American Journal of Psychiatry,* 131, 1012-1014.

Cohen, Bruce M., Ferdinando Buonanno, Paul E. Keck, Seth P. Finkelstein & Francine M. Benes. 1988. Comparison of MRI and CT scans in a group of psychiatric patients. *American Journal of Psychiatry,* 145, 1084-1088.

Cohen, Stanley. 1988. *Against Criminology.* New Brunswick, NJ: Transaction Books.
Cohn, Ellen, G. 1990. Weather and violent crime: A reply to Perry and Simpson. *Environment & Behavior,* 22, 280-294.
Coid, Jeremy. 1984. Relief of diazepam withdrawal syndrome by shoplifting. *British Journal of Psychiatry,* 145, 552-554.
Cole, K.D., G. Fisher & S.S. Cole. 1968. Women who kill: A sociopsychological study. *Archives of General Psychiatry,* 19, 1-8.
Colligan, Robert C., David Osborne, Wendell M. Swenson & Kenneth P. Offord. 1989. *The MMPI: A Contemporary Normative Study,* 2nd ed. Odessa, FL: Psychological Assessment Resources.
Collins, James J., Jr. 1981. Alcohol careers and criminal careers. In James J. Collins, Jr. (ed.), *Drinking and Crime.* New York: Guilford. Pp. 152-206.
Comstock, George, A. 1986. Sexual effects of movie & TV violence. *Medical Aspects of Human Sexuality,* 20, 96-101.
Conacher, G. Neil. 1988. Pharmacotherapy of the aggressive adult patient. *International Journal of Law & Psychiatry,* 11, 205- 212.
Conacher, G. Neil, & D.G. Workman. 1989. Violent crime possibly associated with anabolic steroid use. *American Journal of Psychiatry,* 146, 679.
Cornell, Dewey. 1989. Causes of juvenile homicide: A review of the literature. In Elissa Benedek & Dewey Cornell (eds.), *Juvenile Homicide.* Washington: American Psychiatric Press. Pp. 1-36.
Cornell, Dewey G., Elissa P. Benedek & David M. Benedek. 1987- a. Characteristics of adolescents charged with homicide: Review of 72 cases. *Behavioral Sciences & the Law,* 5, 11- 23.
Cornell, Dewey G., Elissa P. Benedek & David M. Benedek. 1987- b. Juvenile homicide: Prior adjustment and a proposed typology. *American Journal of Orthopsychiatry,* 57, 383- 393.
Cornell, Dewey G., Elissa P. Benedek & David M. Benedek. 1989. A typology of juvenile homicide offenders. In Elissa Benedek & Dewey Cornell (eds.), *Juvenile Homicide.* Washington: American Psychiatric Press. Pp. 59-84.
Cornell, Dewey G., Carolee Miller & Elissa P. Benedek. 1987. MMPI Profiles of adolescents charged with homicide. *Behavioral Sciences & the Law,* 6, 401-407.
Cornell, Dewey G., Lois Staresina & Elissa P. Benedek. 1989. Legal outcome of juveniles charged with homicide. In Elissa Benedek & Dewey Cornell (eds.), *Juvenile Homicide.* Washington: American Psychiatric Press. Pp. 163-182.
Cosgrove, Judith, & Terry G. Newell. 1991. Recovery of neuropsychological functions during reduction to use of phencyclidine. *Journal of Clinical Psychology,* 47, 159-169.
Coyle, Joseph T. 1988. Neuroscience and psychiatry. In John A. Talbott, Robert E. Hales & Stuart C. Yudofsky (eds.), *American Psychiatric Press Textbook of Psychiatry.* Washington, DC: American Psychiatric Press. Pp. 3-32.
Crittenden, Patricia M., & Susan E. Craig. 1990. Developmental trends in the nature of child homicide. *Journal of Interpersonal Violence,* 1990, 5, 202-216.
Cromwell, Paul F., Jr., George C. Killinger, Hazel B. Kerper & Charles Walker. 1985. *Probation and Parole in the Criminal Justice System.* St. Paul, MN: West.
Cronbach, Lee J. 1971. Test validation. In Robert L. Thorndike (ed.), *Educational Measurement.* Washington: American Council on Education. Pp. 443-507.
Cronbach, Lee J., & Goldine C. Gleser. 1965. *Psychological Tests and Personnel Decisions.* Urbana: University of Illinois Press.
Cullen, Francis T., Bruce G. Link & Craig W. Polanzi. 1982. The seriousness of crime revisited: Have attitudes toward white-collar crime changed? *Criminology,* 20, 83-102.
Cullum, C. Munro, & Erin D. Bigler. 1988. Short form MMPI findings in patients with predominantly lateralized cerebral dysfunction: Neuropsychological and computerized axial tomography-derived parameters. *Journal of Nervous & Mental Disease,* 176, 332-342.
Cupchik, W., & J. Don Atcheson. 1983. Shoplifting: An occasional crime of the moral majority. *Bulletin of the American Academy of Psychiatry & the Law,* 11, 343-354.

Curtiss, Glenn, Mary D. Feczko & Richard C. Marohn. 1979. Rorscach differences in normal and delinquent white male adolescents: A discriminant function analysis. *Journal of Youth & Adolescence,* 8, 379-392.

Cutshall, Charles R., & Paul E. McCold. 1982. Patterns of stock theft victimization & formal response strategies among the Ila of Zambia. *Victimology,* 7, 137-155.

Dabbs, James M., Robert L. Frady, Timothy S. Carr & Norma F. Besch. 1987. Saliva testosterone and criminal violence in young adult prison inmates. *Psychosomatic Medicine,* 49, 174-182.

Dahlstrom, W. Grant, James H. Panton, Kenneth P. Bain & Leona E. Dahlstrom. 1986. Utility of the Megargee & Bohn MMPI typological assessments: Study with a sample of death row inmates. *Criminal Justice & Behavior,* 13, 5-17.

Dallas, Dan. 1978. Savagery, show and tell. *American Psychologist,* 33, 388-390.

Daly, Martin, & Margo Wilson. 1989. Homicide and cultural evolution. *Ethology & Sociobiology,* 10, 99-110.

Daniel, Anasseril E., & Philip W. Harris. 1982. Female homicide offenders referred for pre-trial psychiatric examination: A descriptive study. *Bulletin of the American Academy of Psychiatry & the Law,* 10, 261-269.

Daniel, Anasseril E., Philip W. Harris & Sayed A. Husain. 1981. Differences between midlife female offenders and those younger than 40. *American Journal of Psychiatry,* 138, 1225-1228.

Daniel, Chris. 1992. Anger control bibliotherapy with a convicted murderer under life sentence: A clinical report. *Journal of Offender Rehabilitation,* 18, 301-310.

Danto, Bruce. 1971. Firearms and their role in homicide and suicide. *Life-Threatening Behavior,* 1, 10-17.

Danto, Bruce. 1985. *Identification and Control of Dangerous and Mentally Disordered Offenders.* Laguna Hills, CA: Eagle.

Daradkeh, Tewfik K. 1990. The possible reasons behind a high intentional homicide rate in Jordan. *Dirasat,* 1988, 15, 59-69.

Davidovich, Jessica R. 1990. Men who abuse their spouses: Social and psychological supports. *Journal of Offender Rehabilitation,* 15, 28-30.

Davis, Bruce A., Peter H. Yu, Alan A. Boulton, J. Stephen Wormith & Donald Addington. 1983. Correlative relationships between biochemical activity and aggressive behavior. *Progress in Neuro-psychopharmacology & Biological Psychiatry,* 7, 529-535.

Davis, Glen E., & Harold Leitenberg. 1987. Adolescent sex offenders. *Psychological Bulletin,* 101, 417-427.

Davis, Hilton. 1974. What does the P scale measure? *British Journal of Psychiatry,* 125, 161-167.

Davis, Kenneth L., Rene S. Kahn, Grant Ko & Michael Davidson. 1991. Dopamine in schizophrenia: A review and reconceptualization. *American Journal of Psychiatry,* 148, 1474-1486.

Dawes, Robyn M., David Faust & Paul E. Meehl. 1989. Clinical versus actuarial judgment. *Science,* 243, 1668-1674.

Dawson, E.B, T.D. Moore & W.J. McGanity. 1972. Relationship of lithium metabolism to mental hospital admission and homicide. *Diseases of the Nervous System,* 33, 546-556.

Day, Lincoln H. 1984. Death from non-war violence: An international comparison. *Social Science & Medicine,* 19, 917-927.

Decker, Scott H., & Carol W. Kohlfeld. 1984. A deterrence study of the death penalty in Illinois, 1933-1980. *Journal of Criminal Justice,* 12, 367-377.

Dell, Suzanne. 1983. The detention of diminished responsibility homicide offenders. *British Journal of Criminology,* 23, 50- 60.

Dell, Suzanne, & Alan Smith. 1983. Changes in the sentencing of diminished responsibility homicides. *British Journal of Psychiatry,* 142, 20-34.

Dembo, Richard, Max Dertke, Lawrence LaVoie, Scott Borders *et al.* 1987. Physical abuse, sexual victimization & illicit drug use: a structural analysis among high risk adolescents. *Journal of Adolescence,* 10, 13-34.

Dembo, Richard, Mark Washburn, Eric D. Wish, James Schneider, Alan Getreu, Estellita Berry, Linda Williams & William R. Blount. 1987. Further examination of the association between marijuana use and crime among youths entering a juvenile detention center. *Journal of Psychoactive Drugs,* 19, 361-373.

Demeter, Erzsebet, Kornelia Tekes, Kalman Jaorossy, Miklos Palkovitz *et al.* 1988. Does -sup-3H-imipramine binding asymmetry indicate psychiatric illness? *Acta Psychiatrica Scandinavica,* 77, 746-747.

Demeter, Erzsebet, Kornelia Tekes, Kalman Jaorossy, Miklos Palkovitz *et al.* 1989. The asymmetry of -sup-3H imipramine binding may predict psychiatric illness. *Life Sciences,* 44, 1403-1410.

Denkowski, George C., & Kathryn M. Denkowski. 1985. The mentally retarded offender in the state prison system: Identification, prevalence, adjustment, and rehabilitation. *Criminal Justice & Behavior,* 12, 55-70.

Deuser, William E., Kristina M. DeNeve, Kathryn B. Anderson & Mark D. Wood. 1991. Temperature and aggression: Symmetries and asymmetries. American Psychological Society, Washington, 15 June.

DeYoub, Paul L. 1984. Hypnotic stimulation of antisocial behavior: A case report. *International Journal of Clinical & Experimental Hypnosis,* 32, 301-306.

DiLalla, Lisabeth Fisher, & Irving I. Gottesman. 1991. Biological and genetic contributors to violence: Widom's untold tale. *Psychological Bulletin,* 109, 125-129.

Dix, George E. 1983. A legal perspective on dangerousness: Current status. *Psychiatric Annals,* 13, 243-256.

Dodson, Peter K., & Ellis D. Evans. 1985. A developmental study of school theft. *Adolescence,* 20, 509-523.

Doerner, William G. 1975. A regional analysis of homicide rates in the United States. *Criminology,* 13, 90-101.

Dollard, John. 1937. *Caste and Class in a Southern Town.* New Haven: Yale University Press.

Donnerstein, Edward I., & Daniel G. Linz. 1986. Mass media sexual violence and male viewers: Current theory and research. *American Behavioral Scientist,* 29, 601-618.

Donnerstein, Edward, & Steven Penrod. 1984. The effects of multiple exposures to filmed violence against women. *Journal of Communication,* 34, 130-147.

D'Orban, P.T. 1990. Female homicide. *Irish Journal of Psychological Medicine,* 7, 64-70.

D'Orban, P.T., & Art O'Conner. 1989. Women who kill their parents. *British Journal of Psychiatry,* 154, 27-33.

Douglass, John E., Robert K. Ressler, Ann W. Burgess & Carol R. Hartman. 1986. Criminal profiling from crime scene analysis. *Behavioral Science & the Law,* 4, 401-421.

Dubovsky, Steve L. 1987. Severe nortriptyline intoxication due to change from a generic to a trade preparation. *Journal of Nervous & Mental Disease,* 175, 115-117.

Dull, Thomas R., & David J. Giacopassi. 1988. Dry, damp, and wet: Correlates and presumed consequences of local alcohol ordinances. *American Journal of Drug & Alcohol Abuse,* 14, 499-514.

Edinger, Jack D. 1979. Cross-validation of the Megargee MMPI typology for prisoners. *Journal of Consulting & Clinical Psychology,* 47, 234-242.

Edinger, Jack D., David L. Reuterfors & S. Susan Logue, 1982. Cross- validation of the Megargee MMPI typology: A study of specialized inmate populations. *Criminal Justice & Behavior,* 9, 184- 203.

Edney, Julian J., & Paul A. Bell. 1984. Sharing scarce resources: Group-outcome orientation, external disaster and stealing in a simulated commons. *Small Group Behavior,* 15, 87-108.

Ehrlich, Isaac. 1975-*a.* The deterrent effect of capital punishment: A question of life and death. *American Economic Review,* 65, 397-417.

Ehrlich, Isaac. 1975-*b.* Deterrence: Evidence and interference. *Yale Law Journal,* 85, 209-227.

Elion Victor H., & Edwin I. Megargee, 1975. Validity of the MMPI PD scale among black males. *Journal of Consulting & Clinical Psychology,* 43, 166-172.

Ellis, Robert H., & Joel S. Milner. 1981. Child abuse and locus of control. *Psychological Reports,* 48, 507-510.

Employment Standards Administration, U.S. Department of Labor. 1988. *Notice: Employee Polygraph Protection Act.* Washington: Wage & Hour Division, USDL. WH Publication 1462.

Erikson, Kai. 1966. *Wayward Puritans: A Study in the Sociology of Deviance.* New York: Wiley.

Erlanger, Howard S. 1974-*a.* The empirical status of the subculture of violence thesis. *Social Problems,* 22, 280-292.

Erlanger, Howard S. 1974-*b.* Social class and corporal punishment in childrearing: A reassessment. *American Sociological Review,* 39, 68-65.

Eysenck, Hans J. 1964. *Crime and Personality.* London: Routledge & Kegan Paul.

Eysenck, Hans J. 1967. *Biological Basis of Personality.* Springfield, IL. Charles C. Thomas.

Eysenck, Hans J. 1977-*a. Crime and Personality,* 2nd ed. London: Routledge & Kegan Paul.

Eysenck, Hans J. 1977-*b.* Personality and factor analysis: A reply to Guilford. *Psychological Bulletin,* 84, 405-411.

Eysenck, Hans J., & Sybil B. Eysenck. 1974. An improved short questionnaire for the measurement of extraversion and neuroticism. *Life Sciences,* 3, 1103-1109.

Eysenck, Hans J., & Gisli H. Gundjonsson. 1989. *The Causes & Cures of Criminality.* New York: Plenum Press.

Eysenck, Sybil B., & Hans J. Eysenck. 1977-*a.* Personality differences between prisoners and controls. *Psychological Reports, 40, 1023-1028.*

Eysenck, Sybil B., & Hans J. Eysenck. 1977-*b.* The place of impulsiveness in a dimensional system of personality description. *British Journal of Social & Clinical Psychology,* 16, 57-68.

Eysenck, S.B.G., J. Rust & Hans J. Eysenck. 1977. Personality and the classification of adult offenders. University of London, London. *British Journal of Criminology,* 17, 169-179.

Fagothey, Austin. 1953. *Right and Reason: Ethics in Theory and Practice.* St. Louis: Mosby.

Farley, Frank. 1986. The big T in personality. *Psychology Today,* May, 44-52.

Farley, Frank, & Trevor Sewell. 1976. Test of an arousal theory of delinquency. *Criminal Justice & Behavior,* 3, 315-320.

Fedler, Fred, & Bert Pryor. 1984. An equity theory explanation of bystanders' reactions to shoplifting. *Psychological Reports,* 54, 746.

Farrington, David P., Leonard Berkowitz & Donald J. West. 1982. Differences between individual and group fights. *British Journal of Social Psychology,* 21, 323-333.

Fein, Robert A. 1985. How the insanity acquittal retards treatment. *Law & Human Behavior,* 8, 283-292.

Feldman, Marilyn, Katherine Mallouh & Dorothy Otnow Lewis. 1986. Filicidal abuse in the histories of 15 condemned murderers. *Bulletin of the American Academy of Psychiatry & the Law,* 1986, 14, 345-352.

Feldman, Robert S., & Linda F. Quenzer. 1984. *Fundamentals of Neuro-psychopharmacology.* Sunderland, MA: Sinauer.

Felson, Richard B. 1982. Impression management and the escalation of aggression and violence. *Social Psychology Quarterly,* 45, 245-254.

Felson, Richard B., & Henry J. Steadman. 1983. Situational factors in disputes leading to criminal violence. *Criminology,* 21, 59- 74.

Felson, Richard B., & Henry J. Steadman. 1984. Self-reports of violence. *Criminology,* 22, 321-342.

Felson, Richard B., Stephen A. Ribner & Meryl S. Siegel. 1984. Age and the effect of third parties during criminal violence. *Sociology & Social Research,* 68, 452-462.

Ferdico, John. 1985. *Criminal Procedure for the Criminal Justice Professional.* St. Louis: West.

Fersch, Elsworth A. 1980. *Psychology and Psychiatry in Courts and Corrections: Controversy and Change.* New York: Wiley.

Feuerverger, Andrey, & Clifford D. Shearing. 1982. An analysis of the prosecution of shoplifters. *Criminology,* 20, 273-289.

Fiddes, Dorothy D. Scotland in the seventies: Adolescents in care and custody — A survey of Adolescent murder in Scotland. *Journal of Adolescence,* 4, 47-65.

Finlay, William. 1991. Revelations reassessed — A history of the Hawthorne experiments. *Science,* 254, 1820-1821.

Finley, Wayne H., Clarence E. McDanal, Sara C. Finley & Clarence J. Rosecrans. 1973. Prison survey for the XYY karyotype in tall inmates. *Behavior Genetics,* 1, 97-100.

Finnegan, William. 1990-*a*. A street kid in the drug trade, I: The drug trade. *New Yorker,* 10 September, 51-75.

Finnegan, William. 1990-*b*. A street kid in the drug trade, II: Drugs in New Haven. *New Yorker,* 17 September, 80- 109.

Fishbain, David A. 1986. Suicide pacts and homicide. *American Journal of Psychiatry,* 143, 1319-1320.

Fishbain, David A., James R. Fletcher, Timothy E. Aldrich & Joseph H. Davis. 1987. Relationship between Russian roulette deaths and risk-taking behavior: A controlled study. *American Journal of Psychiatry,* 144, 563-567.

Flanagan, Timothy J., & Katherine M. Jamieson. 1988. *Sourcebook of Criminal Justice Statistics.* Washington, DC: Bureau of Justice Statistics, U.S. Department of Justice.

Flanagan, Timothy J., & Maureen McLeod. 1983. *Sourcebook of Criminal Justice Statistics.* Washington, DC: Bureau of Justice Statistics, U.S. Department of Justice.

Fletcher, Jack M., Linda Ewing-Cobbs, Michael E. Miner, Harvey S. Levin & Lauren Eisenberg. 1990. Behavioral changes after closed head injury in children. *Journal of Consulting & Clinical Psychology,* 1990, 58, 93-98.

Forst, Brian. 1983. Capital punishment and deterrence: Conflicting evidence? *Journal of Criminal Law & Criminology,* 74, 927- 942.

Fowler, Raymond D. 1976. Sweeping reforms ordered in Alabama prisons. *American Psychological Association Monitor,* 7(April), 1, 15.

Fowler, Raymond D. 1985. Landmarks in computer-assisted psychological assessment. *Journal of Consulting & Clinical Psychology,* 1985, 53, 748-759.

Fowler, Raymond D. 1988. Assessment for decision in a correctional setting. In Donald R. Peterson & Daniel B. Fishman (eds.), *Assessment for Decision.* New Brunswick, NJ: Rutgers University Press. Pp. 214-239.

Fowles, George P. 1988. Neuropsychologically impaired offenders: Considerations for assessment and treatment. *Psychiatric Annals,* 18, 692-697.

Frances, Richard J., & John E. Franklin. 1987. Alcohol-induced organic mental disorders. In Robert E. Hales & Stuart C. Yudofsky (eds.), *American Psychiatric Press Textbook of Neuropsychiatry.* Washington, DC: American Psychiatric Press. Pp. 141-156.

Frances, Richard J., & John E. Franklin. 1988. Alcohol and other psychoactive substance abuse disorders. In John A. Talbott, Robert E. Hales & Stuart C. Yudofsky (eds.), *American Psychiatric Press Textbook of Psychiatry.* Washington, DC: American Psychiatric Press. Pp. 313-356.

Franke, Richard H., Edward W. Thomas & Allen J. Queenen. 1977. Suicide and homicide: Common sources and consistent relationships. *Social Psychiatry,* 12, 149-156.

Fransella, F., & D. Bannister. 1977. *A Manual for Repertory Grid Technique.* London: Academic Press.

Franzen, Michael D., & Mark R. Lovell. 1987. Neuropsychological assessment. In Robert E. Hales & Stuart C. Yudofsky (eds.), *American Psychiatric Press Textbook of Neuropsychiatry.* Washington, DC: American Psychiatric Press. Pp. 41-54.

Franzen, Michael D., & Carl Rollyn Sullivan. 1987. Cognitive rehabilitation of patients with neuropsychiatric disabilities. In Robert E. Hales & Stuart C. Yudofsky (eds.), *American Psychiatric Press Textbook of Neuropsychiatry.* Washington, DC: American Psychiatric Press. Pp. 439-450.

Frishtik, Mordechai. 1988. The probation officer's recommendations in his "investigation report." *Journal of Offender Rehabilitation,* 13, 101-132.

Fry, Lincoln J. 1985. Drug abuse and crime in a Swedish birth cohort. *British Journal of Criminology,* 25, 46-59.

Furlong, Michael J., & Donald A. Leton. 1977. The validity of MMPI scales to identify potential child abusers. *Journal of Clinical Child Psychology,* 6, 55-57.

Galski, Thomas, Kirtley E. Thornton & David Shumsky. 1990. Brain dysfunction in sex offenders. *Journal of Offender Rehabilitation,* 16, 65-80.

Gandelman, Ronald. 1980. Gonadal hormones and the induction of intraspecific fighting in mice. *Neuroscience & Biobehavioral Reviews,* 4, 133-140.

Garofalo, James, & Maureen McLeod. 1990. Improving the use and effectiveness of Neighborhood Watch programs. In Larry J. Siegel (ed.), *American Justice: Research of the National Institute of Justice.* St. Paul, MN: West. Pp. 62-66.

Gastil, Raymond D. 1971. Homicide and a regional culture of violence. *American Sociological Review,* 36, 412-427.

Gearing, Milton L. 1979. The MMPI as a primary differentiator and predictor of behavior in prison: A methodological critique and review of the recent literature. *Psychological Bulletin,* 86, 929-963.

Gelberg, Lillian, Lawrence S. Linne & Barbara D. Leake. 1988. Mental health, alcohol and drug use, and criminal history among homeless adults. *American Journal of Psychiatry,* 145, 191-196.

Geller, E. Scott, Timothy A. Koltuniak & Jeffrey S. Shilling. 1983. Response avoidance prompting: A cost-effect strategy for theft deterrence. *Behavioral Counseling & Community Interventions,* 3, 28-42.

Gelles, Richard J., & Ellen F. Hargreaves. 1990. Maternal employment and violence toward children. In Murray A. Straus & Richard J. Gelles (eds.), *Physical Violence in American Families: Risk Factors and Adaptions to Violence in 8145 Families.* New Brunswick, NJ: Transaction Books. Pp. 279-289.

George, Jennifer M. 1991. State or trait: Effects of positive mood on prosocial behaviors at work. *Journal of Applied Psychology,* 76, 299-307.

Gibbs, John J., & Peggy L. Shelly. 1982. Life in the fast lane: A retrospective view by commercial thieves. *Journal of Research in Crime & Delinquency,* 19, 299-330.

Gilandas, Alex, Stephen Touyz, Pierre J.V. Beumont & H.P. Greenberg. 1984. *Handbook of Neuropsychological Assessment.* Sydney: Grune & Stratton.

Gillies, Hunter. 1976. Homicide in the west of Scotland. *British Journal of Psychiatry,* 128, 105-127.

Glaser, Daniel. 1976. Achieving better questions: A half century's progress in correctional research. *Federal Probation,* 4, 3-9.

Glaser, Daniel. 1979. Capital punishment: Deterrent or stimulus to murder? Our unexamined deaths and penalties. *University of Toledo Law Review,* 10, 317-333.

Glueck, Sheldon, & Eleanor Glueck. 1956. *Physique and Delinquency.* New York, Harper.

Godkin, Edwin Lawrence. 1898. *Problems of Modern Democracy: Political and Economic Essays,* 3rd ed. New York: Harcourt.

Goeppinger, H. 1975. Homicide and criminal career: A first provisional report of the investigations of murderers at Tubingen. *Rassegna di Criminologia,* 6, 39-45.

Goetting, Ann. 1988-a. Patterns of homicide among women. *Journal of Interpersonal Violence,* 3, 3-19.

Goetting, Ann. 1988-b. When females kill one another: The exceptional case. *Criminal Justice & Behavior,* 15, 179-189.

Goetting, Ann. 1988-c. When parents kill their young children. *Journal of Family Violence,* 3, 339-346.

Goetting, Ann. 1989-a. Men who kill their mates: A profile. *Journal of Family Violence,* 4, 285-296.

Goetting, Ann. 1989-*b*. Patterns of homicide among children. *Criminal Justice & Behavior,* 16, 63-80.

Goetting, Ann. 1989-*c*. Patterns of marital homicide: A comparison of husbands and wives. *Journal of Comparative Family Studies,* 20, 341-354.

Goffman, Erving. 1963. *Stigma: Notes on the Management of a Spoiled Identity.* Englewood Cliffs, NJ: Prentice-Hall.

Goffman, Erving. 1967. *Interaction Ritual: Essays on Face-to- Face Behavior.* Garden City, NY: Anchor.

Golann, Stuart, & William J. Fremouw (eds.). 1976. *The Right to Treatment for Mental Patients.* New York: Irvington.

Goldman, Marcus J. 1991. Kleptomania: Making sense of the nonsensical. *American Journal of Psychiatry,* 148, 986-996.

Goleman, Daniel. 1985. Violence against women in films. *Victimology,* 8, 21-22.

Gomme, Ian M. 1985. Predictors of status and criminal offences among male and female adolescents in an Ontario community. *Canadian Journal of Criminology,* 27, 147-159.

Gordon, Alistair M. 1983. Drugs and delinquency: A ten-year follow- up of drug clinic patients. *British Journal of Psychiatry,* 142, 169-173.

Gorenstein, Ethan E. 1982. Frontal lobe functions in psychopaths. *Journal of Abnormal Psychology,* 91, 368-379.

Gorenstein, Ethan E., & Joseph P. Newman. 1980. Disinhibitory psychopathology: A new perspective and model for research. *Psychological Review,* 87, 301-315.

Gossop, Michael R., & Sybil B. Eysenck. 1983. A comparison of the personality of drug addicts in treatment with that of a prison population. *Personality & Individual Differences,* 4, 207- 209.

Gottlieb, Peter, G. Gabrielsen & Peter Kramp. 1988. Increasing rates of homicide in Copenhagen from 1959 to 1983. *Acta Psychiatrica Scandinavica,* 77, 301-308.

Graham, John R. 1987. *The MMPI: A Practical Guide,* 2nd ed. New York: Oxford University Press.

Graham, John W., Gary Marks & William B. Hansen. 1991. Social influence processes affecting adolescent substance use. *Journal of Applied Psychology,* 76, 291-298.

Graham, Mary G. 1990. Controlling drug abuse and crime: A research update. In Larry J. Siegel (ed.), *American Justice: Research of the National Institute of Justice.* St. Paul, MN: West. Pp. 101-113.

Grant, Brian L., & Cooons, David J. 1983. Guilty verdict in a murder committed by a veteran with post-traumatic stress disorder. *Bulletin of the American Academy of Psychiatry & the Law,* 11, 355-358.

Grasmick, Harold G., & Wilbur J. Scott. 1982. Tax evasion and mechanisms of social control: A comparison with grand and petty theft. *Journal of Economic Psychology,* 2, 213-230.

Grasmick, Harold G., Robert J. Bursik & Karyl A. Kinsey. 1991. Shame and embarrassment as deterrents to noncompliance wih the law: The case of an anti-littering campaign. *Environment & Behavior,* 23, 233-251.

Greenberg, Jerald. 1990. Employee theft as a reaction to underpayment inequity: The hidden cost of pay cuts. *Journal of Applied Psychology,* 75, 561-568.

Greenberg, Stephanie W. 1981. Alcohol and crime: A methodological critique of the literature. In James J. Collins, Jr. (ed.), *Drinking and Crime.* New York: Guilford. Pp. 70-109.

Greene, Roger L. 1987. Ethnicity and MMPI performance: A review. *Journal of Consulting & Clinical Psychology,* 55, 497-512.

Greene, Roger L. 1988. The relative efficacy of F-K and the obvious and subtle scales to detect overreporting of psychopathology on the MMPI. *Journal of Clinical Psychology,* 44, 152-159.

Greene, Roger L. 1990. Stability of MMPI scale scores within four codetypes across forty years. *Journal of Personality Assessment,* 55, 1-6.

Griswold, David B. 1984. Crime prevention and commercial burglary: A time series analysis. *Journal of Criminal Justice,* 12, 493-501.

Gross, Lawrence S. 1987. Neuropsychiatric aspects of vitamin deficiency states. In Robert E. Hales & Stuart C. Yudofsky (eds.), *American Psychiatric Press Textbook of Neuropsychiatry.* Washington, DC: American Psychiatric Press. Pp. 287-306.

Group for the Advancement of Psychiatry, Committee on Alcoholism and the Addictions. 1991. Substance abuse disorders: A psychiatric priority. *American Journal of Psychiatry,* 148, 1291-1300.

Gunn, John C. 1978-*a.* Epileptic homicide: A case report. *British Journal of Psychiatry,* 132, 510-513.

Gunn, John C. 1978-*b. Psychiatric Aspects of Imprisonment.* New York: Academic.

Gunn, John. 1982. An English psychiatrist looks at dangerousness. *Bulletin of the American Academy of Psychiatry & the Law,* 10, 143-153.

Gur, Raquel E., Susan M. Resnick, Ruben C. Gur, Abass Alavi, Stanley Caroff, Michael Kushner & Martin Reivich. 1987. Regional brain function in schizophrenia: Repeated evaluation with positron emission tomography. *Archives of General Psychiatry,* 44, 126-129.

Haapanen, Rudy A., & Carl F. Jesness. 1982. *Early Identification of the Chronic Offender.* Sacramento: California Youth Correctional Agency, Department of the Youth Authority.

Haines, Allan T. 1982. Intrinsic resistance training of EMR children in hypothetical temptation to steal situations. *Australia & New Zealand Journal of Developmental Disabilities,* 8, 77-84.

Haines, Allan T., M.S. Jackson & J. Davidson. 1983. Children's resistance to the temptation to steal in real & hypothetical situations: A comparison of two treatment programs. *Australian Psychologist,* 18, 289-303.

Hall, Harold V. 1982. Dangerousness prediction and the maligned forensic professional: Suggestions for detecting distortions of true basal violence. *Criminal Justice & Behavior,* 9, 3-12.

Hall, Harold V. 1984. Predicting dangerousness for the courts. *American Journal of Forensic Psychology,* 2, 5-25.

Hall, Harold V., & Douglas McNinch. 1988. Linking crime-specific behavior to neuropsychological impairment. *International Journal of Clinical Neuropsychology,* 10, 113-122.

Hall, Robert W. 1989. A study of mass murder: Evidence of underlying cadmium and lead poisoning and brain involved immunoreactivity. *International Journal of Biosocial & Medical Research,* 11, 144-152.

Hall, Calvin S., & Gardner Lindzey. 1970. *Theories of Personality,* 2nd ed. New York: Wiley.

Halleck, Seymour L. 1987. *The Mentally Disordered Offender.* Washington, DC: American Psychiatric Press.

Hamilton, James W. 1986. Some observations on the motivations of Lee Harvey Oswald. *Journal of Psychohistory,* 14, 43-54.

Hammersley, Richard, & Valerie Morrison. 1987. Effects of polydrug use on the criminal activities of heroin users. *British Journal of Addiction,* 82, 899-906

Hammersley, Richard, & Valerie Morrison. 1988. Crime amongst heroin, alcohol, and cannabis users. *Medicine & Law,* 7, 185-193.

Hansmann, Henry B., & John M. Quigley. 1982. Population heterogeneity and the sociogenesis of homicide. *Social Forces,* 61, 206-224.

Hare, Robert D. 1970. *Psychopathy: Theory and Research.* New York: Wiley.

Hare, Robert D. 1979. Psychopathy and laterality of cerebral function. *Journal of Abnormal Psychology,* 88, 605-610.

Hare, Robert D. 1982. Psychopathy and physiological activity during anticipation of an aversive stimulus in a distraction paradigm. *Psychophysiology,* 19, 266-271.

Hare, Robert D. 1984. Performance of psychopaths on cognitive tasks related to frontal lobe function. *Journal of Abnormal Psychology,* 93, 133-140.

Hare, Robert D. 1985. Comparison of procedures for assessment of psychopathy. *Journal of Consulting & Clinical Psychology,* 53, 7-16.

Hare, Robert D. 1991. *The Hare Psychopathy Checklist — Revised (PCL-R).* North Tonawanda, NY: Multi-Health Systems.

Hare, Robert D., & Leslie M. McPherson. 1984. Psychopathy and perceptual asymmetry during verbal dichotic listening. *Journal of Abnormal Psychology,* 93, 141-149.

Hare, Robert D., & Leslie M. McPherson. 1985. Violent and aggressive behavior by criminal psychopaths. *International Journal of Law & Psychiatry,* 7, 35-50.

Hare, Robert D., Leslie M. McPherson & Adelle E. Forth. 1988. Male psychopaths and their criminal careers. *Journal of Consulting & Clinical Psychology,* 56, 710-714.

Hare, Robert D., Timothy Harpur, A. Ralph Hakstian & Adelle E. Forth. 1990. The revised psychopathy checklist: Reliability and factor structure. *Journal of Personality Assessment,* 2, 338-341.

Harring, Sidney L. 1983. *Policing a Class Society: The Experience of American Cities, 1865-1915.* New Brunswick: Rutgers University Press.

Harris, Jay E., & Anneliese A. Pontius. 1975. Dismemberment murder: In search of the object. *Journal of Psychiatry & Law,* 3, 7-23.

Harry, Bruce. 1983. Movies and behavior among hospitalized mentally disordered offenders. *Bulletin of the American Academy of Psychiatry & the Law,* (4) 359-364.

Hart, Cedric J. 1987. The relevance of a test of speech comprehension deficit to persistent aggressiveness. *Personality & Individual Differences,* 8, 371-384.

Hartman, David E. 1988. *Neuropsychological Toxicity.* New York: Pergamon.

Harvey, O.J. 1962. Personality factors in resolution of conceptual incongruities. *Sociometry,* 25, 336-352.

Haskell, Martin R., & Lewis Yablonsky. 1974. *Crime and Delinquency.* Chicago: Rand McNally.

Hathaway, Starke R., & Paul E. Meehl. 1956. Psychiatric implications of code types. In George S. Welsh & W. Grant Dahlstrom (eds.), *Basic Readings on the MMPI in Psychology and Medicine.* Minneapolis: University of Minnesota Press. Pp. 136-144.

Hawkins, Darnell F. 1989. Intentional injury: Are there no solutions? *Law, Medicine & Health Care,* 17, 32-41.

Hawkins, Richard. 1984. Employee theft in the restaurant trade: Forms of ripping off by waiters at work. *Deviant Behavior,* 5, 47-69.

Hays, J. Ray, Kenneth S. Solway & Donna Schreiner. 1978. Intellectual characteristics of juvenile murderers versus status offenders. *Psychological Reports,* 43, 80-82.

Heath, Linda, Candace Kruttschnitt & David Ward. 1986. Television and violent criminal behavior: Beyond the bobo doll. *Violence & Victims,* 1, 177-190.

Heather, Nick. 1976. Specificity of schizophrenic thought disorder: A replication and extension of previous findings. *British Journal of Social & Clinical Psychology,* 15, 131-137.

Heather, Nick. 1977. Personal illness in 'lifers' and the effects of long- term indeterminate sentences. *British Journal of Criminology,* 17, 378-386.

Heberling, Jon L. 1973. Judicial review of the guilty plea. *Lincoln Law Review,* 7, 137-150.

Heilbrun, Alfred B. 1978. Psychopathy and violent crime. *Journal of Consulting & Clinical Psychology,* 47, 509-516.

Heilbrun, Alfred B. 1979. Psychopathy and violent crime. *Journal of Consulting & Clinical Psychology,* 47, 509-516.

Heilbrun, Alfred B. 1982. Cognitive models of criminal violence based upon intelligence and psychopathy levels. *Journal of Consulting & Clinical Psychology,* 50, 546-557.

Heilbrun, Alfred B. 1990. Differentiation of death-row murderers and life-sentence murderers by antisociality and intelligence measures. *Journal of Personality Assessment,* 54, 617-627.

Heilbrun, Alfred B., & Mark R. Heilbrun. 1985. Psychopathy and dangerousness: Comparison, integration, and extension of two psychopathic typologies. *British Journal of Clinical Psychology,* 24, 181-195.

Heinrichs, Douglas W., & Robert W. Buchanan. 1988. Significance and meaning of neurological signs in schizophrenia. *American Journal of Psychiatry,* 145, 11-18.

Heller, Melvin S., William H. Taylor, Saundra M. Ehrlich & David Lester. 1984. The association between psychosis and violent crime: A study of offenders evaluated at a court psychiatric clinic. *Journal of General Psychology,* 110, 263-266.

Henderson, Monika. 1983. An empirical classification of non-violent offenders using the MMPI. *Personality & Individual Difference,* 4, 671-677.

Henderson, Monika, & Miles Hewstone. 1984. Prison inmates' explanations for interpersonal violence: Accounts and attributions. *Journal of Consulting & Clinical Psychology,* 52, 789-794.

Hennessy, James J., & Laurie Kepecs-Schlussel. 1992. Psychometric scaling techniques applied to rates of crimes and victimization, I: Major population centers. *Journal of Offender Rehabilitation,* 18, 5-78.

Hennigan, Karen M. 1982. Impact of the introduction of television on crime in the United States: Empirical findings and theoretical implications. *Journal of Personality & Social Psychology,* 42, 461-477.

Herrnstein, Richard. 1990. Biology and crime. In Larry J. Siegel (ed.), *American Justice: Research of the National Institute of Justice.* St. Paul, MN: West. Pp. 11-14.

Hindler, C.G. 1989. Epilepsy and violence. *British Journal of Psychiatry,* 155, 246-249.

Hinsie, Leland E., & Robert Jean Campbell. 1970. *Psychiatric Dictionary,* 4th ed. New York: Oxford University Press.

Hirsch, Charles S., Norman B. Rushforth, Amasa B. Ford & Lester Adelson. 1973. Homicide and suicide in a metropolitan county: Long- term trends. *Journal of the American Medical Association,* 223, 900-905.

Hirschi, Travis, & H. Charles Selvin. 1973. *Principles of Survey Analysis.* New York, Free Press.

Hoffman, Michelle. 1991. NMDA receptor cloned — twice. *Science,* 254, 801-89\02.

Hofmann, Frederick G., & Adele D. Hofmann. 1975. *A Handbook on Drug and Alcohol Abuse: The Biomedical Aspects.* New York: Oxford University Press.

Holcomb, William R., & Nicholas Adams. 1982. Racial influences on intelligence and personality measures of people who commit murder. *Journal of Clinical Psychology,* 38, 793-796.

Holcomb, William R., & Nicholas A. Adams. 1985. Personality mechanisms of alcohol-related violence. *Journal of Clinical Psychology,* 41, 714-722.

Holcomb, William R., Nicholas A. Adams & Howard M. Ponder. 1984. Are separate black and white MMPI norms needed? An IQ- controlled comparison of accused murderers. *Journal of Clinical Psychology,* 40, 189-193.

Holcomb, William R., Nicholas A. Adams & Howard M. Ponder. 1985. The developmental and cross-validation of an MMPI typology of murderers. *Journal of Personality Assessment,* 49, 240- 244.

Holcomb, William R., Nicholas A. Adams, Howard M. Ponder & Wayne P. Anderson. 1984. Cognitive and behavioral predictors of MMPI scores in pretrial psychological evaluations of murderers. *Journal of Clinical Psychology,* 40, (2) 592-597.

Holinger, Paul C. 1979. Violent deaths among the young: Recent trends in suicide, homicide, and accidents. *American Journal of Psychiatry,* 136, 1144-1147.

Holinger, Paul C. 1980. Violent deaths as a leading cause of mortality: An epidemiologic study of suicide, homicide, and accidents. *American Journal of Psychiatry,* 137, 472-476.

Holinger, Paul C., & Elaine H. Klemen. 1982. Violent deaths in the United States, 1900-1975: Relationships between suicide, homicide, and accidental deaths. *Social Science & Medicine,* 16, 1928- 1938.

Holinger, Paul C., Daniel Offer & Eric Ostrov. 1987. Suicide and homicide in the United States: An epidemiologic study of violent death, population changes, and the potential for prediction. *American Journal of Psychiatry,* 144, 215-219.

Holland, James G., & B.F. Skinner. 1961. *The Analysis of Behavior.* New York: McGraw-Hill.

Holland, Terrill R., & Bill McGarvey. 1985. Crime specialization, seriousness progression, and Markov chains. *Journal of Consulting & Clinical Psychology,* 52, 837-840.

Holland, Terrill R., Gerald B. Beckett & Norman Holt. 1982. Prediction of violent versus nonviolent recidivism from prior violent and nonviolent criminality. *Journal of Abnormal Psychology*, 91, 178-182.

Holland, Terrill R., Gerald E. Beckett & Mario Levi. 1981. Intelligence, personality, and criminal violence: A multivariate analysis. *Journal of Consulting & Clinical Psychology*, 49, 106-111.

Holland, Terrill R., Norman Holt & Gerald E. Beckett. 1982. Prediction of violent versus nonviolent recidivism from prior violent and nonviolent criminality. *Journal of Abnormal Psychology*, 91, 178-182.

Holland, Terrill R., Mario Levi & Gerald E. Beckett. 1983. Associations between violent and non-violent criminality: A canonical contingency-table analysis. *Multivariate Behavioral Research*, 16, 237-241.

Holland,Terrill R., Norman Holt, Mario Levi & Gerald E. Beckett. 1983. Comparison and combination of clinical and statistical predictions of recidivism among adult offenders. Journal of Applied Psychology, 68, (2) 203-211.

Hollin, Clive R. 1990. *Cognitive-Behavioral Interventions with Young Offenders*. New York: Pergamon.

Hollinger, Richard C., & John P. Clark. 1983. Deterrence in the workplace: Perceived Certainty, perceived severity, and employee theft. *Social Forces*, 62, 398-418.

Holmes, Ronald M., & James E. deBurger. 1985. Profiles in terror: The serial murderer. *Federal Probation*, 49, 29-34.

Holzman, Harold R. 1982. The serious habitual property offender as "moonlighter": An empirical study of labor force participation among robbers and burglars. *Journal of Criminal Law & Criminology,*73, 1774-1792.

Hosch, Harmon M., & D. Steven Cooper. 1982. Victimization as a determinant of eyewitness accuracy. *Journal of Applied Psychology*, 67, 649-652.

Hotaling, Gerald T., & David B. Sugarman. 1986. An analysis of risk markers in husband to wife violence: The current state of knowledge. *Violence & Victims*, 1, 101-124.

Howard, Richard C. 1984. The clinical EEG and personality in mentally abnormal offenders. *Psychological Medicine*, 14, 569-580.

Howard, Richard C., Roger Bailey & Alison Newman. 1984. A preliminary study of Hare's "Research Scale for the Assessment of Psychopathy" in mentally-abnormal offenders. *Personality & Individual Differences*, 5, 389-396.

Hucker, S., R. Langevin, G. Wortzman & J. Bain. 1986. Neuropsychological impairment in pedophiles. *Canadian Journal of Behavioural Science*, 18, 440-448.

Huff-Corzine, Lin, Jay Corzine & David C. Moore. 1986. Southern exposure: Deciphering the south's influence on homicide rates. *Social Forces*, 64, 906-924.

Hull, Debra B., & Jacqueline Burke. 1991. The religious right, attitudes toward women, and tolerance for sexual abuse. *Journal of Offender Rehabilitation*, 17, 1-12.

Humphrey, John A., & Harriet J. Kupferer. 1977. Pockets of violence: An exploration of homicide and suicide. *Diseases of the Nervous System*, 38, 833-837.

Humphrey, John A., & Stuart Palmer. 1987. Stressful life events and criminal homicide. *Omega: Journal of Death & Dying*, 17, 299-308.

Hunt, Dana E., Douglas S. Lipton & Barry Spunt. 1984. Patterns of criminal activity among methadone clients and current narcotics users not in treatment. *Journal of Drug Issues*, 14, 687-702.

Husain, Arshad, Daniel E. Anasseril & Phillip W. Harris. 1983. A study of young age and mid-life homicidal women admitted to a psychiatric hospital for pretrial evaluation. *Canadian Journal of Psychiatry*, 28, 109-113.

Inciardi, James A. 1982. The production and detection of fraud in street studies of crime and drugs. *Journal of Drug Issues*, 12, 285-291.

Inciardi, James A., Anne E. Pottieger & Charles E. Faupel. 1982. Black women, heroin, and crime: Some empirical notes. *Journal of Drug Issues*, 12, 241-250.

Jackson, Merrill S. 1984. The measurement of simulated stealing behavior and moral judgment. *Australian Psychologist*, 19, 263-269.

Jackson, Merrill S., & Allan T. Haines. 1982. A comparative study of the responses of young normal children and older retarded children in hypothetical temptation to steal situations. *Australian & New Zealand Journal of Developmental Disabilities,* 8, 85-91.

Janeskela, Galan M., & Martin G. Miller. 1985. An exploratory study of delinquency, criminal offenses, and juvenile status offenders via the cross-validation design. *Adolescence,* 20, 161-170.

Jarvinen, Liisa. 1977. Personality characteristics of violent offenders and suicidal individuals. *Annals of the Finnish Academy of Sciences,* 19-30.

Jason, Janine. 1984. Centers for Disease Control and the epidemiology of violence. *Child Abuse & Neglect,* 8, 279- 283.

Javitt, Daniel C., & Stephen R. Zubin. 1991. Recent advances in the phencyclidine model of schizophrenia. *American Journal of Psychiatry,* 148, 1301-1308.

Jensen, Arthur R. 1965. Maudsley Personality Inventory. In Oscar K. Buros (ed.), *The Sixth Mental Measurement Yearbook.* Highland Park, NJ: Gryphon. Pp. 288-291.

Johnson, Dennis L., James G. Simmons & B. Carl Gordon. 1983. Temporal consistency of the Meyer-Megargee inmate typology. *Criminal Justice & Behavior,* 10, 263-268.

Johnson (Hon.) Frank M. 1976. Minimum constitutional standards for inmates of Alabama penal system. Appendix A, *Pugh v. Locke. 406 Federal Supplement,* 1976, 332-337.

Johnston, Lloyd D., Patrick M. O'Malley & Jerald G. Bachman, 1987. Psychotherapeutic, licit, and illicit use of drugs among adolescents: An epidemiological perspective. *Journal of Adolescent Health Care.* 8, 36-51.

Jones, John W., & William Terris. 1983. Prediction of employee theft in home improvement center. *Psychological Reports,* 52, 187-201.

Jones, Taz, William B. Beidelman & Raymond O. Fowler. 1981. Differentiating violent and non-violent prison inmates by use of selected MMPI scales. *Journal of Clinical Psychology,* 37, 673-678.

Joseph, Rhawn. 1990. *Neuropsychology, Neuropsychiatry, and Behavioral Neurology.* New York: Plenum.

Jutai, Jeffrey W., Robert D. Hare & John F. Connolly. 1987. Psychopathy and event-related brain potentials (ERPs) associated with attention to speech stimuli. *Personality & Individual Differences,* 8, 175-184.

Kagan, Jerome, & Howard A. Moss. 1962. *Birth to Maturity: A Study in Psychological Devlopment.* New York: John Wiley.

Kahn, Marvin W. 1959. A comparison of personality, intelligence, and social history of two criminal types. *Journal of Social Psychology,* 49, 33-40.

Kahn, Marvin W. 1967. Correlates of Rorschach reality adherence in the assessment of murderers who plead insanity. *Journal of Projective Techniques & Personality Assessment,* 31, 44-47.

Kahn, Marvin W. 1971. Murderers who plead insanity: A descriptive factor-analytic study of personality, social, and history variables. *Genetic Psychology Monographs,* 84, 275-360.

Kahn, Marvin W., & W.E. Kirk. 1968. The concepts of aggression: A review and reformation. *Psychological Record,* 18, 559-573.

Kahn, Marvin W., & Lawrence Raifman. 1981. Hospitalization versus imprisonment and the insanity plea. *Criminal Justice & Behavior,* 8, 483-490.

Kalichman, Seth C. 1988. MMPI profiles of women and men convicted of domestic homicide. *Journal of Clinical Psychology,* 44, 847-853.

Kallis, M. Jeffrey, & Dindo J. Vanier. 1985. Consumer shoplifting: Orientations and deterrents. *Journal of Criminal Justice,* 13, 459-473.

Kalmuss, Debra S., & Murray A. Straus. 1990. Wife's marital dependency and wife abuse. In Murray A. Straus & Richard J. Gelles (eds.), *Physical Violence in American Families: Risk Factors and Adaptions to Violence in 8145 Families.* New Brunswick, NJ: Transaction Books. Pp. 360-382.

Kandel, Elizabeth, Sarnoff A. Mednick, Lisa Kirkegard-Sorensen, Barry Hutchings *et al.* 1988. I.Q. as a protective factor for subjects at high risk for antisocial behavior. *Journal of Consulting & Clinical Psychology,* 56, 224-226.

Kanekar, Suresh, Nirmala J. Pinto & Deepa Mazumdar. 1985. Causal and moral responsibility of victims of rape and robbery. *Journal of Applied Social Psychology,* 15, 622-637.

Kaplan, David A., Peter McKillop & Bob Cohn. 1990. The noose for an American? Malaysia's stiff justice for possession of pot. *Newsweek,* 15 October, 42.

Kaplan, Edith. 1990. The process approach to neuropsychological assessment of psychiatric patients. *Journal of Neuropsychiatry & Clinical Neurosciences,* 2, 72-87.

Kaplun, David, & Robert Reich, 1976. The murdered child and his killers. *American Journal of Psychiatry,* 133, 809-813.

Kaufman, Joan, & Edward Zigler. 1987. Do abused children become abusive parents? *American Journal of Orthopsychiatry,* 57, 186-192.

Kelley, Katherine A. 1985. Nine social indicia as functions of population size or density. *Bulletin of the Psychonomic Society,* 23, 24-26.

Kelly, George A. 1955. *The Psychology of Personal Constructs.* New York: Norton.

Kelly, George A. 1963. *A Theory of Personality: The Psychology of Personal Constructs.* New York: Norton.

Kelly, George A. 1967. A psychology of the optimal man. In Brendan H. Maher (ed.), *The Goals of Psychotherapy.* New York: Appleton-Century-Crofts.

Kelly, George A. 1969. *Clinical Psychology and Personality: The Selected Papers of George Kelly.* Edited by Brendan Maher. New York: Wiley.

Kelly, George A. 1970. Behavior is an experiment. In D. Bannister (ed.), *Perspectives in Personal Construct Theory.* London: Academic. Pp. 255-269.

Kelly, George A. 1980. A psychology of the optimal man. In Alvin W. Landfield & Larry M. Leitner (eds.), *Personal Construct Psychology.* New York: Wiley. Pp. 33-34.

Keltikangas-Jarvinen, Liisa. 1978. Personality of violent offenders and suicidal individuals. *Psychiatrica Fennica,* 14, 57-63.

Keltikangas-Jarvinen, Liisa. 1980. Rorschach and TAT protocols of violent identical twins: A case report. *Psychiatria Fennica,* 16, 77-80.

Keltikangas-Jarvinen, Liisa. 1982. Alexithymia in violent offenders. *Journal of Personality Assessment,* 46, 462-467.

Kemp, Simon. 1987. Perception of the rate of increase of crime. *New Zealand Journal of Psychology,* 16, 3-8.

Kendall, Philip C., & Lauren Braswell. 1985. *Cognitive-Behavior Therapy for Impulsive Children.* New York: Guilford.

Kennedy, Thomas D. 1986. Trends in inmate classification: A status report of two computerized psychometric approaches. *Criminal Justice & Behavior,* 13, 165-184.

Kessler, Ronald C., Geraldine Downey, J. Ronald Milavsky & Horst Stipp. 1988. Clustering of teenage suicides after television news stories about suicides; A reconsideration. *American Journal of Psychiatry,* 145, 1379-1383.

Kinard, E. Milling. 1982. Child abuse and depression: Cause or consequence? *Child Welfare,* 61, 403-413.

King, D.P. 1973. Firearms and crime. *Criminologist,* 8, 50- 58.

King, David R. 1978. The brutalization effect: Execution publicity and the incidence of homicide in South Carolina. *Social Forces,* 57, 683-687.

Kitahara, Michio. 1986. Dietary tryptophan ratio and homicide in western and southern Europe. *Journal of Orthomolecular Medicine,* 1, 13-16.

Klaus, Patsy A., Michael R. Rand & Bruce M. Taylor. 1983. The victim. *Report to the Nation on Crime and Justice: The Data.* Washington: Bureau of Justice Statistics, U.S. Department of Justice. NCJ-87068.

Klein, David, Maurice S. Reizen, George H. van Amburg & Scott A. Walker. 1977. Some social characteristics of young gunshot fatalities. *Accident Analysis & Prevention,* 9, 177-182.

Klein, Lawrence, Brian Forst & Victor Filatov. 1978. The deterrent effect of capital punishment: An assessment of the estimates. In Alfred Blumstein (ed.), *Deterrence and Incapacitation: Estimating the Effects of Criminal Sanctions on Crime Rates.* Washington: National Academy of Sciences. Pp. 336-360.

Klein, Stephen, Joan Petersilia & Susan Turner. 1990. Race and imprisonment decisions in California. *Science,* 247, 812-816.

Klemke, Lloyd W. 1982. Exploring juvenile shoplifting. *Sociology & Social Research,* 67, 59-75.

Kochkin, Sergei. Personality correlates of a measure of honesty. 1987. *Journal of Business & Psychology,* 1, 236-247.

Kokkevi, Anna, & Helen Agathonos. 1988. Intelligence and personality profile of battering parents in Greece: A comparative study. *Child Abuse & Neglect,* 11, 93-99.

Korbin, Jill E. 1989. Fatal maltreatment by mothers: A proposed framework. *Child Abuse & Neglect,* 13, 481-489.

Korchin, Sheldon J. 1976. *Modern Clinical Psychology.* New York: Basic Books.

Kozol, Harry L., R. Boucher & R. Garofalo. 1972. The diagnosis and treatment of dangerousness. *Crime & Delinquency,* 18, 371-392.

Krakowski, Menahem I., Antonio Convit, Judith Jaeger & Shang Lin. 1989. Neurological impairment in violent schizophrenic inpatients. *American Journal of Psychiatry,* 146, 849-853.

Kramer, Morton. 1977. *Psychiatric Services and the Changing Institutional Scene, 1970-1985.* Washington, DC: U.S. Government Printing Office.

Kruesi, Markus J., Judith L. Rapoport, E. Mark Cummings & Carol J. Berg. 1987. Effects of sugar and aspartame on aggression and activity in children. *American Journal of Psychiatry,* 144 1487-1490.

Kudryavtsev, V.N. 1974. The structure of criminality and social change. *United Nations Social Defence Research Institute,* 8, 23-39.

Kunce, Joseph T., Joseph J. Ryan & C. Cleary Eckelman. 1976. Violent behavior and differential WAIS characteristics. *Journal of Consulting & Clinical Psychology,* 44, 42-45.

Kundu, Ramanath, & Gita Bhaumik. 1982. Some affective personality qualities of murderer: A research note. *Personality Study & Group Behavior,* 2, 36-43.

Lalli, M., & S.H. Turner. 1968. Suicide and homicide: A comparative analysis by race and occupational levels. *Journal of Criminal Law, Criminology, Police Science,* 59, 191-200.

Lamb, H. Richard. 1988. Community psychiatry and prevention. In John A. Talbott, Robert E. Hales & Stuart C. Yudofsky (eds.), *American Psychiatric Press Textbook of Psychiatry.* Washington, DC: American Psychiatric Press. Pp. 1141-1160.

Lamb, H. Richard, & Robert W. Grant. 1982. The mentally ill in an urban county jail. *Archives of General Psychiatry,* 39, 17- 22.

Lancaster, Neville P. 1978. Necrophilia, murder, and high intelligence: A case report. *British Journal of Psychiatry,* 132, 605-608.

Landau, Simha F. 1988. Violent crime and its relation to subjective social stress indicators: The case of Israel. *Aggressive Behavior,* 14, 337-362.

Landesman, Sharon, & Earl C. Butterfield. 1987. Normalization and deinstitutionalization of mentally retarded individuals: Controversy and facts. *American Psychologist,* 42, 809-816.

Landfield, A.W. 1977. Interpretive man: The enlarged self-image. In J. K. Cole & A.W. Landfield (eds.), *1976 Nebraska Symposium on Motivation: Personal Construct Psychology.* Lincoln, NE: University of Nebraska Press. Pp. 127-178.

Landfield, A.W., & L.M. Leitner. 1980. *Personal Construct Psychology: Psychotherapy and Personality.* New York: Wiley.

Lang, Reuben A., Roger Holden, Ron Langevin, George M. Pugh *et al.* 1987. Personality and criminality in violent offenders. *Journal of Interpersonal Violence,* 2, 179-195.

Langan, Patrick A. 1991. America's soaring prison population. *Science,* 251, 1568-1573.

Langevin, Ron. 1982. Diagnosis of killers seen for psychiatric assessment: A controlled study. *Acta Psychiatrica Scandinavica,* 66, 216-228.

Langevin, Ron, Mark Ben-Aron, George Wortzman & Robert Dickey. 1987. Brain damage, diagnosis, and substance abuse among violent offenders. *Behavioral Sciences & the Law,* 5, 77-94.

Langevin, R., D. Paitich, B. Orchard, L. Handy & A. Russon. 1982- *a*. Diagnosis of killers seen for psychiatric assessment. *Acta Psychiatrica Scandinavica,* 66, 216-228.

Langevin, R., D. Paitich, B. Orchard, L. Handy & A. Russon. 1982- *b*. The role of alcohol, drugs, suicide attempts and situational strains in homicide committed by offenders seen for psychiatric assessment. *Acta Psychiatrica Scandinavica,* 66, 229-242.

Larrance, Deborah T., & Craig T. Twentyman. 1983. Maternal attributions and child abuse. *Journal of Abnormal Psychology,* 92, 449-457.

Laufer, William S., Dagna K. Skogg & James M. Day. 1982. Personality and criminality: A review of the California Psychological Inventory. *Journal of Clinical Psychology,* 38, 562-573.

Laybourn, Ann. 1986. Traditional strict working class parenting: An undervalued system. *British Journal of Social Work,* 16, 625-644.

Leibman, Faith H. 1989. Serial murderers: Four case histories. *Federal Probation,* 53, 41-45.

Leippe, Michael R. 1985. The influence of eyewitness non- identification on mock-jurors' judgments of a court case. *Journal of Applied Social Psychology,* 15, 656-672.

Lesco Philip A. 1989. Murder-suicide in Alzheimer's disease. *Journal of the American Geriatrics Society,* 37, 167-168.

Lester, David. 1973. Variation in homicide rate with latitude and longitude in the United States. *Perceptual & Motor Skills, 36, 532.*

Lester, David. 1977. The relationship between suicide and homicide. *Corrective & Social Psychiatry & Journal of Behavior Technology, Methods & Therapy,* 23, 83-84.

Lester, David. 1980. Variation in suicide and homicide by latitude and longitude. *Perceptual & Motor Skills,* 51, 1346.

Lester, David. 1981. Freedom of the press and personal violence: A cross-national study of suicide and homicide. *Journal of Social Psychology,* 114, 267-269.

Lester, David. 1986-*a*. Interaction of divorce, suicide, and homicide. *Journal of Divorce,* 9, 103-109.

Lester, David. 1986-*b*. The distribution of sex and age among victims of homicide: A cross-national study. *International Journal of Social Psychiatry,* 32, 47-50.

Lester, David. 1987-*a*. National distribution of blood groups, personal violence (suicide and homicide), and national character. *Personality & Individual Differences,* 8, 575-576.

Lester, David. 1987-*b*. Religion, suicide, and homicide. *Social Psychiatry,* 22, 99-101.

Lester, David. 1987-*c*. Religiosity and personal violence: A regional analysis of suicide and homicide rates. *Journal of Social Psychology,* 127, 685-686.

Lester, David. 1987-*d*. Substitution of method in suicide and homicide: A regional analysis. *Psychological Reports,* 60, 278.

Lester, David. 1988-*a*. A regional analysis of suicide and homicide rates in the USA: Search For broad cultural patterns. *Social Psychiatry & Psychiatric Epidemiology,* 23, 202-205.

Lester David. 1988-*b*. Economic factors and suicide. *Journal of Social Psychology,* 128, 245-248.

Lester, David. 1988-*c*. Gun control, gun ownership, and suicide prevention. *Suicide & Life-Threatening Behavior,* 18, 176-180.

Lester, David. 1989. The deterrent effect of executions on homicide. *Psychological Reports,* 64, (1) 306.

Lester, David, & Murrell, Mary E. 1982. The preventive effect of strict gun control laws on suicide and homicide. *Suicide & Life- Threatening Behavior,* 12, 131-140.

Levin, Jerome D. 1987. *Treatment of Alcoholism and Other Addictions.* Northvale, NJ: Jason Aronson.

Lewis, Collins E., C. Robert Cloninger & John Pais. 1983. Alcoholism, antisocial personality, and drug use in a criminal population. *Alcohol and Alcoholism,* 18, 53-60.

Lewis, Dorothy Otnow. 1990. Neuropsychiatric and experiential correlates of violent juvenile delinquency. *Neuropsychology Review,* 1, 125-136.

Lewis, Dorothy O., Richard Lovely, Catherine Yeager & George Ferguson. 1988. Intrinsic and environmental characteristics of juvenile murderers. *Journal of the American Academy of Child & Adolescent Psychiatry,* 27, 582-587.

Lewis, Dorothy O., Shelley S. Shanok, Madeline Grant & Eva Ritvo. 1983. Homicidally aggressive young children: Neuropsychiatric and experiential correlates. *American Journal of Psychiatry,* 140, 148-153.

Lewontin, Richard C., & Daniel L. Hartl. 1991. Population genetics in forensic DNA typing. *Science,* 254, 1745-1750.

Lidberg, Lars. 1985. Platelet monoamine oxidase activity and psychopathy. *Psychiatry Research,* 16, 339-343.

Lieber, Arnold L. 1978. Human aggression and the lunar synodic cycle. *Journal of Clinical Psychiatry,* 39, 385-392.

Lieber, Arnold L., & Carolyn R. Sherin. 19 1972. Homicides and the lunar cycle: Toward a theory of lunar influence on human emotional disturbance. *American Journal of Psychiatry,* 129, 69-74.

Liederman, Jacqueline. 1988. Misconceptions and new conceptions abut early brain damage, functional asymmetry, and behavioral outcome. In Dennis L. Molfese & Sidney J. Segalowitz (eds.), *Brain Lateralization in Children.* New York: Guilford. Pp. 375-400.

Lilienfeld, Scott O., & Irwin D. Waldman. 1990. The relationship between childhood attention-deficit hyperactivity disorder and adult antisocial behavior re-examined: The problem of heterogeneity. *Cinical Psychology Review,* 10, 699-725.

Lindgren, Scott D., Dennis C. Harper, Lynn C. Richman & James A. Stebbens. 1986. Mental imbalance and the prediction of recurrent delinquent behavior. *Journal of Clinical Psychology,* 42, 821-825.

Lindner, Robert M. 1947. *Handbook of Correctional Psychology.* New York: Philosophicl Library.

Lindner, Robert M. 1961. *The Fifty-Minute Hour.* New York: Bantam.

Lindquist, Charles A., Terry D. Smusz & William Doerner. 1985. Causes of conformity: An application of control theory to adult misdemeanant probationers. *International Journal of Offender Therapy & Comparative Criminology,* 29, 1-14.

Lindqvist, Per. 1986. Criminal homicide in northern Sweden, 1970- 1981. Alcohol intoxication, alcohol abuse, and mental disease. *International Journal of Law & Psychiatry,* 8, 19-37.

Linz, Daniel G., Edward Donnerstein & Steven Penrod. 1984. The effects of multiple exposures to filmed violence against women. *Journal of Communication,* 34, 130-147.

Litwack, Thomas R., & Louis B. Schlesinger. 1987. Assessing and predicting violence: Research, law, and applications. In Irving B. Weiner & Allen K. Hess (eds.), *Handbook of Forensic Psychology.* New York: Wiley. Pp. 205-257.

Loeber, Rolf. 1982. The stability of antisocial and delinquent child behavior: A review. *Child Development,* 53, 1431-1446.

Loeber, Rolf. 1990. Families and crime. In Larry J. Siegel (ed.), *American Justice: Research of the National Institute of Justice.* St. Paul, MN: West. Pp. 15-18.

Loeber, Rolf, & Karen B. Schmaling. 1985. The utility of differentiating between mixed and pure forms of antisocial child behavior. *Journal of Abnormal Child Psychology,* 13, 315- 334.

Loeber, Role, Wendy Weissman & John B. Reid. 1983. Family interactions of assaultive adolescents, stealers, and nondelinquents. *Journal of Abnormal Child Psychology,* 11, 1-14.

Loftin, Colin, & Robert H. Hill. 1974. Regional subculture and homicide: An examination of the Gastil-Hackney thesis. *American Sociological Review,* 39, 714-724.

Loftin, Colin, & David McDowall. 1984. The deterrent effects of the Florida felony firearm law. *Journal of Criminal Law & Criminology,* 75, 250-259.

Loftin, Colin, Milton Heumann & David McDowall. 1983. Mandatory sentencing and firearms violence: Evaluating an alternative to gun control. *Law & Society Review,* 17, 287-318.

Louscher, P. Kent, Ray E. Hosford & C. Scott Moss. 1983. Predicting dangerous behavior in a penitentiary using the Megargee typology. *Criminal Justice & Behavior,* 10, 269-284.

Lowenstein L.F. 1988. Licence to kill: Is there a case for the death penalty? *Journal of Rehabilitation, 252, 32-36.*

Lowenstein, L.F. 1989. Homicide: A review of recent research (1975- 1985). *Criminologist,* 13, 74-89.

Luckenbill, David F. 1977. Criminal homicide as a situated transaction. *Social Problems,* 25, 175-186.

Lukianowicz, N. 1971. Infanticide. *Psychiatria Clinica,* 4, 145-158.

Lukianowicz, N. 1972. Attempted infanticide. *Psychiatria Clinica,* 5, 1-16.

Luxenbrg, Jay S., Susan E. Swedo, Martine F. Flament, Robert P. Friedland, Judith Rapoport & Stanley L. Rapoport. 1988. Neuroanatomical abnormalities in obsessive compulsive disorder detected with quantitative X-ray computed tomography. *American Journal of Psychiatry,* 145, 1089-1093.

Maguire, Kathleen, & Timothy J. Flanagan. 1991. *Sourcebook of Criminal Justice Statistics.* Washington, DC: Bureau of Justice Statistics, U.S. Department of Justice.

Maher, Brendan H. 1969. *Clinical Psychology and Personality: The Selected Writings of George Kelly.* New York: Wiley.

Mahoney, Michael J. 1976. *Scientist as Subject: The Psychological Imperative.* Cambridge, MA: Ballinger.

Main, Mary, & Ruth Goldwyn. 1984. Predicting rejection of her infant from mother's representation of her own experience: Implications for the abused-abusing intergenerational cycle. *Child Abuse & Neglect,* 8, 203-217.

Malamuth, Neil M. 1983. Factors associated with rape as predictions of laboratory aggression against women. *Journal of Personality & Social Psychology,* 50, 953-962.

Malamuth, Neil M. 1986. Predictors of naturalistic sexual aggression. *Journal of Personality & Social Psychology,* 50, 953-962.

Malamuth, Neil M. 1988. Predicting laboratory aggression against female and male targets: Implications for sexual aggression. *Journal of Research in Personality,* 22, 474-495.

Malamuth, Neil M., & John Briere. 1986. Sexual violence in the media: Indirect effects on aggression against women. *Journal of Social Issues,* 42, 75-92.

Malamuth, Neil M., & Paul Centi. 1986. Repeated exposure to violent and non-violent pornography: Likelihood or raping ratings and laboratory aggression against women. *Aggressive Behavior,* 12, 129-137.

Malamuth, Neil M., & James V. Check. 1985. The effects of aggressive pornography on beliefs in rape myths: Individual differences. *Journal of Research in Personality,* 19, 299-320.

Malamuth, Neil M., Maggie Heim & Seymour Feshbach. 1980. Sexual responsiveness of college students to rape depictions. *Journal of Personality & Social Psychology,* 38, 399-408.

Malmquist, Carl P. 1990. Depression in homicidal adolescents. *Bulletin of the American Academy of Psychiatry & the Law,* 18, 23-26.

Malmquist, Carl P., & Paul E. Meehl. 1978. Barabbas: A study in guilt-ridden homicide. *International Review of Psychoanalysis,* 5, 149-174.

Maloney, Michael P., & Michael P. Ward. 1979. *Psychological Assessment: A Conceptual Approach.* New York: Oxford University Press.

Manderscheid, Ronald W., Michael J. Witkin, Marilyn J. Rosenstein, Laura J. Milazzo-Sayre, Helen E. Bethel & Robin L. MacAskill. 1985. Specialty mental health services: System and patient characteristics. In Carl A. Taube & Sally A. Barrett (eds.), *Mental Health, United States 1985.* Rockville, MD: Division of

Biometry & Epidemiology, National Institute of Mental Health, U.S. Department of Health & Human Services. Pp. 7-69.

Mann, Coramae R. 1990. Black female homicide in the United States. *Journal of Interpersonal Violence,* 5, 176-201.

Marohn, Richard C. 1987. John Wesley Hardin, adolescent killer: The emergence of a narcissistic behavior disorder. *Adolescent Psychiatry,* 14, 271-296.

Marohn, Richard C., Ellen M. Locke, Ronald Rosenthal & Glenn Curtiss. 1982. Juvenile delinquents and violent death. *Adolescent Psychiatry,* 10, 147-170.

Marolla, Joseph A., & Diana Scully. 1986. Attitudes toward women, violence, and rape: A comparison of convicted rapists and other felons. *Deviant Behavior,* 7, 337-355.

Marshall, William L., & William Lawrence Clark. 1962. *A Treatise on the Law of Crimes,* 7th ed. (Marian Quinn Barnes, revising ed.). Mundelein, IL: Callaghan.

Martin, Martha B., Cynthia M. Owen & John M. Morisha. 1987. An overview of neurotransmitter and neuroreceptors. In Robert E. Hales & Stuart C. Yudofsky (eds.), *American Psychiatric Press Textbook of Neuropsychiatry.* Washington, DC: American Psychiatric Press. Pp. 55-87.

Martin, Ronald L., C. Robert Cloninger & Samuel B. Guze. 1982. The natural history of somatization and substance abuse in women criminals: A six year follow-up. *Comprehensive Psychiatry,* 23, 528-537.

Martinius, Joest. 1983. Homicide of an aggressive adolescent boy with right temporal lesion. *Neuroscience & BioBehavioral Reviews,* 7, 419-422.

Master, Franklin D. 1984. Punishment of the mentally ill offender: The state of Nevada v. Patrick Henry Lizotte. *American Journal of Forensic Psychiatry,* 5, 17-27.

Mawson, A.R., & Keith W. Jacobs. 1978. Corn consumption, tryptophan, and cross-national homicide rates. *Journal of Orthomolecular Psychiatry,* 7, 227-230.

Mayer, Connie. 1990. *Survey of Case Law Establishing Constitutional Minima for the Provision of Mental Health Services to Psychiatrically Involved Inmates.* Albany, NY: Albany Law School.

Mayhew, Pat, & David Elliott. 1990. Self-reported offending, victimization, and the British crime survey. *Violence & Victims,* 5, 82-96.

McCauley, Clark, & Robert F. Forman. 1988. A review of the Office of Technology Assessment report on polygraph validity. *Basic & Applied Social Psychology,* 9, 73-84.

McClain, Paula D. 1982. Black female homicide offenders and victims: Are they from the same population? *Death Education,* 6, 265-278.

McCreary, Charles P. 1976. Trait and type differences among male and female assaultive and non-assaultive offenders. *Journal of Personality Assessment,* 40, 617-621.

McDaniel, Michael A., & John W. Jones. 1986. Meta-analysis of the validity of the Employee Attitude Inventory theft scales. *Journal of Business & Psychology,* 1, 31-50.

McDonald, Angus, & Daniel Paitich. 1981. A study of homicide: The validity of predictive test factors. *Canadian Journal of Psychiatry,* 26, 549-554.

McDowall, David. 1986. Poverty and homicide in Detroit, 1926-1978. *Violence & Victims,* 1, 23-34.

McElroy, Susan L., Harrison G. Pope, Jr., James I. Hudson, Paul E. Keck & Kerrin L. White. 1991. Kleptomania: A report of 20 cases. *American Journal of Psychiatry,* 148, 1991, 652-657.

McEwan, Alexander W. 1983. Eysenck's theory of criminality and the personality types and offenses of young delinquents. *Personality & Individual Differences,* 4, 201-204.

McFarland, Sam G. Is capital punishment a short-term deterrent to homicide? A study of the effects of four recent American executions. *Journal of Criminal Law & Criminology,* 74, 1014-1032.

McGahey, Richard. 1990. Jobs and crime. In Larry J. Siegel (ed.), *American Justice: Research of the National Institute of Justice.* St. Paul, MN: West. Pp. 24-27.

McGarrell, Edmund F., & Timothy J. Flanagan. 1985. *Sourcebook of Criminal Justice Statistics.* Washington, DC: Bureau of Justice Statistics, U.S. Department of Justice.

McGlothlin, William H. 1985. Distinguishing effects from concomitants of drug use: The case of crime. In Lee N. Robins (ed.), *Studying Drug Abuse: Series in Psychosocial Epidemiology, VI.* New Brunswick, NJ: Rutgers University Press. Pp. 153-172.

McGovern, Francis J., & Jeffrey S. Nevid. 1986. Evaluation apprehension on psychological inventories in a prison-based setting. *Journal of Consulting & Clinical Psychology,* 54, 576-578.

McGreevy, Margaret A., Henry J. Steadman & Lisa Callahan. 1991. The negligible effects of California's 1982 reform of the insanity defense test. *American Journal of Psychiatry,* 148, 744-750.

McGurk, Barry J. 1978. Personality types among homicides. *British Journal of Criminality,* 18, 146-161.

McGurk, Barry J. 1981. Validity and utility of a typology of homicides based on Megargee's theory of control. *Personality & Individual Differences,* 2, 129-136.

McGurk, Barry J., & Neil Bolton. 1981. A comparison of the Eysenck Personality Questionnaire and the Psychological Screening Inventory in a delinquent sample and a comparison group. *Journal of Clinical Psychology,* 37, 874-879.

McGurk, Barry J., & Cynthia McDougall. 1981. A new approach to Eysenck's theory of criminality. *Personality & Individual Differences,* 2, 338-340.

McKee, Christopher. 1978. Fantasies of mutiny and murder: A suggested psycho-history of the seaman in the United States Navy, 1798-1815. *Armed Forces & Society,* 4, 293-304.

McKinley, J. Charnley, & Starke R. Hathaway. 1956. Scales 3 (Hysteria), 9 (Hypomania), and 4(Psychopathic deviate). In George S. Welsh & W. Grant Dahlstrom (eds.), *Basic Readings on the MMPI in Psychology and Medicine.* Minneapolis: University of Minnesota Press. Pp. 87-103.

McManus, Michael, Norman E. Alessi, W. Lexington Grapentine & Arthur S. Brickman. 1984. Psychiatric disturbances in serious delinquents. *Journal of the American Academy of Child Psychiatry,* 23, 602-615.

McNeil, Dale E., & Renee L. Binder. 1991. Clinical assessment of risk of violence among psychiatric patients. *American Journal of Psychiatry,* 148, 1317-1321.

Mears, Frederick, & Robert J. Gatchel. 1979. *Fundamentals of Abnormal Psychology.* Chicago: Rand McNally,

Mechanic, David. 1980. *Mental Health and Social Policy,* 2d ed. Englewood Cliffs: Prentice-Hall.

Medlicott, R.W. 1976. Psychiatric aspects of murder and attempted murder. *New Zealand Medical Journal,* 83, 5-9.

Mednick, Sarnoff A. & Karl O. Christiansen. 1977. *Biosocial Bases of Criminal Behavior.* New York: Gardner.

Meehl, Paul E. 1954. *Clinical versus Statistical Prediction: A Theoretical Analysis and a Review of the Evidence.* Minneapolis: University of Minnesota Press.

Megargee, Edwin I. 1966. Undercontrolled and overcontrolled personality types in extreme antisocial aggression. *Psychological Monographs,* 80, 3 (Number 611).

Megargee, Edwin I. 1970. The prediction of violence with psychological tests. In Charles S. Spielberger (ed.), *Current Topics in Clinical and Community Psychiatry.* New York: Academic Press.

Megargee, Edwin I. 1976. The prediction of dangerous behavior. *Criminal Justice & Behavior,* 3, 3-22.

Megargee, Edwin I. 1977. New classification system for criminal offenders. *Criminal Justice & Behavior,* 4, 1-116.

Megargee, Edwin I. 1984. A new classification system for criminal offenders: VI differences among the types on the Adjective Checklist. *Criminal Justice & Behavior,* 11, 349-376.

Megargee, Edwin I. 1986. A psychometric study of incarcerated presidential threateners. *Criminal Justice & Behavior,* 13, 243-260.

Megargee, Edwin I., & Martin J. Bohn. 1977. Empirically-determined characteristics of the ten types. *Criminal Justice & Behavior*, 4, 149-210.

Megargee, Edwin I., & Martin J. Bohn. 1979. *Classifying Criminal Offenders: A New System Based on the MMPI*. Beverly Hills: Sage.

Megargee, Edwin I., & Joyce L. Carbonell. 1985. Predicting prison adjustment with MMPI correctional scales. *Journal of Consulting & Clinical Psychology*, 53, 874-883.

Megargee, Edwin I., & Patrick E. Cook. 1975. Negative response bias and the MMPI overcontrolled hostility scale. *Journal of Consulting & Clinical Psychology*, 43, 725-729.

Megargee, Edwin I., J.C. Cook & H.T. Mendelsohn. 1967. The development and validation of an MMPI scale of assaultiveness in overcontrolled individuals. *Journal of Abnormal Psychology*, 72, 519-528.

Meloy, J. Reid. 1988. *The Psychopathic Mind: Origins, Dynamics, Treatment*. Northvale, NJ: Jason Aronson.

Menninger, W. Walter. 1984. Guns and violence: An American phenomenon. *American Journal of Social Psychiatry*, 4, 37- 40.

Messer, Stephen C., Tracy L. Morris & Alan M. Gross. 1990. Hypoglycemia and psychopathology: A methodological review. *Clinical Psychology Review*, 10, 631-648.

Messick, Samuel. 1900. Test validity and the ethics of assessment. *American Psychologist*, 25, 1012-1027.

Messner, Steven F. 1982. Poverty, inequality, and the urban homicide rate: Some unexpected findings. *Criminology*, 20, 103-114.

Messner, Steven F. 1983. Regional and racial effect on the urban homicide rate: The subculture of violence revisited. *American Journal of Sociology*, 88, 997-1007.

Messner, Steven F. 1985. Regional differences in the economic correlates of urban homicide rate: Some evidence on the importance of cultural context. *Criminology*, 21, 477-488.

Miceli, Marcia P., Janelle B. Dozier & Janet P. Near. 1991. Blowing the whistle on data fudging: A controlled field experiment. *Journal of Applied Social Psychology*, 21, 271-295.

Michael, Richard P., & Doris Zumpe. 1983-a. Annual rhythms in human violence and sexual aggression in the United States and the role of temperature. *Social Biology*, 30, 263-278.

Michael, Richard P., & Doris Zumpe. 1983-b. Sexual violence in the United States and the role of season. *American Journal of Psychiatry*, 140, 883-886.

Milavsky, J. Ronald. 1990. TV and violence. In Larry J. Siegel (ed.), *American Justice: Research of the National Institute of Justice*. St. Paul, MN: West. Pp. 11-14.

Milburn, Thomas W. 1963. Design for the study of deterrence. In S.B. Sells (ed.), *Stimulus Determinants of Behavior*. New York: Ronald. Pp. 224-235.

Milgram, Stanley. 1963. Behavioral study of obedience. *Journal of Abnormal & Social Psychology*, 67, 371-378.

Milgram, Stanley. 1965. Some conditions of obedience and disobedience to authority. *Human Relations*, 18, 57-85.

Miller, Neal E., & John Dollard. 1950. *Social Learning and Imitation*. New Haven: Yale University Press.

Miller, S.J., Simon Dinitz & J. P. Conrad. 1982. *Careers of the Violent*. Lexington, MA: Heath.

Milliken, A. Donald. 1982. Homicidal transsexuals: Three cases. *Canadian Journal of Psychiatry*, 27, (1) 43-46.

Milner, Joel S., & Catherine Ayoub. 1980. Evaluation of "at risk" parents using the Child Abuse Potential Inventory. *Journal of Clinical Psychology*, 36, 945-948.

Milner, Joel S., & Ronald C. Wimberly. 1979. An inventory for the identification of child abusers. *Journal of Clinical Psychology*, 35, 95-100.

Milner, Joel S., & Ronald C. Wimberly. 1980. Prediction and explanation of child Abuse. *Journal of Clinical Psychology*, 36, 875-884.

Mischel, Walter. 1973-a. On the empirical dilemmas of psychodynamic approaches: Issues and alternatives. *Journal of Abnormal Psychology*, 82, 335-344.

Mischel, Walter. 1973-*b*. Toward a cognitive social learning reconceptualization of personality. *Psychological Review,* 80, 252-253.

Mischel, Walter. 1979. On the interface of cognition and personality: Beyond the person-situation debate. *American Psychologist,* 34, 740-754.

Monahan, John. 1976. The prediction of violence. In John Monahan (ed.), *Community Mental Health and the Criminal Justice System.* New York: Pergamon. Pp. 13-34.

Monahan, John. 1981-a. *The Clinical Prediction of Violent Behavior.* Washington, DC: U.S. Department of Health & Human Services.

Monahan, John. 1981-b. *Predicting Violent Behavior: An Assessment of Clinical Techniques.* Beverly Hills: Sage.

Monahan, John, & Henry J. Steadman. 1982. Crime and mental disorder: An epidemiological approach. In Michael Tonry & Norval Morris (eds.), *Crime and Justice,* IV. Chicago: University of Chicago Press.

Montanile, Joseph. 1986. Bernhard Goetz as group-fantasy object. *Journal of Psychohistory,* 14, 545-63.

Moore, Richard H. 1983. College shoplifters. *Psychological Reports,* 1983, 53, 1111-1116.

Moore, Richard H. 1984. Shoplifting in middle America: Patterns and motivational correlates. *International Journal of Offender Therapy & Comparative Criminology,* 28, 53-64.

Morand, Claud, Simon M. Young & Frank R. Ervin. 1983. Clinical response of aggressive schizophrenics to oral tryptophan. *Biological Psychiatry,* 18, 575-578.

Morris, Desmond. 1969. *The Naked Ape.* New York: Dell.

Morris, Norval. 1974. *The Future of Imprisonment.* Chicago: University of Chicago Press.

Morris, Norval, & Michael Tonry. 1990. Between prison and probation — Intermediate punishments in a rational sentencing system. *Correctional Psychologist,* 22, 1-7.

Moss, C. Scott, Mark E. Johnson & Ray E. Hosford. 1984. An assessment of the Megargee typology in lifelong criminal violence. *Criminal Justice & Behavior,* 11, 225-234.

Motiuk, Laurence L., James Bonta & Don A. Andrews. 1986. Classification in halfway houses: The relative and incremental predictive criterion validities of the Megargee MMPI and LSI systems. *Criminal Justice & Behavior,* 13, 33-46.

Mouridsen, Svend E., & Kai Tolstrup. 1988. Children who kill: A case study of matricide. *Journal of Child Psychology & Psychiatry & Allied Disciplines,* 29, 511-515.

Mrad, David F., Robert I. Kabacoff & Paul Duckro. 1983. Validation of the Megargee typology in a halfway house setting. *Criminal Justice & Behavior,* 10, 252-262.

Mueller, Gerhard O. W. 1961-a. The failure of concepts of criminal theory in judging the psychopathic offender. *Archives of Criminal Psychodynamics,* 4, 558-588.

Mueller, Gerhard O. W. 1961-b. The public law of wrongs — Its concepts in the world of reality. *Journal of Public Law,* 10, 203-244.

Mullen, P.E. 1984. Mental disorder and dangerousness. *Australian & New Zealand Journal of Psychiatry,* 18, 8-17.

Myers, Steven A. 1967. The child slayer. *Archives of General Psychiatry,* 17, 211-213.

Myers, Steven A. 1970. Maternal filicide. *American Journal of Diseases of Children,* 120, 534-536.

Myers, Steven Lee. 1991. Student opens fire at U. of Iowa, killing 4 before shooting himself. *New York Times,* November 2, A- 8.

Myers, Wade C., & Anthony Caterine. 1990. Tarasoff and threats of patricide by a 9-year-old boy. *American Journal of Psychiatry,* 147, 535-536.

Myers, Wade C., & John P. Kemph. 1990. DSM-III--R classification of murderous youth: Help or hindrance? *Journal of Clinical Psychiatry,* 51, 239-242.

Nathan, Peter E., & Sandra L. Harris. 1980. *Psychopathology and Society,* 2nd ed. New York: McGraw Hill.

Nathan, Peter E., & Anne-Helene Skinstad. 1987. Outcomes of treatment for alcohol problems: Current methods, problems, and results. *Journal of Consulting & Clinical Psychology,* 55, 332-340.

National Center for State Courts, U.S. Department of Justice. 1979. *State Court Caseload Statistics.* Washington, DC: National Criminal Justice Statistics and Information Service.

Nemeroff, Charles B., Michael J. Owens, Garth Bissette, Anne C. Andorn & Michael Stanley. 1988. Reduced corticotropin releasing factor binding sites in the frontal cortex of suicide victims. 1988. *Archives of General Psychiatry,* 45, 577-579.

Newcomb, Michael D., & P.M. Bentler. 1988. Impact of adolescent drug use and social support on problems of young adults: A longitudinal study. *Journal of Abnormal Psychology,* 97, 64-75.

Newman, Donald E. 1974. The personality of violence: Conversations with protago-nists. *Mental Health & Society,* 1, 328-344.

Newman, Graeme. 1974. Acts, actors, and reactions to deviance. *Sociology & Social Research,* 58, 434-440.

Newman, Graeme. 1975. A theory of deviance removal. *British Journal of Sociology,* 26, 203-217.

Newman, Graeme. 1976. *Comparative Deviance: Perception and Law in Six Cultures.* Amsterdam: Elsevier.

Nicholson, Robert A., & Karen E. Kugler. 1991. Competent and incompetent criminal defendants: A quantitative review of comparative research. *Psychological Bulletin,* 109, 355-370.

Niemeyer, Robert A. 1985. *The Development of Personal Construct Theory. Lincoln, NE: University of Nebraska Press.*

Niemeyer, Robert A. 1988. Integrative directions in personal construct therapy. *International Journal of Personal Construct Psychology, 1, 283-297.*

Niemeyer. Robert A. 1990. George A. Kelly: In memoriam. *History of Psychology Newsletter,* 22, 3-14.

Niemeyer, Robert A., & Gregory J. Niemeyer. 1987. *Personal Construct Therapy Casebook.* New York: Springer.

Norton, K.R., A.H. Crisp & A.V. Bhat. 1985. Why do some anorexics steal? Personal, social, and illness factors. *Journal of Psychiatric Research,* 19, 385-390.

Nurco, David N., John C. Ball, John W. Shaffer & Thomas E. Hanlon. 1985. The criminality of narcotic addicts. *Journal of Nervous & Mental Disease,* 173, 94-102.

Nurco, David N., John W. Shaffer, John C. Ball & Timothy W. Kinlock. 1984. Trends in the commission of crime among narcotic addicts over successive periods of addiction and nonaddiction. *American Journal of Drug & Alcohol Abuse,* 10, 481-489.

O'Brien, Robert M. 1987. The interracial nature of violent crimes: A re-examination. *American Journal of Sociology,* 92, 817- 835.

O'Carroll, Patrick W. 1990. Homicides among Black males 15-24 years of age, 1970-84. *Public Health Surveillance of 1990: Injury Control Objectives of the Nation,* 37, 53-60.

O'Carroll, Patrick W., & James A. Mercy. 1989. Regional variation in homicide rates: Why is the West so violent? *Violence & Victims,* 4, 17-25.

O'Connor, Frank. 1982. *Collected Stories.* New York: Vintage.

O'Connor, Michael E. 1984. The perception of crime and criminality: The violent criminal and swindler as social types. Deviant Behavior, 5, 255-274.

Oetting, E.R., & Fred Beauvais. 1990. Adolescent drug use: Findings of national and local surveys. *Journal of Consulting & Clinical Psychology,* 58, 385-394.

Ogloff, James R. 1987. The juvenile death penalty: A frustrated society's attempt for control. *Behavioral Sciences & the Law,* 5, 447-455.

Ojesjo, Leif. 1983. Alcohol, drugs, and forensic psychiatry. *Psychiatric Clinics of North America,* 6, 733-749.

O'Leary, K. Daniel, & G. Terence Wilson. 1975. *Behavior Therapy: Application and Outcome.* Englewood Cliffs: Prentice- Hall.

Olfson, Mark. 1987. Weir Mitchell and lithium bromide. *American Journal of Psychiatry,* 144, 1101-1102.

Opton, Edward W. 1971. It never happened — and besides they deserved it. In Nevitt Sanford & Craig Comstock (eds.), *Sanctions for Evil.* San Francisco: Jossey-Bass. Pp. 49-70.

Ornstein, Anna, Cheryl Gropper & Janice Z. Bogner. 1983. Shoplifting: An expression of revenge and restitution. *Annual of Psychoanalysis,* 11, 311-331.

Orvaschel, Helen, Diane Sholomskas & Myrna Weissman. 1980. Assessing children in psychiatric epidemiological studies: A review of interview techniques. In Felton Earls (ed.), *Studies of Children: Psychosocial Epidemiology.* New York: Prodist/Neal Watson. Pp. 84-95.

Otto, Mary L. 1990. Treating abusive parents in outpatient settings. *Journal of Offender Rehabilitation,* 15, 57-64.

Oysterman, Daphna, & Hazel Markus. 1990. Possible selves in balance: Implications for delinquency. *Journal of Social Issues,* 46, 141-157.

Owens, David J., & Murray A. Straus. 1975. The social structure of violence and approval of violence as an adult. *Aggressive Behavior,* 1, 193-211.

Painton, Priscilla. 1991. Miracle in Brooklyn: The rescue of a desperate 12-year-old girl's abandoned baby shows that hope can survive on even the meanest streets. *Time,* April 8, 31.

Pallone, Nathaniel J. 1986. *On the Social Utility of Psychopathology: A Deviant Majority and Its Keepers?* New Brunswick, NJ: Transaction Books.

Pallone, Nathaniel J. 1988. Advocacy scholarship on the death penalty in the USA. *Transaction/Society,* 26, 177-180.

Pallone, Nathaniel J. 1989. Controlled dangerous substances and felony crime: Data from recent studies in the US. In Raagnar Waahlberg (ed.), *Prevention and Control: Realities and Aspirations,* Volume III. Oslo: National Directorate for the Prevention of Alcohol & Drug Problems. Pp. 498-507.

Pallone, Nathaniel J. 1990-*a*. Drug use and felony crime: Biochemical credibility and unsettled questions. *Journal of Offender Rehabilitation,* 15, 85-109.

Pallone, Nathaniel J. 1990-*b*. *Rehabilitating Criminal Sexual Psychopaths: Legislative Mandates, Clinical Quandaries.* New Brunswick, NJ: Transaction Books.

Pallone, Nathaniel J. 1991. *Mental Disorder among Prisoners.* New Brunswick, NJ: Transaction Books.

Pallone, Nathaniel J. 1992. The MMPI in police officer selection: Legal constraints, case law, empirical data. *Journal of Offender Rehabilitation,* 17 (3/4), 199-216.

Pallone, Nathaniel J., & James J. Hennessy. 1977. Some correlates of recidivism among misdemeanants and minor felons. *Journal of Social Psychology,* 101, 321-322.

Pallone, Nathaniel J., & Daniel S. LaRosa. 1979. Mental health specialists and services in correctional facilities: Who does what? *Journal of Offender Rehabilitation,* 4, 33-41.

Pallone, Nathaniel J., & Richard J. Tirman. 1978. Correlates of substance abuse remission in alcoholism rehabilitation: Effective treatment or symptom abandonment? *Journal of Offender Rehabilitation,* 3, 7-18.

Pallone, Nathaniel J., James J. Hennessy & Daniel S. LaRosa. 1980. Professional psychology in state correctional institutions: Present status and alternate futures. *Professional Psychology,* 11, 755-763.

Palmer, Stuart. 1981. Sex differences in criminal homicide and suicide in England & Wales and in the United States. *Omega,* 11, 255-270.

Pankratz, Loren D. 1984. Murder and insanity: 19th century perspectives from the "American Journal of Insanity." *International Journal of Offender Therapy & Comparative Criminology,* 28, 37-43.

Panton, James H. 1976. Personality characteristics of death-row prison inmates. *Journal of Clinical Psychology,* 32, 306-309.

Panton, James H. 1977. Personality characteristics of drug pushers incarcerated within a state prison population. *Quarterly Journal of Corrections,* 1, 11-13.

Panton, James H. 1978. Personality differences between rapists of adults, rapists of children, and non-violent sexual molesters of female children. *Research Communications in Psychology, Psychiatry & Behavior,* 3, 385-393.

Panton, James H. 1979. MMPI profile configurations associated with incestuous and non-incestuous child molesting. *Psychological Reports,* 45, 335-338.

Paretsky, Sara. 1991. Soft spot for serial murderers. *New York Times, April 28, 1991,* E-17.

Parisi, Nicolette, Michael R. Gottfredson, Michael J. Hindelang & Timothy J. Flanagan. 1979. *Sourcebook of Criminal Justice Statistics.* Washington, DC: Bureau of Justice Statistics, U.S. Department of Justice.

Parkchester Journal. 1991. Risk lures teen-agers to "surf" on the subways. *New York Times,* 28 November, B-8.

Parker, Kevin C., R. Karl Hanson & John Hunsley. 1988. MMPI, Rorschach, and WAIS: A meta-analytic comparison of reliability, stability, and validity. *Psychological Bulletin,* 103, 367-373.

Parrington, Vernon Louis. 1930. *Main Currents in American Thought.* New York: Harcourt Brace.

Parwatikar, S.D., William R. Holcomb & Karl A. Menninger. 1985. The detection of malingered amnesia in accused murderers. *Bulletin of the Academy of Psychiatry & the Law,* 13, (1) 97-103.

Pasamanick, Benjamin. 1962. A survey of mental disease in an urban population. *American Journal of Psychiatry,* 119, 299-305.

Pasewark, Richard A., Mark L. Pantile & Henry J. Steadman. 1982. Detention and rearrest rates of persons found not guilty by reason of insanity and convicted felons. *American Journal of Psychiatry,* 139, 892-897.

Passell, Peter, & John B. Taylor. 1977. The deterrent effect of capital punishment: Another view. *American Economic Review,* 67, 445-458.

Patrick, Christopher, & William G. Iacono. 1991. Validity of the control question polygraph test: The problem of sampling bias. *Journal of Applied Psychology,* 76, 229-238.

Paulson, Morris J., Abdelmonen A. Afifi, Anne Chalef & Mary L. Thomas. 1974. The MMPI: A descriptive measure of psychopathology in abusive parents. *Journal of Clinical Psychology,* 30, 387-390.

Paulson, Morris J., Abdelmonon A. Afifi, Anne Chaleff, Vinnie Y. Liu & Mary L. Thomason. 1975. A discriminant function procedure for identifying abusing parents. *Suicide,* 1975, 5, 104-114.

Pennsylvania appeals court says patient's psychologist and counselor not liable for failing to warn victim strangled by patient. 1991. *Register Report: Newsletter for Psychologist Health Service Providers,* 17(1), 19.

Penrose, Lionel S. 1939. Mental disease and crime: Outline of a comparative study of European statistics. *Medical Psychology,* 19, 1-15.

Perdue, William C., & David Lester. 1974. Racial differences in the personality of murderers. *Perceptual & Motor Skills,* 38, 726.

Pernanen, Kai. 1981. Theoretical aspects of the relationship between alcohol use and crime. In James J. Collins, Jr. (ed.), *Drinking and Crime.* New York: Guilford. Pp. 1-69.

Perry, Josephus D., & Miles E. Simpson. 1987. Violent crimes in a city: Environmental determinants. *Environment & Behavior,* 19, 77-90.

Perry, Samuel. 1987. Substance-induced organic mental disorders. In Robert E. Hales & Stuart C. Yudofsky (eds.), *American Psychiatric Press Textbook of Neuropsychiatry.* Washington, DC: American Psychiatric Press. Pp. 157-176.

Pervin, Lawrence. 1976. A free-response description approach to the analysis of person-situation interaction. *Journal of Personality & Social Psychology,* 34, 465-474.

Pervin, Lawrence. 1980. *Personality: Theory, Assessment, and Research,* 2nd ed. New York: Wiley.

Petersen, K.G. Ingemar, M. Matousek, Sarnoff A. Mednick, J. Volavka & V. Pollock. 1982. EEG antecedents of thievery. *Acta Psychiatrica Scandinavica,* 65, 331-338.

Petersilia, Joan. 1980. Criminal career research: A review of recent evidence. In Norval Morris & Michael Tonry (eds.), *Crime and Justice, II*. Chicago: University of Chicago Press. Pp. 321-379.

Peterson, Donald R. 1988. The role of assessment in professional psychology. In Donald R. Peterson & Daniel B. Fishman (eds.), *Assessment for Decision*. New Brunswick, NJ: Rutgers University Press. Pp. 5-43.

Peterson, Ruth D., & John Hagan. 1984. Changing conceptions of race: Towards an account of anomalous findings of sentencing research. *American Sociological Review*, 49, 56-70.

Petrunik, Michael. 1982. Crime & delinquency prevention: An overview of current approaches. *Impact*, 1, 21-31.

Petti, Theodore A., & Leonard Davidman. 1981. Homicidal school- age children: Cognitive style and demographic features. *Child Psychiatry & Human Development*, 12, 82-89.

Petursson, Hannes, & Gisli H. Gundjonsson. 1981. Psychiatric aspects of homicide. *Acta Psychiatrica Scandinavica*, 64, 363-371.

Pfuhl, Edwin H. 1983. Police strikes and conventional crime: A look at the data. *Criminology*, 21, 489-503.

Phillips, David P. 1983. The impact of mass media violence in U.S. homicides. *American Sociological Review*, 48, (4) 560-568.

Phillips, David P., & John E. Hensley. 1984. When violence is rewarded or punished: The impact of mass media stories on homicide. *Journal of Communication*, 34, 101-116.

Phillips, Michael R., Aron S. Wolf & David J. Coons. 1988. Psychiatry and the criminal justice system: Testing the myths. *American Journal of Psychiatry*, 145, 605-610.

Pichot, Pierre. 1978. Psychopathic behaviour: A historical overview. In Robert D. Hare & Daisy Schalling (eds.), *Psychopathic Behaviour: Approaches to Research*. New York: John Wiley. Pp. 56-70.

Pierce, Lois H., & Robert L. Pierce. 1987. Incestuous victimization by juvenile sex offenders. *Journal of Family Violence*, 2, 351- 364.

Pinizzoto, Anthony J. 1984. Forensic psychology: Criminal personality profiling. *Journal of Police Science & Administration*, 12, 32-40.

Pitchard, D.A. 1979. Stable predictors of recidivism: A summary. *Criminology*, 17, 15-21.

Pokorny, Alex D., & Joseph Jachimczyk. 1974. The questionable relationship between homicides and the lunar cycle. *American Journal of Psychiatry*, 131, 827-829.

Pollock, V.E., John Briere, Lon Schneider & Joachim Knop. 1990. Childhood antecedents of antisocial behavior: Parental alcoholism and physical abusiveness. *American Journal of Psychiatry*, 147, 1290-1293.

Pontius, Anneliese A. 1987. "Psychotic Trigger Reaction" — Neuropsychiatric and neuro-Biological (limbic?) aspects of homicide, reflecting on normal action. *Integrative Psychiatry*, 5, 116- 124.

Pontius, Anneliese A. 1989. Subtypes of limbic system dysfunction evoking homicide in limbic Psychotic Trigger Reaction and temporal lobe epilepsy — Evolutionary constraints. *Psychological Reports*, 65, 659-671.

Pope, Harrison G., & David L. Katz. 1990. Homicide and near- homicide by anabolic steroid users. *Journal of Clinical Psychiatry*, 51, 28-31.

Poussaint, Alvin F. 1983. Black-on-black homicide: A psychological- political perspective. *Victimology*, 8, 161-169.

Poythress, Norman G. 1990. Avoiding negligent release: Contemporary clinical and risk management strategies. *American Journal of Psychiatry*, 147, 994-997.

President's Commission on Law Enforcement and Administration of Justice. 1967. *Task Force Report: Science and Technology*. Washington, DC: U.S. Government Printing Office.

Pritchard, David. 1986. Homicide and bargained justice: The agenda setting effect of crime news on prosecutors. *Public Opinion Quarterly*, 50, 143-159.

Pruesse, M., & Vernon L. Quinsey. 1977. Dangerousness of patients released from maximum security — A replication. *Journal of Psychiatry & Law,* 5, 217-224.

Pruitt, Charles R., & James Q. Wilson. 1983. A longitudinal study of the effect of race on sentencing. *Law & Society Review,* 17, 613-635.

Public Health Service, U.S. 1984. *Vital Statistics of the United States — Vital and Health Statistics: Mortality Data.* Washington: National Center for Health Statistics.

Putnins, Aldis L. 1982. The Eysenck Personality Questionnaires & delinquency prediction. *Personality & Individual Differences,* 3, 339-340.

Quay, Herbert Q. 1965. Psychopathic personality as pathological stimulation seeking. *American Journal of Psychiatry,* 122, 180-183.

Quay, Herbert C. 1987. *Handbook of Juvenile Delinquency.* New York: Wiley.

Quinsey, Vernon L., & Douglas Upfold. 1985. Rape completion and victim injury as a function of female resistance strategy. *Canadian Journal of Behavioural Science,* 17, 40-50.

Quinsey, Vernon L., Terry C. Chaplin, & Douglas Upfold. 1984. Sexual arousal to non-sexual violence and sadomasochistic themes among rapists and non-sex offenders. *Journal of Consulting & Clinical Psychology,* 52, 651-657.

Rachlin, Stephen, Abraham L. Halpern & Stanley L. Portnow. 1984. The volitional rule, personality disorders and the insanity defense. *Psychiatric Annals,* 14, 139-141, 145-147.

Rada, Richard T., & Robert Kellner. 1976. Thiothixene in the treatment of geriatric patients with chronic organic brain syndrome. *Journal of the American Geriatrics Society,* 24, 105-107.

Rada, Richard, D.R. Laws, Robert Kellner, Laxmi Stivasta & Glenn Peake. 1983. Plasma androgens in violent and non-violent sex offenders. *Bulletin of the American Academy of Psychiatry & the Law,* 11, 149-158.

Rafuls, William A., Irl Extein, Mark S. Gold & Frederick C. Goggins. 1987. Neuropsychiatric aspects of endocrine disorders. In Robert E. Hales & Stuart C. Yudofsky (eds.), *American Psychiatric Press Textbook of Psychiatry.* Washington, DC: American Psychiatric Press. Pp. 307-325.

Raine, Adrian, & Peter H. Venables. 1988. Enhanced P3 evoked potentials and longer P3 recovery times in psychopaths. *Psychophysiology,* 25, 30-38.

Raine, Adrian, Mary O'Brien, Norine Smiley & Angela Scerbo. 1990. Reduced lateralization in verbal dichotic listening in adolescent psychopaths. *Journal of Abnormal Psychology,* 99, 272-277.

Ram, P. Kodanda. 1987. A comparative study of murderers and recidivists using Eysenck's personality inventory. *Indian Journal of Clinical Psychology,* 14, 100-101.

Rascovsky, Arnaldo. 1974. Filicide and the unconscious motivation for war. *Adolescent Psychiatry,* 3, 54-67.

Raskin, David C. 1989. Polygraph techniques for the detection of deception. In David C. Raskin (ed.), *Psychological Methods in Criminal Investigation and Evidence.* New York: Springer. Pp. 247-296.

Rattner, Arye. 1990. Social indicators and crime rate forecasting. *Social Indicators Research,* 22, 83-95.

Ray, John J. 1983. Race and climate as influences on anxiety. *Personality & Individual Differences,* 4, 699-701.

Ray, Joseph B., Gary S. Solomon, Maria G. Doncaster & Richard Mellina. 1983. First offender adult shoplifters: A preliminary profile. *Journal of Clinical Psychology,* 39, 769-770.

Reason, James, & Deborah Lucas. 1984. Absent-mindedness in shops: Its incidence, correlates, and consequences. *British Journal of Clinical Psychology,* 23, 121-131.

Redl, Fritz, & David Wineman. 1957. *The Aggressive Child.* New York: Free Press.

Reid, Sue Titus. 1976. *Crime and Criminology.* Hinsdale, IL: Dryden.

Reinehr, Robert C., Harold K. Dudley & John V. White. 1985. Dangerousness review boards: Their composition and their functions. *Journal of Psychiatry & Law,* 13, 449-456.

Resnick, P.J. 1969. Child murder by parents: A psychiatric review of filicide. *American Journal of Psychiatry,* 126, 325-334.

Richardson, Philip, Mark J. Morein & John G. Phin. 1978. *Criminal Justice Drug Abuse Surveillance System.* Arlington, VA: Creative SocioMedics.

Rieber, Robert W. 1990. In search of the impertinent question: An overview of Bateson's theory of cummunication. In Robert W. Rieber (ed.), *The Individual, Communication, and Society.* New York: Cambridge University Press.

Roberts, Leslie. 1991. More pieces in the dioxin puzzle. *Science,* 254, 277.

Rogers, Richard. 1986. *Conducting Insanity Evaluations.* New York: Van Nostrand Reinhold.

Rogers, Richard. 1987. APA's position on the insanity defense: Empiricism versus emotionalism. *American Psychologist,* 42, 840-848.

Rogers, Richard, William Seman & Orest E. Wasyliw. 1983. The RCRAS [Rogers Criminal Responsibility Assessment Scale] and legal insanity: A cross-validation study. *Journal of Clinical Psychology,* 39, (4) 554-559.

Rogers, Richard, James L. Cavanaugh, William Seman & M. Harris. 1984. Legal outcomes and clinical findings: A study of insanity evaluations. *Bulletin of the American Academy of Psychiatry & the Law,* 12, 75-83.

Rohrbeck, Cynthia A., & Craig T. Twentyman. 1986. Multimodal assessment of impulsiveness in abusing, neglecting, and nonmaltreating mothers and their preschool children. *Journal of Consulting & Clinical Psychology,* 54, 231-236.

Roizen, Judy. 1981. Alcohol and criminal behavior among blacks: The case for research on special populations. In James J. Collins, Jr. (ed.), *Drinking and Crime.* New York: Guilford. Pp. 207-252.

Rose, D., & E.J. Bitter. 1982. The Palo Alto destructive content scale as a predictor of physical assaultiveness in men. *Journal of Personality Assessment,* 44, 228-233.

Rosen, Lee A., Sharon R. Booth, Mary E. Bender, Melanie L. McGrath, Sue Sorrell & Ronald S. Drabman. 1988. Effects of sugar (sucrose) on children's behavior. *Journal of Consulting & Clinical Psychology,* 56, 583-589.

Rosenthal, Barry J., & Kareem Nakkash. 1982. Drug addiction and criminality: A model for predicting the incidence of crime among a treatment population. *Journal of Drug Issues,* 12, 293-303.

Rosenthal, Robert. 1966. *Experimenter Effects in Behavioral Research.* New York: Appleton.

Rosenthal, Robert. 1987. Pygmalion effects: Existence, magnitude, and social importance. *educational Researcher,* 16, 37-41.

Rosenthal, Robert, & Lenore Jacobsen. 1968. *Pygmalion in the Classroom: Teacher Expectation and Pupil's Intellectual Development.* New York: Holt, Rinehart & Winston.

Rosner, Lydia S. 1992. System beating: Structural impediments to the public good. *Journal of Offender Rehabilitation,* 18, 239- 252.

Rosse, Richard B., & John M. Morisha. 1988. Laboratory and other diagnostic tests in psychiatry. In John A. Talbott, Robert E. Hales & Stuart C. Yudofsky (eds.), *American Psychiatric Press Textbook of Psychiatry.* Washington, DC: American Psychiatric Press. Pp. 247-277.

Rosse, Richard B., Cynthia M. Owen & John M. Morisha. 1987. Brain imaging and laboratory testing in neuropsychiatry. In Robert E. Hales & Stuart C. Yudofsky (eds.), *American Psychiatric Press Textbook of Neuropsychiatry.* Washington, DC: American Psychiatric Press. Pp. 17-40.

Rotton, James, & James Frey. 1985. Air pollution, weather, and violent crimes: Concomitant time-series analysis of archival data. *Journal of Personality & Social Psychology,* 49, 1207-1220.

Roueche, Berton. 1991. Annals of medicine: A good, safe tan. *New Yorker,* 11 March, 69-74.

Roundtree, George A., Dan W. Edwards & Jack B. Parker. 1984. A study of the personal characteristics of probationers as related to recidivism. *Journal of Offender Rehabilitation,* 8, 53-61.
Rowley, John C., Charles P. Ewing & Simon I. Singer. 1987. Juvenile homicide: The need for an interdisciplinary approach. *Behavioral Sciences & the Law,* 5, (1) 1-10.
Royal College of Psychiatrists. 1987. *Drug Scenes: A Report on Drugs and Drug Dependence.* London: The College.
Ruback, R. Barry, & Timothy S. Carr. 1984. Crowding in a woman's prison: Attitudinal and behavioral effects. *Journal of Applied Social Psychology,* 14, 57-68.
Rubin, Bernard. 1972. Prediction of dangerousness in mentally ill criminals. *Archives of General Psychiatry,* 25, 397-407.
Rubinson, Eileen, Gregory M. Asnis & Jill H. Friedman. 1988. Knowledge of the diagnostic criteria for major depression: A survey of mental health professionals. *Journal of Nervous & Mental Disease,* 176, 480-484.
Ruff, Carol F., Joyce L. Ayers & Donald I. Templer. 1977. The Watson and the Hovey MMPI scales: Do they measure organicity or functional psychopathology? *Journal of Clinical Psychology,* 33, 732-734.

Sacco, Vincent F. 1985. Shoplifting prevention: The role of communication-based intervention strategies. *Canadian Journal of Criminology,* 27, 15-29.
Saklofske, D.H., D.W. McKerracher & Sybil B.G. Eysenck. 1978. Eysenck's theory of criminality: A scale of criminal propensity as a measure of antisocial behavior. *Psychological Reports, 43, 683- 686.*
Saks, Michael J. 1990. Expert witnesses, nonexpert witnesses, and nonwitness experts. *Law & Human Behavior,* 14, 291-313.
Sampson, Robert J. 1983. Structural density and criminal victimization. *Criminology,* 21, 276-293.
Schatzberg, Alan F., & Jonathan O. Cole. 1986. *Manual of Clinical Psychopharmacology.* Washington: American Psychiatric Press.
Scheff, Thomas J. 1964. The societal reaction to deviance: Ascriptive elements in the psychiatric screening of mental patients in a midwestern state hospital. *Social Problems,* 11, 401-413.
Scheff, Thomas J. 1966. *Being Mentally Ill: A Sociological Theory.* Chicago: Aldine.
Schneider, A.L., P.R. Schneider & S.G. Bazemore. 1981. In-program reoffense rates for juveniles in restitution projects. In *Oversight Hearing on Juvenile Restitution Programs,* NIJ Document 82247. Rockville, MD: National Institute for Juvenile Justice & Delinquency Prevention, U.S. Department of Justice. Pp. 286-368.
Schoenthaler, Stephen J. 1982. The effect of sugar on the treatment and control of antisocial behavior: A double-blind study of an incarcerated juvenile population. *International Journal of Biosocial Research,* 3, 1-9.
Schoenthaler, Stephen J. 1983-*a.* Diet and crime: An empirical examination of the value of nutrition in the control and treatment of incarcerated juvenile offenders. *International Journal of Biosocial Research,* 4, 23-59.
Schoenthaler, Stephen J. 1983-*b.* The Los Angeles probation department diet-behavior program: An empirical analysis of six institutional settings. *International Journal of Biosocial Research,* 5, 88-98.
Schoenthaler, Stephen J. 1983-*c.* The northern California diet-behavior program: An empirical examination of 3000 incarcerated juveniles in Stanislaus County juvenile hall. *International Journal of Biosocial Research,* 5, 99-106.
Schoenthaler, Stephen J. 1983-*d.* Types of offenses which can be reduced in an institutional setting using nutritional intervention. *International Journal of Biosocial Research,* 4, 74-84.
Schopp, Robert F. 1991. *Automatism, Insanity, and the Psychology of Criminal Responsibility: A Philosophical Inquiry.* New York: Cambridge University Press.
Schwitzgebel, Robert L., & R. Kirkland Schwitzgebel. 1980. *Law and Psychological Practice.* New York: John Wiley.
Scott, P.D. 1973-*a.* Fatal battered baby cases. *Medicine, Science, & the Law,* 13, 197-206.

Scott, P.D. 1973-*b*. Parents who kill their children. *Medicine, Science, & the Law,* 13, 120-126.

Scott, P.D. 1978. Non-accidental injury in children: Memorandum of evidence to the Parliamentary Select Committee on Violence in the Family. *British Journal of Psychiatry,* 131, 366-380.

Scully, Diana, & Joseph Marolla. 1985. "Riding the bull at Gilley's": Convicted rapists describe the rewards of rape. *Social Problems,* 31, 530-544.

Sechrest, Lee, Susan O. White & Elizabeth D. Brown. 1979. *The Rehabilitation of Criminal Offenders: Problems and Prospects.* Washington: National Academy of Sciences.

Sellin, Thorsten. 1959. *The Death Penalty.* Philadelphia: American Law Institute.

Sells, Saul B. 1963. Dimensions of stimulus situations which account for behavior variance. In S.B. Sells (ed.), *Stimulus Determinants of Behavior.* New York: Ronald. Pp. 3-15.

Seymour, Richard, & David E. Smith. 1987. *The Physician's Guide to Psychoactive Drugs.* Binghamton: Haworth.

Shapiro, David. 1984. Criminal responsibility: The historical background. In David L. Shapiro, Psychological Evaluation and Expert Testimony. New York: Van Nostrand Reinhold. Pp. 28-50.

Sheldon, William H. 1942. *The Varieties of Temperament: A Psychology of Constitutional Differences.* New York: Harper & Brothers.

Sheldon, William H. 1949. *Varieties of Delinquent Youth: An Introduction to Constitutional Psychiatry.* New York: Harper & Brothers.

Sheley, Joseph F., & Kenneth D. Bailey. 1985. New directions for anti- theft policy: Reductions in stolen goods buyers. *Journal of Criminal Justice,* 13, 399-415.

Sherif, Muzafer, & Carolyn Sherif. 1953. *Groups in Harmony and Tension: An Integration of Studies in Intergroup Relations.* New York: Octagon.

Shoham, Shlomo G., Giora Rahav, Rachel Markowski, Frances Chard *et al.* 1987. Family parameters of violent prisoners. *Journal of Social Psychology,* 127, 83-91.

Siever, Larry J., & Kenneth L. Davis. 1991. A psychobiological perspective on the personality disorders. *American Journal of Psychiatry,* 148, 1647-1658.

Sila, Ante. 1977. Psychopathologic traits of perpetrators of felonious homicides. *Socijalna Psichijatrija,* 5, 3-81.

Silver, Jonathan M., Stuart C. Yudofsky & Robert E. Hales. 1987. Neuropsychiatric aspects of traumatic brain injury. In Robert E. Hales & Stuart C. Yudofsky (eds.), *American Psychiatric Press Textbook of Neuropsychiatry.* Washington, DC: American Psychiatric Press. Pp. 179-190.

Silver, Stuart B., & Michael K. Spodak. 1983. Dissection of the prongs of ALI [American Law Institute]: A retrospective assessment of criminal responsibility by the psychiatric staff of the Clifford T. Perkins Hospital Center. *Bulletin of the American Academy of Psychiatry & the Law,* 11, 383-391.

Silverman, Robert A., & Leslie W. Kennedy. 1988. Women who kill their children. *Violence & Victims,* 3, 113-127.

Simon, Robert I. 1987. *Clinical Psychiatry and the Law.* Washington, DC: American Psychiatric Press.

Singh, Arvinder. 1980. Study of personality of murderers and the psychosocial factors related to murder. *Indian Journal of Criminology,* 8, 15-20.

Sivak, Michael. 1983. Society's aggression level as a predictor of traffic fatality rate. *Journal of Safety Research,* 14, 93-99.

Skinner, B.F. 1938. *The Behavior of Organisms: An Experimental Analysis.* New York: Appleton-Century-Crofts.

Skinner, B.F. 1957. *Verbal Behavior.* New York: Appleton- Century-Crofts.

Skinner, B.F. 1961. *Cumulative Record.* New York: Appleton-Century-Crofts.

Skinner, B.F. 1974. *About Behaviorism.* New York: Appleton-Century-Crofts.

Sloan, John H., Arthur L. Kellermann, Donald T. Reay, James A. Ferris *et al.* 1989. Handgun regulations, crime, assaults, and homicide: A tale of two cities. *New England Journal of Medicine,* 319, 1256-1262.

Slobogin, Christopher, Gary B. Melton, & C. Robert Showalter. 1984. The feasibility of a brief evaluation of mental state at the time of the offense. *Law & Human Behavior,* 8, 305-320.

Smeaton, George, & Donn Byrne. 1987. The effects of R-rated violence & erotica, individual differences, & victim characteristics on acquaintance rape proclivity. *Journal of Research in Personality,* 21, 171-184.

Smith, Brian. 1988. Personality: Multivariate systems theory. In James or Joseph Nesseleroade & Raymond B. Cattell (eds.), *Handbook of Multivariate Experimental Psychology,* 2d ed. New York: Plenum. Pp. 687-736.

Smith, Lynda B., David E. Silber & Stephen A. Karp. 1988. Validity of the Megargee-Bohn MMPI typology with women incarcerated in a state prison. *Psychological Reports,* 62, 107-113.

Snyder, Solomon H. 1988. Psychotogenic drugs as models for schizophrenia: Comments on the current status of the dopamine hypothesis of schizophrenia. *Neuropsycho-pharmacology,* 1, 197-199.

Solomon, Gary S., & Joseph B. Ray. 1984. Irrational beliefs of shoplifters. *Journal of Clinical Psychology,* 40, 1075-1077.

Sommers, Evelyn K., & James V. Check. 1987. An empirical investigation of the role of pornography in the verbal and physical abuse of women. *Violence & Victims,* 2, 189-209.

Sorrells, James M. 1977. Kids who kill. *Crime & Delinquency,* 23, 312-320.

Spellacy, Frank J. 1978. Neuropsychological discrimination between violent and nonviolent men. *Journal of Clinical Psychology,* 34, 49-52.

Spellacy, Frank J., & W.G. Brown. 1984. Prediction of recidivism in young offenders after brief institutionalization. *Journal of Clinical Psychology,* 40, 1070-1074.

Srivastava, Shri O. 1976. A social psychological study of the condemned prisoners in Uttar Pradesh. *Social Defence,* 11, 38-49.

Srole, Leo, Thomas S. Langer, Stanley T. Michael, Marvin K. Opler & Thomas A.C. Bennie. 1962. *Mental Health in the Metropolis.* New York: McGraw-Hill.

Srole, Leo, & Anita Kassen Fischer. 1986. The Midtown Manhattan longitudinal study: Aging, generations, and genders. In Myrna M. Weissman, Jerome K. Myers & Catherine E. Ross (eds.), *Community Surveys of Psychiatric Disorders.* New Brunswick, NJ: Rutgers University Press. Pp. 77-108.

Stack, Steven. 1989. The effect of publicized mass murders and murder-suicides on lethal violence, 1968-1980: A research note. *Social Psychiatry & Psychiatric Epidemiology,* 24, 202-208.

Stalans, Loretta J., Karyl A. Kinsey & Kent W. Smith. 1991. Listening to different voices: Formation of sanction beliefs and taxpaying norms. *Journal of Applied Social Psychology,* 21, 119-138.

Steadman, Henry J. 1982. A situational approach to violence. *International Journal of Law & Psychiatry,* 5, 171-186.

Steadman, Henry J., & Joseph Cocozza. 1978. Psychiatry, dangerousness, and the repetitively violent offender. *Journal of Criminal Law & Criminology,* 69, 226-231.

Steadman, Henry J., Lydia Keitner, Jeraldine Braff & Thomas M. Arranites. 1983. Factors associated with a successful insanity plea. *American Journal of Psychiatry,* 140, 401-405.

Steadman, Henry J., Marilyn J. Rosenstein, Robin L. MacAskill & Ronald W. Manderscheid. 1988. A profile of mentally disordered offenders admitted to inpatient psychiatric services in the United States. *Law & Human Behavior,* 12, 91-99.

Steffensmeier, D.J., & R.H. Steffensmeier. 1977. Who reports shoplifters? Research opportunities and further developments. *International Journal of Criminology & Penology,* 5, 79-95.

Steinmetz, Suzanne K. 1980. Women and violence: Victims and perpetrators. *Journal of Psychotherapy,* 34, 334-350.

Stenross, Barbara. 1984. Police response to residential burglaries: Dusting for prints as a negative rite. *Criminology,* 22, 389- 402.

Stern, Daniel, & Nathaniel J. Pallone. 1971. Effects of brief exposure to photographic vs. rose reporting of racial aggression or harmony upon certain racial attitudes. *Journal of Social Psychology,* 85, 93-101.

Stewart, C.H.M., & D.R. Helmsley. 1979. Risk perception and likelihood of action in criminal offenders. *British Journal of Criminology*, 19, 105-119.

Stewart, C.H., & D.R. Helmsley. 1984. Personality factors in the taking of criminal risks. *Personality & Individual Differences*, 5, 119-122.

Stone, Alan A. 1976. *Mental Health and Law: A System in Transition*. New York: Jason Aronson.

Stone, Alan A. 1984. *Law, Psychiatry, and Morality*. Washington, DC: American Psychiatric Press.

Stone, Evelyn M. 1988. *American Psychiatric Glossary*. Washington, DC: American Psychiatric Press.

Stoudemire, G. Alan. 1987. Selected organic mental disorders. In Robert E. Hales & Stuart C. Yudofsky (eds.), *American Psychiatric Press Textbook of Neuropsychiatry*. Washington, DC: American Psychiatric Press. Pp. 125-140.

Straus, Murray A. 1979-a. Family patterns and child abuse in a nationally representative American sample. *Child Abuse & Neglect*, 3, 213-225.

Straus, Murray A. 1979-b. Measuring intrafamily conflict and violence: The Conflict Tactics (CS) scales. *Journal of Marriage & the Family*, 41, 75-88.

Straus, Murray A. 1980-a. *Behind Closed Doors: Violence in the American Family*. Garden City, NY: Anchor- Doubleday.

Straus, Murray Arnold. 1980-a. Stress and physical child abuse. *Child Abuse & Neglect*, 4, 75-88.

Straus, Murray Arnold, & Richard J. Gelles. 1990. *Physical Violence in American Families: Risk factors and Adaptations*. New Brunswick. NJ: Transaction.

Strauss, Abbey. 1989. Homicidal psychosis during the combined use of cocaine and an over-the-counter preparation. *Journal of Clinical Psychiatry*, 50, 147.

Suinn, Richard M. 1960. The Shipley-Hartford Retreat Scale as a screening test of intelligence. *Journal of Clinical Psychology*, 16, 419.

Sutker, Patricia B., Albert N. Allain & Scott Geyer. 1978. Female criminal violence and differential MMPI characteristics. *Journal of Consulting & Clinical Psychology*, 46, 1141-1143.

Swett, Chester, & Stuart C. Hartz. 1984. Antecedents of violent acts in a prison hospital. *American Journal of Social Psychiatry*, 4, 24-29.

Szasz, Thomas. 1987. *Insanity: The Idea and Its Consequences*. New York: John Wiley.

Szymusik, A. 1972. Studies on the psychopathology of murderers. *Polish Medical Journal*, 11, 752-757.

Tardiff, Kenneth J. 1988. Violence. In John A. Talbott, Robert E. Hales & Stuart C. Yudofsky (eds.), *American Psychiatric Press Textbook of Psychiatry*. Washington, DC: American Psychiatric Press. Pp. 1037-1058.

Tarter, Ralph E., Andrea M. Hegedus & Arthur T. Alterman. 1983. Cognitive capacities of juvenile, violent, nonviolent, and sexual offenders. *Journal of Nervous & Mental Disease*, 171, 564- 567.

Tarter, Ralph E., Andrea M. Hegedus, Nancy E. Winsten & Arthur T. Alterman. 1984. Neuropsychological, personality, and familial characteristics of physically abused delinquents. *Journal of the American Academy of Child Psychiatry*, 23, 668-674.

Taylor, Michael Alan, Frederick S. Sierles, & Richard Abrams. 1987. The neuropsychiatric evaluation. In Robert E. Hales & Stuart C. Yudofsky (eds.), *American Psychiatric Press Textbook of Neuropsychiatry*. Washington, DC: American Psychiatric Press. Pp. 3-16.

Taylor, Pamela J. 1986. Psychiatric disorder in London's life- sentenced offenders. *British Journal of Criminology*, 26, 63- 78.

Tennenbaum, David J. 1978. Personality and criminality: A summary and implications of the literature. *Journal of Criminal of Justice*, 5, 225-235.

Teplin, Linda A. 1983. The criminalization of the mentally ill: Speculation in search of data. *Psychological Bulletin*, 94, 54-67.

Terman, Lewis M. 1916-a. The Binet scale and the diagnosis of feeblemindedness. *Journal of Criminal Law & Criminology*, 7, 530-543.

Terman, Lewis M. 1916-*b*. Mentality tests. *Journal of Educational Psychology,* 7, 348-361.

Terman, Lewis M. 1925. *Genetic Studies of Genius: Mental and Physical Traits of a Thousand Gifted Children.* Palo Alto: Stanford University Press.

Terman, Lewis, & Matitah Oden. 1940-*a*. Significance of deviates: Status of the California gifted group at the end of the 16 years. *Yearbook of the National Society for the Study of Education,* 39, (1) 67-74.

Terman, Lewis M., & Matitah Oden. 1940-*b*. Sign of deviates: The correlates of adult achievement in the California gifted group. *Yearbook of the National Society for the Study of Education.* 39, 67-74.

Terman, Lewis M., & Matitah Oden. 1947. *The Gifted Child Grows Up: A 25 Year Follow-up of a Superior Group.* Palo Alto: Stanford University Press.

Terman, Lewis M., & Maud A. Merrill. 1960. *Stanford-Binet Intelligence Scale: Manual for the Third Revision, Form L-M.* Boston: Houghton-Mifflin.

Terris, William, & John Jones. 1982. Psychological factors related to employees' theft in the convenience store industry. *Psychological Reports,* 51, 1219-1238.

Thomas, Charles W. 1987. Pride and purpose as antidotes to Black homicidal violence. *Journal of the National Medical Association,* 79, 155-160.

Thorndike, Robert L. 1968. Pygmalion in the classroom. *American Educational Research Journal,* 5, 708-711.

Thornton, William E., & Bonnie J. Pray. 1975. The portrait of a murderer. *Diseases of the Nervous System,* 36, 176-178.

Thrasher, Frederic, M. 1936: *The Gang: A Study of 1313 Gangs in Chicago,* 2nd ed. Chicago: University of Chicago Press.

Toborg, Mary A., & John P. Bellassai. 1987. *Assessment of Pretrial Urine Testing in the District of Columbia, I: Background and Description of the Urine Testing Program; IV: Analysis of Drug Use Among Arrestees.* Washington, DC: Toborg Associates.

Toch, Hans. 1975. *Men in Crisis: Human Breakdowns in Prison.* Chicago: Aldine.

Toch, Hans, & Kenneth Adams. 1988. *Coping: Maladaptation in Prisons.* New Brunswick, NJ: Transaction.

Toch, Hans, Kenneth Adams & Ronald Greene. 1987. Ethnicity, disruptiveness, and emotional disorder among prison inmates. *Criminal Justice & Behavior,* 14, 93-109.

Torrey, E. Fuller. 1988. *Nowhere to Go: The Tragic Odyssey of the Homeless Mentally Ill.* New York: Harper & Row.

Torstensson, Marie. 1987. *Drug Abusers in a Metropolitan Cohort.* Stockholm: Department of Sociology, University of Stockholm.

Tuchfeld, Barry S., Richard R. Clayton & John A. Logan. 1982. Alcohol, drug use, and delinquent criminal behavior among male adolescents and young adults. *Journal of Drug Issues,* 12, 185-198.

Turns, Danielle M., & Ernest M. Gruenberg. 1973. An attendant is murdered: The state hospital responds. *Psychiatric Quarterly,* 47, 487-494.

Tyler, Leona E. 1965. *The Psychology of Human Differences.* New York: Appleton-Century-Crofts.

Tyler, Leona E. 1978. *Individuality: Human Possibilities and Personal Choice in the Psychological Development of Men and Women.* San Francisco: Jossey-Bass.

U.S. Public Health Service. 1989. *International Classification of Diseases, 9th Revision, Clinical Modification: Third Edition.* Washington: U.S. Department of Health & Human Services. Publication No.(PHS) 89-1260.

Vaisanen, Leena, & Erkki Vaisanen. 1983. Matricide where the daughter was an instrument for the suicide of her mother. *Psychiatria Fennica, Supplement 15,* 119-122.

van Praag, Herman M. 1988. Biological psychiatry audited. *Journal of Nervous & Mental Disease,* 176, 195-199.

Veneziano, Carol A. 1986. Prison inmates and consent to treatment: Problems and issues. *Law & Psychology Review,* 10, 129- 146.

Veneziano, Carol A. 1986. Prison inmates and consent to treatment: Problems and issues. *Law & Psychology Review,* 10, 129- 146.

Veneziano, Carol A., & Louis Veneziano. 1986. Classification of adolescent offenders with the MMPI: An extension and cross- validation of the Megargee typology. *International Journal of Offender Therapy & Comparative Criminology,* 30, 11-23.

Vigderhous, Gideon. 1975. Suicide and homicide as causes of death and their relationship to life expectancy: A cross-national comparison. *Social Biology,* 22, 338-343.

Villanueva, Michael R., Deborah D. Roman & Michael R. Tuley. 1988. Determining forensic rehabilitation potential with the MMPI: Practical implications for residential treatment populations. *American Journal of Forensic Psychology,* 6, 27-35.

Violence Epidemiology Branch, U.S. Department of Health & Human Services. 1984. *Homicide Surveillance.* Washington, DC: U.S. Government Printing Office.

Virkkunen, Matti. 1974. Suicide linked to homicide. *Psychiatric Quarterly,* 48, 276-282.

Virkkunen, Matti. 1979. Alcoholism and antisocial personality. *Acta Psychiatrica Scandinavica,* 59, 493-501.

Virkkunen, Matti. 1982-a. Evidence for abnormal glucose tolerance test among violent offenders. *Neuropsychobiology,* 8, 30-34.

Virkkunen, Matti. 1982-b. Reactive hypoglycemic tendency among habitually violent offenders: A further study by means of the glucose tolerance test. *Neuropsychobiology,* 8, 35-40.

Virkkunen, Matti. 1983-a. Insulin secretion during the glucose tolerance test in antisocial personality. *British Journal of Psychiatry,* 142, 598-604.

Virkkunen, Matti. 1983-b. Serum cholesterol levels in homicidal offenders: A low cholesterol level is connected with a habitually violent tendency under the influence of alcohol. *Neuropsychobiology,* 10, 65-69.

Virkkunen, Matti. 1984. Reactive hypoglycemic tendency among arsonists. *Acta Psychiatrica Scandinavica,* 69, 445-452.

Virkkunen, Matti. 1985. Urinary free cortisol secretion in habitually violent offenders. *Acta Psychiatrica Scandinavica,* 72, 40- 44.

Virkkunen, Matti. 1986. Insulin secretion during the glucose tolerance test among habitually violent and impulsive offenders. *Aggressive Behavior,* 12, 303-310.

Virkkunen, Matti, & M.O. Huttunen. 1982. Evidence for abnormal glucose tolerance test among violent offenders. *Neuropsychobiology,* 8, 30-34.

Virkkunen, Matti, & Eila Kallilo. 1987. Low blood glucose nadir in the glucose tolerance test and homicidal spouse abuse. *Aggressive Behavior,* 13, 59-66.

Virkkunen, Matti, & S. Narvanen. 1987. Plasma insulin, tryptophan, and serotonin levels during the glucose tolerance test among habitually violent and impulsive offenders. *Neuropsychobiology,* 17, 19-23.

Virkkunen, Matti, Arto Nuutila & Simo Huusko. 1976. Effect of brain injury on social adaptability: Longitudinal study on frequency of criminality. *Acta Psychiatrica Scandinavica,* 53, 168-172.

Virkkunen, Matti, David F. Horrobin, Douglas K. Jenkins & Mehar S. Manku. 1987. Plasma phospholipid essentially fatty acids and prostaglandins in alcoholic, habitually violent, and impulsive offenders. *Biological Psychiatry,* 22, 1087-1096.

Virkkunen, Matti, Judith de Jong, John J. Bartko & Frederick K. Goodwin. 1989. Relationship of psychobiological variables to recidivism in violent offenders and impulsive fire setters: A follow-up study. *Archives of General Psychiatry,* 46, 600-603.

Virkkunen, Matti, Arto Nuutila, Frederick K. Goodwin, & Markku Linnoila. 1987. Cerebrospinal fluid monamine metabolite levels in male arsonists. *Archives of General Psychiatry,* 44, 241-247.

Volavka, Jan. 1991. Aggression, electroencephalography, and evoked potentials: A critical review. *Neuropsychiatry, Neuropsychology & Behavioral Neurology,* 3, 249-259.

Volkow, Nora D., & Laurence R. Tancredi. 1991. Biological correlates of mental activity studied with PET [positron emisssion tomography]. *American Journal of Psychiatry,* 148, 439- 443.

von Hirsch, Andrew. 1976. *Doing Justice: The Choice of Punishments.* New York: Hill & Wang.

von Hirsch, Andrew. 1985. *Past or Future Crimes: Deservedness and Dangerousness in the Sentencing of Criminals.* New Brunswick, NJ: Rutgers University Press.

von Hirsch, Andrew. 1988. *Federal Sentencing Guidelines: The United States and Canadian Schemes Compared.* New York: Center for Research in Crime & Justice, School of Law, New York University.

Vuocolo, Alfred B. 1968. *The Repetitive Sex Offender.* Menlo Park: New Jersey State Diagnostic Center.

Wahl, Otto F., & J. Yonatan Lefkowits. 1989. Impact of a television film on attitudes toward mental illness. *American Journal of Community Psychology,* 17, 521-528.

Wakshlag, Jacob, Virginia Vial & Ronald Tamborini. 1983. Selecting crime drama and apprehension about crime. *Human Communication Research,* 10, 227-242.

Walker, Nigel. 1968. *Crime and Insanity in England: The Historical Perspective.* Edinburgh: Edinburgh University Press.

Walters, Glenn D. 1986-*a*. Correlates of the Megargee criminal classification system: A military correctional setting. *Criminal Justice & Behavior,* 13, 19-32.

Walters, Glenn D. 1986-*b*. Screening for psychopathology in groups and black and white prison inmates by means of the MMPI. *Journal of Personality Assessment,* 50, 257-264.

Walters, Glenn D., Thomas A. Scrapansky & Glenn A. Marlow. 1986. The emotionally disturbed military criminal offender: Identification, background, and institutional adjustment. *Criminal Justice & Behavior,* 13, 261-285.

Walters, Glenn D., Thomas W. White & Roger L. Greene. 1988. Use of the MMPI to identify malingering and exaggeration of psychiatric symptomatology in male prison inmates. *Journal of Consulting & Clinical Psychology,* 56, 111-117.

Wass, Hannelore, Jane L. Raup, Karen Cerullo, Linda G. Martel *et al.* 1988-89. Adolescents' Interest in and views of destructive themes in rock music. *Omega: Journal of Death & Dying,* 19, 177-186.

Wauchope, Barbara A., & Murray A. Straus. 1990. Physical punishment and physical abuse of American children: Incidence rates by age, gender, and occupational class. In Murray A. Straus & Richard J. Gelles (eds.), *Physical Violence in American Families: Risk Factors and Adaptions to Violence in 8145 Families.* New Brunswick, NJ: Transaction Books. Pp. 133-148.

Waugh, Evelyn. 1983. *Work Suspended and Other Stories.* London: Penguin.

Webley, Paul, Henry Robben, Henk Effers & Dick Hessing. 1991. *Tax Evasion: An Experimental Approach.* New York: Cambridge University Press.

Webster, Rhonda L., Jay Goldstein & Alexander Segall. 1985. A test of the explanatory value of alternative models of child abuse. *Journal of Comparative Family Studies,* 16, 295-317.

Wechsler, David. 1958. *The Measurement and Appraisal of Adult Intelligence,* 4th ed. Baltimore: Williams & Wilkins.

Welte, John W., & Ernest L. Abel. 1989. Homicide: Drinking by the victim. *Journal of Studies on Alcohol,* 50, 197-201.

Welte, John W., & Brenda A. Miller. 1987. Alcohol use by violent and property offenders. *Drug & Alcohol Dependence,* 19, 313- 324.

Wenk, Ernst A., James O. Robison & Gerald W. Smith. 1972. Can violence be predicted? *Crime & Delinquency,* 18, 393-402.

West, Donald J., & Alexander Walk (eds.). 1977. *Daniel McNaughton: His Trial and the Aftermath.* Ashford, Kent: Royal College of Psychiatrists.

Wettstein, Robert M. 1987. Legal aspects of neuropsychiatry, In Robert E. Hales & Stuart C. Yudofsky (eds.), *American Psychiatric Press Textbook of Neuropsychiatry.* Washington, DC: American Psychiatric Press. Pp. 451-463.

Wettstein, Robert M. 1988. Psychiatry and the law. In John A. Talbott, Robert E. Hales & Stuart C. Yudofsky (eds.), *American Psychiatric Press Textbook of Psychiatry.* Washington, DC: American Psychiatric Press. Pp. 1059-1084.

Wheeler, Stanton. 1976. Trends and problems in the sociological study of crime. *Social Problems,* 23, 525-534.

White, Garland F. 1989. Media and violence: The case of professional football championship games. *Aggressive Behavior,* 15, 423-433.

Whitman, Steven, Tina E. Coleman, Cecil Patmon, Bindu T. Desai, Robert Cohen & Lambert N. King. 1984. Epilepsy in prison: Elevated prevalence and no relationship to violence. *Neurology,* 34, 775-782.

Widom, Cathy S. 1989--a. Does violence beget violence? A critical examination of the literature. *Psychological Bulletin,* 106, 3-28.

Widom, Cathy S. 1989-b. A tail on an untold tale: Response to "Biological and genetic contributors to violence: Widom's untold tail." *Psychological Bulletin,* 109, 130-132.

Widom, Cathy S. 1989-c. The cycle of violence. *Science,* 244, 160-166.

Wiens, Arthur N., & William H. Banaka. 1960. Estimating WAIS IQ from Hartford-Shipley scores. *Journal of Clinical Psychology,* 16, 452.

Wiggins, Jerry. 1973. *Personality and Prediction.* Reading, MA: Addison-Wesley.

Wilbanks, William. 1980. Relationships among victimization rates for accidents, suicide, and homicide. *Victimology,* 7, 213-217.

Wilbanks, William. 1982. Fatal accidents, suicide, and homicide: Are they related? *Victimology,* 7, 213-217.

Wilbanks, William. 1983. Female homicide offenders in the U.S. *International Journal of Women's Studies,* 6, 302-310.

Wilcox, David E. 1985. The relationship of mental illness to homicide. *American Journal of Forensic Psychiatry,* 6, 3-15.

Wilk, Rita J. 1988. Implications of involuntary outpatient commitment for community mental health agencies. *American Journal of Orthopsychiatry,* 58, 580-591.

Wilkes, John. 1986. Murder in mind. *Psychology Today,* 21, 26-32.

Williams, Arhtur H. 1982. Adolescents, violence, and crime. *Journal of Adolescence,* 5, 125-134.

Williams, Denis. 1969. Neural factors related to habitual aggression: Consideration of differences between those habitual aggressives and others who have committed crimes of violence. *Brain,* 92, 501-520.

Williams, Euphemia G. 1983. Adolescent loneliness. *Adolescence,* 18, 51-66.

Williams, Frank P. 1985. Deterrence and social control: Rethinking the relationship. *Journal of Criminal Justice,* 13, 141-151.

Williams, Kirk R. 1984. Economic sources of homicide: Re-estimating the effects of poverty and inequality. *American Sociological Review,* 49, 283-289.

Williams, Ruth M. 1985. Children's stealing: A review of theft control procedures for parents and teachers. *Remedial & Special Education,* 6, 17-23.

Williams, Joyce F., & Karen A. Holmes. 1982. In judgment of victims: The social context of rape. *Journal of Sociology & Social Welfare,* 9, 154-169.

Williams, Wright, & Kent S. Miller. 1977. The role of personal characteristics in perceptions of dangerousness. *Criminal Justice & Behavior,* 4, 241-252.

Wilmotte, J.N., & J.P. Plat-Mendlewicz. 1973. Epidemiology of suicidal behavior in one thousand Belgian prisoners. In Bruce L. Danto (ed.), *Jail House Blues: Studies of Suicidal Behavior in Jail and Prison.* Detroit: Epic. Pp. 57-82.

Wilson, G. Terence, & K. Daniel O'Leary. 1980. *Principles of Behavior Therapy.* Englewood Cliffs: Prentice-Hall.

Wilson, James Q., & Richard J. Herrnstein. 1985. *Crime & Human Nature: The Definitive Study of the Causes of Crime.* New York: Simon & Schuster.

Wilson, Margo, & Martin Daly. 1985. Competitiveness, risk taking, and violence: The young male syndrome. *Ethology & Sociobiology,* 6, 59-73.

Wilson, Paul R. 1987. "Stranger" child murder: Issues related to causes and controls. *International Journal of Offender Therapy & Comparative Criminology,* 31, 49-59.

Wineburg, Samuel S. 1987. The self-fulfillment of the self-fulfilling prophecy: A critical appraisal. *Educational Researcher,* 16, 28-37.

Wish, Eric D. 1990. Drug testing. In Larry J. Siegiegel (ed.), *American Justice: Research of the National Institute of Justice.* St. Paul, MN: West. Pp. 109-113.

Wish, Eric D., & Joyce Ann O'Neil. 1989. Drug use forecasting (DUF) research update. *Research in Action: Drug Use Forecasting.* National Institute of Justice, U.S. Department of Justice, September 1989.

Wish, Eric D., Elizabeth Brady & Mary Cuadrado. 1986. *Urine Testing of Arrestees: Findings from Manhattan.* New York: Narcotic and Drug Research, Inc.

Witte, Ann D., & Peter Schmidt. 1980. Evaluating correctional programs: Models of criminal recidivism and an illustration of their use. *Evaluation Review,* 4, 585-600.

Wolfe, David A. 1985. Child-abusive parents: An empirical review and analysis. *Psychological Bulletin,* 97, 462-482.

Wolfe, David A., John A. Fairbank, Jeffrey A. Kelly & Andrew S. Bradlyn. 1983. Child abusive parents' physiological responses to stressful and non-stressful behavior in children. *Behavioral Assessment,* 5, 363-371.

Wolfgang, Marvin E. 1958. *Patterns in Criminal Homicide.* Philadelphia: University of Pennsylvania Press.

Wolfgang, Marvin E., & Franco Ferracuti. 1967. *The Subculture of Violence.* London: Tavistock.

Wolpe, Joseph. 1969. *The Practice of Behavior Therapy.* New York: Pergamon.

Wood, Nollie P. 1990. Black homicide: A public health crisis. *Journal of Interpersonal Violence,* 5, 147-150.

Wood, Nollie P., & James A. Mercy. 1990. Unintentional firearm- related fatalities, 1970-84. *Public Health Surveillance of 1990: Injury Control Objectives of the Nation,* 37, 47-52.

Wood, Rodger Llewellyn. 1987. *Brain Injury Rehabilitation: A Neurobehavioral Approach.* Rockville, MD: Aspen.

Wood, Wendy, Frank Y. Yong & J. Gregory Chachere. 1991. Effects of media violence on viewers' aggression in unconstrained social interaction. *Psychological Bulletin,* 109, 371-383.

Wormith, J. Stephen. 1984. The controversy over the effects of long- term incarceration. *Canadian Journal of Criminology,* 26, 423-437.

Wormith, J. Stephen, & C.S. Goldstone. 1984. Clinical and statistical prediction of recidivism. *Criminal Justice & Behavior,* 11, 3- 34.

Wright, Kevin N. 1991. The violent and the victimized in the male prison. *Journal of Offender Rehabilitation,* 16, 1-25.

Yablonsky, Lewis. 1959. The delinquent gang as a near-group. *Social Problems,* 7, 108-117.

Yablonsky, Lewis. 1970. *The Violent Gang,* 2nd ed. New York: Penguin.

Yang, Bijou, & David Lester. 1988-*a*. The participation of females in the labor force and rates of personal violence (suicide and homicide). *Suicide & Life-Threatening Behavior,* 18, 270- 278.

Yang, Bijou, & David Lester. 1988-*b*. Predicting execution rates in the U.S.A. *Psychological Reports,* 62, 305-306.

Yesevage, Jerome A., Michel Benezech, Roland Larrieu-Arguille & Marc Bourgeois. 1986. Recidivism of the criminally insane in France: A 22-year follow-up. *Journal of Clinical Psychiatry,* 47, 465- 466.

Yeudall, Lorne T., & D. Fromm-Auch. 1979. Neuropsychological impairments in various psychopathological populations. In John Gruzelier & Pierre Flor-Henry (eds.), *Hemisphere Asymmetries of Function in Psychopathology.* Amsterdam: Elsevier/North Holland Biomedical Press. Pp. 401-428.

Yeudall, Lorne T., Orestes Fedora & DaLee Fromm. 1987. A neuropsychological theory of persistent criminality: Implications for assessment and treatment. *Advances in Forensic Psychology & Psychiatry,* 2, 119-191.

Yochelson, Samuel, & Stanton E. Samenow. 1976. *The Criminal Personality.* New York: Jason Aronson.

Yohman, J. Robert, Kim W. Schaeffer & Oscar A. A. Parsons. 1988. Cognitive retraining in alcoholic men. *Journal of Consulting & Clinical Psychology,* 56, 67-72.

Zachary, Robert A. 1990. *Shipley Institute of Living Scale — User's Guide to the Microcomputer Edition,* 2d ed., Version 2.000. Los Angeles: Western Psychological Services.

Zager, Lynne D. 1988. The MMPI-based criminal classification system: A review, current status, and fu fu future directions. *Criminal Justice & Behavior*, 15, 39-57-57.

Zaleski, Zbigniew. 1984. Sensation-seeking and risk-taking behaviour. *Personality & Individual Differences,* 5, 607- 608.

Zastrow, C., & R. Navarre. 1979. Self-talk: A new criminological theory. *International Journal of Comparative & Applied Criminal Justice,* 3, 167-176.

Zillman, Dolf, & Jennings Bryant. 1983. Pornography and social ssscience research: Higher moralities. *Journal of Communication,* 33, 111-114.

Zimbardo, Philip G., & Ebbe B. Ebbesen. 1969. *Influencing Attitudes and Changing Behavior.* Reading, MA: Addison- Wesley.

Zimring, Franklin E. 1990. Gun control. In Larry J. Siegel (ed.), *American Justice: Research of the National Institute of Justice.* St. Paul, MN: West. Pp. 32-36.

Zimring, Franklin, & Gordon Hawkins. 1986. *Capital Punishment and the American Agenda.* New York: Cambridge University Press.

Index of Authors and Names

Index of Topics

Adjudication, defined 381; acquittal 73; conviction 73; indictment prior to 73-74; incarceration 74; plea by defendant 73; probation 74; sanctions following 73-74; schematic representation of steps leading to 75

Alexithymia, defined 381

Aggravating factors [in assessing criminal culpability] 51-53

Aggression: as anti-social behavior 40; character contest and 262; criminal behavior as distinct from 40; intermale, in infrahuman species 256; laboratory analogues 101; as learned behavior 207, 376; neurology in relation to 138-160, 349-361; territoriality 139; psychological model for 40; psychopathology 376; sadism, 167; somatotypes and 156

Ake, U.S. Supreme Court 267

Alcohol 241-250; abuse of 350, as self-medication for neuropsychological dysfunction 155, among juvenile homicide offenders 197, neurogenesis of 350; arrests related to use of 72; character contest, use of as lubricant in 258-262; criminogenesis 243, 248, 249; hypoglycemia and 249; intergenerational transmission in patterns of use and abuse 233; Korsakov's psychosis, as causative of 52; as mental disorder 350; offense of record, use of, prior to, 240 organic mental disorders, 52; paradoxical effects 248; prevalence among adolescents, use of 332; psychopathy and 151; ubiquity of 248; use of, as exculpatory 52, 151-153; use of, as voluntary misbehavior 52; use of, by homicide victims 259

Alcoholism, defined 381

Allen v. Illinois, 59

Alzheimer's disease 141, 155

American Bar Association: and insanity defense 51-53; mitigating factors 51; severity of disorder 51

American Law Institute: and insanity defense 51; model legislation 51; model penal code 51

Analogue studies of criminal behavior: personal victimization 100; research fraud 100; robbery 100; stealing 100; whistle-blowing in 100

American Psychiatric Association 2, 53, 56, 60, 62, 63, 64, 115

American Psychological Association 1, 102, 115, 317

Anomie, defined 381; vs. synomie 132

Arrest: consequences following 77; funneling effect following 77; rarity of intrusive sanctions following 77; rates, by category of crime 72, during Victorian era 73; sequelae to 78-87

Assessment, actuarial [of personality]: methods 169; MMPI validity 168; of child abusers 168; pattern analysis in 169; prediction 286; and standardization 169; superiority as assessment method 169 *See also* Differential psychology

Attention deficit disorder, as neurogenic 353

Attribution theory *See* Labeling

Autonomic nervous system, defined 389 *See* Central nervous system

"Baggage, psychological," defined 8

Barabbas (Film) 214

Barefoot, U.S. Supreme Court 267

Batson, U.S. Supreme Court 267

Bazelon Rule in exculpation of criminal responsibility 51

Behavior: psychogenesis 37; origins 9; recurrent patterns 37

Behavior therapy: clinical techniques of, in correctional institutions 362

Belly of the Beast, In the (Autobiography; Abbott) 268

Biochemical substances: addiction to 382; arrest rates for 242; in character contests 300; corn consumption 245; Dioxin (Agent Orange) 274; as disin-

NATHANIEL J. PALLONE is University Distinguished Professor, Psychology & Criminal Justice, at Rutgers — The State University of New Jersey, where he previously served as dean and as academic vice president. A fellow of the American Psychological Association, the American Psychological Society, and the American College of Forensic Psychology and a diplomate of the American Board of Professional Psychology, since 1976 he has chaired the Classification Review Board for Sex Offenders in New Jersey's Department of Corrections, a statutory "dangerousness review" body charged with assessing the therapeutic progress of criminal sexual psychopaths confined for treatment under the state's habitual sex offender act. He has treated adjudicated heroin addicts at the New York State Narcotics Addiction Control Commission and has been a consultant to the Criminal Justice Research Center (Albany) and the Connecticut Department of Corrections. Pallone is senior editor of *Current Psychology* (Transaction Periodicals Consortium) and editor of the *Journal of Offender Rehabilitation;* his most recent books are *Rehabilitating Criminal Sexual Psychopaths: Legislative Mandates, Clinical Quandaries* (Transaction, 1990) and *Mental Disorder among Prisoners: Toward an Epidemiological Inventory* (Transaction, 1991). He has collaborated with Hennessy in studies of criminal recidivism and of professional roles in offender rehabilitation services since 1972.

JAMES J. HENNESSY chairs the Division of Psychological & Educational Services in the Graduate School of Education at Fordham University, Lincoln Center, where he previously served as director of the PhD program in counseling psychology. Active in the scientific programs of the American Psychological Association, the American Psychological Society, and the American Educational Research Association, he has served as a research consultant to the Connecticut Department of Corrections and, between 1973-91, as consulting psychologist at a network of publicly funded day treatment centers in two New York counties that provide educational services for adjudicated delinquents and adolescents diagnosed with conduct and behavior disorders. An editor of *Current Psychology* (Transaction Periodicals Consortium) and of *Comprehensive Mental Health Care* and a member of the editorial board of the *Journal of Offender Rehabilitation,* Hennessy is a frequent contributor to scholarly and professional journals on psychometric methodology and advanced data analysis techniques. He has collaborated with Pallone in studies of criminal recidivism and of professional roles in offender rehabilitation services since 1972.